Communications
in Computer and Information Science 306

Manish Parashar   Dinesh Kaushik
Omer F. Rana   Ravi Samtaney
Yuanyuan Yang   Albert Zomaya (Eds.)

Contemporary Computing

5th International Conference, IC3 2012
Noida, India, August 6-8, 2012
Proceedings

 Springer

Volume Editors

Manish Parashar
Rutgers University
Piscataway, NJ, USA
E-mail: parashar@rutgers.edu

Dinesh Kaushik
Argonne National Laboratory, IL, USA
E-mail: kaushik@mcs.anl.gov

Omer F. Rana
Cardiff University, UK
E-mail: o.f.rana@cs.cardiff.ac.uk

Ravi Samtaney
King Abdullah University of Science and Technology
Thuwal, Makkah, Saudi Arabia
E-mail: ravi.samtaney@kaust.edu.sa

Yuanyuan Yang
Stony Brook University, NY, USA
E-mail: yang@ece.sunysb.edu

Albert Zomaya
The University of Sydney, NSW, Australia
E-mail: albert.zomaya@sydney.edu.au

ISSN 1865-0929   e-ISSN 1865-0937
ISBN 978-3-642-32128-3   e-ISBN 978-3-642-32129-0
DOI 10.1007/978-3-642-32129-0
Springer Heidelberg Dordrecht London New York

Library of Congress Control Number: 2012942856

CR Subject Classification (1998): C.2, I.2, H.4, H.3, F.1, I.4

Typesetting: Camera-ready by author, data conversion by Scientific Publishing Services, Chennai, India

Printed on acid-free paper

Springer is part of Springer Science+Business Media (www.springer.com)

Preface

Welcome to the 2012 International Conference on Contemporary Computing (IC3). This was the fifth conference in the series, held annually at the Jaypee Institute of Information Technology, and organized jointly by the hosts and the University of Florida, Gainesville, USA. The conference focuses on issues of contemporary interest in computing, spanning systems, algorithms and applications. I hope you find the conference and these proceedings exciting and rewarding.

The IC3 call for papers received a respectable response, attracting 162 submissions. I worked with the Track Chairs and the Program Committee to put together an outstanding technical program consisting of the 42 regular papers and seven short papers that appear in these proceedings. The submissions were subjected to a rigorous peer-review process by an international team of about 95 experts serving as Technical Program Committee members. The Program Committee was led by five Program Track Chairs, themselves representing an eclectic mix of distinguished international experts – Albert Zomaya for Algorithms, Dinesh Kaushik and Ravi Samtaney for Applications, and Omer Rana and Yuanyuan Yang for Systems.

In addition to the contributed papers, the technical program was complemented by eight distinguished keynote speakers:

- Chandrajit Bajaj, Professor of Computer Sciences at the University of Texas at Austin
- Nageswara S.V. Rao, Corporate Fellow in Computer Science and Mathematics Division at Oak Ridge National Laboratory, USA
- M. Balakrishnan, Professor in the Department of Computer Science & Engineering, I.I.T. Delhi, India
- Sunil D. Sherlekar, Principal Engineer and Director of Parallel Computing Research at Intel Labs in Bangalore, India
- H.T. Kung, William H. Gates Professor of Computer Science and Electrical Engineering at Harvard University
- Ramesh Hariharan, Chief Technology Officer, Strand Life Sciences, Bangalore, India
- Alok Choudhary, John G. Searle Professor of Electrical Engineering and Computer Science, Northwestern University, USA
- Ishwar Parulkar, CTO of Provider Access Business Unit of Cisco Systems, Bangalore, India

I am grateful to the authors of all the submitted papers for choosing this conference to present their work. The conference would not be possible without your efforts and valuable contributions. I am grateful to the Program Committee for providing thoughtful and timely reviews. Their collective expertise allowed the Track Chairs and myself to conduct a fair evaluation of contributions spanning diverse areas of contemporary computer science research. I would like to thank the General Chairs, Sartaj Sahni and Sanjay Goel, for giving me the opportunity to lead this year's technical program. They kept tabs on the timelines, and provided guidance and invaluable assistance throughout the process. I would also like to thank the rest of the IC3 team for all their support and assistance.

Manish Parashar

Organization

Chief Patron

Jaiprakash Gaur

Patron

Manoj Gaur

Steering Committee

Yaj Medury	Jaypee Institute of Information Technology, India
Sartaj Sahni	University of Florida, USA
S.C. Saxena	Jaypee Institute of Information Technology, India
Sanjay Ranka	University of Florida, USA
Srinivas Aluru	Iowa State University, USA and IIT Bombay, India
Manish Parashar	Rutgers, The State University of New Jersey, USA
Guna Seetharaman	Air Force Research Laboratory, Rome, NY, USA
Narendra Ahuja	University of Illinois at Urbana-Champaign, USA and ITRA, MCIT India
Pankaj Jalote	Indraprastha Institute of Information Technology (IIIT), Delhi
Sanjay Goel	Jaypee Institute of Information Technology, India

Advisory Committee

Hari Om Gupta	Jaypee Institute of Information Technology, India
Krishna Gopal	Jaypee Institute of Information Technology, India
Krishna Kant	Jaypee Institute of Information Technology, India
R.C. Jain	Jaypee Institute of Information Technology, India

General Co-chairs

Sartaj Sahni	University of Florida, USA
Sanjay Goel	Jaypee Institute of Information Technology, India

Program Chair

Manish Parashar	Rutgers, The State University of New Jersey, USA

Track Co-chairs

Algorithms

Albert Zomaya	University of Sydney, Australia

Applications

Dinesh Kaushik	KAUST, Saudi Arabia
Ravi Samtaney	KAUST, Saudi Arabia

Systems (Hardware and Software)

Omer Rana	Cardiff University, UK
Yuanyuan Yang	Stony Brook University, USA

Special Session

Biomedical Informatics

Dinesh P. Mittal	University of Medicine and Dentistry of New Jersey, USA

Algorithms

Ahmed Al-Dubai	Napier University, Scotland, UK
Alexey Lastovetsky	University College Dublin, Ireland
Azzedine Boukerche	University of Ottawa, Canada
Bella Bose	Oregon State University,USA
Bernabé Dorronsoro	University of Luxembourg, Luxembourg
Bertil Schmidt	University of Mainz, Germany
Cevdet Aykanat	Bilkent University, Turkey
Chen Wang	CSIRO, Australia
Denis Trystram	ENSIMAG, Grenoble Institute of Technology, France
E.-G. Talbi	University of Lille - INRIA - CNRS, France
Flavia Delicato	Federal University of Rio de Janeiro, Brazil

Franciszek Seredynski	Cardinal Stefan Wyszynski University, Poland
Hamid Sarbazi-azad	Sharif University of Technology, Iran
H.S. Dagar	JIIT, India
Javid Taheri	University of Sydney, Australia
Jianer Chen	Texas A&M University, USA
Joanna Kolodziej	University of Bielsko-Biala, Poland
Keqin Li	State University of New York, USA
Keqiu Li	Dalian University of Technology, China
K. Kant	JIIT, India
Nasro Min-Allah	COMSATS Institute of Information Technology, Pakistan
Oliver Sinnen	The University of Auckland, New Zealand
Olivier Beaumont	Université Bordeaux 1, France
Paulo Pires	Federal University of Rio de Janeiro, Brazil
Samee U. Khan	University of North Dakota State University, USA
Stephan Olariu	Old Dominion University, USA
Zahir Tari	RMIT University, Australia

Systems (Hardware and Software)

Bharat Madan	Penn State University, USA
Bhardwaj Veeravalli	University of Singapore, Singapore
Bin Xiao	Hong Kong Polytechnic University, Hong Kong
Bo Hong	Georgia Institute of Technology, USA
Box Leangsuksun	Louisana Tech, USA
Bruno Schulze	LNCC, Brazil
Dan Li	Tsinghua University, China
David Bader	Georgia Tech, USA
David W. Walker	Cardiff University, UK
Gagan Agrawal	The Ohio State University, USA
Geyong Min	University of Bradford, UK
Haiying Shen	Clemson University, US
Hewu Li	Tsinghua University, China
Hongyi Wu	University of Lousiana, USA
Ivan Rodero	Rutgers University, USA
Jianping Wang	City University of Hong Kong, Hong Kong
Jie Li	University of Tsukuba, Japan
Jose Cunha	New University of Lisbon, Portugal
Jun Wang	University of Central Florida, USA
Kartik Gopalan	SUNY-Binghamton, USA
Lu Peng	Louisiana State University, USA
Madhusudhan Govindaraju	SUNY-Binghamton, USA
Miao Zhao	Multimedia Networking Research Lab of Huawei Technologies, USA

Mo Li   Nanyang Technological University, Singapore
Mukaddim Pathan   CSIRO, Australia
Olav Lysne   Simula Research Laboratory and University of
                               Oslo, Norway
Parimala Thulasiraman   University of Manitoba, Canada
Peter Varman   Rice University, USA
Rafael Tolosana   University of Zaragoza, Spain
Rajiv Ranjan   UNSW, Australia
Simon Caton   Karlsruhe Institute of Technology, Germany
Tor Skeie   Simula Research Lab, Norway
Tridib Mukherjee   Xerox Research Centre, India
Umit V. Catalyurek   Ohio State University, USA
Weisong Shi   Wayne State Universiry, USA
Xiao Qin   Auburn University, USA
Xiaolin (Andy) Li   University of Florida, USA
Xin Yuan   Florida State University, USA
Yang Qin   HIT Shenzhen Graduate School, China
Yavuz Oruc   University of Maryland at College Park, USA
Yifeng Zhu   University of Maine, USA

Applications

Ananth Kalyanaraman   Washington State University, USA
Francesco Masulli   University of Genova, Italy
Gerrit Voss   NTU, Singapore
Hatem Ltaief   KAUST Supercomputing Laboratory,
                               Saudi Arabia
Kalyan Kumaran   Argonne National Laboratory, USA
Kuntal Ghosh   Indian Statistical Institute, Kolkata, India
Lars Kaderali   University of Heidelberg, Germany
Lois Curfman McInnes   Argonne National Laboratory, USA
Mona Mathur   STMicroelectronics, India
Nicolas Pasquier   University of Nice, France
Pabitra Mitra   Indian Institute of Technology, Kharagpur,
                               India
Pallav Kumar Baruah   Sri Sathya Sai Institute of Higher Learning,
                               India
Pavan Balaji   Argonne National Laboratory, USA
Rajat De   Indian Statistical Institute, Kolkata, India
Rajkumar Kettimuthu   Argonne National Lab, USA
Rio Yokota   KAUST, Saudi Arabia
Sheetal Saini   Louisiana Tech University, USA
Sumantra Dutta Roy   Indian Institute of Technology Delhi, India
Sung-Bae Cho   Yonsei University, Korea

Utpal Garain	Indian Statistical Institute, Kolkata, India
Weiguo Liu	Nanyang Technological University, Singapore
Xiangliang Zhang	King Abdullah University of Science, Saudi Arabia
Ying Qian	King Abdullah University of Science and Technology, Saudi Arabia

Biomedical Informatics

Chakresh K. Jain	JIIT, Noida
Satish Chandra	JIIT, Noida
Vikas Saxena	JIIT, Noida

Publicity Co-chairs

Rajkumar Buyya	University of Melbourne, Australia
Paolo Bellavista	University of Bologna, Italy
Koji Nakano	Hiroshima University, Japan
Masoud Sadjadi	Florida International University, USA
Bhardwaj Veeravalli	University of Singapore, Singapore
Alok Aggarwal	JIIT, India

Publications Committee

Vikas Saxena	JIIT, Noida, India (Publication Chair)
Satish Chandra	JIIT, India
Maneesha Srivastava	JIIT, India
Chetna Gupta	JIIT, India
Rakhi Hemani	JIIT, Noida, India
Gagandeep Kaur	JIIT, India

Web Administration

| Sandeep K. Singh | JIIT, Noida, India |
| Shikha Mehta | JIIT, Noida, India |

Graphic Design

| Sangeeta Malik | JIIT, Noida, India |

Registration and Local Arrangements Co-chairs

Sangeeta Mittal	JIIT, India
Prakash Kumar	JIIT, India
Saurabh K. Raina	JIIT, India
Manish K. Thakur	JIIT, India

Local Arrangements Committee

Ravneesh Aujla	JIIT, Noida, India
S.J.S. Soni	JIIT, Noida, India
Akhilesh Sachan	JIIT, Noida, India
Sanjay Kataria	JIIT, Noida, India
S. Bhaseen	JIIT, Noida, India
Adarsh Kumar	JIIT, Noida, India
Anuja Arora	JIIT, Noida, India
Archana Purwar	JIIT, Noida, India
Arti Gupta	JIIT, Noida, India
Chetna Dabas	JIIT, Noida, India
Hema N.	JIIT, Noida, India
Indu Chawla	JIIT, Noida, India
K. Rajalakshmi	JIIT, Noida, India
Kavita Pandey	JIIT, Noida, India
Megha Rathi	JIIT, Noida, India
Minakshi Gujral	JIIT, Noida, India
Mukta Goyal	JIIT, Noida, India
Niyati Agarwal	JIIT, Noida, India
Parmeet Kaur	JIIT, Noida, India
Pawan Kumar Upadhyay	JIIT, Noida, India
Prashant Kaushik	JIIT, Noida, India
Pritee Parwekar	JIIT, Noida, India
Purtee Kohli	JIIT, Noida, India
Sangeeta	JIIT, Noida, India
Shikha Jain	JIIT, Noida, India
Suma Dawn	JIIT, Noida, India
Tribhuvan Kumar Tewari	JIIT, Noida, India
Vimal Kumar K.	JIIT, Noida, India
Vivek Mishra	JIIT, Noida, India

Table of Contents

Track: Applications

Track: Systems (Hardware & Software)

Track: Biomedical Informatics

Poster Papers

Erratum

Computational Modeling and Visualization in the Biological Sciences

Chandrajit Bajaj

Department of Computer Science,
Institute of Computational Engineering and Sciences,
The University of Texas, Austin
bajaj@cs.utexas.edu

Abstract. Discoveries in computational molecular cell biology and bioinformatics promise to provide new therapeutic interventions to disease. With the rapid growth of sequence and structural information for thousands of proteins, and hundreds of cell types computational processingare a restricting factor in obtaining quantitative understanding of molecular-cellular function. Processing and analysis is necessary both for input data (often from imaging) and simulation results. To make biological conclusions, this data must be input to and combined with results from computational analysis and simulations. Furthermore, as parallelism is increasingly prevalent, utilizing the available processing power is essential to development of scalable solutions needed for realistic scientific inquiry. However, complex image processing and even simulations performed on large clusters, multi-core CPU, GPU-type parallelization means that nave cache unaware algorithms may not efficiently utilize available hardware. Future gains thus require improvements to a core suite of algorithms underpinning the data processing, simulation, optimization and visualization needed for scientific discovery. In this talk, I shall highlight current progress on these algorithms as well as provide several challenges for the scientific community.

M. Parashar et al. (Eds.): IC3 2012, CCIS 306, p. 1, 2012.

Analytical and Experimental Methods for High-Performance Network Testing

Nageswara S.V. Rao

Computer Science and Mathematics Division,
Oak Ridge National Laboratory,
Oak Ridge, TN 37831, USA
raons@ornl.gov

Abstract. There has been an increasing number of large-scale science and commercial applications that produce large amounts of data, in the range of petabytes to exabytes, which has to be transported over wide area networks. Such data transport capability requires high performance protocols together with complex end systems and network connections. A systematic analysis and comparison of such data transport methods involves the generation of the throughput profiles from measurements collected over connections of different lengths. For such testing, the connections provided by production networks and testbeds are limited by the infrastructures, which are typically quite expensive. On the other hand, network emulators provide connections of arbitrary lengths at much lower costs, but their measurements only approximate those on physical connections. We present a differential regression method to estimate the differences between the performance profiles of physical and emulated connections, and then to estimate "physical" profiles from emulated measurements. This method is more general and enables: (i) an objective comparison of profiles of different connection modalities, including emulated and physical connections, and (ii) estimation of a profile of one modality from measurements of a different modality by applying a differential regression function. This method is based on statistical finite sample theory and exploits the monotonicity of parameters to provide distribution-free probabilistic guarantees on error bounds. We present an efficient polynomial-time dynamic programming algorithm to compute the underlying differential regression function. We provide a systematic analysis of long-haul InfiniBand and TCP throughput measurements over dedicated 10Gbps connections of several thousands of miles. These results establish the closeness of throughput profiles generated over plain, encrypted, physical and emulated connections. In particular, our results show that robust physical throughput profiles can be derived using much less expensive emulations, thereby leading to significant savings in cost and effort.

M. Parashar et al. (Eds.): IC3 2012, CCIS 306, p. 2, 2012.

Power Consumption in Multi-core Processors

M. Balakrishnan

Professor, Deptt of Computer Science and Engineering,
I.I.T. Delhi, India
mbala@cse.iitd.ernet.in

Abstract. Power consumption in processors has become a major concern and clearly that has been one key factor behind growth of multi-core processors to achieve performance rather than single core with increased clock frequency. In this talk we would start by describing the processor power consumption issues as well as motivation for low power multi-core processors. We would also briefly trace the impact on power consumption as the processor architecture evolution mainly focussed on increasing performance. We would finally describe our recent research efforts focussed on multi-core power estimation.

M. Parashar et al. (Eds.): IC3 2012, CCIS 306, p. 3, 2012.

Parallel Computing Goes Mainstream

Sunil D. Sherlekar

Intel Labs,
Bangalore, India
sunil.d.sherlekar@intel.com

Abstract. For several decades now (since Gordon More conjectured his Moore's "Law"), the computing industry has benefited from ever-increasing processor speed. Application developers, therefore, had the privilege of planning ahead for more powerful application software with the assurance that the computing power required will be available. Processor manufacturers could also plan to keep increasing processor speeds with the assurance that application developers were ready to use them. In terms of programmer productivity, the most important implication was that most programmers could write sequential code; the only exceptions being those who wrote operating systems or application software for "supercomputers". A few years ago, this convenient symbiotic relationship began to unravel. The main "culprit" was limitations of technology. It was no longer feasible to make processors faster because it was not possible to handle the heat generated by the faster circuitry. Fortunately, Moore's Law continues to hold, hence it is possible to keep packing an increasing number of transistors on a chip. Given the continued opportunity provided by Moore's Law and faced with the heat dissipation problem, the industry stopped increasing the speed of processors and, instead, started designing chips with multiple processors. This meant that the industry could still bring out chips which had increasing computing power albeit with each processor "core" not getting any faster. The downside of this development is that all programmers — and not just a few select ones — need to write parallel programs to be able to actually use the computing power of multi-processor or multi-core chips. Parallel Programming has to go mainstream. There are two challenges a programmer faces when designing parallel programs: ensuring correctness and extracting the maximum possible performance. Over the last few decades, the Computer Science community has addressed the challenge of correctness fairly well. Besides developing alternative programming paradigms — shared-memory and message-passing — programming languages have been designed with appropriate constructs to help (but not necessarily ensure) absence of typical parallel-programming bugbears such as deadlocks and race conditions. What is still sorely lacking, however, is any systematic methodology to improve the performance of programs. Getting the best possible performance for a given parallel program from the underlying hardware is still an art, bordering on "black magic". The industry is in a dire need to create such a systematic methodology. The primary obstacle to creating such a systematic methodology is that we do not yet have a programming

M. Parashar et al. (Eds.): IC3 2012, CCIS 306, pp. 4–5, 2012.

model of hardware at the right level of abstraction. We have the ISA (Instruction Set Architecture) that is excellent for addressing functionality but has no information about hardware performance. At the other end of the spectrum, we have the RTL (Register-Transfer Level) model of hardware that provides information about hardware performance but is too detailed (not abstract enough) to be useful to programmers (at least those who are not experts). The industry today is witnessing acceleration in the rate of reduction of hardware costs, an example being the one teraflops double-precision performance of Intel's KNC chip. This has created the exciting opportunity to bring high-performance computing into the mainstream. However, to make this happen needs a large number of engineers who can design correct and efficient parallel programs. Today we have a fairly good systematic methodology to design parallel programs that are functionally correct. Programmer productivity is being further enhanced with the development of Domain-Specific Languages (DSL's). This needs to be urgently complemented with a systematic methodology to enhance performance on a given target hardware platform. The development of such a methodology must form one of the core themes of research for the computing community.

Big Data and Compressive Sensing

H.T. Kung

William H. Gates Professor,
Computer Science and Electrical Engineering,
Harvard University, USA

Abstract. Data is growing very fast. Today one can spot business trends, detect environmental changes, predict forthcoming social agendas and combat crime, by analyzing large data sets. However, this so-called "Big Data" analytics is challenging because they have unprecedentedly large volumes. In this presentation, we describe a new approach based on the recent theory of compressive sensing to address the issue of processing, transporting and storing large data sets of enormous sizes gathered from high-resolution sensors and the Internet.

M. Parashar et al. (Eds.): IC3 2012, CCIS 306, p. 6, 2012.

Data-Driven Biology and Computation

Ramesh Hariharan

Computer Scientist, Engineer and Entrepreneur,
Chief Technology Officer, Strand Life Sciences, Bangalore, India
ramesh@strandls.com

Abstract. The last decade has seen tremendous advances in our ability
to interrogate biological systems at the molecular level. As these technologies mature and reduce in cost, the prospect that one day we could
use these to understand disease on a personal rather than a population
basis becomes a possibility. The talk will describe this landscape and also
outline the central role that computing plays in this endeavour.

M. Parashar et al. (Eds.): IC3 2012, CCIS 306, p. 7, 2012.

Dynamic Model of Blended Biogeography Based Optimization for Land Cover Feature Extraction

Lavika Goel[1], Daya Gupta[1], and V.K. Panchal[2]

[1] Department of Computer Engineering,
Delhi Technological University (DTU), Delhi, India
goel_lavika@yahoo.co.in, dgupta@dce.ac.in
[2] Defence Terrain & Research Lab, Defence & Research Development Organisation (DRDO),
Metcalfe House, Delhi, India
vkpans@ieee.org

Abstract. This paper presents a dynamic model of the blended biogeography based optimization (BBO) for land cover feature extraction. In the blended BBO, the habitats represent the candidate problem solutions and the species migration represents the sharing of features (SIVs) between candidate solutions according to the fitness of the habitats which is called their HSI value [9]. However, it is assumed that these SIVs i.e. the number of solution features, remain constant for every habitat [10] and the HSI for each habitat depends only on the immigration and the emigration rates of species [9]. This paper extends the blended BBO by considering the fact that the no. of SIVs or the decision variables may not remain constant for all candidate solutions (habitats) that are part of the Universal habitat. Since the characteristics of each habitat vary greatly hence, comparing all the habitats using the same set of SIVs may be misleading and also may not lead to an optimum solution. Hence, in our dynamic model, we consider the fact that HSI of a solution is affected by factors other than migration of SIVs i.e. solution features, also. These other factors can be modeled as several definitions of HSI of a habitat, each definition based on a different set of SIVs which simulates the effect of these other factors. We demonstrate the performance of the proposed model by running it on the real world problem of land cover feature extraction in a multi-spectral satellite image.

Keywords: Biogeography based optimization, species population modeling, evolutionary algorithms, remote sensing.

1 Introduction

Biogeography based Optimization (BBO) is a new evolutionary optimization method which is inspired from the science of biogeography [9]. Motivated by the migration mechanisms of ecosystems, various extensions to biogeography- based optimization (BBO) were proposed including the blended BBO algorithm [12]. As a global optimization method, BBO is an original algorithm based on the mathematical model of organism distribution in biological systems. In the original BBO paper, it was

M. Parashar et al. (Eds.): IC3 2012, CCIS 306, pp. 8–19, 2012.

illustrated that BBO is competitive with other EAs. It could become a popular EA if it continues to improve with additional modifications and extensions, for example, oppositional BBO [3] and the blended BBO [12], and if it is applied to additional practical engineering problems such as the ECG diagnosis [8], power system optimization [6], economic load dispatch [7], ground water detection [14] and satellite image classification [1], [2], [4].

BBO is an application of biogeography to EAs. Biogeography not only gives a description of species distributions, but also a geographical explanation. Biogeography is modeled in terms of such factors as habitat area and immigration and emigration rates, and describes the evolution, extinction and migration of species. However, the extensions of BBO that have been proposed till date do not consider the factors of evolution and extinction of species in determining the no. of species in a habitat at a time instant and only considers the immigration and the emigration rates as the deciding factor for the determination of no. of species at a time instant. We introduce two additional factors, population evolution rate and population extinction rate, besides immigration and emigration in the calculation of the species count, for the characterization of a habitat with a high or a low HSI value. Also, the extensions to the original BBO (mainly, the blended BBO) that have been proposed till now have assumed that the SIVs i.e. solution features remain constant for every habitat [10]. However, the no. of SIVs or the decision variables may not remain constant for all candidate solutions (habitats) since the characteristics of each habitat vary greatly as is reported in the natural biogeography theory [15] and hence, comparing all the habitats using the same set of SIVs may be misleading and also may not lead to an optimum solution. Hence, the HSI value of a habitat should be considered as a function of different sets of SIVs depending upon the characteristics of the habitat under consideration.

Hence, the contribution of this paper is twofold. First, motivated by natural biogeography and species population demographical literature, we extend the species abundance model originally proposed by Dan Simon [9]. Second, using the concept of dynamic HSI function, we formulate the modified version of the original biogeography based land cover feature extraction algorithm [4] and demonstrate its performance on the dataset of Alwar area in Rajasthan where it proves itself to be an efficient feature extractor as an extension to the original biogeography based land cover feature extractor [4]. The rest of the paper is organized as follows. Section 2 reviews the blended BBO algorithm as an optimizing approach and proposes the extended form of the blended BBO. Section 3 extends the species abundance model originally proposed by Dan Simon [9], [11], [13]. Section 4 presents the proposed dynamic model of the blended BBO algorithm for land cover feature extraction [4]. Section 5 presents the simulation results. In section 6, we present the conclusion and directions for future research.

2   Blended Biogeography Based Optimization

In biogeography, migration is the movement of species between different habitats. In BBO, migration is a probabilistic operator that adjusts each solution H_i by sharing features between solutions. In blended BBO, a blended migration operator which is a generalization of the standard BBO migration operator, motivated by the blended crossover in GAs [12]. In blended migration in BBO, a solution feature of solution H_i is not simply replaced by a feature from solution H_j. Instead, a new solution feature in a BBO solution is comprised of two components: the migration of a feature from another solution, and the migration of a feature from itself. Blended migration is defined as

$$H_i(SIV) \leftarrow \alpha H_i(SIV) + (1 - \alpha)H_j(SIV)$$

Where α is a real number between 0 and 1. In blended migration, the new solution feature (SIV) of H_i comes from a combination of its own SIV and the emigrating solution's SIV. The immigration and the emigration rates are functions of the species count of the habitat and are calculated as

$$\lambda_i = I \left(1 - \frac{k(i)}{n}\right) \tag{1}$$
$$\mu_i = E \left(\frac{k(i)}{n}\right) \tag{2}$$

where I is the maximum possible immigration rate; E is the maximum possible emigration rate; $k(i)$ is the fitness rank of the ith individual (1 is worst and n is best); and n is the number of candidate solutions in the population. Blended migration is an attractive BBO modification from a couple of different viewpoints. On the one hand, good solutions will be less likely to be degraded due to migration. On the other hand, poor solutions can still accept a lot of new features from good solutions. That is, if the solution H_i is much more fit than solution H_j, it would make sense to have α close to 1; but if solution H_i is much less fit than the solution H_j, it would make sense to have α close to 0. The mutation probability is as was given by the original BBO algorithm inversely proportional to the solution probability [9], [12] and is defined by

$$m_i = m_{max} \left(1 - \frac{P_i}{P_{max}}\right)$$

where m_{max} is the user defined maximum mutation probability, $P_{max} = argmax\, P_i$, $i = 1, ..., n$ (n is population size), and P_i is the solution probability. For more details refer [12].

3   Extended Species Abundance Model of Blended BBO

The extensions of BBO that have been proposed till date do not consider the factors of evolution and extinction of species in determining the no. of species in a habitat at a time instant and only considers the immigration and the emigration rates as the deciding factor for the determination of no. of species at a time instant. We introduce two additional factors, population evolution rate (α_k) and population extinction rate (β_k), besides immigration (λ_k) and emigration (μ_k) in the calculation of the species count, for the characterization of a habitat with a high or a low HSI value. Hence, the population growth is determined by four factors, births (B), deaths (D), immigrants (I), and emigrants (E) [16], [17] also suggested by [15]. Using a formula expressed as

$$\Delta P \equiv B - D + I - E \tag{3}$$

In other words, the population growth of a period can be calculated in two parts, natural growth of population (B-D) and mechanical growth of population (I-E) [16], [17].In the original as well as in the extensions of BBO, the HSI value of a habitat was only characterized by the emigration and immigration rates. We introduce two additional factors, population evolution rate and population extinction rate, besides immigration and emigration in the calculation of the species count, for the characterization of a habitat with a high or a low HSI value.

Population evolution rate (α_k) is a governing factor in determining the no. of species in a habitat at a time instant since the no. of species in a habitat may increase due to several reasons besides immigration such as cross-breeding utilizing the biotic potential of the species, bringing in new species by natural causes such as wind, etc. or by human activities, plentiful resources, optimal environmental conditions, etc. [17].

Population extinction rate (β_k) is a governing factor in determining the no. of species in a habitat at a time instant since the no. of species in a habitat may decrease due to several reasons besides emigration such as the:

- Density-Independent Checks on Population Growth such as the vagaries of the physical environment [16], [18] for example
— drought
— freezes
— hurricane
— floods
— forest fires
- Density-Dependent Checks on Population Growth [16], [18]
— Intraspecific competition
— Interspecific competition
— Reproductive competition
— Predation
— Parasitism
- Population Cycles- Some populations go through repeated and regular periods of boom followed by bust.
- The Carrying Capacity of the Environment- The limiting value of the population that can be supported in a particular environment is called its carrying capacity. As the carrying capacity of the environment decreases, after a period of exponential growth, the size of the population begins to level off and soon reaches a stable value.

Therefore, we define species growth rate (σ_k) when there are 'k' species in the habitat under consideration, by equation (10).

Species growth rate (σ) = Immigration rate (λ) + Evolution rate (α)

i.e. $\qquad \sigma_k = (\lambda_k + \alpha_k)$

Substituting the value of λ_k from Simon's model (1) [9, 12],

$$\sigma_k = I\left(1 - \frac{k}{No}\right) + \alpha_k \qquad (4)$$

We define species decline rate (β_k) when there are 'k' species in the habitat under consideration, by equation (5).

Species decline rate (ρ) = Emigration rate (μ) + Extinction rate (β)

$$i.\,e. \qquad \rho_k = \left(\mu_k + \beta_k\right)$$

Substituting the value of μ_k from Simon's model (2) [9, 12],

$$\rho_k = \frac{kE}{No} + \beta_k \tag{5}$$

Hence, we establish the significance of the additional factors governing the population of species at a time instant. Hence, we can generate a generalized species population model by extending the migration model of Simon [9], [12] by considering the additional factors of species evolution and extinction rates in addition to the immigration and the emigration rates and study their influence on the species count at a given time instant. In the Simon's model of species abundance, the immigration rate λ_k and the emigration rate μ_k are considered as linear functions of the number of species k. However, in our model, we propose that the species count at a given time instant is not a linear function of immigration and emigration rates (as was also established in [10], [18]), but it is also dependent upon the evolution and extinction rates of species. Hence, we can see how the inclusion of the two additional factors which characterize the population growth rates and the decline rates [16], [17] can affect the species abundance model.

4   Dynamic Model of BBO for Land Cover Feature Extraction

In the blended BBO, the HSI of a habitat is determined by the immigration and emigration rates solely. The habitats with a high HSI value are characterized by a high immigration rate and habitats with a low HSI are characterized by a high emigration rate. However, the above HSI calculation does not take into account the population evolution and extinction rates which play a significant role in the determination of the species count on a habitat at a given time instant as explained in the previous section.

We extend the blended BBO by considering the fact that HSI of a solution is affected by factors other than migration of SIVs i.e. solution features, also. These other factors are modeled in the extended form of blended BBO as several definitions of HSI of a habitat, each definition based on a different set of SIVs which simulates the effect of these other factors. In each iteration of the optimization process, one of these definitions of HSI is chosen for the purpose of HSI calculation, the decision of choice of HSI function being based on these other factors. The result of applying the extended form of blended BBO on an optimization problem is that the no. of SIVs or the decision variables may not remain constant for a candidate solutions (habitats) in every iteration as opposed to the classical BBO [9]. Also, since the characteristics of each habitat vary greatly and hence, comparing all the habitats using the same set of SIVs may also be misleading and may not lead to an optimum solution.

We therefore propose the following biogeography based algorithm in order to extract land cover features from the satellite image as an extension to the original biogeography based feature extraction algorithm [4]. The input to the proposed algorithm is the multi-spectral satellite image and the output is the extracted features from the image. The algorithm for the proposed extended biogeography based land cover feature extraction is presented in figure 1. In the extended form of blended BBO for land cover feature extraction, we exploit the proposed fact that the number of solution features i.e. *SIVs* of a given habitat, may not remain constant during the problem optimization process and they may in fact vary dynamically during optimization. Making use of the proposed hypotheses, we calculate the *HSI* of each of the habitat H_i in the Universal habitat H_u using two different functions namely entropy and standard deviation. We calculate the difference between the HSI of the selected species H_i and each of the feature habitats H_j based on entropy and standard deviation separately and find out the feature habitat with which H_i has the minimum difference. We also calculate the percentage of this minimum difference value with the HSI of the species habitat H_i based on entropy and standard deviation and assume the feature index of the function which has the smaller percentage difference value. This means that the HSI function which decides the classified feature for each species habitat H_i changes based on the classification efficiency that is provided by it since for each species habitat H_i, we recalculate the HSI of the feature habitat based on the HSI function (entropy / standard deviation) which maximizes the classification efficiency (smaller is the percentage difference value, greater is the classification accuracy provided by the function). Hence, the proposed algorithm adapts to dynamic changes in the HSI (its definition / function) during the optimization process.

Get the multi-spectral satellite image.
Cluster the pixels of image randomly (using rough set theory) and consider each cluster as a species of the Universal habitat.
Take each of the 5 land cover features as a feature habitat. Hence, we have 5 feature habitats each for Water, Urban, Rocky, Barren and Vegetation features, having members produced by experts.
   Calculate HSI of each of the feature habitat.
While $(H_u \; ! = NULL)$
     For each species H_i in the Universal habitat H_u
       Select a species from H_u
         For each of the feature habitat H_j.
         Migrate the specie H_i to H_j.
         Recalculate the *HSI* of the feature habitat H_j after the migration of the
         species H_i to it based on *entropy* and *standard deviation* separately.
       End for
         Calculate the percentage of the minimum difference obtained between the
         species H_i and the feature habitat H_j based on *entropy* and
         standard deviation both.
       If (% Difference$_{entropy}$ < % Difference $_{std\ deviation}$)
         HSI$_{current}$ = {Entropy};
         Feature$_{Index}$(HSI$_{current}$) = Feature$_{Index}$(Entropy);
      Else
         HSI$_{current}$ = {Standard Deviation};
         Feature$_{Index}$(HSI$_{current}$) = Feature$_{Index}$(Standard Deviation);
      End
        Absorb the species H_i in the feature habitat H_j.
     End For
End While

Fig. 1. Algorithm for dynamic biogeography based land cover feature extraction

5 Detailed Framework of the Dynamic Biogeography Based Feature Extractor

This section demonstrates the concept of dynamic HSI function proposed in our extended BBO through the case study of Alwar region in Rajasthan. The case study has two sections, the first section begins with the description of the dataset used and the second section presents the proposed methodology and finally the feature extraction results of the proposed extended BBO based feature extractor on the Alwar image.

5.1 Dataset Used

We have used a multi-spectral, multi resolution and multi sensor image of Alwar area in Rajasthan with dimensions 472 X 576. The satellite image for seven different bands is taken. The Bands are Red, Green, Near Infra-Red (NIR), Middle Infra-Red (MIR), Radarsat-1 (RS1), Radarsat-2 (RS2) and Digital Elevation Model (DEM) [5]. The Red, Green, NIR, and MIR band images is taken from LISS (Linear Imaging Self Scanning Sensor)-III, sensor of Resource-sat an Indian remote sensing satellite. RS1and RS2 are the images from Canadian satellite Radar-sat. Digital elevation model is derived by using images from RS1 and RS2 [5]. The area is selected as it contains hilly track, water, agriculture land, urban zone, barren lands. The 7-Band image satellite image of Alwar area in Rajasthan is shown in figure 2 is taken.

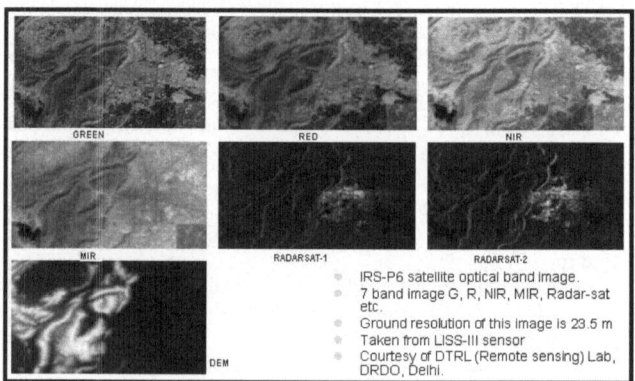

Fig. 2. 7-band satellite image of Alwar region in Rajasthan

5.2 Proposed Methodology

We calculate the percentage difference values for the average entropies calculated in the multi-spectral bands for each rough sets generated equivalence class with the equivalence class has minimum difference with [4], obtained on the Alwar image. The image is subjected to 'n' (here, we take n=20) simple partitions., for the sake of simplicity. (The image may be partitioned into any number as per the individual preference.). We demonstrate the proposed methodology and the calculations on one out of these 'n' partitions. The considered portion of the image is the 16th partition (z=16) since this region contains the maximum number of land cover features and hence best suits for the demonstration of the proposed methodology of dynamic feature extraction. The values are normalized so that both the HSI function based on entropy return the percentage difference values that are scaled in the interval of the percentage difference values returned by the HSI function based on standard deviation. Scaling factor for each of the table entries i.e. for the percentage difference values for each equivalence class used is defined as below:

$$Scaling\ factor_i$$
$$= \frac{Max(Percentage\ diff(Stddev)) - Min(Percentage\ diff(Stddev))}{Max(Percentage\ diff(Entropy)) - Min(Percentage\ diff(Entropy))}$$
$$\times Percentage\ diff_i\ (Entropy)$$

where i represents the ith equivalence class. Table 1 & 2 summarize the percentage difference values calculated for each of the equivalence class for the considered partitions based on entropy and standard deviation respectively as explained in the previous section.

Table 1. Percentage Difference matrix based on the HSI function 'Entropy' for the Alwar image

% difference values based on Entropy for equivalence class $(U_{i=1}^{9} i)$ in the considered partition (z=16)	1	2	3
1	3.5487	2.3784	2.6645
2	2.3874	1.0133	0.8855
3	1.4097	0.8060	0.4897

Table 2. Percentage Difference matrix based on the HSI function 'Standard deviation' for the Alwar image

% difference values based on Standard Deviation for equivalence class $(U_{i=1}^{9} i)$ in the considered partition (z=16)	1	2	3
1	3.1387	0.3156	2.9329
2	4.9893	4.0612	3.3435
3	6.9197	0.3414	0.3197

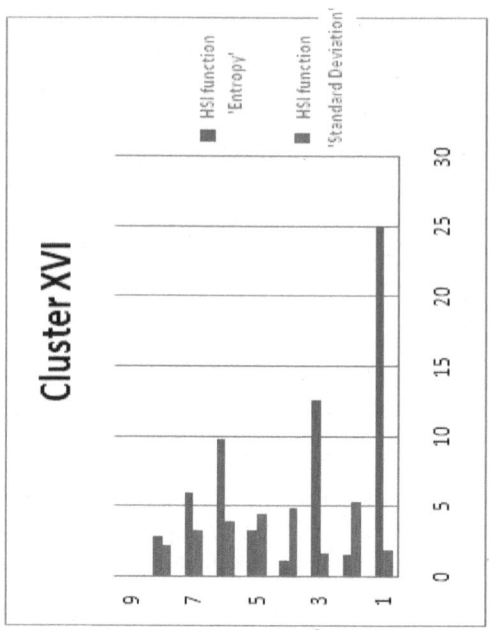

Fig. 3. Bar graph representing the percentage Difference Matrix based on HSI function 'Entropy' and 'Standard Deviation' for the Alwar Image. Color codes are: Red- Entropy and Blue-Standard Deviation.

Figure 3 presents the bar graph representing the percentage Difference Matrix based on HSI function 'Entropy' and 'Standard Deviation' for the Alwar Image. The color codes are red for entropy and blue for standard deviation. Table 3 presents the table of the output percentage difference values which will be mapped to the corresponding feature indices which will form the classified image. The output percentage difference values are dynamically decided based on the HSI function chosen for the equivalence class under consideration. In other words, the function (entropy or standard deviation) which yields smaller percentage difference value is chosen as the HSI function and the corresponding feature index into which this HSI function classifies the equivalence class is taken as the output feature index into which the equivalence class will be classified finally. Table 4 represents the final feature index values for each of the equivalence classes. These feature index values are the values into which the equivalence class is classified into based on the dynamically decided HSI function. The feature index codes are 1-Barren, 2-Rocky, 3-Urban, 4-Vegetation and 5-Waterbody. Table 5 carries the information about the HSI function that was chosen for each of the equivalence classes based on the criteria of maximization of classification accuracy at runtime. The HSI function codes are 1 is for entropy and 2 is for standard deviation.

Table 3. Resultant Percentage Difference matrix based on the dynamically decided HSI function for the considered portion of the Alwar image.

Result % difference matrix (based on dynamic HSI function) for equivalence class $(U_{i=1}^{9}\, i)$ in the considered partition (z=16)	1	2	3
1	1.8155	1.4522	1.5695
2	1.0300	3.2664	3.8690
3	3.1855	2.1780	0.0000

Table 4. Classified feature index matrix based on dynamically decided HSI function for a portion of the Alwar image. The feature index codes are 1-Barren, 2-Rocky, 3-Urban, 4-Vegetation and 5-Waterbody.

Classified Feature Index based on dynamic HSI function for equivalence class $(U_{i=1}^{9}\, i)$ in the considered partition (z=16)	1	2	3
1	5	2	4
2	2	2	3
3	3	3	0

Table 5. HSI functions chosen dynamically for each equivalence class in the considered portion of the Alwar image. The HSI function codes are 1-Entropy and 2-Standard Deviation.

Dynamic HSI function for equivalence class $(U_{i=1}^{9}\, i)$ in the considered partition (z=16)	1	2	3
1	1	2	1
2	2	2	1
3	1	1	2

5.3   Feature Extraction Results on the Portion of Alwar Image

The classified image of the considered portion of the Alwar image (z=16th partition) is obtained in figure 4 which clearly shows the extraction of land cover features of water, urban, rocky and vegetation (barren feature is absent in the input image, hence its extraction cannot be shown for the considered portion) . The yellow color represents rocky area, green color represents vegetation area, black color represents barren area and red color represents the urban area.

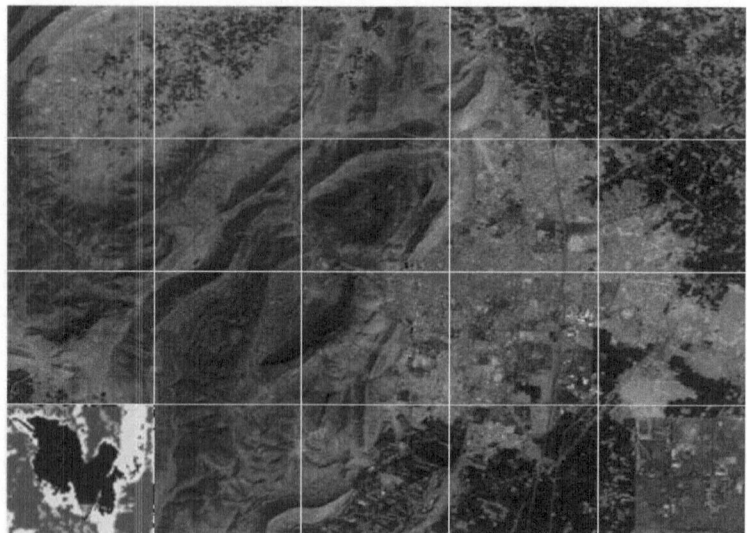

Fig. 4. Final Classified image of the portion of Alwar region after applying dynamic biogeography based land cover feature extractor

6   Conclusion and Future Scope

The main argument in the paper is to propose an algorithm that adapts to dynamic changes in the definition of HSI due to changes in species population during the optimization process. This is required since the mix of species and their evolution pattern has significant effect on physical characteristics of habitat and their contribution to HSI. Thus, there is change in HSI function due to factors other than migration also. This means that HSI function is required to be dynamic reflecting changes in population mix due to migration as well as factors other than migration during optimization process. This implies that if different population mixes characterize different habitats, then HSI function for these habitats will be different and the no. of SIVs for each of these habitats will also be different based on their population mixes.

We demonstrate the performance of the extended BBO by running it on the real world problem of land cover feature extraction in a satellite image. The proposed technique of dynamic selection of the applicable HSI function has been demonstrated on a portion of the dataset of Alwar region in Rajasthan for achieving maximal classification accuracy that is possible with the available operators. The results of applying the proposed extended biogeography based optimization algorithm for the purpose of land cover feature extraction in multi-spectral satellite images in this paper are preliminary and can be refined in future developments for the extraction of more land cover features and for a more efficient extraction by setting a threshold level and refining the results with each iteration, thus increasing the kappa coefficient (classification efficiency) further.

References

1. Goel, L., Gupta, D., Panchal, V.K.: Hybrid bio-inspired techniques for land cover feature extraction: A remote sensing perspective. Applied Soft Computing Journal 12, 832–849 (2012)
2. Goel, L., Panchal, V.K., Gupta, D.: Embedding Expert knowledge to Hybrid Bio-Inspired Techniques- An Adaptive Strategy Towards Focused Land Cover Feature Extraction. International Journal of Computer Science & Information Security 8(2), 244–253 (2010)
3. Ergezer, M., Simon, D.: Oppositional biogeography-based optimization for combinatorial problems. In: IEEE Congress on Evolutionary Computation (2011)
4. Panchal, V., Singh, P., Kaur, N., Kundra, H.: Biogeography based satellite image classification. International Journal of Computer Science and Information Security 6(2), 269–274 (2009)
5. Kiefer, R.W., Lillesand, T.M.: Principles of Remote Sensing (2006)
6. Rarick, R., Simon, D., Villaseca, F.E., Vyakaranam, B.: Biogeography-based optimization and the solution of the power flow problem. In: Proceedings of the IEEE Conference on Systems, Man, and Cybernetics, pp. 1029–1034 (2009)
7. Bhattacharya, Chattopadhyay, P.: Application of biogeography-based optimization for solving multi-objective economic emission load dispatch problems. Electric Power Components and Systems 38(3), 340–365 (2010)
8. Rashid, B.K., Khambampati, A., Kim, S., Kim, K.: An oppositional biogeography-based optimization technique to reconstruct organ boundaries in the human thorax using electrical impedance tomography. Physiological Measurement 32(7), 767–796 (2011)
9. Simon, D.: Biogeography Based Optimization. IEEE Transactions on Evolutionary Computation 12(6) (2008)
10. Simon, D.: A Dynamic System Model of Biogeography based Optimization 11(8), 5652–5661 (2011)
11. Ma, H.: An analysis of the equilibrium of migration models for biogeography-based optimization. Information Sciences 180, 3444–3464 (2010)
12. Ma, H., Simon, D.: Blended Biogeography based optimization for constrained optimization. Engineering Applications of Artificial Intelligence 24(3), 517–525 (2011)
13. Ma, H., Ni, S., Sun, M.: Equilibrium Species Counts and Migration Model Tradeoffs for Biogeography based Optimization. In: IEEE Conference on Decision and Control, pp. 3306–3310 (2009)
14. Kundra, H., Kaur, A., Panchal, V.: An integrated approach to biogeography based optimization with case based reasoning for retrieving groundwater possibility. In: Proceedings of the Eighth Annual Asian Conference and Exhibition on Geospatial Information, Technology and Applications (2009)
15. Briggs, J.C.: Biogeography and Plate Tectonics (1987)
16. http://users.rcn.com/jkimball.ma.ultranet/BiologyPages/P/Populations2.html
17. http://en.wikipedia.org/wiki/Population_growth
18. Gupta, S., Arora, A., Panchal, V.K., Goel, S.: Extended Biogeography Based Optimization for Natural Terrain Feature Classification from Satellite Remote Sensing Images. In: Aluru, S., Bandyopadhyay, S., Catalyurek, U.V., Dubhashi, D.P., Jones, P.H., Parashar, M., Schmidt, B. (eds.) IC3 2011. CCIS, vol. 168, pp. 262–269. Springer, Heidelberg (2011)

Grenade Explosion Method for Maximum Weight Clique Problem

Manohar Pallantla and Alok Singh

Department of Computer and Information Sciences,
University of Hyderabad, Hyderabad 500 046, India
pmanohar_mvgr@yahoo.co.in
alokcs@uohyd.ernet.in

Abstract. Maximum weight clique problem is an NP-Hard problem which seeks the fully connected subgraph of maximum weight in a given vertex weighted graph G. In this paper, we have used a recently proposed metaheuristic technique called Grenade Explosion Method (GEM) to solve the maximum weight clique problem. GEM was originally designed for continuous optimization problems. We have suitably modified the GEM so that it can be applied to a discrete optimization problem. To our knowledge this is the first approach which uses GEM for the discrete optimization. Computational results on the benchmark instances show the effectiveness of our proposed GEM approach.

Keywords: Combinatorial Optimization, Grenade Explosion Method, Heuristic, Maximum Weight Clique Problem.

1   Introduction

A clique in an undirected graph $G = (V, E)$ is a subset S of the vertex set V, such that for every two vertices in S, there exists an edge connecting the two. This is equivalent to saying that the subgraph induced by S is complete. A maximal clique is a clique that cannot be extended further, that is, a clique which does not exist exclusively within the vertex set of a larger clique. A maximum clique is a maximal clique of the largest possible size in a given graph. Maximum weight clique problem is an extension of maximum clique problem where the vertices are assumed to have positive weights and the aim is to find a clique with maximum weight. Both Maximum clique and maximum weight clique problems are NP-Hard [1]. These problems are also hard to approximate [2]. . Both maximum clique and maximum weight clique problem find practical applications in diverse domains such as computer vision, pattern recognition, robotics, fault tolerance etc.

Many exact and heuristic algorithms have been proposed for the maximum weight clique problem. Among the heuristic technique, Balas and Niehaus [3] proposed a steady-state genetic algorithm that uses a specially designed crossover operator called optimized crossover. The optimized crossover takes two cliques as input and produces a single offspring by finding the maximum weight clique in the subgraph induced by union of vertices present in the two input cliques. The maximum weight clique in the subgraph is found by solving the maximum flow problem in the complement of the

M. Parashar et al. (Eds.): IC3 2012, CCIS 306, pp. 20–27, 2012.
© Springer-Verlag Berlin Heidelberg 2012

subgraph. Bomze et al. [4] proposed an approximation method based on replicator dynamics. Massaro et al. [5] developed a complementary pivoting based heuristic called PBH using the continuous formulation of maximum weight clique problem based on Motzkin-Struss theorem [6]. Busygin [7] also used continuous formulation to develop a new trust region based technique called QUALEX-MS. Singh and Gupta [8] developed WT-HSS, a hybrid evolutionary approach combining a steady-state genetic algorithm with a greedy heuristic. The WT-HSS was compared with PBH and QUALEX-MS and it outperformed both these approaches.

In this paper we have developed a hybrid approach combining a new metaheuristic technique called Grenade Explosion Method (GEM) with a heuristic. Ahrari and Atai [9] proposed GEM after carefully observing the process of grenade explosion. We have compared our approach against the best heuristic approach reported in the literature. Computational results show the effectiveness of our approach.

The remainder of this paper is organized as follows: Section 2 provides a brief introduction to grenade explosion method. Our hybrid approach is presented in Section 3. Computational results are presented in Section 4, whereas section 5 provides some concluding remarks.

2 Grenade Explosion Method (GEM)

Grenade Explosion Method (GEM) is a population based new metaheuristic technique designed by Ahrari and Atai [9] by observing the grenade explosion phenomenon. Actually, when a grenade explodes, pieces of shrapnel can damage the objects which are within a certain distance L_e from explosion site. This distance is called the length of explosion. The loss due to each piece of shrapnel is computed and a high value of loss per shrapnel indicates the presence of valuable objects in the vicinity of the explosion site. Therefore, to inflict more loss, the next grenade should be thrown where we got maximum loss. In this method the fitness is the loss occurred at the collision location.

GEM is an iterative algorithm that begins by generating a population of solutions randomly where each solution point represent the location of a grenade. So number of grenades N_g is same as the population size. Only restriction on initial population is that each member should be at a distance of R_t from other members. R_t is called the agent territory radius and is an important parameter of the algorithm. A higher value of R_t ensures that solution points are widely separated in search space, whereas a low value of R_t may yield solution points close to one another. The parameter R_t can be adjusted during the iterations of the algorithm. Once initial population is generated, the iterative phase of the GEM begins. During each iteration, grenades are processed one-by-one according to non-increasing order of their fitness by producing N_q pieces of shrapnel around each grenade, i.e., N_q new solution points are generated in the neighborhood of each solution point i, i.e., the location of grenade i. Each of these solution points has to be within distance L_e of solution point i and has to be at least a distances of R_t from other population members. The best among these N_q solution points will be the new location grenade i in the next iteration. Like R_t, the value of L_e can also be adjusted during the iterations of the algorithm. Ahrari and Atai [9] suggested to use higher values of L_e and R_t during initial iterations and then decrease their values gradually. The method for generating neighboring solution varies from one problem to another. As Ahrari and Atai originally designed GEM for continuous optimization, they generated the neighboring solution points by adding a random quantity in each coordinate of the current solution point. Once the new location for all grenades are determined the next iteration of GEM begins. The whole process is repeated till the termination condition is satisfied. For further details of the GEM, please refer to [9].

3   Hybrid GEM for Maximum Weight Clique Problem

We have developed a hybrid approach combining GEM with a heuristic. The heuristic first converts the subgraph obtained through into GEM into a clique and then extends it into a maximal weight clique. Actually, the GEM algorithm is originally designed for the continuous optimization, but we are using it for discrete optimization, so we have made some suitable changes in the algorithm in order to use it to solve the maximum weight clique problem. The main features of our hybrid approach are described below:

3.1   Solution Encoding and Fitness

We have encoded a solution by the set of nodes of the clique it represents. Fitness of a solution is equal to the sum of the weights of the node present in the clique represented by it, i.e., the fitness function is same as the objective function.

3.2   Generating New Cliques in the Neighborhood of a Clique

The procedure of generating new population around each clique (grenade) work as follows: We randomly replace some nodes in that clique with some other nodes that are not already there in that clique. Parameter L_e controls the number of nodes that will be replaced. Now, the resulting subgraph might not be a clique, so we first convert it into a clique and then further extend it into a maximum weight clique using a heuristic which is described in the next subsection. Now, we have to check whether the newly generated clique is at a distance of R_t apart from all the existing cliques, i.e., whether the newly generated clique differs at R_t nodes from other cliques or not. If it is closer than R_t then ignore that solution, otherwise accept that solution. In this manner, we will generate N_q number of solutions around each solution where N_q is the parameter of the algorithm.

3.3   The Heuristic

We have used the same procedures as used in [8] to convert a subgraph into a clique and then extend it into a maximal weight clique. There are two reasons for making such a choice. First of all, our primary aim was to demonstrate the applicability of GEM on a discrete optimization problem. By choosing the same procedures as used in [8], we can attribute the improvements, if any, in solution quality over those reported in [8] to the use of GEM. Second reason was that these procedures work so well that whatever alternative procedures we tried, we were not able to outperform them. These two procedures are described below.

A subgraph is transformed into a clique iteratively. During each iteration, a node, say v, is selected randomly and the set S of all those nodes present in the subgraph which are not connected to v is computed. With probability p_d we delete the nodes in S from the subgraph, otherwise, we compute the average of the product of the weight and the degree of the nodes in S. This average is multiplied with a constant factor c_f. If the result is greater than the product of the weight and the degree of v then v is deleted from the subgraph, otherwise the nodes in S are deleted. This process is repeated till the subgraph is transformed into a clique.

In order to extend a clique to a maximal weight clique, we begin by computing the set S_{ad} of those nodes which are adjacent to all nodes in the clique. Then we add a node from S_{ad} to the clique. This node is selected either randomly or it is a node that has the maximum product of weight and local degree (degree in the subgraph induced by S_{ad}). The parameter p_r determines the probability of random selection. S_{ad} is recomputed and if it is non empty then the whole process is repeated, otherwise the procedure stops.

3.4   Initial Population Generation

In order to generate each member of the initial population, we first generate a subgraph were each node is included in the subgraph with probability of p_e. Then this subgraph is transformed into a maximal weight clique by using the heuristic described in the previous section.

For each newly generated solution, it is checked whether this new solution is at least at a distance of R_t apart from the existing population members. If it is so then it is included in the initial population, otherwise it is discarded.

4   Computational Results

The GEM approach for Maximum Weight Clique Problem has been coded in C and executed on an Intel core 2 quad system with 4 GB RAM running at 2.83 GHz under Ubuntu 9.04. In all our experiments, in order to generate a neighboring solution we replace two nodes, i.e., L_e=2. We have used Number of grenades (N_g) = 50, number of shrapnel (N_q) = 20, Agent territory radius (R_t) = 1, p_d = 0.5, c_f = 1.1, p_r = 0.4 and p_e = 0.2. All the parameter values were chosen empirically after a large number of trials. The values of last 4 parameters were found to be equal to those used in [8]. We have executed our GEM approach until either the optimal solution is found (if known) or for a maximum of 500 iterations. If a solution does not improve over 200 iterations, we replace that solution with a new solution that is generated in the same manner as a solution for initial population.

We have compared our GEM approach against WT-HSS [8] which is the best heuristic approach known so far on the same instances as used in [8]. These instances are divided into three classes – normal, irregular and Östergard. First two classes consist of normal and irregular graphs of different node sizes and edge densities. These two classes of graphs are used to test the performance of different approaches proposed in [4, 5, 7, 8]. Irregular graphs were generated using algorithm 4.1 of [4]. Node weights were integers distributed uniformly at random in the range [1, 10]. For each of the two classes of graphs, a family of 20 random graphs was generated for a particular node size and edge density, For each graph of a family the ratio of largest weight clique found by an algorithm to the actual maximum weight clique expressed in percentage was calculated. The performance of an algorithm was measured in terms of average ratio over the whole family. Actual maximum weight cliques were found using the exact algorithm proposed in [10].

Table 1. Performance of GEM and WT-HSS on normal random weight graphs

N	Density	GEM Avg. Ratio	WT-HSS Avg. Ratio
100	0.10	100.00%	100.00%
100	0.20	100.00%	100.00%
100	0.30	100.00%	100.00%
100	0.40	100.00%	100.00%
100	0.50	100.00%	100.00%
100	0.60	100.00%	100.00%
100	0.70	100.00%	100.00%
100	0.80	100.00%	100.00%
100	0.90	100.00%	99.94%
100	0.95	100.00%	99.98%
200	0.10	100.00%	100.00%
200	0.20	100.00%	100.00%
200	0.30	100.00%	100.00%
200	0.40	100.00%	100.00%
200	0.50	100.00%	100.00%
200	0.60	100.00%	100.00%
200	0.70	100.00%	99.92%
200	0.80	100.00%	99.91%
300	0.10	100.00%	100.00%
300	0.20	100.00%	100.00%
300	0.30	100.00%	100.00%
300	0.40	100.00%	100.00%
300	0.50	100.00%	100.00%
300	0.60	99.91%	99.86%
300	0.70	100.00%	99.15%
300	0.80	99.80%	99.39%

Tables 1 and 2 compare the performance of GEM with WT-HSS on normal and irregular graphs respectively. Both GEM and WT-HSS were executed once on each instance. Data for WT-HSS is taken from [8]. Table 1 clearly shows the superiority of GEM. GEM is able to solve optimally all instances upto the size 200. There are only two graph families of size 300 where GEM is not able to solve all instances optimally. Even on these two families average ratio of GEM is better. Both GEM and WT-HSS are able to solve all irregular instances optimally as shown in the table 2. Execution times are not reported as they are less than a second for all instances.

There are 15 benchmark instances for the maximum weight clique problem based on real life coding theory problems. These instances were proposed by Östergard [10]. Number of nodes varies from 132 to 8914 in these instances. Table 3 shows the performance of GEM and WT-HSS on these benchmark instances. Both GEM and WT-HSS were executed 20 independent times on each benchmark instance. Table 3 reports the best and average cliques found by GEM and WT-HSS on each instance. It also reports the percentage number of times (%Opt.), the optimal solution was found by GEM and WT-HSS over all their runs and the average execution time in seconds to find the best solution. Data for WT-HSS is taken from [8]. Both GEM and WT-HSS were able to find the optimal value at least once for all instances. However, the GEM is superior to WT-HSS in terms of solution quality. There are 13 and 9 instances respectively for GEM and WT-HSS for which %Opt is 100% indicating that

Table 2. Performance of GEM and WT-HSS on irregular random weight graphs

N	Density	GEM	WT-HSS
		Avg. Ratio	Avg. Ratio
100	0.10	100.00%	100.00%
100	0.20	100.00%	100.00%
100	0.30	100.00%	100.00%
100	0.40	100.00%	100.00%
100	0.50	100.00%	100.00%
100	0.60	100.00%	100.00%
100	0.70	100.00%	100.00%
100	0.80	100.00%	100.00%
100	0.90	100.00%	100.00%
100	0.95	100.00%	100.00%
200	0.10	100.00%	100.00%
200	0.20	100.00%	100.00%
200	0.30	100.00%	100.00%
200	0.40	100.00%	100.00%
200	0.50	100.00%	100.00%
200	0.60	100.00%	100.00%
200	0.70	100.00%	100.00%
200	0.80	100.00%	100.00%
300	0.10	100.00%	100.00%
300	0.20	100.00%	100.00%
300	0.30	100.00%	100.00%
300	0.40	100.00%	100.00%
300	0.50	100.00%	100.00%
300	0.60	100.00%	100.00%
300	0.70	100.00%	100.00%
300	0.80	100.00%	100.00%

Table 3. Performance of GEM and WT-HSS on Östergard benchmark instances

Instance	n	opt	GEM				WT-HSS			
			Best	Avg.	%Opt.	Time	Best	Avg.	%Opt.	Time[a]
11-4-4	150	34	34	34.00	100%	0.03	34	34.00	100%	0.03
12-4-6	230	110	110	110.00	100%	0.49	110	109.30	95%	0.26
14-4-7	223	282	282	280.30	75%	1.50	282	277.70	65%	0.41
14-6-6	807	42	42	42.00	100%	0.20	42	42.00	100%	0.28
16-4-5	156	322	322	322.00	100%	0.29	322	321.65	95%	0.19
16-8-8	2246	30	30	30.00	100%	0.04	30	30.00	100%	0.06
17-4-4	132	156	156	156.00	100%	0.03	156	156.00	100%	0.02
17-6-6	558	70	70	70.00	100%	1.09	70	67.50	50%	0.71
19-4-6	263	1448	1448	1448.00	100%	0.96	1448	1437.20	70%	0.67
19-8-8	2124	62	62	62.00	100%	0.90	62	62.00	100%	2.13
20-6-5	1302	84	84	84.00	100%	0.06	84	84.00	100%	1.70
20-6-6	1490	190	190	189.00	90%	10.71	190	187.50	75%	11.60
20-8-10	2510	83	83	83.00	100%	0.06	83	83.00	100%	0.18
20-10-9	5098	26	26	26.00	100%	0.56	26	26.00	100%	6.58
20-10-10	8914	46	46	46.00	100%	1.70	46	46.00	100%	6.92

[a]Execution time on a Pentium 4 system with 512 MB RAM running at 2.6 GHz under Red Hat Linux 9.0

these algorithms were able to find the optimal solutions in all 20 runs for these instances. For the two instances were GEM was not able to find optimal solution in all 20 trials, the average solution quality of GEM is better. As far as comparison of execution times are concerned, they are not directly comparable as WT-HSS is executed on a Pentium 4 system with 512MB RAM running at 2.6GHz under Red Hat Linux 9.0, which is different from the system used to execute GEM. However, a rough comparison can always be made which indicates that on some instances GEM is faster, whereas on other instances WT-HSS is faster. Overall, WT-HSS seems to be slightly faster than GEM, but GEM compensates it by returning solutions of better quality.

5   Conclusions

In this paper we have proposed a hybrid approach for the Maximum Weight Clique Problem combining a new metaheuristic technique called Grenade Explosion Method (GEM) with a heuristic. Computational results on the benchmark instances show the effectiveness of the proposed approach. Our approach outperformed the previous best approach on both Östergard as well as randomly generated instances.

GEM was originally designed for continuous optimization problems. To our knowledge this is the first approach which uses GEM for the discrete optimization. Approaches similar to our approach can be designed for other discrete optimization problems.

References

1. Garey, M.R., Johnson, D.S.: Computers and Intractability: A Guide to the Theory of NP-Completeness. W. H. Freeman, San Francisco (1979)
2. Khot, S.: Improved inapproximability results for maxclique, chromatic number and approximate graph coloring. In: Proc. of the 42nd Annual IEEE Symposium on the Foundations of Computer Science, pp. 600–609 (2001)
3. Balas, E., Niehaus, W.: Optimized crossover-based genetic algorithms for the maximum cardinality and maximum weight clique problems. Journal of Heuristics 4, 107–122 (1998)
4. Bomze, I.M., Pelillo, M., Stix, V.: Approximating the maximum weight clique using the replicator dynamics. IEEE Transactions on Neural Networks 11, 1228–1241 (2000)
5. Massaro, A., Pellilo, M., Bomze, I.M.: A complementary pivoting approach to the maximum weight clique problem. SIAM Journal of Optimization 12, 928–948 (2002)
6. Motzkin, T.S., Strauss, E.G.: Maxima for graphs and a new proof of theorem of turan. Canadian Journal of Mathematics 17, 533–540 (1965)
7. Busygin, S.: A new trust region technique for the maximum weight clique problem. Discrete and Applied Mathematics 154, 2080–2096 (2006)
8. Singh, A., Gupta, A.K.: A hybrid evolutionary approach to the maximum weight clique problem. International Journal of Computational Intelligence Research 2, 349–355 (2006)
9. Ahrari, A., Atai, A.A.: Grenade explosion method – a novel tool for optimization of multimodal functionds. Applied Soft Computing 10, 1132–1140 (2010)
10. Östergard, P.R.J.: A new algorithm for the maximum weight clique problem. Nordic Journal of Computing 8, 424–436 (2001)

A Greedy Heuristic and Its Variants for Minimum Capacitated Dominating Set

Anupama Potluri and Alok Singh

Department of Computer and Information Sciences,
University of Hyderabad, Gachibowli, Hyderabad - 500046, India
{apcs,alokcs}@uohyd.ernet.in

Abstract. The Minimum Capacitated Dominating Set (CAPMDS) problem is the problem of finding a dominating set of minimum cardinality with the additional constraint that the nodes dominated do not exceed the capacity of the dominating node. The capacity can be uniform across all nodes or variable. Being a generalization of the Minimum Dominating Set problem, this problem also $\mathcal{NP}$-hard. In this paper, we present a heuristic and a couple of its variants for solving the CAPMDS problem. Our heuristics work for both uniform and variable capacity graphs. We show that the heuristic proposed is better than the variants, in general. However, for Unit Disk Graphs with high degree of connectivity and uniform capacity, one of the variants performs better. For general graphs, the proposed heuristic is far superior to the variants.

Keywords: Minimum Capacitated Dominating Set, Heuristics, Clustering, Wireless Networks.

1   Introduction

The concept of clustering or allocating centers and assigning nodes to these centers is very much in use in many applications, especially communication networks but also in distributed databases and distributed data structures [1]. Clustering in wireless networks has mostly been done using the concept of Minimum Dominating Set (MDS) or Minimum Independent Dominating Set (MIDS). However, nodes have limited bandwidth as well as limited battery power. Hence, load balancing when forming clusters is an important consideration. This leads to the concept of a bounded capacity for every node, where the capacity represents the number of nodes that the node in question can service at the most. Such a dominating set, where the number of dominated nodes does not exceed a capacity, is called the Capacitated Dominating Set (CAPDS). The problem of finding a capacitated dominating set with the minimum cardinality (CAPMDS) is proven to be $\mathcal{NP}$-hard [2]. The capacity of a node can be uniform, i.e., every node in the graph has the same capacity or it can be variable. In homogeneous networks with similar nodes, the capacity of each node is same, whereas in heterogeneous networks with nodes containing different types of network interfaces, the bandwidth or the capacity of the node is variable. Similarly, the battery life of the nodes can vary depending on their type as well as their power consumption.

M. Parashar et al. (Eds.): IC3 2012, CCIS 306, pp. 28–39, 2012.

Formally, the capacitated dominating set is defined as follows: a graph $G = (V, E)$ is given. Every node $v \in V$ has a capacity denoted by $cap(v) \geq 1$. The open neighborhood of a node is defined as $\Gamma(v) = \{u : (u, v) \in E\}$. A capacitated dominating set is a subset $S \subseteq V$ such that there is a mapping $\phi : V \to S$ such that $\phi(v) \in \Gamma(v)$ and $|\{u \mid \phi(u) = v\}| \leq cap(v)$ for all $v \in S$.

A graph $G = (V, E)$ is said to be a Bounded-Independence Graph (BIG) if the size of the Maximum Independent Set of the r-hop neighborhood of a node v, $\Gamma_r(v)$, is bounded by a function $f(r), \forall r \geq 0$. If the function $f(r)$ is a polynomial $O(r^c)$, where $c \geq 1$, such graphs are called polynomially bounded growth graphs [3], [4]. BIGs, especially, polynomially-bounded growth graphs are typically used to model wireless communication networks.

Bar-Ilan et. al. [1] present many approximation algorithms for the problems of network center allocation such that the allocation does not exceed a capacity L on the nodes, i.e., the allocation is balanced. Here, centers are the dominating nodes. In particular, they consider two types of center allocation problems with load balancing: first, where the number of centers is fixed, say k, and the problem is to minimize the maximum distance between any center and an assigned node. The second problem is to fix a bound ρ on the maximum distance of a node from a dominating node and minimizing the number of centers, given the capacity. The latter is called the ρ-dominating set by Bar-Ilan et al. It is this problem that we consider in this paper. They present a greedy algorithm for the case of uniform capacity nodes which is proven to be an approximation algorithm with a ratio of $\lceil \ln N \rceil$ where N is the total number of nodes in the graph. A distributed approximation algorithm has been presented by Kuhn and Moscibroda [5], where they prove that, in general graphs, even with uniform capacity, the problem is non-local in nature. They present an approximation local algorithm for the case where the capacity may be violated by some parameter $\epsilon > 0$. They also present a constant factor distributed approximation algorithm for the special case of capacitated domination in Bounded-Independence Graphs (BIGs) with uniform capacity [5].

In this paper, we present a greedy heuristic and its variants to compute the solution to the ρ-dominating set problem defined by Bar-Ilan et al., with $\rho = 1$. We show that the results of these heuristics vary quite a bit, especially with general graphs. The rest of this paper is organized as follows: we review the related work in section 2, describe the heuristic algorithms in section 3, experimentation and discussion of the results in section 4 and conclude with section 5.

2 Related Work

The algorithm proposed by Bar-Ilan et. al. for the ρ-dominating set of a graph with uniform capacity is as follows: construct a bi-partite graph with dominating nodes forming one partition and the unassigned nodes the second partition. Now, two new vertices s and t are added to the graph. s is connected to every dominating node and t to every unassigned node. If the uniform capacity of each node is c, the edge from s is given a weight of $c - 1$ and every edge from dominating nodes to other nodes as well as every edge coming into t have a weight of 1. The integral max-flow algorithm is run on this bi-partite graph. Every node v, whose flow $f(u, v) > 0$, chooses u to be its dominating node. In each iteration, the algorithm selects a node not yet in the dominating set, adds it temporarily to the set of dominating nodes and repeats the above process. At the end of the iterations, the node which yields the minimum number of unassigned nodes is added to the dominating set being constructed and the nodes covered by it are added to its cluster. The construction of the bi-partite graph and the whole process is then repeated until there are no more unassigned nodes in the graph. As stated earlier, this algorithm is proven to return a cardinality not more than $OPT \times \ln N$, where OPT is the cardinality of the optimal solution. However, the algorithm does not work for variable capacity graphs.

In [5], a constant distributed approximation algorithm is presented for BIGs with uniform capacity. The algorithm has two phases: in the first phase, a Maximal Independent Set (MIS) is found. It is well-known that any MIS is a dominating set. It is assumed that this MIS algorithm returns clusters of the form (u_i, C_i) where u_i is the center and C_i is the cluster associated with it, i.e., it is the set of all neighbors of u_i, which have been assigned to it. In a capacitated dominating set, we also need to ensure that capacity constraints are not violated. Hence, for every u_i whose capacity is violated, the second phase of the algorithm recursively computes an MIS such that a capacitated dominating set of size $O(|C_i| / cap)$ is computed. One of the proposed variants in this paper (in section 3.2) is similar to this algorithm, but does not use recursion. Hence, it is much simpler to implement.

3   Proposed Greedy Heuristic Algorithm and Its Variants

In this section, we describe three variants of a heuristic for the computation of a capacitated dominating set. These heuristics work for both uniform as well as variable capacity graphs. In all these heuristics, all the nodes in the graph are initially colored WHITE. Any node added to the dominating set is colored BLACK and the nodes covered by the dominating node are colored GREY. The heuristics terminate when there are no more WHITE nodes in the graph. The next three sub-sections describe our heuristics.

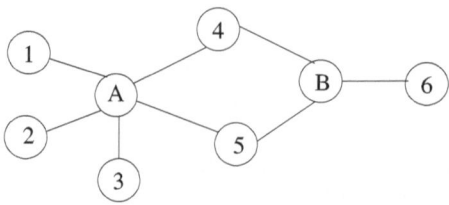

Fig. 1. Example Topology to illustrate the advantage of choosing a node with lower absolute degree as the dominating node when two nodes have the same $min(c_u, d_u)$ value, where c_u and d_u are the capacity and WHITE degree of node u respectively

3.1 Maximum Coverage-Lowest Degree Heuristic

This heuristic is based on the standard heuristic used for the Minimum Dominating Set problem, which is also the optimal approximation algorithm as described in [6]. Our algorithm works as follows: the node with the maximum number of WHITE neighboring nodes, d_v, that can be covered, given its capacity, c_v, is determined. This node is added to the dominating set. The nodes that are covered by this dominating node are chosen randomly from its set of neighbors. This process is repeated until there are no more WHITE nodes in the graph.

$$v \leftarrow \operatorname{argmax}_{u \in V} min(c_u, d_u) \tag{1}$$

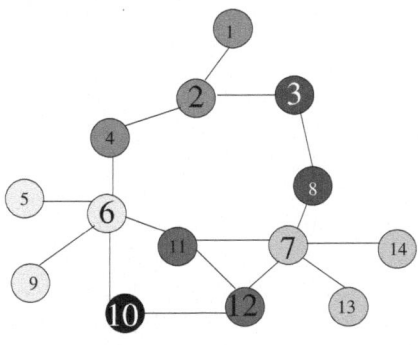

$$CapMDS = \{2, 3, 6, 7, 10, 12\}$$

Fig. 2. Example Topology with the CapMDS formed by the MC-LDEG algorithm

If two nodes have the same number of WHITE nodes that can be covered given their capacities, we can break the tie in many ways: choosing the first node found or choosing the node with the absolute lower degree are two such methods. We experimented with both these methods on various graphs. We found that in general graphs, as the size of the graph increases, the difference in cardinality between these two schemes becomes as large as 50-150 nodes with the latter giving better results. The reason for this difference can be explained as follows: consider the following scenario given in Fig. 1. Let each node have a uniform capacity of 3 (excluding itself) and all nodes are WHITE. Nodes A and B have the maximum number of WHITE nodes that can be covered given the capacity. If we choose A as the dominating node, we have a choice of covering nodes 4 and 5 or excluding them. If nodes 4 and 5 are included in the cluster of node A, then, we will need to include 3 more nodes in the dominating set - either B or 6, and let us say the two neighbors of A, 1 and 2. On the other hand, if B is chosen as the dominating node, it covers nodes 4, 5 and 6. Now, A will cover nodes 1, 2 and 3. Thus, the cardinality of the dominating set is two, whereas in the other case, it would have been four. We break the tie in the heuristic presented in this paper by selecting the node with the lower absolute degree.

Algorithm 1. *Maximum-Coverage Lowest-Degree Heuristic (MC-LDEG)(G = (V, E))*

$\overline{D} := \phi$
$maxCap := 0$
$maxDegree := 0$
$s := -1$
while $V \neq \phi$ **do**
  $v := \text{argmax}_{u \in V} \min(c_u, d_u)$
  if $((maxCap < \min(c_v, d_v)) \bigvee ((maxCap = \min(c_v, d_v)) \bigwedge (d_v < maxDegree)))$ **then**
    $maxCap := \min(c_v, d_v)$
    $maxDegree := d_v$
    $s := v$
  end if
  $\overline{D} := \overline{D} \cup \{v\}$
  $V := V \setminus s$
end while
return $\overline{D}$

An example topology with the solution returned by this algorithm is given in Fig. 2 when the capacity is uniform and is equal to 2. Nodes 2, 3, 4, 6, 7, 8, 10, 11, 12 all have 2 WHITE neighbors in the beginning and the capacity = 2. Thus, any of them can be included in the dominating set. However, of these the nodes with lowest absolute degree are 3, 4, 8, 10. Let us assume that it is the node with the lowest index that is chosen as the dominating node to break the tie this time. Thus, 3 becomes part of the dominating set. Its neighbors, 2 and 8 are colored GREY. At this point of time, the nodes which have ≥ 2 WHITE neighbors are 2, 6, 7, 10, 11, 12. The process is now repeated with these nodes and the final dominating set is shown with each cluster in a different color (shade) and the dominating nodes in a larger font as shown in Fig. 2.

The pseudo-code for this heuristic is given in Algorithm 1. In the rest of the paper, we refer to this heuristic as MC-LDEG heuristic.

3.2 Cluster-Subdivision Heuristic

This heuristic is based on the distributed approximation algorithm proposed for Bounded-Independence Graphs (BIGs) with uniform capacity in [5]. In this heuristic, we first calculate the Maximal Independent Set (MIS) of the given graph which is nothing but a dominating set of the graph exactly as in [5]. The non-dominating nodes in the graph are assigned to different dominating nodes to form clusters that are mutually disjoint. This is shown in Fig. 3, with the clusters being $\{2, \{1, 3, 4\}\}$, $\{6, \{5, 9, 10, 11\}\}$ and $\{7, \{8, 12, 13, 14\}\}$. If the capacity of a dominating node is not exceeded, the cluster is retained as it is and the dominating node is retained in the final capacitated dominating set. If the capacity of the dominating node is exceeded, the MC-LDEG algorithm is run on the cluster, i.e., on the subgraph induced by the dominating node and the nodes covered by it. Thus, we sub-divide the cluster into further clusters such that the capacity is not exceeded for any dominating node in the sub-clusters. We call this the C-SUBD heuristic in the

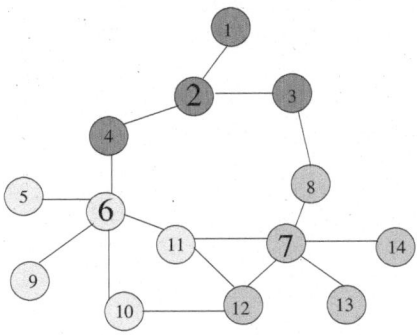

Maximal Independent Set MIS = {2, 6, 7}

Fig. 3. Example Topology with disjoint clusters formed using MIS. The MIS nodes are numbered in a bigger font.

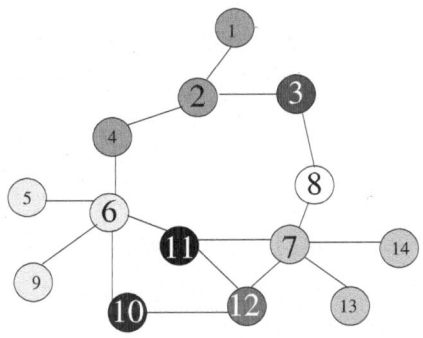

CapMDS = {2, 6, 7, 3, 8, 10, 11, 12}

Fig. 4. Running algorithm of C-SUBD now gives a dominating set whose members are numbered in a bigger font

rest of this paper. The pseudo-code for this heuristic is given in Algorithm 2. The result of running this heuristic on the topology of Fig. 3 is shown in Fig. 4. Since the nodes in each cluster are not connected to each other except through the cluster head, we end up with a large capacitated dominating set in this case.

3.3 Relax MIS Heuristic

This heuristic is similar to the C-SUBD heuristic, but differs in the procedure where the capacity of the dominating node is exceeded. As in C-SUBD heuristic, we find the

---

Algorithm 2. *Cluster-Subdivision Heuristic (C-SUBD)($G = (V, E)$)*

$\overline{D} := \phi$

Compute MIS, I of G and form disjoint Clusters (v, C_v) where v is the dominating node and C_v is the set of nodes that are dominated by v.

for all $v \in I$ **do**

   if $\mid C_v \mid \, > \, cap(v)$ **then**

      $\overline{D} := \overline{D} \cup \text{MC-LDEG}(C_v)$

   else

      $\overline{D} := \overline{D} \cup v$

   end if

end for

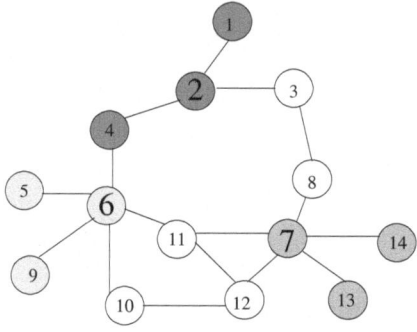

Maximal Independent Set MIS = {2, 6, 7}

Fig. 5. The excess nodes of the members of MIS are deleted from the clusters formed and colored WHITE

MIS of the graph initially. Then, unlike in C-SUBD where each cluster is further subdivided, we remove the excess nodes covered by any dominating node from its cluster by changing their color back to WHITE as shown in Fig. 5. The nodes to be removed from the cluster are selected randomly. We, now, run the MC-LDEG algorithm on the entire graph until there are no more WHITE nodes in the graph. We call this heuristic the DS-RELAX heuristic in the rest of the paper. The pseudo-code for this is given in Algorithm 3.

This heuristic differs from C-SUBD heuristic in that if there are excess nodes in two adjacent clusters which are adjacent to each other, they will be able to form a cluster together. In the previous heuristic, such nodes could not combine to form a single cluster. This can be seen in Fig. 6. Nodes 10, 11, 12 are removed from their respective clusters whose centers are 6, 7. These are adjacent to each other and can form a single cluster of their own without violating the capacity constraint. This is what happens in this heuristic. However, in C-SUBD, since they are part of different clusters, they cannot combine into a single cluster. The same is true for nodes 3, 8.

Algorithm 3. *Relax MIS Heuristic (DS-RELAX)*$(G = (V, E))$

$\overline{D} := \phi$

Compute MIS, $\overline{D}$ of G and form Clusters (v, C_v) where v is the dominating node and C_v is the set of nodes that are dominated by v.

for all $v \in \overline{D}$ **do**

  if $| C_v | > cap(v)$ **then**

    Mark all excess nodes of v WHITE

  end if

end for

$\overline{D} := \overline{D} \cup$ MC-LDEG(G)

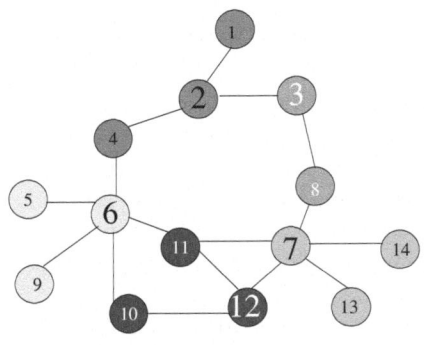

$$\text{CapMDS} = \{2, 6, 7, 3, 12\}$$

Fig. 6. Running algorithm DS-RELAX now gives a dominating set whose members are numbered in a bigger font

4   Experimentation and Discussion of Results

We have done extensive experimentation with both Unit Disk Graphs (UDGs) generated using the topology generator provided in [7] and general graph instances which have been taken from the Type I instances in [8]. We present the results of applying all the heuristics presented in this paper in Tables 1 - 4.

Capacitated dominating set finds use in wireless networks where the bandwidth may be the capacity of a node. The ratio of bandwidth of 802.11 (WiFi) interface to that of 802.16 (WiMAX) interface or a 3G/4G mobile interface is approximately 2:5. Hence, we have chosen the ratio of 2:5 for variable capacity of nodes in a graph. We use $(2, 5)$ or $(\alpha/5, \alpha/2)$ as the capacities of the nodes, where α is the average degree of the graph. We also tested our heuristics assuming that the capacity can be a value in the interval $[1 \cdots \alpha]$ as an additional test case. In the case of uniform capacity, we generated three different uniform capacities, viz., 2, 5 and average degree reperesented by α.

We experimented with six different graph sizes - 50, 100, 250, 500, 800 and 1000 nodes. In the case of UDGs, we used two different ranges - 150 and 200 units - in an area of 1000×1000 units to study the effect of degree of connectivity on the solutions. In the case of general graph instances, we experimented with different number of edges for each graph size. For every nodes/range combination in UDGs and nodes/edges combination in general graphs, the results presented are an average of the runs of the algorithm over 10 different instances.

4.1   Uniform Capacity Results

Table 1 lists the results of the heuristics for uniform capacity of 2, 5 and average degree (α) on UDG graphs. Table 2 lists the results for similar experimentation on general graph Type I instances from [8]. Given below are some of the observations on the results obtained.

1. In UDGs with node capacity = 2, the C-SUBD heuristic performs better than both the DS-RELAX and MC-LDEG heuristics as the graph size increases. Also, the difference in the cardinality increases as the degree of connectivity increases. DS-RELAX heuristic is the worst of the three for UDG instances for this capacity.

   For capacity = 5, MC-LDEG performs best of all three except for range=200 and nodes=800, 1000. Thus, when the degree of connectivity is very high, C-SUBD does slightly better than MC-LDEG for this capacity. DS-RELAX is also better than C-SUBD up to graphs of size 250 nodes. Beyond this size C-SUBD performs better than DS-RELAX.

   For capacity = α, the C-SUBD heuristic performs worse than the other two heuristics in all cases. MC-LDEG is the best heuristic in this case.

2. For general graphs, MC-LDEG always performs better than the other two heuristics. It becomes significantly better as the graph size, degree of connectivity and capacity increase. DS-RELAX is always better than C-SUBD for general graphs. C-SUBD heuristic is significantly worse than the other two heuristics for general graphs as the size of the graph and degree of connectivity increase.

This can be explained by the fact that the number of independent nodes is bounded in UDGs. As seen in topology in Fig. 4, having too many independent nodes in a cluster leads to larger dominating sets with the C-SUBD heuristic.

4.2   Variable Capacity Results

Table 3 lists the results obtained by the heuristics with variable capacity of (2, 5), ($\alpha/5$, $\alpha/2$) and in the range $[1 \cdots \alpha]$ for the nodes in UDG graphs. Table 4 compares the cardinality returned by the various heuristics with variable capacity on Type I graph instances from [8]. Given below are some of the observations on the results obtained.

1. The MC-LDEG heuristic performs best among the three for all variable capacity ranges in both UDG and general graphs.
2. When the capacity of nodes is either 2 or 5 in UDG graphs, the DS-RELAX heuristic does better than C-SUBD for graphs of sizes up to 250 nodes. With higher capacities such as $\alpha/2$ and $\alpha/5$, DS-RELAX does better for all sizes of graphs. For capacity in the closed interval $[1 \cdots \alpha]$, DS-RELAX and C-SUBD perform similarly.

Table 1. Cardinality (γ) of CAPMDS using C-SUBD, DS-RELAX and MC-LDEG for UDG Instances with a uniform capacity of 2, 5, average degree=α for every node

N	Range	C-SUBD			DS-RELAX			MC-LDEG		
		2	5	α	2	5	α	2	5	α
50	150	25	17.8	21.2	23.5	17.8	20.6	21.1	15.6	17.9
50	200	22.6	15.1	15.1	22.5	14.8	14.8	20.4	12.7	12.7
100	150	45.8	30.6	30.6	44.8	28.9	28.9	41.2	23.3	23.3
100	200	42.1	26.3	19.5	44.6	24.4	18.2	41.4	21	14.1
250	150	99.7	60.7	33.8	111.4	54.4	31.9	104	48.4	25.1
250	200	94.2	53.8	21.4	110.8	51	20	106.4	47.8	15.3
500	150	184.5	104.8	37.6	223.5	102.5	35	212.7	95.7	26.3
500	200	178.1	96.7	23	219.5	99	21.1	213.5	95.4	15.7
800	150	286.1	155.8	37.8	352.9	159.7	35.9	343.4	152.7	27.4
800	200	278.1	146.3	24.6	350.4	157.4	22.7	344.3	152	16.3
1000	150	352.3	190.4	39.2	438.2	199.4	36.6	428.4	190.8	27.2
1000	200	343.9	180.3	24	437.3	196.4	22.5	430.5	190.6	17

Table 2. Cardinality (γ) of CAPMDS using C-SUBD, DS-RELAX and MC-LDEG for Graph Instances in [8] with a uniform capacity of 2, 5 and average degree=α for every node

N	Edges	C-SUBD			DS-RELAX			MC-LDEG		
		2	5	α	2	5	α	2	5	α
50	100	26.7	17.9	18.6	23.2	17.9	18.6	20.3	14.2	15.2
50	250	26.8	18.4	11.2	22.3	13.8	11.2	19.9	10.1	7
50	500	22.3	14.1	7.4	21.7	11.6	7.1	19.3	9.5	4.2
100	100	43.8	43.4	43.8	43.8	43.4	43.8	43.6	39.5	43.6
100	250	56.3	35.6	35.6	46.3	34.9	34.9	39.3	26.1	26.1
100	500	60.6	36.3	24.1	44.4	27.8	23.7	39.6	21.1	15.3
250	250	109	108.6	109	109	108.6	109	108.8	100	108.8
250	500	133.5	91.4	95.6	116.8	91.3	94.8	99.4	71.1	77.7
250	1000	155.9	93	71.1	112.8	76.9	69.1	98.3	55.8	45.4
500	500	216.4	216.2	216.4	216.4	216.2	216.4	216.5	201.2	216.5
500	1000	271.1	185.7	195.5	237.2	185.5	192.5	199.2	141.2	153.4
500	2000	316.1	185.2	141.7	225.7	153.5	138.2	197	109.4	91.2
800	1000	380	332.5	380	374.5	332.5	374.5	330.8	281.3	330.8
800	2000	460.8	286.6	286.6	370.5	280.9	280.9	317.1	209.4	209.4
800	5000	550.4	354.9	182.4	358.4	214.7	173.9	313	156.8	104.3
1000	1000	431.8	431.4	431.8	431.8	431.4	431.8	431.7	399.5	431.7
1000	5000	670.5	412.5	255.4	450.7	287	245.5	391.6	205.7	152.6
1000	10000	722.4	513.3	164	444.2	238.9	157.9	391.3	187.7	88.7

3. For general graphs, with all variable capacities experimented with, the DS-RELAX heuristic performs better than C-SUBD heuristic. The difference becomes significant as the size of the graph as well as the average degree of connectivity increase.

Table 3. Cardinality (γ) of CAPMDS using C-SUBD, DS-RELAX and MC-LDEG for UDG Instances with a VARIABLE capacity of (2, 5), ($\alpha/5$, $\alpha/2$) and [1..α] for every node

N	Range	C-SUBD			DS-RELAX			MC-LDEG		
		(2,5)	**($\alpha/5,\alpha/2$)**	**[1..α]**	**(2,5)**	**($\alpha/5,\alpha/2$)**	**[1..α]**	**(2,5)**	**($\alpha/5,\alpha/2$)**	**[1..α]**
50	150	20.8	31.2	23.6	20.6	33.4	24.6	16.1	31	19.1
50	200	16.6	23.4	17.6	17.1	24.2	18.9	12.7	21.1	13.7
100	150	35	43	33.3	35	41.9	34	25.8	37.4	25.6
100	200	28.5	28	21.9	26.9	26.7	22.2	21.3	21	15.2
250	150	63.8	53.5	40	59.9	48.1	40.5	49.7	37.6	26.8
250	200	56.4	32.5	26	55.1	30.2	26.1	47.6	22.6	16.9
500	150	107.5	56.6	45.5	108	52.5	46.4	95.8	39.2	30
500	200	99.1	34.6	27.4	102.7	32.4	27.8	95.2	24.2	17.6
800	150	159.6	60.2	47.4	164.2	55.7	48.3	151.7	40.4	29.7
800	200	151.2	37	28.8	158.6	33.9	29.5	151.7	24.3	18
1000	150	194.6	62.8	48.1	201.3	57.6	49.7	189.2	41	29.8
1000	200	185.2	35.3	29.6	196.9	33.4	28.5	189	25.1	18.4

Table 4. Cardinality (γ) of CAPMDS using C-SUBD, DS-RELAX and MC-LDEG for Graph Instances in [8] with a VARIABLE capacity of (2, 5), ($\alpha/5$, $\alpha/2$) and [1..α] for the nodes

N	Edges	C-SUBD			DS-RELAX			MC-LDEG		
		(2,5)	**($\alpha/5,\alpha/2$)**	**[1..α]**	**(2,5)**	**($\alpha/5,\alpha/2$)**	**[1..α]**	**(2,5)**	**($\alpha/5,\alpha/2$)**	**[1..α]**
50	100	19.8	30.1	23.4	19.5	26.1	21.5	15.1	21.7	16.3
50	250	20.4	21.7	16.1	14.8	16	13.2	10.3	10.5	8.6
50	500	15.9	12.9	8	12.2	9.9	7.4	9.8	6	4.5
100	100	43.5	64.4	52	43.5	62.9	51.5	41.6	63.9	47.6
100	250	45.3	63.8	50.3	39.4	51.9	41.7	26.8	42.6	28.5
100	500	49.1	49.2	42	31.1	31.6	29.2	21.4	21.4	16.2
250	250	108.7	161.4	132.6	108.7	156.4	131.6	103.3	156.4	113.4
250	500	115.8	155.8	127.7	106.3	130.7	114.6	75.4	107.6	82.2
250	1000	125.7	150.7	107	87.3	97.2	82.5	57.6	65.6	49.5
500	500	216.3	324.6	274.3	216.3	316.4	272.4	209.4	314	231.2
500	1000	234.4	310.1	268.9	215.9	264.5	237	153.1	214	166.2
500	2000	260.3	290.4	231.4	175.3	190.7	168.7	115	131.1	98.6
800	1000	357.5	543	461.1	355.8	510	441.1	298.7	496.7	356.6
800	2000	371.9	527.5	409.5	324.1	413.2	340.3	222.4	339.6	228.7
800	5000	469.6	434.8	341.4	244.1	230.6	211.1	162.8	146.6	109.3
1000	1000	431.7	647.3	543.1	431.7	630.5	538.5	413	628.7	457.5
1000	5000	540.3	539.6	444.6	320.3	319.8	297.5	213.1	213.2	164.7
1000	10000	615.2	440.4	354.7	261.2	203	192.3	191.4	118.4	92.9

5   Conclusions

We have presented a heuristic for CAPMDS problem, MC-LDEG, which is based on the heuristic for MDS. We have also presented two other variants of this heuristic: C-SUBD, based on the algorithm proposed in [5] and DS-RELAX which is a variant of both the algorithm proposed in [5] as well as MC-LDEG. We have done extensive experimentation on UDG and general graph instances with both uniform and variable capacity. We find that the C-SUBD heuristic performs pretty well for UDGs with low uniform capacity, especially for those with higher degree of connectivity. On the other hand, it has extremely poor performance for general graphs and hence should never be used for general graphs. The DS-RELAX heuristic performs better than C-SUBD in general graphs and in UDGs with higher capacity. MC-LDEG heuristic is the best of the three variants. It performs significantly better than the other two heuristics for general graph instances with both uniform and variable capacity. It also performs better than them for UDGs with variable capacity and high uniform capacity. Thus, we can say that, in general, it is better to use the MC-LDEG algorithm for computing CAPMDS than the other two variants.

References

1. Bar-Ilan, J., Kortsarz, G., Peleg, D.: How to allocate network centers. Journal of Algorithms 15, 385–415 (1993)
2. Garey, M., Johnson, D.: Computers and tractability, a guide to the theory of np-completeness (1979)
3. Nieberg, T., Hurink, J.L.: A PTAS for the Minimum Dominating Set Problem in Unit Disk Graphs. In: Erlebach, T., Persinao, G. (eds.) WAOA 2005. LNCS, vol. 3879, pp. 296–306. Springer, Heidelberg (2006)
4. Schneider, J., Wattenhofer, R.: A log-star distributed maximal independent set algorithm for growth-bounded graphs. In: Proceedings of the Twenty-Seventh ACM Symposium on Principles of Distributed Computing, PODC 2008, pp. 35–44 (2008)
5. Kuhn, F., Moscibroda, T.: Distributed approximation of capacitated dominating sets. In: Proceedings of the Nineteenth Annual ACM Symposium on Parallel Algorithms and Architectures, SPAA 2007, pp. 161–170 (2007)
6. Wattenhoffer, R. (Distributed dominating set approximation),
   http://www.disco.ethz.ch/lectures/ss04/
   distcomp/lecture/chapter12.pdf
7. Mastrogiovanni, M.: The clustering simulation framework: A simple manual (2007),
   http://www.michele-mastrogiovanni.net/
   software/download/README.pdf
8. Jovanovic, R., Tuba, M., Simian, D.: Ant colony optimization applied to minimum weight dominating set problem. In: Proceedings of the 12th WSEAS International Conference on Automatic Control, Modelling and Simulation (ACMOS 2010), pp. 322–326 (2010)

Developing Heuristic for Subgraph Isomorphism Problem

Saifuddin Kaijar and S. Durga Bhavani

Department of Computer & Information Sciences,
University of Hyderabad, Hyderabad, India

Abstract. Subgraph isomorphism problem is an NP-hard problem and
the available algorithms are of exponential time complexity. Hence these
are not efficient for real world applications. A number of heuristic methods are proposed in the literature in this field. Ullmann[6] proposed a
solution for subgraph isomorphism problem in 1976, which is being referred till today. Ullmann's algorithm is refined to get better algorithms
in current literature. Cordella et al.[7] proposed an algorithm VF2, that
improves Ullmann's refinement. In this project, we propose a heuristic to
be applied to Ullmann's algorithm in order to reduce the search space.
We show that the proposed heuristic performs better than both Ullmann's and VF2 algorithm. The testing is done using a graph generation
software[12]. Further the heuristic algorithm is tested on the benchmark
data set [4]. Both the experiments show that our proposed heuristics
perform better for all type of graphs given in the benchmark data set.

Keywords: backtrack programming, graph similarity measure, isomorphism, graph matching.

1 Introduction

Graphs are universal data structures to represent human-understanding structures. Many real-life problems can be solved by modeling the underlying structure as a graph. In computer science, graphs are used to represent component
structures, networks of communication, data organization, the flow of computation, etc. Graph-theoretic methods have been applied in a variety of fields:
Analysis of chemical structures, pattern recognition, representation of Chinese
characters, recognition of 3-D objects in images and robotic vision. When graphs
are used to represent the object structure, comparison of two different objects can
be formulated by the search of correspondence between two attributed graphs,
representing the objects. So, by means of graph matching we can generalize the
structural matching or pattern matching problem.

Finding the correspondence between two graphs can be done using various
graph algorithm techniques. The most popular technique is isomorphism, which
detects the 1:1 correspondence between every pair of vertices of two input graphs.
Sometimes, due to noise of the real life data, we are only interested in approximate matching techniques. However matching is expensive from computational

M. Parashar et al. (Eds.): IC3 2012, CCIS 306, pp. 40–52, 2012.
© Springer-Verlag Berlin Heidelberg 2012

point of view. So, many algorithms are published in literature to reduce both time and space complexity.

In order to find the matching between two graphs, the correspondence between their structure and labels is to be determined. Two graphs which contain the same number of vertices connected in the same way are said to be isomorphic. A graph $G_1 = (V_1, E_1, \mu_1, \nu_1)$ is isomorphic to a subgraph of a graph $G_2 = (V_2, E_2, \mu_2, \nu_2)$, say $G_2' = (V_2', E_2', \mu_2', \nu_2')$, if there is a bijective function $f : V_1 \rightarrow V_2'$ such that, for every pair of vertices $v_i, v_j' \in V_1$, if $(v_i, v_j') \in E_1$, then $(f(v_i), f(v_j')) \in E_2'$. And this mapping must also preserve the labels on the vertices and edges. The function f is called a subgraph matching function. Subgraph isomorphism problem is a decision problem in which, given two graphs $G_1 = (V_1, E_1, \mu_1, \nu_1)$ and $G_2 = (V_2, E_2, \mu_2, \nu_2)$ as input, one must determine whether G_2 contains a subgraph that is isomorphic to G_1 or not, where G_1 is called a input graph and G_2 is called a target graph.

In this paper, we first give a detailed discussion about Ullmann refinement algorithm and VF2 algorithm that is required for gaining better understanding of the proposed technique. The algorithm proposed in this paper introduces new heuristics which make an improvement to these two existing algorithms. In the second part of the paper, we explain the basic outline of our proposed method and detail the method in further sections. We conclude by giving all the experimentation results and discussion.

2   Existing Approaches

Most of the earlier algorithms for subgraph isomorphism problems are based on the tree search with backtracking method. The main idea of backtracking based search tree algorithm is to build an isomorphic mapping from $G_1(k)$ (initially k=0) to a subgraph of G_2 and iteratively expand the matching $G_1(K+1)$ by adding an unused vertex that satisfies the necessary condition with respect to the previous matched pair of vertices. The backtrack procedure is called recursively in order to make further extensions to expand all the possible mappings. It is obvious that the efficiency of direct backtracking algorithm depends exponentially on the number of recursive calls it makes. In order to reduce the complexity, using some heuristic, we can easily prune unfruitful branches of search tree as early as possible.

Hence to reduce complexity Ullmann [6] proposed a tree search technique that starts with all the possible mappings between two input graphs and searching the entire search space.

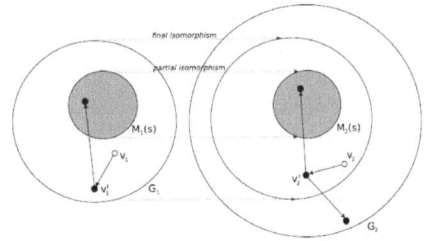

Fig. 1. Example of the additional checks executed by VF2. A vertex in G_1 will have to be mapped to a compatible vertex in G_2 in the future steps. If no compatible vertex in G_2 is available the partial mapping is doomed [11].

In order to calculate all possible mappings, Ullmann defines an *initial matrix* that holds all the possible correspondences between each of the pairs of vertices of the two input graphs. In order to reduce complexity a refinement procedure is used by Ullmann that eliminates some of the false positive entries from initial matrix. To define the refinement procedure he used a condition that for every pair of vertices in the initial matrix, if v_i is mapped to v_j then all the adjacencies of v_i of input graph should correspond to any of the adjacencies of vertex v_j of target graph. VF2 [7] is a procedure that improves Ullmann's refinement by reducing the number of backtracks with the help of a forward checking technique. It reduces total search space by using advanced data structures. They proposed a deterministic matching method for verifying both graph and subgraph isomorphism, which explores the search space by means of depth-first search technique. To represent the total search space they used a state space representation(SSR). To cope with large graphs they use adjacency list representation in place of Ullmann's adjacency matrix. The process of finding the mapping function can be suitably described by means of a set of rules, called *feasibility rules* that prune the search tree initially. Each time search tree holds only for those branches that satisfy these rules. Each state S of the matching process can be associated to a partial mapping solution. Each time it adds a new *pair(v, w)* to the partial solution and checks the validity of partial mapping.

That validity checking is done by feasibility rules. Those feasibility rules are dependent on the structure of the input graphs.

3   Motivation

VF2 [7] algorithm generally works efficiently. But a close walk through the algorithm reveals a shortcoming that increases the algorithmic computation time. According to VF2 the mapping is expressed as a set of $pair(i, j)$ (with $i \in G_1$ and $j \in G_2$) each representing the mapping of vertex i of G_1 with a vertex j of G_2. Now let's consider the following situation given in Figure 2:

According to VF2 algorithm v_i corresponds to anyone of $\{v_{j1}, v_{j2}, v_{j3}\}$, because all the pairs i.e. $\{(v_i, v_{j1}), (v_i, v_{j2}), (v_i, v_{j3})\}$ satisfy the *feasibility rules*, proposed by Cordella[7], but VF2 in any way does not give an optimum solution i.e it does not point the efficient pair among the available. This shortcoming is the central motivation of our proposed method. In the case of big graphs the number of pairs increase dramatically which decreases the algorithmic efficiency. To overcome this problem, we introduce a similarity measure that computes pair wise vertex distances by which we can select the vertices which are close to a given vertex. We can explore our search with $max\{ sm(v_i, v_{jk}) | 1 \leq k \leq n$, where n is the no of possibilities}. Here sm indicates the similarity measure.

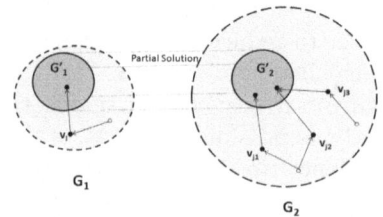

Fig. 2.   Shortcoming   of   VF2 Algorithm

It is clear that the efficiency of the algorithm depends on the similarity measure which indicates that a more precise similarity measure increases the efficiency. In this paper we use one of the popular similarity measures proposed by Blondel [13].

4 Outline of Proposed Method

In order to reduce computation we make use of heuristics which are detailed in later sections.

1. Calculate Similarity_Matrix
2. Calculate modified Initial_Matrix
   (a) Remove inconsistency
   (b) Calculate depth-k look-ahead degree weightage
3. Get next-pair
   (a) Select efficient pair for explore further
4. Check partial solution
5. Refine Initial_Matrix
6. Recursive call

4.1 Calculate Similarity_Matrix

Graph similarity measure presents a related measure of similarity for two different sets of vertices. If vertex similarity score is high then we can assume that those two vertices are similar. It is a relative measure so there really may not be an exact matching between two graphs. But it gives a better approximation of similarity of two graphs. There are classical approaches to measure the structural similarity of graphs in literature. Here we are using one of the best techniques that is proposed by Blondel et al.[13]. In their paper they introduce a concept of similarity between vertices of directed graphs. Assume that we have two directed graphs $G_1 = (V_1, E_1)$ and $G_2 = (V_2, E_2)$ with $A_{n \times n}$ and $B_{m \times m}$ as their adjacency matrices respectively. Now we are defining X_k to be the $m \times n$ similarity matrix of entries $x_{i,j}$ at iteration k. Then Blondel computes and updates this similarity matrix using an iterative approach that is given by the linear mapping.

$$X_{k+1} = BX_k A^T + B^T X_k A, \qquad k = 0, 1, 2, ..., \qquad (1)$$

Initialize the similarity matrix with some positive value and then update the mentioned formula accordingly. The basic algorithm is as follows:

Here k is a parameter that application dependent.

Algorithm 1. Computing similarity matrix of graphs:

Set $X_0 = 1$;
for $i \leftarrow 1$ *to* k **do**

$\quad \left\lfloor\; X_{k+1} \leftarrow \dfrac{BX_k A^T + B^T X_k A}{\|BX_k A^T + B^T X_k A\|} \right.$

return X_k

4.2   Calculate Modified Initial_Matrix

For subgraph isomorphism problem we use backtracking which initially needs to know the possible correspondence between every pair of vertices of input and target graph (to define a pair we use the notation $pair(i, j)$, where i and j are the vertices of input and target graph respectively). To store this information we use an *Initial Matrix*, $M^0 = [m_{i,j}^0]_{n \times m}$, where n and m are the order of input and target graph respectively. In this matrix if $m^0[i, j] = 1$, which indicates that the vertex i from input graph corresponds to vertex j in target graph. So, if we can remove some of the $1's$ from *initial matrix* then search space will be reduced, for which we use a heuristic that is one step improvisation to that of Ullmann.

– To define the refinement procedure, Ullmann used a condition in which for every pair of vertices in initial matrix, if v_i corresponds to v_j then all the adjacencies of v_i of input graph should correspond to any of the vertices that are adjacent to vertex v_j in the target graph. But let's consider following situation:

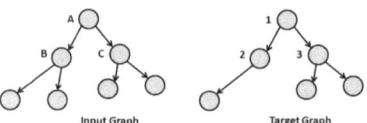

Input Graph   Target Graph

Fig. 3. Example : calculate modified initial_matrix

In this example given in 3, according to Ullmann, for checking the correspondence between $pair(A, 1)$, for all the adjacent vertices of A i.e. B and C of input graph may correspond to any of the adjacent of vertex 1 i.e.3, but both B and C cannot correspond to a single vertex i.e. 3. We addressed this situation in different way.

– To check the correspondence, Ullmann made use of another heuristic i.e. if two vertices correspond to each other than their adjacency vertex set should also correspond with each other. But this is not sufficient as this property of correspondence should also be preserved recursively for all the adjacent vertices for all levels of adjacency. Let's take an example:

In this above example of figure 4, according to Ullmann's heuristic A may correspond to 1 because B can correspond to 2. But if we look one step further then we see that C cannot correspond to 3 as $degree(C) > degree(3)$. So, B cannot correspond to 2 as well as A cannot correspond to 1. Similarly

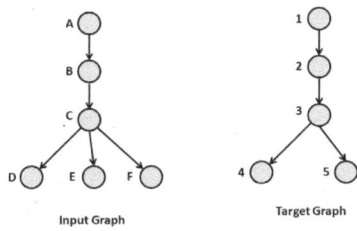

Fig. 4. Example : check correspondence

we need to check to a depth of k to take a decision. For that we are using following steps :

1. Calculate degree weightage of each vertex of both graphs. To calculate degree weightage we are using this formula: $weightage(A) = weightage (A) + weightage(adjacent(A))$, initially weightage is the degree of that vertex.
2. Calculate that degree weightage for k iterations.
3. If weightage(A_i) > weightage(B_i) then $M^0[A, B] = 0$, where $1 \leq i \leq k$ and $A \, \epsilon \, G_1$ and $B \, \epsilon \, G_2$.

For directed graph we need to calculate both in-degree and out-degree.

5   Get Next_Pair

To explore our search further, each time we select one $pair(i, j)$ and adding the newly selected pair into the partial solution and expanding the search tree. For every vertex from input graph there should be one vertex from target graph so that $m[i, j] = 1$ in refined initial matrix. Now instead of selecting random pair like other existing algorithms, we are using some prior knowledge so that our search will be more faster and we will expand our search tree in correct path. To get the next pair, we are selecting one vertex from input graph and one vertex from target graph in different way. For this we are using following heuristics:

1. To get the next vertex from input graph we are checking the immediate adjacent vertices of the last matched vertex from input graph. Among them we need to select the highest priority vertex. The priority is defined such that vertex with less number of 1s in a row of initial matrix has higher priority over other vertices, where each row defines a vertex of input graph. That can be done by the following steps:

   (a) Expand and generate all the adjacent vertices of last matched vertex and append those vertices into FIFO
   (b) Sort the FIFO based on priority
   (c) Extract one vertex from FIFO for next pair
   Lets take an example , G_1 be a input graph.

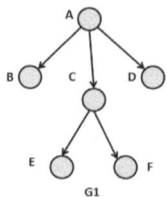

Fig. 5. Example : get next_pair

In Figure 5 A is already matched with 1. Now for the next recursive call we need to get next matching pair. Instead of looking at all the non-matched vertices of input graph i.e.$\{B, C, D, E, F\}$, we are only interested in the immediate adjacent vertices of A, i.e. $\{B, C, D\}$. Among them we need to select the proper one. Here we are always adding the new vertex from input graph such that partial graph of the input graph remains connected, which helps to check the partial solution.

2. On the other hand, to select a vertex from target graph for each $pair(i, j)$, we are using the similarity value from similarity matrix. The basic idea to calculate the similarity matrix is to get similarity measure between a pair of vertices. Higher similarity value means those two vertices are more similar. So, for a particular vertex from input graph, we are checking entire row of similarity matrix of corresponding vertex. After that, we are selecting the winner vertex of target graph based on the higher similarity value and the possibility of correspondence from initial matrix.

If v_i is the vertex of input graph, $M^0 = [m(i, j)]_{n \times m}$ is the initial matrix and $S_0 = [s(i, j)]_{n \times m}$, is the similarity matrix where n and m is the order of input and target graph respectively. Then

$$pair(v_i, v_j) = max_{1 \leq j \leq m} \{s_{i,j} * m_{i,j}\})$$

If $pair(v_i, v_j)$ is not satisfying the isomorphic condition then we need to take the second highest value and so on. The search efficiency depends on the correct choice of the vertex of target graph.

6   Algorithm

Our proposed idea is based on a recursive procedure. In pre-computation phase, we first calculate the similarity matrix and modify initial matrix, that takes only polynomial time. After that the actual matching procedure is called, which returns a permutation matrix, i.e. the mapping of isomorphism. It is a recursive procedure. It returns isomorphic mapping after the first match is found or returns FAIL after checking all possibilities(i.e. no isomorphism present). Algorithm of our proposed method is as follows:

Algorithm 2. Proposed Subgraph_Isomorphism Algorithm

Data: $G_1 = (V_1, E_1), G_2 = (V_2, E_2)$, M^0, such that M^0, an Initial Matrix
Result: M' is an permutation matrix
begin

$\quad M' \leftarrow \Phi$
$\quad S_M \leftarrow$ Calculate_Similarity_Matrix(G_1, G_2)
$\quad M^0 \leftarrow$ Calculate_Modified_Initial_Matrix(G_1, G_2)
$\quad M' \leftarrow$ call Proposed_Match(G_1, G_2, S_M, M^0, M')

Procedure Proposed_Match(G_1, G_2, S_M, M^0, M')
begin

$\quad$ **if** *visit all the vertices of G_1* **then**
$\quad\quad$ **if** *Check_Iso(G_1, G_2, M')* **then**
$\quad\quad\quad$ print "Match Found"
$\quad\quad\quad$ return M'
$\quad$ **else**
$\quad\quad$ $(v_i, v_j) \leftarrow$ Get_Next_Pair(S_M, M^0)
$\quad\quad$ $M' \leftarrow M' \cup (v_i, v_j)$
$\quad\quad$ **if** *Partial_Solution(G_1, G_2, M')* **then**
$\quad\quad\quad$ Refine(M^0)
$\quad\quad\quad$ **if** *Dead_State(M^0)* **then**
$\quad\quad\quad\quad$ return
$\quad\quad\quad$ call Proposed_Match(G_1, G_2, S_M, M^0, M')

In our proposed algorithm, we always make sure that the search will not go to a state twice and we try to detect a false positive branch as early as possible so that that branch is not explored further.

7   Experiments and Results

The data set used in this experimentation has been constructed by Foggia et al.[4]. The dataset contains categories of Randomly Connected Graphs, Regular Meshes (2D, 3D and 4D), Bounded Valence Graphs, Irregular Meshes and Irregular Bounded Valence Graphs. The dataset has sufficient pairs of graphs to check both graph isomorphism and subgraph isomorphism problem. We are only interested on subgraph pairs. For that, we have mainly three category of pairs - *i*) Pairs of graph-subgraph isomorphic graphs; the subgraph size is 20% of the full graph, defined as **si2**. *ii*) the subgraph size is 40% of the full graph, defined as **si4**. and *iii*) the subgraph size is 60% of the full graph, defined as **si6**. We did our experiments for all three types of pairs.

We implemented our proposed method in *C*-Programming Language. Graph is represented as an adjacency matrix, that is dynamically allocated in the run time. We compared the performance of our proposed algorithm with the two other programs of reference: Ullmann and VF2, which are publicly available. For the time being, we compared the performance by means of the number of recursive calls. Because less number of recursive calls means the program will reach the actual solution by less computation. Here in this project, we concentrated only for the first match. So our algorithm will stop after getting the first match. We don't bother about all the matches, and also we check the isomorphism only for directed graphs because our proposed heuristics work only for directed graphs. In the next section, we give all the experimentation results and discussion.

7.1 Performance Evolution

In this section, we compare the performance of our proposed algorithm with VF2 and Ullmann's algorithm. The performance gain is calculated over VF2 and Ullmann's algorithm as: $\frac{P}{VF2}$ and $\frac{P}{Ull}$ respectively, where P is the proposed method. If $\frac{P}{VF2} < 0.1$, that means our algorithm if 10 times efficient than VF2 and so on. In order to assess the efficiency of our proposed method over VF2 and Ullmann, we divided the interval into "beans".

7.2 Randomly Generated Graphs

For the first set of experiments, we used simple randomly generated graphs, where graphs are the edges to connect nodes without any structural regularity. It is assumed that the probability of an edge connecting two nodes of the graph is independent to the nodes themselves. The probability that an edge is present between two distinct vertices v and v' is defines by η. We experimented with three different sizes of subgraphs i.e. si2, si4, si6. The actual database contains 1000 pairs of graphs of each size, here we used 600 pairs of graph of each size. The results are as follows:

In this type of graphs of **Table1**, the first few rows cover a large percentage of graphs, which means that our algorithm is more efficient for this type of graph. Approximately for 65% of graphs, Proposed $<<$ VF2, and the last row shows that for 6 percent of graphs, our algorithm is less efficient than VF2. In the case of Ullmann's algorithm only for a few graphs, our algorithm is less efficient.

In **Table2** proposed algorithm performance if same as previous, but here more number of instances are present {2,3,4,5} row that means VF2 and Ullmann's algorithm are more closer than previous set of graphs.

In **Table3** more instances are present in rows 3,4 and 5. From this result, it is easy to see that if difference between input graph size and target graph size is more, then our search is faster. In this experiment, we can see that sometimes VF2 is taking more time than Ullmann, because VF2 improves only the data-structure but overlooks a few iterations for actual solution. Another important thing to notice is that their feasibility function is not working so well as it prunes false positive branch early, that may be the reason VF2 for running more number of iterations. We ensure that our heuristic takes care of both these aspects.

Table 1. Ramdomly generated Graph : The subgraph size is 20% of the full graph

si2_rand	r01		r001		r005	
	Count	%	Count	%	Count	%
$\frac{P}{VF2} < .01$	67	13	6	1	84	17
$.01 \leq \frac{P}{VF2} < .1$	153	31	96	19	160	32
$.1 \leq \frac{P}{VF2} < .3$	104	21	136	27	85	17
$.3 \leq \frac{P}{VF2} < .6$	58	12	129	26	58	12
$.6 \leq \frac{P}{VF2} < .9$	48	10	36	7	39	7
$\frac{P}{VF2} \cong 1$	32	6	44	9	42	8
$1 < \frac{P}{VF2} \leq 2$	7	1	5	1	4	1
$\frac{P}{VF2} > 2$	31	6	48	10	28	6

si2_rand	r01		r001		r005	
	Count	%	Count	%	Count	%
$\frac{P}{Uu} < 0.01$	60	12	0	0	52	11
$0.01 \leq \frac{P}{Uu} < 0.1$	167	33	30	6	146	29
$0.1 \leq \frac{P}{Uu} < 0.3$	103	21	93	19	105	21
$0.3 \leq \frac{P}{Uu} < 0.6$	58	11	128	26	62	13
$0.6 \leq \frac{P}{Uu} < 0.9$	40	8	132	26	51	10
$\frac{P}{Uu} \cong 1$	53	11	106	21	71	14
$1 < \frac{P}{Uu} \leq 2$	13	3	10	2	11	2
$\frac{P}{Uu} > 2$	6	1	1	0	2	0

Table 2. Randomly generated graph : The subgraph size is 40% of the full graph

si4_rand	r01		r001		r005	
	Count	%	Count	%	Count	%
$\frac{P}{VF2} < 0.01$	22	4	1	0	50	10
$0.01 \leq \frac{P}{VF2} < 0.1$	163	33	57	12	139	28
$0.1 \leq \frac{P}{VF2} < 0.3$	156	31	191	38	143	28
$0.3 \leq \frac{P}{VF2} < 0.6$	94	19	134	27	99	20
$0.6 \leq \frac{P}{VF2} < 0.9$	43	8	45	9	39	8
$\frac{P}{VF2} \cong 1$	8	2	32	6	14	3
$1 < \frac{P}{VF2} \leq 2$	4	1	0	0	4	1
$\frac{P}{VF2} > 2$	10	2	40	8	12	2

si4_rand	r01		r001		r005	
	Count	%	Count	%	Count	%
$\frac{P}{Uu} < 0.01$	18	4	0	0	16	3
$0.01 \leq \frac{P}{Uu} < 0.1$	179	36	5	1	114	23
$0.1 \leq \frac{P}{Uu} < 0.3$	159	32	58	12	141	28
$0.3 \leq \frac{P}{Uu} < 0.6$	93	19	183	37	113	23
$0.6 \leq \frac{P}{Uu} < 0.9$	27	5	174	35	83	17
$\frac{P}{Uu} \cong 1$	16	3	78	15	26	5
$1 < \frac{P}{Uu} \leq 2$	6	1	2	0	5	1
$\frac{P}{Uu} > 2$	2	0	0	0	2	0

Table 3. Randomly generated graph : The subgraph size is 60% of the full graph

si6_rand	r01		r001		r005	
	Count	%	Count	%	Count	%
$\frac{P}{VF2} < 0.01$	6	1	0	0	11	2
$0.01 \leq \frac{P}{VF2} < 0.1$	59	12	37	7	60	12
$0.1 \leq \frac{P}{VF2} < 0.3$	145	29	167	34	148	30
$0.3 \leq \frac{P}{VF2} < 0.6$	171	34	191	38	169	34
$0.6 \leq \frac{P}{VF2} < 0.9$	100	20	56	11	93	18
$\frac{P}{VF2} \cong 1$	5	1	16	3	8	2
$1 < \frac{P}{VF2} \leq 2$	1	0	0	0	0	0
$\frac{P}{VF2} > 2$	13	3	35	7	11	2

si6_rand	r01		r001		r005	
	Count	%	Count	%	Count	%
$\frac{P}{Uu} < 0.01$	2	0	0	0	0	0
$0.01 \leq \frac{P}{Uu} < 0.1$	49	10	3	1	16	3
$0.1 \leq \frac{P}{Uu} < 0.3$	154	31	18	3	103	21
$0.3 \leq \frac{P}{Uu} < 0.6$	170	34	189	38	183	37
$0.6 \leq \frac{P}{Uu} < 0.9$	105	21	232	46	177	35
$\frac{P}{Uu} \cong 1$	18	3	58	12	20	4
$1 < \frac{P}{Uu} \leq 2$	2	1	0	0	1	0
$\frac{P}{Uu} > 2$	0	0	0	0	0	0

7.3   Mesh Graph

For the second set of experiments, we use mesh graphs. It is generally agreed that graphs having a regular structure represent the worst case for general graph matching algorithms. This problem gave birth to specialized graph matching methods, with kind of algorithms able to efficiently perform the matching for given graph structures. The database includes, as regular graphs, the mesh connected graphs (2D, 3D and 4D). The considered 2D mesh are graphs in which each node (except those belonging to the border of the mesh) is connected with its 4 neighborhood nodes. Similarly, each node of a 3D and 4D graph has respectively connections with its 6 and 8 neighborhood nodes. For all three size of graphs we experiment our algorithm. The experimental results are as follows:

Table 4. Mesh Graph : The subgraph size is 20% of the full graph

si2_m2D	m2D Count	%	m2Dr2 Count	%	m2Dr4 Count	%	m2Dr6 Count	%
$\frac{P}{VF2} < 0.01$	0	0	13	3	19	4	28	6
$0.01 \le \frac{P}{VF2} < 0.1$	7	1	127	25	159	32	176	35
$0.1 \le \frac{P}{VF2} < 0.3$	36	7	109	22	99	20	111	22
$0.3 \le \frac{P}{VF2} < 0.6$	82	17	78	16	76	15	73	15
$0.6 \le \frac{P}{VF2} < 0.9$	91	18	42	8	45	9	35	7
$\frac{P}{VF2} \cong 1$	151	30	71	14	56	11	52	10
$1 < \frac{P}{VF2} \le 2$	43	9	21	4	18	3	13	3
$\frac{P}{VF2} > 2$	90	18	39	8	28	6	12	2

si2_m2D	m2D Count	%	m2Dr2 Count	%	m2Dr4 Count	%	m2Dr6 Count	%
$\frac{P}{UU} < 0.01$	0	0	0	0	3	1	3	1
$0.01 \le \frac{P}{UU} < 0.1$	1	0	79	16	109	22	148	30
$0.1 \le \frac{P}{UU} < 0.3$	8	2	127	25	124	25	138	28
$0.3 \le \frac{P}{UU} < 0.6$	74	15	73	15	96	19	76	15
$0.6 \le \frac{P}{UU} < 0.9$	127	25	71	14	59	12	55	11
$\frac{P}{UU} \cong 1$	199	40	104	21	77	15	59	12
$1 < \frac{P}{UU} \le 2$	45	9	32	6	20	4	15	3
$\frac{P}{UU} > 2$	46	9	14	3	12	2	6	1

Table 5. Mesh Graph : The subgraph size is 40% of the full graph

si4_m2D	m2D Count	%	m2Dr2 Count	%	m2Dr4 Count	%	m2Dr6 Count	%
$\frac{P}{VF2} < 0.01$	0	0	10	2	11	2	21	4
$0.01 \le \frac{P}{VF2} < 0.1$	34	7	168	33	147	29	138	28
$0.1 \le \frac{P}{VF2} < 0.3$	121	24	144	29	138	28	142	28
$0.3 \le \frac{P}{VF2} < 0.6$	102	20	64	13	85	17	93	19
$0.6 \le \frac{P}{VF2} < 0.9$	51	10	30	6	50	10	47	9
$\frac{P}{VF2} \cong 1$	95	19	58	12	46	9	40	8
$1 < \frac{P}{VF2} \le 2$	38	8	3	1	2	1	6	1
$\frac{P}{VF2} > 2$	59	11	23	4	21	4	13	3

si4_m2D	m2D Count	%	m2Dr2 Count	%	m2Dr4 Count	%	m2Dr6 Count	%
$\frac{P}{UU} < 0.01$	0	0	0	0	1	0	1	0
$0.01 \le \frac{P}{UU} < 0.1$	9	2	64	13	59	12	67	13
$0.1 \le \frac{P}{UU} < 0.3$	68	14	146	29	157	31	166	33
$0.3 \le \frac{P}{UU} < 0.6$	123	25	140	28	122	24	143	29
$0.6 \le \frac{P}{UU} < 0.9$	101	20	62	12	91	18	61	12
$\frac{P}{UU} \cong 1$	122	24	79	16	67	14	53	11
$1 < \frac{P}{UU} \le 2$	43	9	8	2	4	1	8	2
$\frac{P}{UU} > 2$	34	7	1	0	0	0	1	0

Table 6. Mesh Graph : The subgraph size is 60% of the full graph

si6_m2D	m2D Count	%	m2Dr2 Count	%	m2Dr4 Count	%	m2Dr6 Count	%
$\frac{P}{VF2} < 0.01$	6	1	1	0	1	0	3	1
$0.01 \le \frac{P}{VF2} < 0.1$	153	26	74	15	56	12	81	16
$0.1 \le \frac{P}{VF2} < 0.3$	178	30	168	34	157	31	164	33
$0.3 \le \frac{P}{VF2} < 0.6$	127	21	166	33	165	33	162	32
$0.6 \le \frac{P}{VF2} < 0.9$	36	6	58	12	99	20	57	11
$\frac{P}{VF2} \cong 1$	44	7	17	3	7	1	13	3
$1 < \frac{P}{VF2} \le 2$	18	3	1	0	5	1	2	0
$\frac{P}{VF2} > 2$	38	6	15	3	10	2	18	4

si6_m2D	m2D Count	%	m2Dr2 Count	%	m2Dr4 Count	%	m2Dr6 Count	%
$\frac{P}{UU} < 0.01$	0	0	0	0	0	0	0	0
$0.01 \le \frac{P}{UU} < 0.1$	75	13	9	2	23	5	5	1
$0.1 \le \frac{P}{UU} < 0.3$	164	27	104	21	126	25	104	21
$0.3 \le \frac{P}{UU} < 0.6$	156	26	182	36	193	39	220	44
$0.6 \le \frac{P}{UU} < 0.9$	88	15	164	33	132	26	136	27
$\frac{P}{UU} \cong 1$	77	13	36	7	21	4	32	6
$1 < \frac{P}{UU} \le 2$	20	3	5	1	5	1	3	1
$\frac{P}{UU} > 2$	20	3	0	0	0	0	0	0

In the case of mesh graphs of **Table 4,5,6** our algorithm is also performing much better than existing algorithm. Here most of the graphs are fallen in 2,3,4,5 rows. Approximately 80% of all graphs are only in that region.

7.4 Bounded Valence Graphs

Third set of experiment we did with bounded valence graphs, in which every node has a number of edges (among ongoing and outgoing) lower than a given threshold, called Valence. A particular case occurs when the number of edges are equal for all the nodes; in this case the graph is commonly called fixed valence graph. The database includes graphs with a fixed valence, that have been generated by inserting random edges (using an uniform distribution) with

Table 7. Bounded Valence Graphs : The subgraph size is 20% of the full graph

si2_bvg	b03	
	Count	%
$0.1 \leq \frac{P}{VF2} < 0.5$	0	0
$\frac{P}{VF2} \cong 1$	483	97
$1 < \frac{P}{VF2} \leq 2$	16	3
$\frac{P}{VF2} > 2$	1	0

si2_bvg	b03	
	Count	%
$0.6 \leq \frac{P}{Ull} < 0.5$	0	0
$\frac{P}{Ull} \cong 1$	483	97
$1 < \frac{P}{Ull} \leq 2$	16	3
$\frac{P}{Ull} > 2$	1	0

Table 8. Bounded Valence Graphs : The subgraph size is 40% of the full graph

si4_bvg	b03	
	Count	%
$0.6 \leq \frac{P}{VF2} < 0.5$	0	0
$\frac{P}{VF2} \cong 1$	487	97
$1 < \frac{P}{VF2} \leq 2$	12	3
$\frac{P}{VF2} > 2$	1	0

si4_bvg	b03	
	Count	%
$0.6 \leq \frac{P}{Ull} < 0.5$	0	0
$\frac{P}{Ull} \cong 1$	488	98
$1 < \frac{P}{Ull} \leq 2$	12	2
$\frac{P}{Ull} > 2$	0	0

Table 9. Bounded Valence Graphs : The subgraph size is 60% of the full graph

si6_bvg	b03	
	Count	%
$0.6 \leq \frac{P}{VF2} < 0.5$	0	0
$\frac{P}{VF2} \cong 1$	499	100
$1 < \frac{P}{VF2} \leq 2$	1	0
$\frac{P}{VF2} > 2$	0	0

si6_bvg	b03	
	Count	%
$0.6 \leq \frac{P}{Ull} < 0.5$	0	0
$\frac{P}{Ull} \cong 1$	499	100
$1 < \frac{P}{Ull} \leq 2$	1	0
$\frac{P}{Ull} > 2$	0	0

the constraint that the valence of a node cannot exceed a selected value; edge insertion continues until all the nodes reach the desired valence.

From the experimental result of Table 7,8,9 it is clear that for bounded valence graphs our algorithm is performing as same as VF2 and Ullmann's algorithm. For every graphs all algorithms are taking same number of iteration and all iterations are same as the number of vertex present in input graph that means all this three algorithms are calculating each vertex in input graph only once (i.e. no backtracking).

8   Conclusion and Future Work

This paper addresses the problem of subgraph isomorphism. Pair wise comparison of graphs has become more interesting. We have compared its practical performance with the worlds most acknowledged package for subgraph isomorphism testing, VF2. Our algorithm has outperformed it for a number of graph families, that shows the efficiency of our proposed heuristics. Approximately for 80% of graphs of benchmark data set, our proposed heuristics are shown to take the same number of iterations as the size of input graph.

Based on the work done in this paper there are a number of issues to be considered for future work. Another way to improve the performance of the algorithm would be to add more efficient data-structure in order to reduce the execution time and also new refinement techniques may be considered. i.e. new invariants that might help eliminate some backtracking points. The current status of the work has progressed enough for developing efficient heuristics for exact algorithm. The natural extension for future of this problem is approximate graph/subgraph isomorphism problem.

References

1. Corneil, D.G., Gotlieb, C.C.: An Efficient Algorithm for Graph Isomorphism. Journal of the ACM (JACM) 17(1) (1970)
2. Qiu, M., Hu, H., Jiang, Q., Hu, H.: A New Approach of Graph Isomorphism Detection based on Decision Tree. In: Second International Workshop on Education Technology and Computer Science, vol. 2, pp. 32–35 (2010)
3. Zager, L.A., Verghese, G.C.: Graph Similarity Scoring and Matching. Applied Mathematics Letters 21(1), 86–94 (2008)
4. Foggia, P.: A Database of Graphs for Isomorphism and Sub-Graph Isomorphism, http://amalfi.dis.unina.it/graph/
5. Lipets, V., Vanetik, N., Gudes, E.: Subsea: an efficient heuristic algorithm for subgraph isomorphism. In: Data Mining and Knowledge Discovery, vol. 19(3), pp. 320–350 (2009)
6. Ullmann, J.R.: An Algorithm for Subgraph Isomorphism. Journal of the ACM 23(1) (1976)
7. Cordella, L.P., Foggia, P., Sansone, C., Vento, M.: A (Sub)Graph Isomorphism Algorithm for Matching Large Graphs. IEEE Transactions on Pattern Analysis and Machine Intelligence 26, 1367–1372 (2004)
8. Randi, M.: On Canonical Numbering of Atoms in a Molecule and Graph Isomorphism. Journal of Chemical Information and Computer Sciences, 171–180 (1977)
9. Kuramochi, M., Karypis, G.: An Efficient Algorithm for Discovering Frequent Subgraphs. IEEE Transactions on Knowledge and Data Engineering 16(9) (2004)
10. Messmer, B.T., Bunke, H.: A Decision Tree Approach to Graph and Subgraph Isomorphism Detection. Pattern Recognition 32(12), 1979–1998 (1999)
11. Battiti, R., Mascia, F.: An Algorithm Portfolio for the Sub-graph Isomorphism Problem. In: Stützle, T., Birattari, M., Hoos, H.H. (eds.) SLS 2007. LNCS, vol. 4638, pp. 106–120. Springer, Heidelberg (2007)
12. Viger, F., Latapy, M.: Efficient and Simple Generation of Random Simple Connected Graphs with Prescribed Degree Sequence. In: Computing and Combinatorics Conference (2005), http://www-rp.lip6.fr/~latapy/FV/generation.html
13. Blondel, V.D., Gajardo, A., Heymans, M., Senellart, P., Van Dooren, P.: A Measure of Similarity between Graph Vertices: Applications to Synonym Extraction and Web Searching. Applications to Synonym Extraction and Web Searching. SIAM Review 46, 647–666 (2004)

0-1 Integer Programming for Generation Maintenance Scheduling in Power Systems Based on Teaching Learning Based Optimization (TLBO)

Suresh Chandra Satapathy[1], Anima Naik[2], and K. Parvathi[3]

[1] ANITS, Vishakapatnam
sureshsatapathy@ieee.org
[2] MITS, Rayagada, India
animanaik@gmail.com
[3] CUTM, Paralakhemundi
Kparvati16@gmail.com

Abstract. This paper presents optimal solution of the unit maintenance scheduling problem in which the cost reduction is as important as reliability. The objective function of the algorithms used to address this problem, considers the effect of economy as well as reliability. Various constraints such as spinning reserve, duration of maintenance crew are being taken into account while dealing with such type of problems. In our work we apply the Teaching learning based optimization algorithm on a power system with six generating units. Numerical results reveal that the proposed algorithm can find better and faster solutions when compared to other heuristic or deterministic methods.

Keywords: Maintenance scheduling, TLBO, integer programming.

1 Introduction

The major responsibility of power station maintenance department is to maximize plant reliability, availability and efficiency by determining both short and long term maintenance requirements. It also complies with statutory and mandatory requirements and investigates into plant problems. The aim of the department is to make the most economic use of its available resources; this is achieved, in part, by having a level of staff (engineering, supervisory, craft) to deal with the general day-to-day steady workload and by making alternative arrangements to cater for work load peaks [1]. To achieve the above goal, periodic servicing must take place and normally falls under the wing items [1]: Planned maintenance: overhaul, preventive maintenance and Unplanned maintenance: emergency maintenance.

Preventive maintenance requires shop facilities, skilled labor, keeping records and stocking of replacement parts and hence expensive. The cost of downtime resulting from avoidable outages may amount to ten or more times the actual cost of repair. The high cost of downtime makes it imperative to economic operation that maintenance be scheduled into the operating schedule [1]. Thus the maintenance

M. Parashar et al. (Eds.): IC3 2012, CCIS 306, pp. 53–63, 2012.

scheduling problem is to determine the period for which generating units of an electric power utility should be taken off line for planned preventive maintenance over the course of a one or two year planning horizon, in order to minimize the total operating cost while system energy, reliability requirements and a number of other constraints are satisfied [10].

Many efforts have been put by researchers, in past, to solve this maintenance scheduling problem. These approaches have been based on many heuristics/stochastic and deterministic algorithms. Few are mentioned below for examples: Lagrangian relaxation [11], Linear programming [12], Mixed integer programming [13], Decomposition methods [14], Goal programming [15], Tabu search [16], Simulated annealing [17], Genetic algorithm [18], Fuzzy logic [19], Neural networks [20], Particle swarm optimization [21], Ant colony optimization [22], Harmony Search [23].

In this paper, we have used yet one more stochastic approach recently developed know as Teaching-learning based Optimization (TLBO)[5] in the maintenance scheduling field. The attractive feature of TLBO is based on the fact that unlike other techniques like GA, PSO, and harmony Search, it has no parameters for tuning and hence can find the optimal solution in less computational time [5, 2]. TLBO has been recently used in various applications [23, 24, 25] with very fast convergence characteristics. The simulation results in our work reveal that the TLBO approach not only outperforms all other approaches in terms of producing good result but also able to do so in quicker times.

The rest of this paper is structured as follows. Section 2 presents the Concepts of Teaching learning based Optimization technique. Section 3 discusses the fundamentals of 0-1 integer programming problem. Section 4 presents the maintenance scheduling problem. Section 5 details the result with the simulation strategy and experimentation carried out and presents the discovered results. The paper concludes with a discussion on the observations and highlights the scope for future work in this area.

2   Teaching Learning Based Optimization

This optimization method is based on the effect of the influence of a teacher on the output of learners in a class. Like other nature-inspired algorithms, TLBO [5] is also a population based method that uses a population of solutions to proceed to the global solution. A group of learners are considered as the population. In TLBO, different subjects offered to learners are considered as different design variables for the TLBO. The learning results of a learner is analogous to the 'fitness', as in other population-based optimization techniques. The teacher is considered as the best solution obtained so far.

There are two parts in TLBO: 'Teacher Phase' and 'Learner Phase'. The 'Teacher Phase' means learning from the teacher and the 'Learner Phase' means learning through the interaction between learners.

2.1   Teacher Phase

In our society the best learner is mimicked as a teacher. The teacher tries to disseminate knowledge among learners, which will in turn increase the knowledge level of the whole class and help learners to get good marks or grades. So a teacher increases the mean learning value of the class according to his or her capability i.e.

say the teacher T_1 will try to move mean M_1 towards their own level according to his or her capability, thereby increasing the learners' level to a new mean M_2. Teacher T_1 will put maximum effort into teaching his or her students, but students will gain knowledge according to the quality of teaching delivered by a teacher and the quality of students present in the class. The quality of the students is judged from the mean value of the population. Teacher T_1 puts effort in so as to increase the quality of the students from M_1 to M_2, at which stage the students require a new teacher, of superior quality than themselves, i.e. in this case the new teacher is T_2.

Let M_i be the mean and T_i be the teacher at any iteration i. T_i will try to move mean M_i towards its own level, so now the new mean will be T_i designated as M_{new}. The solution is updated according to the difference between the existing and the new mean given by

$$Difference\_mean_i = r_i(M_{new} - T_F M_i) \tag{1}$$

where T_F is a teaching factor that decides the value of mean to be changed, and r_i is a random number in the range [0, 1]. The value of T_F can be either 1 or 2, which is again a heuristic step and decided randomly with equal probability as

$$T_F = round[1 + rand(0,1) * (2 - 1)] \tag{2}$$

This difference modifies the existing solution according to the following expression

$$X_{new,i} = X_{old,i} + Difference\_mean_i \tag{3}$$

2.2   Learner Phase

Learners increase their knowledge by two different means: one through input from the teacher and the other through interaction between themselves. A learner interacts randomly with other learners with the help of group discussions, presentations, formal communications, etc. A learner learns something new if the other learner has more knowledge than him or her. Learner modification is expressed as

$$For\ i = 1{:}P_n$$
Randomly select two learners X_i and X_j, where $i \neq j$
$$If\ f(X_i) < f(X_j) \qquad X_{new,i} = X_{old,i} + r_i (X_i - X_j)$$
$$Else \qquad X_{new,i} = X_{old,i} + r_i (X_j - X_i)$$
$$End\ If$$
$$End\ For$$
Accept X_{new} if it gives a better function value.

3   The Integer Programming Problem

Many power systems areas such as, short-term hydro scheduling, optimal reconfiguration and capacitor allocation, reactive power market clearing, transmission network expansion planning, etc. require the variables to be integers. These problems are called Integer Programming problems. Optimization methods developed for real search spaces can be used to solve Integer Programming problems by rounding off the real optimal values to the nearest integers.

Maintenance scheduling problem is kind of 0-1 Integer Programming. Importance of TLBO is in solving the problems of nonlinear optimization in the space of real numbers and has applications in the problems related to engineering optimization[2][3][4]. In order to expand the above mentioned matter in 0-1 integer programming, consider the real numbers of the problem, which at the beginning of TLBO algorithm are chosen randomly in the interval [0, 1]. For solving the problem, values equal to or higher than 0.5 are rounded to 1 and values less than 0.5 are rounded to 0.

4   Maintenance Scheduling Model

We have used Leou's model two objective functions [1], [6] in our work. Due to the binary nature of the maintenance scheduling problem, integer programming optimization method can be better suited. This method is computationally acceptable even for problem is scaled up with a large number of variables and constraints. In this paper, the beginning time of maintenance is adopted as the state variable. The maintenance scheduling problem can be set up as a 0-1 integer programming whose general form is: find the n-vector x^* which minimizes the cost function

$$Z = c^T x \tag{4}$$

Subjected to

$$Ax \leq b \tag{5}$$

Where $x_i = 0 \ or \ 1, \quad i = 1,2,\ldots\ldots,n.$

A feasible solution satisfies the constraints. A feasible n-vector x^* is optimal if and only if solution $c^T x^* \leq c^T x$ for all feasible x. Each x_i is associated with beginning maintenance on some unit j during some week k if and only if $x_i = 1$ for each problem tables relating i, j and k are developed.

Let us take an example of group of six units that must be maintained during a ten week period. The sample machine input data are shown in table 1.

Table 1. Machines input data for six unit system

Unit No.	Allowed Period	Capacity (MW)	Maintenance crew	Outage duration
1	1-4	200	10	3
2	3-6	300	15	4
3	5-7	300	15	4
4	6-9	300	15	4
5	12-14	500	20	4
6	14-16	500	20	4

It can been seen that only four units (unit 1 to 4) should be maintained during the ten week period. Table 2 gives variables associated with each unit that should be maintained. In this table i, j, and k respectively shows "Associated unknown", "Unit No." and "Maintenance starts in week". For instance, if $x_6 = 1$, maintenance on unit 2 begins on the fourth week.

Table 2. State variables for six unit system during 10 week period

x_i	x_1	x_2	x_3	x_4	x_5	x_6	x_7	x_8
(j,k)	(1,1)	(1,2)	(1,3)	(1,4)	(2,3)	(2,4)	(2,5)	(2,6)

	x_9	x_{10}	x_{11}	x_{12}	x_{13}	x_{14}	x_{15}
	(3,5)	(3,6)	(3,7)	(4,6)	(4,7)	(4,8)	(4,9)

4.1   Objective Function

The deferring maintenance of units may cause damage on the machines. In order to improve the reliability of the power system and save the maintenance expense of the damaged machines, the objective function adopted in this paper, was to maintain the units as earlier as possible. In our above example, only four units should be maintained during the following ten week period. The objective functions can be expressed as the following forms:

$$c_1 = [\ 1\ 2\ 3\ 4\ 1\ 2\ 3\ 4\ 1\ 2\ 3\ 1\ 2\ 3\ 4\ ] \qquad (6)$$

$$c_2 = [\ 0\ 1\ 2\ 3\ 0\ 1\ 2\ 3\ 0\ 1\ 2\ 0\ 1\ 2\ 3\ ] \qquad (7)$$

According to (4), values in the c_1 vector [1] and c_2 vector [6], [7] are the coefficients of objective functions and express the maintenance cost of each one of unit generators.

For each unit there is a cost of 1 associated with the beginning of the maintenance during the first allowed week. There is a cost of 2 imposed for beginning maintenance in the second week. The schedule that minimizes this cost function is the "earliest possible" maintenance schedule.

4.2   Constraints

4.2.1 Spinning Reserve
In order to maintain the electric power supply normally, there must have a lot of spinning reserve to compensate for the outage of the generating units. The spinning reserve constraint can be expressed as

Capacity for maintenance + load capacity + spinning reserve
$$\leq \text{generating capacity} \qquad (8)$$

4.2.2 Maintenance Crew
For each period, numbers of the people, who to perform maintenance schedule, cannot exceed the available crew. Assume the number of people available for maintenance is P. The maintenance crew should satisfy the following constraint for each period.

Numbers of people are performing maintenance $\leq$ P   (9)

4.2.3 Duration of Maintenance

In order to let the units operate in good condition, the units should be maintained after a period of operation.

5   Case Study

5.1   Input Data

In this section, test results of the six-unit test system mentioned previously is reported.

As indicated in Table 1, the six-unit system can generate 2100 MW, and the number of people available for maintenance is 50. During the maintenance period (ten week interval), only four units (unit 1 to unit 4) need to perform maintenance. The machines input data are shown in Table 1.

Figure 2 shows the load curve of the system. The spinning reserve is 400 MW.

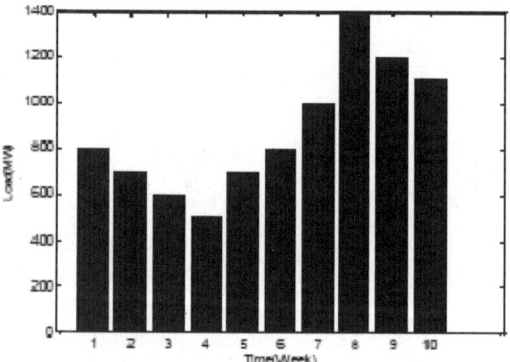

Fig. 1. Load curve of the six unit system

1st to 4th constraints of (10) indicate the beginning maintenance constraint for unit 1 to unit 4. 5th to 14th constraints of (10) represent the spinning reserve constraints. From the machine input data of Table 1, in period 1 and period 2 only unit 1 is possible to perform the maintenance. The 6th constraint contains two items, which are $200x_1$ and $200x_2$. $200x_2$ describes the possibility of unit 1 start maintaining in period 2. 200 is the capacity of unit 1. Since the outage duration of unit 1 lasting 3 periods, hence $200x_1$ is included in the 6th constraint. For the same consideration, the spinning reserve constraint of period 3 is included in the 7th constraint. In addition to consideration of spinning reserve constraints, the available people to perform maintenance are also important. 15th to 24th constraints of (10) describe the consideration of crew constraints. In this case, the available people to perform maintenance are 50 people. In period 1, from the machine data shown in Table 1, only unit 1 is possible in maintenance. The crew constraint of period 1 is shown in the 15th constraint. Numbers of people needed to perform maintenance for unit 1 are 10 people. In period 2, also only unit 1 is possible for maintenance, but unit 1 may start to maintain between period 1 and period 4. Therefore, in period 2, the crew constraint is demonstrated in the 16th constraint. Following the same rule, we build the crew constraints for all periods.

Integrate with these input data, the model is shown as follows:

Min
$$Z = x_1 + 2x_2 + 3x_3 + 4x_4 + x_5 + 2x_6 + 3x_7 + 4x_8 + x_9 + 2x_{10} + 3x_{11} + x_{12}$$
$$+ 2x_{13} + 3x_{14} + 4x_{15}$$

s.t

$$x_1 + x_2 + x_3 + x_4 = 1$$
$$x_5 + x_6 + x_7 + x_8 = 1$$
$$x_9 + x_{10} + x_{11} = 1$$
$$x_{12} + x_{13} + x_{14} + x_{15} = 1$$
$$200x_1 + 800 + 400 \leq 2100$$
$$200x_1 + 200x_2 + 700 + 400 \leq 2100$$
$$200x_1 + 200x_2 + 200x_3 + 300x_5 + 600$$
$$+400 \leq 2100$$
$$200x_2 + 200x_3 + 300x_5 + 200x_4 + 300x_6$$
$$+500 + 400 \leq 2100$$
$$200x_3 + 300x_5 + 200x_4 + 300x_6 + 300x_7$$
$$+300x_9 + 700 + 400 \leq 2100$$
$$300x_5 + 200x_4 + 300x_6 + 300x_7 + 300x_9 +$$
$$300x_8 + 300x_{10} + 300x_{12} + \quad 800 + 400 \leq 2100$$
$$300x_6 + 300x_7 + 300x_9 + 300x_8 + 300x_{10} +$$
$$300x_{12} + 300x_{11} + 300x_{13} + \quad 1000 + 400 \leq 2100$$
$$300x_7 + 300x_9 + 300x_8 + 300x_{10} + 300x_{12} + 300x_{11}$$
$$+300x_{13} + 300x_{14} + \quad 1400 + 400 \leq 2100$$
$$300x_8 + 300x_{10} + 300x_{12} + 300x_{11} + 300x_{13} + 300x_{14}$$
$$+300x_{15} + 1200 + 400 \leq 2100$$
$$300x_{11} + 300x_{13} + 300x_{14} + 300x_{15} + 1100 + 400 \leq 2100$$
$$10x_1 \leq 50$$
$$10x_1 + 10x_2 \leq 50$$
$$10x_1 + 10x_2 + 10x_3 + 15x_5 \leq 50$$
$$10x_2 + 10x_3 + 15x_5 + 10x_4 + 15x_6 \leq 50$$
$$10x_3 + 15x_5 + 10x_4 + 15x_6 + 15x_7 + 15x_9 \leq 50$$
$$15x_5 + 10x_4 + 15x_6 + 15x_7 + 15x_9 + 15x_8 + 15x_{10}$$
$$+15x_{12} \leq 50$$
$$15x_6 + 15x_7 + 15x_9 + 15x_8 + 15x_{10} + 15x_{12} + 15x_{11}$$
$$+15x_{13} \leq 50$$
$$15x_7 + 15x_9 + 15x_8 + 15x_{10} + 15x_{12} + 15x_{11} + 15x_{13}$$
$$+15x_{14} \leq 50$$
$$15x_8 + 15x_{10} + 15x_{12} + 15x_{11} + 15x_{13} + 15x_{14}$$
$$+15x_{15} \leq 50$$
$$15x_{11} + 15x_{13} + 15x_{14} + 15x_{15} \leq 50$$

(10)

6   Output Result

6.1   Simulation Strategy

In this paper, while comparing the performance of algorithms, we focus on computational time required to find the solution. For comparing the speed of the algorithms, the first thing we require is a fair time measurement. The number of iterations or generations cannot be accepted as a time measure since the algorithms perform different amount of works in their inner loops. Hence, we choose the number of *fitness function evaluations (FEs)* as a measure of computation time instead of generations or iterations. Since the algorithms are stochastic in nature, the results of two successive runs usually do not match. Hence, we have taken 20 independent runs (with different seeds of the random number generator) of each algorithm. The results have been stated in terms of the mean values and standard deviations over the 20 runs in HAS and TLBO case.

Finally, we would like to point out that all the experiment codes are implemented in MATLAB. The experiments are conducted on a Pentium 4, 1GB memory desktop in Windows XP 2007 environment.

6.2   Experimental Results

For comparing the results of scheduling problem here we have considered Fuzzy 0-1 Integer Programming, Implicit enumeration, Harmony search algorithm and teaching learning based optimization. To judge the accuracy for optimal solution obtained by HSA and TLBO algorithm, each of them run for a very long time. Then, we note the result as found. The results obtained from the algorithms and the values reported are averages over *20* simulations, with standard deviations to indicate the range of values to which the algorithms converge. Result for Fuzzy 0-1 integer programming and Implicit Enumeration are taken from paper [1][9]. All detail for the result is given in the table 3 for 1st objective function and in the table 4 for 2nd objective function

Table 3. Objective function with c_1 vector

x	Fuzzy 0-1 Integer Programming	Implicit Enumeration	Harmonic Search Algorithm	TLBO Algorithm
x_1	0	1	1	1
x_2	0	0	0	0
x_3	1	0	0	0
x_4	0	0	0	0
x_5	1	1	1	1
x_6	0	0	0	0
x_7	0	0	0	0
x_8	0	0	0	0
x_9	1	1	1	1
x_{10}	0	0	0	0

Table 3. *(Continued)*

x_{11}	0	0	0	0
x_{12}	0	0	0	0
x_{13}	0	0	0	0
x_{14}	0	0	0	0
x_{15}	1	1	1	1
Z	9	7	7	7
No of fitness evaluation in Mean std	-	-	Fitness evaluation more than 30,000	1483 187.76

Table 4. Objective function with c_2 vector

X	Fuzzy 0-1 Integer Programming	Implicit Enumeration	Harmonic Search Algorithm	TLBO Algorithm
x_1	0	1	1	1
x_2	0	0	0	0
x_3	1	0	0	0
x_4	0	0	0	0
x_5	1	1	1	1
x_6	0	0	0	0
x_7	0	0	0	0
x_8	0	0	0	0
x_9	1	1	1	1
x_{10}	0	0	0	0
x_{11}	0	0	0	0
x_{12}	0	0	0	0
x_{13}	0	0	0	0
x_{14}	0	0	0	0
x_{15}	1	1	1	1
Z	5	3	3	3
No.of fitness evalution in Mean std	-	-	Fitness evaluation more than 70,000	2941 307.962

From the table 3 and table 4 it is clear that the compared with Leou's method (Fuzzy 0-1 Integer Programming) that calculates Z in 9 and 5 values [1], [9], HSA and TLBO are more proper and simpler. Also, in comparison to implicit enumeration that calculates Z in 7 and 3 values [1], HSA and TLBO are faster. Again if we will compare TLBO and HSA then TLBO is more faster, as it converges in less fitness evaluation.

7   Conclusion

In this paper, 0-1 Integer Programming based on the Teaching learning based optimization (TLBO) for finding an optimal generation maintenance schedule is presented. The purpose of objective function is to make units maintain as earlier as possible. Constraints are spinning reserve, crew and duration of maintenance. Comparing the optimal schedule with other optimization methods indicates that ours is better than others.

References

1. Mohammadi Tabari, N., Pirmoradian, M., Hassanpour, S.B.: Implicit enumeration based 0-1 integer programming for generation maintenance scheduling. In: Proceedings of the International Conference on Computational Technologies in Electrical and Electronics Engineering, IEEE REGION 8 SIBIRCON 2008, pp. 151–154 (2008)
2. Rao, R.V., Savsani, V.J., Vakharia, D.P.: Teaching-Learning-Based Optimization: An optimization method for continuous non-linear large scale problems. Information Sciences 183(1), 1–15 (2012)
3. Rao, R.V., Savsani, V.J., Vakharia, D.P.: Teaching-learning-based optimization: A novel method for constrained mechanical design optimization problems. Computer-Aided Design 43(3), 303–315 (2011)
4. Rao, R.V., Savsani, V.J., Balic, J.: Teaching-learning-based optimization algorithm for unconstrained and constrained real parameter optimization problems. Engineering Optimization (in press, 2012),
   http://dx.doi.org/10.1080/0305215X.2011.652103
5. Rao, R.V., Savsani, V.J., Vakharia, D.P.: Teaching–learning-based optimization: A novel method for constrained mechanical design optimization problems. Elsevier, Computer-Aided Design 43, 303–315 (2011)
6. Leou, R.C., Yih, S.A.: A flexible unit maintenance scheduling using fuzzy 0-1 integer programming. In: Proceedings of IEEE Power Engineering Society Summer Meeting, pp. 2551–2555 (2000)
7. Leou, R.C.: A flexibleunit maintenance scheduling considering uncertainties. IEEE Transactions on Power Systems 16, 552–559 (2001)
8. Fetanat, A., Shafipour, G.: Harmony Search Algorithm Based 0-1 Integer Programming For Generation Maintenance Scheduling in Power Systems. Journal of Theoretical and Applied Information Technology
9. Huang, C.J., Lin, C.E., Huang, C.L.: Fuzzy approach for generator maintenance scheduling. Electr. Power Syst. Res. 24, 31–38 (1992)
10. Marwali, M.K.C., Shahidehpour, S.M.: Integrated generation and transmission maintenance scheduling with network constraints. IEEE Transactions on Power Systems 13, 1063–1068 (1998)
11. Geetha, T., Shanti Swarup, K.: Coordinated preventive maintenance scheduling of GENCO and TRANSCO in restructured power systems. International Journal of Electrical Power & Energy Systems 31, 626–638 (2009)
12. Chattopadhyay, D.: A practical maintenance scheduling program: mathematical model and case study. IEEE Transactions on Power Systems 13, 1475–1480 (1998)

13. Dailva, E.L., Schilling, M.T., Rafael, M.C.: Generation maintenance scheduling considering transmission constraints. IEEE Transactions on Power Systems 15, 838–843 (2000)
14. Marwali, M.K.C., Shahidehpour, S.M.: Short-term transmission line maintenance scheduling in a deregulated system. IEEE Transactions on Power Systems 15, 1117–1124 (2000)
15. Moro, L.M., Ramos, A.: Goal programming approach to maintenance scheduling of generating units in large scale power systems. IEEE Transactions on Power Systems 14, 1021–1028 (1999)
16. El-Amin, I., Duffuaa, S., Abbas, M.: A Tabu search algorithm for maintenance scheduling of generating units. Electric Power Systems Research 54, 91–99 (2000)
17. Daha, K.P., Burt, G.M., McDonald, J.R., Galloway, S.J.: Ga/sa based hybrid techniques for the Scheduling of generator maintenance in power systems. In: Proceedings of Congress on Evolutionary Computation, pp. 547–567 (2000)
18. Huang, S.: Generator maintenance scheduling: a fuzzy system approach with genetic enhancement. Electric Power Systems Research 41, 233–239 (1997)
19. El-Sharkh, M.Y., El-Keib, A.A., Chen, H.: A fuzzy evolutionary programming-based solution methodology for security-constrained generation maintenance scheduling. ElectricPower Systems Research 67, 67–72 (2003)
20. Kim, H., Moon, S., Choi, J., Lee, S., Do, D., Gupta, M.M.: Generation maintenance scheduling considering air pollution based on the fuzzy theory. In: Proceedings of IEEE International Fuzzy System, pp. III-1759–III-1764 (1999)
21. Siahkali, H., Vakilian, M.: Electricity generation scheduling with large-scale wind farms using particle swarm optimization. Electric Power Systems Research 79, 826–836 (2009)
22. Foong, W.K.: Ant colony optimization for power plant maintenance scheduling. PhD thesis, The University of Adelaide (2007)
23. Satapathy, S.C., Naik, A.: Data Clustering Based on Teaching-Learning-Based Optimization. In: Panigrahi, B.K., Suganthan, P.N., Das, S., Satapathy, S.C. (eds.) SEMCCO 2011, Part II. LNCS, vol. 7077, pp. 148–156. Springer, Heidelberg (2011)
24. Krishnanand, K.R., Panigrahi, B.K., Rout, P.K., Mohapatra, A.: Application of Multi-Objective Teaching-Learning-Based Algorithm to an Economic Load Dispatch Problem with Incommensurable Objectives. In: Panigrahi, B.K., Suganthan, P.N., Das, S., Satapathy, S.C. (eds.) SEMCCO 2011, Part I. LNCS, vol. 7076, pp. 697–705. Springer, Heidelberg (2011)
25. Rao, R.V., Savsani, V.J.: Mechanical design optimization using advanced optimization techniques. Springer, London (2012)

Time Series Quanslet: A Novel Primitive for Image Classification

Tusar Kanti Mishra[1] and Arun K. Pujari[2]

[1] National Institute of Technology Rourkela, India
[2] Central University of Hyderabad, India
{tusar.k.mishra,arun.k.pujari}@gmail.com

Abstract. successful indexing/categorization of images greatly enhance the performance of content based retrieval systems by filtering out irrelevant classes. This rather difficult problem has not been adequately addressed in current image database systems. In this paper we have introduced a novel feature for classification of image data by taking the one dimensional representation of it (time series) as our input data. Here we have chosen local shape feature instead of global shape feature for the said purpose which enhances its consistency in case of distorted and mutilated shapes.

Keywords: classification, data mining, quanslet.

1 Introduction

Grouping images into semantically meaningful categories is a challenging and important problem in content based image retrieval. As image shapes can be converted into time series [1] the simple nearest neighbor algorithm [2][3] has been suggested as a good tool for solving many time series problems for its simplicity. On the other hand, the simple nearest neighbor algorithm is found to posses some drawbacks while solving for time series problems. First, the nearest neighbor algorithm requires storing and searching the entire dataset, resulting in a time and space complexity that limits its applicability. Second, beyond mere classification accuracy, we often wish to gain some insight into the data unlike simple nearest neighbor algorithm which is unable to reason for why a particular object it assigns to a particular class. In this work we introduce a new time series primitive, time series quanslets, which is able to overcome these limitations. Again, it is also capable of classifying somehow distorted or mutilated time series. Informally, quanslets are quantized time series subsequences which are in some sense maximally representative of a class.

The straight forward problem is to properly classify different images into their corresponding classes in a given dataset. For simplicity, consider a set of image objects $D = d_1, d_2, \ldots, d_n$ even though D might be a multi-class object collection, we'll initially assume each object d_i is either of type class-I or Not class-I. Our primary task is to extract some local feature q_1 among the d_i's that is maximally representative of the class-1 objects and particularly discriminating

M. Parashar et al. (Eds.): IC3 2012, CCIS 306, pp. 64–72, 2012.

them from the rest in D (a case of binary classification). Next, we generalize this concept to rest of the d_is and find q_2 which will discriminate the objects of class-2 from the rest in D. similarly, we find all the q_i's where i is the total number of different classes. That is, in the later part we generalize the binary classification approach into multiple one. These local features are to be used as classifiers for distinguishing between objects in a database. Simultaneously we'll put emphasis on increasing the time as well as space efficiency.

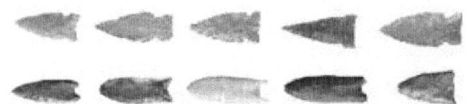

Fig. 1. Top: Clovis Projectile Points, Bottom: Avonlea Projectile Points

For an illustration consider Fig-1 representing projectile points of two different classes *Avonlea* and *Clovis*. Suppose we want to build a classifier to distinguish between these two arrowheads: what features should we use? Well, for this we better go for the shapes because the color and size within each class limits the inter variability. Further, the differences in the global shapes are very subtle and the distortion due to damages by external forces is also apparent for which taking global shape for the classification is not suggested. So, we attempt the following. We convert each projectile point image into quantized one dimensional representation. In recent years simple one dimensional representation has been successfully implemented for classification and clustering non-noisy shapes [4]. Now, instead of comparing the entire shapes we may compare a small quantized subsection of a shape which still serves the same objective saving time as well as space. This subsection should be of the nature of particularly discriminating two classes. We can term such subsections as *quanslets* (Quantized Shapelets/sub-shapes).

The particular difference between *avonlea* and *clovis* Arrowhead is that there is a un-notched hafting (Fig-2) area near the bottom connected by a deep concave bottom end in *clovis*. After we find the *quanslet* and recorded its distance to the nearest matching subsequence in all the objects in the database, we can build a simple decision tree classifier. With this we may have idea about several advantages of *quanslet* that:

1. *Quanslet* can give interpretable results.
2. As *quanslets* are local features, they can be significantly more accurate on classification, because taking global features can be brittle to a small distortion also.
3. The rate of classification is very fast, i.e. less than $O(ml)$, here m is the length of the query time series and l is the length of the *quanslet*.

Fig. 2. Local feature of the clovis arrowhead that particularly discriminates it from avonlea

2   Related Works and Background

The problem we intend to solve here is believed to be unique. Our work is somehow closer to that of [5] and [6]. In [6] the authors have taken all sub-signals as candidate patterns which can be observed as a form of supervised motif discovery algorithm [7], however we believe that the time and space consumed here can be reduced efficiently without hampering the quality of the outcome.

3   Definitions

1. *Time Series*: A Time Series $T = t_1, t_2, \ldots, t_m$ is an ordered set of m real val-
    ued variables. Data points $t_1, t_2, \ldots, t_m$ are typically arranged by temporal
    order, spaced at equal time intervals. We are interested in the local proper-
    ties of a time series rather than the global properties. A local subsection of
    time series is termed as a subsequence.
2. *Subsequence*: Given a time series T of length m, a subsequence S of T is
    a sampling of length $l = m$ of contiguous positions from T, that is, $S = t_p, \ldots, t_p + l - 1$, for $1 = p = ml + 1$. Our algorithm needs to extract all
    of the subsequences of a certain length. This is achieved by using a sliding
    window of the appropriate size.
3. *Sliding Window*: Given a time series T of length m, and a user-defined
    subsequence length of l, all possible subsequences can be extracted by sliding
    a window of size l across T and considering each subsequence $S_p l$ of T. Here
    the superscript l is the length of the subsequence and subscript p indicates
    the starting position of the sliding window in the time series. The set of
    all subsequences of length l extracted from T is defined as $S_T l$, $S_T l = S_p lofT, for 1 < p < ml + 1$. As with virtually all time series data mining
    tasks, we need to provide a similarity measure between the time series Dist
    (T, R).
4. *Distance between the time series*: *Dist (T, R)* is a distance function that
    takes two time series T and R which are of the same length as inputs and
    returns a non negative value d, which is said to be the distance between T
    and R. We require that the function *Dist* be symmetrical; that is, $Dist(R, T)$
    $= Dist (T, R)$. The Dist function can also be used to measure the distance
    between two subsequences of the same length, since the subsequences are of
    the same format as the time series. However, we will also need to measure

the similarity between a short subsequence and a (potentially much) longer time series.

5. *Distance from the time series to the subsequence*: $SubsequenceDist(T, S)$ is a distance function that takes time series T and subsequence S as inputs and returns a nonnegative value d, which is the distance from T to S. $SubsequenceDist(T, S) = min(Dist(S, S'))$, Intuitively, this distance is simply the distance between S and its best matching location somewhere in T.

6. *Entropy*: A time series dataset D consists of two classes, A and B. Given that the proportion of objects in class A is $p(A)$ and the proportion of objects in class B is $p(B)$, the entropy of D is: $I(D) = -p(A)log(p(A)) - p(B)log(p(B))$.

4 Finding the Quanslet

The quanslet approach suggested by us, on the other hand beautifully resolves the above mentioned two major drawbacks of the *shapelet* approach. Again, this maintains the important data mining feature like getting into the depth of the data. In general *quanslet* returns the same *gain* values, even in some cases *quanslet* approach found to be returning better *gain* values than the best so far published technique-the *shapelet* approach. The proposed algorithm for finding the *quanslet* is mentioned as in table 8 along with its related sub procedures in 9, 10 and 11 respectively.

Algorithm 1. FindQuanslet(dataset D)

1: $Candidates \leftarrow GenerateCandidates(D)$
2: $bsf\_gain \leftarrow 0$
3: **for** Each Q in *candidates* **do**
4:      $gain \leftarrow CheckCandidate(D, Q)$
5:      **if** $gain > bsf\_gain$ **then**
6:          $bsf\_gain \leftarrow gain$
7:          $bsf\_Quanslet \leftarrow Q$
8:      **end if**
9: **end for**
10: Return $bsf\_quanslet$

Given a combined dataset D, in which each quantized time series object is labeled either *class A* or *class B*, along with the candidate subsequences as generated using a *trie* data structure in algorithm-2. Then, it stores them in the unordered list called the candidates. After initializing the best information gain bsf_gain to be zero (line 2), it checks how well each candidate in candidates can separate objects in *class A* and *class B*(line 3 to 7). For each candidate it obtains the information gain achieved if that candidate is used to separate the data (line 4). As illustrated in Fig-3 we can visualize this as placing class annotated points on the real number line, representing the distance of each time series to the candidate. Intuitively, we hope to find that this mapping produces two well separated pure groups.

Fig. 3. Objects arranged in the number line as per their distance to the quantized time series subsequence, dotted line represents split point

If the information gain is higher than the *bsf_gain* then the algorithm updates the *bsf_gain* and the corresponding best *quanslet* to be *bsf_quanslet*. Finally it returns the candidate with highest information gain (line 10).

The two subroutines GenerateCandidates() and CheckCandidate() called in the algorithm are outlined in algorithm2 and algorithm3, respectively. Algorithm2 begins by considering empty *trie* and empty *pool*. It inserts the individual quantized time series into the *trie*(line-4). Then, using *voting experts* it segments the series into appropriate number of candidates [8].

Algorithm 2. Generate_Candidates(dataset D)

1: $Trie \leftarrow \phi, pool \leftarrow \phi$
2: **for** T in D **do**
3:        Insert(Trie, t)
4: **end for**
5: **for** t in T **do**
6:        $vote(loc(t)) \leftarrow VotingExpert(Trie, t)$
7:        **if** $vote(loc(t)) \geq threshold\_vote$ **then**
8:              $pool \leftarrow pool \cup segments(loc(t), T)$
9:        **end if**
10: **end for**
11: Return pool

Algorithm-3 inserts all of the quantized time series objects into the histogram object_histogram according to the distance from the object to the candidate in line 1 to 4. After that, the algorithm returns the utility of that candidate by calling CalculateInformationGain() in line 6.

After building the distance histogram for all of the time series objects to a certain candidate, the algorithm will find a split point that divides the time series objects into two sub sets (denoted by dashed line in Fig-3). As noted in definition-g, an optimal split point is a distance threshold. Comparing the distance from each quantized time series objects in the dataset to the candidate with the threshold, we can divided the dataset into two sub sets, which achieves the highest information gain among all of the possible partitions. Any point

---

Algorithm 3. Generate_Candidates(dataset D)

1: $objects\_histogram \leftarrow \phi$
2: **for** each T in D **do**
3:      $dist \leftarrow SubsequenceDist(Q, S)$
4:      insert Q into objects_histogram by the key dist
5: **end for**
6: ReturnCalculateInformationGain(objects_histogram)

Algorithm 4. CalculateInformationGain(distance histogram objhist)

1: split_dist$\leftarrow$ OptimalSplitPoint(obj_hist)
2: $D_1 \leftarrow \phi, D_2 \leftarrow \Phi$
3: **for** d in obj_hist **do**
4:      **if** $d.dist < split\_dist$ **then**
5:          $D_1 \leftarrow D_1 \cup d.objects$
6:      **else**
7:          $D_2 \leftarrow D_2 \cup d.objects$
8:      **end if**
9: **end for**
10: Return $I(D) - I'(D)$

---

on the positive real number line could be a split point, so there are infinite possibilities from which to choose. To make the search space smaller, we check only the mean values of each pair of adjacent points in the histogram as a possible split point. This reduction still finds all of the possible information gain values since the information gain cannot change in the region between two adjacent points. Furthermore, in this way, we maximize the margin between two sub sets.

5   Experimental Evaluation

5.1   Spanish vs Polish War Shiels

War shields classification is an important topic in Anthropology. War shields can be divided into different classes based on the location they are found, the human mass that created them, and the date they were in use, we show some samples of the war shields used in our experiments.

We convert the shapes of the Shields to a time series using the angle-based method taking the following parameters. We then randomly created a 16/113 training/test split. For the training phase we simply took 8/8 training data. With angular method corresponding time series were generated and further quantized. Using the proposed algorithms the time series were segmented and some quanslets were generated.

Fig. 4. Top: Polish war shields, Bottom: Spanish war shields

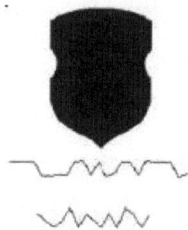

Fig. 5. Top: Polish war shields, Middle: Shape Descriptor, Bottom: Quantized Time series

The results thus obtained were compared with that of the shapelet approach [6] as shown in Fig-6. The quanslet approach was found utilizing too less of time for its overall execution. Also due to use of proper segmentation algorithm it also reduced the size of the total candidate pool. Back referring to the original image, the proper pieces of local shapes that are responsible for identifying each class were also found to be apparent. Thus, giving us a mining capability.

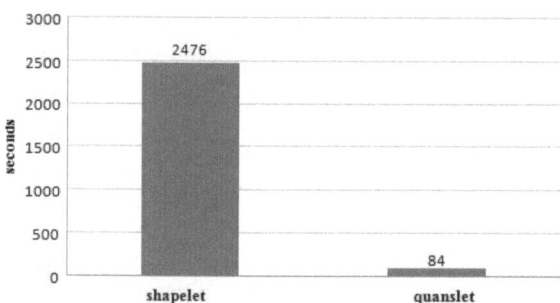

Fig. 6. Execution time comparison: shapelet vs quanslet

5.2   Clovis vs Avonlea Arrowheads

The examples cited at the beginning of this paper discusses about these arrowheads. For this 22/158 strain/test samples were taken. While experimenting

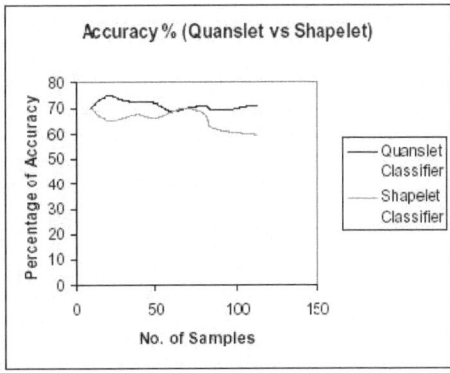

Fig. 7. Accuracy comparison: shapelet vs quanslet

with these, it was found that the accuracy of the proposed approach exactly approximated the shapelet approach. But, it got accomplished in a very little time as compared to the later one proving its time efficiency. We achieved the same discriminating local feature (Fig-2).

6 Conclusion

The proposed method is found to be time efficient, yet having some mining capability. It is also proving itself to be a good classifier. Our further work includes using quanslets for classification of optical characters (ocr).

References

1. Keogh, E., Wei, L., Xi, X., Lee, S.-H., Vlachos, M.: Lb_keogh supports exact indexing of shapes under rotation invariance with arbitrary representations and distance measures. In: Proceedings of the 32nd International Conference on Very Large Data Bases. VLDB Endowment, pp. 882–893 (2006)
2. Ding, H., Trajcevski, G., Scheuermann, P., Wang, X., Keogh, E.: Querying and mining of time series data: experimental comparison of representations and distance measures. In: Proc. VLDB Endow., vol. 1(2), pp. 1542–1552 (2008)
3. Salzberg, S.L.: On comparing classifiers: Pitfalls to avoid and a recommended approach. In: Data Mining and Knowledge Discovery, vol. 1(3), pp. 317–328 (1997)
4. Phillips, D.: Image Processing in C, 2nd edn. R and D publication (2000)
5. Geurts, P.: Pattern Extraction for Time Series Classification. In: Siebes, A., De Raedt, L. (eds.) PKDD 2001. LNCS (LNAI), vol. 2168, pp. 115–127. Springer, Heidelberg (2001)

6. Ye, L., Keogh, E.: Time series shapelets: a new primitive for data mining. In: Proceedings of the 15th ACM SIGKDD International Conference on Knowledge Discovery and Data Mining, pp. 947–956. ACM (2009)
7. Chiu, B., Keogh, E., Lonardi, S.: Probabilistic discovery of time series motifs. In: Proceedings of the Ninth ACM SIGKDD International Conference on Knowledge Discovery and Data Mining, ser. KDD 2003, pp. 493–498. ACM (2003)
8. Cohen, P., Heeringa, B., Adams, N.: Unsupervised segmentation of categorical time series into episodes. In: Proceedings of the 2002 IEEE International Conference on Data Mining, pp. 99–106. IEEE Computer Society (2002)

A Fast Algorithm for Learning Weighted Ensemble of Roles

Abdullah Almutairi, Sanjay Ranka, and Manas Somaiya

Computer Information Science & Engineering Department, University of Florida
{aalmutai,ranka}@cise.ufl.edu,
manas@computer.org

Abstract. The POWER (PrObabilistic Weighted Ensemble of Roles) model[1] is a Bayesian mixture model where a single data point is generated by multiple components with varying degrees of influence. This is unlike standard mixture models where each data point is generated by a single mixture component. The POWER model allows for capturing various hidden and complexly overlapping components and roles of entities that contribute to generating the data points. However, the POWER model suffers from a very slow learning time. The highest complexity time of the parameters' learning steps is $O\left(n \cdot k \cdot d^2\right)$, with n being the number of data points, k the number of components of the model and d the number of data attributes.

In this paper, we propose an approximation to the POWER model weight parameter learning algorithm that reduces the computational time significantly. The overall complexity of the new algorithm is $O\left(n \cdot k \cdot d \cdot p\right)$ in practice (where p is an approximation parameter much smaller than d). This allows the model learning time to be linear in the number of attributes of the data and provides a significant speedup over the original algorithm.

We demonstrate the accuracy of our approximation technique using synthetic and real datasets. We also provide experimental results of the approximate POWER model on a dataset of NIPS papers and a dataset of wireless web access patterns and show that the model learnt are similar. An implementation of the approximate POWER model on the dataset of NIPS papers is about 27 times faster than the original version.

Keywords: Mixture Model, Data Mining, Approximation.

1 Introduction

Mixture models have been used to model and cluster data for several decades. A probabilistic mixture model uses a combination of probability distributions (components) to model complex data. The Gaussian Mixture Model [GMM], one of the most popular mixture models, assumes that data points are generated by sampling from a mixture of 'k' Gaussians.

The PrObabilistic Weighted Ensemble of Roles model or "POWER" model[1] for short, is a new class of mixture models where multiple components compete with a varying degree of influence to produce a single data point. This class of mixture models helps in discovering hidden complex patterns in the data.

M. Parashar et al. (Eds.): IC3 2012, CCIS 306, pp. 73–85, 2012.

However, the POWER model suffers from a very long learning time in order to detect these complex overlapping data patterns. It has been shown that it takes around 300 hours to learn the 21-component model on a large data set called the NIPS papers data set. The NIPS papers dataset represents the top 1000 non-trivial words collected from 1500 conference papers. The long learning time is mainly due to the time complexity of the model which is $O\left(n \cdot k \cdot d^2\right)$ where n is the number of data points, k is the number of components and d the number of attributes. This computational cost is specifically inflicted in the weight parameter update step of the Gibbs sampler that is used to learn the model. Such high execution time prohibits scaling the application of the POWER framework for high-dimensional datasets.

In this paper, we propose an approximation to the POWER model weight parameter learning algorithm that reduces the computational time significantly. The overall complexity of the new algorithm is $O\left(n \cdot k \cdot d \cdot p\right)$ in practice, where p is the number of partitions used in our approximation and is much smaller than d. This allows the model learning time to be linear in the number of attributes of the data and provides a significant speedup over the original algorithm.

We demonstrate the accuracy of our approximation technique using synthetic and real datasets. We also provide experimental results of the approximate POWER model on the NIPS dataset and the wireless datasets and show that the model learned is similar. An implementation of the approximate POWER model on the NIPS papers dataset with 1000 dimensions is about 27 times faster than the original version.

2   Method

Bayesian inference for the POWER model is accomplished via Gibbs sampling. This algorithm is used to generate samples from a joint probability distribution of many random variables. This is especially useful when it is easy to sample from the conditional distributions of the random variables. The Gibbs sampler is a Monte Carlo Markov Chain that when it is run for numerous iterations reaches the steady state where the samples closely approximate the joint probability distribution of the random variables.

The compute intensiveness of the overall algorithm is in the portion that learns the weight matrix. Due to the paper size restrictions, the description of the POWER model and some other details of our method can be found in our technical report in the following link http://www.cise.ufl.edu/tr/DOC/REP-2012-541.pdf.

2.1   Weight Learning in the POWER Model

The POWER model uses the Gibbs sampling algorithm to learn the parameters of the model. Gibbs sampling is used to generate samples from a joint probability distribution of many random variables. It is especially used when it is hard to sample the joint probability distribution of the random variables but it is simpler to sample from the conditional distribution of those random variables. The Gibbs sampler is an iterative algorithm, it starts from a random initialization and updates the value of each random variable by sampling from its conditional distribution w.r.t all other random variables.

The conditional distribution of the mask value m (the non-normalized weight w) is represented as,

$$F(m_{i,j} \mid X, c, w, \theta, \alpha) \propto \gamma(w_{i,j} \mid q, r) \cdot \prod_a \prod_j \frac{w_{g_{a,j},j} \cdot I(c_{a,g_{a,j}} = 1)}{\sum_i w_{i,j} \cdot I(c_{a,i} = 1)}. \qquad (1)$$

Where q and r are user defined prior parameters for m, $I()$ is an indicator function that evaluates to 1 if the logical argument provided to it is true, and 0 otherwise, and,

$$w_{i,j} = \frac{m_{i,j}}{\sum_j m_{i,j}}. \qquad (2)$$

The second term of the RHS in (1) is the likelihood function, which takes $O(n \cdot d)$ time to update the value of one weight $w_{i,j}$. Then, the time to update the $k \times d$ values of W is $O(n \cdot k \cdot d^2)$. To clearly show the time requirement of each weight update, the Log Likelihood function (LL) of (1) is going to be used from now on. It is also what is being approximated in our proposed method. The Log Likelihood function is obtained by first taking the log of the RHS in (1):

$$\log\left(\gamma(w_{i,j} \mid q, r) \cdot \prod_a \prod_j \frac{w_{g_{a,j},j} \cdot I(c_{a,g_{a,j}} = 1)}{\sum_i w_{i,j} \cdot I(c_{a,i} = 1)}\right). \qquad (3)$$

Then focusing on the likelihood function part in (3) and converting the products into sums using the log properties.

$$\sum_{a=1}^{n} \sum_{j=1}^{d} \log\left(\frac{w_{g_{a,j},j} \cdot I(c_{a,g_{a,j}} = 1)}{\sum_i w_{i,j} \cdot I(c_{a,i} = 1)}\right). \qquad (4)$$

The weights are going to be divided to the active weight of component i and the sum of active weights for all other components. Below is the Log Likelihood function that we are going to use to update the weights:

$$LL_{i,j} = \sum_{a=1}^{n} \sum_{j2=1}^{d} (\log(\underbrace{\frac{w_{i,j2}}{\overline{w}_{a,j2} + w_{i,j2}}}_{g_{a,j2}=i}) + \log(\underbrace{\frac{\overline{w}_{a,j2}}{\overline{w}_{a,j2} + w_{i,j2}}}_{g_{a,j2}\neq i})). \qquad (5)$$

Where $\overline{w}_{a,j2}$ are elements of the $n \times d$ matrix called the Against Weight $\overline{W}$. elements of this matrix represent the sum of active weights from all components beside i,

$$\overline{w}_{a,j2} = \sum_{i2=1}^{k} \underbrace{w_{i2,j2}}_{c_{a,i2}\neq i}. \qquad (6)$$

After each weight $w_{i,j}$ is updated, all of the other elements of W_i vector is modified to maintain the constraint that $\sum_{j=1}^{d} w_{i,j} = 1$. The change to the other elements of W_i

is by a factor of $\frac{1-w'_{i,j}}{1-w_{i,jPREV}}$, where $w'_{i,j}$ is the new updated $w_{i,j}$ and $w_{i,jPREV}$ is the previous value in $w_{i,j}$. We call this factor an Update Ratio (UR_j). We will show below the changes happening to W_i after each weight update. $W_i^{(j)}$ denotes W_i after updating the jth weight.

The original W_i vector:

$$W_i = \langle w_{i,1}, w_{i,2}, \cdots, w_{i,d} \rangle .$$

After updating the value of $w_{i,1}$ using (1) W_i becomes:

$$W_i^{(1)} = \langle w'_{i,1}, UR_1 \cdot w_{i,2}, \cdots, UR_1 \cdot w_{i,d} \rangle .$$

where,

$$UR_1 = \frac{1 - w'_{i,1}}{1 - w_{i,1}}. \tag{7}$$

After updating the value of $w_{i,2}$:

$$W_i^{(2)} = \langle UR_2 \cdot w'_{i,1}, w'_{i,2}, \cdots, UR_2 \cdot UR_1 \cdot w_{i,d} \rangle .$$

where,

$$UR_2 = \frac{1 - w'_{i,2}}{1 - UR_1 \cdot w_{i,2}}. \tag{8}$$

In general, after updating the value of $w_{i,j}$:

$$W_i^{(j)} = \left\langle \prod_{t=2}^{j} UR_t \cdot w'_{i,1}, \prod_{t=3}^{j} UR_t \cdot w'_{i,2}, \cdots, UR_j \cdot w'_{i,j-1}, w'_{i,j}, \right.$$
$$\left. \prod_{t=1}^{j} UR_t \cdot w_{i,j+1}, \cdots, \prod_{t=1}^{j} UR_t \cdot w_{i,d} \right\rangle .$$

where,

$$UR_j = \frac{1 - w'_{i,j}}{1 - w_{i,j} \cdot \prod_{t=1}^{j-1} UR_t}. \tag{9}$$

After updating the values of the whole vector:

$$W_i^{(d)} = \left\langle \prod_{t=2}^{d} UR_t \cdot w'_{i,1}, \prod_{t=3}^{d} UR_t \cdot w'_{i,2}, \cdots, UR_d \cdot w'_{i,d-1}, w'_{i,d} \right\rangle .$$

where,

$$UR_d = \frac{1 - w'_{i,d}}{1 - w_{i,d} \cdot \prod_{t=1}^{d-1} UR_t}. \tag{10}$$

Approximation Algorithm: In this section, we propose an approximation to Equation (1) reducing the time requirements to update W_i. Let us first simplify equation 5:

$$LL_{i,j} = \sum_{a=1}^{n} \sum_{j2=1}^{d} (\underbrace{\log(w_{i,j2})}_{g_{a,j2}=i} + \underbrace{\log(\overline{w_{a,j2}})}_{g_{a,j2}\neq i}) - \sum_{a=1}^{n} \sum_{j2=1}^{d} \log(\overline{w_{a,j2}} + w_{i,j2}). \quad (11)$$

During the update of W_i elements using equation (1), $\overline{W}$ elements do not change between updates since they are not dependent on W_i, W_i elements on the other hand change after each update. Since some values in computing $LL_{i,j}$ for W_i do not change ($\overline{W}$), and other values ($w_{i,\star}$ except $w_{i,j}$) change by a certain factor (UR_j) after updating $w_{i,j}$, it is possible to use a computed value of $LL_{i,j}$ to compute $LL_{i,j+1}$ in a lesser time. Therefore, $LL_{i,1}$ can be first computed to update $w_{i,1}$ then their values can be used to compute $LL_{i,2}$ without restarting the whole computation, and so on until $LL_{i,d}$ is computed from $LL_{i,d-1}$ and $w_{i,d-1}$, to finally update $w_{i,d}$. But the following term needs to addressed in order to achieve this idea,

$$\sum_{a=1}^{n} \sum_{j2=1}^{d} \log(\overline{w_{a,j}} + w_{i,j}). \quad (12)$$

Since the W_i elements are summed with elements of $\overline{W}$ inside the log, we have to recompute this term after each update of a W_i element. If the W_i term can be removed or separated out then it is possible to reuse a computed value of $LL_{i,j}$ to compute $LL_{i,j+1}$ by just adding the terms that have the updated W_i values. An approximation is proposed to achieve this incremental computation of all $LL_{i,j}$ values in a lesser time than the original POWER model. The approximation comprises of a set of p chosen elements $\overline{x}$ with corresponding counts n_x. The p-elements of $\overline{x}$ will be modified after each weight $w_{i,j}$ update. We will denote the p-elements of $\overline{x}$ corresponding to $w_{i,j}$ by $\overline{x}_j$. The p is chosen to be much smaller than the number of attributes d. These elements and corresponding counts will be chosen to satisfy the following:

$$\sum_{p=1}^{P} n_{x_p} \cdot \log(\overline{x}_{j,p}) \approx \sum_{a=1}^{n} \sum_{j2=1}^{d} 1 + \frac{\overline{w_{a,j2}}}{w_{i,j2}}. \quad (13)$$

This transforms the second term of equation (11) to the following:

$$\sum_{a=1}^{n} \sum_{j2=1}^{d} -\log(w_{i,j2}) - \sum_{p=1}^{P} n_{x_p} \cdot \log(x_{j,p}). \quad (14)$$

The technical report will discuss in detail the process of computing the p elements of x and n_x. But it should be noted that in the POWER model, $F(m_{i,j})$ is approximated using a Beta distribution. This requires three computations of the conditional in order to fit values for each of the Beta parameters, the two shape parameters and one scale parameter. For this reason, we update each weight three times obtaining three samples of each weight. The three Beta parameters can then be solved. We will show in the next sections the steps of computing our approximate Log Likelihood ($LLapp_{i,j}$) for the first weight update and for the following incremental computation for the second update of the first weight. The computations for the third update of the first weight and for the remainder weights follow the same idea and are discussed in the report.

2.2   The Initial $LLapp$ Computation for the First Weight $w_{i,1}$

We will define new variables used in $LLapp$ for $w_{i,1}$, let $CW = \langle cw_1, cw_2, \cdots, cw_d \rangle$ be a vector of positive integers that represent the number of times $g_{a,j} = i$ for attribute j. So cw_1 is the number of times $g_{a,1} = i$. Another variable used is $sumCW$, which is the sum of all cw elements, $sumCW = \sum_{j=1}^{d} cw_j$. These variables are used to simplify the $LLapp$ equations and to help update the value of $LLapp$ between weight updates. The CW vector computation requires scanning the G matrix once, it is only computed once in the initial $LLapp$ computation. The time then to compute the vector is $O(n \cdot d)$. The equation to compute $LLapp$ for $w_{i,1}$ which will be denoted by $LLapp_{i,1}$ is shown below:

$$LLapp_{i,1} = \sum_{j2=1}^{d} cw_{j2} \cdot \log(w_{i,j2}) + \sum_{a=1}^{n} \sum_{j2=1}^{d} \underbrace{(\log(\overline{w_{a,j2}}) - \log(w_{i,j2}))}_{g_{a,j2} \neq i}$$

$$- \sum_{p=1}^{P} n_{x_p} \cdot \log(\overline{x}_{1,p}). \quad (15)$$

From the computed $LLapp_{i,1}$, a first update of $w_{i,1}$ will be sampled. The first update of $w_{i,1}$ will be denoted by $\acute{w}_{i,1}$, this will be used in $L\acute{L}app_{i,1}$ which is the $LLapp_{i,1}$ equation to find the second update of $w_{i,1}$.

Time Complexity for Computing $LLapp_{i,1}$:   To compute $LLapp_{i,1}$ The CW vector needs to be computed first, which as mentioned will take $O(n \cdot d)$. Also, p-elements of x and n_x needs to be computed, this will take $O(n \cdot d \cdot p)$. The report will describe the time for computing $\overline{x}$ and n_x. The $\overline{x}$ and n_x elements are only computed once in $LLapp_{i,1}$, in the other $LLapp_{i,*-1}$ computations, the p elements of x will only be updated in constant time for each x. Making the total time of $\overline{x}$ updates is $O(p)$, this is handled in the other computations of $LLapp$.

After computing all the values of the needed variables, computing the value for $LLapp_{i,1}$ requires $O(d)$ time to compute the value of the first term. The second and third term of the equation takes $O(n \cdot d)$ time for computing the sum of $\log(\overline{W})$ over all of its elements. The final term that represent our approximation obviously takes $O(d)$ time to compute.

The total time for computing the variables needed and then all of the terms of $LLapp_{i,1}$ is:

$$TotalTime : O(\underbrace{n \cdot d + n \cdot d \cdot p}_{computing\ CW\ and\ \overline{x}} + \underbrace{d + n \cdot d + p}_{computing\ LLapp_{i,1}}) = O(n \cdot d \cdot p). \quad (16)$$

$LLapp_{i,1}$ will take a longer time to compute than $LL_{i,1}$ which had a time of $O(n \cdot d)$. This is due to the overhead of computing our approximation p-elements $\overline{x}$ and n_x. Even though it takes a longer time to compute these elements in $LLapp_{i,1}$, these elements will allow the other computations $LLapp_{i,*-1}$ to just take $O(p \cdot d)$ time altogether to be computed. Making the total time to update all the elements of W_i to be $O(n \cdot d \cdot p)$.

2.3 $LLapp$ for the Second Update of $w_{i,1}$

The original POWER model updates each weight $w_{i,j}$ three times to find three estimates of the beta distribution in order to approximate $F(m_{i,j})$. This leads to somewhat different $LLapp$ equations used for the second and third update of $w_{i,1}$ and for the second and third update of the other weights $w_{i,*-1}$. The $LLapp_{i,j}$ of any second update of $w_{i,j}$ will be denoted with $L\acute{L}app_{i,j}$. $L\acute{L}app_{i,j}$ uses $LLapp_{i,1}$ to compute it's value. $L\acute{L}app_{i,j}$ will also use the same CW and $sumCW$ that was computed in $LLapp_{i,1}$, it also uses $\dot{w}_{i,1}$ which is the first update of $w_{i,1}$ that was computed from $LLapp_{i,1}$. $\dot{U}R_1$ which is the Update Ratio between the first and second update will be used also, this equals:

$$\dot{U}R_1 = \frac{1 - \dot{w}_{i,1}}{1 - w_{i,1}}. \tag{17}$$

Modified values of the p-elements of $\overline{x}_1$ will be computed to find $L\acute{L}app_{i,1}$, they will be denoted by $\dot{\overline{x}}_1$. The report will describe computing those modified values. The term corresponding to the old values of $\overline{x}_1$ then needs to be removed from the $L\acute{L}app_{i,1}$. This is done by adding the term $\sum_{p=1}^{P} n_{x_p} \cdot \log(\overline{x}_p)$, since this term was subtracted from $LLapp_{i,1}$. Finally, the same term with the modified values of $\overline{x}_1$ is incorporated into $L\acute{L}app_{i,1}$ by adding their negative values. It should be noted that the p-elements of n_x will not be modified between weight updates. This will be also be discussed in the report. $L\acute{L}app_{i,1}$ is shown below:

$$L\acute{L}app_{i,1} = LLapp_{i,1} + cw_1 \cdot \log(\dot{w}_{i,1}) + (sumCW - cw_1) \cdot \log(\dot{U}R_1) -$$
$$cw_1 \cdot \log(w_{i,1}) + n \cdot \log(\dot{w}_{i,1}) + (n \cdot d - d) \cdot \log(\dot{U}R_1) - n \cdot \log(w_{i,1}) \tag{18}$$
$$+ \sum_{p=1}^{P} n_{x_p} \cdot \log(\overline{x}_{1,p}) - \sum_{p=1}^{P} n_{x_p} \cdot \log(\dot{\overline{x}}_{1,p}).$$

A second update to $w_{i,1}$ will be sampled from computing $L\acute{L}app_{i,1}$, this will be denoted by $\ddot{w}_{i,1}$. This value will be used similarly in the next update to $w_{i,1}$. The corresponding $LLapp$ will be denoted by $L\tilde{L}app_{i,1}$.

Time Complexity for Computing $L\acute{L}app_{i,1}$: Computing p elements of $\dot{\overline{x}}_1$ will take $O(p)$ time altogether as will be shown in the report. All the other variables in $L\acute{L}app_{i,1}$ are already available, making the time to compute $L\acute{L}app_{i,1}$ is $O(p)$.

The total time for computing the variables needed and then all of the terms of $LLapp_{i,1}$ is:

$$TotalTime : O(\underbrace{p}_{\text{computing } p\text{-elements of } \overline{x}_1} + \underbrace{p}_{\text{computing } LL\acute{a}pp_{i,1}}) = O(p). \qquad (19)$$

The third update follows the same idea as the second update so we omit its details. Then, the total time to find $\acute{w}_{i,1}$ after the three updates to $w_{i,1}$ is:

$$O(n \cdot d \cdot p + p + p) = O(n \cdot d \cdot p).$$

Which is larger than $O(n \cdot d)$ the time to find $\acute{w}_{i,1}$ in the original POWER model. This extra time is important to compute the p-elements of $\overline{x}$ and n_x in the initial computation of $LLapp_{i,1}$, which will help in reducing the time greatly for all the other updates of $w_{i,\star-1}$.

$LLapp$ for the the remainder weights $w_{i,\star-1}$ follow the same idea with a slight change in the indices and will be discussed in the technical report.

What is missing now is how the $LLapp$ equations were constructed from LL. Due to paper size restrictions these details will be discussed in the technical report. But we will show the parts that equation (11) was divided to, leaving the details of handling each part to the report.

$$LL_{i,j} = \sum_{a=1}^{n}\sum_{j2=1}^{d} \underbrace{(\log(w_{i,j2})}_{\substack{g_{a,j2}=i \\ A_{i,j}}} + \underbrace{\log(\overline{w_{a,j2}}))}_{\substack{g_{a,j2}\neq i \\ B_{i,j}}} - \underbrace{\sum_{a=1}^{n}\sum_{j2=1}^{d} \log(\overline{w_{a,j2}} + w_{i,j2})}_{C_{i,j}}. \qquad (20)$$

3   Experiments

This section will show and discuss the results of our approximation on both synthetic and real world data. The POWER model algorithm and approximation was written in C++ and was run on the CISE department's storm AMD64 CPU server as a single thread program.

3.1   Synthetic Data Set Results

We ran our approximate method on synthetic data. The dataset was of size 1500 data points with 20 attributes generated from the mixture of 4 simple patterns. Table 1 shows the original generated patterns and the learned patterns after running our approximate method with 16 partitions. Our method learned all the patterns correctly.

3.2   NIPS Papers Data Set

We tested the approximate version of the POWER model on the NIPS papers data set and compare the results with the original version. The data set consists of words collected from 1500 papers. The vocabulary covers 12419 words, and a total of approximately 6.4 million words can be found in the paper. The top 1000 non-trivial words

Table 1. The generated and learned 4 patterns used for the synthetic dataset. the underbrace under a number is the string length of the number.

Generated pattern 1	$\underbrace{1\cdots1}_{10}\underbrace{0\cdots0}_{10}$
Learned pattern 1	$\underbrace{0.99\cdots0.99}_{10}\underbrace{0\cdots0}_{10}$
Generated pattern 2	$\underbrace{1\cdots1}_{20}$
Learned pattern 2	$\underbrace{0.99\cdots0.99}_{20}$
Generated pattern 3	$\underbrace{0\cdots0}_{10}\underbrace{1\cdots1}_{10}$
Learned pattern 3	$\underbrace{0\cdots0}_{10}\underbrace{0.99\cdots0.99}_{10}$
Generated pattern 4	$\underbrace{1\cdots1}_{5}\underbrace{0\cdots0}_{10}\underbrace{1\cdots1}_{5}$
Learned pattern 4	$\underbrace{0.99\cdots0.99}_{5}\underbrace{0\cdots0}_{10}\underbrace{0.99\cdots0.99}_{5}$

were considered. Each paper was converted to a row of zeros and ones corresponding to the absence and presence of the word respectively. A 0/1 matrix of size 1500 by 1000 was obtained. The number of components k was set to 21.

As per the original paper, KL divergence is used on the results from learning the model to rank the attributes according to importance for all components. Table 2 shows the highly ranked words for some of the components learned from the NIPS data set.

Discussion. As in the original POWER model, each learned component has a clear and intuitive meaning. For example, Component 1 represents words related to theory and proofs. Component 4 represents words related to hardware and electronics. Component 8 represents words related to the brain and the nervous system. Component 9 is concerned with words related to classification and data mining. Component 10 relates to neural networks. Component 12 relates to natural language processing (NLP). Component 13 relates to statistical and Bayesian methods. Component 17 relates to computer vision and image processing. Component 19 is related to robotics and moving objects. Finally, component 20 is concerned with speech processing.

The original version of the POWER model learning for the NIPS data set took 300 hours (431 seconds on average for one iteration of the Gibbs sampling). Our version of the POWER model learning with 16 partitions of the approximation took 8.8 hours (16 seconds on average for one iteration of the Gibbs sampling). This, our version is around 27 times faster than the original version.

3.3 Wireless Data Set

We will run the approximate POWER model on data gathered from the wireless network in the University of Southern California. The method of obtaining the data can be

Table 2. The highest ranked words for some of the components learned from the NIPS data set

Id	Words
1	symbol, turn, variables, definition, proof, unique, mathematical, linearly, implies, exact
3	predictor, predicted, deviation, validation, randomly, true, heuristic, test, smaller, modified
4	chip, vlsi, transistor, hardware, analog, digital, gate, circuit, pulse, voltage, processor, implementation, array, design, winner
8	cortical, cortex, evidence, synaptic, cognitive, orientation, stimuli, mechanism, brain, population, sensory, responses, selective, stimulus, receptive
9	dimensionality, ica, principal, pca, unsupervised, cluster, mixture, kernel, diagonal, clustering, images, nearest, reduction, covariance, decomposition
10	inhibitory, oscillation, synapses, neuronal, excitatory, synapse, synaptic, hebbian, strength, oscillator, inhibition, activity, firing, active, spike
12	language, text, interpretation, similarity, structure, context, string, focus, description, assignment
13	likelihood, posterior, probabilistic, markov, mixtures, probabilities, hmm, bayesian, conditional, bayes, densities, monte, mixture, carlo, belief
17	images, object, pixel, vision, scene, image, contour, resolution, detection, edge, segmentation, translation, visual, invariant, edges
19	reinforcement, reward, policy, sutton, agent, controller, action, programming, exploration, robot, learner, trajectory, environment, starting, strategy
20	acoustic, speaker, phoneme, speech, classifier, vowel, window, mlp, database, segmentation, language, forward, sound

found in [2]. The data represents the wireless Internet users' activity in the campus on march 2008, where the access of the top 100 most visited web domains in campus were observed for 22,816 users. Each user's access pattern was converted to a row of zeros and ones corresponding to the access or non-access of the web domain respectively. A 0/1 matrix of size 22816 by 100 was obtained. The number of components k was set to 21 and the number of partitions for the approximation were chosen to be 16.

KL divergence is again used on the results from learning the model to rank the web domains according to importance for all components. Table 3 shows the highly ranked web domains for some of the components learned from the wireless data set.

Discussion. The approximate version of the POWER model discovers obvious patterns of web domain components. Component 2 captures the domains related to microsoft windows applications. Component 7 represents a group of web domains that are always

Table 3. The highest ranked web domains for some of the components learned from the wireless data set using the approximate version of the POWER model

Id	Web Domains
2	windowsmedia, gridserver, microsoft, microsoftoffice2007, ln, yahoo, adrevolver, youtube, llnw, veoh
7	washingtonpost, cnet, mac, apple, facebook, doubleclick, mediaplex
14	ebayrtm, ebayimg, ebay, adrevolver, tribalfusion, mediaplex, yahoo, panthercdn, doubleclick
17	hotmail, live, net, quiettouch, coremetrics, ln, windowsmedia, microsoft, doubleclick, bankofamerica
18	mcafee, hackerwatch, ln, aol, llnw, doubleclick, mediaplex, facebook

clustered together in [2] and was seen to identify mac users web access patterns. Component 14 discovers the cluster of ebay related domains. Component 17 clusters microsoft email domains, it also captures the relationship between the bank of america domain and the coremetrics domain, which is the online analytics tool it uses. Finally, Component 18 clusters the digital web security web domains together. Component 11 is the cluster of news web domains.

The runtime of the model learning for the approximate POWER model was 16.23 hours, with the weight resampling step taking 11.6 seconds on average per iteration, one complete iteration of the approximate POWER takes 23.38 seconds. This is in contrast to the original POWER model taking 125 seconds on average per iteration, which makes our model about 5.34 times faster.

The overhead of our approximate method appears on data with a small number of attributes, but this overhead disappears when handling data with a large number of attributes since our method is linear with the number of attributes instead of quadratic as the original version. As the number of attributes increase in the data the speedup gain increases also.

4   Related and Future Work

Performance issues arise in Data Mining methods due to the methods' nature of working on very large data sets. This is more so the case in current scientific and commercial applications where there is a higher volume of data processed. Among the techniques used to improve the speed of Data Mining methods are parallel structures and techniques[3]. Parallel techniques have been used on many popular Data Mining algorithms to improve upon. Ye et al. [4] developed a parallel version of the Apriori algorithm where the input is distributed among the nodes and each node computes its local candidate k-itemsets. Each node then sends its local k-itemsets to a master node that computes the sum of all candidates and prunes them resulting in the frequent k-itemsets. Parallelizing k-means clustering has received an extensive amount of study [5,6,7]. Many of the parallel techniques in k-means clustering relied on partitioning the tasks and data among the nodes, some used the map-reduce framework for the same purpose. In computing the averages in our approximation the data was also partitioned among the large number of threads to speed up the operation. Monte Carlo algorithms have also been shown to be suited for parallel computation [8].

Also, data reduction[9] techniques are used to improve the performance of Data Mining methods when working on very large data sets. The technique reduces the number of data points for the input by removing points that are seen to not be a part of any cluster. One way of reducing the data is density bias sampling[10] where the points have different probabilities of being part of the input. This probability depends on the value of prespecified data characteristics and the specific analysis requirements.

We have also designed a straightforward parallel version of the approximation running on a CUDA GPU that further improved on the runtime performance. The improvement was achieved by utilizing the SIMD nature of CUDA and using this to exploit some of the parallelization available in updating parameters of the model and computing the partitions of the approximation faster. The GPU version allowed for around a 40 times speed up over the original model on the NIPS data.

5   Conclusions

In this paper, we proposed an approximation to the POWER model that reduced the complexity time of learning the model to $O(n \cdot k \cdot d)$. The approximation allowed the model learning to be linearly scalable with the number of attributes. This also reduced the running time to a big degree allowing a serial implementation of the model learning to be about 27 times faster than the original POWER model on the NIPS data set. This is the first work done on speeding up the POWER model and improving its complexity time. We have also shown the speed up gain and the correctness of the results using experiments on a couple of real-life datasets.

References

1. Somaiya, M., Jermaine, C., Ranka, S.: A POWER Framework for Multi-Class Membership in Bayesian Mixture Models. In: ACM Conference on Knowledge Discovery and Data Mining (2010)
2. Moghaddam, S., Helmy, A., Ranka, S., Somaiya, M.: Data-driven Co-clustering Model of Internet Usage in Large Mobile Societies. In: 13th ACM Int'l Conf. on Modeling, Analysis and Simulation of Wireless and Mobile Systemss (MSWIM) (2010)
3. Zaki, M.J.: Data mining parallel and distributed association mining: A surray. In: IEEE Concurrency (1999)
4. Ye, Y., Chiang, C.: A Parallel Apriori Algorithm for Frequent Itemsets Mining. In: Proceedings of the Fourth International Conference on Software Engineering Research, Management and Applications (SERA 2006), pp. 87–94. IEEE Computer Society, Washington, DC (2006)
5. Zhao, W., Ma, H., He, Q.: Parallel K-Means Clustering Based on MapReduce. In: Jaatun, M.G., Zhao, G., Rong, C. (eds.) Cloud Computing. LNCS, vol. 5931, pp. 674–679. Springer, Heidelberg (2009)

6. Zhang, Y., Xiong, Z., Mao, J., Ou, L.: The Study of Parallel K-Means Algorithm. In: The Sixth World Congress on Intelligent Control and Automation, WCICA, vol. 2, pp. 5868–5871 (2006)

7. Lv, Z., Hu, Y., Zhong, H., Wu, J., Li, B., Zhao, H.: Parallel K-Means Clustering of Remote Sensing Images Based on MapReduce. In: Wang, F.L., Gong, Z., Luo, X., Lei, J. (eds.) WISM 2010. LNCS, vol. 6318, pp. 162–170. Springer, Heidelberg (2010)

8. Rosenthal, J.S.: Parallel computing and Monte Carlo algorithms. Far East Journal of Theoretical Statistics 4, 207–236 (2000)

9. Barbara, D., Faloutsos, C., Hellerstein, J., Ioannidis, Y., Jagadish, H.V., Johnson, T., Ng, R., Poosala, V., Ross, K., Sevcik, K.C.: The new jersey data reduction report. In: Data Engineering Bulletin (1996)

10. Kollios, G., Gunopoulos, D., Koudas, N., Berchtold, S.: An Efficient Approximation Scheme for Data Mining Tasks. In: Proc. IEEE Int. Conf. on Data Engineering (ICDE 2001), pp. 453–462 (2001)

Retracted: Dynamic Optimization Algorithm for Fast Job Completion in Grid Scheduling Environment

Monika Choudhary and Sateesh Kumar Peddoju

Electronics and Computer Science Department, IIT Roorkee, Roorkee, India
monika.ch13@gmail.com, drpskfrc@iitr.ernet.in

Abstract. Grid environment is a type of parallel and distributed system that provides resources for computing and storage. Grid Scheduling is the technique of mapping jobs to resources such that resources are utilized efficiently to meet user demands. But minimization of time experienced by user for task completion is a thought provoking issue today for optimal scheduling in the grid network. This paper presents a dynamic optimization algorithm for minimizing the average turnaround time resulting in fast completion of jobs submitted to the grid. The algorithm considers arrival time of job and the waiting time encountered at resource while selecting the target resource for execution.

Keywords: scheduling, Optimal grid scheduling, dynamic job execution.

1 Introduction

The rapid development in computing resources has enhanced the performance of computers and reduced their costs. This availability of low cost powerful computers coupled with the popularity of the Internet and high-speed networks has led the computing environment to be mapped from distributed to Grid environments. Grid computing has emerged as a potential next generation platform for solving large-scale problems in several domains of science and engineering. It generally involves millions of heterogeneous resources scattered across multiple organizations, administrative domains, and policies[1, 2].The management and scheduling of resources in such a large-scale distributed systems are complex activities. Grid provides information services such as storage and application services and utilize the available resources to meet user demands[3]. Scheduling deals with the allocation of resources like processor nodes to user requests for mostly computational applications.

The grid system can broadly be classified under three layers[4]. The first layer is the user application layer in which the jobs are submitted to the scheduler by the user. The second layer contains scheduler and Grid Information System (GIS). All the resources reside in third layer where user's jobs are executed. Various steps involved from job submission to passing the results to user are presented in Fig 1. A Grid scheduler (GS) receives applications from Grid users, selects feasible resources for these applications according to the information from the Grid Information Service

M. Parashar et al. (Eds.): IC3 2012, CCIS 306, pp. 86–94, 2012.
© Springer-Verlag Berlin Heidelberg 2012

module. Finally it generates application-to-resource mappings, based on certain objective functions. Unlike their counterparts in traditional distributed systems, Grid schedulers usually cannot control Grid resources directly, but work like brokers or agents or even tightly coupled with the applications [3]. In this paper a scheduling algorithm is demonstrated to minimize average turnaround time in heterogeneous resource environment.

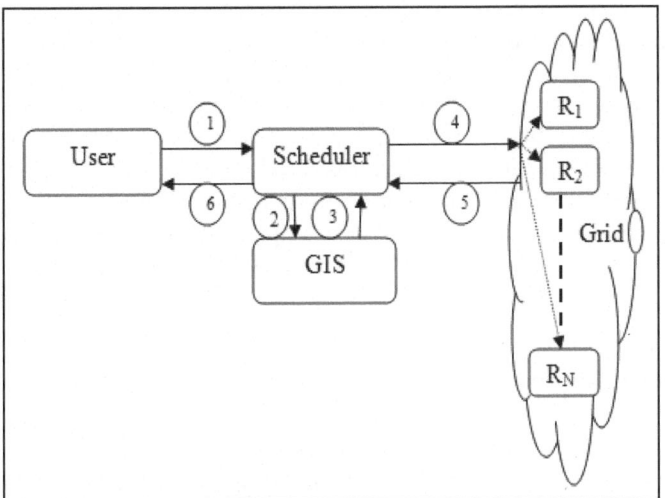

Fig. 1. Job Submission and Execution in Grid Environment

The rest of this paper is organized as follows: Section 2 briefly discusses related work, followed by Section 3 which describes scheduling model. Next, Section 4 presents the proposed scheduling algorithm and its strategy. In Section 5 the experimental details and results of experiments are presented with comparison with some existing algorithms. Finally, Section 6 concludes the paper and proposes future improvements.

2   Related Work

Grid resource management and task scheduling are hot research points for domestic and foreign scholars [5]. Scheduling process in grid can be generalized into three stages – resource discovery and filtering, resource selecting and scheduling according to certain objectives, and job submission[6]. This paper tries to explore the second stage of resource selection and scheduling. Several scheduling policies have been proposed by researchers. In one of them, machines collectively arrive at a decision that describes the task allocation that is collectively best for the system, ensuring that the allocations are both energy and makespan optimized [14]. Independent batch scheduling can be employed in Computational Grid with make span and energy consumption as the scheduling criteria [15]. Another approach uses non-cooperative, semi-cooperative and cooperative methods for scheduling. The non-cooperative sealed-bid method is one where tasks are auctioned off to the highest bidder. In the semi-cooperative n-round sealed-bid method each site delegate its work to others if it cannot perform the work itself. Lastly, in the cooperative method all of the sites deliberate with one another to execute all the tasks as efficiently as possible [16]. Goal programming can be used for scheduling purpose in Grid [17].

Resources in a grid environment can be selected in various ways. The selection of resources can be either random, sequential, according to its processing power or any other means[7]. In random algorithm jobs are submitted on the scheduler and the scheduler contacts GIS to obtain the resource information and then it chooses a resource randomly. The job is submitted on this chosen resource. This algorithm is very simple to implement and has less overhead on the scheduler[8]. In the sequential assignment as the jobs are submitted to the scheduler, the resources are allocated in order in which the request is made. For example if there are three resources (i.e. R0, R1, R2). The J0 is submitted to R0, J1 is to R1, and so on. In this algorithm the resources have equal distribution of jobs.

3   Scheduling Model

Schedule is an allocation of system resources to individual jobs for certain time. To arrive at a valid schedule, scheduling model is used. The architecture comprises of three main modules which are [9]

1. A Scheduling policy
2. An objective function
3. A Scheduling Algorithm

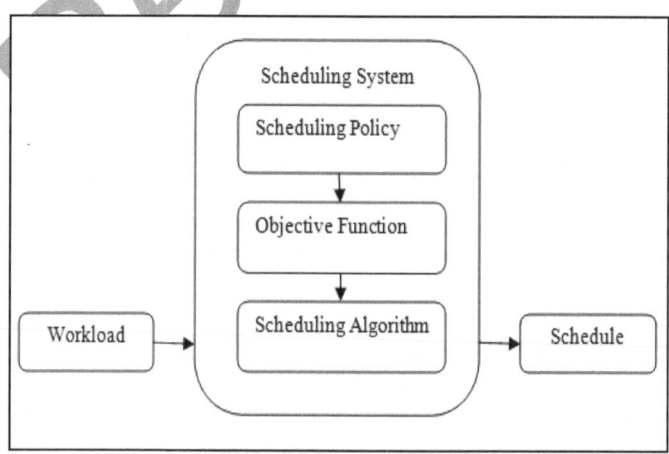

Fig. 2. Scheduling Model

1. Scheduling policy – It is a collection of rules to determine the resource allocation for all submitted jobs and act as a strategy to settle resource conflicts, if any. The policy laid before listing the algorithm is

- Jobs are prioritized in the order of their arrival.
- If more than one resource is available for job execution, resource which gives minimum turnaround time is chosen.

2. Objective Function – It determines the objective or goal of the scheduling algorithm. This makes it possible to compare two schedules which are based on same job set. For example, minimal turnaround time is used as objective function to compare few existing algorithm with the proposed one.

3. Scheduling Algorithm – This lists the various steps which are to be followed to generate a valid schedule for actual jobs submitted. It is expected to produce optimal schedules with respect to objective function and in accordance with time and resource constraints.

4   Proposed Algorithm

The proposed algorithm is suitable for dynamic heterogeneous resource environment. It uses greedy approach to select resource for the jobs submitted. An algorithmic approach is called "greedy" when it makes decisions for each step based on what seems best at the current step to reach the final goal [10].

Each incoming job is considered as independent of other and scheduled on chosen resource such that it gives minimum turnaround time for that job. After calculating the turnaround time of each resource, the resource with minimum turnaround time is selected and job is executed there. The overall turnaround time of jobs is thus minimized. For each job the greedy scheduler takes into consideration.

- Arrival time of job
- job size
- processing power of resource

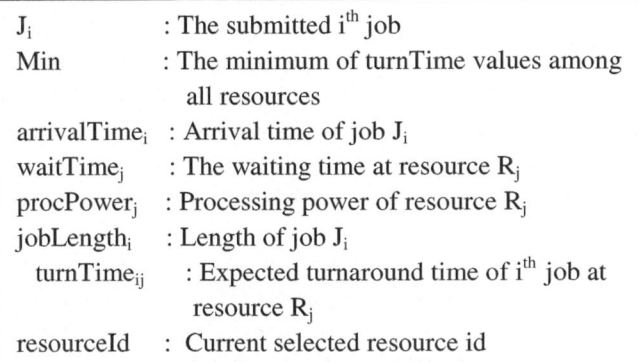

J_i	: The submitted i^{th} job
Min	: The minimum of turnTime values among all resources
arrivalTime$_i$	: Arrival time of job J_i
waitTime$_j$	: The waiting time at resource R_j
procPower$_j$	: Processing power of resource R_j
jobLength$_i$	: Length of job J_i
turnTime$_{ij}$	: Expected turnaround time of ith job at resource R_j
resourceId	: Current selected resource id

Fig. 3. List of terms used

In the Job_Schedule algorithm shown in Figure 4, the waitTime of all resources is set to zero at the beginning. All the incoming jobs are entered into queue along with their parameters like their arrival time and length. Now, a job is removed from queue and its target resource determined on the basis of Resource_Selection algorithm (Figure 5). The resource will remain in processing state for some time to process the job submitted. So the resource parameters are updated according to the new waiting time of the resource selected. This process cycle repeats until the job queue becomes empty. As jobs are independent of each other it is assumed that they are scheduled in the order of their arrival on first come, first serve (FCFS) basis.

Other QoS factors can be incorporated to change the scheduling sequence of jobs according to user needs. This can be done by queuing on the basis of deadline, profit or job priority etc [11]. Further, the proposed algorithm can be merged with job grouping for better results [12].

1. Initialize wait time of all resources to zero
waitTime = 0.0

2. For each new job arrived
i. Set arrival time of job(arr_time)
ii. Insert the job in queue Q

3. While queue Q is not empty
i. Delete the job J_i
ii. Call Resource_Selection Algorithm
iii. UPDATE
iv. Advance the Q pointer

4. End

Fig. 4. Job_Schedule Algorithm

To select a resource for job execution, turnaround time of job for each resource is considered and the one resulting in the minimum turnaround time is selected. Turnaround time is the time taken by task to complete execution after it is scheduled to a resource. This includes waiting time at resource and the execution time. Once target resource is selected, its waitTime is updated according to the turnTime computed. By this scheduler knows when that resource will next be available next for job execution.

The time complexity of the proposed algorithm is O(mn) where m is the number of jobs submitted and n is the number of resources. Thus, it is directly proportional to number of resources and jobs. In certain dynamic systems, the number of active resources can be adjusted according to user need and demands.

1.Initialize minimum to ∞

2. For every resource R_j
    i. If waitTime$_j$ is nonzero
       a. Calculate expected waiting time
          waitTime$_j$ = waitTimetime- arrival_time
       b. Calculate expected turnaround time
          turn_time$_{ij}$ = wait_time$_j$ +
(Job_req/Proc_power$_j$)
       else
       turn_time$_{ij}$ = Job_req/Proc_power$_j$
    ii. If minimum >turn_time$_{ij}$
       minimum = turn_time$_{ij}$ and res_id=R_j

3. Submit job J_i to resource R_j

4. Update wait time of resource R_j
    Start_time = arrival_time$_i$ + turn_time$_{ij}$

5. End

Fig. 5. Resource_Selection Algorithm

5   Simulation Results

GridSim toolkit is used to conduct the simulations based on the developed scheduling algorithm[13]. The GridSim toolkit provides facilities for the modeling and simulation of resources and network connectivity with different capabilities, configurations, and domains. It supports primitives for application composition, information services for resource discovery, and interfaces for assigning application tasks to resources and managing their execution. These features can be used to simulate resource brokers or Grid schedulers for evaluating performance of scheduling algorithms or heuristics[1].

The experiments are performed and results are compared with two existing algorithms – Random Resource Selection[8] and Sequential Assignment[8] as they are usually used in a generalized scenario. The architecture and configuration of resources used in simulation is shown in Table 1. Input parameters to be provided by user include the number of users, number of gridlets and n. The length of gridlets is generated using random function. The algorithms use meta- scheduler where resource failure is not considered.

Table 1. Resources with their architecture and processing power

Resources	R0	R1	R2
Architecure	Sun Ultra	Sun Ultra	Sun Ultra
OS	Unix	AIX	Unix
Proc_power (in MIPS)	48000	43000	54000

The scheduler submits jobs to these resources and the results obtained after using the three different scheduling algorithms are compared.

A. Random Resource Selection – In this allocation policy, job is sent to any of the resource chosen randomly[8]. The turnaround time experienced cannot be predicted in random resource selection.
B. Sequential Assignment – Resources are selected in round robin fashion. There is no consideration of efficient scheduling. A cyclic sequence of resource is predefined and resource for next job is chosen accordingly[8].
C. Proposed Algorithm – As discussed, proposed dynamic and optimized algorithm result in fast job execution by taking waiting time encountered by job at resource into consideration. Individual turnaround time of job is minimized to reduce the overall turnaround time. Thus by introducing little computation of turnaround time the performance of the system has improved significantly.

Table 2. Algorithms with their average turnaround time

Algorithms	Avg. Turnaround time (in ms)
Random Resource Selection	231.64
Sequential Assignment	207.62
Proposed Algorithm	177.38

The experiment is repeated with different number of jobs each time and average of all is computed to get better results. It is evident from Table 2 that the proposed algorithm gives minimum turnaround time in a given time slot by more than 14% which is a significant amount. Hence, user experience an improved turnaround time when jobs are scheduled using optimized algorithm for fast job completion as compared to random and sequential resource assignment techniques.

6   Conclusions and Future Work

The proposed greedy algorithm for grid reduces the average turnaround time of submitted jobs in a given time slot. This was proved by simulation with GridSim on different resources that proposed algorithm has improved average turnaround as compared to Random and Sequential Assignment.

This algorithm can be improved further by prioritizing the jobs on the basis of their QoS factors and deadline while queuing them.

References

1. Murshed, M., Buyya, R., Abramson, D.: Gridsim:A toolkit for the modeling and simulation of global grids. Technical Report, Monash-CSSE 2001/102, Monash University, Australia (2001)
2. Foster, I., Kesselman, C.: The Grid: Blueprint for a New Computing Infrastructure. Morgan Kaufmann Publishers, San Francisco (1999)
3. Baker, M., Buyya, R., Laforenza, D.: Grids and Grid technologies for wide-area distributed computing. Software: Practice and Experience 32(15), 1437–1466 (2002)
4. Buyya, R., Abramson, D., Giddy, J.: An economy driven resource management architecture for global computational power grids. In: The 7th International Conference on Parallel and Distributed ProcessingTechniques and Applications (PDPTA 2000), Las Vegas, USA (2000)
5. Lu, B., Zhang, H.: Grid load balancing scheduling algorithm based on statistics thinking. In: The 9th International Conference for Young Computer Scientist, pp. 288–292 (2008)
6. Dong, F., Akl, S.G.: Scheduling algorithms for grid computing: State of the art and open problems. Technical Report of the Open Issues in Grid Scheduling Workshop, School of Computing, University Kingston, Ontario (2006)
7. Buyya, R., Abramson, D., Giddy, J.: Nimrod/G: An architecture for a resource management andscheduling system in a global computational grid. In: International Conference on High Performance Computing in Asia-Pacific Region (HPC Asia 2000), vol. 1, pp. 283–289. IEEE Computer Society Press, USA (2000)
8. Hamscher, V., Schwiegelshohn, U., Streit, A., Yahyapour, R.: Evaluation of Job-Scheduling Strategies for Grid Computing. In: Buyya, R., Baker, M. (eds.) GRID 2000. LNCS, vol. 1971, pp. 191–202. Springer, Heidelberg (2000)
9. Krallmann, J., Schwiegelshohn, U., Yahyapour, R.: On the Design and Evaluation of Job Scheduling Algorithms. In: Feitelson, D.G., Rudolph, L. (eds.) JSSPP 1999. LNCS, vol. 1659, pp. 17–42. Springer, Heidelberg (1999)
10. Cormen, T.H., Leiserson, C.E., Rivest, R.L.: Introduction to algorithms, 2nd edn., pp. 16, 370–16, 403. The MIT press, McGrawHill Book Company, Boston, Massachusetts (2001)
11. Cao, Q., Wei, Z.B., Gong, W.M.: An optimized algorithm for task scheduling based on activity based costing in cloud computing. In: Proc. 2009 3rd International Conference on Bioinformatics and Biomedical Engineering (iCBBE 2009), pp. 1–3. IEEE Press (2009)
12. Ang, T., Ng, W., Ling, T., Por, L., Liew, C.: A bandwidth-aware job grouping-based scheduling on grid environment. Information Technology Journal 8(3), 372–377 (2009)
13. Murshed, M., Buyya, R.: Using the GridSim toolkit for enabling grid computing education. In: Proc. of the Int. Conf. on Communication Networks and Distributed Systems Modeling and Simulation, CNDS 2002, San Antonio, Texas, USA (2002)
14. Khan, S.U., Ahmad, I.: A Cooperative Game Theoretical Technique for Joint Optimization of Energy Consumption and Response Time in Computational Grids. IEEE Transactions on Parallel and Distributed Systems 20(3), 346–360 (2009)

15. Kolodziej, J., Khan, S.U., Xhafa, F.: Genetic Algorithms for Energy-aware Scheduling in Computational Grids. In: 6th IEEE International Conference on P2P, Parallel, Grid, Cloud, and Internet Computing (3PGCIC), Barcelona, Spain, pp. 17–24 (October 2011)
16. Khan, S.U., Ahmad, I.: Non-cooperative, Semi-cooperative, and Cooperative Games-based Grid Resource Allocation. In: 20th IEEE International Parallel and Distributed Processing Symposium (IPDPS), Rhodes Island, Greece (April 2006)
17. Khan, S.U.: A Goal Programming Approach for the Joint Optimization of Energy Consumption and Response Time in Computational Grids. In: 28th IEEE International Performance Computing and Communications Conference (IPCCC), Phoenix, AZ, USA, pp. 410–417 (December 2009)

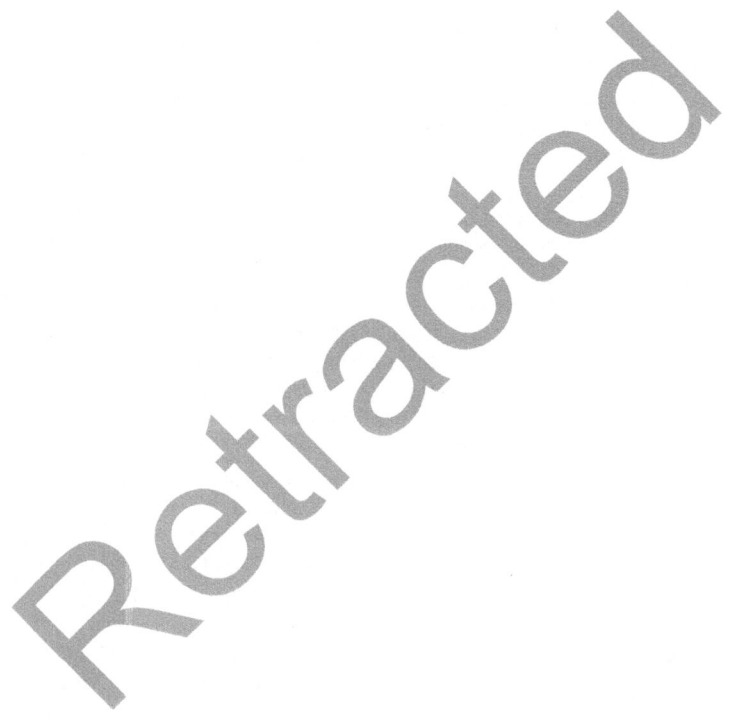

Range Grouping for Routing in Dynamic Networks

Prachi Badera, Akanksha Bhardwaj, and K. Rajalakshmi

Department of Computer Science,
Jaypee Institute of Information Technology, Noida
{prachbadera,busy.akanksha}@gmail.com, k.rajlakshmi@jiit.ac.in

Abstract. Most of the networks that we see in our day to day lives today are types of dynamic networks i.e. networks which keep on changing in very short period of time. One example of such a network is the network formed by Bluetooth connectivity. Due to limited range of wireless trans-receivers, a mobile node can communicate with the mobile nodes that lie within its range. Hence, in order to communicate with nodes in far-off regions, forwarding of data have to be done. Our methodology is based on this concept. Our proposition will first apply an algorithm to cluster the existing nodes in two types of clusters called INTER and INTRA clusters and then perform routing with the help of routing algorithm as proposed by us. The information regarding change in topology is maintained in the form of lists [data structure] which helps in routing the data effectively.

Keywords: clustering, routing, dynamic network, gateway, hoping, Quality of Service.

1 Introduction

The networks in which the nodes keep on moving randomly or the ones whose topology keeps on changing due to change in position of the nodes are called Dynamic Networks [2]. Dynamic networks with users from heterogeneous networks, different operator, provider or technology domains, today, are needed for scenarios such as emergency and disaster recovery, field work among others. One of the major challenges that one faces is to design routing protocols that satisfy the consequent requirements [11]. The examples of such networks are ad-hoc wireless local area networks [8]. The term ad-hoc network is in conformance with current usage within the IEEE 802.11 subcommittee [13].

One such network can be formed by using the Bluetooth connectivity. As described by Suri and Rani in [12], the original idea of Bluetooth concept was that of cable replacement between portable and/or fixed electronic device. According to the specification, when two Bluetooth devices come into each other's communication range, one of them assumes the role of master of the communication and the other becomes the slave. However, the range of a Bluetooth enabled devices is very limited.

This paper investigates an approach on how to route the data in a wide network formed by Bluetooth usage using the concept of clusters and then forwarding the data.

M. Parashar et al. (Eds.): IC3 2012, CCIS 306, pp. 95–105, 2012.

Also, the information regarding change in topology due to node's movement will be stored and maintained time to time. Section 2 related work done in this field is described in short summary. Section 3 explains the proposed approach with cluster algorithm and routing algorithm. Section 4 explains the security issues related to this application and Section 5 describes the analysis and Section 6 concludes the paper.

2   Related Work

The Bluetooth technology works on the principal of formation of piconets and scatternet [1]. The Bluetooth enabled nodes decide their masters and respective slaves by themselves. Hence, it becomes a little difficult to track down the changing masters and slaves with time passage. Therefore, there arises a necessity to apply clustering algorithm to cluster or form groups of nodes based on their ranges in a given network.

In past, a lot of different clustering algorithms have been used to cluster the similar type of data (based on different types) in mobile networks such as in [5], [6].Also, many routing protocols have been proposed and implemented. Out of these, the famous ones are Distance Vector and Link State protocols. In Distance Vector, as explained in [8], [15], [13], each host maintains an estimated distance to each node and periodically checks for the shortest path. For routing purpose, it hops the data to the next node from where it is expected to get the shortest path. In this protocol, the nodes do not have information about the whole network.

In Link state Protocol, as in [6], [3], every node has the information about the whole network topology. The path is directly related to cost. Based on this cost, the shortest path is calculated from each node. And hence, the routing takes place. Since, every node has information about the whole network in Link State, the processing overhead and the bandwidth overhead is much higher for *Link state* than *Distance Vector*.

The problems with the application of Distance Vector and Link State have been explained in detail is [2], [8], [13]. Some of the problems are as such:

a.   Computational overhead in these protocols in terms of battery power and in wireless network, in terms of network bandwidth.
b.   The convergence characteristics of these protocols may not be good enough to suit the necessities of dynamic networks.

The other problem [9] in mobile ad hoc networks that has received considerable attention is the broadcast storm problem [7]. Multiple forwarders try to relay packets simultaneously. This is an important issue in mobile networks especially when the node density is high. Several routing schemes have been proposed to overcome the broadcast storm problem. One solution is to select the farthest node from the source in order to make multi-hop forwarding more efficient [10]. The concept of multi-hop cellular network is introduced in [14], where IEEE 802.11 protocol is applied. Only recently, some research on IEEE 802.16j has been conducted.

3   Proposed Approach

This paper proposes an algorithm to first cluster the nodes of the network which are lying in the range of one or the other nodes and then apply our proposed algorithm for routing [forwarding] the data. A change in the network topology implies a change in the cluster membership i.e. nodes move from one cluster to another, hence deletion in one cluster and addition in another.

3.1   Cluster Classification

The clusters defined follow the following assumptions:

1. A cluster is defined as a group of nodes in which there exist at least one path to reach from one node to other.
2. A cluster can have size maximum upto seven as Bluetooth master at once can detect only upto 7 slaves.
3. Edges of the cluster are defined as the edges joining the nodes forming a cluster.
4. The whole network should lie in one or the other cluster.

The clusters are independently controlled and are dynamically reconfigured as nodes move. The clustering algorithm as described below is a very simplistic approach to solve this problem; hence, it may not be applicable to every routing problem.

Given: A Dynamic Network with 8 nodes.

Problem: Find clusters which accommodates all the nodes in the network and hence, allow routing.

Let the given network be explained as the one given in figure 1. The problems needs to find out the clusters based on their range. Let node A be the master and suppose it first runs the application to detect its nearby devices. Node A finds out nodes B, C, D in its cluster and store the address and the name in their data structures. Similarly, nodes B, C, D, E, F, G, H, I will find the nodes lying in its range and store this information in their lists respectively. Figure 2 explains how the network given in figure 1 will store the information.

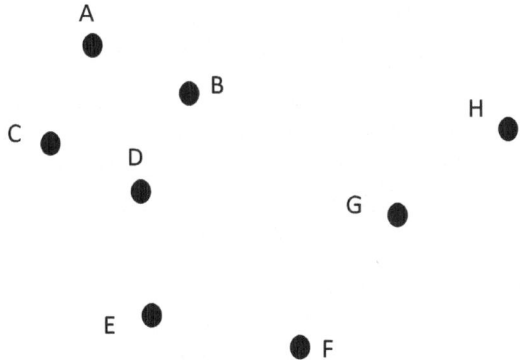

Fig. 1. Dynamic Network Nodes

Table 1. A's list of nearby devices

NODE	ADDRESS
B	00:15:83:15:A3:10
C	00:15:87:45:DC:3D
D	18:86:AC:96:46:1E

Similarly, node B → A, C, D in its list.

     Node C → A, B, D.
     Node D → A, C, B
     Node E → D, F, G
     Node F → E, G
     Node G → E, H

Next, these lists are exchanged with the nearby nodes. At each node, a comparison between the nodes of its list and the list received from its neighbors takes place. A node that is found to be different is appended in its list i.e. after comparison, the list becomes as follows:

     Node A → B,C,D
     Node B → A,C,D
     Node C → A,B,D
     Node D → A,B,C,E,F,G
     Node E → A,B,C,D,F,G
     Node F → D,E,G,H
     Node G → D,E,G,H
     Node H → E, F, G

Now, the master node A forms a cluster containing nodes B,C,D. Then node B checks in for the uncommon node and finds no such node. Therefore, no new cluster formation takes place at B. Similarly, nodes C and D form a part of cluster formed by node A. Figure 3 explains the above.

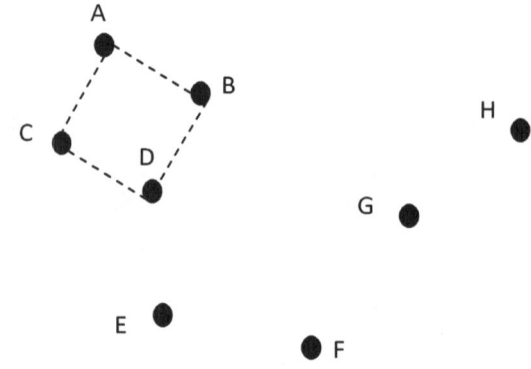

Fig. 2. Formation of cluster with nodes A, B, C, D

However, at node D, new nodes are found after comparing the lists. Therefore, it puts the newly found nodes in one cluster other than the one formed earlier with nodes A, B, C, D and forms an INTER cluster with nodes E takes place. Figure 4 shows the formation of INTER cluster.

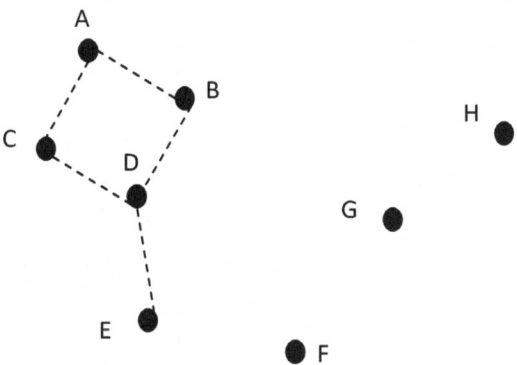

Fig. 3. Cluster formation among nodes D and E

As it is clear from figure 4 that all the nodes have not yet been covered by the clusters, hence again the lists exchange and comparison takes place. And in the similar fashion as described above, the whole network in divided into 4 clusters. Figure 5 and 6 give a clear picture of the clusters.

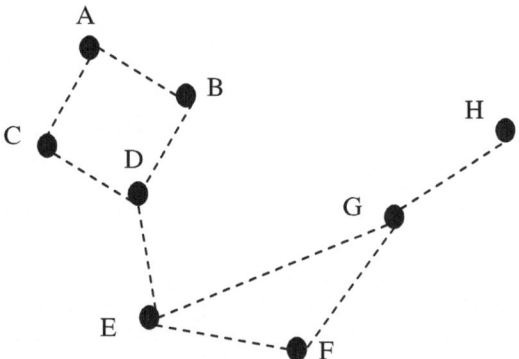

Fig. 4. Clusters covering all the nodes in the network

A particular formation of a cluster can be unique only to a particular time limit. Since, we talk about dynamic networks; the nodes are bound to move in every second or even earlier than that. Hence, addition and deletion of nodes has to be taken into account. Also, there will be a possibility of addition of new nodes in the network. All these possibilities are covered in the following figures.

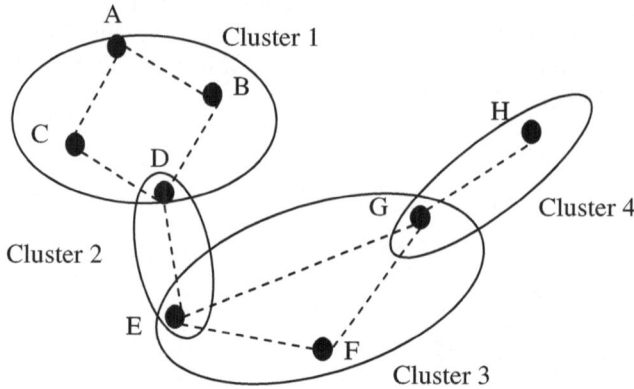

Fig. 5. Four clusters are formed covering all the nodes in the network

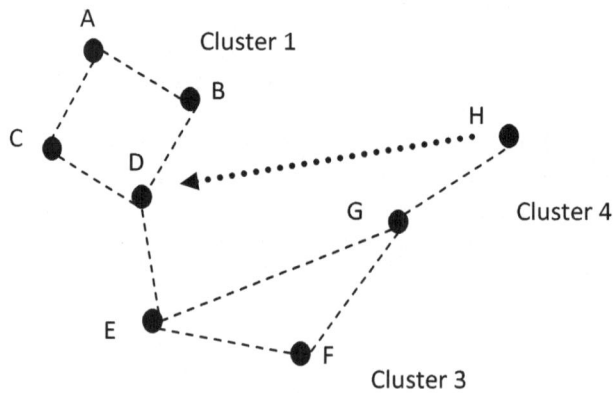

Fig. 6(a). Movement of Node H to cluster ABCD

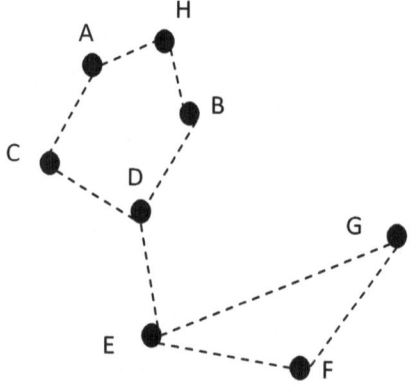

Fig.6(b). Addition of Node H to cluster ABCD and deletion from cluster GH

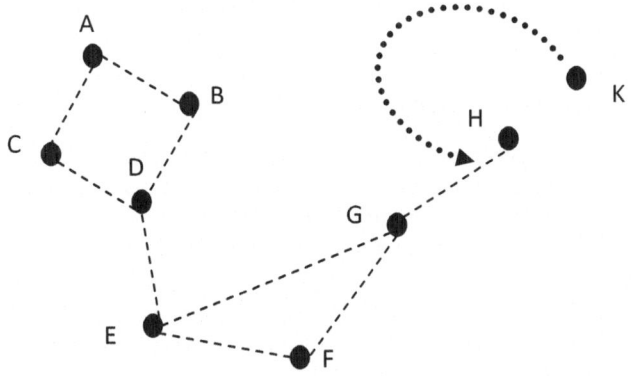

Fig. 7(a). Addition of a new node in the network

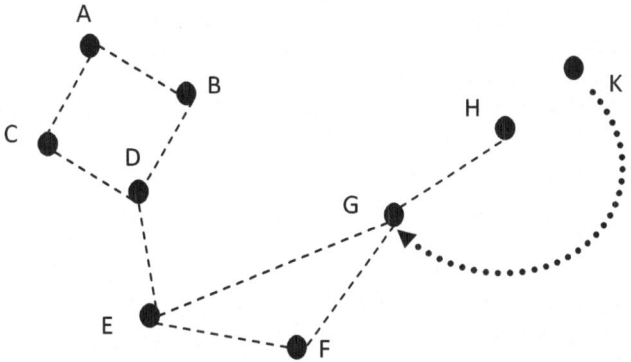

Fig. 7(b). The new node gets added in the already existing cluster

Note : in the above example, the new Node K has been added to the cluster GH as K was lying in the range of G and H. if it would have been lying in the range of some other node, then it would have formed the cluster with that node correspondingly.

This network architecture has three main advantages. First, it provides spatial reuse of the bandwidth due to node clustering. Secondly, bandwidth can be shared or reserved in a controlled fashion in each cluster. Finally, the cluster algorithm is robust in the face of topological changes caused by node motion, node failure and node insertion/removal.

3.2   Routing Protocol

After the formation of the clusters, the main task that remains is forwarding of the data.

In order to accomplish this, the nodes have the list available with itself which it can refer to know if the node exists in the network or not. After mentioning the destination node, the node looks at the list. The data are sent to the neighboring node via *hoping*. When the data reach the **gateway** node (i.e. the node which is a part of more than one cluster), it looks for the route with the help of the lists again and then again routes the data.

For example:

A wants to send data to H. [refer fig 5]

a) Data to be sent are *packetized* and it also contains the address of the destination node. Therefore, at every node, comparison with the address of the node and that carried with the data take place in order to identify whether to forward the data or to announce that the data have been received.

b) Firstly data are sent to node B or C depending on the outcome of implementation of Dijikstra's algorithm as explained in [4] and also the connectivity sensitivity among nodes [since, it is an ad-hoc network].

c) From that node, it is sent to node D.

d) Node D, as it is clear from the figure, is the Gateway for cluster 1 and cluster 2 [figure 6], it routes the data to the next cluster.

e) Then, again according to the traffic intensity, it is routed to the node F or G.

f) If routed to F, comparison takes place and again forwarded to node G.

g) If already sent to G, comparison of the address takes place and then it is finally sent to node H.

h) At node H, comparison of the addresses returns TRUE and hence, the data are delivered at the right place.

3.3   Implementation Details

The detection of nearby devices takes place periodically in order to take in view the change in topology frequently. Mainly, the application is developed in the language Python version 2.5. Python doesn't support Bluetooth directly. Therefore, its module PyBluez is used. Python is chosen because of its simplicity and the fact that it is compatible with any Operating System i.e. it has no specific system requirements.

After the correct destination has received the data, it replies to the network with proper GUI. Following are the screenshots of some of the user interfaces.

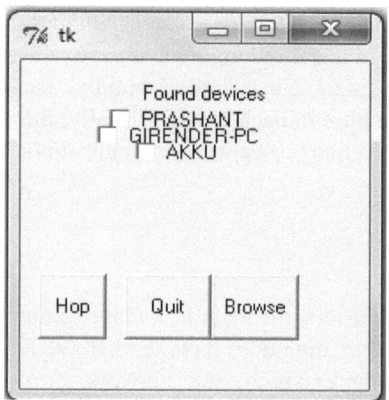

Screenshot 1: Interface after detecting nearby devices

The user is now given an option to

1. Hop (i.e. increase the nodes in network)
2. Quit from application
3. Browse files to be sent.

If 'Hop' button is clicked, then the comparison between the lists takes place which is followed by clustering. The appended list is then passed to interface like Screenshot 1. If 'Quit' button is clicked, then the application quits and everything thing that was under processing is turned off.

If 'Browse' button is clicked, then file browser like screenshot 2 is opened. The user needs to select the destination node first and then select the file to be sent. He has the option to send *.txt, *.jpg, *.py, *.tcl files.

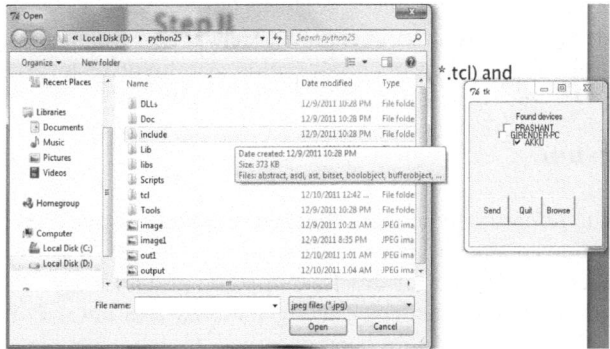

Screenshot 2: Browsing options with selected destination Node

4 Security Issues

Since it is an ad-hoc network, the security of the data is an issue. For this purpose, the data before sending is *encrypted* and when it is received by the correct destination node, it is *decrypted*. If it is, by any chance, delivered on wrong node, it will not be decrypted. Also, to ensure the participation of slave node in the network, an *authentication query* is run to ask for the permission of the user first and then let him participate in the network.

5 Analysis

In this section, we explain the analysis done after implementing this approach. The biggest advantage of this algorithm is that it starts its detecting protocol after every 10 seconds since it is a dynamic network which is prone to changes in topology frequently.

Another point is that while using various Bluetooth enabled devices, we observed that the algorithm designed works the best in laptops of only few companies such as HP, Compaq and Dell. In rest of the laptops, the Bluetooth power is little lower. However, the application doesn't itself consume any power.

The third aspect is time taken i.e. computational time. The application may take time to start since in the beginning of the algorithm, it has to find the nearby devices which may result in large time consumption, but once it detects the nearby devices, it takes even lesser than 60 seconds to execute it completely. Also it doesn't take time for running the detecting algorithm after the first time.

The Multi channel Link State Routing protocol as described by Cheolgi Kim et al [3] divides the nodes into cluster heads and its dependents. The cluster head is responsible for gathering the link state information periodically. The drawback of this approach is high memory consumption. In our approach, the memory used is very less as compared to former approach due to very little nesting of tables.

The routing protocols designed for vehicular networks as in [4], [9], are efficient and provide good Quality of Service in vehicular networks. However, computations performed for every packet introduces delay in our scenario as the network doesn't suffer from rapid random variation in channel. Hence, performing these computations periodically is more beneficial as in our algorithm as it involves less overhead.

6   Conclusion

Until recently, the research on network theory has mainly focused on graphs with the assumption that they remain static, i.e. they do not change over time. A wealth of knowledge has been developed for this type of static graph theory. Work on dynamic graph theory has been motivated by finding patterns and laws. Power laws, small diameters, shrinking diameters have been observed. Graph generation models that try to capture these properties are proposed to synthetically generate such networks.

Our study mainly focuses on the deep study of change of topology in such networks. For that purpose, we introduced a new algorithm to cluster the far away spread nodes and then route the message to the furthest of nodes with help of *Gateways, Packetization* and *Hoping*.

The algorithm proposed is an easy to understand and implement. It leads to easy formation of clusters and then routing. Also, it is simple to maintain the clusters, their lists and hence the whole network with this approach.

References

1. Amin, M.S., Bhuyan, F.A., Rahman, M.L.: Bluetooth Scatternet Formation Protocol: A Comparative Performance Analysis. In: Asia-Pacific Conference Communications, APCC 2006, pp. 1–5 (August-September 2006)
2. Bilgin, C.C., Yener, B.: Dynamic Network Evolution: Models, Clustering, Anomaly detection. IEEE Networks (2006)
3. Kim, C., Koy, Y.-B., Vaidya, N.H.: Link-state routing protocol for multi-channel multi-interface wireless networks. In: Military Communications Conference, MILCOM 2008, pp. 1–7. IEEE (November 2008)
4. Fan, Y.-Z., Lu, D.-M., Wang, Q.-C., Jiang, F.-C.: An improved Dijkstra algorithm used on vehicle optimization route planning. In: Second International Conference on Computer Engineering and Technology (ICCET), pp. V3-693–V3-696 (April 2010)

5. Forero, P.A., Cano, A., Giannakis, G.B.: Distributed Clustering Using Wireless Sensor Networks. IEEE Journal Selected Topics in Signal Processing 5(4), 707–724 (2011)
6. Guizani, B., Ayeb, B., Koukam, A.: Hierarchical cluster-based link state routing protocol for large self-organizing network. In: 2011 IEEE 12th International Conference High Performance Switching and Routing (HPSR), pp. 203–208 (July 2011)
7. Wisitpongphan, N., Tonguz, O.K., Parikh, J.S., Mudalige, P., Bai, F., Sadekar, V.: Broadcast storm mitigation techniques in vehicular ad hoc networks. IEEE Wireless Communications 14(6), 84–94 (2007)
8. Usop, N.S.M., Abdullah, A., Abidi, A.F.A.: Performance Evaluation of AODV, DSDV & DSR Routing Protocol in Grid Environment. IJCSNS International Journal of Computer Science and Network Security 9(7) (July 2009)
9. Nurul Nazirah, M.I.M., Satiman, N., Anis Izzati, A.Z., Fisal, N., Syed Yusof, S.K., Ariffin, S.H.S., Abbas, M.: Cross-layer Routing Approach in Highly Dynamic Networks. In: 4th International Conference Modeling, Simulation and Applied Optimization (ICMSAO), pp. 1–5 (April 2011)
10. Chen, R., Jin, W.L., Regan, A.: Broadcasting safety information in vehicular networks: Issues and approaches. Network Magazine of Global Internetworking 24(1), 20–25 (2010)
11. Silva, A., Silva, T., Gomes, R., Oliveira, L., Cananea, I., Sadok, D., Johnsson: Routing Solutions for Future Dynamic Networks. In: 10th International Conference on Advanced Communication Technology, ICACT 2008, pp. 212–217 (February 2008)
12. Suri, P.R., Rani, S.: Bluetooth network-the adhoc network concept. In: SoutheastCon. Proceedings, pp. 720–720. IEEE (March 2007)
13. Diepstraten, W., Ennis, G., Bellanger, P.: DFWMAC - Distributed Foundation Wireless Medium Access Control. IEEE Document P802.11-93/190 (November 1993)
14. Lin, Y., Hsu, Y.: Multihop cellular: A new architecture for wireless communications. In: Proc. of IEEE INFOCOM 2000, vol. 3, pp. 1273–1282 (March 2000)
15. Hu, Y.-C.: Johnson, D.B., Perrig, A.: SEAD: secure efficient distance vector routing for mobile wireless ad hoc networks. In: Proceedings Fourth IEEE Workshop on Mobile Computing Systems and Applications, pp. 3–13 (2002)

Intensity Modeling for Syllable Based Text-to-Speech Synthesis

V. Ramu Reddy and K. Sreenivasa Rao

School of Information Technology,
Indian Institute of Technology Kharagpur
Kharagpur - 721302, West Bengal, India
ramu.csc@gmail.com, ksrao@iitkgp.ac.in

Abstract. The quality of text-to-speech (TTS) synthesis systems can be improved by controlling the intensities of speech segments in addition to durations and intonation. This paper proposes linguistic and production constraints for modeling the intensity patterns of sequence of syllables. Linguistic constraints are represented by positional, contextual and phonological features, and production constraints are represented by articulatory features associated to syllables. In this work, feedforward neural network (FFNN) is proposed to model the intensities of syllables. The proposed FFNN model is evaluated by means of objective measures such as average prediction error (μ), standard deviation (σ), correlation coefficient ($\gamma_{X,Y}$) and the percentage of syllables predicted within different deviations. The prediction performance of the proposed model is compared with other statistical models such as Linear Regression (LR) and Classification and Regression Tree (CART) models. The models are also evaluated by means of subjective listening tests on the synthesized speech generated by incorporating the predicted syllable intensities in Bengali TTS system. From the evaluation studies, it is observed that prediction accuracy is better for FFNN models, compared to other models.

Keywords: Syllable intensities, Intensity prediction, LR, CART, FFNN, Phonological, Contextual, Positional, Articulatory, Linguistic, Production, Naturalness, Intelligibility.

1 Introduction

Prosody strongly influences the quality of the synthesized speech, and it refers to acoustical attributes such as intonation, duration and intensity. The acoustic correlate of loudness is referred as intensity. Intensity is also treated as an important acoustic parameter in various speech processing tasks such as text-to-speech synthesis (TTS), speech recognition, emotion recognition, speaker recognition and verification, language recognition etc. However, there was not much effort was made in modeling the intensity compared to other prosodic parameters such as intonation and duration. For different languages, rule-based and data-based models were developed for both intonation [1, 2] and duration [3, 4]. However,

M. Parashar et al. (Eds.): IC3 2012, CCIS 306, pp. 106–117, 2012.

with respect to text-to-speech synthesis, some attempts were made by Robert Mannel [5] and Fabio Tesser [6] in modeling the intensity. In [5], intensities were modeled for a sequence of diphones in diphone based speech synthesis system. Tesser developed intensity model for diphone based emotional TTS system in addition to intonation and duration models [6].

In this work, syllable based Bengali TTS system [7] was developed, with the help of Festival framework. Syllable is chosen as the basic unit as it is the most appropriate unit for the Indian languages. Hence, for modeling intensity patterns, we need to explore syllable specific features, which can capture the inherent relationship between the linguistic and production constraints of speech and intensity variation patterns. In this work, to model the intensities of sequence of syllables, the features representing the linguistic and production constraints are proposed. The linguistic and production constraints can be represented by using positional, contextual, phonological and articulatory (PCPA) features associated to syllables. In this paper, we proposed feedforward neural network to model the intensities of the syllables. The main intuition to use neural network model is that it can capture the functional relationship between input-output pattern pairs [8]. It has generalization ability to predict the values for the patterns which are not present in the learning phase.

Rest of the paper is organized as follows: Following section discusses the details of speech database used in this work. Section 3 discusses the proposed PCPA features to model the intensities of sequence of syllables. Section 4 presents the proposed FFNN model for predicting the intensities of the sequence of syllables using proposed features. Evaluation of the FFNN model along with other statistical models such as LR and CART is explained in section 5. Summary and conclusions of this paper is laid in the final section.

2   Speech Database

The text utterances of speech database used for this study is collected from Bengali Anandabazar newspaper, various text books and story books which covers wide range of domains. The collected text corpus covers 7762 declarative sentences with 4372 unique syllables and 22382 unique words. The text is recorded with a professional female artist in a noiseless chamber. The duration of total recorded speech is around 10 hrs. The speech signal was sampled at 16 kHz and represented as 16 bit numbers. The speech utterances are segmented and manually labeled into syllable-like units. For every utterance a labeled file is maintained which consists of syllables of the utterance and their timing information. The syllable structures considered here are V, CV, CCV, CVCC and CCVC, where C is a consonant and V is a vowel. The average intensities of syllables are computed as follows:

$$I = 10 log_{10} \left(\frac{\sum_{i=1}^{N} x_i^2}{N P_0^2} \right)$$

where I is intensity of syllable expressed in decibel, N is number of speech samples of syllable, x_i is the amplitude of ith speech sample and P_0 is auditory threshold pressure expressed in Pascals ($P_0 = 2 \times 10^{-5}$ Pa). It is observed that the intensities of syllables in speech database vary from 55-83 dB, with mean and standard deviations of 70.92 dB and 4.78 dB respectively.

3   Proposed Features

It is known that there exists some inherent relationship between linguistic and production constraints of speech to the intensity variation patterns in speech. The linguistic constraints of syllables can be expressed using positional, contextual and phonological (PCP) features and production constraints of syllables can be expressed using articulatory features (A). In this study we use 35 dimensional feature vector representing the linguistic constraints and production constraints of each syllable. Out of 35 features, 24 features represents the linguistic constraints in the form of positional, contextual and phonological information and remaining 11 features represents articulatory information of production constraints of each syllable. The positional features are further classified based on syllable position in a word and sentence, and word position in a sentence.

3.1   Linguistic Constraints

The linguistic constraints used in this work are as follows:

Syllable position in the sentence: The position of syllable in the sentence is represented by three features. The first feature represents the distance of the syllable from the starting position of the sentence. It is measured in number of syllables which are ahead of present syllable. The second feature indicates the distance of the syllable from the end of the sentence. The third feature represents the total number of syllables present in a sentence.

Syllable position in the word: Words are separated by the delimiter space. The syllable position in a word is characterized by three features, similar to syllable position in the sentence. Here, syllable position in a word from the starting and ending positions are considered as two features. Third feature indicates the total number of syllables in a word.

Word position in the sentence: The position of word in the sentence is represented by three features. The first feature represents the distance of the word from the starting position of the sentence. It is measured in number of words which are ahead of present word. The second feature indicates the distance of the word from the end of the sentence. The third feature represents the total number of words present in a sentence.

Syllable identity: Each syllable constitutes combination of consonants (C) and vowels (V) representing phonological information. Here, segment refer to either consonant or vowel. In this analysis more than four segment syllables are ignored. The segments are then encoded, so that each syllable is represented by four features indicating its identity.

Context of a syllable: Contextual information is represented by previous syllable and following syllable. Each of these syllables is represented by a four dimensional feature vector, representing the identity of the syllable.

Syllable nucleus: In a syllable, vowel is treated as a nucleus. Within each syllable, the number of segments before and after the vowel and total number of segments in a syllable are also important. This is represented by three independent codes specifying three distinct features.

The detailed list of features used for modeling the intensities of syllables is given in Table 1.

Table 1. List of factors affecting the intensities of syllables, features representing the factors and the number of nodes needed for neural network to represent the features

Factors	Features	# Nodes
Syllable position in the sentence	Position of syllable from beginning of the sentence	3
	Position of syllable from end of the sentence	
	Number of syllables in the sentence	
Syllable position in the word	Position of syllable from beginning of the word	3
	Position of syllable from end of the word	
	Number of syllables in the word	
Word position in the sentence	Position of word from beginning of the sentence	3
	Position of word from end of the sentence	
	Number of words in the sentence	
Syllable identity	Segments of the syllable (consonants and vowels)	4
Context of the syllable	Previous syllable	4
	Following syllable	4
Syllable nucleus	Number of segments before the nucleus	3
	Number of segments after the nucleus	
	Number of segments in a syllable	

3.2 Production Constraints

The intensities of speech segments are also influenced by the production mechanism of speech sounds in addition to the linguistic constraints. Each sound unit has specific articulatory movements and positions while producing the sound. These production constraints in turn depends on the language. In this study the features related to different articulatory positions and manners of speech segments (consonants and vowels) are considered as production constraints. These production constraints are represented as articulatory features to predict the durations of syllables. The manner of articulation describes the involvement of speech organs such as tongue, lips, jaw in producing a sound. The place of articulation of a consonant is the point of contact where an obstruction occurs in the vocal tract between an active (moving) articulator (typically some part of the tongue) and a passive (stationary) articulator (typically some part of the roof of the mouth). Place of articulation gives the consonant its distinctive sound along with the manner of articulation. For any place of articulation, there may be several manners, and therefore several homorganic consonants. The quality of the vowel depends on the articulatory features that distinguish different vowel sounds [9]. Daniel Jones developed the cardinal vowel system to describe vowels in terms of the common articulatory features *height* (vertical dimension), *backness* (horizontal dimension) and *roundedness* (lip position) [9]. Height relates to position of tongue and to degree of lowering of jaw. Backness relates to the position of the body of the tongue in oral cavity. Rounding refers to the position of the lips. In this paper, 11 dimensional feature vector representing the articulatory features is used. The features used to represent the articulatory information are vowel length, vowel height, vowel frontness, vowel roundness (lip rounding), consonant type, consonant place, consonant voicing, aspiration, nukta (diacritic mark), type of first phone and type of last phone in a syllable.

The detailed list of production constraints represented in the form of articulatory features is given in Table 2.

Table 2. List of articulatory features

Features	Description
vlen	Length of the vowel in a syllable (short, long, dipthong and schwa).
vheight	Height of the vowel in a syllable (high, mid and low).
vfront	Frontness of the vowel in syllable (front, mid and back).
vrnd	Lip roundness (no rounding and rounding).
ctype	Type of consonant (stop, fricative, affricative, nasal, and liquid).
cplace	Place or position of the production of the consonant (labial, alveolar, palatal, labio-dental, dental and velar).
cvox	Whether consonant is voiced or unvoiced (voiced and unvoiced).
asp	Whether consonant is aspirated or unaspirated (aspirated and unaspirated).
nuk	Whether consonant with nukta or not nukta (withnukta and withoutnukta).
fph	Type of first phone in a syllable (vowel, voiced consonant, unvoiced consonant, nasal, semivowel, nukta and fricative).
lph	Type of last phone in a syllable (vowel, voiced consonant, unvoiced consonant, nasal, semivowel, nukta and fricative).

4　Proposed Intensity Model

In this work, a four layer feedforward neural network (FFNN) [10] with input layer, two hidden layers and output layer is used to model the intensities of the

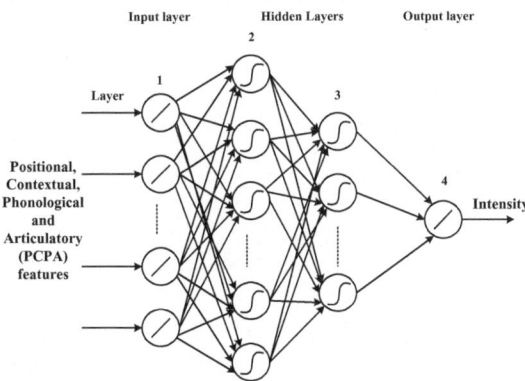

Fig. 1. Architecture of four layer feedforward neural network

syllables. The structure of the four layer FFNN is shown in Fig. 1. Different structures were explored to obtain the optimal four layer FFNN, by incrementally varying the hidden layers neurons in between 5 to 100. The optimal structure 35L 71N 17N 1L is obtained with minimum generalization error after exploring several structures, where L denotes linear unit and N denotes non-linear unit. The activation function used for non-linear unit (N) is hyperbolic tangent i.e., $\tanh(s)$ function. Here, the input and output features are normalized between [-1, 1] before giving to the neural network. The mapping function is between the 35-dimensional input vector and the 1-dimensional output vector. Two hidden layers which comprise 71 and 17 hidden units in the first and second hidden layers can capture the local and global variations across the features. The FFNN operates from left to right and training was carried using Lavenberg-Marquardt backpropagation algorithm.

In this work, the total data consists of 177820 syllables is used for modeling the intensities. The data is divided into two parts namely design data and test data. The design data is used to determine the network topology. The design data in turn is divided into two parts namely training data and validation data. Training data is used to estimate the weights (includes biases) of the neural network and validation data is used to minimize the overfitting of network, to verify the performance error and to stop training once the non-training validation error estimate stops decreasing. The test data is used once and only once on the best design, to obtain an unbiased estimate for the predicted error of unseen non-training data. The percentages of data divided for training, validation and testing the network are 70%, 15% and 15% respectively.

The mean squared error for training, validation and testing of the FFNN is shown in Fig. 2. The number of epochs needed for training depends on the behavior of the validation error. The training of the network stops once the validation error stops decreasing continuously. The validation error is monitored by keeping the validation checks at every epoch. The decreasing nature of the error

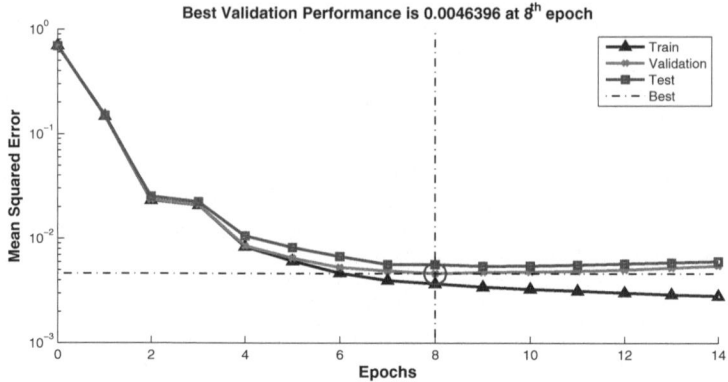

Fig. 2. Train, validation and test errors of the FFNN model developed for modeling the intensity values of syllables

shown in Fig. 2 represents, network is capturing the implicit relation between the input and the output.

5   Evaluation of Proposed Intensity Model

The prediction performance of the proposed FFNN model is evaluated by means of objective and subjective tests. In addition to FFNN model we also explored other non-linear statistical model like Classification and Regression Tree (CART) and linear statistical model like Linear Regression (LR) models in predicting the intensities. The performance of the FFNN model is compared with LR and CART models developed by PCPA features. The details of objective and subjective tests of the models are discussed in the following subsections.

5.1   Objective Evaluation

The proposed intensity model is evaluated with the syllables in the test set. The intensities of each syllable in the test set is predicted using FFNN by presenting the feature vector of each syllable as input to the network. The prediction performance of the FFNN model with the proposed features is given in Table 3. Columns 2-5 of Table 3 indicate the percentage of syllables predicted within different deviations from their actual intensity values. The deviation (D_i) is calculated as follows:

$$D_i = \frac{|x_i - y_i|}{x_i} \times 100$$

where x_i and y_i are the actual and predicted intensity values, respectively.

The prediction accuracy is evaluated by means of objective measures such as average prediction error (μ), standard deviation (σ) and correlation coefficient

$(\gamma_{X,Y})$ between actual and predicted intensity values shown in columns 6-8 of Table 3.

The formulae used to compute objective measures are given below:

$$\mu = \frac{\sum_i |x_i - y_i|}{N}$$

$$\sigma = \sqrt{\frac{\sum_i d_i^2}{N}}, d_i = e_i - \mu, e_i = x_i - y_i$$

where x_i, y_i are the actual and predicted intensity values respectively, and e_i is the error between the actual and predicted intensity values. The deviation in error is d_i, and N is the number of observed intensity values of the syllables. The correlation coefficient is given by

$$\gamma_{X,Y} = \frac{V_{X,Y}}{\sigma_X . \sigma_Y}, \text{ where } V_{X,Y} = \frac{\sum_i |x_i - \bar{x}|.|y_i - \bar{y}|}{N}$$

where σ_X, σ_Y are the standard deviations for the actual and predicted intensity values respectively, and $V_{X,Y}$ is the correlation between the actual and predicted intensity values.

The prediction performance of the LR and CART models is also given in Table 3. From the Table 3, it is observed observed that among LR, CART and

Table 3. Performance of the CART, LR and FFNN models for predicting the intensity values of syllables using PCPA features for Bengali language

Model	% Predicted syllables within deviation				Objective measures		
	1%	3%	5%	7%	μ (dB)	σ (dB)	γ
LR	13.97	37.96	60.89	76.2	3.40	2.66	0.69
CART	16.67	48.22	71.63	85.53	2.80	2.38	0.80
FFNN	**18.02**	**49.24**	**73.23**	**87.16**	**2.60**	**2.03**	**0.81**

FFNN models, the prediction accuracy is low for LR model compared to other models. From this we can hypothesize that the input features are nonlinearly related to syllable intensities rather than simple linear combination of features. From the results it is observed that FFNN model outperformed other models in predicting the intensity patterns of sequence of syllables. This indicate that neural network model captures the inherent relationship which exist between the PCPA features and intensities of syllables reasonably well compared to other models.

The prediction performance of the intensity models are also examined by using scatter plots shown in Fig. 3. The scatter plot is generated by jointly plotting the actual and the predicted syllable intensity values. In ideal case, the predicted

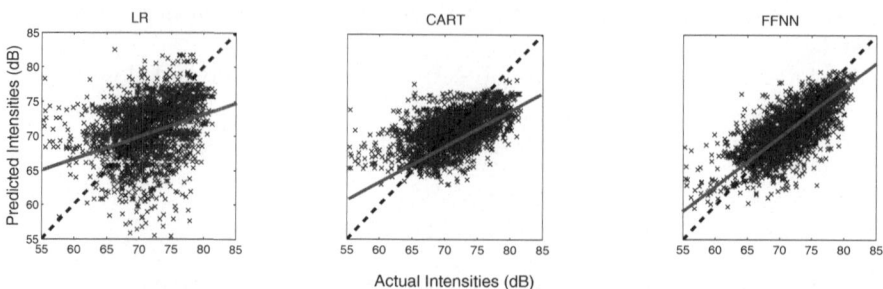

Fig. 3. Prediction performance of LR, CART and FFNN models using scatter plots

values should coincide with the actual values, with that all the points should fall on the diagonal, represented by dotted line in Fig. 3. The thick solid line in Fig. 3 represents the predicted intensity vs. actual intensity of the syllables. The angle between the solid line and dotted line (diagonal) is inversely proportional to accuracy in prediction. From the scatter plots, it is observed that the angle between solid and dotted lines is less in case of FFNN, compared to LR and CART models. It is observed from the Fig. 3, that the predicted intensity values are more deviated from the actual values at lower and higher intensities. From the Fig. 3, it is also observed that the predicted intensity values of LR and CART models are more deviated from actual intensity values compared to FFNN model. The prediction accuracy of FFNN model seems to be better in the range of 65-81 dB.

For demonstrating the accuracy of prediction of the intensities of the sequence of syllables at the utterance level, the actual and predicted syllable intensities of an utterance *"bArAmotI eArsTriper pAsh die kud~i pon~chish kimi gele gaond"*, are plotted in Fig. 4. From Fig. 4, it is observed that the predicted intensity pattern by the proposed FFNN model is very close to the original contour compared to LR and CART models. It indicates that the proposed

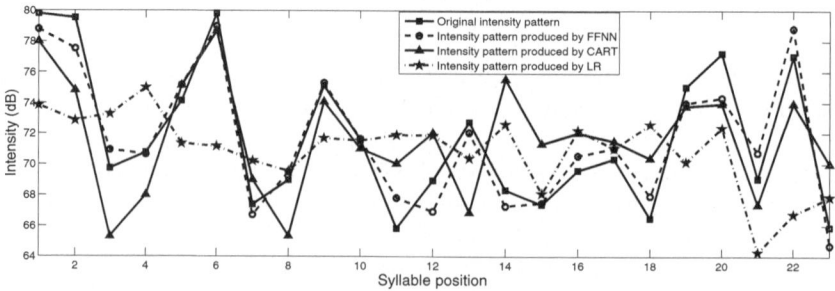

Fig. 4. Comparison of predicted intensity patterns from LR, CART and FFNN models with original intensity pattern for the utterance *"bArAmotI eArsTriper pAsh die kudi~ pon~chish kimi gele gaond"*

model predicts the intensities of sequence of syllables reasonably well compared to other models.

5.2   Subjective Evaluation

The prediction accuracy of the intensity models is also evaluated by analyzing the quality of the synthesized speech by incorporating the predicted intensity values of the syllables. The quality of the synthesized speech is evaluated by naturalness and intelligibility. In this work, 20 subjects within the age group of 23-35 were considered for evaluation of the synthesized speech. After giving appropriate training to the subjects, evaluation of TTS system is carried out in a laboratory environment. Randomly 10 sentences were selected and played the synthesized speech signals through headphones to evaluate the quality. Here, the subjects were asked to assess both the naturalness and the intelligibility of syntheiszed speech based on the 5-point scale [2]. The subjective evaluation is carried for the synthesized sentences generated by incorporating FFNN, CART and LR intensity models in festival based TTS system. The architecture of the intensity models incorporated in the TTS system is shown in Fig. 5. The mean opinion scores (MOS) for naturalness and intelligibility of the synthesized speech are shown in Table 4. From the Table 4, it is observed that the MOS values for both naturalness and intelligibilty of synthesized speech using predicted intensity values by FFNN model seems to be better than the MOS values of other models.

For analyzing the accuracy of the prediction of intensity models, we also conducted the listening tests for assessing the intelligibility and naturalness on the speech without incorporating the intensities. Here, the synthesized waveform will be generated at the time of synthesis using only linguistic features provided by linguistic module, without using intensity information from prosodic module for

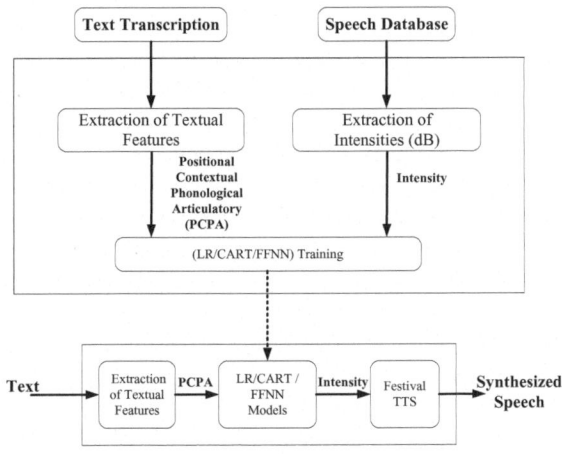

Fig. 5. Integration of intensity models in TTS

Table 4. Mean opinion scores and confidence levels for the quality of synthesized speech of Bengali TTS after incorporating the intensity models

Model with input features	Mean opinion score(Confidence level)	
	Intelligibility	*Naturalness*
(1) Without using intensity model	3.16 (> 99.5)	2.52 (> 99.5)
(2) LR model using PCPA	3.23 (> 99.0)	2.56 (> 99.0)
(3) CART model using PCPA	3.36 (> 95.0)	2.66 (> 95.0)
(4) FFNN model using PCPA	**3.41**	**2.73**

picking the units from the speech database. The MOS values of these listening tests are given in the first row in Table 4. It is observed, that the MOS values without considering intensity information is low compared to the MOS values using predicted intensity features for selecting the units. The significance of the differences in the pairs of the mean opinion scores for intelligibility and naturalness is tested using hypothesis testing. The level of confidence for the observed differences in the pairs of MOSs between FFNN model and other models are given in brackets in Table 4. From the Table 4, it is observed that the level of confidence is high (> 95.0) in all cases. This indicates that the differences in the pairs of MOS in each case is significant. From this study, we conclude that prediction accuracy by the proposed FFNN model is significantly better than LR and CART models at perceptual level.

6   Summary and Conclusions

In this work, the prediction of intensities of syllables is explored using FFNN model. Positional, contextual and phonological and articulatory features representing linguistic and production constraints of speech are proposed for developing the FFNN model. The model is evaluated by computing objective measures such as average prediction error, standard deviation and correlation coefficient. The accuracy in prediction was also analyzed in terms of percentage of syllables predicted within different deviations with respect to their actual intensities. The prediction performance of proposed FFNN model is also compared with CART and LR models. Verification of the prediction performance of the intensity model was also carried by conducting the perceptual tests on the synthesized speech utterances with incorporating the derived intensities from the FFNN model. The mean opinion scores of the perceptual tests indicate, that the quality of speech synthesized speech with the predicted intensity by FFNN model was better than the speech synthesized without the intensity information as well as speech synthesized using intensity information of other models. Both objective and subjective results indicates good performance of proposed FFNN model. The performance may be further improved if phrase break information is also included.

Acknowledgements. We would like to acknowledge Department of Information Technology (DIT), Government of India for offering this project. We also acknowledge the research scholars of IIT Kharagpur for their voluntary participation in listening tests to evaluate the Bengali TTS system developed in this work.

References

1. Jilka, M., Mohler, G., Dogil, G.: Rules for generation of TOBI-based American English intonation. Speech Communication 28, 83–108 (1999)
2. Reddy, V.R., Rao, K.S.: Intonation Modeling using FFNN for Syllable based Bengali Text To Speech Synthesis. In: Proc. Int. Conf. Computer and Communication Technology, MNNIT, Allahabad, pp. 334–339 (2011)
3. Klatt, D.H.: Synthesis by rule of segmental durations in English sentences. In: Lindblom, B., Ohman, S. (eds.) Frontiers of Speech Communication Research, pp. 287–300. Academic Press, New York (1979)
4. Rao, K.S., Yegnanarayana, B.: Modeling durations of syllables using neural networks. Computer Speech and Language 21, 282–295 (2007)
5. Mannel, R.H.: Modelling of the segmental and prosodic aspects of speech intensity in synthetic speech. In: Proc. Int. Conf. Speech Science and Technology, Melbourne, pp. 538–543 (December 2002)
6. Tesser, F.: Emotional Speech Synthesis: from theory to application. PhD thesis, International Doctorate School in Information and Communication Technologies. DIT - University of Trento, Italy (February 2005)
7. Narendra, N.P., Rao, K.S., Ghosh, K., Reddy, V.R., Maity, S.: Development of syllable-based text to speech synthesis system in Bengali. Int. J. of Speech Technology 14(3), 167–181 (2011)
8. Haykin, S.: Neural Networks: A Comprehensive Foundation. Pearson Education Aisa, Inc., New Delhi (1999)
9. I. P. Association, Handbook of the International Phonetic Association: A Guide to the Use of the International Phonetic Alphabet. Cambridge University Press (1999)
10. Tamura, S., Tateishi, M.: Capabilities of a Four-Layered Feedforward Neural Network: Four Layers Versus Three, vol. 8, pp. 251–255 (March 1997)

Data-Driven Phrase Break Prediction
for Bengali Text-to-Speech System

Krishnendu Ghosh and K. Sreenivasa Rao

School of Information Technology
Indian Institute of Technology Kharagpur
Kharagpur, India
ghosh.krrish@gmail.com, ksrao@sit.iitkgp.ernet.in

Abstract. In this paper, an approach is proposed to accurately predict
the locations of phrase breaks in a sentence for a Bengali text-to-speech
(TTS) synthesis system. Determining the positions of phrase breaks is
one of the most important tasks for generating natural and intelligible
speech. In order to approximate the break locations, a feed-forward neural network (FFNN) based approach is proposed in the current study.
For acquiring prosodic phrase break knowledge, morphological information along with widely-used positional and structural features are
analyzed. The importance of all the features is demonstrated using a
model-dependent feature selection approach. Finally the phrase break
predicting model is implemented with the selected optimal set of features
and incorporated inside a Bengali TTS system built using Festival framework [1]. The proposed FFNN model is developed using the optimally
selected morphological, positional and structural features. The performance of the proposed FFNN model is compared with widely used Classification and Regression Tree (CART) model for prediction of breaks
and no-breaks. The FFNN model is evaluated objectively on the basis
of precision, recall and a harmonized measure - F score. The significance
of the phrase break module is further analyzed by conducting subjective
listening tests.

Keywords: Phrase break prediction, morphological, positional and
structural features, CART, FFNN.

1   Introduction

Phrase breaks poses an important role in structuring an utterance and implying
the purpose of its existence. A phrase is a syntactic structure with one or more
words but does not possess the grammatical organization of a sentence. While
speaking, phrase breaks are used as the limit of words that can be spoken at once.
Phrase breaks decompose a sentence into some meaningful prosodic chunks, making the sentence natural, pleasant, intelligible and meaningful. Without proper
phrasing, speech generated by a synthesis module, cannot achieve required degree of naturalness. Hence, phrase break prediction is one of the most important
modules in a text-to-speech (TTS) synthesis system. The phrasing model also

M. Parashar et al. (Eds.): IC3 2012, CCIS 306, pp. 118–129, 2012.
© Springer-Verlag Berlin Heidelberg 2012

serves as input to other modules of a TTS system like segmentation module [2,3] and fundamental frequency contour generation module [4]. Hence, accurate phrase break prediction is mandatory to achieve good quality synthesized speech out of a TTS system.

The phrase break prediction is one of the most indispensable modules which instills the naturalness and intelligibility in the synthesized speech waveform. Early approaches to develop a quality phrasing model used hand-crafted rules based on punctuation and simple syntactic features [2]. Recent trend of using robust machine-learning tools is observed for highly-researched languages. For Indian languages, building an accurate phrase break prediction model is difficult due to the unavailability of a standard corpus annotated with relevant morphological, positional and other features. Simple CART based phrase break prediction systems is modeled recently for primary Indian languages. The present study proposes a feed forward neural network (FFNN) to capture the complex non-linear characteristics of the breaks.

The paper is organized as follows: Section 2 describes existing approaches used for predicting the phrase breaks. Section 3 describes the details of the database used in the current study. Section 4 discusses the architecture of the proposed neural network model. In section 5, relevant features are analyzed to select the optimal feature set for phrase break prediction. Section 6 describes the implementation methodology for developing the phrasing model. Section 7 discusses both the subjective and objective performance evaluation for the proposed approach. Finally, the paper concludes with the outlines for further improvements of the current study.

2   Literature Survey

The approaches, used for predicting the phrase breaks, can be classified in two major classes: rule-based and data-driven or stochastic methods [5].

One of the earliest rule-based phrase break prediction approaches was focused on the syntactic structure and the psychological organization of a sentence [6]. 'Psychological organization of a sentence' segments a sentence considering where human beings tend to introduce pauses while uttering that sentence. Phrase breaks can be predicted from the relations between psychologically introduced phrases and syntactical phrases. The phrasing model had been further improved with the introduction of punctuation [7]. But, casual texts, without proper punctuation, cannot be handled using this method. Further enhancements were observed with the introduction of morphological analysis [8]. The rule-based methods are basically simple in structure and heuristic in nature. These methods consider mainly syntactic, prosodic and structural information from an engineering or linguistic viewpoint to predict the position of the phrase breaks [4,9]. Writing such hand-crafted rules is difficult for predicting phrase break locations due to the variations present in any language. Moreover, the rules are language and domain specific.

Data-driven approaches can surpass the limitations of the rule-based methods with the help of rich corpus and statistical techniques. Data-driven models are self-learning approaches which are trained with the attribute-value pairs for the input-output. The models can interpret the knowledge obtained in the training procedure later in testing phase for various purposes e.g., classification, identification or diagnosis. Earlier data-driven models used for phrase break prediction consists of mainly simple approaches such as CART [10], memory-based learning (MBL) method [11] and window method [7]. The attributes, also known as features, are information on which the locations of the phrase break depends. For phrase break prediction, mainly word level features and sometimes sentence level features are considered. The data-driven models require corpus annotated with significant phrase-related knowledge [5]. Simple data-driven approaches like CART or decision trees may not capture the feature variability of a unseen linearly non-separable problem such as, phrase break prediction. On the other hand, non-linear classifiers like HMM, SVM and ANN, can classify new data with better accuracy. Specially, ANNs are well known for classification problems as they can relate the input-output pairs [12].

3   Database

The database is collected mainly from Anandabajar Patrika, a Bengali news corpus that consists of political news, entertainment, sports and stories. The other sources are story and text books of various domains such as history, geography, travelogue, drama and science. Prior to use, the corpus is thoroughly corrected manually. The corpus is finally tagged with punctuation to indicate phrase breaks manually. The main goal of an unrestricted TTS system is to synthesize any text. Therefore, the corpus should address maximum possible variations of vocabulary in Bengali. We collected a total of 60,000 sentences to attain 7,762 optimal sentences [13,14]. Optimal sentences have selected to capture the most frequent intonational phenomena.

Finally, 6,210 sentences, with 59,567 words and 24,638 manually added phrase breaks, are used for training purpose. Remaining 1,552 sentences, consisting of 14,492 words and 6,338 manually tagged phrase breaks, are used for evaluating the proposed model.

4   Features

For phrase break prediction, generally word level features are used. Traditionally positional, structural and morphological features have been proved to be significant for phrase break prediction [4]. Morphological features are hard to extract due to lack of proper morphological analyzer in Indian languages. In context of developing a syllable-based Bengali TTS system, systematic analysis on the significance of the available features for phrase break prediction is not observed in the literature. The present study tries to analyze the significance of the word-level features for phrase break prediction. Traditional positional and structural features are proposed in this work. Moreover, one well-known and significant morphological feature - parts-of-speech (POS) is also proposed. The current study proposes another morphological feature, namely phonetic strength. The feature "**phonetic strength** of a word" is explored in order to identify phrase boundaries more accurately. A word is said to have phonetically weak or strong form if it has more than one pronunciation. The weak form is the normal and unstressed pronunciation for a word. On the other hand, strong form is the pronunciation that is used for introducing emphasis, contrast and citation. For making emphasis or contrast, it is a natural tendency to put stress on the word. Stress introduces phrase breaks in the utterance to make the sense of emphasis or contrast prominent. Hence, the phonetically strong words significantly assign phrase breaks before or after it based on contexts [15]. The positional and structural features are collected automatically and the morphological features are collected manually. These features are tagged in the training data. The set of features are:

1. Positional:
   - Number of words from beginning of sentence
   - Number of words to end of sentence
   - Number of words in the focus sentence
2. Structural:
   - Number of phones in a word
   - Number of syllables in a word
   - Number of phones in the focus sentence
3. Morphological:
   - POS of this word
   - Phonetic strength

A phrase is constructed with more than one word in most of the cases. Therefore, the phrase related information lies inside the phrase structure and dependence between the word under study and its context words. Hence, the features of the context words are also significant to predict the phrase level information. A 5-gram window is proposed in the current study to extract contextual information for phrase break prediction. The 5-gram window is a [-2,+2] window which represents the previous two and following two words and the focus word. The contextual information is collected for 4 features (number of syllables in a word, number of phones in a word, POS of the word and phonetic strength of the word). For other 4 features, context information is redundant, as the context information lies embedded in the feature of the focus word. Therefore, contextual information of the proposed 8 features generates a feature set of 24 features. Each of the 24 features may not be significant in predicting accurately the locations of the phrase breaks. Therefore, the general practice is to select an optimal feature set.

Feature selection is one of the important issues of a classification problem. Feature selection is the process that selects an optimally performing subset from the total feature set [16]. The optimal feature selection is important due to presence of redundant, ambiguous and irrelevant features in the training set. Those attributes or features can be segregated from the data set, even if the exact governing rules are not known. A typical feature selection method consists of four basic steps - (i) subset generation, (ii) subset evaluation, (iii) stopping criterion and (iv) result validation [17]. Common classical model independent methods for feature selection consists of scoring or ranking approaches based on information gain (IG), cross entropy, mutual information, weight of evidence, odds ratio and frequency [18,19]. Classifiers like decision tree and neural network models generally use backward search technique to discard redundant features [20]. A backward search technique for feature selection uses the total feature set for classification procedure in the first step. Later, it starts discarding features until the stop criterion reaches. The current study proposes the simple backward search technique with deletion of one feature at each step provided the following two conditions stand: (i) the overall classification accuracy, for predicting breaks and no-breaks together, should not decrease, and (ii) at each step, the less scoring or less significant feature will be discarded.

The proposed FFNN based phrase break prediction module is built using all the 24 features in the first step. The proposed model achieves an overall accuracy of 81.06% for predicting the breaks and no-breaks. The second step deletes the features and checks whether the accuracy is improved after deletion of the corresponding feature or not. The feature, after deleting which, the accuracy is improved the most, is deleted from the feature list permanently. For the remaining feature set, the second step is repeatedly carried out until a) improvement in accuracy is not noted or b) the feature set contains only one feature. In course of building the optimal feature set using the proposed backward feature selection technique, five features are deleted. The features and improvement in overall accuracy after deleting the corresponding features is discussed in Table 1. The notation "pp.x" used in the following table represents the feature x of the previous to previous word of the target word. Similarly, "nn.x" is used to mention the feature x of the next to next word of the focused word.

Table 1. Redundant Feature Deletion for Optimal Subset Selection

Deleted Features	Improvement in Accuracy after deleting the Feature
pp.Number of syllables in a word	1.5%
nn.Number of syllables in a word	1.24%
pp.Number of phones in a word	1.16%
nn.Number of phones in a word	0.84%
pp.Phonetic strength	0.34%

Among all the 24 features, 5 features are deleted as mentioned in Table 1 and remaining 19 features are selected in the optimal feature set.

5   Modeling of FFNN Based Approach

An artificial neural network (ANN) is a mathematical model which is basically formed to capture the relation between the input and output pair. A neural network (NN) is formed with some layers of neurons which are connected with the input and output to model the function of the ANN to generate the output from the input. The basic parameters of an ANN are: (i) the interconnection, (ii) the learning function and (iii) the activation function. A feed forward neural network (FFNN) is a NN model where each layer feeds input to the next layer in a feed forward fashion [12]. A multi-layer FFNN model is preferred for non-linearly separable classification or pattern recognition problems.

The phrase breaks can be modeled by using a multi-layer feed-forward neural network. Three layer feed-forward neural network with an input layer, an output layer and the hidden layer are well-known for simple classification problems [21,22]. The general structure of a three-layer FFNN is shown in Figure 1. The basic parameters of a neural network are explored and the best fitted parameters are selected for prediction purpose. The optimal network structure is chosen based on minimum training error, after exploring several structures by varying number of units in the hidden layer.

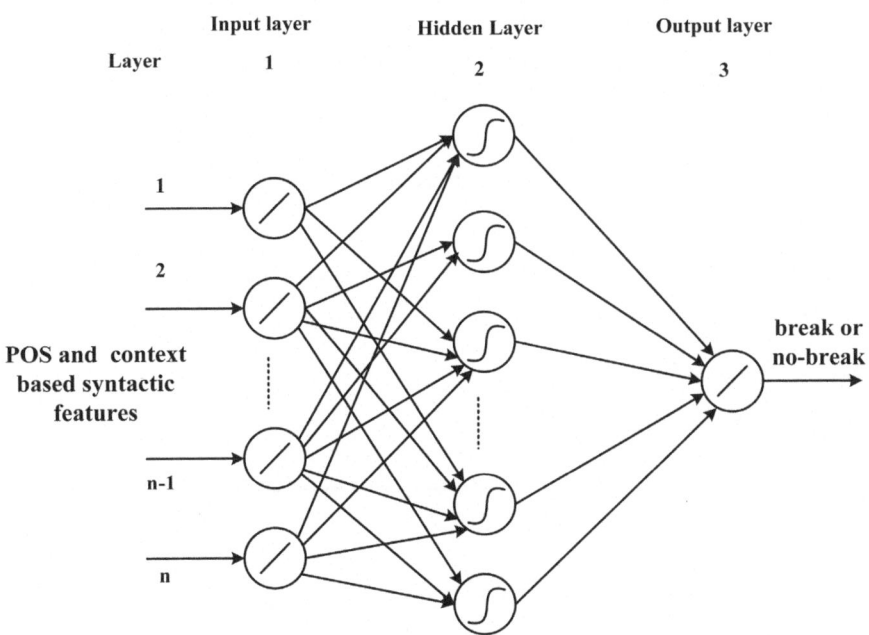

Fig. 1. Example of a three-layer feed-forward neural network

6   Implementation

A three-layer feed forward neural network (FFNN) is used for modeling the phrase breaks. The first layer is the input layer with linear units. The second layer is the hidden layer having more units than the input layer to capture local features from the input space. It has been noted that, for phrase break prediction problem, features of other than [-2,+2] context window are not significant for localizing breaks and no-breaks. Therefore, capturing the local variability is the primary issue here. Hence, the proposed model performs well with one hidden layer [12]. The third layer is the output layer having one unit predicting whether it is a break or a no-break. The mapping function is applied between the 19-dimensional input vector and the one-dimensional output. At the input layer, the activation function for the units is linear and at the hidden layers, it is nonlinear.

The final optimal network structure is 19L 38N 1N, where L represents a linear unit, and N represents a non-linear unit. The integer values indicate the number of units used in corresponding layer. The nonlinear units use tanh(s) as the activation function, where s is the activation value of that unit. All the input and output features have been normalized to the range [-1, +1] before using in the neural network. Back propagation learning algorithm is used to adapt the weights of the network in order to minimize the error for each prediction [12].

Since the number of training samples are significantly larger than the number of weights, the possibility of over-fitting of the training data is rare. The training errors for neural network models for phrase break prediction are shown in Figure 2. The decreasing trend in the training error indicates that the network is capturing the implicit relation between the input and output.

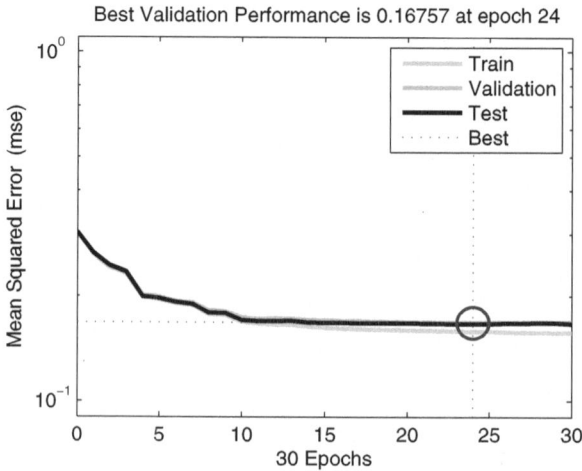

Fig. 2. Training errors for the proposed four-layer feed forward neural network model for phrase break prediction

7   Evaluation

The accuracy of the phrasing model is evaluated using objective and subjective measures. The objective measure consists of percentage of correct prediction for the breaks and no-breaks. But, the ultimate goal of a phrasing model is to attain natural and intelligible synthesized speech output from a TTS system. To capture the perception based qualities, subjective listening test is conducted to determine the significance of the phrasing model in the Bengali TTS system.

7.1   Objective Evaluation

Error may occur while predicting phrase breaks in two cases: (1) Insertion error (I): If a break is predicted where there is a no-break in the test set. (2) Deletion error (D): If a break is not predicted where there is a break in the test set. In most of the cases, one insertion error while predicting the phrase breaks generates another deletion error and vice-versa.

The overall accuracy of a phrase break prediction model is measured using the following variables:

BC=Breaks correctly predicted= B-D,
NBC=No-breaks correctly predicted= NB-I,
BA=Breaks actually present in the test set,
NBA=No-breaks actually present in the test set,
BP=Breaks predicted totally,
NBP=No-breaks predicted totally.

Considering, NB is the number of no-breaks and B is the number of breaks present in the test set. D and I stands for the number of deletion and insertion errors respectively.

In [23], a CART based phrase break prediction model has been proposed. Being trained on 6,210 sentences and tested with 1,552 sentences and using 7 optimally selected features from the same 24 feature set, the phrase break prediction model predicts the locations of the 6,338 breaks (B) with 75.07% and 8,154 no-breaks (NB) with 80.94% accuracy. On the other hand, the performance of the proposed phrasing model surpasses the referred result. The reason is: a multi-layer FFNN model with back propagation method for error correction can change the weights of the interconnected neurons to approximate the relation between the input-output pairs and therefore, predict the outcome with better accuracy [24]. Another intriguing property of the FFNN based approach is the ability to handle the unseen and new data using new features which are not mentioned explicitly in the training data [25]. The proposed approach predicts the locations of the 6,338 breaks (B) with 79.87% and 8,154 no-breaks (NB) with 88.94% accuracy. The details of the result is mentioned in Table 2.

The performance of the phrase break prediction models, discussed in [23] and in the current study, are analyzed by calculating results in terms of precision and recall, and using an F score. Precision is used to measure how many of the phrase breaks or no-breaks predicted by the model are correct, and recall measures what percentage of the phrase breaks or no-breaks in the test data are correctly predicted. The F score gives a balanced measure of overall quality by harmonizing precision and recall.

For breaks,
Precision $= P_B = \frac{BC}{BP}$

Recall $= R_B = \frac{BC}{BA}$

F score $= F_B = \frac{2P_B R_B}{P_B + R_B}$

Similarly for no-breaks,
Precision $= P_{NB} = \frac{NBC}{NBP}$

Recall $= R_{NB} = \frac{NBC}{NBA}$

F score $= F_{NB} = \frac{2P_{NB} R_{NB}}{P_{NB} + R_{NB}}$

Table 2. Objective Evaluation of the CART based and proposed FFNN based phrase break prediction model

	Precision		Recall		F Score	
	CART	FFNN	CART	FFNN	CART	FFNN
Break	80.66%	82.66%	75.07%	79.87%	77.76%	81.06%
No-break	77.23%	84.23%	80.94%	88.94%	79.04%	86.04%

7.2   Subjective Evaluation

The significance of a phrase break prediction module in the TTS system is evaluated by conducting listening tests on 20 synthesized sentences before and after incorporating both the CART based and FFNN based phrasing model. Listening tests are conducted using 20 subjects to judge the quality of speech on 5 point scale for each sentence. The details of the 5 point scale is mentioned in Table 3:

Table 4 shows the mean opinion scores for the following cases:

MOS 1: MOS for baseline TTS system without any phrase break model.
MOS 2: MOS for baseline TTS system with the CART based phrasing model.
MOS 3: MOS for baseline TTS system with the FFNN based phrasing model.

The significance of increment in the MOS scores is tested using hypothesis testing [26]. The level of confidence for the observed increment was obtained by using sample variances and values of Student-t distribution. The levels of confidence achieved for all the transitions are high(99.5% and 95% for the transitions MOS

Table 3. Instruction for evaluating speech quality through mean opinion score method

Point	Quality of sentence
1	Poor speech with very low intelligibility
2	Poor speech but intelligible
3	Good speech and intelligible
4	Very good speech quality but less naturalness
5	As good as natural speech

Table 4. Comparison of TTS system without and with the phrasing model

MOS for different models	MOS	Standard Deviation
MOS 1	2.92	0.78
MOS 2	3.3	0.54
MOS 3	3.42	0.47

1-2 and MOS 2-3 respectively). This confirms the significance of the increment in the MOS scores. Subjects also perceived notable improvements in the naturalness and intelligibility with incorporation of proposed phrasing models in the Bengali TTS system.

8 Conclusion

This paper presents FFNN based approach for phrase break prediction. For this purpose, positional, structural and morphological features are collected from the database. Model dependent backward feature selection process is used for selecting the optimal feature set. The basic parameters of FFNN model such as, network structure, learning and activation functions are determined using the selected features. Finally, the well-suited parameters are selected for prediction purpose. The proposed model is evaluated using both objective and subjective tests. Our main contribution is exploring the available features to select optimal feature set and FFNN model for building the phrasing model. Both the objective and subjective performances confirm the significance and accuracy of the proposed model in generating natural and intelligible speech from the TTS system.

Further improvements are expected using following ideas.

1. With the help of machine learning tools and information retrieval, more features as well as model independent feature selection processes may be explored. It is expected to have better phrasing model using optimal and more significant feature set.

2. General stochastic models such as CART, work at the word level. Hence, all context information cannot be used. Exploring a model which considers the

full sentence at once (such as -gram models), may improve the phrase prediction precision [5].

3. Other probabilistic methods like HMM and Bayesian network can be used if proper tagged database is ready [5,27].

4. Along with the prosodic and syntactic features, signal based features like F0 and pitch reset may be used to determine the phrase break positions [28].

Acknowledgement. The work presented in this paper has been performed at IIT Kharagpur as a part of the project "Development of text to speech synthesis in Indian languages" supported by the Department of Information Technology, Government of India. Our special thanks to research scholars of School of Information Technology, IIT Kharagpur for participating in the listening tests.

References

1. Narendra, N.P., Rao, K.S., Ghosh, K., Reddy, V.R., Maity, S.: Development of Syllable-based Text to Speech Synthesis System in Bengali. International Journal of Speech Technology 14(3), 167–181 (2011)
2. Hirschberg, J.: Pitch accent in context: Predicting intonational prominence from text. Artificial Intelligence (63) (1993)
3. Fordyce, C.S., Ostendorf, M.: Prosody Prediction for Speech Synthesis Using Transformational Rule Based Learning. In: Proceedings of International Conference of Spoken Language Processing, pp. 682–685 (1998)
4. Krishna, N.S., Murthy, H.A.: A New Prosodic Phrasing Model for Indian Language Telugu. In: Proceedings of Interspeech, pp. 793–796 (2004)
5. Sun, X., Applebaum, T.H.: Intonational Phrase Break Prediction Using Decision Tree and N-Gram Model. In: Proceedings of Eurospeech (2001)
6. Gee, J.P., Grosjean, F.: Performance structures: a psycholinguistic and linguistic appraisal. Cognitive Psychology (15), 411–458 (1983)
7. Taylor, P., Black, A.W.: Assigning phrase breaks from part-of-speech sequences. Computer Speech and Language (12), 99–117 (1998)
8. Silverman, K.: The Sructure and Processing of Fundamental Frequency Contours. Ph.D. thesis, University of Cambridge (1987)
9. Hirschberg, J., Prieto, P.: Training intonational phrasing rules automatically for English and Spanish Text-to-Speech. Speech Communication 18, 281–290 (1996)
10. Breiman, L., Friedman, J., Olshen, R., Stone, C.: Classification and Regression Trees. Chapman and Hall, New York (1984)
11. Busser, G., Daelemans, W., van den Bosch, A.: Predicting phrase breaks with memory-based learning. In: Proceedings of 4th ISCA Tutorial and Research Workshop on Speech Synthesis, Perthshire, Scotland, pp. 29–34 (2001)
12. Yegnanarayana, B.: Artificial Neural Networks. Prentice-Hall, New Delhi (1999)
13. Kishore, S.P., Black, A.W.: Unit size in unit selection speech synthesis. In: Proceedings of Eurospeech, pp. 1317–1320 (2003)
14. Thomas, H.S., Rao, M.N., Ramalingam, C.: Natural Sounding TTS based on Syllable like Units. In: Proceedings of European Signal Processing Conference, Florence, Italy (2006)
15. Roach, P.: English Phonetics and Phonology. Cambridge University Press, Cambridge (1991)

16. Gabrilovich, E., Markovitch, S.: Feature Generation for Text Categorization using World Knowledge. In: IJCAI, pp. 1048–1053 (2005)
17. Dash, M., Liu, H.: Feature Selection for Classification. In: Intelligent Data Analysis, vol. 1, pp. 131–156 (1997)
18. Mladenic, D., Grobelnik, M.: Feature Selection for Classification Based on Text Hierarchy. In: Proceedings of Text and the Web, Conference on Automated Learning and Discovery (1998)
19. Kwak, N., Choi, C.H.: Input Feature Selection for Classification Problems. IEEE Transactions on Neural Networks 13(1), 143–159 (2002)
20. Leray, P., Gallinari, P.: Feature selection with neural networks. Pattern Recognition Letters Archive 23(11) (September 2002)
21. Tamura, S., Tateishi, M.: Capabilities of a Four-Layered Feedforward Neural Network: Four Layers Versus Three. IEEE Transactions on Neural Networks 8, 251–255 (1997)
22. Sontag, E.D.: Feedback stabilization using two hidden layer nets. IEEE Transactions on Neural Networks 3, 981–990 (1992)
23. Ghosh, K., Reddy, V.R., Rao, K.S.: Phrase Break Prediction for Bengali Text to Speech Synthesis System. In: Proceedings of International Conference of Natural Language Processing, Chennai (2011)
24. Rao, K.S., Yegnanarayana, B.: Modeling durations of syllables using neural networks. Computer Speech & Language 21(2), 282–285 (2007)
25. Mitchell, T.M.: Machine Learning, 123 p. McGraw Hill, New York (1997)
26. Hogg, R.V., Ledolter, J.: Engineering Statistics. Macmillan, New York (1987)
27. Schmidt, H., Atterer, M.: New statistical methods for phrase break prediction. In: Proceedings of the 20th International Conference on Computational Linguistics (2004)
28. Pfitzinger, H., Reichel, U.: Text-based and Signal-based Prediction of Break Indices and Pause Durations. In: Proceedings of Speech Prosody, Dresden, pp. 133–136 (2006)

Behaviour of Torsional Surface Wave in a Homogeneous Substratum over a Dissipative Half Space

Sumit Kumar Vishwakarma[*] and Shishir Gupta

Department of Applied Mathematics, Indian School of Mines
Dhanbad-826004, Jahrkhand, India
sumo.ism@ismu.ac.in

Abstract. The present paper studies the propagation of torsional surface wave in a homogeneous isotropic substratum lying over a viscoelastic half space under the influence of rigid boundary. Dispersion relation has been obtained analytically in a closed form. The effect of internal friction, rigidity, wave number and time period on the phase velocity has been studied numerically. Dispersion equation thus obtained match perfectly with the classical dispersion equation of Love wave when derived as a particular case.

Keywords: Homogeneous substratum, rigid boundary, Internal friction, Torsional wave.

1   Introduction

Torsional surface wave is a wave with amplitudes decaying exponentially with distance from the free surface. These waves are horizontally polarized but give a twist to the medium when it propagates. Although much information is available on the propagation of surface waves such as Rayleigh waves, Love waves and Stonely waves etc., the torsional wave has not drawn much attention and very little literature is available on the propagation of this wave. The propagation of seismic waves in anisotropic medium are of great practical importance. They are not only helpful in investigating the internal structure of the Earth but also very useful in exploration of natural resources buried inside the earth's surface, e.g., oils, gases, deposits, and other useful hydrocarbons and minerals. Elastic wave problems are usually formulated for convenience under the restricted assumptions of inhomogeneity, perfect elasticity, plane parallel boundaries and isotropy. A layered medium by its very nature is anisotropic in the large, but the individual layers may also be anisotropic in a manner which cannot be handled by a further subdivision into finer layers. Heterogeneous media with random grain orientation tend to be isotropic. A straight mathematical attack may produce explicit or numerical solutions even for rather complex solid media. The mathematical expression provides the bridge between modeling results and field application. Any disturbance in earth's interior may serve as the basic reason

---

[*] Corresponding author.

M. Parashar et al. (Eds.): IC3 2012, CCIS 306, pp. 130–140, 2012.
© Springer-Verlag Berlin Heidelberg 2012

of seismic wave propagation. The theoretical study of wave propagation consists of finding the solution of a partial differential equation or a system of partial differential modeling under initial and boundary conditions The earth being highly anisotropic in nature has some of its part viscoelastic. Therefore the present paper studies the torsional surface wave propagation in an elastic layer lying over a viscoelastic half space. In this paper, sattempt has been made to come up with the significant effect of viscoelastic material on the phase velocity of torsional wave along with the influence of other elastic parameters. These waves often propagate during the earthquakes and become responsible to some extent for the destruction on the earth's crustal layer. Therefore seismologists have started taking a keen interest in the propagation of torsional surface wave in various geo-media. Inside the Earth, a very hard layer (also known as "rigid") is present. Since the composition of the Earth is heterogeneous including a very hard layer, the inhomogeneous medium and the rigid interface play significant roles in the propagation of the seismic waves. Imperfect elastic bodies can be considered as having properties intermediate between those of elastic and viscous bodies, and are called viscoelastic bodies.

In the present paper, study has been made on the propagation of torsional surface wave in a homogeneous isotropic layer overlying a viscoelastic half space under the effect of rigid boundary plane. Harmonic wave propagation in viscoelastic media with stochasticity by Manolis and Shaw (1996) whereas investigation has been made on shear wave in viscoelastic medium at irregular boundaries (Chattopadhyay et al 2010). He (Chattopadhyay et al 2010) has also shown the effect of point source and heterogeneity on SH wave propagation. Inhomogeneous harmonic plane waves in viscoelastic anisotropic media have been studied by Červený (2004). References have also been made to Sethi and Gupta (2011), Park and Kausel (2004), Romeo (2003), Sari and Salk (2002) and Chattopadhyay et al. (2011) for their excellent contribution in investigating elastic wave in various medium under various circumstances. The works done by Davini et al. (2008), Gupta et al. (2012) and Akbarov et al. (2011) cannot be overlooked as their contributions are commendable towards torsional wave propagation. In the present paper, the dispersion equation has been obtained using variable separable technique. It is observed that the phase velocity of Torsional surface wave decreases with the decrease in the internal friction while decreases with the increase in the rigidity of the half space under consideration. Graphs have also been plotted for dimensionless phase velocity against time period to get the effect of internal friction and rigidity.

2   Statement of the Problem

For the study of torsional surface waves, a cylindrical coordinate system has been considered. The model consists of an homogeneous crustal layer of thickness H overlying a vertically dissipative (viscoelastic) half-space. The origin of the cylindrical co-ordinate system (r, θ, z) is located at the interface separating the layer from the half-space, and the z-axis is directed downwards (as shown in Figure 1). In the layer, rigidity and density has been taken as μ_0 and ρ_0 respectively, which are constant throughout whereas in the viscoelastic half space μ, ρ and μ' represents the rigidity, density and internal friction (viscoelastic parameter) respectively.

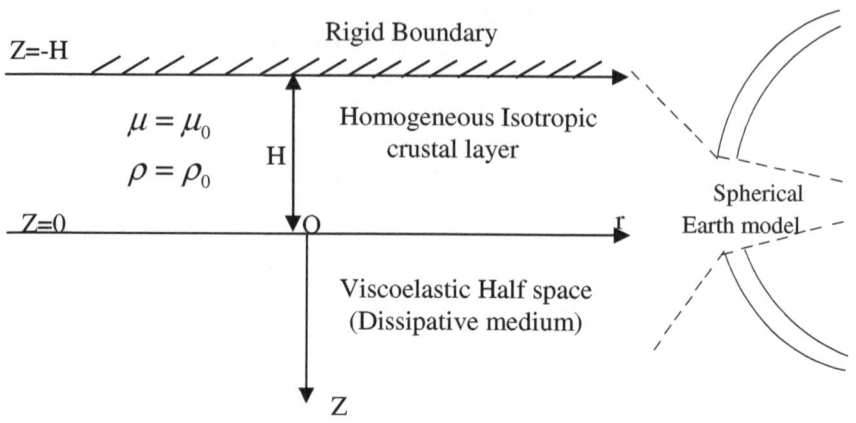

Fig. 1. Geometry of the problem

3   Solution of the Layer

The dynamical equations of motion for torsional surface waves propagating in radial direction as given by Biot (1965) can be written as

$$\frac{\partial \sigma_{r\theta}}{\partial r} + \frac{\partial \sigma_{z\theta}}{\partial z} + \frac{2}{r}\sigma_{r\theta} = \rho\frac{\partial^2 v}{\partial t^2} \tag{1}$$

where $v(r, z, t)$ is the displacement along θ direction.

For an elastic medium, the stresses are related to displacement by

$$\sigma_{r\theta} = \mu\left(\frac{\partial v}{\partial r} - \frac{v}{r}\right) \text{ and } \sigma_{z\theta} = \mu\frac{\partial v}{\partial z}$$

If the material parameters which are involved in torsional wave propagation are

$$\mu = \mu(z) \text{ and } \rho = \rho(z) \tag{2}$$

Eq. (1) takes the form

$$\mu\left(\frac{\partial^2}{\partial r^2} + \frac{1}{r}\frac{\partial}{\partial r} - \frac{1}{r^2}\right)v + \frac{\partial}{\partial z}\left(\mu\frac{\partial v}{\partial z}\right) = \rho\frac{\partial^2 v}{\partial t^2} \tag{3}$$

We may assume the solution of (3) as

$$v = V(z)J_1(kr)e^{i\omega t} \qquad (4)$$

where V is the solution of

$$\frac{d^2V}{dz^2} + \frac{\mu'}{\mu}\frac{dV}{dz} - K^2\left(1 - \frac{c^2}{c_s^2}\right)V = 0 \qquad (5)$$

in which $c = \dfrac{\omega}{k}$ and $c_s = \left(\dfrac{\mu}{\rho}\right)^{1/2}$ and $J_1(kr)$ is the Bessel function of first kind and fist order.

Now, since the layer is homogeneous and isotropic, Eq. (5) reduces to

$$\frac{d^2V}{dz^2} - K^2\left(1 - \frac{c^2}{c_0^2}\right)V = 0 \qquad (6)$$

The Solution of Eq. (6) may be given as

$$V = A_1e^{m_1 kz} + A_2e^{-m_1 kz}$$

where $m_1 = \sqrt{1 - \dfrac{c^2}{c_0^2}}$. A_1 and A_2 are arbitrary constants and hence the displacement in the upper homogeneous layer is

$$v = v_0(say) = \left(A_1e^{m_1 kz} + A_2e^{-m_1 kz}\right)J_1(kr)e^{i\omega t} \qquad (7)$$

4   Solution of the Half Space

In the half space, the Torsional surface wave travels in radial direction and therefore all the mechanical properties associated with it are independent of θ. For torsional surface wave, $u = w = 0$ and $v = v(r, z, t)$ and the equation of motion for viscoelastic voigt type may be written as (Biot 1965)

$$\left(\mu + \mu'\frac{\partial}{\partial t}\right)\left(\frac{\partial^2}{\partial r^2} + \frac{1}{r}\frac{\partial v}{\partial r} + \frac{d^2v}{dz^2}\right) = \rho\frac{\partial^2v}{\partial t^2} \qquad (8)$$

where μ is the modulus of rigidity of the medium and μ' is the internal friction or viscoelastic parameter.

For the wave propagating along r direction one may assume the solution of Eq. (8) as

$$v = V(z) J_1(kr) e^{i\omega t} \tag{9}$$

where V is the solution of

$$\frac{d^2 V}{dz^2} - K^2 \left\{ 1 - \frac{c_1^2}{c_2^2(1+iA)} \right\} V(z) = 0 \tag{10}$$

in which $c_1 = \dfrac{\omega}{k}$, $c_2 = \left(\dfrac{\mu}{\rho}\right)^{1/2}$, $A = \dfrac{\omega \mu'}{\mu}$ and $\omega = \dfrac{2\pi}{T}$

The solution of Eq. (10) satisfying the condition $\lim\limits_{z \to \infty} V(z) = 0$ is

$$V = \left[B_1 \cos(\alpha_1 \alpha_3 z) - B_2 \sin(\alpha_1 \alpha_3 z) \right] e^{-\alpha_1 \alpha_2 z} \tag{11}$$

where

$$\alpha_1 = \left[\frac{k^2 \gamma_1}{c_2^2(1+A^2)} \right]^{1/2}, \quad \alpha_2 = \cos\left(\frac{\theta}{2}\right), \quad \alpha_3 = \sin\left(\frac{\theta}{2}\right)$$

$$\gamma_1 = \left[\left\{ c_2^2(1+A^2) - c_1^2 \right\}^2 + \left(Ac_1^2\right)^2 \right]^{1/2}, \quad \theta = \tan^{-1} \left[\frac{A}{\left(\dfrac{c_2^2}{c_1^2} + A \dfrac{c_2}{c_1} - 1 \right)} \right]$$

Therefore the final solution of Eq. (8) may be written as

$$v = v_1 \,(say) = \left[B_1 \cos(\alpha_1 \alpha_3 z) - B_2 \sin(\alpha_1 \alpha_3 z) \right] J_1(kr) e^{i\omega t - \alpha_1 \alpha_2 z} \tag{12}$$

5   Boundary Conditions

The following boundary conditions must be satisfied

1. At the rigid surface $z = -H$, the displacement is vanishing so that

$$v_0 = 0 \text{ at } z = -H \tag{13a}$$

2. At the interface $z = 0$, the continuity of the stress require that

$$\mu_0 \frac{\partial v_0}{\partial z} = \left(\mu + \mu' \frac{\partial}{\partial t} \right) \left(\frac{\partial v_1}{\partial z} \right) \text{ at } z = 0 \tag{13b}$$

3. The continuity of the displacement requires that

$$v_0 = v_1 \text{ at } z = 0 \tag{13c}$$

4. $\left(\mu + \mu'\dfrac{\partial}{\partial t}\right)\left(\dfrac{\partial v_1}{\partial r} - \dfrac{v_1}{r}\right) = 0 \text{ at } z = 0 \tag{13d}$

Now, Using Eq. (7), Eq. (13a) becomes

$$A_1 e^{-\sqrt{1-\frac{c^2}{c_0^2}}kH} + A_2 e^{\sqrt{1-\frac{c^2}{c_0^2}}kH} = 0 \tag{14a}$$

Using Eq. (7), Eq. (12) and Eq. (13b), we have

$$A_1\mu_0\sqrt{1-\frac{c^2}{c_0^2}}k - A_2\mu_0\sqrt{1-\frac{c^2}{c_0^2}}k = B_1\left(-\mu_1\alpha_1\alpha_2 - \mu'\alpha_1\alpha_2 i\omega\right) + B_2\left(-\mu\alpha_1\alpha_3 - \mu'\alpha_1\alpha_3 i\omega\right) \tag{14b}$$

Similarly, we have from Eq. (13c) and Eq. (13d)

$$A_1 + A_2 = B_1 \tag{14c}$$

$$\cot\left(\frac{\theta}{2}\right)B_1 + B_2 = 0 \tag{14d}$$

Eliminating the arbitrary constants A_1, A_2, B_1 and B_2, we have

$$\begin{vmatrix} e^{-\sqrt{1-\frac{c^2}{c_0^2}}kH} & e^{\sqrt{1-\frac{c^2}{c_0^2}}kH} & 0 & 0 \\ \mu_0\sqrt{1-\frac{c^2}{c_0^2}}k & -\mu_0\sqrt{1-\frac{c^2}{c_0^2}}k & \left(-\mu\alpha_1\alpha_2 - \mu'\alpha_1\alpha_2 i\omega\right) & \left(-\mu\alpha_1\alpha_3 - \mu'\alpha_1\alpha_3 i\omega\right) \\ 1 & 1 & 1 & 0 \\ 0 & 0 & \cot\left(\frac{\theta}{2}\right) & 1 \end{vmatrix} = 0$$

Expanding the above determinant, we get

$$\cot\left(\sqrt{1-\frac{c^2}{c_0^2}}kH\right) = \frac{\mu\alpha_1\left(\alpha_3\cot\left(\frac{\theta}{2}\right) + \alpha_2\right) + i\mu'\alpha_1\omega\left(\alpha_3\cot\left(\frac{\theta}{2}\right) + \alpha_2\right)}{\mu_0 k\sqrt{1-\frac{c^2}{c_0^2}}}$$

Equating the real part of above equation, we get

$$\cot\left(\sqrt{1-\frac{c^2}{c_0^2}}kH\right) = \frac{\mu}{\mu_0}\frac{\left[\left\{(1+A^2)-\frac{c^2}{c_1^2}\right\}^2+\left(A\frac{c^2}{c_1^2}\right)^2\right]^{1/4}}{\sqrt{1+A^2}\sqrt{\frac{c^2}{c_0^2}-1}}\left[\sin\left(\frac{\theta}{2}\right)\cot\left(\frac{\theta}{2}\right)+\cos\left(\frac{\theta}{2}\right)\right] \quad (15)$$

Eq. (15) is the required dispersion equation of torsional surface wave in homogeneous isotropic layer over a viscoelastic half space under the influence of rigid boundary.

6 Particular Case

When the internal friction μ' is neglected, the half space becomes perfectly elastic, homogenous and isotropic. Then the Eq. (15) reduces to

$$\cot\left(kH\sqrt{\frac{c^2}{c_0^2}-1}\right) = \left(\frac{\mu}{\mu_0}\right)\left(\sqrt{\frac{c^2}{c_1^2}-1}\bigg/\sqrt{1-\frac{c^2}{c_0^2}}\right)$$

which is a well known classical result of Love wave in a homogeneous layer over an elastic homogeneous half space under the effect of rigid boundary and hence validating the solution of the problem discussed.

7 Numerical Computation and Discussion

The significant effect of internal friction, rigidity of the layer and half space, wave number and the time period on the phase velocity of torsional surface wave have been studied using euation (15). The numerical data has been taken from Gubbin (1990). The value of c_0/c_1 has been kept fixed to 1.2 in all the figures. In figure 2 and Figure 3, plotting has been obtained for dimensionless phase velocity against dimensionless wave number whereas figure 4 and figure 5 has been plotted with horizontal axis as Time period (in second) against vertical axis as dimensionless phase velocity.

Figure 2 shows the effect of dimensionless internal friction on torsional wave velocity when the upper boundary plane of the layer is rigid. The value of dimensionless internal friction (μ/μ') for curve no. 1, curve no.2 and curve no. 3 has been taken as 10, 50 and 100 respectively. The value of T has been taken as 0.15 second whereas the value of μ/μ_0 has been taken as 0.4. It has been found that as the internal friction μ' decreases the phase velocity also decreases for a particular wave number. It also shows that the phase velocity decreases as the wave number increases. Thus one can conclude that the phase velocity of torsional wave is directly proportional to internal friction when the upper boundary plane of the layer is rigid.

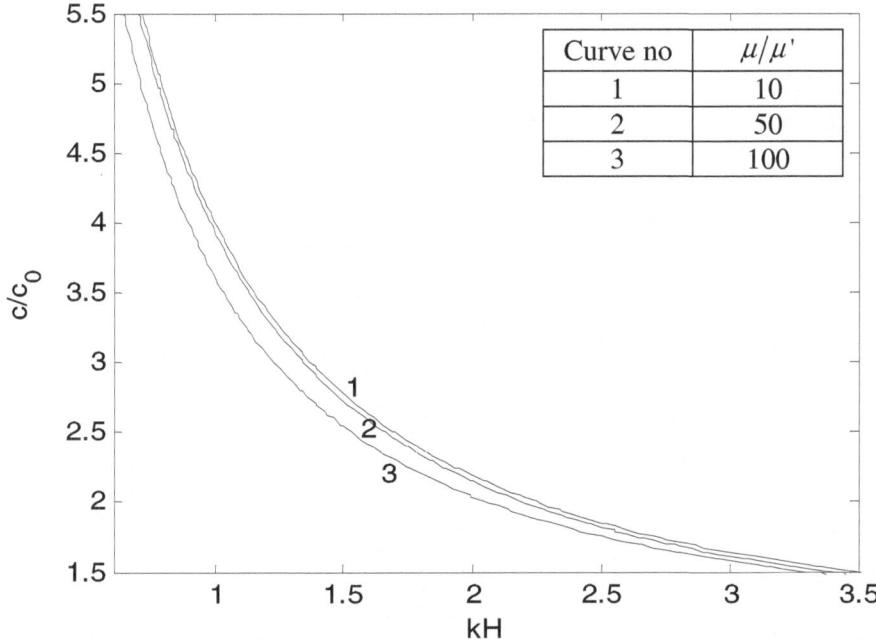

Curve no	μ/μ'
1	10
2	50
3	100

Fig. 2. Dimensionless phase velocity against dimensionless wave number for $T = 0.15$ and $(\mu/\mu_0) = 0.4$

Figure 3 reflects the influence of rigidity of the layer and the half space on the torsional surface wave propagation. The value of (μ/μ') has been taken as 10 whereas the value of T has been kept fixed at 0.15. The value of rigidity ratio (μ/μ_0) has been taken as 0.2, 0.4, 0.6 and 0.8 for curve no. 1, curve no. 2, curve no. 3 and curve no.4 respectively. It is observed that as the rigidity of the half space increases the phase velocity decreases uniformly at a particular wave number keeping the upper boundary of the layer overburdened.

Figure 4, Studies the impact of internal friction and time period on the torsional wave propagation. The value of kH has been taken as 0.5 whereas the value of (μ/μ_0) has been taken as 0.5. For curve no. 1, curve no. 2, curve no. 3 and curve no. 4, the value of dimensionless internal friction (μ/μ') has been taken as 30, 50, 70 and 100 respectively. It has been found that as the time period increases the phase velocity decrease while as the internal friction of the half space decreases the phase velocity also decreases under the significant effect of rigid boundary plane.

In Figure 5, curves have been plotted for the dimensionless phase velocity against time period for different value of rigidity ratio. The value of kH and (μ/μ') are taken as 0.5 and 10 respectively whereas the value of (μ/μ_0) for curve no. 1, curve no.2,

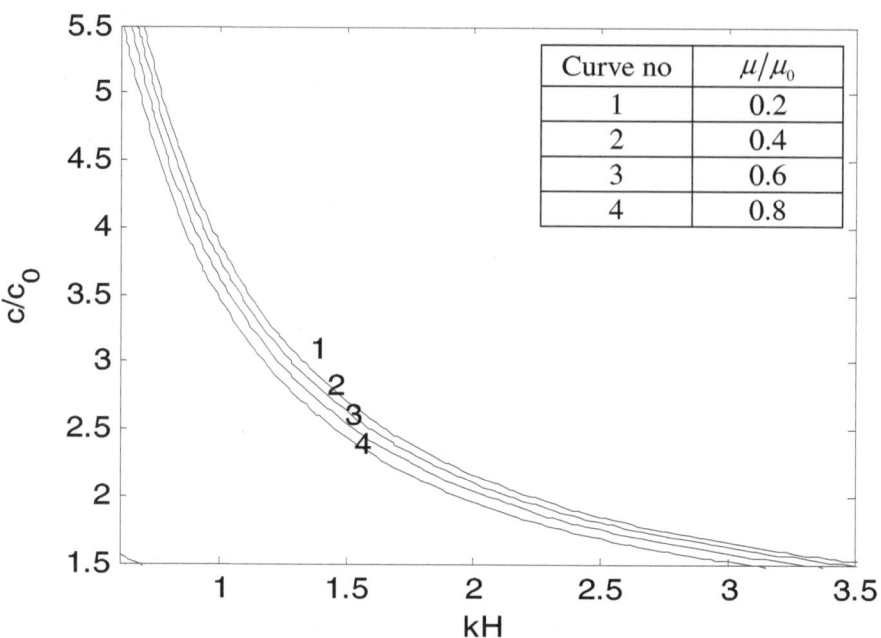

Fig. 3. Dimensionless phase velocity against dimensionless wave number for $T = 0.15$ and $(\mu/\mu') = 10$

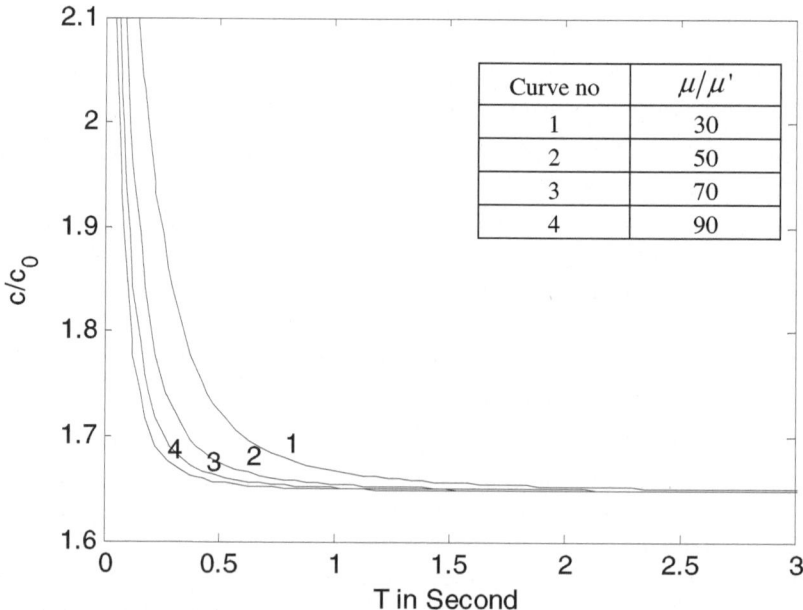

Fig. 4. Dimensionless phase velocity against Time period (in second) for $kH = 0.5$ and $(\mu/\mu_0) = 0.5$

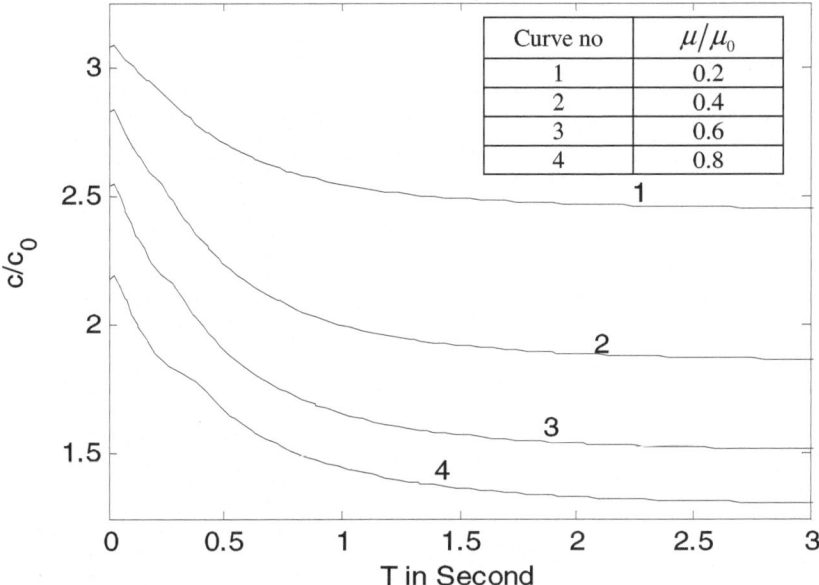

Fig. 5. Dimensionless phase velocity against Time period (in second) for $kH = 0.5$ and $(\mu/\mu') = 10$

curve no. 3 and curve no. 4 are 0.2, 0.4, 0.6 and 0.8 respectively. The effect found here is almost same as that of the previous one, but the curves here are more apart thereby reflects that as the rigidity of the viscoelastic half space increases, the phase velcocity decreases and as the rigidity of the layer decreases the phase velocity also decreases. This concludes that the phase velocity of torsional surface wave in a layer sandwiched between an overburdened layer and a half space is inversely proportional to the rigidity of the half space.

8   Conclusions

In this problem, propagation of torsional surface wave in homogeneous layer sandwiched between an overburdened boundary and a viscoelastic half space has been studied. Variable separable method has been employed to find the displacement in both the media in terms of Whittaker's function. Dispersion equation is derived and the same has been justified for special case when viscoelastic half space has been replaced by elastic half space. The dimensionless phase velocity c/c_0 is plotted against dimesnsionless wave number kH and time period T for the given geometry. Effect of the variation in magnitude of non-dimensional rigidity and internal friction on phase velocity has also been shown graphically. The internal friction has found to have pronounced effect on the propagation of Torsional surface wave. It has been observed that as the internal friction decreases the phase velocity also decreases whereas as the rigidity of the half space increases the phase velocity decreases for the same frequency under the effect of rigid boundary plane. It has also been found that at a fixed value of dimensionless internal friction and rigidity ratio, the phase velocity decreases as the dimensionless wave number increases. The effect of Time period on the Torsional wave propagation has also come out prominently. We have obtained that as the Time period increases the phase velocity also decreases. Similar result has been obtained for different value of rigidity ratio and the internal friction except the few once which is self explained graphically.

Acknowledgement. The authors are thankful to anonymous reviewers for their constructive comments and valuable suggestions in improving the quality of the paper.

References

1. Monolis, G.D., Shaw, R.P.: Harmonic wave propagation through viscoelastic heterogeneous media exhibiting mild stochasticity – II. Applications. Soil Dyn. Earthq. Eng. 15(2), 129–139 (1996)
2. Chattopadhyay, A., Gupta, S., Sharma, V., Kumari, P.: Propagation of shear waves in viscoelastic medium at irregular boundaries. Acta Geophysica 58(2), 195–214 (2010)
3. Chattopadhyay, A., Gupta, S., Sharma, V.K., Pato, K.: Effect of Point Source and Heterogeneity on the Propagation of SH-Waves. International Journal of Applied Mathematics and Mechanics 6(9), 76–89 (2010)
4. Červen, V.: Inhomogeneous harmonic plane waves in viscoelastic anisotropic media. Stud. Geophys. Geod. 48(1), 167–186 (2004)
5. Sethi, M., Gupta, K.C.: Surface Waves in Homogeneous, General Magneto-Thermo, Visco-Elastic Media of Higher Order Including Time Rate of Strain and Stress. International Journal of Applied Mathematics and Mechanics 7(17), 1–21 (2011)
6. Park, J., Kausel, E.: Impulse response of elastic half space in the wave number-time domain. J. Eng. Mech. ASCE 130(10), 1211–1222 (2004)
7. Romeo, M.: Interfacial viscoelastic SH waves. Int. J. Solid Struct. 40(9), 2057–2068 (2003)
8. Sari, C., Salk, M.: Analysis of gravity anomalies with hyperbolic density contrast: An application to the gravity data of Western Anatolia. J. Balkan Geophys. Soc. 5(3), 87–96 (2002)
9. Gubbins, D.: Seismology and Plate Techtonics. Cambridge University Press, Cambridge (1990)
10. Biot, M.A.: Mechanics of Incremental Deformation. John Willey and Sons, New York (1965)
11. Chattopadhyay, A., Sahu, S.A., Singh, A.K.: Dispersion of G-type seismic wave in magnetoelastic self reinforced layer. International Journal of Applied Mathematics and Mechanics 8(9), 79–98 (2011)
12. Davini, C., Paroni, R., Puntle, E.: An asymptotic approach to the Torsional problem in thin rectangular domains. Meccanica 43(4), 429–435 (2008)
13. Gupta, S., Majhi, D., Kundu, S., Vishwakarma, S.K.: Propagation of Torsional surface waves in a homogeneous layer of finite thickness over an initially stressed heterogeneous half-space. Applied Mathematics and Computation 218, 5655–5664 (2012)
14. Akbarov, S.D., Kepceler, T., Mert, E.M.: Torsional wave dispersion in a finitely pre-strained hollow sandwich circular cylinder. Journal of Sound and Vibration 330, 4519–4537 (2011)

Financial Application as a Software Service on Cloud

Saurabh Kumar Garg, Bhanu Sharma,
Rodrigos N. Calheiros, Ruppa K. Thulasiram*,
Parimala Thulasiraman**, and Rajkumar Buyya

Department of Computing and Information Systems
University of Melbourne
Melbourne, Australia
{sgarg,raj}@csse.unimelb.edu.au,
rodrigo.calheiros@gmail.com,
{bsharma,tulsi,thulasir}@cs.umanitoba.ca

Abstract. In this work, we propose a SaaS model that provides service to ordinary investors, unfamiliar with finance models, to evaluate the price of an option that is currently being traded before taking a decision to enter into a contract. In this model, investors may approach a financial Cloud Service Provider (CSP) to compute the option price with time and/or accuracy constraints. The option pricing algorithms are not only computationally intensive but also communication intensive. Therefore, one of the key components of the methodology presented in this paper is the topology-aware communication between tasks and scheduling of tasks in virtual machines with the goal of reducing the latency of communication between tasks. We perform various experiments to evaluate how our model can map the tasks efficiently to reduce communication latency, hide network latency ensuring that all virtual machines are busy increasing response time of users.

1 Introduction

Cloud computing offers on-demand software service to customers without having the customer know the inner details of the software or IT infrastructure used for their service. Businesses outsource their computing needs to the Cloud to avoid investing in infrastructure and maintenance. The charges they pay to Cloud providers are generally seen as economical while considering the cost that they would incur having the infrastructure in-house. One sector that can significantly benefit from Cloud is the financial sector.

For example, an investor would be interested in obtaining information that would help in making decision whether to buy a stock at a future date, at a particular price based on some basic information available in public such as Yahoo!Finance. This kind of future investment is referred to as a *option*. This requires knowledge of the current

---

* The author was visiting from Department of Computer Science, University of Manitoba, Canada.
** The author was visiting from Department of Computer Science, University of Manitoba, Canada.

M. Parashar et al. (Eds.): IC3 2012, CCIS 306, pp. 141–151, 2012.
© Springer-Verlag Berlin Heidelberg 2012

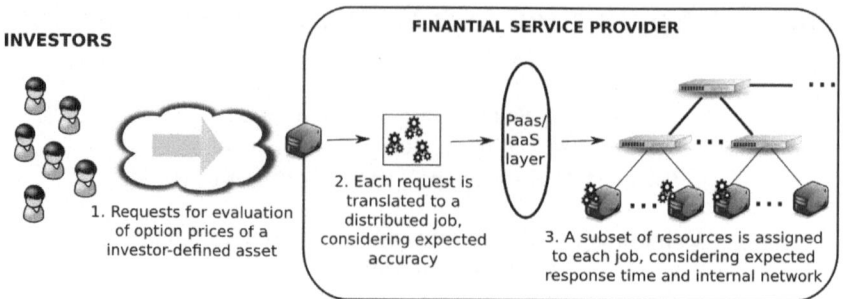

Fig. 1. Financial Service Provisioning in the Cloud

stock price, stock volatility and the proper time to exercise the stock for profit. There are many algorithms [5,7,3] to *price an option*. In finance, this problem is called an *option pricing problem*.

Investors interested in pricing an option would need to have working knowledge of these algorithms to help them take an informative decision on computing the option prices. The algorithms used in the option pricing problem are computationally intensive and require parallel processing to obtain results in real time. These computations are very complicated for an investor who is not familiar with the algorithms. The option pricing problem, falls under the category high performance computing applications and several works have already been done in this area [12].

In this study, we propose a SaaS model that provides service to ordinary investors, unfamiliar with finance models, to evaluate an option that is currently being traded before taking a decision to enter into a contract. This provider owns the data center infrastructure and uses it to host the Financial SaaS.

In our SaaS Model (Figure 1), decision on the kernel (option pricing algorithm) to be deployed for a user request, number of tasks to be generated for such request, number of resources to be assigned to the request, and which resources to serve the request is performed at the PaaS level: SaaS requests received from users are forwarded to the PaaS component that make such decisions, which in turn deploys the tasks to the available infrastructure (IaaS). Note that if the SaaS service were offered by a provider that does not own the infrastructure, a fine control over the platform that enables better QoS for investors would be hard to achieve.

To our knowledge no work exists that addresses the need for decision making service involving financial instruments on Cloud. Contributions of the paper are: (a) Making decision on a particular financial model to use that would best fit the user's requirements and constraints. (b) Satisfying investors constraints on time deadline and accuracy. (c) Mapping the tasks to appropriate VMs considering various latencies. (d) Optimizing the number of request processed per second considering HPC nature of the particular algorithm being considered for option pricing.

We organize the rest of the paper as follows. In section 2 we discuss financial option and task scheduling on Cloud. In Section 3, we describe our system model and in Section 4 we present our algorithm for evaluation of the algorithms on Cloud. In Section 5 we describe the results and conclude in Section 6.

2   Background and Related Work

In this section, we discuss financial options and a literature survey of task scheduling on Clouds.

Financial Options: Formally, an *option* is a contract in which the buyer (generally known as the option *holder*) of an option has the right but without any obligation to buy (with *call* option) or sell (with *put* option) an underlying asset (for example, a stock) at a predetermined price (*strike price, K*) on or before a specified date (*expiration date, T*). The seller (known as *writer*) has the obligation to honor the terms specified in the option contract. The holder pays a premium to the writer (see for example [8]). An European option can be exercised only at the expiration date whereas an American option may be exercised on any date before the expiration date. We have considered four different algorithms in this study for implementing on the CSP side to render option pricing services: Binomial Lattice [7,13], Monte-Carlo simulation [3], Fast Fourier Transform [5] and Finite-Difference technique [14].

Task Scheduling on Cloud: A key component of the methodology presented in this paper is the topology-aware communication between tasks and scheduling of tasks in VMs with the goal of reducing the latency of communication between tasks. Kandalla *et al.* [9] proposed topology-aware algorithms for communication between MPI tasks. However, this approach does not consider virtualized data centers as the underlying hardware infrastructure supporting the application and therefore, cannot be directly applied in our proposed solution. Volckaert *et al.* [15], proposed a network-aware task scheduling algorithm on grids following an embarrassingly parallel (bag of tasks) approach, which is not applicable to financial applications that introduce communication overhead between tasks. Lee *et al.* [10] proposed a topology-aware resource allocation mechanism for IaaS Clouds using genetic algorithm to find the optimal placement of tasks to machines which again follows an embarassignly parallel approach. Coti *et al.* [6] proposed topology-aware scheduling of MPI applications on Grids which cannot be directly applicable to Cloud.

3   System Model

Customers of SaaS provider (CSP) are investors who need to evaluate (the price of) an option that is currently being traded before taking a decision to enter into a contract or not. Our proposed system model will be able to provide information as whether the entering the option contract could be profitable. For this purpose, the CSP in our model uses one of the four algorithms for option pricing: fast Fourier transform (FFT), finite-difference (FD), binomial lattice, and Monte-Carlo simulation. Each of these algorithms is representative of typical HPC applications with their different computation and communication needs. The customers' request for resource contains: service description, required accuracy, and deadline for service response. Each of the option pricing algorithms has different processing times which affects service deadline. Also, each algorithm provides an accuracy different from another. Therefore, customers are charged for the service depending on the required accuracy and service deadline. Each customer may have their own parameters or input for an option. For example, the current stock price (S), strike price in the contract (K), volatility of the asset (σ), expiration time in years T, and current interest rate (r). These parameters are provided as service description to the CSP. Another important parameter is the number of time steps N. For example, in the binomial lattice algorithm, increasing the number of time steps, makes the problem more fine-grained providing more accurate results. However, this increases processing time. The CSP executes customers' requests at its own data center. With this

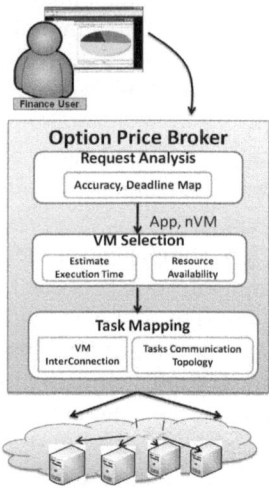

Fig. 2. System Model

model, the service provider can ensure the secrecy of the models they use to provide service to their customers, which can be more accurate than models available with other CSP.

The system architecture that can support the described scenario is depicted in Figure 2, and contains two main components, namely *option price broker* and *data center*.

The option price broker receives user requests, analyzes them, and submits them to the data center. It keeps information about resource availability and number of requests being processed. It processes each request in three distinct phases: (i) defines the preferred order of execution of algorithms based on request's accuracy and deadline; (ii) searches for a mapping of tasks to VMs considering the preferred order of algorithms: that is, if it is unable to accommodate a set of VMs for its first choice algorithm, it evaluates the possibility of the second algorithm; (iii) maps the tasks based on their communication requirement, on the VM's network topology, and on memory requirements.

The data center handles the actual execution of tasks that represent user requests. The data center network topology considered in this paper assumes servers placed in racks are connected using edge and aggregation switches and core routers. In this paper, we assume static routing inside the data center. The fat tree topology on which the servers are organized can be over-subscribed depending on the number of servers connected to the edge switch. Moreover, each server hosts 2^k VMs where k can be predetermined by the provider.

4 Algorithm and Evaluation

In this section, we discuss the mechanism for processing user requests. Each request has the form $(OptVariables_i, A_i, d_i)$, where $OptVariables_i$ are the variables for calculating option pricing, A_i is the required accuracy and d_i is the service deadline by which user is expecting the results. The option price broker performs three phases of computations:

4.1 Phase 1: Algorithm Decision

In this step, the broker decides which algorithm to use to service the customers request. This depends on the desired accuracy and service deadline.

Table 1. Rank of techniques for accuracy requirements

	Low (0-50%)	Medium (50-70%)	High (70-100%)
Binomial	2	1	3
Monte-Carlo	1	2	4
Finite Diff.	3	3	1
FFT	4	4	2

To determine which algorithm provides better accuracy, the CSP considers a pre-computed table, derived from benchmark results of the algorithms. In Table 1, each of the algorithm used in this study is ranked (1 is highest and 4 is lowest) according to three accuracy levels: low, medium and high. This is derived from our previous experience [11] of running these algorithms on different platforms. Similarly, Table 2 depicts the ranks of these algorithms in terms of the execution time. For example, if a customer requires high accuracy but has a relaxed (large) deadline, then finite-difference technique is chosen as the preferred algorithm to compute the option prices. However, if a user needs high accuracy and has a tight deadline, the request is rejected. Note, that the four algorithms are ranked based on the request characteristics and this is the order that will be considered.

Since these algorithms are also communication intensive, some thought needs to be given to the communication structure of the algorithms to better schedule them on the VMs. For FFT, we follow the Cooley-Tukey butterfly algorithm [2]. The parallel FFT algorithm requires $logP$ communications and $logN - logP$ computations. Therefore, the execution time of each task is given by $t_{computation} * (logN - logP) + t_{communication} * logP$, where N is number of elements (or time steps) and P is the number of VMs.

The option price broker also makes a decision on the number of VMs required to execute tasks for ensuring its completion within the deadline.

Table 2. Rank of techniques for timing requirements

	Low (quicker)	Medium (moderate)	High (large)
Binomial	1	2	4
Monte-Carlo	2	1	3
Finite Diff.	4	4	1
FFT	3	3	2

4.2 Phase 2: Virtual Machines Selection

In this phase, the option price broker decides on the set of VMs needed to execute the algorithm selected in phase 1. As mentioned earlier, each server in the data center hosts 2^k VMs. Moreover, each algorithm has communication and computation needs that have to be met by the internal network topology and server resources, respectively. Since the data center runs several requests/algorithms simultaneously, the broker selects a set of VMs for an incoming request in such a way that the communication overhead is minimized. For example, if FFT is being considered to be executed, the broker tries to select VMs that belong to the same server or whose servers are positioned in the same rack. This ensures data locality. Therefore, the broker adopts the following strategy for VM selection. Let the number of VMs required by the request i for given accuracy level A_i and deadline d_i, be $numVmReq_i$. This is assumed to be a power of two. Let $EstExTime_i$ be the estimated execution time of each task. The following mapping strategies are used to schedule different algorithms.

For FFT, tasks have to be confined to the same server or rack. The selection of VMs for this algorithm is described in Algorithm 1. For Finite-Difference technique, since communication is only between neighbouring taks, there is no restriction about VM placement, and the mapping is described in Algorithm 2. Finally, in the case of Monte-Carlo and Binomial Lattice, that are loosely-coupled algorithms, tasks are distributed in a round-robin strategy.

4.3 Phase 3: Mapping Tasks to Selected VMs

In this phase, the actual scheduling of each task from various applications to VMs takes place, following the decisions made in the previous phases. The mapping considers communication between tasks.

5 Results and Discussions

This section presents the performance results of our proposed algorithm to enable Option Pricing as Cloud Software service. We simulated a SaaS Cloud scenario using CloudSim [4]. We compare our mechanism to a general approach of deploying the VMs across a data center without any knowledge of network and application requirements. We call this approach as $BlindMethod$. In phase 2 using this mehtod, tasks are randomly assigned to VMs. The simulation design reflects configurations that are similar to actual data centers and can determine the performance of our proposed mechanism (computation strategy).

Algorithm 1. Mapping of tasks to VMs in the FFT algorithm

$numHostReq_i = numVmReq_i/2^k$;

foreach *edge switch* **do**

    Search $numHostReq_i$ available servers that can process the job within deadline;

    if *servers are found* **then**

        map tasks to VMs based on network topology required for communication;

        exit;

    end

    else

        search for $numVmReq_i$ available VMs in a same rack;

        if *VMs are found* **then**

            map tasks to VMs based on network topology required for communication;

            exit;

        end

        else

            try the next algorithm in the priority list;

        end

    end

end

Algorithm 2. Mapping of tasks to VMs in the FD algorithm

$numHostReq_i = numVmReq_i/2^k$;

foreach *edge switch* **do**

    search for $numVmReq_i$ available VMs in a same rack;

    if *VMs are found* **then**

        map tasks to VMs based on network topology required for communication;

    end

    else

        search for $numHostReq_i$ servers that can process the job within deadline;

        if *servers are found* **then**

            map tasks to VMs based on network topology required for communication;

        end

        else

            try the next algorithm in the priority list;

        end

    end

end

5.1   Option Pricing SaaS Provider's Configuration

Current Cloud data centers generally contain commodity hardware with hierarchical tree network topology [1]. Therefore, in our experiments each simulated server is equivalent to a Intel Core i7-920 with 4 cores and 8 threads (virtual cores), 2.66 Ghz with 8 GB RAM. We have deployed two VMs per server each with 4 cores and 4 GB RAM. Each server is connected to the edge network with 1 Gigabit Ethernet link. Servers are placed in racks, and each rack has one edge switch. We have one 4-port root switch, four 2-port aggregate switch with one up link and eight edge switches. The edge and aggregate switches are connected by 10 Gigabit Ethernet links. The network bandwidth between aggregate switches is 20 Gbps. The default number of servers in each rack is 10, therefore 160 VMs are simulated. The switching delays for different number of hops are based on the work by Kandalla et al. [9], i.e. intra rack communication delay is $1.57 \mu sec$, delay due to communication through aggregate switch is $2.45 \mu sec$ and delay due to communication through root switch is $2.85 \mu sec$. To estimate the execution time of different algorithms we run different set of experiments using all four option pricing algorithms on a Intel Core i7-920 4cores/8thread (virtual cores), 2.66 Ghz with 8GB RAM machine.

5.2   Option Pricing Request Generation

Since there is no trace available from data centers running financial applications, we generated different types of requests using uniform distribution for varying option pricing inputs, accuracy (low, medium, high) and deadline (low, medium, high) requirements. The arrival rate of customer requests is 10000 requests per second.

5.3   Performance Metrics and Experimental Scenarios

We use two metrics to evaluate our computation strategy: average processing time and network overhead. The average processing time indicates how fast our mechanism can process user requests, which is an important quality of service metric for any SaaS provider. The network overhead indicates how much data is transferred through the edge switches and it shows the importance of the network topology and application for scheduling tasks. We considered the following aspects in the experiments: (i) Effect of different mixture of requests in terms of accuracy, and (ii) Effect of different arrival rates of requests.

5.4   Analysis of Results

Effect of Change in Accuracy Requirements. Figure 3 presents how accuracy requirement of requests affect the performance of our proposed algorithm. Figure 3(a) , (b) and (c) present respectively data transfer, response time, and option algorithms used for our strategy (called $NetAwareSaaS$ in the figure), respectively, in comparison to $BlindMethod$, considering different rate of requests for accuracy levels. In these figures, x%,y%,z% represents the scenario where x% of requests are for low accuracy results, y% of requests are for medium accuracy results and z% of requests are for high accuracy results.

Results show that our strategy reduces network overhead due to data transfer and response time of requests, and response times and data transfers are barely affected by different mixes of accuracy, compared to the $BlindMethod$ strategy. This is due to network aware allocation of resources to serve the customer requests. Since most of the requests in BlindMethod strategy are assigned to VMs which belongs to different switches, more data communication delays resulted in more processing time. Other

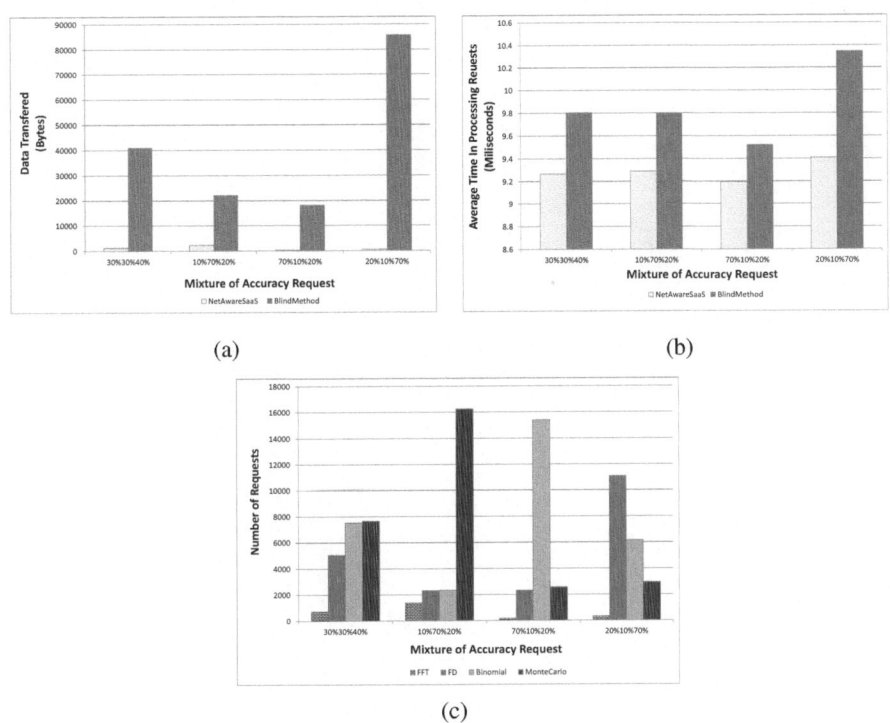

(a)

(b)

(c)

Fig. 3. Effect of Accuracy Requirements of Requests

than this, Figure 3(c) also indicate how different ratio of accuracy requested by customers affect the choice of algorithms used for computing the option price. For instance, when 70% of requests asks for low accuracy, the large data communication is due to binomial lattice algorithm which requires about four VMs to process the customer's request. When 70% of requests is for medium accuracy, the monte carlo algorithm is used which has low communication needs but high computation time. When 70% of request required high accuracy, the amount of data transferred across the switches is quite high in case of BlindMethod strategy due to finite-difference algorithm which has much higher data transfer requirement than any other algorithm. This also has impact on the average processing time for a request due to delays in data transfer.

Effect of Change in Request Arrival Rate. Figure 4 presents how arrival rate of requests affect the performance of our proposed algorithm. Figure 4(a) , (b) and (c) present respectively data transfer, response time, and option algorithms used for our strategy (called $NetAwareSaaS$ in the figure) and $BlindMethod$, considering different arrival rate of requests. In the figure, low , medium, high represents the scenario where 100 requests/sec, 1000 requests/sec and 1000request/sec respectively, are received by the SaaS provider. The incoming requests have 30% low ,30% medium, 40% high accuracy requirements.

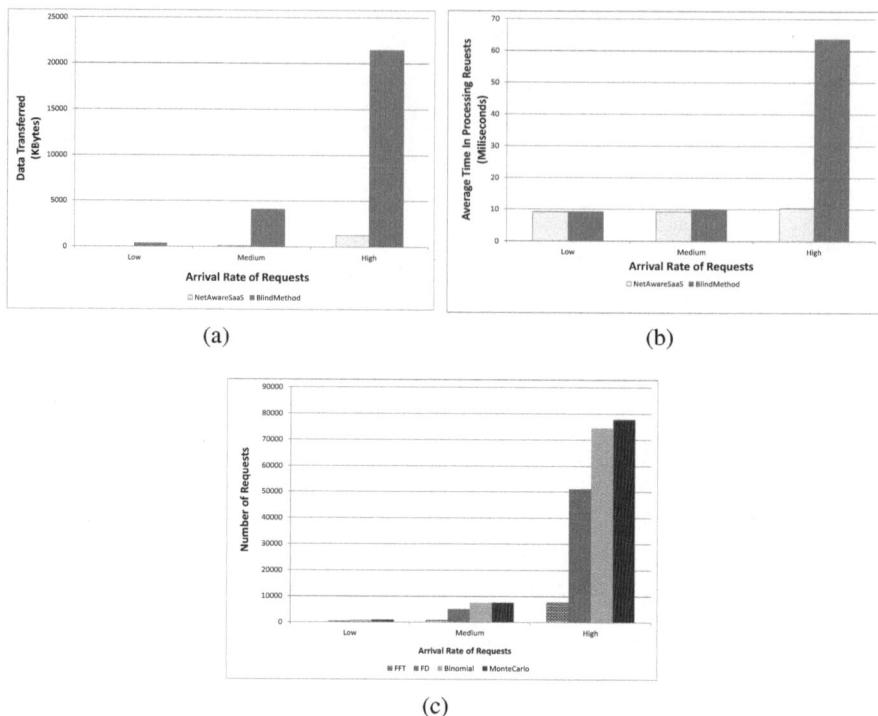

(a)   (b)

(c)

Fig. 4. Effect of Request Arrival Rate

With the increase in arrival rate, the number of requests to be processed increases, and the data transferred and response time increases drastically. The reason for increase in response time is not just the time taken to transfer data between VMs but also the queuing delay on each VM. For low and medium arrival rate the increase in response time is not as much as when arrival rate is high. This behaviour is observed due to the number of resources utilized by each strategy. For low and medium arrival rate there were enough resources to process the requests and keep the response time quite low. However, when the arrival rate increases to high, all the resources in data centers are being utilized to process each requests which also resulted in high queuing and data transferred delays. Nevertheless, the impact on the performance of NetAwareSaaS strategy is almost negligible and in all cases it leads to minimum network overhead due to data transfers and also low processing time.

6   Conclusions

In this work, we proposed a SaaS model that provides service to ordinary investors, unfamiliar with finance models, to evaluate the price of an option that is currently being traded before taking a decision to enter into a contract. The model computed as a first step, based on required accuracy and service time, an appropriate algorithm to be applied. Since these are communication intensive, we considered the communication pattern between tasks for efficient mapping to virtual machines.

Our simulation results showed that our strategy helps in reducing response time and data transfers in the internal network, compared to an approach where SaaS does not have access to the infrastructure and thus cannot apply the techniques described in this paper. Our intention is to expand the current scope of a CSP to devise algorithms for pricing such instruments as well in the near future. Portfolio optimization is another large area of service that could utilize Cloud resources.

References

1. Al-Fares, M., Loukissas, A., Vahdat, A.: A scalable, commodity data center network architecture. SIGCOMM Computer Communication Review 38(4), 63–74 (2008)
2. Barua, S., Thulasiram, R.K., Thulasiraman, P.: High Performance Computing for a Financial Application Using Fast Fourier Transform. In: Cunha, J.C., Medeiros, P.D. (eds.) Euro-Par 2005. LNCS, vol. 3648, pp. 1246–1253. Springer, Heidelberg (2005)
3. Boyle, P.: Options: A Monte Carlo approach. J. of Finan. Econ. 4, 223–238 (1977)
4. Calheiros, R.N., Ranjan, R., Beloglazov, A., De Rose, C.A.F., Buyya, R.: CloudSim: A toolkit for modeling and simulation of cloud computing environments and evaluation of resource provisioning algorithms. Software: Practice and Experience 41(1), 23–50 (2011)
5. Carr, P., Madan, D.B.: Option valuation using the fast Fourier transform. The Journal of Computational Finance 2(4), 61–73 (1999)
6. Coti, C., Herault, T., Cappello, F.: MPI Applications on Grids: A Topology Aware Approach. In: Sips, H., Epema, D., Lin, H.-X. (eds.) Euro-Par 2009. LNCS, vol. 5704, pp. 466–477. Springer, Heidelberg (2009)
7. Cox, J.C., Ross, S.A., Rubinstein, M.: Options pricing: A simplified approach. Journal of Financial Economics 7, 229–263 (1979)
8. Hull, J.: Options, Futures, and other Derivative Securities. Prentice-Hall (May 2008)
9. Kandalla, K., Subramoni, H., Vishnu, A., Panda, D.: Designing topology-aware collective communication algorithms for large scale InfiniBand clusters: Case studies with scatter and gather. In: 10th Workshop on Comm. Arch. for Clusters (CAC 2010), Atlanta, USA (April 2010)
10. Lee, G., Tolia, N., Ranganathan, P., Katz, R.H.: Topology-aware resource allocation for data-intensive workloads. SIGCOMM Comp. Comm. Review 41, 120–124 (2011)
11. Sharma, B., Thulasiram, R.K., Thulasiraman, P.: Option pricing: A mosaic of experiments and results (Technical Memo CFD058-W10, Computational Financial Derivatives Lab, Department of Computer Science, University of Manitoba (2010), http://www.cs.umanitoba.ca/~tulsi
12. Solomon, S., Thulasiraman, R.K., Thulasiraman, P.: Option pricing on the gpu. In: The 12th IEEE Int. Conf. on High Perf. Comp. and Comm., Melbourne, Australia (2010)
13. Thulasiram, R.K., Litov, L., Nojumi, H., Downing, C., Gao, G.: Multithreaded algorithms for pricing a class of complex options. In: Proceedings (CD-RoM) of the IEEE/ACM International Parallel and Distribued Processing Symposium (IPDPS), San Francisco, CA (2001)
14. Thulasiram, R.K., Zhen, C., Chhabra, A., Thulasiraman, P., Gumel, A.: A second order L0 stable algorithm for evaluating European options. Intl. J. of High Performance Computing and Networking (IJHPCN) 4, 311–320 (2006)
15. Volckaert, B., Thysebaert, P., De Leenheer, M., De Turck, F., Dhoedt, B., Demeester, P.: Network aware scheduling in grids. In: Proceedings of the 9th European Conference on Networks & Optical Communications (NOC 2004), Eindhoven, Netherlands (June 2004)

An Automated Metamorphic Testing Technique for Designing Effective Metamorphic Relations

Gagandeep[1] and Gurdeepak Singh[2]

[1] Department of Computer Science, Punjabi University, Patiala
[2] Infosys Technologies, Mysore
{gdeep.pbi,gurdeepak.88}@gmail.com

Abstract. Creation of metamorphic relations, and building up a dynamic system to carry out automated metamorphic testing has been aimed. Modeling notation has been adopted to design and extract metamorphic properties of the system, which have been tested during run time. Real time data for system execution has been used to generate follow up test data. Thus, parallel execution and testing system properties helps to achieve reduction in testing cost and effort. The complete methodology and its effectiveness for testing systems for which no reliable test oracle exists, has been demonstrated with the help of suitable case study, and the results have been verified.

Keywords: metamorphic testing, metamorphic relations, follow-up test data, test oracle.

1 Introduction

In the theory of testing, an assumption by the name of 'oracle' exits. It is a mechanism against which one can determine whether the outcome of a program or test case is correct or not. But there are some situations where the availability of oracle is either not there or is excessively expensive. For instance, assuring the quality of applications such as those in the fields of scientific calculations, simulations, optimizations, data mining, etc. presents a challenge because conventional software testing processes do not always apply. The general class of software systems for which no reliable test oracle is available is known as "non-testable programs". The oracle problem gives rise to a new form of testing known as metamorphic testing. Though manual forecasting and comparing of test result is the possibility, it certainly needs more time and chances of error are exceedingly high.

Metamorphic testing produces follow up test cases based on metamorphic relations extracted from the program. It is a methodology of reusing input test data to create additional test cases. Good metamorphic relations give effective results whereas bad relations can make this technique worthless. In this paper, emphasis is on detecting effective metamorphic relations which are able to detect high number of failures in the system. The contributions of this paper includes: (i) Utilization of original test data for system execution and metamorphic testing. (ii) Creation of Follow-up test

M. Parashar et al. (Eds.): IC3 2012, CCIS 306, pp. 152–163, 2012.
© Springer-Verlag Berlin Heidelberg 2012

cases with the aid of original test data and metamorphic properties. (iii) Automated metamorphic testing at run time within the context of the system and, (iv) Practical experimentation and verification of results. The rest of this paper is organized as follows: Section 2 gives a brief description of metamorphic testing, and the modeling notation, Section 3 mentions proposed methodology for implementation, Section 4 incorporates case study and finally, the paper is concluded with some future work in Section 5.

2   Related Work

2.1   Metamorphic Testing

Metamorphic testing is a property-based testing strategy. It has been proposed to employ successful test cases and alleviate the oracle problem. It states that, even if a test case (known as the *original* test case) does not reveal any failure, follow-up test cases should be constructed to check whether the software satisfies some necessary conditions of the target solution of the problem. These necessary conditions are known as Metamorphic Relations. A metamorphic relation is the relationship among the test input data and could be used to create additional test inputs based on existing one and to predict the relations among the test outputs [5].

Chen et al. [2] brought forward a semi proving method capable of verifying expected necessary conditions in regard to the correctness of the program symbolic evaluation. Metamorphic testing techniques are integrated to envisage this method. Both structural and functional information are considered when performing global symbolic evaluation and identifying metamorphic relations. Thus, combination of black and white box information helps in better tackling of subtle errors. Nevertheless, the verification of Metamorphic relations for majority of the test inputs is a compulsion regarding the correctness of a program but still not sufficient in itself. Metamorphic testing makes the check of relations among most of the executions instead of making a check about the correctness of individual outputs. Chen et al. [3] harnessed metamorphic testing to solve partial differential equations of different programs. This results into removing the oracle problem while testing numerical component.

To check a class of metamorphic relations Gotlieb and Botella [4] put forth an automated framework. The basis of usual techniques for automatic test data generation is the assumption that we should have a complete oracle when testing a process. This paper brings forth a framework for automatic test data generation even without the presence of oracle during testing process. It is capable of checking metamorphic relations. The framework takes the course of constraint logic programming techniques to find test data that is feared to be violating metamorphic relations in question. An approach has been presented by Chan et al. [6] to test online service oriented applications. It involves formulation of metamorphic service that contains the characteristic of an access wrapper and as an agent for conducting metamorphic testing. It contains services under test along side the implementation of metamorphic relations. This approach involves making use of successful test case for offline testing as if they are the original test case for online testing.

2.2   Modeling Notation

The combination of expressiveness and versatility of UML has enabled model-based paradigm to become popular in today's era of software development. Unified Modeling Language (UML) provides the possibility to describe the system from different perspectives like static view by class diagram; dynamic view by interaction and state chart diagrams. With the advent of model-based specification and design method, researchers are trying to find out the importance of UML in terms of designing and testing; when a model evolves from an initial to a subsequent version. Due to lack of assistance in modeling process creating useful model for a system is a difficult task. To produce graphical model representation of a system Snook and Butler [1] suggested adaptation of a graphical design notation (UML) for formal specification and support this with a prototype tool to perform automatic translation into a B specification. It has been found that graphical modeling tool is important for developing structural models of systems.

Pilskalns et al. [7] adopted Graph-based approach to combine the information from structural and behavioral diagrams (Class Diagram and Sequence Diagrams). In this approach, each sequence diagram is transformed into an Object-Method Directed Acyclic Graph (OMDAG). The OMDAG is created by mapping object and sequence method calls from a Sequence Diagram to vertices and arcs in a directed acyclic graph. However, this approach does not take into account the pre and post conditions of the operations which affect behavior of a class. Ali et al. [8] proposed a methodology for identifying changes and test case selection based on UML designs of the system. The work is based on the existing work on control flow analysis with some extensions to regression testing. They included class diagram to get more information while testing and capturing the changes. Though, the approach is simple it needs to be automated.

3   Testing Framework

Main emphasis has been laid upon creation of effective metamorphic relations. In metamorphic testing we need only those relations which yield maximum number of failures in order to detect maximum faults with least amount of test data. The proposed framework incorporates the following steps:

(i) **Analysis and Specification Phase.** Due to increasing complexity and evolution of software systems, this phase is regarded as the most vital phase of problem solving and software development process. The objective is to clearly understand customer requirements and to systematically organise them. In context of metamorphic testing, correct and complete analysis of requirements is of utmost importance as they lay strong foundation for extracting system properties, which later on transform into metamorphic relations.

(ii) Conversion of Specifications into Class Diagram. Graphical or modeller representation of a system is easier to understand than the textual representation, as it gives the best overview of the system requirement specification document. Class diagram has been adopted to depict the design of the system. It depicts static view of the system as a collection of classes and interfaces, along with the collaborations and relationships among classes and interfaces. The idea behind use of class diagram is that classes, interfaces and their relationships help to identify constraints and properties of the system, thereby assist in system development and testing.

(iii) Inheritance of Metamorphic Relations. Identification of good metamorphic relations requires analysis of individual modules of the system and determination of their target function. To identify properties of the target function control flow of a module is traversed. Modelling Notation of a system helps to get information about main target functions, their properties and constraints of a system.

(iv) Automated Metamorphic Testing at Runtime. After successful detection of metamorphic relations, metamorphic testing of the system is carried out. Input used during the original execution of a system is considered as test data and concurrent metamorphic testing is carried out with the help of that test data. Follow up test cases are generated from original test cases with the help of metamorphic relations. Every instance of the system in which any change is brought up to the system can be tested with the help of metamorphic testing.

4   Experimental Setup

For practical experimentation example of Banking system has been considered. The system is dynamic and operates in real time. The software has been developed in C#. Metamorphic testing has been performed on varying transactions. We started with requirement gathering activity for Banking system. The system four modules viz. Deposit module, Withdraw module, Loan module and Fixed Deposit module have been considered. An important activity in banking system is calculation of interest that needs to be correct. The important information analysed form the system is as follows:

i. The system initiates with creation of employees and investors, and assigns them a unique ID.
ii. Investors are provided with four services viz. Deposit, Withdraw, Loan and Fixed Deposit.

iii.   In Deposit module, Investors can deposit amount they wish to add. Interest money should be updated accordingly.

Rate of Interest =3%

iv.   In Withdraw module, Investors can get their money withdrawn from their account. After the transaction, the interest on amount is updated.

v.   In Loan module, make loan is a sub-module where constraints are applied on age and amount which must be followed for grant of a loan.

Constraint 1:- Loan Granted *iff 25<=age<=65* **&& Amount<=1,00,000**

vi.   To pay the instalments person has to pay instalment more than interest amount calculated. Rate of interest (ROF) applied also varies according to time period.

Constraint 2:- ROF= 12% *for 30 day*
15% after 30 days

vii.   In Fixed deposit module, age constraints are applied during deciding rate of interest in make deposit module.

Constraint 3:- age>=60   *ROF= 9%;*
<60   *ROF= 8.75%.*

viii.   In payment of Fixed deposits these constraints are taken care of-

Constraint 4:- time <=45   *Principal amt paid, Interest=0;*
45<time<Mature date   *ROF=3%;*
time>=Mature date   *Full amt according to ROF paid.*

After thorough analysis of the system and its specification, system is designed using UML notation that helps to detect properties of system. Figure 1 represents class diagram of Banking System. Effective Metamorphic Relations leads to real application of Metamorphic Testing and from the properties inherited from class diagram of the system deduction of effective metamorphic system can be done. Metamorphic relations are the necessary conditions but not sufficient.

For Banking system eleven metamorphic relations are inherited as represented in Table 1. These relations help to test the system by generating follow up test data from original test data. After detecting metamorphic relations for Bank Testing System next step is to move towards the selection of MRi's suitable to individual module. For example parameter time (T_i) is fixed in Fixed Deposit module and hence it is not useful to check all relations for transactions of this module.   Selection of Metamorphic relations for each module is shown in Table 2. Metamorphic testing is applied after detection of Metamorphic Relations. Here in Bank testing system, there are four different modules. Each transaction carried out in each module is considered as an original test case and is checked for any fault.

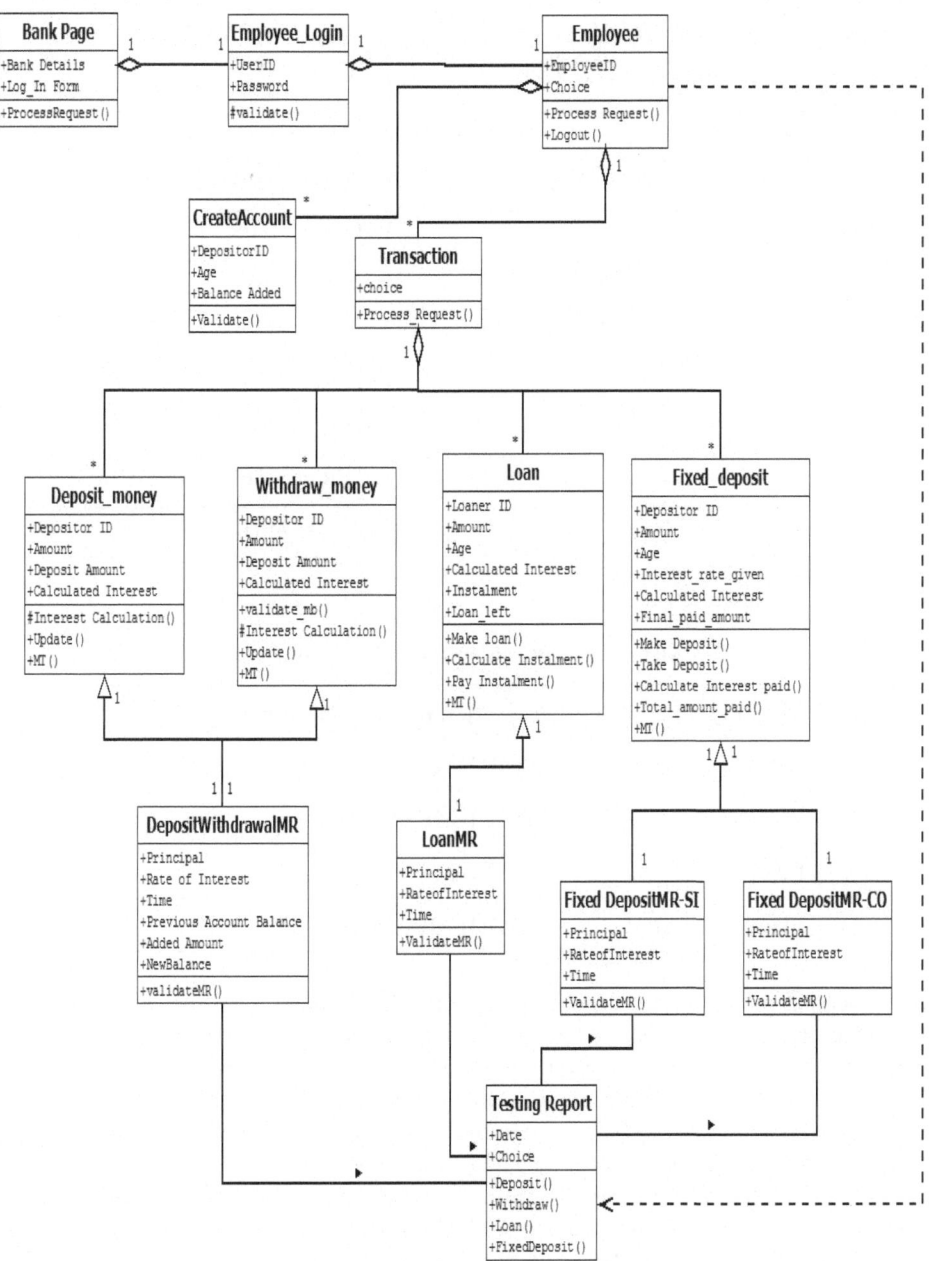

Fig. 1. Banking System showing Different Modules and Corresponding Relationship between classes

Table 1. Metamorphic Relations

MR_i	Property	To Prove
MR1	$P_i'= (INTER_i \times 36500) \div (ROF \times T_i)$	$P_i' == P_i$
MR2	$P_i' = P_i \times 2$	$INTER_i' = 2 \times INTER_i$
MR3	$ROI' = 0.75; ROI'' = ROI + ROI'$	$INTER_i = INTER_i'' - INTER_i'$
MR4	$T_i' = T_i \div 2$	$INTER_i' = INTER_i \div 2$
MR5	$a = INTER_i, b = (P_i \times ROI \times T_i) \div 36500$	$Log\ (a) = Log\ (b)$
MR6	$T_i' = (INTER_i \times 36500) \div (ROI \times P_i)$	$T_i' = T_i$
MR7	$P_i = P_i1 + P_i2 + P_i3$	$INTER_i = INTER_i1 + INTER_i2 + INTER_i3$
MR8	$P_i' = P_i \times 2; T_i' = T_i \div 2$	$INTER_i' = INTER_i$
MR9	$ROI' = 0.75; ROI'' = ROI + ROI'; T_i' = T_i \div 2$	$INTER_i = (INTER_i' \div 2) - INTER_i''$
MR10	$a = INTER_i; b = (INTER_i' \div 2) - INTER_i''$	$Log\ (a) =\ Log(b)$
MR11	$a = 1.75*(OLD\_BAL + NEW\_DEP); b = 1.75*P_i$	$a = b$

Table 2. Metamorphic Relations for Different System Modules

Modules	Metamorphic Relations
Deposit	MR1-MR11
Withdraw	MR1-MR11
Loan	MR1-MR10
Fixed Deposit	MR1, MR2, MR3, MR5, MR7

In Deposit module, after validating customer Id, Amount to be deposited is asked. From the date on which last update in account was made to the current date, days are calculated and for that time period interest is credited to customers account. Rate of Interest taken is 3% for this module. Concurrently active transaction is tested and its result is stored in Testing Report. Similarly in withdraw module, the first applied constraint is that minimum currency balance in account must not be less then Rs.500. After fetching the account details from the database, amount to be withdrawal is subtracted from the account balance .Calculation of time period for which Interest amount is updated, is done before withdrawal of money. For each active transaction testing is carried out and results are saved for further use. Figure 2 represents snapshot of Deposit module and Figure 3 represents snapshot of Withdraw module of the system.

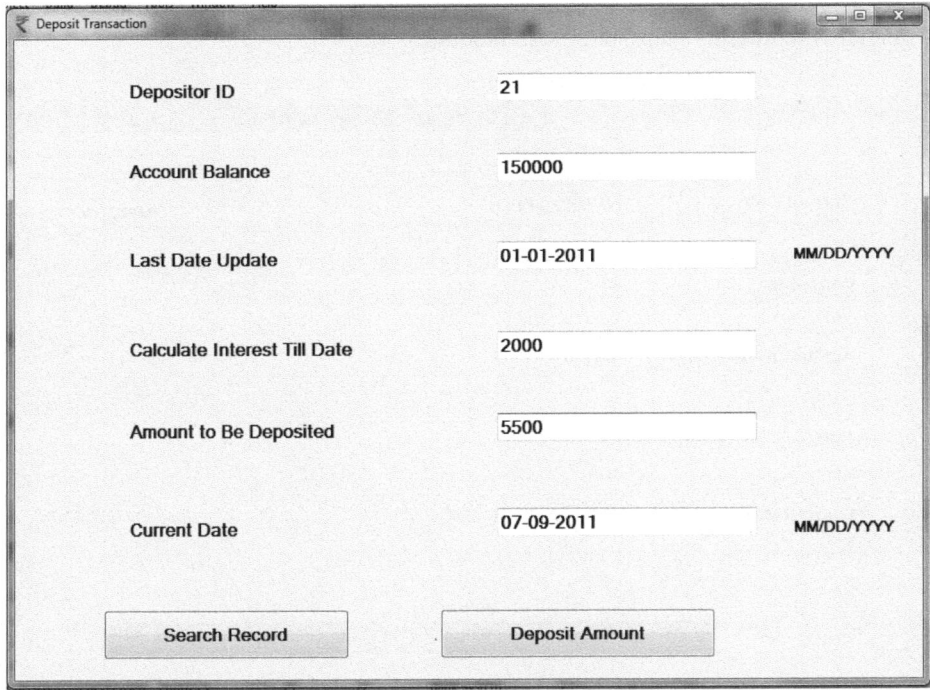

Fig. 2. Snapshot of Deposit Module

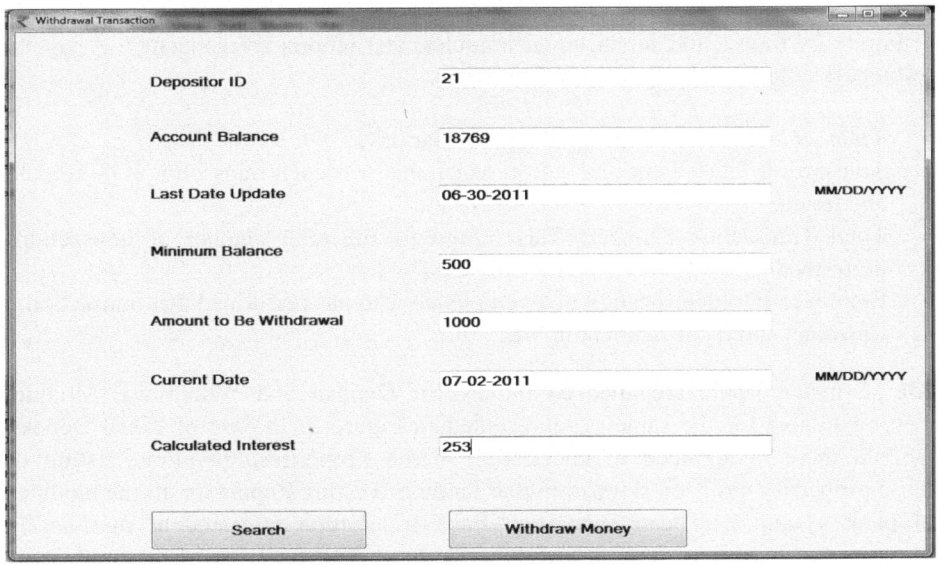

Fig. 3. Snapshot of Withdrawal Module

Figure 4 represents snapshot of loan module.

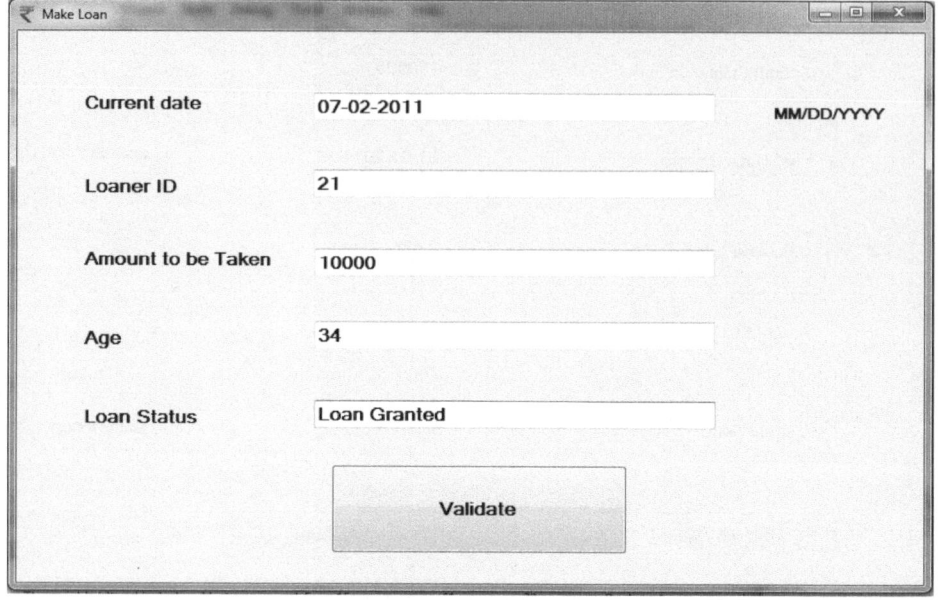

Fig. 4. Snapshot of Loan Module

For every transaction for different modules, test reports are generated. A typical test report includes the following information:

- Transaction Number: This is for a particular day.
- Transaction Time: Time and date at which that particular transaction is performed and tested.
- Total Transaction Number: This represents the total number of transactions performed.
- Employee ID: Identification of an employee who has performed that transaction.
- Customer ID: ID of Account holder.

All 11 metamorphic are checked in case of Deposit and Withdrawal Module. Testing Report for the same is represented in Figure 5. In case of Fixed Deposit module there is no need to check time based properties, therefore, testing of those properties has been skipped in that module. Testing Report for all the modules of bank system has been generated. Each transaction is tested at runtime by using its parameters as original test data. Sample result for some of the modules is represented below:

1. Module 1: Deposit Money (Checking relation MR1)

T1: Deposit Rs.1000 in account   T2: Deposit Rs.1000 in account

Parameters: P_i=1700, ROI=3%, T_i=30   Parameters: P_i=36500, ROI=3%, T_i=100
MR1:- Calculated Inter$_i$:-4 on P_i:1700   **MR1:-** Calculated Inter$_i$:-300 on P_i:36500
P_i'= (Inter*36500)/ (ROI*T_i)=1622   Pi'= (Inter*36500)/ (ROI*T_i)=36500
$P_i \neq P_i'$: **False**   => P_i=P_i' : **True**

For transaction T1 MR1 fails, New Principal Amount calculated is less then old Principal Amount. That means interest calculated is not correct. Transaction T2 succeeds for MR1.

2. Module 1: Deposit Money (Checking relation MR5)

T1: Deposit Rs.1000 in account   T2: Deposit Rs.1000 in account

Parameters: P_i=2190, ROI=3%, T_i=100   Parameters: P_i=3500, ROI=3%, T_i=100
MR5:- Calculated Inter$_i$:- 18   **MR5:-** Calculated Inter$_i$:- 28.76
a= log(Interi) =1.25   a= log(Interi) =1.45
b=log(Pi)+log(ROI)+log(Ti)-   b=log(Pi)+log(ROI)+log(Ti)-
log(36500)=1.25   log(36500)= 1.46
⇨ a=b : **True**   a≠b : **False**

For transaction T1 MR5 succeeds while it fails for transaction T2.

3. Module 2: Withdraw Money (Checking Relation MR6)

T1: Deposit Rs.1000 in account   T2: Deposit Rs.1000 in account

Parameters: P_i=1700, ROI=3%, T_i=30   Parameters: P_i=4380, ROI=3%, T_i=100
MR6:- Calculated Inter$_i$:-4 on Ti:30   **MR6:-** Calculated Inter$_i$:-36 on Ti:100
Ti'= (Inter*36500)/ (ROI*Pi)=28.6   Ti'= (Inter*36500)/ (ROI*Pi)=100
Ti≠Ti' : **False**   Ti=Ti' : **True**

Interest calculated in transaction T1 is not correct as there is difference between old Time and new time calculated. Therefore relation MR6 fails for transaction T1 and succeeds for transaction T2.

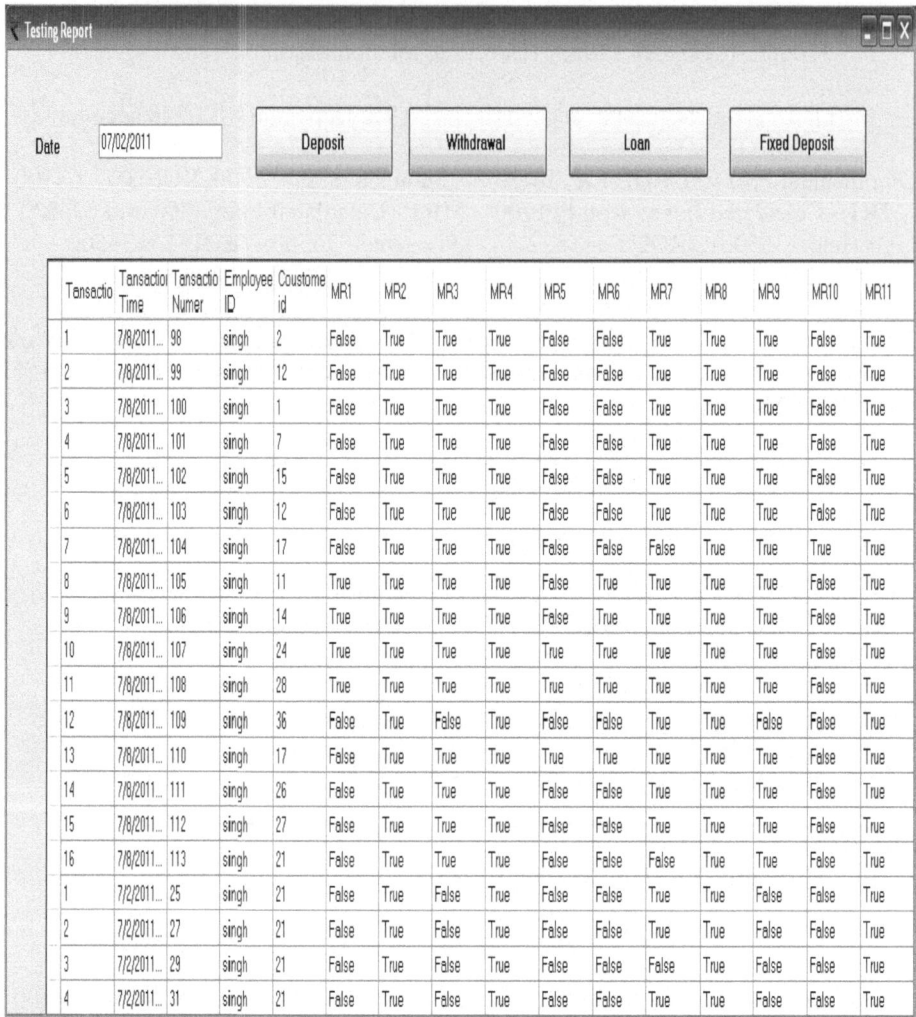

Fig. 5. Snapshot of Testing Report 1

5   Conclusion

Automated Metamorphic testing at runtime is carried out on Bank Testing system. Testing Report for each module represents the date wise transactions for each module. The automation of test data generation in Bank system helps us to reduce the overload of creating test data and testing the system efficiently as each transaction of an account uses the original data used during its execution as test data. It has been observed that strong metamorphic relations can detect maximum number of failures. There is maximum change in parameters in deposit, withdrawal and loan module when the next test case is generated. Hence test data in these modules have maximum variations. The complete process of designing and testing metamorphic relations incurs minimal cost. The experiment we have carried out has a large scope of improvement as it is only the demonstration of this approach. Developing full software by considering more modules of this case study like Money Exchange, and performing run time testing, is another challenging task. Moreover, interaction between various modules of a system needs to be checked.

References

1. Snook, C., Butler, M.: Using a Graphical Design Tool for Formal Specification. In: 13th Workshop of the Psychology of Programming Interest Group, Bournemouth, UK, pp. 311–321 (2001)
2. Chen, T.Y., Tse, T.H., Zhou, Z.Q.: Semi-proving: An Integrated Method Based on Global Symbolic Evaluation and Metamorphic Testing. In: Proceedings of the ACM SIGSOFT International Symposium on Software Testing and Analysis (ISSTA 2002), pp. 191–195. ACM Press, New York (2002)
3. Chen, T.Y., Feng, J., Tse, T.H.: Metamorphic Testing of Programs on Partial Differential Equations: A Case Study. In: Proceedings of the 26th Annual International Computer Software and Applications Conference (COMPSAC 2002), pp. 327–333. IEEE Computer Society Press (2002)
4. Gotlieb, A., Botella, B.: Automated Metamorphic Testing. In: Proceedings of the 27th Annual International Computer Software and Applications Conference (COMPSAC 2003), pp. 34–40. IEEE Computer Society Press, California (2003)
5. Chen, T.Y., Huang, D.H., Tse, T.H., Zhou, Z.Q.: Case Study on the Selection of Useful Relations in Metamorphic Testing. In: 4th Ibero-American Symposium on Software Engineering and Knowledge Engineering (JIISIC 2004), pp. 569–583. Polytechnic University of Madrid, Spain (2004)
6. Chan, W.K., Cheung, S.C., Leung, K.R.P.H.: Towards a Metamorphic Testing Methodology for Service-Oriented Software Applications. In: 1st International Workshop on Services Engineering (SEIW 2005), pp. 470–476. IEEE Computer Society (2005)
7. Pilskalns, O., Williams, D., Aracic, D.: Security Consistency in UML Designs. In: Proceedings of 30th International Conference on Computer Software and Applications (COMPSAC 2006), pp. 351–358. IEEE Press (2006)
8. Ali, A., Nadeem, A., Zohaib, M., Iqbal, Z., Usman, M.: Regression Testing based on UML Design Models. In: Proceedings of 13th IEEE International Symposium on Pacific Rim Dependable Computing, pp. 85–88 (2007)

Service Oriented Architecture Adoption Trends: A Critical Survey

Ashish Seth[1,*], Ashim Raj Singla[2], and Himanshu Aggarwal[1]

[1] Punjabi University, Patiala, India
[2] Indian Institute of Foreign Trade, New Delhi, India
{ashish_may13,himagrawal}@rediffmail.com, arsingla@iift.ac.in

Abstract. Analyst reports are confirming that adoption of SOA is growing; the actual goal of SOA is to help align IT capabilities with business goals. In today's competitive scenario where business demand changes very frequently, the expectation from technology is raised to level where we are expecting the business processes are developed in such a manner that they can adapt the frequent changes without affecting the overall organization business architecture. Thus the need to assume business processes as a smart services that can be loosely coupled. Thus need of service oriented architecture arises. This paper is a review of articles and research work that have undergone in the past 1 decade (i.e. from 2001 - 2011). The source of data is from most prestigious journal and website covering area of SOA, In this paper we have identified the factors that are relevant to SOA implementation and up to how much extents each factor is crucial to SOA implementation is also identified.

Keywords: SOA, SOA implementation, change management, SOA market trends, adhoc needs, web services, governance, migration.

1 Introduction

In the early years of computing, we had only monolithic applications running on stand-alone machines. From the era of monolithic systems of early '60s, we have seen the development of structured, object based, client/server, 3-tier, N-tier, distributed systems, component based and finally the service-oriented architectures of the modern age (see fig 1).

Service Oriented Architecture (SOA) is a computer system's architectural style for creating and using business processes, throughout their lifecycle. SOA allow exchange of data between applications and become a part of business process. The market for "core" service-oriented architecture (SOA) technology will reach $43 billion by 2010(www.searchwebservices.com, Dec2003) According to WinterGreen Research, Service oriented architecture (SOA) markets at $450 million in 2005 are expected to reach $18.4 billion by 2012. This growth is expected because SOA enables the flexible IT architecture and adhoc on demand features that is needed to respond to market shifts brought by speeded product cycles and competitive challenges.

---

* Corresponding author.

M. Parashar et al. (Eds.): IC3 2012, CCIS 306, pp. 164–175, 2012.
© Springer-Verlag Berlin Heidelberg 2012

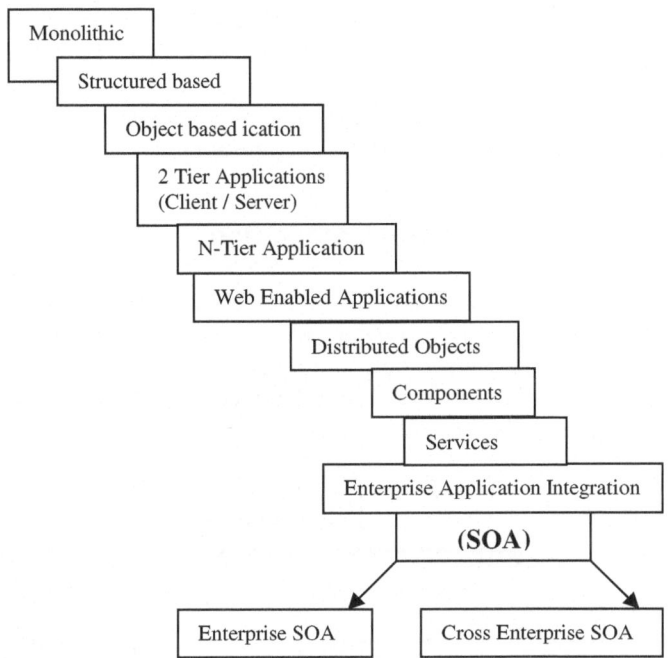

Fig. 1. SOA Evolution

According to Gartner estimates, by 2010, at least 65% of large enterprises will have more than 35% of their application portfolios based on SOA, up from fewer than 5% of organizations in 2005. Another report from Springboard Research estimates that the SOA market in India would have grown at a CAGR of 49% from 2006-2009, making it one of the fastest growing markets in the APAC region.

According to a report dated Aug 2009 by Frost and Sullivan, the SOA market in India is at a nascent stage and it largely remains untapped by major vendors although numerous opportunities exist. Dhruv Singhal, Senior Director – Fusion Middleware Sales Consulting, Oracle India, pointed out, "Today, the primary driver for SOA adoption is the business demand that forces enterprise data centers to deliver more with minimal resources. SOA adopts open standards to reduce integration costs, provide composite applications, and reduce custom coding through configuration and enable self-sufficiency for the end user. It is expected to be a critical business enabler rather than a mere IT tool."

IBM is the defacto industry standard market leader in SOA. IBM dominates SOA with 64% of the market; the rest of market is divided between 12 other participants with measurable market share, none of whom have even been able to garner as much as 8% of the market. IBM stands alone as the leader in SOA, inventing the concept of refining reusable solutions that have been around for a long time, while the IBM SOA can be a solution to be used on a global business works; the SOA services as a middleware infrastructure are implemented flexible enough to give to local differences.

Forrester surveyed enterprises – from the Global 2000 to large companies of at least 1,000 – about their experience with SOA and their plans for future investments: "Sixty-eight percent of enterprises say they are using SOA or will be using it by the end of 2010. Fifty-six percent are using SOA now, and that number jumps to 74 percent when considering only Global 2000 organizations.

2   Approaches to SOA Implementation

Broadly it is found that there are two approaches of SOA implementation i.e. Theoretical Approach and Empirical Approach. We too divided each of the 95 papers selected for this study into theoretical and empirical study; the detailed analysis is given in next section. It is further observed that most of the approaches are empirical based. These two approaches be categorized into different level (see figure 2).

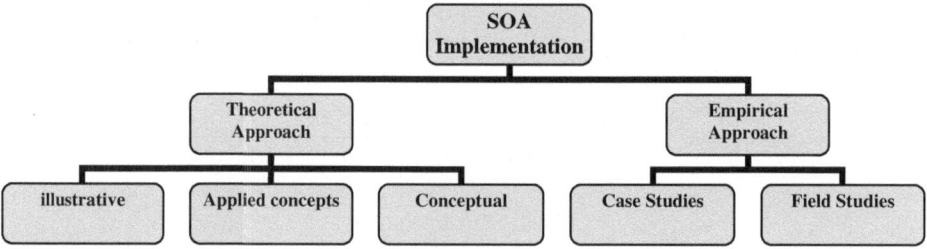

Fig. 2. SOA implementation categorized view

At its core, SOA is a strategy for business agility, because SOA uses loosely coupled services— reusable components that represent business tasks—it can deliver applications that are cost-effective, enable integration and leverage legacy investments, it is said that. "SOA is not just technology play but business agility". According to Douglas W. Frye et al. The typical enterprise implementation environment is highly complex, seldom does an organization implement all of its business processes using a single software product, and this compels organizations to understand how their business processes are enabled by multiple systems within the enterprise. Enterprise integration is the alignment of strategies, business processes, information systems, technologies, and data across organizational boundaries to provide competitive advantage. The process of achieving enterprise integration includes all managerial and technological factors that enable cross-functional process integration.

SOA gives you the ability to more easily integrate IT systems, provide multi channel access to our systems, and to automate business process. Like any new investment in technology and infrastructure, it's important to understand the right way to do it and what you can and can't do. SOA and web services are great, but they can't do everything However, our experience from working with current and potential adopters of SOA is that they often have a variety of misconceptions that lead them to oversimplify the effort required to implement SOA. Chief among these misconceptions is the belief that if we adopt SOA, an organization will achieve all its IT goals. In reality, SOA is not architecture, but an architectural pattern from which an infinite number of architectures can be derived—both good and bad. To efficiently and effectively utilize SOA we must start to begins with thinking differently – from how to build effective systems to how to get business done most effectively.

Moreover the latest study conducted during past year by different research agencies for SOA adoption and issues (see table 1), suggest the widespread interest in SOA, the collected statistics is further analyzed and divided into three views of interest i.e. Developers perspective, companies perspective and higher management perspective.

Table 1. Current Statistics by research agencies in current trends in SOA adaptation

Companies Perspective
15% of small companies (with fewer than 100 employees) have SOA efforts underway, compared to 35% of companies with more than 500 employees. (*Nucleus Research*)
12% — that's the average growth rate of companies with "well-aligned IT-business operations," versus 4% overall. (*BTM Institute*)
40% of companies with SOA spend between 10 and 30 percent of their overall IT budgets on SOA projects. Most have increased their SOA budgets over last year. (*IBM*)
37% of companies implementing SOA report seeing positive return on investment from SOA — which, by the way, isn't too shabby (*Nucleus Research*)
29% of companies with advanced SOA deployments are using SOA governance software, compared of 17% of companies still in earlier stages of SOA. (*Aberdeen*)
25% of mainframe companies have SOA efforts now in progress and another one-third are planning or considering SOA. At least half say they are or will employ mainframes in a central role in SOA. (*Unisphere Research/SHARE*)
50% of new mission-critical operational applications and business processes were designed this year around SOA, a number will jump to more than 80 percent by 2010. (*Gartner*)
Developers Perspective
49% of developers working with SOA say they can now complete a typical SOA project within three months – more than twice as many as a year ago. Plus, more than 60% of all SOA projects are now developed and deployed within just six months. (*Evans Data*)
61% of advanced SOA deployers saw a reduction in the number of software defects discovered in production, compared to 18% of non-deploying companies could say they were able to reduce defects. (*Aberdeen*)
61% of advanced SOA deployers saw a reduction in the number of software defects discovered in production, compared to 18% of non-deploying companies could say they were able to reduce defects. (*Aberdeen*)
75% of mainframe developers said they want to modernize their systems. But 52%, also said they had concerns about their system's ability to actually support SOA. (*Software AG*)
24% of developers said that they've used SOA techniques, up 85% from the previous year (*Evans Data*)

Table 1. (*Continued*)

Higher Management Perspective
48% of CIOs are planned to open their SOAs "to the cloud" in 2007 — the cloud being "where their current and potential trading partners are." (*McKinsey*)
55% of executives view SOA as "the best way to support the use of social networking and Web 2.0 development techniques in their IT infrastructure." (*BEA*)
56% of executives at companies deploying SOA admit that at least half of the code or artifacts developed under their roofs are not reviewed for compliance before moving into production. (*SOA Forum*)
57% of executives expect to see cost reductions as a result of SOA, while 27% cite code reuse and 23% expect to increase business agility. (*Saugatuck*)

3   Data Collection

The study has been focused on reputed journals and websites of computer science, information technology, and information systems covering research articles on service oriented computing, service oriented architecture and issues related to SOA. The survey is limited to time frame from year 2000 to year 2011. We further divide the period into three blocks to better analyze their growth and compare certain factors The articles were searched with search term *SOA implementation issues/ SOA Research* .After filtering from total 200 papers we have identified 95 articles and paper which are relevant for this study. The following figure (fig 3) shows the number of article published in different span of time.

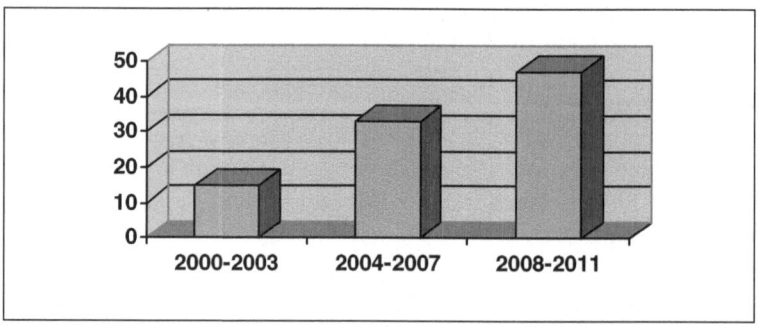

Fig. 3. Number of articles on SOA Implementation

The bar chart drawn for the number of research articles published during different interval clearly shows that interest for SOA is increasing drastically. It is identified through literature survey that SOA is evolving as organization are moving from their legacy systems to SOA environment, it is further identified that this growth is further expected to grow for the benefits that SOA provides and adhoc nature it provides to changing needs of business.

4   Research Methodology

For the analysis of data collected for the purpose, we have classified the data as theoretical studies and empirical studies. Theoretical studies are further splitted into illustrative, conceptual and applied concepts. Conceptual studies describe structure, models or theories and provide explanation or reasons. Illustrative studies , basically try to guide the practice, offer recommendations for actions and explain action to be fulfilled whereas applied concept studies are a mixture of both conceptual and illustrative studies. They are mainly based on ideas , structures and speculations rather than on the systematic and direct observation of reality. Empirical studies have been divided into case studies and field studies.

Table 2 below shows the number of paper reviewed under different categories, out of total 95 papers, the majority of articles in our review is empirical (52), compared to theoretical (43).

Table 2. Number of paper reviewed under different categories

	2000-2003	2004-2007	2008-2011
Theoretical Approach (43)			
Illustrative	4	9	6
Applied Concept	3	6	4
Conceptual	3	4	4
Empirical Approach (52)			
Case Studies	5	7	9
Field Studies	7	11	13
Total (95)	**22**	**37**	**36**

Figure 4 below shows that most of the articles are covering field studies followed by case studies. It is also analyzed that most of papers categorized as theoretical get published during year 2004-2007. Similarly in Empirical category maximum paper were found in year 2007-2011. It further indicates that among the theoretical studies, illustrative concept studies were most common followed by applied concept ones and the conceptual ones. The field study stands out as the most often used among the empirical methods.

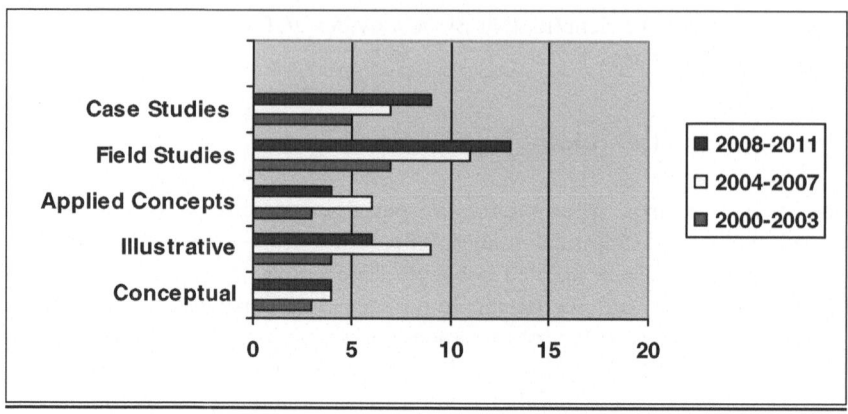

Fig. 4. Different studies on SOA covered during 2000-2011

5   SOA Implementation Factors

Most of the articles /paper published on the area of SOA discusses the following factors (see table 3) which needs to taken care of while implementing SOA. We have identified each factor in different papers and find out the percentage of each factor out of total articles published .The resulting factors were neither mutually exclusive nor collectively exhaustive; so an article could be classified into one or more categories and occurrence of given factor could increase with the increase in numbers of reviewed articles . Here our purpose is not to rank various factors in terms of their importance but to identify and analyze critical factors of SOA implementation. Table below shows the number of articles dealing with each factor and the percentage of the total that they represent. Here total of each factor comes out to be 167, not 95, since articles reviewed may dealt with more than one factors.

Table 3. Figures in respective columns represent number of articles; their percentages out of total

Factors	2000-2003	2004- 2007	2008-2011	Total
Governance Issues	6;3.5	10;5.9	8;4.7	24;14.3
Migration factors	5;2.9	8;4.7	9;5.3	22;13.1
Legacy Systems Integration	6;3.5	11;6.5	5;2.9	22;13.1
Change Management	3;1.7	4;2.3	4;2.3	11;6.5
Adhoc requirements	8;4.7	9;5.3	10;5.9	27;16.1
Resource Competences	1;0.5	2;1.1	3;1.7	6;3.5
Security Risk	2;1.1	3;1.7	3;1.7	8;4.7
Risk Management	1;0.5	3;1.7	2;1.1	6;3.5

Table 3. (*Continued*)

Challenges in scope understanding	0;0.0	3;1.7	1;0.5	4;2.3
Integration Business and IT	3;1.7	3;1.7	5;2.9	11;6.5
Return on Investment	3;1.7	2;1.1	3;1.7	8;4.7
BPM and business agility	3;1.7	1;0.5	2;1.1	6;3.5
User involvement and Organizational Commitment	3;1.7	0;0.0	2;1.1	5;2.9
Training and Teaching Methodology	2;1.1	2;1.1	3;1.7	7;4.1
Total	**46;27.5**	**61;36.5**	**60;35.9**	**167;100**

Description of some of the key factors identified is as follows

Governance Issues. A generic SOA Governance model comprises a policy framework, organizational entities, a metrics system, and a catalog of best practices. These adjust the sets of policies, according to best practice recommendations, to the current needs of the system. Several software companies propose different perspectives on SOA Governance, including, e.g., SOA maturity models or service lifecycle management. For IT Governance, many accepted approaches exist. In many aspects they provide guidance for SOA Governance frameworks.

Migration issues. The problem that accompanies a major shift in the way business functionality is packaged and offered is that it threatens to make what already exists obsolete, even when existing systems represent massive investment. This effect is compounded in the case of services because they appear to offer freedom from such a legacy "tie-in": if a new service provider offers a new improved service, you simply change service provider. Of course, much of the hype surrounding the arrival of service. and service-oriented marketplace both fuels and feeds upon these issues.

Change Management. The change management primarily deals with the strategies for the realization of new structures, systems, processes or behaviour patterns. From Crnkovic et al. (1995) point of view, it has two main goals, supporting the processing of changes –and enabling traceability of changes. Beginning with the identification and description of the problem that causes the change, one or more solution alternatives will be drafted, and the required changes will be defined. In the creation phase, the planned and wanted change activities will be effectively applied. These could lead to new change in the manufacturing processes, like new or changed parts, processes or organization forms

Security Risk. Security of Information and risk of business continuity has been the critical issues that need to be handled while adapting to SOA. *Information Security* is to ensure that information security weaknesses and events are highlighted in a timely manner. Information security is achieved be implementing, amongst others, controls. For governance, control means to ensure that adequate measures are in place to provide assurance that objectives will be achieved and undesirable events will be prevented or detected and corrected (IT Governance Institute, 2007). Da Veiga and

Eloff (2008) demonstrate that ISO/IEC 17799 (2005) addresses a comprehensive set of information security controls for governance. *Business Continuity* is to ensure that interruptions to business activities can be handled appropriately and timely.

Challenges in scope understanding. It is always very important to understand the architecture and the technology that is to be used in the right way and must understand and identify the capabilities it provides and what you can and can't do. It is further found that many of the articles are targeted to clarify the concept of service oriented technology. SOA success may hinge on a meeting of the minds between the architects and developers of web services and business process modelers who map out corporate requirements. Understanding the SOA in respect to above points is very important, it requires a fresh approach, clear vision and a multi dimensional view to understand the SOA scope. In order to undertake a project to develop a service or an application from services there is a need to know the scope and size of the work involved. This will help in determining the cost and effort for such a project.

Return on Investment. Setting up the people, training, processes, tools, and components that fit into that architecture requires an initial investment and commitment from the development organization. Jeffrey Poulin ,et al named this investment as the "Relative Cost of Writing for Reuse (RCWR)." Based on data collected over the past 10 years, this investment is approximately 1.5 times (meaning 50% more) cost over building software for one-time use. As with RCWR, data shows that the "Relative Cost of Reuse (RCR)" during development is only 20% of the cost of development without reuse; i.e., traditional reuse provides an 80% development savings.

BPM and business agility. Business Process Management (BPM) empowers a business analyst to align IT systems with strategic goals by creating well defined enterprise business processes, monitoring their performance, and optimizing for greater operational efficiencies. Each business process is modeled as a set of individual processing tasks. These tasks are typically implemented as *services* within the enterprise. The BPM system provides a toolset that allows the business analyst to create process models, and then performs the business process automation, or execution of the model, by invoking the services. Additionally, the BPM system may provide monitoring and management capabilities.

Pie chart drawn for the factors important for SOA adaptation (see fig 5), clearly shows the importance of SOA governance followed by issues of migration and legacy systems.

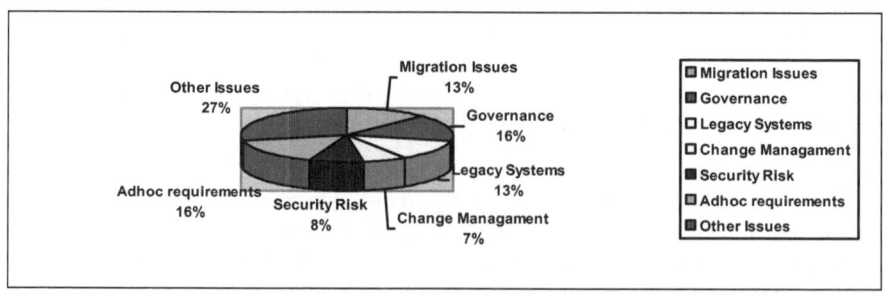

Fig. 5. Proportion of factors that are mostly covered in the SOA article published during 2000-2011

6   Conclusion

This survey is based on information from industry sources, journal, web articles, and magazines. The forecasts in this report are from the top down and bottom-up analysis to ensure that it examined similarity in that perspective. The conclusion that emerges with this survey is that one can identify the different aspects of implementation of SOA, one can also identify the factors critical to SOA, understanding of these factors will be great help for researchers and organizations working in area of SOA and able to find answers to questions like how do organizations choose which SOA infrastructure to acquire? How does an organization test the infrastructure sufficiently to guarantee the level of security, governance and management provided meets their requirements? How is interoperability between different vendor infrastructures handled? After reviewing through large number of paper we conclude in general factors that are keys to SOA success are understanding what SOA can do and what it can' t. In a nutshell it is derived that management, planning and Implementation must be go hand in hand to achieve successful SOA implementation. In the coming years, SOA will move from its inception phase to a build phase, and blend into the mainstream in application development and integration.

References

1. Alaa, G.: Derivation of Factors Facilitating Organizational Emergence based on Complex Adaptive Systems & Social Autopoiesis Theories. Emergence: Complexity & Organization Journal 11(1), 19–34 (2009)
2. Maurizio, A., Girolami, L., Jones, P.: EAI and SOA: factors and methods influencing the integration of multiple ERP systems (in an SAP environment) to comply with the Sarbanes-Oxley Act. Journal of Enterprise Information Management 20(1), 28–36 (2007)
3. Granebring, A., Révay, P.: Service-Oriented architecture is a driver for daily decision support. Emerald 36(5/6), 622–635 (2007)
4. Mukhija, A., Glinz, M.: Runtime adaptation of applications through dynamic recomposition of components. In: Proc. of 18th International Conference on Architecture of Computing Systems, pp. 99–112 (2005)
5. Shishkov, B., van Sinderen, M., Quartel, D.: SOA-Driven Business-Software Alignment. In: Proceedings of the IEEE International Conference on e-Business Engineering (ICEBE 2006), pp. 86–94 (2006)
6. Bieberstein, N.: Application Development as an Engineering Discipline: Revolution or Evolution? IBM Systems Journal 36 (1997)
7. Nott, C., Stockton, M.: Chose an ESB Topology to Fit Your Business Model, IBM developerWorks. IBM Corporation (2006)
8. Chen, Y., Zhou, L., Zhang, D.: Ontology- supported Web service composition: An approach to service-oriented knowledge management in corporate financial services. Journal of Database Management 17(1), 67–84 (2006)
9. Crawford, C., Bate, G., Cherbakov, L., Holley, K., Tsocanos, C.: Toward an on demand service architecture. IBM Systems Journal 44(1), 81–107 (2005)
10. Chryssolouris, G.: Manufacturing Systems – Theory and Practice, 2nd edn. Springer, New York (2006)

11. Chryssolouris, G., Lee, M.: An assessment of flexibility in manufacturing systems. Manufacturing Review 5(2), 105–116 (1992)
12. Erickson, J., Lyytinen, K., Siau, K.: Agile modeling, agile software development, and extreme programming: The state of research. Journal of Data- base Management 16(4), 80–89 (2005)
13. Irmert, F., Fischer, T., Meyer-Wegener, K.: Runtime Adaptation in a Service-Oriented Component Model. In: Proceedings of the 2008 International Workshop on Software Engineering for Adaptive and Self-Managing Systems, SEAMS 2008, pp. 97–104. ACM (2008)
14. Ferguson, D., Stockton, M.: Service oriented architecture: Programming model and product architecture. IBM Systems Journal 44(4), 753–780 (2005)
15. Satoh, F., Hirose, S.: Pattern-based Policy Configuration for SOA Applications. In: Proceedings of the 2008 IEEE International Conference on Services Computing, vol. 1, pp. 13–20. IEEE (2008)
16. Heineman, G.T., Councill, W.T.: Component-Based Software Engineering Putting the Pieces Together, p. 880. Addison-Wesley, Boston (2001)
17. Georgoulias, K., Papakostas, N., Makris, S., Chryssolouris, G.: A toolbox approach for flexibility measurements in diverse environments. In: Annals of CIRP, vol. 56(1), pp. 423–426 (2007)
18. Hess, H.M.: Aligning technology and business: Applying patterns for legacy transformation. IBM Systems Journal 44 (2005)
19. Hu, J., Luo, F.E., Li, J., Tong, X., Liao, G.: SOA-based Enterprise Service Bus. In: Proceedings of the 2008 International Symposium on Electronic Commerce and Security, ISECS, pp. 536–539 (2008)
20. Hu, J., Luo, F.E., Li, J., Tong, X., Liao, G.: Cooperative Middleware Specialization for Service Oriented Architectures. In: Proceedings of the 13th International World Wide Web Conference on Alternate Track Papers & Posters, pp. 206–215 (2004)
21. Kontogiannis, K., Lewis, G.A., Smith, D.B., Litoiu, M.: The Landscape of Service-Oriented Systems: a Research Perspective. In: Proceedings of the 29th International Conference on Software Engineering Workshops (SDSOA 2007), pp. 108–116 (2007)
22. Krappe, H., Stanev, S., Ovtcharova, J.: Integration of flexible manufacturing and change management processes in a service-oriented architecture. In: Proceedings of the IEEE International Joint Conferences on Computer, Information, and Systems Sciences and Engineering. Springer, Dordrecht (2006)
23. Lewis, G., Morris, E., O'Brien, L., Smith, D., Wrage, L.: SMART: The service-oriented migration and reuse technique. Technical Report CMU/SEI-2005-TN-029, Software Engineering Institute, Carnegie Mellon University, Pittsburgh, PA (2005)
24. O'Brien, L., Jon Gray, P.: Business Transformation to SOA: Aspects of the Migration and Performance and QoS Issues. In: Proceedings of the 2nd International Workshop on Systems Development in SOA Environments, pp. 35–40 (2008)
25. Keen, M., Bishop, S., Hopkins, A., Milinski, S.: Patterns: Impelmenting an SOA using an enterprise service bus. IBM Corporation (2004)
26. Marks, E.A., Bell, M.: Service-oriented Architecture A Planning and Implementation Guide for Business and Technology. Wiley (2006)
27. Papazoglou, M.P., van den Heuvel, W.-J.: Service oriented architectures: approaches, technologies and research issues. The International Journal on Very Large Data Bases 16(3), 389–415 (2006)

28. Niemann, M., Eckert, J., Repp, N., Steinmetz, R.: Towards a Generic Governance Model for Service-Oriented Architectures. In: Proceedings of Americas Conference on Information Systems, pp. 190–205 (2008)
29. Niemann, M.: Governance for Service-oriented Architectures: An Implementation Approach (2008),
http://ftp.informatik.rwthaachen.de/Publications/
CEUR-WS/Vol-374/I-
30. Zimmermann, O., Doubrovski, V., Grundler, J., Hogg, K.: Service-Oriented Architecture and Business Process Choreography in an Order Management Scenario: Rationale, Concepts, Lessons Learned. In: Conference on Object Oriented Programming Systems Languages and Applications (OOPSL 2005), October 16-20, pp. 301–312 (2005)
31. Pulier, E., Taylor, H.: Security in a Loosely Coupled SOA Environment (2006),
http://www.developer.com/design/print.php/10925_3605836_1
32. Ravichandran, T., Leong, Y., Teo, H., Oh, L.: Service-Oriented Architecture and Organizational Integration: An Empirical Study of IT-Enabled Sustained Competitive Advantage. In: Proceedings of International Conference on Information Systems (ICIS), pp. 108–122 (2007)
33. Ren, M., Lyytinen, K.: Building Enterprise Architecture Agility and Sustenenace with SOA. The Communications of the Association for Information Systems (CAIS) 22, Article 4, 75–86 (2008)
34. Ricadela, A.: The dark side of SOA. Information Week, 54–58 (2006)
35. Rahaman, M.A., Schaad, A., Rits, M.: Towards Secure SOAP MessageExchange in a SOA. Available from: ACM 1-59593-546-0/06/0011 (2006)
36. Navabpour, S., Soltan Ghoraie, L., Malayeri, A.A., Chen, J., Lu, J.: An Intelligent Traveling Service Based on SOA. In: IEEE Congress on Services 2008, Part I, pp. 102–120 (2008)
37. Schmidt, M., Hutchinson, B., Lambros, P.: Enterprise service bus: making service oriented architecture real. IBM Systems Journal 44(4), 781–797 (2005)
38. Seth, A., Seth, K., Singla, A.R.: Aspect of Service Oriented computing, JCT Journal of Computing (2010)
39. Seth, A., Agarwa, H., Singla, A.R.: Designing a SOA Based Model. ACM SIGSOFT Software Engineering Notes 36(5), 1–5 (2011)
40. Bose, S., Walker, L., Lynch, A., Bieberestein, N.: Impact of Service Oriented Architecture on Enterprise Systems, Organizational Structures, and Individuals. IBM System Journal 44(4), 127–138 (2005)
41. Anand, S., Padmanabhuni, S., Ganesh, J.: Perspectives on Service Oriented Architecture. In: Proceedings of the 2005 IEEE International Conference on Services Computing, vol. 02, p. 17. IEEE Computer Society (2005)
42. Reisig, W.: Modeling- and Analysis Techniques for Web Services and Business Processes. In: Steffen, M., Zavattaro, G. (eds.) FMOODS 2005. LNCS, vol. 3535, pp. 243–258. Springer, Heidelberg (2005)

Gender Classification Based on Lip Colour

Anand Gupta[1], Sundeep Narang[2], and Tasha Chandolia[2]

[1] Department of Computer Engineering
[2] Department of Instrumentation and Control Engineering
Netaji Subhas Institute of Technology, Dwarka
{omaranand,sundeepnrng,tasha.101091}@gmail.com

Abstract. Much research has been reported in the field of gender classification through face recognition techniques making use of variation in skin textures and distances between the nose, eyes and mouth and so forth. However, to the best of our knowledge, no work has yet been done on recognition of males and females on the basis of lip colour. In this paper, we have proposed a two-stage methodology on the above subject. In the first stage, termed as the Lip Contour Extraction Stage, the colour contrast between the skin and the lip enables the lip contour extraction. The mask so obtained is made noiseless thus perfecting the contour. The next stage, termed as the Gender Classification stage, the extracted contour is classified for genders on the basis of pronounced variation in the hue and saturation values of the lip colour. These variations, though not discernible through the naked eyes, are analysed using training machines like SVM and Neural Network. The promising experimental results showing an overall accuracy of 85 % while an accuracy of 90% for Asian and 80% for White, for gender classification, can pave way to the future of lip recognition in Biometric systems.

Keywords : Gender Classification, Lip Recognition, model-based approach.

1   Introduction

Gender classification systems find varied applications ranging from criminology to biometric validation. These applications require characteristics recognition which is made possible using clearly discernible facial features like the eyes, the face structure and the texture of the skin between the two genders. One of these facial features is the lip region which can be used to distinguish between the two genders. The lip region is roughly the lower one third part of the face, comprising basically of the lips and region between the lips and nose. Apart from lip shape recognition systems, we believe that the applications of the lip region (such as lip based biometric identification) have not been investigated thoroughly.

Through this paper, we have investigated another arena of lip region application which is gender classification using lip colour. Though, the difference in the lip colour is not discernible through the naked eye, however, using the proposed model, a clear difference in the hue and saturation values of the lip colour has been observed. These observations have been mentioned in the later section of the paper.

M. Parashar et al. (Eds.): IC3 2012, CCIS 306, pp. 176–187, 2012.

For an emphatic apprehension of the proposed model, the remaining part of this Section 1 is divided into the following sub-sections: Sub-section 1.1 incorporates the previous related works on the applications of lip region; Sub-section 1.2 brings forth such observations that have helped us in developing the proposed model after reviewing the prior works; Sub-section 1.3 spells out our contribution; Section 2 gives the framework for classification which is further divided into sub-sections 2.1 and 2.2 explaining the two stage methodology; Section 3 contains the experimental results while Section 4 consists of the discussion on the results and finally Section 5 draws the conclusion and future work on our model.

1.1   Related Work

There have been several approaches for Lip Contour Detection like [1], [2], [3], [4], [5] and for Gender Classification like [6], [7], [8]. Another study in lip colour has been for medical purposes as described in [9] and lip as a biometric as described in [10].

Lip Contour Detection has been carried out using several approaches, the two important ones being Active Contour Model (ACM) and Colour Segmentation. In the former approach as is done in [1] and [2], the lip contour is extracted by minimizing the associated energy while the latter approach as shown in [3], [4] and [5] presents a colour segmentation approach in which the red hue of the lip information is combined with Markov Random Field (MRF) model and then ACM has been used to get the perfect contours after the MRF modelling.

Study on gender classification has been done for facial features recognition and classification as well as for behavioural characteristics like that based on gait. Facial features like forehead, eyebrows, eyes, nose, lip and chin areas are easily differentiable for males and females. Methods like Principal Component Analysis for dimension reduction and Fisher Linear Discriminant algorithm for gender determination have been used in [7] and texture normalisation as intermediate methods for classification in [8]. Training machines like Support Vector Machine (SVM), Neural Network (NN), Adaboost and LDA have been used for classification purpose. [6] and [7] make use of the facial features, wherein the colour images are detected by converting the inherent RGB colour space into YCbCr colour space and then the lip region, mouth region and the nose regions are located. For gait based gender classification as done in [8], prior information is extracted from the psychological experiments which when combined with an automatic method increases the classification accuracy.

An altogether different application of lip colour has been studied in [9]. The Hue (H), Saturation (S) and Intensity (I) values of the various images are stored in the form of bins and then trained for five different lip colours namely pale red, light red, deep red, normal red and purple. The test images are then compared with the trained images and a good efficiency is obtained.

As mentioned in [10], the lip features have been confirmed as unique through studies by Yasuo Tsuchihasi and Kazuo Suzuki [11, 12]. Making use of Zemike and Hu moments as well as colour features, lips biometric system has been presented.

Thus, making use of Lip Contour Detection method as shown in [3], [4] and [5] and Colour based classification as shown in [9], a Gender Classification method can be developed to classify males and females on the basis of lip colour and shape. This very combination we have tried to achieve through our investigation and work.

1.2 Motivation

The following observations from the previous related works have led us to develop the proposed model for Gender Classification:

1. Lip Detection methods as shown in [3], [4], and [5] have led us to develop a method based on colour segmentation which has been explained in the later sections.
2. Gender Classification makes use of training machines like SVM, NN, LDA and Adaboost.
3. In [9], the HSI values of the lips are used to create bins and train and test the images using the aforementioned training machines. Using this method, the colour aspects of the lip can be used to distinguish the males and females.

Use of the lip features for classification purpose has the following advantages over the previous methods of gender classification, described in the prior section:

1. The lip region is generally visible; not hidden.
2. This type of classification is anatomical in nature; better accuracy is expected as against the behavioural type of classification.

Taking into consideration these advantages and the fact that this field of gender classification has not been studied well, we have proposed a system based on lip colour.

1.3 Contribution

We have developed a novel methodology for gender classification based on lip colour. Moreover, to our knowledge, the lip contour detection method used in this paper is a novel method as well. The method, which is a prerequisite to classification, creates a mask by Hue selection of the image and then removing the noise from the mask by using the method as explained later in this paper. The Gender classification stage makes use of the H, S, and I values of the extracted contour. Finally the trained images are compared with the test images and the likewise results are obtained. The highlight of this approach lies in its simplicity and cogent efficiency. Our contributions include:

1. Development of a colour based segmentation approach for lip contour extraction using the Hue values of the region of interest (ROI).
2. Development of a colour specification model for classification based on lip colour for both males and females.

The proposed method of lip contour detection is similar to [3] and [4]. The contour detection method, though a prerequisite, can be implemented as a plug-in, i.e. the prior methods can be used for the same purpose but with a varied efficiency. The final stage of gender classification only depends on the mask obtained from the contour; hence better the contour, more the accuracy.

2   Framework for Classification

The following assumptions are taken into account for classification purpose:

1. The ROI is the lower one third portion of the face;
2. The mouth of the subject is closed; teeth and tongue are not visible.
3. The race and age of the person are known which are critical in determining the efficiency of the proposed model.

According to the two-stage model we have proposed, the first stage as the Lip contour Detection stage and the second stage as the Gender Classification stage, the latter being further sub-divided into two stages viz. the Colour Specification and Testing of Images. The last sub-stage uses the three training machines for testing and training viz. Support Vector Machine (SVM), Neural Network (NN) and Perceptron respectively.

The stages are described in detail as follows:

2.1   The Lip Detection Stage

In this stage (as shown in Figure 1), the input is the image of the region of interest and the output is the mask of the image which is then used for classification purpose. The intermediate stages are Lip Region Masking and Noise Removal. The intermediate stages are explained as follows:

1. Lip Region Masking: This method is used to calculate the hue values of the inherent RGB and they are normalized. The hue values greater than 0.5 are folded back onto $0.5 - 0$ range and then the values between 0 and 0.04 are extracted to create a mask (which has noise). Folding is done to shift right half region of the hue to 0 as lip pixels are in both the left and right extremes of hue range. The next stage is used to remove the noise and get a perfect contour for classification.

   The algorithm is as follows:

```
Input: RGB Mouth Region Image.
Step 1: Convert RGB image to HSI Color space.
Step 2: If Hue value (H) > 0.5 Then H = H - 2(H-0.5)
Step 3: If H < 0.04 Then H = 1
        Else H = 0
Output: H that is Lip Region Mask (with Noise)
```

2. Noise Removal: In this stage, all the single non-connected pixels in the image are filled and then the region with the largest area is used as contour while the rest of the regions are discarded.

The algorithm is as follows:

```
Input: H that is Mask from lip region masking stage
Step 1: Fill all not connected, single pixels in mask
Step 2: Label all connected regions extracted in mask
        with Natural numbers, i.e. make value of all
        pixels in that region equal to label number (#).
Step 3: A# = area for # Labelled region; X = # of max(A# ∀ #)
Step 5: For all regions in mask H If # == X Then # = 1
        Else # = 0
Output: H that is Lip region mask (without noise)
```

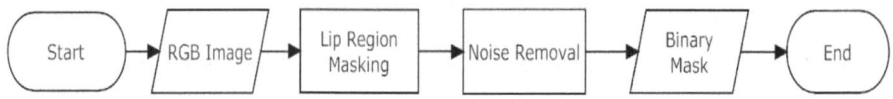

Fig. 1. Lip Contour Extraction

Finally the mask of the lip region is obtained and sent as an input to the next stage i.e. Gender Classification stage as shown in Figure 2.

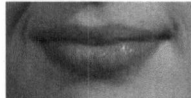   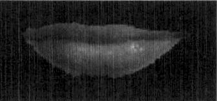

2(a). Original Image   **2(b).** Imageafter Stage 1   **2(c).** Image after Stage 2   **2(d).** Mask overlaid on original

Fig. 2. Mask Obtained after Lip Contour Detection Stage

2.2   The Gender Classification Stage

The mask of the image obtained in the first stage is an input to the first sub-stage, i.e. Colour Specification. The output of this stage is colour specific bins which are then sent to the second sub-stage which tests the given images. Training and testing are done via three training machines, SVM, Neural Network and Perceptron. The various sub-stages are explained as below:

Colour Specification. In this sub-stage (refer to Figure 3), formation of bins of H, S and I is taking place. These bins are then sent to each of the training networks.

$$H = \{\theta \text{ if } B<=G, 360 - \theta \text{ if } B>G\} \tag{1}$$

where $\theta = \cos^{-1}(((0.5*(R-G)+(R-B))/((R-G)^2+((R-B)(G-B))^{1/2})$

$$S = 1-(3/(R+G+B))*(\min(R,G,B)) \tag{2}$$

$$I = 1/3*(R+G+B) \tag{3}$$

H, S and I values are calculated according to equations (1), (2) and (3). These values are then normalised and the single matrices of the three values of size 13, 13 and 17 respectively are concatenated to form a bin of size 43 for each image. These bins are then sent to each of the training machines aforementioned as inputs and are trained according to their gender.

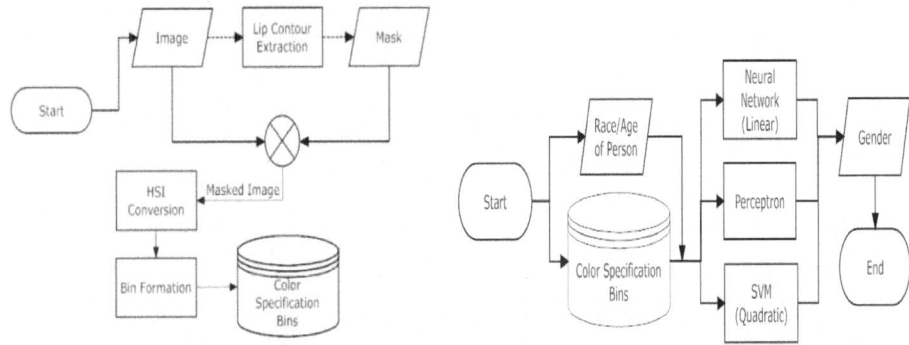

Fig. 3. Colour Specification Stage-H, S, I values of the lip contours obtained are sent to the Bin Formation process and trained according to the respective genders

Fig. 4. The Testing Stage-For testing, the bins are also trained according to race and age of the subjects and then trained according to the respective genders

Testing of Images. The trained database for both colour specification and lip shape detection is then used to test the images using the aforementioned training machines as shown in Figure 4.

3   Experimental Results

The implementation of the algorithm is carried out on AMD Athlon™ 2.4 GHz Processor, 4 GB RAM, Windows 7 Ultimate in MATLAB® Release 2010a. The algorithm is implemented on 125 subjects taken from FERET database [13] since it is one of the largest database of facial images (1199 individuals), hence appropriate for our experimentation. It consists of images collected between August 1993 and July 1996. However, only the images taken in 1994 of the 125 subjects are processed since the particular database has better lighting conditions, thus befitting our algorithm. The dataset used for the experimentation consists of only those images in which the subjects are facing front towards the camera. The dataset also contains information about the age and race of the subjects. The training images are sent to the Colour Specification Stage for formation of bins as explained in the previous section. The bins formed in this stage are trained using SVM, Neural Network and Perceptron. As mentioned in the earlier sections, there is a significant difference in the hue and saturation of the lip colour of males and females belonging to White and Asian races. Following results indicate this difference by plotting the number of pixels occupied by each bin versus the range of each bin for both genders and races:

1. Hue and Saturation variation in lip colour of males and females belonging to Asian race.

From Figure 5, it is evident that the hue values of the both genders are centralized in the bins 0.04 – 0.12 which is around the red region. However there is a difference in the percentage of the number of pixels occupied by the lip colour of respective genders. While from Figure 6, the number of pixels occupied by both the genders has a definite pattern.

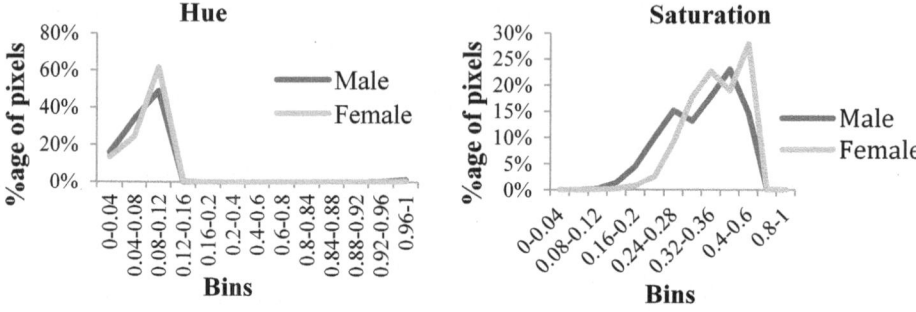

Fig. 5. Hue Variation in lip colour of both genders (Asian Race)

Fig. 6. Saturation Variation in lip colour of both genders (Asian Race)

2. Hue and Saturation variation in lip colour of males and females belonging to White race.

From Figure 7, it is evident that the hue values of the both genders are centralized in the bins 0.04 – 0.12 which is around the red region. However, there is no significant distinction between the two.

While from Figure 8, the number of pixels occupied by both the genders has a definite pattern different from the Asian race.

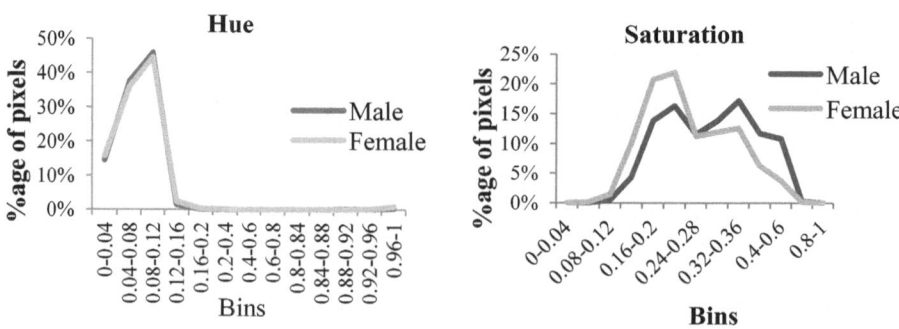

Fig. 7. Hue Variation in lip colour of both genders (White Race)

Fig. 8. Saturation Variation in lip colour of both genders (White Race)

Thus making use of the aforesaid distinct variations, the test images are tested for the following cases:

1. Race and Age are taken as the classification parameters:
    a) The age and race of the subject are not known;
    b) The race of the subject is considered while the age is not known;
    c) The age of the subject is considered while the race is not known;
    d) The race and age of the subject, both are considered.

2) Different kernel functions in SVM are taken as classification parameters:

3) Different layers and neurons in Neural Network are taken as classification parameters:

On the basis of the aforementioned cases, the following results are obtained:

I. Race and Age are taken as the classification parameters

   a) The age and race of the subject are not known:

Fig 9 shows the accuracy of the various training machines i.e. SVM, NN and Perceptron while the race or the age of the subjects is unknown. Time taken for testing is 51.55 seconds.

   b) The race of the subject is considered while the age is not known:

Fig 10 shows the accuracy of the various training machines i.e. SVM, NN and Perceptron when the race of the subject is known, however the age is not known. The various races taken into consideration were Asian, Hispanic, White and Middle-Eastern. Time taken for testing is 1 minute and 14.14 seconds.

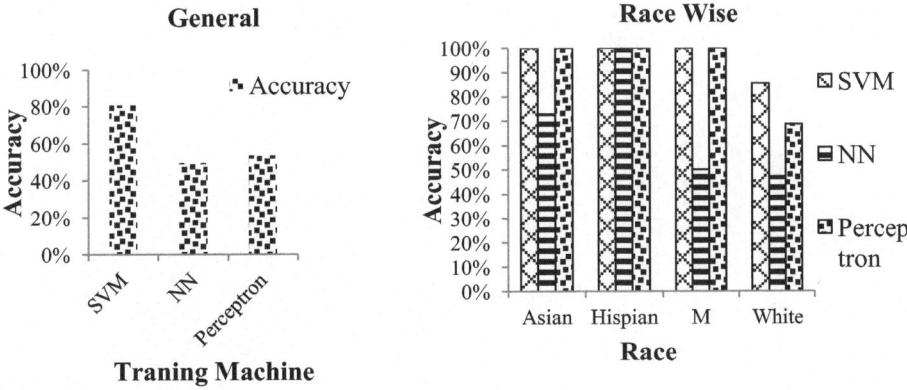

Fig. 9. Gender Classification (race/age not known)

Fig. 10. Gender Classification (race is known)

*M – Middle Eastern

   c) The age of the subject is considered while the race is not known:

Fig 11 shows the accuracy of the various training machines i.e. SVM, NN and Perceptron when the age of the subject is known, while race is not known. The various age groups taken into consideration were 15-24, 25-34, 35-44 and 45-54. Time taken for testing is 53.58 seconds.

d) The age and race of the subject , both are considered:

Fig 12 shows the accuracy of the various training machines i.e. SVM, NN and Perceptron when both the race and the age of the subject are known. Time taken for testing is 51.51 seconds.

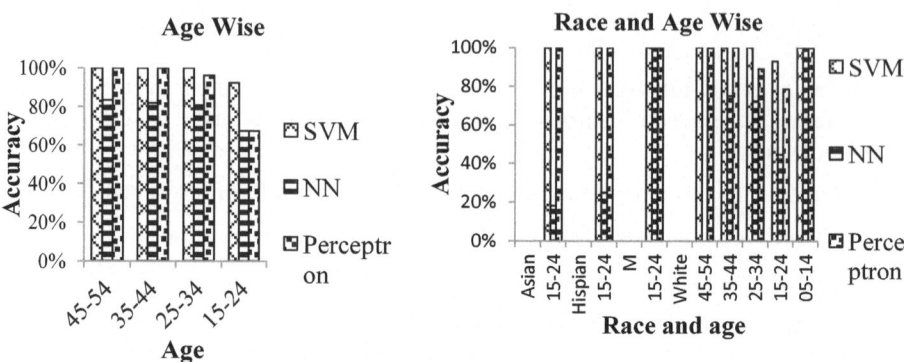

Fig. 11. Gender Classification (age is known)   **Fig. 12.** Gender Classification (age/race known)

II. *Different Kernel Functions in SVM are taken as classification parameters*

Fig 13 shows the accuracy with the different types of Kernel functions in SVM when race of the person is not known while Fig 14 shows the accuracy when the race of the person is known. The time taken is 28.32 seconds for the first while 1 minute 14 seconds for the second result.

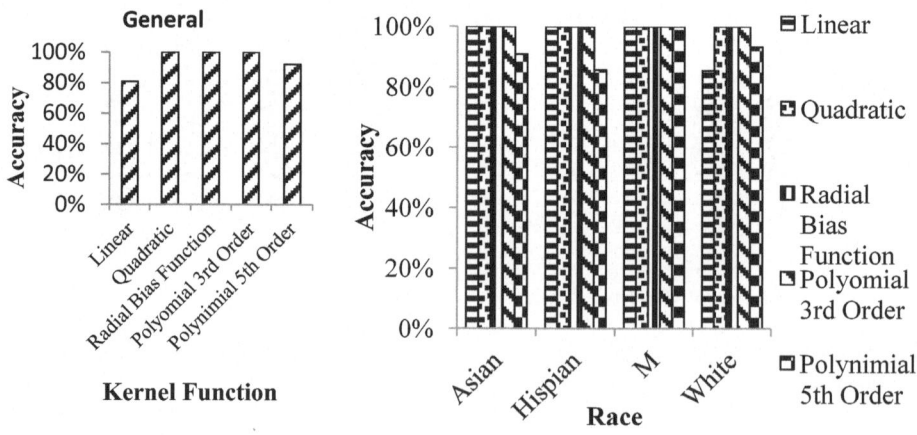

Fig. 13. Gender Classification using different Kernel Function (race not known)   **Fig. 14.** Gender Classification using different Kernel Function (race is known)

III. Different number of layers and Neurons in Neural Network are taken as classification

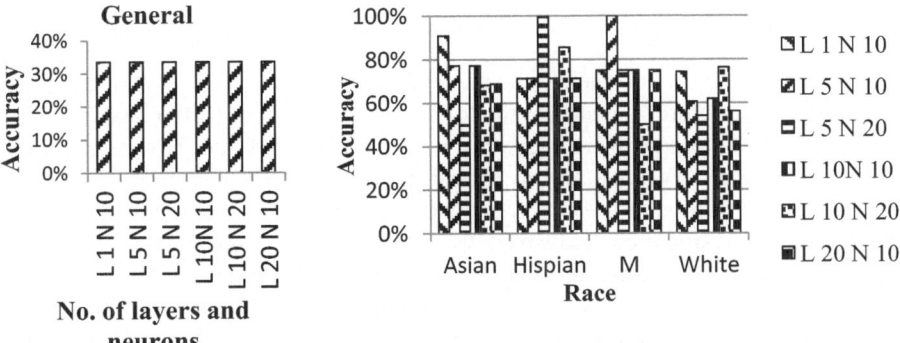

Fig. 15. Gender Classification with different layers and neurons (race not known)

Fig. 16. Gender Classification with different layers and neurons (race known)

Figures 15 and 16 show the accuracy of classification with different number of layers and neurons when the race is not known and when the race is known, respectively.

- Where L is the number of layers and N is the number of neurons

4   Discussion

The experimental results as presented in the previous section can be summarised as follows:

1. SVM shows the highest accuracy while classifying with or without the knowledge of age and race as against NN and Perceptron.
2. While making use of different Kernel functions in SVM, Quadratic, Radial Basis (RBF) and 3rd order Polynomial have the maximum accuracy both while classifying with or without the knowledge of age and race as against the other kernel functions.
3. In case of Neural Network based classification, almost equal and low (less than 35%) accuracy is obtained for different layers and different number of neurons, when the race is not known. However, very good accuracy is obtained when the race is known. Increasing the number of neurons and layers to an optimum value enhances the accuracy of classification.

5   Conclusion

In this paper, we have presented a novel method for gender classification based on lip colour. This method makes use of Colour Segmentation based Lip Contour Detection which has been used to classify males and females on the basis of lip colour. Experimental Results indicate that the accuracy as well as efficiency of classification increases if the race and age of the subject is taken into consideration. Thus, our assumption that race and age of the subject should be a prerequisite has been confirmed.

However, in order to make our methodology more effective and useful for automation in the future, we address the following issues. Firstly, after analysis, it was found out that the model works for only a few races i.e. Asian, Hispanic, Middle-Eastern and White. We thus, aim to extend the proposed methodology to recognise the subjects irrespective of their race. Secondly, in our model, the lip colour feature is only used for classification. However, we intend to widen our research on gender classification based on other lip features such as the shape and texture, which can further increase the accuracy for classification. Moreover, the images used for experimentation are static images. We, thus seek to develop a model that has a real-time database having good resolution lip region as the region of interest. We, thus, hope to increase the efficiency of the model once the aforementioned issues are resolved.

References

1. Delmas, P., Coulon, P.Y., Fristot, V.: Automatic snakes for robust lip boundaries extraction. In: Proceedings of IEEE International Conference on Acoustics, Speech, and Signal Processing, Civic Plaza, Hyatt Regency - Phoenix, Arizona, March 15-19, vol. 6, pp. 3069–3072 (1999)
2. Liew, A.W.C., Leung, S.H., Lau, W.H.: Lip contour extraction using a deformable model. In: International Conference on Image Processing, Vancouver, BC, Canada, September 10-13, vol. 2, pp. 255–258 (2000)
3. Lievin, M., Delmas, P., Coulon, P.Y., Luthon, F., Fristol, V.: Automatic lip tracking: Bayesian segmentation and active contours in a cooperative scheme. In: IEEE International Conference on Multimedia Computing and Systems, Florence, Italy, June 7-11, vol. 1, pp. 691–696 (1999)
4. Zhang, X., Mersereau, Z.M.: Lip feature extraction towards an automatic speechreading system. In: International Conference on Image Processing, Vancouver, BC, Canada, September 10-13, vol. 3, pp. 226–229 (2000)
5. Eveno, N., Caplier, A., Coulon, P.Y.: New color transformation for lips segmentation. In: IEEE Fourth Workshop on Multimedia Signal Processing, Cannes, France, October 3-5, pp. 3–8 (2001)
6. Zhiguang, Y., Li, M., Ai, H.: An Experimental Study on Automatic Face Gender Classification. In: 18th International Conference on Pattern Recognition, Hong Kong, August 20-24, vol. 3, pp. 1099–1102 (2006)
7. Zbudak, Ö., Kırcı, M., Akir, Y.Ç., Güneş, E.O.: Effects of the facial and racial features on gender classification. In: 15th IEEE Mediterranean Electrotechnical Conference, Valletta, Malta, April 26-28, pp. 26–29 (2010)
8. Yu, S., Tan, T., Huang, K., Jia, K., Wu, X.: A Study on Gait-Based Gender Classification. IEEE Transactions on Image Processing 18, 1905–1910 (2009)

9. Zheng, L., Li, X., Yan, X., Li, F., Zheng, X., Li, W.: Lip color classification based on support vector machine and histogram. In: 3rd International Conference on Image and Signal Processing, Quebec, Canada, October 16-18, vol. 4, pp. 1883–1886 (2010)
10. Choras, M.: The lip as a biometric. In: Proceeding of Pattern Analysis and Application, vol. 1, pp. 105–112 (2010)
11. Kasprzak, J., Cheiloscopy, L.B.: Human identification on the basis of lip prints. CLK KGP Press, Warsaw (2001) (in Polish)
12. Tsuchihasi, Y.: Studies on personal Identification by means of lip prints. Forensic Sci. 3(3), 3:233–3:248 (1974)
13. Color FERET database, http://face.nist.gov/colorferet/

Using Strong, Acquaintance and Weak Tie Strengths for Modeling Relationships in Facebook Network

Arnab Kumar, Tushar Rao, and Sushama Nagpal

Netaji Subhas Institute of Technology, Delhi, India
{arnabkumar225,rao.tushar}@nsitonline.in,
sushmapriyadarshi@yahoo.com

Abstract. Predicting strength of a relationship (also known as Tie Strength Problem) has been a trivial research area amongst sociologists for decades. However, considering the recent trends in internet behavior of people along with the development of so called *social web*, makes it popular amongst web scientists to work on this as a potential research topic with new perspectives. Real life is a complex social dynamic system comprising individuals starting of either as *strong acquaintances* or *weak acquaintances* and move towards *strong* or *weak ties* with passage of time. In this paper we validate the existence of varying degree of relationship individuals have on Facebook using unsupervised machine learning techniques like divisive hierarchical clustering and statistical techniques like SSE ; analyzing strength of the boundaries that distinguish them. We have realized this on a feature rich dataset of more than 100 nodes collected during 10th of July, 2011 to the 9th of September 2011 using a Facebook application. We provide descriptive error analysis interviews focussing on the clustered structure, obtaining it with an accuracy of 90%. The paper concludes by illustrating how modeling tie strength can improve social media design elements, including privacy controls, message routing and information prioritization in databases. Potential usage of this work can be in making complex recommender systems, lead generation marketing and in organizational or telecom network.

Keywords: social network analysis, Facebook, relationship, ties, social web, machine learning.

1   Introduction

Relationships have always played a very important role in everybody's life. Recent rise in popularity of OSNs(Online Social Networks) is based upon their ability to provide a platform for people with ease to connect. As Jennifer L. Berman from CBIZ, Chicago had once remarked, by using social media we have all opened our rolodex for the whole world to see[1]. However, as every relation is not equal, understanding relationships in online social networks (OSNs) and consequently connecting the theory behind tie strength (strength of a relationship) with the data

---

[1] Facebook friends as job references?: http://www.msnbc.msn.com/id/26223330

M. Parashar et al. (Eds.): IC3 2012, CCIS 306, pp. 188–200, 2012.

behind social media is now an upcoming area of research that merges both sociologists and data scientists. According to Mark Granovetter, tie Strength is defined as a linear combination of the amount of time, emotional intensity, intimacy (or mutual confiding), and reciprocal services which characterize each relationship [10]. Researchers working on online social networks (OSNs) have also found out that understanding tie strengths can improve behavior prediction in tasks such as fraud detection [15] and viral marketing [5]. As a result of all these developments, understanding various types of tie strength has become really important in modelling various networks as well as societies in general.

There is wide acceptance in the sociology community for broadly two types of ties- strong ties and *weak ties*. Strong Ties are defined as the people that the candidate would trust, people whose social circle would overlap with the candidate being analyzed. Often, due to coincidence of both social as well as topographical circles, people with whom you share strong ties are the set of people having higher network similarity to you[8]. Trusted friends and family, called strong ties, can affect emotional health [17] and can often join together during times of crisis and struggle. Weak ties, on the other hand, are those whom a person may have met once, maybe just for purpose or at a given event, but the person may not know the latter personally. It is argued, that weak ties are responsible for the majority of the embeddedness and structure of social networks in society as well as the transmission of information through networks [12]. In fact, research work in this field even points to the fact that weak ties expedite the transmission of knowledge across different workgroups [12], which help people to come across creative ideas [4] or find a job [9].

However, there may be relationships which possess characteristics intermediate between strong and weak ties, or a transitional tie strength undergoing its transition from strong to weak ties or vice versa. Consequently, we introduce and subsequently validate the presence of a third type of tie strength→ acquaintances. A recently met fellow colleague may be an example of an acquaintance, as they are people with whom a person comes in contact daily, but may not be bound to him emotionally or ask for his help during the time of need.As an extension of this, we further propose to further classify this third type of tie strength (acquaintances) into two categories- *Strong and Weak acquaintances*. The further classification of Acquaintances into two categories-*Strong and Weak Acquaintances* is done with the belief that all acquaintances are not same, with some of the acquaintances undergoing their transition from acquaintances to strong ties (Strong acquaintances) and others undergoing a degradation in relationship with the subject from an acquaintance to a weak tie (Weak Acquaintances).

This paper is organized as related prior research in section 2 and data collection process along with description of the predictive variables in section 3. Further in section 4 we discuss the techniques and describe results as summarized in Table 1. In section 5 we discuss the 4 types of ties strengths with potential use in industry and academia and conclude the work in section 6.

2   Related Work

The concept of tie strength was first introduced by Mark Granovetter -"The Strength of Weak Ties" which he proposed 4 dimensions of tie strength-*amount of time, intimacy, intensity and reciprocal services.* [10]. Ronald Burt proposed that structural factors shape tie strength[3]. Similarly, Wellman and Wortley had argued that providing emotional support, such as offering advice on family problems, indicated a stronger tie between a set of people [19].Further, Nan Lin, et al.,introduced various other parameters which could be used for the prediction of tie strength,such as social distance,socioeconomic status, education level, political affiliation, race and gender[14]. Zhao et al. have used tie strength as basis of proposing information dissipation model [21].

Many researchers in the past have made use of clustering techniques [18], [13]. Facebook data has also been used for sociological analysis in context of tie strengths [7]. Interaction data has been used to give a quantitative estimate of tie strength, although we believe that quantitative estimation of tie strength is difficult to validate, as the number assigned to a relationship is itself time variant [8]. Similarly, research work has also been done in this field to formulate a link- based latent variable model[20],along with algorithms based on Supervised Random Walks being proposed that combines the information from network structure with nodes and edge level attributes [1].

3   Data Collection and Processing

The data set used for the purpose of this research work has been collected over a time period of 2 months, from the 10th of July, 2011 to the 9th of September 2011 using an automated application. The application designed collected data for each of the participants (seed nodes) using OAuth 2.0 to collect data from the user through the application used on Facebook, ensuring anonymity of data with the consent of the participants who had participated in that collection (who had agreed to donate their data for the research work).

As an incentive, the people who participated as a part of the dataset collection were promised that the results of the research work would be shared with them. Finally, 20 participants were willing to participate and data of 5 friends were collected from each, therefore providing us with a dataset of 100 participants (20 seed nodes, 100 edges). The 20 participants involved in the process of data collection were students from the college, brought together from around 6 departments of the college. The sample consisted of 12 men and 8 women ranging between 18 and 25 years old. The minimum number of friends that a participant had was 135, whereas the maximum was 450. Since the mean age of the participants was 22.5, the minimum of friends taken were 135 and the participants were connected to an average of 86 community pages, groups and events; it ensured that our participants fall within the mainstream of Facebook users. For sample coherence, we have considered only the participants who are two years old on Facebook.

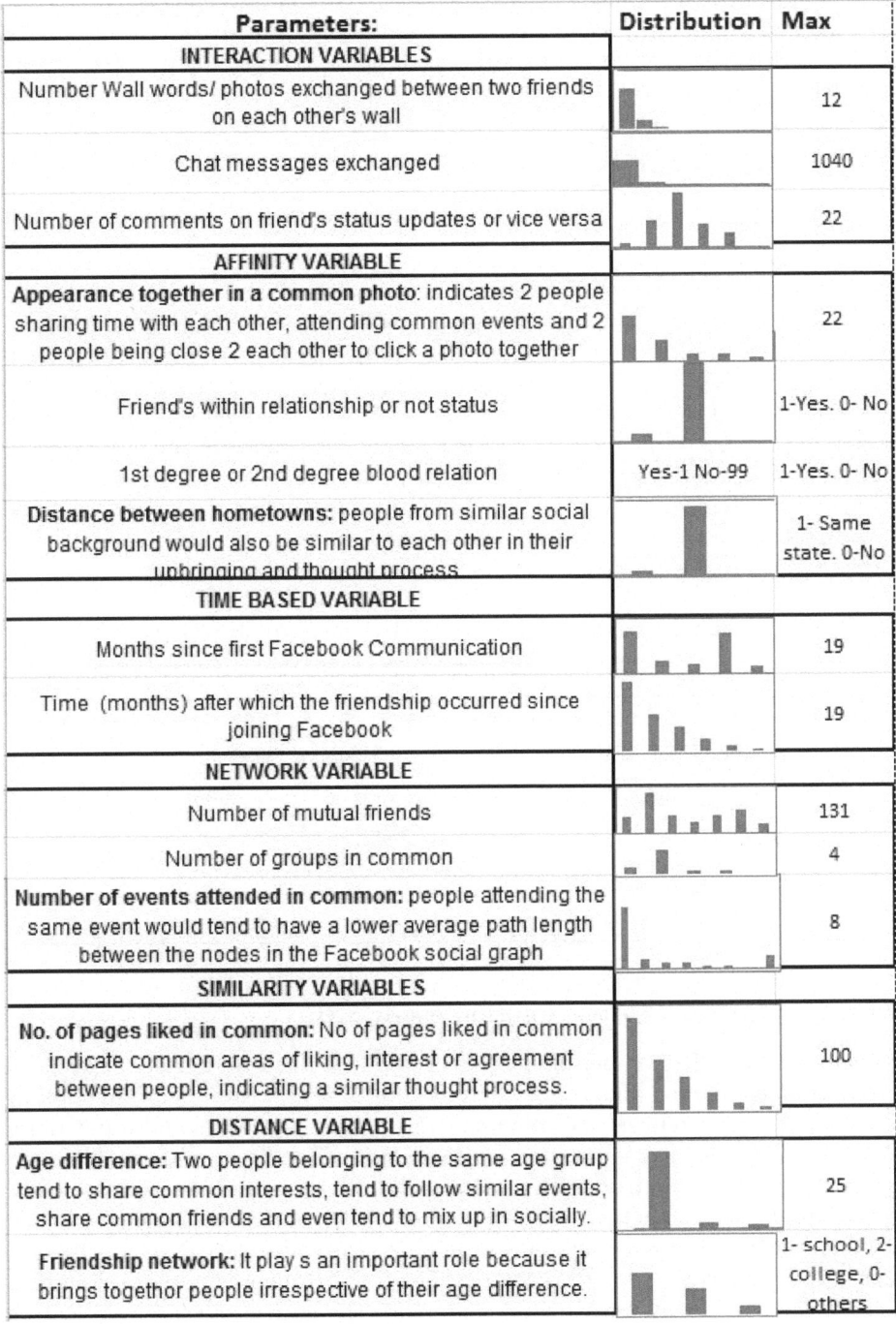

Parameters:	Distribution	Max
INTERACTION VARIABLES		
Number Wall words/ photos exchanged between two friends on each other's wall		12
Chat messages exchanged		1040
Number of comments on friend's status updates or vice versa		22
AFFINITY VARIABLE		
Appearance together in a common photo: indicates 2 people sharing time with each other, attending common events and 2 people being close 2 each other to click a photo together		22
Friend's within relationship or not status		1-Yes. 0- No
1st degree or 2nd degree blood relation	Yes-1 No-99	1-Yes. 0- No
Distance between hometowns: people from similar social background would also be similar to each other in their upbringing and thought process		1- Same state. 0-No
TIME BASED VARIABLE		
Months since first Facebook Communication		19
Time (months) after which the friendship occurred since joining Facebook		19
NETWORK VARIABLE		
Number of mutual friends		131
Number of groups in common		4
Number of events attended in common: people attending the same event would tend to have a lower average path length between the nodes in the Facebook social graph		8
SIMILARITY VARIABLES		
No. of pages liked in common: No of pages liked in common indicate common areas of liking, interest or agreement between people, indicating a similar thought process.		100
DISTANCE VARIABLE		
Age difference: Two people belonging to the same age group tend to share common interests, tend to follow similar events, share common friends and even tend to mix up in socially.		25
Friendship network: It play s an important role because it brings togethor people irrespective of their age difference.		1- school, 2- college, 0- others

Fig. 1. Parameters under study

Validation of our inference from the Facebook data collected had been performed by asking each and every candidate to submit a questionnaire given in Table 4, mailed to them in which the candidate was questioned regarding the relationship that the candidate shared with the person with whom his/her relationship had been analysed using our model and machine learning analysis. Features considered for prediction of the tie strengths in our model are given in figure 1.

4   Results

In this paper,we first try to validate the number of clusters present in the data,which is performed by using Statistical technique like SSE[2].After the number of clusters are determined,we use the unsupervised machine learning technique of clustering to cluster relationships into various categories of tie strength. Determination of the tie strength category to which each relationship would fall would be followed by a validation of the clusters determined in the data used,by using the widely used parameters of Dunn Index,Silhoutte Width etc. Finally we conclude the results by computing intercluster distance,ensuring that none of the clusters analyzed as a part of our research are statistically non-significant. Table 1 provides a summary of the techniques used in this paper.

Table 1. Summary of the statistical and Machine Learning techniques used

Technique Used		Comments	Results
SSE	vs within group SSE	Evaluating proper cluster solution	SSE decreases fatser then 250 randomized dataset. Cluster size 4.
	vs (SSE- random SSE)	Validation for same	Largest difference between actual and random SSE is at 4
Heirarchial clustering		Find patterns in the feature rich dataset	Dendogram- Cluster feature map
clValid- cluster validation		Cluster solution using hierarchical technique is validated.	For cluster solution 4, Dunn index- 0.28, silhouette- 0.68 and connectivty 11.15
Intercluster distance		Relevance of 4 clusters and redundancy	Intercluster distances are statistically significant.

4.1   Appropriate Cluster Solution Using SSE

To help compute the number of clusters in the data used, the script we wrote in language R conducted additional analysis to evaluate cluster solutions. Specifically, the script produced 250 randomized versions of the original input data, and calculates SSE against cluster solutions for the randomized data. The data is randomized by column, so each variable will have the same mean and standard deviation in both the actual and randomized matrices. If a data set has strong clusters, the SSE of the actual data should decrease more quickly than the random data as than cluster level goes up. Thus, the R algorithm used plots SSE against the number of tested clusters for both the actual and 250 randomized matrices. The plots for this treatment has been presented in figure 4.1.

---

[2] K-Means Cluster Analysis in R: http://www.mattpeeples.net/kmeans.html

In our analysis of the data, the SSE for the actual data does decrease faster than the 250 randomized data sets. This suggests that the data set has structure and clusters are present. There is somewhat of a reduction in the rate of SSE decreases after the 4 cluster solution. However, the "elbow" in the plot is not extreme and thus, further evaluation would be appropriate.

Another way to evaluate the appropriate cluster solution is to examine the absolute difference between the actual and random SSE against the tested cluster solutions. An appropriate cluster solution could be defined as the solution at which the actual SSE differs the most from the mean of the random SSE. To facilitate this comparison, the absolute difference between the actual and random (mean of all runs) SSE against the cluster solutions is also displayed. One standard deviation above and below the mean absolute difference are also shown. The plot for this treatment is as follows-

In the plots above, the greatest absolute difference between actual and random SSE occurs at the 4 cluster solution. This suggests that this cluster solution may be an appropriate level to test. The fact that this cluster solution also coincides with the possible "elbow" in the plot of SSE against random SSE shown above provides additional information supporting this cluster solution. These methods therefore gives an idea of the number of clusters that may be present in the data we are dealing with to be about 4.Moreover,this is also in confirmation with the hypothesis that we had started with, that relationships(tie strength) should fall into 4 criteria-strong ties, acquaintance (strong and weak acquintance ties) and weak ties.

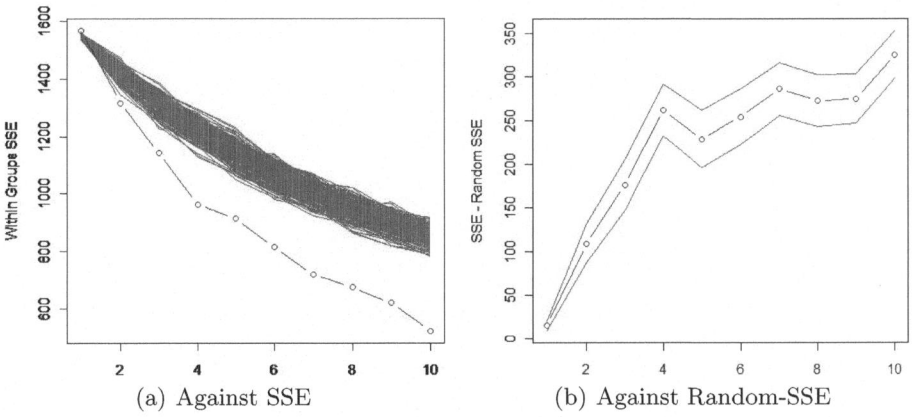

(a) Against SSE   (b) Against Random-SSE

Fig. 2. Cluster solution against (a) and (b)

4.2   Identifying Tie-Strength Using Hierarchial Clustering

Connectivity based clustering, also known as hierarchical clustering, is based on the core idea of objects being more related to nearby objects than to objects farther away. As such, these algorithms connect "objects" to form "clusters" based on their distance, a cluster can be described largely by the maximum distance needed to connect parts of the cluster,providing an extensive hierarchy of clusters that divide at certain distances, represented in the form of a dendogram. In a dendrogram, the y-axis marks the distance at which the clusters divide, while the objects are placed along the x-axis such that the clusters don't mix. In cluster analysis, single linkage, nearest neighbor or shortest distance is a method of calculating distances between clusters in hierarchical clustering, where the distance between two clusters is computed as the distance between the two closest elements in the two clusters. Mathematically, the linkage function - the distance D(X, Y) between clusters X and Y - is described by the expression

$$D(X,Y) = \min_{x \epsilon X, y \epsilon Y} d(x,y) \tag{1}$$

Where X and Y are any two sets of elements considered as clusters, and d (x, y) denotes the distance between the two elements x and y. As it is evident from the dendogram obtained by us, the relationship a person shares with any person could be classified into any one of the 4 types of tie strength. However, even though the relationships falling into the 4 clusters of tie strength have been determined, we are faced with the problem of determining which cluster corresponds to which type of tie strength. To solve this problem, normalized values of parameters like wall words exchanged, comments exchanged etc. are evaluated, after which the clusters are identified by the way that the normalized values of parameters like number of wall posts,number of mutual friends etc. would be characterized in strong ties, followed by acquaintance(strong and weak respectively) and weak ties.

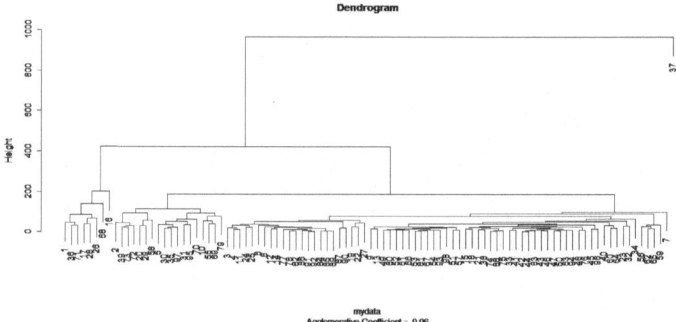

Fig. 3. Dendogram

4.3   Validating Cluster Solution by clValid

The clValid package offers three types of cluster validation, "internal", "stability", and "biological"[2]. Internal validation measures take only the dataset and the clustering partition as input and use intrinsic information in the data to assess the quality of the clustering. For internal validation, we selected measures that reflect the compactness, connectedness, and separation of the cluster partitions. Connectedness relates to what extent observations are placed in the same cluster as their nearest neighbors in the data space, and is here measured by the connectivity [11]. Compactness assesses cluster homogeneity, usually by looking at the intra-cluster variance, while separation quantities the degree of separation between clusters (usually by measuring the distance between cluster centroids). Since compactness and separation demonstrate opposing trends (compactness increases with the number of clusters but separation decreases), popular methods combine the two measures into a single score. The Dunn Index [6] and Silhouette Width[16] are both examples of non-linear combinations of the compactness and separation, and with the connectivity comprise the three internal measures available in clValid .

Connectivity

Let N denote the total number of observations (rows) in a dataset and M denote the total number of columns, which are assumed to be numeric (e.g., a collection of samples, time points, etc.). Define $nn_{i(j)}$ as the jth nearest neighbor of observation i, and let $x_{i,nn_{i(j)}}$ be zero if i and j are in the same cluster and $1 = j$ otherwise. Then, for a particular clustering partition $Ç = \{C_1, ..., C_K\}$ of the N observations into K disjoint clusters, the connectivity is given in equation 2.

$$Conn(C) = \sum_{i=1}^{N} \sum_{j=1}^{L} x_{i,nn_{i(j)}} \qquad (2)$$

where L is a parameter giving the number of nearest neighbors to use. The connectivity has a value between zero and 1 and should be minimized.

Silhouette Width

The Silhouette Width is the average of each observation's Silhouette value and is defined as given in equation 3.

$$S(i) = \frac{b_i - a_i}{max(b_i, a_i)} \qquad (3)$$

where a_i is the average distance between i and all other observations in the same cluster, and b_i is the average distance between i and the observations in the nearest neighboring cluster", i.e.

$$a_i = \frac{1}{n(C(i))} \sum_{j \epsilon C_i} dist(i,j) \quad , \quad b_i = \min_{C_k \epsilon C \backslash C(i)} \sum_{j \epsilon C_k} \frac{dist(i,j)}{n(C_k)} \qquad (4)$$

where C(i) is the cluster containing observation i, dist(i; j) is the distance (e.g. Euclidean, Manhattan) between observations i and j, and n(C) is the cardinality of cluster C. The Silhouette Width thus lies in the interval [-1,1], and should be maximized.

Dunn Index

The Dunn Index is the ratio of the smallest distance between observations not in the same cluster to the largest intra-cluster distance as given in equation 5.

Table 2. Features derived from various clustering techniques

Method	Parameter	Value	Method	Parameter	Value
	Connectivity	11.1528		Connectivity	24.2992
Hierarchical	Dunn	0.2767	Pam	Dunn	0.0131
	Silhoutte	0.6763		Silhoutte	0.4262
	Connectivity	11.2603		Connectivity	15.0131
K-means	Dunn	0.1574	Sota	Dunn	0.1681
	Silhoutte	0.6302		Silhoutte	0.639
	Connectivity	19.0611		Connectivity	20.556
Dianna	Dunn	0.0905	Clara	Dunn	0.0385
	Silhoutte	0.6062		Silhoutte	0.429
	Connectivity	26.4448		Connectivity	22.8246
Fanny	Dunn	0.0117	Som	Dunn	0.0085
	Silhoutte	0.4202		Silhoutte	0.4291

$$D(C) = \frac{\min\limits_{C_k, C_l \in C, C_k \neq C_l} \left(\min\limits_{i \in C_k, j \in C_l} dist(i,j) \right)}{\max\limits_{C_m \in C} diam(C_m)} \tag{5}$$

where $diam(C_m)$ is the maximum distance between observations in cluster Cm. The Dunn Index has a value between zero and 1, and should be maximized.

4.4 Intercluster Distance and Cluster Size

The Intercluster distance between the 4 clusters determined in the dataset used is evaluated to confirm that there aren't any redundant cluster being analyzed as a part of our research. Here, as a part of our work, 3 types of inter cluster distances are studied and presented.

- Single Distance or the shortest distance between 2 clusters
- Average Distance or the distance between the means of the 2 clusters
- Centroidal Distance or the distance between the centroids of 2 clusters.

Moreover,the size of each and every cluster determined as- 8, 17, 29 and 44 further confirm that none of the clusters analyzed is statistically insignificant to other clusters.

5 Discussion

After the process of data collection is completed, every participant is mailed a questionnaire, questioning them regarding the relation or the tie strength they share with the friends with whom their relation has been analyzed, which enables us to validate our work by comparing the tie strength predicted by us and the tie strength as told by the participant. As represented in the dendogram, the dendogram predicts that there are 8 weak ties, 18 strong ties, 24 strong acquaintances and 50 weak acquaintances. After validation it was confirmed that the number of weak ties were 11, number of strong ties were 20 strong acquaintances were

Table 3. Intercluster Distances

Shortest Inter-Cluster Distance			
Clusters	C1	C2	C3	C4
C1	0	84.71	328.68	372.86
C2	84.71	0	41.19	82.35
C3	328.67	41.19	0	8.3
C4	372.86	82.35	8.30	0

Inter Cluster Distance(Average Distance)			
Clusters	C1	C2	C3	C4
C1	0	346.03	538.22	541.85
C2	346.03	0	207.72	206.63
C3	538.22	207.71	0	83.69
C4	541.86	206.63	83.69	0

Inter Cluster Distance(Centroidal)			
Clusters	C1	C2	C3	C4
C1	0	340.96	536.17	539.6
C2	340.96	0	199.7	199.25
C3	536.17	199.7	0	70.67
C4	539.6	199.25	70.67	0

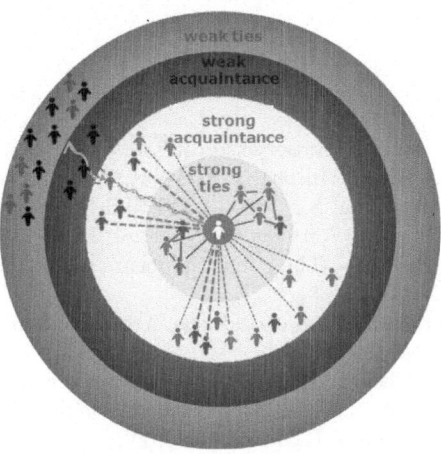

Fig. 4. Types of Tie Strengths

22 and the number of weak acquaintances were 47, thereby giving us an accuracy of 90% in predicting tie strength between individuals. A confidence interval gives an estimated range of values which is likely to include an unknown population parameter, the estimated range being calculated from a given set of sample data which is 100 nodes out of total population size 800 million people who are part of Facebook. However, as discussed in earlier sections, the confidence interval obtained for our dataset is 5.88%, due to which accuracy of tie strength predictability of our method is from $84.12\%(90 - 5.88)$ to $95.88(90 + 5.88)$.

Figure 4 illustrates the classification of relationships into various categories-strong,strong acquaintances,weak acquaintances and weak ties. Moreover, it also illustrates how relationships start as acquaintances, and then undergo transition to strong or weak ties with the progress of time.

6   Conclusion and Future Work

In this paper, we have worked upon identifying and calculating strengths of different kind of relationships, (*ties*) exhibited by individuals on the social network Facebook and draw some concrete analogies about how these are similar to real life relationships. Our results based on 15 edge to edge features (friend to friend network in Facebook's context) show that there are 4 different kinds of tie-strengths visible in a network i.e. strong, weak, strong- acquaintance and weak acquaintance. We have also investigated the process of finding optimum number of clusters based on variety of techniques as discussed in section 4 and further make primary attempts to measure the boundary strengths between 4 kinds of tie-strengths. Our proposed approach brings radicle change in the understanding of the relationship behavior of the people based on online activity and makes us realize how a particular relationship matures from kind of tie-strengths to another over the period of time. However, due to certain limitations of the time period of dataset collection process, in future we wish to replicate this study over larger and complex dataset from variety of other social networks like Twitter, LinkedIn etc.

References

1. Backstrom, L., Leskovec, J.: Supervised random walks: predicting and recommending links in social networks. In: 4th WSDM, WSDM 2011 (2011)
2. Brock, G., Pihur, V., Datta, S., Datta, S.: clvalid: An r package for cluster validation. Journal of Statistical Software 25(4), 1–28 (2008)
3. Burt, R.S.: Structural Holes: The Social Structure of Competition, vol. 58. Harvard University Press (1992)
4. Burt, R.S.: Structural holes and good ideas. American Journal of Sociology 110(2), 349–399 (2004)
5. Domingos, P., Richardson, M.: Mining the network value of customers. In: Proceedings of the Seventh ACM SIGKDD International Conference on Knowledge Discovery and Data Mining, KDD 2001 (2001)
6. Dunn, J.C.: Well separated clusters and optimal fuzzy-partitions. Journal of Cybernetics 4, 95–104 (1974)
7. Espinoza, F.A., Oliver, J.M., Wilson, B.S., Steinberg, S.L.: Using hierarchical clustering and dendrograms to quantify the clustering of membrane proteins. Bulletin of Mathematical Biology (2011)
8. Gilbert, E., Karahalios, K.: Predicting tie strength with social media. In: 27th HFCS, CHI 2009 (2009)
9. Granovetter, M.S.: Getting a job: A study of contacts and careers. University of Chicago Press (1995)
10. Granovetter, M.S.: The strength of weak ties. American Journal of Sociology, 1360–1380 (1973)
11. Handl, J., Knowles, J., Kell, D.B.: Computational cluster validation in post-genomic data analysis. Bioinformatics 21 (August 2005)
12. Hansen, M.T.: The search-transfer problem: The role of weak ties in sharing knowledge across organization subunits. Administrative Science Quarterly 44(1), 82 (1999)

13. Kossinets, G., Watts, D.J.: Empirical analysis of an evolving social network. Science 311(5757), 88–90 (2006)
14. Lin, N., Ensel, W.M., Vaughn, J.C.: Social resources and strength of ties: Structural factors in occupational status attainment. American Sociological Review 46(4), 393–405 (1981)
15. Neville, J., Simsek, O., Jensen, D., Komoroske, J., Palmer, K., Goldberg, H.: Using relational knowledge discovery to prevent securities fraud. In: 11th ACM SIGKDD, KDD 2005 (2005)
16. Rousseeuw, P.: Silhouettes: a graphical aid to the interpretation and validation of cluster analysis. J. Comput. Appl. Math. 20 (November 1987)
17. Schaefer, C., Coyne, J.C., Lazarus, R.S.: The health-related functions of social support 4(4), 381–406 (1981)
18. Tichy, N.M., Tushman, M.L., Fombrun, C.: Social network analysis for organizations. Academy of Management Review 4(4) (1979)
19. Wellman, B., Wortley, S.: Different strokes from different folks: Community ties and social support. American Journal of Sociology 96(3), 558–588 (1990)
20. Xiang, R., Neville, J., Rogati, M.: Modeling relationship strength in online social networks. In: 19th WWW, WWW 2010 (2010)
21. Zhao, J., Wu, J., Feng, X., Xiong, H., Xu, K.: Information propagation in online social networks: a tie-strength perspective

Appendix

Error Analysis

The model described above performed relatively well in predicting tie strength; however, it is not perfect, especially in differentiating between a weak tie and an acquaintance. To understand its limitations, we conducted seven interviews, out of which two are presented in the paper to give an idea as to the problems faced by the model in estimating tie strength, with some problems being fundamental to all social networks, irrespective of the model adopted to analyze them-

1. I don't know why he befriended me on Facebook ? Inspite of going to the same school and have a few friends in common, as a result of us belonging to the same school and class in particular, but there hasn't been any interaction between us aside from befriending each other on Facebook.

Rating: Weak Prediction: Acquaintance: This case illustrates the error induced in our model due to the fact that even though there is no contact between the members currently. Model predicts the relationship between them to be that of acquaintances due to the two people sharing a common school, thereby leading to a common network and a set of mutual friends.

2. Ah Yes! This friend is an old ex? We haven't spoken to each other in about 7 years after our split, although we ended up befriending each other on Facebook when I first joined it a few years ago. But the relationship maybe still important to me as we were best friends for 4 years even before we dated.Optimistically hoping we will recover and maybe regain some of the friendship we had. However, it hasn't happened yet though.

Rating: Acquaintance Prediction: Weak: This case illustrates the error induced in our model due to the fact that even though the relationship we are dealing with, in this case is that of an acquaintance, the model predicts a weak relationship because the real world relationship between the 2 people existed before the existence of Facebook and the real world relationship between them never translated into a virtual relation on Facebook.

Table 4. Questionnaire

Q1. How Strong is your relationship with this person?
a) Barely know him/her (Weak)
b) He/She is an acquaintance
c) We are very close
Answer:
Q2. How would you feel asking this friend to loan you Rs.1000?
a) Would never ask
b) Very comfortable
Answer:
Q3. How helpful would this person be if you were looking for a job?
a) No help at all
b) Very helpful
Answer:
Q4. How upset would you be if this person unfriended you?
a) Not upset at all
b) Very upset
Answer:
Q5. How likely would you migrate to another social networking website with your friend??
a) Would not matter
b) Would matter due to professional relationship
c) Must bring them along due to close friendship
Answer:

Context Based Relevance Evaluation of Web Documents

Pooja Gupta

Maharaja Agrasen Institute of Technology,
GGSIPU, NewDelhi
poojaguptamait@gmail.com

Abstract. Focused crawling is considered to be an important strategy to reduce search space and give more relevant links to a user, based on search queries. Existing web crawlers work only on the basis of full string matching of query keywords with words present in various tags or fields in the web pages. But a particular keyword can have different meanings in different contexts depending on its usage as verb, noun etc. For example *'fly' refers to an insect if used as a noun and refers to an act of moving in the air if used as a verb.* Most of the existing search engines work on semantic context, based on string matching of keywords but not based on contextual senses of keywords. Further, general crawling strategy of various crawlers is forward oriented, giving less consideration to the backward links of the page. There is a strong need to work on a crawling strategy that overcomes these gaps. In this paper a mechanism that evaluates the web document on the basis of contextual senses (verb, noun etc.) of the keywords contained in the downloaded page is being proposed. Moreover back-link to a web page has also been analyzed with reference to a specific page providing links related to the page. Consequently, more number of relevant links related to one topic is displayed to the user.

Keywords: Context, Web documents, Back-links, WWW, Relevance, Search Engine, Contextual Senses, Query Response.

1 Introduction

A focused crawler traverses the web only in the relevant sub domain to find out the more specific web pages related to a user query. It has been observed that a particular keyword has various contextual senses in which that word can be used and most of the search engines do not consider [15] this aspect of the context present in various tags or fields in the web page. For Instance a keyword called 'Spider' can be used in many contexts such as arachnid, wanderer (a computer program), computer game and a skillet made of cast iron etc.

In this paper a mechanism that evaluates the web document on the basis of various contextual senses of the keywords contained in the downloaded page is being proposed. Further, general crawling strategy of various crawlers is forward oriented, giving less consideration to the backward links of the page[15]. Whereas it has been observed that if the back-links of a particular web document of interest is also being

M. Parashar et al. (Eds.): IC3 2012, CCIS 306, pp. 201–212, 2012.
© Springer-Verlag Berlin Heidelberg 2012

listed at the same place, web surfer will get more related information [8]. The proposed mechanism also analyses the back-links in reference with the associated link and if found fairly relevant, the web page in question is considered important and stored in the database for future reference along with its more relevant back-links. In this paper, the integrated back-links relevance evaluation technique is used to further refine crawling that provides more number of relevant results in the user specified area of interest. It has been observed that using these technique web pages related to other topic/s but within the same scope is also displayed in top 10 results replenishing with more appropriate information.

2   Related Work

The available research in the area implicate that most of the search engines find the context of the document considering the web page in which the link to this document is presented as hyperlink [14], using some anchor text surrounding the hyperlink. M. Diligenti [16] had proposed a focused crawling strategy using context graphs, in which the documents related to the same topics are arranged in the single layer of the graph using the standard TF-IDF, the separate graph is generated first for each seed URL and then merged with each other when completed. It also allows back-ward crawling using this graph, but no contextual sense is considered. Bhagwat et al [13] has compared the various clustering algorithms that cluster the web pages or documents, concerning the similarities between the documents based on the semantic of the keywords and then discuss the context disambiguation. The context of a keyword may relate to the semantic meaning of the keyword according to the grammar but the context sense is the sense in which that word may be used. So, the context sense of the user search is important in order to satisfy his need efficiently.

Further, the hyperlink structure of WWW plays a potential role in deciding relevancy of a web page helping the search engine to take decision for satisfying the user query. There are two types of such links present in a web page named as in-links (back-links) and out-links (forward-links). Existing studies on various focused/topical crawlers by various researchers use techniques that select certain text appearing around the hyperlink. The selected text is called as the link context [1], [2], [3].

The back-links of a web page are important in the sense that they help in establishing the relative importance of the source document with the current document. At present comparatively less work has been reported towards this relationship. S. Chakarbarti [8] found that if back-link information is provided to web surfer; the process of information sighting will be much more effective.

The Page Rank algorithm [4], [5] assigns a score to each page considering the number of back-links to this page, more the number of back-links to a web page the more popular it is considered. HITS algorithm [10] assigns a score to a web page based on the authority and hub score, which is in fact the count of forward links from and back-links to that web page. Moreover, HITS algorithm works at query evaluation time, so scores assigns to a web page are query dependent. Guang et al in [7] has proposed a level-based link analysis technique to assign a rank to a web page by using the back-link count to this web page, which is the crawling priority of the web page. N. Chauhan has used the hyperlink anchor text to evaluate the context of the associated page in [9] and applied a filtering mechanism based on linguistic analysis of all context sentences to get the best illustrated context of associated page.

A critical review of the available literature indicates that the search engines suffer from the following major drawbacks.

1. The contextual senses of keywords are not considered to be important.
2. All back-links are considered of equal importance without considering the relevance of source document with regards to the target documents.
3. Many back-links may be emanating from irrelevant web pages and therefore number of quantity of such links alone can not be the criterion of measuring relevance or importance of the web pages.

In this paper a context based relevance evaluation technique that not only evaluate the context of a web page in respect to the contextual senses of the keywords embedded in it but also finds contextually related back-links, that helps maintaining the list of contextually related web documents to serve a user query more efficiently by providing more relevant pages in top positions.

3   The Proposed Mechanism for Contextual Sense Based Relevance Evaluation

The WWW is a potential source of huge amount of information in diverse topics, putting a challenge for search engines to make only the relevant information resources available to the user whenever needed, thus the need to get the topic/contextual sense of the information present in hyperlinked web documents. In this paper a mechanism 'contextual sense based relevance evaluation' is being presented in which keywords' frequency and their various contextual senses are taken into consideration to compute the contextual sense/topic of the web document and to analyze the relevance of back-links with the associated document. In order to implement this mechanism the hyperlink structure of web documents is used as an inherent source of information to get frequencies of keywords at various places in hypertext web document and their different contextual senses. The block diagram of architecture framework is shown in Fig. 1. The architecture framework provides the functionality to evaluate a web document in respect to various contextual senses of keywords and to compute the relevance score of back-links to a web documents. The respective updates are made to the repository for further usage.

The architecture consists of six major components; the brief functionality of these components is manifested in Table 1.

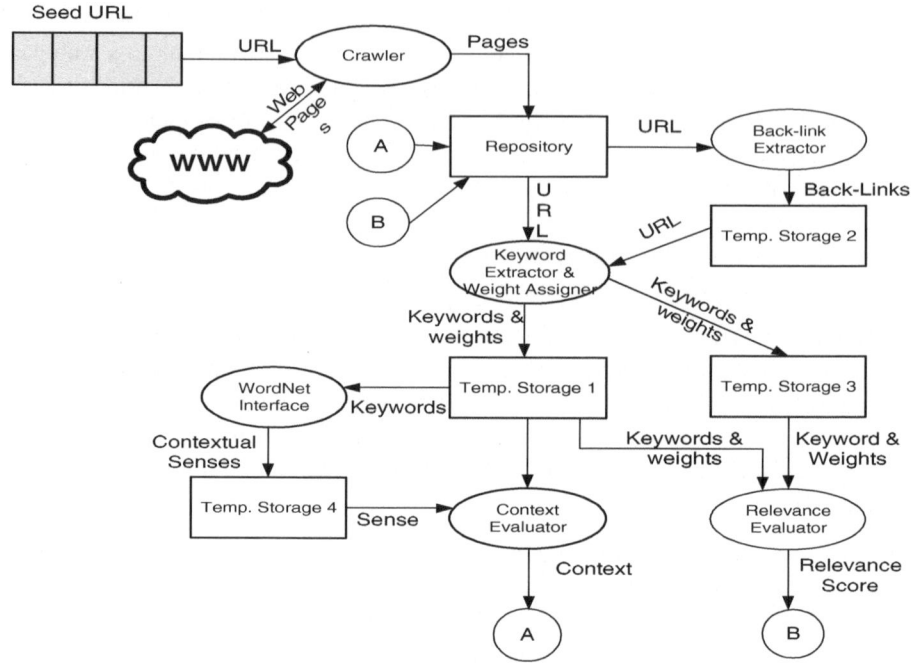

Fig. 1. Architecture Framework

Table 1. Architecture Components and Functionality

Components	Functionality
Crawler	It takes the input URLs from the seed URL list and download the respective web document from WWW and then extracts all out-links from the web documents, stores the downloaded web pages to repository
Back-link Extractor	It takes the URL from the repository and extract all the back-links of that URL
Keyword Extractor and Weight Assigner	It takes the input in the form of URL from the repository and back-link repository, results with extraction of keywords with their occurrence frequency, assigns weights to all keywords corresponding to their occurrences in various HTML tags and computes the accumulated weights
WordNet Interface	This designed interface is used to pass the list of keywords to wordnet dictionary and to get the different contextual senses of keywords
Context Evaluator	It evaluates the context of the web document by taking the list of keywords with corresponding accumulated weights as one input and various contextual senses of keywords from the WordNet Interface as second input. It updates the repository with computed context of the web page.
Relevance Evaluator	It computes the relevance score of back-links w.r.t the associated web page by taking the list of keywords and corresponding accumulated weights of back-links web page and associated web page and update the repository with this information

The architecture framework shown in Fig.1 has two main plug-in components 'context evaluator' and 'relevance evaluator'. The process of context evaluation is explained in section 3.1.1 and of relevance evaluation is explained in section 3.1.2.

3.1   Extraction of Contextual Senses

The occurrence of various keywords at various tags in a hypertext web document is quite significant. For instance, a keyword present in the HEAD Tag of the web page is highly significant as compared to the keywords present in MetaKeyword Tag or in MetaD Tags. After careful observation, in this work the various HTML Tags have been assigned weights on the basis of their significance. Further, the context of the web page is a piece of text that contributes towards assigning meaning of a web document in view of its embedded keywords. However, a keyword may have more than one contextual sense or meanings known as 'polysemy'. For example, the word 'wood' has 8 different contextual senses as listed in Table 2.

Table 2. Contextual Senses of Word, *Wood*

S. No.	Contextual sense
1	Plant material
2	Forest
3	US film actress
4	Henry Wood (writer)
5	US Painter
6	Wind instrument
7	Golf Club
8	English Conductor

It has been observed that if the web pages for 'wood' are searched without any contextual sense, search engine may return all or most of the web pages containing word 'wood' but in different senses and if contextual senses are considered during the search more relevant pages will be returned in response to a submitted query. In this work, for the purpose of getting the various contextual senses of a keyword the WordNet dictionary tool [12] has been used.

3.1.1 Evaluation of Web Documents Using Contextual Senses

On the basis of the frequency of occurrence of various keywords in various HTML tags; the web page can be analyzed corresponding to different contextual senses of keywords present within the web page to get the context/topic of that web page. The data flow between the components of framework, for computing the context of a web page w.r.t. various contextual senses is shown in Fig 2.

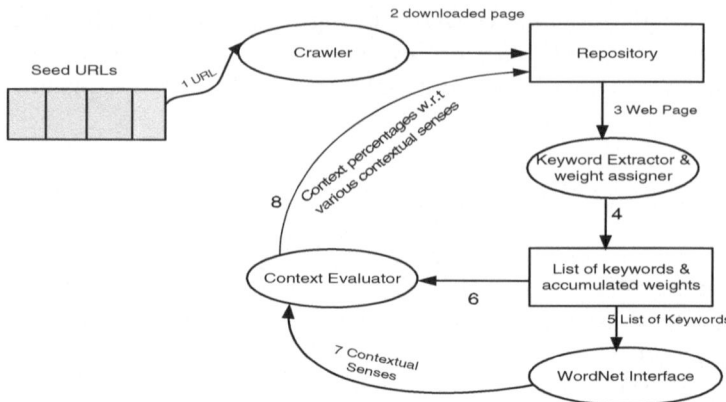

Fig. 2. Context Evaluation

The context evaluation process considers different contextual senses of the keywords (refer Fig. 2) to find out the topic of the web page based on the occurrence frequency and accumulated weight of the keywords. Keyword extractor provides the list of keywords and assigns the weight corresponding to their occurrence frequency at various HTML tags. The top few higher weighted keywords are then processed to get their different contextual senses and corresponding definitions. The context evaluator matches the contextual sense definitions with the list of keywords in the web page under consideration. The contextual sense to which the highest number of keyword is matched is considered as the context of that web page. This context is used to decide whether the page will be displayed to the user for a particular contextual sense or not.

3.1.2 Evaluation of Web Documents Using Back-Links' Relevance

As discussed in section 2, the back-links play an important role while serving the user query with a set of relevant documents. With the help of the weights assigned to keywords present in back-link page in various HTML Tags, the relevancy of back-links of a web page can be computed. The data flow between architecture framework's components for computing the relevance of back-links to a web page is as shown in Fig. 3

The back-link relevance evaluator module finds the relevance score of a back-link page with respect to the web page under consideration. The lists of keywords with corresponding accumulated weight for back-link page and for the web page are taken as input. Relevance evaluator analyzes these lists of keywords in order to get a match within back-link page and web page and computes the fraction to which back-link page is related to the same topical area as of web page. The relevance score is assigned based on this matching fraction. It has been observed that back-link with a higher relevance score is more relevant to the same topical area as of web page and considered as a high-quality link to display to the user interested in that topic. Thus, the back-link with a significantly high relevance score are acknowledged as an acceptable source of information in same topical area.

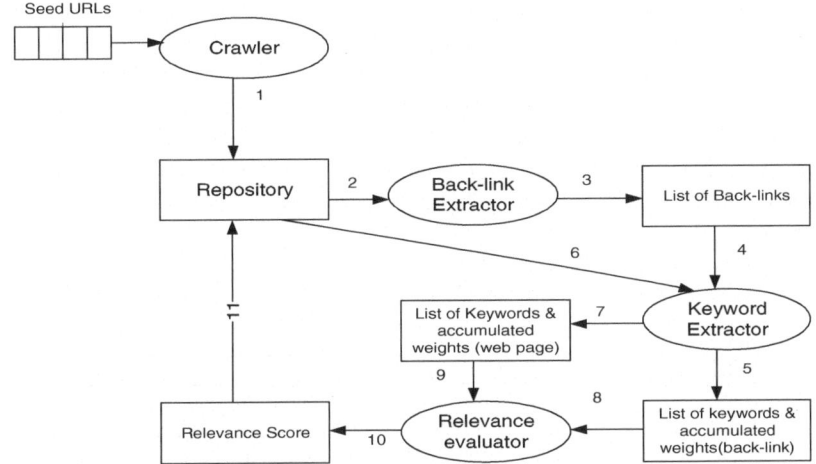

Fig. 3. Back-link Relevance Evaluation

The context of the web page in respect to the contextual senses of the various keywords present in the web page has been evaluated. The web pages having high match value are considered to be more contextually related to that sense and given query; the relevance score of back-links to these web pages is computed to find out the more relevant back-links to be displayed to the user. Thus if a particular web page is evaluated to best suited a query, its back-links with significant relevance fraction can also be displayed to the user, providing more specific information in desired topical area.

4   Experimentation/Results

Based on the processes mentioned in section 3 (Fig. 2, Fig. 3), experiments are performed on some set of URLs taken from the list of URLs crawled by the crawler, for both sections 3.1.1 and 3.1.2. Section 4.1 is showing results for context evaluation of a web page and section 4.2 is showing the results for relevance evaluation of back-links of a web page respectively. The data test for both the sections consisted of an initial set of 50 URLs and each URL consist of an average 1729 number of keywords. It has been observed from the results that for each keyword in a web document average number of contextual senses are '8'. It has also been examined from the results that a particular web document may serve 2 to 3 almost related contextual senses but more appropriate to one contextual sense only.

4.1   Results of Using Contextual Senses in Evaluation of a Web Document

Further, based on the process discussed in section 3.1.1, to compute the context of a web page, dataset containing 20 initial URLs has been taken. For the purpose of showing results while considering the space constraint, for instance, the URL 'http://en.wikipedia.org/wiki/Spider' is picked as initial URL and a total of '2586' different keywords are found in the corresponding web page. For top 5 weighted keywords 'Spider', 'Species', 'Web', 'Prey' and 'Silk' total 16 different contextual senses are obtained from the WordNet. The web page is then analyzed for these senses and it has been observed for the first sense 'Arachnid' of top most keyword 'Spider' the context match percentage obtained is 0.51. On similar basis another web page related to 'mouse' is analyzed, the experimental result sets obtained are as shown in Table 3.

Table 3. Results Set for Web Page Related to 'Mouse'

Set No.	Number of records
Set 1	'20' initial URLs has been taken
Set 2	'1658' keywords are found in one particular web page
Set 3	For top '5' highest weight keywords present in the same page, total '18' different contextual senses are obtained
Set 4	Context match percentage varies from '0.43' to '0.039' and even 'Zero' for some contextual senses

The above analysis on the web page shows that it suited the best to one contextual sense, and may also contextually related to other senses. For example, the web page for 'mouse_computing' is relating 'mouse' in sense of 'computer mouse' to 43% and in sense of 'computer manipulation' to 23% . It means that this document can be used in the sense 'computer mouse' and can also be considered in sense 'computer manipulation'.

4.2   Results of Prioritizing Back-Links in Evaluation of Web Documents

Based on the relevance evaluator module mentioned in section 3.1.2, to show the evaluation process for computing the relevance of back-links for a particular web page, back-links up to a level of 4 are considered. The experimental result sets for a particular web page and its back-links are as shown in Table 4.

Table 4. (Results for Back-Link Relevance Evaluation for Page Related to 'Mouse')

Set No.	Number of records
Set 1	Out of number of back-links obtained for result analysis purpose back-links to level 4 are considered
Set 2	'723' keywords obtained in back-link at level 1
Set 3	'1658' keywords in associated web page
Set 4	About '210' common keywords
Set 5	Relevance score varies from '0.13', '0.23', '0.39' to '0.37'

On similar basis to show the results, URLs related to different topics 'Mouse Computing', 'Kuk-war', 'Academics', and 'Web Crawler' are taken as input, the analysis in respect to relevance score (RS) is done . Due to the limitation regarding showing the calculations for all the considered back-links up to level 4, only the final results obtained by proposed mechanism has been shown in Table 5.

Table 5. RS of Back-Links up to Level 4

Back-link Level	RS (Mouse Computing)	RS (KUK War)	RS (Academic)	RS (WebCrawler)
1	0.134631	0.577223	1.05	0.273
2	0.23655042	0.350524	0.40	0.039735
3	0.39145715	0.145044	0.43	0.054184
4	0.376317924	0.373086	0.567233	0.004816

A graph is plotted for back-links up to level 4 and their respective relevance score as shown in Fig 4.

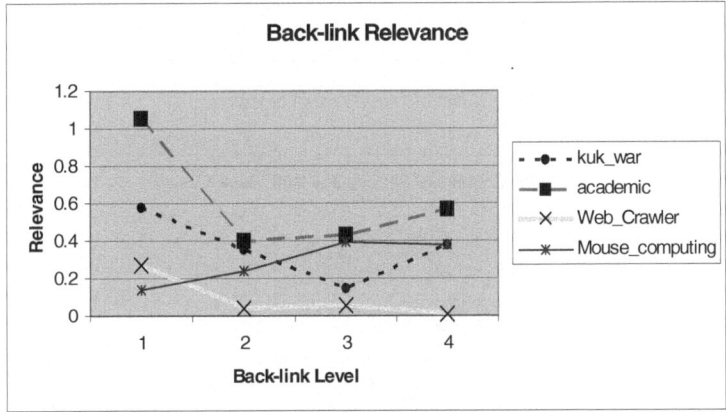

Fig. 4. Back-link Relevance

Further, the back-links contextual relevance score analysis shows that not all the back-links to a web page are equally important i.e. only some of them are more relevant to the web page and can be a good source of information in that particular area. The list of documents related to one topic thus obtained are stored in database with their respective contextual senses and scores for future reference; that helps in resolve the user query with more number of relevant documents.

The analysis of top 10 results displayed in response to a query in two different scenarios is done. First is called 'Without Contextual Senses and Without Back-Link' where, no contextual sense information and no back-link information is being used and second is called 'With Contextual Senses and With Back-links' where contextual senses as well as back-links information is provided. It is cleared that the results displayed to the user in the second scenario are better. The resultant web pages are prorated in 3 categories as 'Related to topic', 'Related to other Useful topics in the same Area' and 'Unrelated'. The graphs plotted for both scenarios are as shown in Fig. 5 and Fig. 6 respectively.

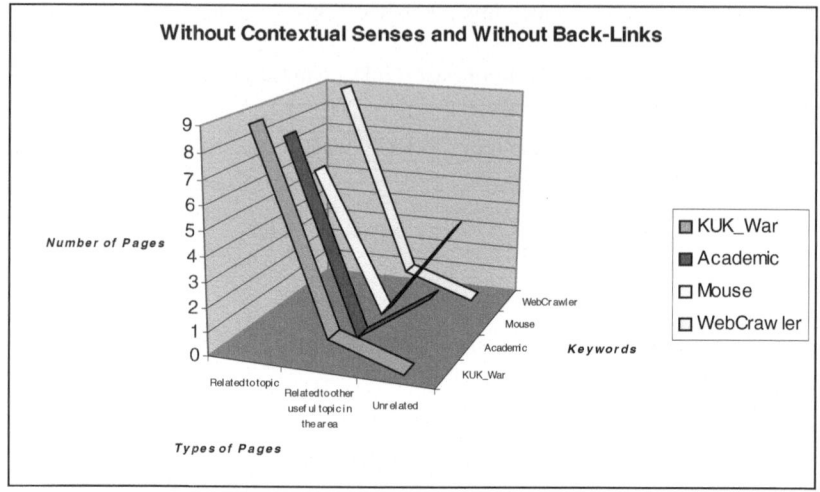

Fig. 5. Result Analysis in Scenario '1'

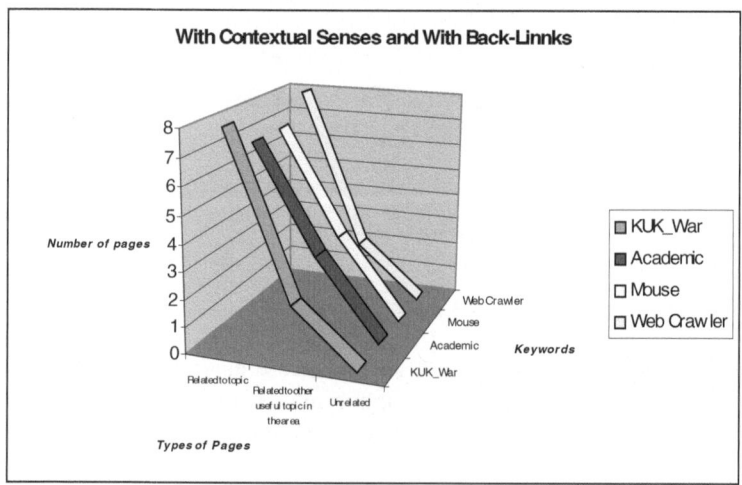

Fig. 6. Result Analysis in Scenario '2'

It is illuminated from Fig. 6 that number of unrelated web pages in top 10 results displayed to the user in scenario '2' for every topic is 'Zero' whereas in scenario '1' unrelated results may occur in some cases (Fig. 5). Thus, if contextual sense present to the user it helps in providing more relevant results and added information in the same area is provided using highly related back-links.

5   Conclusions

The context based focused search engine works to get contextually related documents to serve a user query in order to result with more number of relevant documents related to the user interest. It has been observed that if a document serves a user query well, its parent documents may also serve well. Therefore, back-links of URLs are considered important in order to retrieve more relevant documents for a given query. In addition, not all the back-link URLs are important. Thus, in this work a technique has also been proposed which finds the relevant back-links by computing their relevance score. The proposed technique first finds out the web pages that are contextually more related to the query keyword and then compute the relevance score of back-links of those web pages to find out the more relevant back-links, to be displayed to the users. It has been observed from the results that a pair of URLs having significant high relevance score(RS) score are more related to the web page as compared to those having less significant relevance score, thus are less related to the topic of the web page (WP) taken into consideration. Thus only the important pairs of URLs are stored for the future reference to serve the query.

Acknowledgement. I would like to express my deep and sincere gratitude to my supervisor, Dr. Sandeep Singh for his support and constant supervision as well as for providing necessary information and guidance required in writing this paper. His detailed and constructive comments during the result analysis and editing of the paper have provided a good basis for the present paper.

References

1. Chakarbarti, S., Punera, K., Subramanyam, M.: Accelerated Focused Crawling through Online Relevance Feedback. In: Proc. 11th Int'l World Wide Web Conf. (2002)
2. Hersovici, M., Jacovi, M., Maarek, Y.S., Pelleg, D., Shtalhaim, M., Ur, S.: The Shark-Serach Algorithm –An Application: Tailored Web Site Mapping. In: Proc. Seventh Int'l World Wide Web Conf. (1998)
3. Pant, G., Menczer, F.: Topical Crawling for Business Intelligence. In: Koch, T., Sølvberg, I.T. (eds.) ECDL 2003. LNCS, vol. 2769, pp. 233–244. Springer, Heidelberg (2003)
4. Brin, S., Page, L.: The Anatomy of a Large-Scale Hypertextual Web Search Engine. In: Seventh Int'l World Wide Web Conf. (1998)
5. Craven, P.: Google's Page Rank Explained, Copyright Web Workshop
6. Davison, B.D.: Topical Locality in the Web. In: Proc. Int'l ACM SIGIR Conf. Research and Development in Information Retrieval (2000)
7. Feng, G., Liu, T.-Y., Zhang, X.-D., Qin, T., Gao, B., Ma, W.-Y.: Level-Based Link Analysis. In: Zhang, Y., Tanaka, K., Yu, J.X., Wang, S., Li, M. (eds.) APWeb 2005. LNCS, vol. 3399, pp. 183–194. Springer, Heidelberg (2005)
8. Chakrabarti, S., Gibson, D.A., McCurley, K.S.: Surfing the Web Backwards. In: The Proceedings of 8th World Wide Web Conferences (1999)
9. Chauhan, N., Sharma, A.K.: A framework to derive web pages context from hyperlink structure. IJICT 1(3/4), 329–346 (2008)

10. Lecture No. 4, HITS Algorithm – Hubs and Authorities on the Internet,
    `http://www.math.cornell.edu/~mec/Winter2009/RalucaRemus/Lecture4/lecture4.html`
11. Gupta, P., Sharma, A.K.: Novel Technique For Back-Link Extraction And Relevance Evaluation. IJCSIT 3(3), 227–238
12. WordNet dictionary
13. Bhagwani, J., Hande, K.: Context Disambiguation in Web Search Results using Clustering Algorithms. IJCSC 2(1), 119–123 (2011)
14. Pant, G.: Deriving Link-Context from HTML Tag Tree. In: Proc. Eighth ACM SIGMOD Workshop Research Issues in Data Mining and Knowledge Discovery (DMKD 2003) (2003)
15. Novak, B.: A Survey of Focused Web Crawling Algorithms. In: Proc. of SIKDD (2004)
16. Diligenti, M., Coetzee, F.M., Lawrence, S., Giles, C.L., Gori, M.: Focused Crawling Using Context Graphs. In: Proceedings of the 26th VLDB Conference, Cairo, Egypt (2000)

A Novel Faster Approximate Fuzzy Clustering Approach with Highly Accurate Results

Gargi Aggarwal and M.P.S. Bhatia

Department of Computer Science, Netaji Subhas Institute of Technology (NSIT)
New Delhi, India
{agg.gargi07,bhatia.mps}@gmail.com

Abstract. Clustering has been used extensively for exploratory data analysis. GK clustering algorithm can provide a data partition that is more meaningful than the standard fuzzy c-means and its variants. In this paper we propose a novel approach towards fuzzy clustering which reduces the processing time significantly while keeping the results highly accurate. It is a matrix based approach using the concept of equivalent samples and the weighting samples. Equivalence is measured in terms of proximity of the samples and then weighted samples are used as an input to the modified GK clustering algorithm. Objective function and validation index estimates are used to assess the goodness of partition. Experimental results are shown to emphasize the benefits of the proposed technique in domains like Telecom where we have massive data sets to be processed for real time clustering and recommendation engines.

Keywords: Fuzzy Clustering, Gustafson Kessel Algorithm, Matrix formation, Validation index.

1 Introduction

Clustering is a major tool for data analysis [1,2] and interpretation. Fuzzy Set theory proposed by Zadeh [3] was a major breakthrough in 1965. It helped us to look at membership values instead of just "yes" or "no" in terms of a data point being a member of a set or not. Now a point had a 'degree' of closeness or degree of membership towards the clusters identified. In real world scenario, it may not be feasible to have this black and white assignment for every point to a cluster and thus this concept has direct application in real environment [4] where we can have degrees of grey.

The most widely used fuzzy clustering algorithm is the Fuzzy C-means Algorithm (FCM) [2]. But this has a major drawback in the sense that the distance metric used is the Euclidean distance and hence it does not respond well in identifying non-spherical clusters. To detect varied geometrical shaped clusters, Fuzzy c-means algorithm was extended by Gustafson and Kessel [5] by using an adaptive distance function.

A major issue with these algorithms is that they have a lot of iterations (due to multiple computations done for each and every point) and thus with large data sets the process becomes time consuming thereby impacting the clustering performance.

M. Parashar et al. (Eds.): IC3 2012, CCIS 306, pp. 213–224, 2012.
© Springer-Verlag Berlin Heidelberg 2012

For instance in telecom domain, we need to analyze data sets with millions of data points. We need an approach which retains the key benefits of the GK algorithm while greatly reducing the computational time.

We propose a novel approach towards reducing the processing time, where we modify the GK algorithm to accommodate weighted representative points of the given data set. Experimental results show that this method can give highly accurate clustering results (corroborated via objective function and validation index estimates) while greatly reducing the computational time.

This paper is organized into six sections. Section 2 briefly discusses the related work. Section 3 discusses the datasets that we have used for our experiments. Section 4 discusses our proposed approach where we give the details of the pre-processing done on the data, how the data is reduced, modifications that have been made in the GK clustering algorithm, etc. Section 5 presents experimental results, while Section 6 gives the conclusions.

2   Literature Survey

With the advancements in business analytics, personal computing technology, image processing mechanisms and easy and cheap access to the storage media, we now have humongous data in front of us which needs real time analysis to derive meaning out of it. Researchers lately have tried to speed up the processing of such huge data sets by employing various techniques.

One of the tangents that researchers have explored is through the training of artificial neural networks. Here the gradient between the two iterations of clustering algorithm is considered [7]. In [8] an approximation method for fuzzy and possibilistic kernel c-means clustering algorithm is proposed. It constrains the cluster centers to be linear combinations of a size m randomly selected subset of the n input objects, where m ≪ n. It causes significant memory savings and up to 3 orders of magnitude of speedup are possible.In [9], data is reduced to speed up the clustering process. To reduce the work space Principal Component Analysis (PCA) is used here. The proposed reduction can be used as a pre-processing technique before any clustering task. Initialization of the cluster centers is another way to speed up clustering. This helps in reduction of the number of iterations to be done by the clustering algorithm. [10] Proposes such a technique. It deals with quadratic entropy fuzzy c-means using regularization function, quadratic terms, mean distance functions and kernel distance functions. It uses silhouette method to obtain the cluster validity and choosing the number of clusters. It is a major problem to cluster such data as such a large data set does not usually fit in the memory at the same time. [11] Compares methods used to cluster large data i.e. online fuzzy clustering algorithm and single pass fuzzy clustering algorithms. It uses cluster center location for comparison measurements.

Grid methodology has also got significant attention in order to cluster large databases. They have been used widely in clustering - be it in terms of better initialization or overall approximation. [12] developed a general grid clustering approach that does not require input parameters. It's a combination of divisive and agglomerative clustering algorithms. An incremental clustering algorithm based on grids has been proposed in [13]. It partitions the grid space dynamically to improve clustering. [14] describes an improvement on the mountain method of clustering for non-uniform grids. It uses a p-tree algorithm for the hierarchical partitioning of the data set. [15] developed a simple heuristic approach for approximate estimation of the cluster centers on the basis of the concept of a mountain function. [16] Worked on modifications of mountain method [15] to analyze large data sets and to speed-up the convergence of fuzzy c-means clustering. Original Mountain method was found to be impractical for large data sets.

Fuzzy C-means Clustering has been the prime base methodology underlying varied research work on fuzzy clustering of unsupervised data. Usually with a huge database like that of Telecom sector with millions of records, it is not always possible to identify clear uniform spherical clusters. We in our proposed technique have used a modified version of the GK clustering algorithm which has been identified to work well (owing to the adaptive distance norm – Mahalanobis distance) in such scenarios and hence are able to detect clusters of varied shapes within the same dataset.

We need to consider another issue here – The issue of excessive time consumption in case of larger data sets which is usual in practical domain. Authors have worked on multiple modules to balance these requirements and come up with a solution. This area of research is fairly complex as the two parameters of accuracy and speed, contradict each other.

In order to achieve efficacy, there is a trade-off between accuracy and time saving. The various approaches proposed in this respect so far just help out in initialization or approximations, but their application is limited in large data set domains. Here we propose a novel approach which strives to get faster clustering without much compromise on quality of results (clusters).

3 Data Set Description

Following are the data sets we used for conducting our experiments:

3.1 Iris Data Set

This data set has been taken from the UCI Repository of Machine Learning Databases. It is a very well known database to be used in the pattern recognition literature. There are 3 classes, each having 50 instances. Each class refers to a type of iris plant. The attribute to be predicted after clustering is the class of the iris plant. There are 150 instances and 4 attributes in the data set - sepal length in cm, sepal width in cm, petal length in cm and petal width in cm. For our experiments we are considering only the first two attributes.

3.2 Telecom Data Set

One of the major applications of our approach would be in fields where we have requirements of clustering huge data sets for real time decisions/recommendations. We have taken this data set as a case study from a leading telecom operator in India.

The data is called Site Report in Telecom parlance. The data captures the key parameters of every operational site (Base Transceiver Station). Every Site/Tower is equipped with a capacity which is expressed in Erlangs. So the data set has cell id, location etc along with the key variables – Erlang Equipped and Erlang used which are mapped here for clustering. There are 101450 instances and 11 attributes – Cell ID, Site ID, Location, Date of OnAir, Site Population, FCR, Utilization, Erlang equipped, Erlang used, LAPU Retailer, Tertiary. For the experiments, we are considering two of these - Erlang Equipped and Erlang used.

4   Novel Approach towards Faster Clustering

4.1   Data Preprocessing

As we have seen that the GK clustering algorithm involves multiple iterations and in each iteration, a distance metric is calculated for each and every point with each of the cluster centre as set in previous iteration. These iterations are repeated while reducing the objective function in each step.

Now consider a domain where we have millions of data sets which are to be clustered on real time basis for a recommendation engine. The original approach is just not viable in such cases. Further in such large data sets, many points are very close and form dense clusters. For example in telecom domain, we shall have millions of instances in the form of users/subscribers. The usage shall be mapped on voice, data and VAS services. Now, there will be many users with similar consumption patterns on these variables and it's just not worth doing millions of these repetitive iterations/computations. Our proposed approach is highly effective in such scenarios.

In our matrix approach, we use a cell width and divide the sample space into multiple cells, which are then used to get weighted mean representation of our data set. This approach significantly reduces the computations (especially the repeated computations due to similar data points among a huge data set) while at the same time keeping the benefits of the GK clustering algorithm. The data points are coupled with their weights and then used for clustering. This helps compensate for the loss of information due to data reduction step.

4.2   GK Clustering Algorithm Using Weighted Data

4.2.1   GK Clustering Algorithm Description

Gustafson-Kessel clustering algorithm employs an adaptive distance norm and hence it is able to detect clusters of different geometrical shapes in the same data set. GK algorithm caters to the drawback of FCM which assumes that all clusters are spherical and uses the standard Euclidean distance norm. GK can detect ellipsoidal clusters as it employs the Mahalanobis distance measure as follows [17]:

$$(D_{pqA})^2 = (x_p - v_q)^T A_q (x_p - v_q), \qquad 1<=q<=c, \ 1<=p<=N \qquad (1)$$

Where D_{pq} is the distance between the qth cluster center v_q and the pth data instance x_p. Total number of clusters is represented by 'c' and the total number of instances in the data set is represented by N. The matrices A_q allow each cluster to adapt the distance to the local structure of the data. It's due to this that GK clustering algorithm can detect different shaped clusters in the same data set.

GK algorithm iteratively optimizes an objective function by alternative calculations of the cluster centers and the membership values. The objective function is:

$$ J = \sum_{q=1}^{c} \sum_{p=1}^{N} u_{pq}^{m} D_{pqA_q}^{2} \tag{2} $$

Where u_{pq} is the membership of the pth data instance in the qth cluster. m is the fuzzifier which controls the amount of fuzziness in the clustering. D_{pq} is the same as equation 1.

The cluster centers are calculated using:

$$ V_q = \sum_{p=1}^{N} u_{pq}^{m} x_p \bigg/ \sum_{p=1}^{N} u_{pq}^{m} \tag{3} $$

Where V_q is the center of the qth cluster.

The membership values of the instances in a cluster are calculated using:

$$ \mu_{pq} = 1 \bigg/ \sum_{j=1}^{c} \left(\frac{D_{pqA_q}(x_p, v_q)}{D_{jp}(x_p, v_j)} \right)^{2/(m-1)} \tag{4} $$

4.2.2 Weighted GK Clustering Algorithm Description
Our proposed approach has been divided into three parts:-

-   Dividing the sample space into cells
-   Reducing the data based on density of each cell
-   Clustering the reduced data using modified GK clustering algorithm

4.2.2.1 Dividing the Sample Space into Cells
The prerequisite for our approach is the division of the sample space into cells. Here the selection of the grid size is very crucial. A large grid size can lead to merging of two or more clusters while small size can lead to increase in the computation time. We make use of uniform grids i.e. the number of grid lines per dimension are the same.

In case of dense data we need a finer resolution of the grid and hence closer grid lines per dimension. When the data is sparse the distance between the grid lines can be increased.

4.2.2.2   Data Reduction

Aggregating the sample points in each cell of the grid is the essence of our data reduction approach. Here we combine the samples based on the proximity between them. A cell is taken as the metric for this distance measurement. The instances in the cell are given a representative point with a suitable weighted metric in order to get a more similar representation of the data set and account for loss of data.

4.2.2.3   Clustering Using Modified GK

After the data reduction, we cluster the weighted instances using modified GK clustering algorithm. The GK algorithm has been modified to cater to the weighted instances.

Let set $Z = \{z_1, z_2, z_3 \ldots z_n\}$ having n samples be the data set to be clustered. Let $Z' = \{z_1', z_2' \ldots z_r'\}$ having r samples be the reduced form of the set Z. Here r<<n. Each z_p' has an associated weight, w_p, which is the number of samples in the cell represented by z_p'.

The modified objective function of the GK clustering algorithm based on our proposed approach is:

$$ J = \sum_{q=1}^{c} \sum_{p=1}^{r} w_p u_{pq}^m D_{pqAq}^2 \tag{5} $$

As for the standard GK clustering algorithm, clustering in our proposed approach is also done by the alternative calculations of the cluster centers and the membership values of the instances in different clusters.

The calculation of the cluster centers is done by the following modified equation:

$$ V_q = \sum_{p=1}^{r} w_p u_{pq}^m z'_p \bigg/ \sum_{p=1}^{r} w_p u_{pq}^m \tag{6} $$

The calculation of the membership values is done by the following modified equation:

$$ \mu_{pq} = 1 \bigg/ \sum_{j=1}^{c} \left({}^{w_p D_{pqA_q}(z'_p, v_q)} \big/ {}_{w_p D_{jp}(z'_p, v_j)} \right)^{2/(m-1)} \tag{7} $$

In this case D_{pq} is the distance between z_p', the representative point of a cell, and v_q which is the center of the qth cluster. w_p is the weight associated with z_p'.

5   Experimental Results

Experimental results have been tabulated for the following data sets – Iris data set and the Telecom data set.

The main motivation behind our work is to lower the computational time by the reduction of the number of samples in the data set. But this reduction is meaningful only when the results are comparable to the standard GK algorithm. Thus to judge the performance of our approach, we present experimental results to show that we have achieved significant reduction in the processing time while keeping the results highly accurate. We also show the tradeoff between speedup and similarity to GK. All the experiments were conducted using Matlab 7.10.0(R2010a) on a Windows 7 Ultimate laptop having 2.00 GB RAM and 32- bit OS. Each test is done for 5 times and the mean value is recorded.

5.1   Iris Data Set

This data set contains 3 classes and each class has 50 instances. The entire data space is partitioned into 0.1 x 0.1 size cells. The data is normalized to be in the range 0 to 1.

After the reduction in the data set we are left with 52 instances which is a reduction of 65%. Now weights are assigned to the left over instances in order to compensate for the loss of data. Fig 1 and Fig 2 pictorially depict the results of clustering using the standard GK algorithm and the proposed algorithm [17]. The snapshots clearly depict the correspondence between the two clustering methods.

Table 1 shows the time taken for both the standard GK and the proposed approach implementation. Timing was started when the algorithm to cluster was called and stopped when the function returned.

Table 1. Data Reduction results for the IRIS data set

IRIS Data set	Objective fn value	Time taken	%age reduction in time
Standard GK	7.4023	0.085	8.2%
Proposed Approach	8.49	0.078	

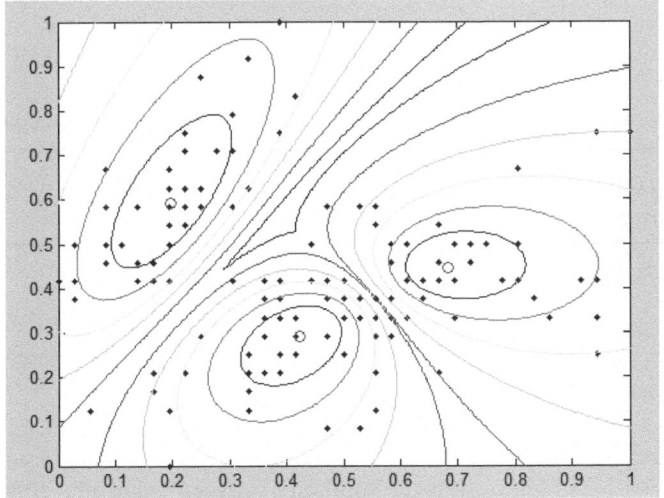

Fig. 1. Clustering with standard GK (IRIS)

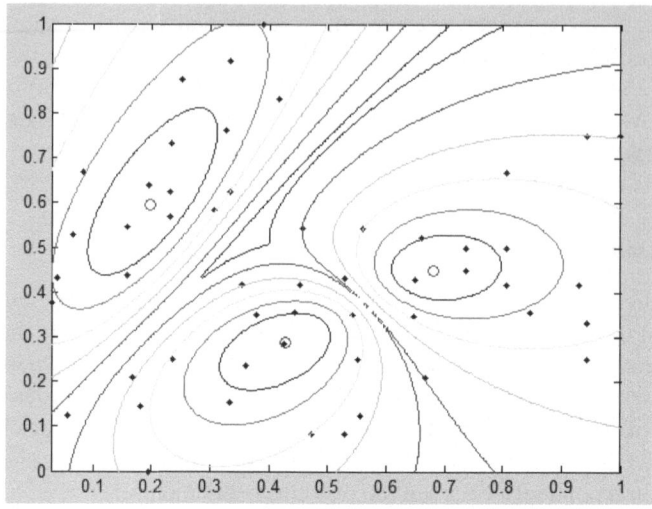

Fig. 2. Clustering with proposed approach (IRIS)

5.2   Telecom Data Set

This data set contains 11 classes having a total of 101450 instances. The entire data space is partitioned into 0.025 x 0.025 size cells. The data are normalized to be in the range 0 to 1.

After the reduction in the data set we are left with 523 instances which is a reduction of 99.48%. Now weights are assigned to the left over instances in order to compensate for the loss of data. Fig 3 and Fig 4 pictorially depict the results of clustering using the standard GK algorithm and the proposed algorithm [17]. The snapshots clearly depict the correspondence between the two clustering methods.

Table 2 shows the time taken for both the standard GK and the proposed approach implementation. Experimental conditions were same as for the Iris data set.

Table 2. Reduction results for the Telecom – Site Report data set

Telecom Data (Site Report)	Objective fn value	Time taken	%age reduction in time
Standard GK	1331.9	11.79	98.22%
Our approach	1432.7	0.2094	

The experimental results depict that the proposed approach is able to achieve highly accurate results with a 98.22% reduction in time as compared with the original algorithm. Fig. 5 and Fig.6 show the similarity between the results obtained using the proposed approach and the standard GK algorithm by comparing the validation

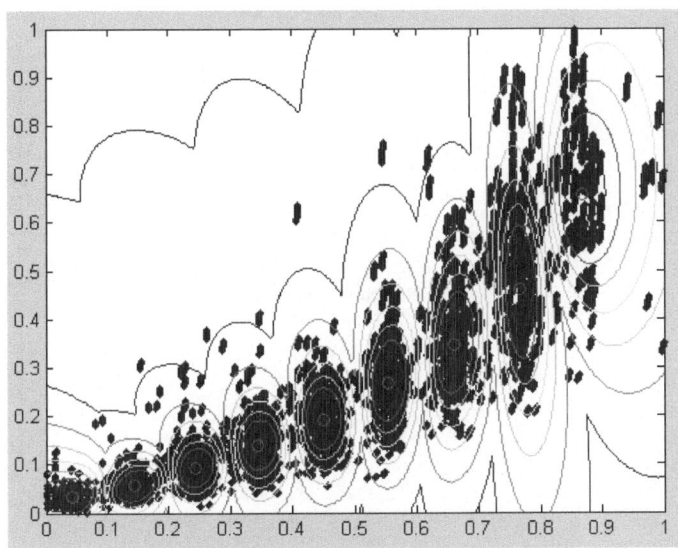

Fig. 3. Clustering with standard GK (TELECOM)

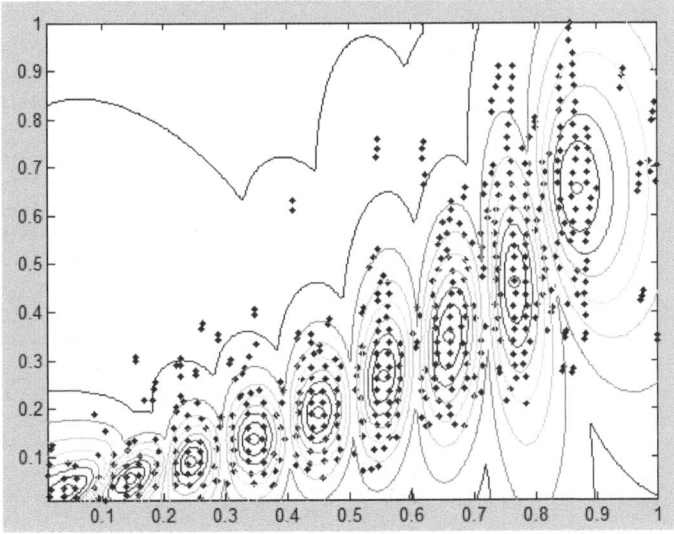

Fig. 4. Clustering with proposed approach (TELECOM)

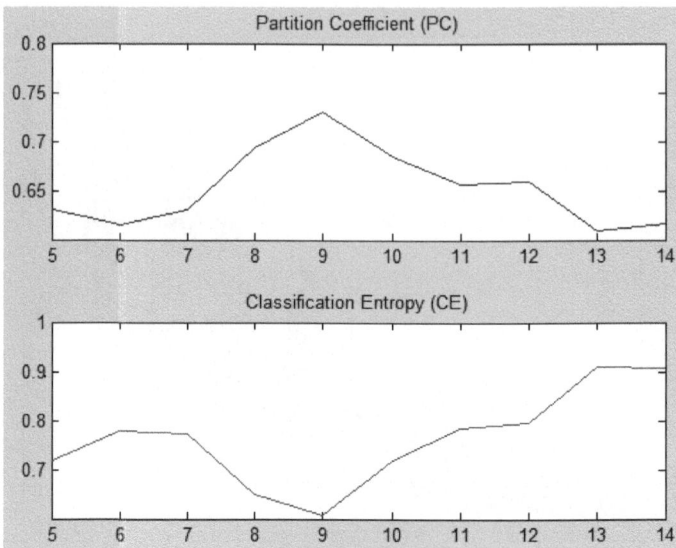

Fig. 5. Validation indexes for standard GK (TELECOM)

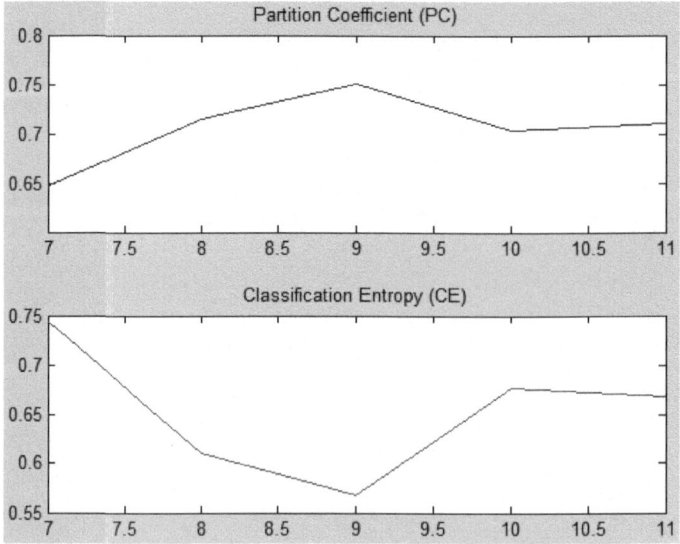

Fig. 6. Validation indexes for proposed approach (TELECOM)

indexes. The largest value of PC and the lowest value of CE is 9 for both the cases. 9 is the ideal number of clusters for the given telecom dataset. This further corroborates that our approach has achieved highly accurate results.

Table 1 and table 2 clearly show the relevance of this algorithm in domains like Telecom. The speedups obtained for the Telecom data are remarkable as compared to the Iris data as the number of instances is much larger in the telecom data set which is usually the scenario with such data intensive domains.

6   Conclusion

We have proposed a technique towards fuzzy clustering which uses a matrix based approach to identify cells and the corresponding weights which are then used as input to an adapted Gustafson Kessel Algorithm. Basis the experimental results we can evidently see the effectiveness of the proposed approach in reducing the computational time while maintaining high accuracy for large datasets as compared to small datasets.

This has direct application in domains like Telecom, where the real time analytics and recommendation engines need to churn out responses fast out of the input data set of millions of points and multiple dimensions.

References

1. Döring, C., Lesot, M.-J., Kruse, R.: Data Analysis with fuzzy clustering methods. Computational Statistics and Data Analysis, 192–214 (2006)
2. Bezdek, J.C.: Pattern Recognition with Fuzzy Objective Function Algorithms. Plenum Press (1981)
3. Zadeh, I.A.: Fuzzy Sets. Information Control 8, 338–353
4. Jain, A.K., Murty, M.N., Flynn, P.J.: Data Clustering: A Review. ACM Computing Surveys 31(3) (1999)
5. Gustafson, D.E., Kessel, W.C.: Fuzzy Clustering with fuzzy covariance matrix. In: Proc IEEE CDC, San Diego,CA, USA, pp. 761–766 (1979)
6. Dunn, J.C.: A Fuzzy relative of the ISODATA process and its use in detecting compact well separated cluster. Journal of Cybernetics 3, 32–57
7. Borgelt, C.: Accelerating Fuzzy Clustering. Information Sciences 179(23), 3985–3997 (2009)
8. Havens, T.C., Chitta, R., Jain, A.K., Jin, R.: Speedup of fuzzy and possibilistic kernel c-means for large-scale clustering. In: International Conference on Fuzzy systems. IEEE (2011)
9. Arfaoui, O., Sassi, M.: Fuzzy Clustering of large scale data sets using Principal Component Analysis. In: International Conference on Fuzzy Systems. IEEE (2011)
10. Kannan, S.R., Ramathilagam, S., Chung, P.C.: Effective fuzzy c-means clustering algorithms for data clustering problems. Expert Systems with Applications (2011)
11. Gu, Y., Hall, L.O., Goldof, D.B.: Evaluating Scalable fuzzy clustering. In: International Conference on Systems man and Cybernetics. IEEE (2010)
12. Yue, S., Wei, M., Wang, J.-S., Wang, H.: A general grid- clustering approach. Pattern Recognition Letters 29 (2008)

13. Lei, G., Yu, X., Yang, X., Chen, S.: An Incremental Clustering Algorithm Based on Grid. In: Eighth International Conference on Fuzzy Systems and Knowledge Discovery (FSKD). IEEE (2011)
14. Rickard, J.T., Yager, R.R., Miller, W.: Mountain Clustering on Nonuniform Grids. In: Proceedings of the 33rd Applied Imagery Pattern Recognition Workshop (AIPR 2004). IEEE (2004)
15. Yager, R.R., Filev, D.P.: Approximate Clustering Via the Mountain Method. IEEE Transactions on Systems, Man and Cybernetics 24(8) (1994)
16. Velthuizen, R.P., Hall, L.O., Clarke, L.P., Silbiger, M.L.: An Investigation of Mountain Method Clustering for Large data sets. Pattern Recognition (1997)
17. Abonyi, J., Balasko, B., Feil, B.: Fuzzy Clustering and Data Analysis Toolbox, http://www.fmt.vein.hu/softcomp/fclusttoolboc/

Materialized View Selection Using Genetic Algorithm

T.V. Vijay Kumar[1] and Santosh Kumar[1,2]

[1] School of Computer and Systems Sciences, Jawaharlal Nehru University,
New Delhi-110067, India
[2] Krishna Institute of Engineering and Technology,
Ghaziabad, UP-201206, India

Abstract. A data warehouse stores historical information, integrated from several large heterogeneous data sources spread across the globe, for the purpose of supporting decision making. The queries for decision making are usually analytical and complex in nature and their response time is high when processed against a large data warehouse. This query response time can be reduced by materializing views over a data warehouse. Since all views cannot be materialized, due to space constraints, and optimal selection of subsets of views is an NP-complete problem, there is a need for selecting appropriate subsets of views for materialization. An approach for selecting such subsets of views using Genetic Algorithm is proposed in this paper. This approach computes the top-T views from a multidimensional lattice by exploring and exploiting the search space containing all possible views. Further, this approach, in comparison to the greedy algorithm, is able to comparatively lower the total cost of evaluating all the views.

Keywords: Data Warehouse, Materialized Views Selection, Genetic Algorithm.

1 Introduction

In most large organizations different departments maintain local databases for supporting sets of applications. With organizational data spreading across different departments, there is a need to provide a common platform over these local databases in order to support global data processing applications. These applications are used to generate consolidated global reports, which are useful for developing a decision support system. These systems are usually built using the eager or in-advance approach [23], which extracts, integrates and stores the information spread across several large, heterogeneous local databases and other information sources, into a central repository referred to as a data warehouse. This data warehouse can be used for answering complex analytical queries in support of decision making [10]. These queries can be answered using the historical data available in the data warehouse. Since data in the data warehouse tends to be very large in size, as it grows continuously with time, and queries posed on it may include a large number of complex aggregates, the organization of data in the data warehouse becomes a crucial factor for processing analytical queries efficiently as also in making it compliant with the underlying data sources[14]. The analytical queries, which are long and complex

M. Parashar et al. (Eds.): IC3 2012, CCIS 306, pp. 225–237, 2012.
© Springer-Verlag Berlin Heidelberg 2012

when processed against a large data warehouse, consume a lot of time for processing and thereby, lead to higher response time. This response time can be reduced by using materialized views [1, 5]. These views are different from virtual views, which are specified in the form of stored queries for generating data from the underlying data repository. The virtual view is computed every time a query uses it. Materialized views, on the other hand store data along with its query specification. It usually contains pre-computed, summarized and relevant information with the aim of providing answers to future queries thereby reducing the query response time. There are several issues associated with materialized views namely view selection, view maintenance, view evolution and answering queries using views. This paper focuses on view selection.

Materialized view selection is the problem of selecting appropriate sets of views for materialization in the data warehouse such that the cost of evaluating queries is minimized subject to given space constraints. According to the definition given in [2] view selection is defined as "given a database schema R, storage space B, and a workload of queries Q, choose a set of views V over R to materialize, whose combined size is at most B". It is not feasible to materialize all possible views as the number of possible views is exponential in the number of dimensions, and for higher dimensions it is not possible to store all possible views within the available storage space. Further, optimal view selection is shown to be an NP Complete problem [7]. Thus there is a need to select an appropriate subset of views, from among all possible views, that can reduce the query response time while fitting within the available space for materialization. There are several view selection approaches proposed in literature, of which most are greedy based or evolutionary based. The greedy based view selection approach, in each iteration, selects the view that would achieve maximum benefit with respect to materialization [1, 5, 6, 7, 15, 17, 18, 19, 20, 21]. The majority of research in the area of materialized views selection is focused around the greedy heuristic based view selection techniques. These techniques are not able to select good quality views for higher dimensional data sets because their total view evaluation cost (TVEC) is high. Several other heuristics have also been proposed in literature that minimize the response time of query processing but compromise on its quality. Alternatively, views can be selected in an evolutionary manner using Genetic algorithm(GA). GA is a widely used evolutionary technique suitable for solving complex problems involving the identification of a good set of solutions from within a large search space[3]. Since the view selection problem is an NP complete problem having complexity of the order $O(2^n)$, where n is the number of dimensions, GA can be adapted to select views for materialization.

Several GA based view selection algorithms have been proposed in literature [8, 9, 11, 12, 22, 24]. These algorithms aim to select views for higher dimensional data sets with the key challenge of selecting views of high quality i.e. low TVEC. In this paper, a GA based algorithm is proposed that attempts to select reasonably good quality views from a multidimensional lattice. The proposed GA based algorithm, unlike existing algorithms, represents a chromosome as a string of views selected for materialization. The length of each chromosome is T for selecting top-T views for materialization. GA is applied with a pre-defined crossover and mutation probability and a good set of top-T views are generated after a pre-specified number of generations. Experimental based comparison of the proposed GA based algorithm, for different crossover and mutation probabilities, with the most fundamental greedy algorithm [7], hereafter in this paper referred to as HRUA, showed that the proposed GA based algorithm is able to select comparatively good quality of views.

The paper is organized as follows: Section 2 discusses the GA based approach and an example based on it is given in section 3. Experimental Results are given in section 4. Section 5 is the conclusion.

2   The Approach

The proposed GA based approach selects top-T views from a multidimensional lattice, which is discussed next.

2.1   Multidimensional Lattice

Views involved in On-Line Analytical Processing (OLAP) queries can be represented as nodes of a multidimensional lattice [7, 14]. The top most view of a lattice, i.e. the root node, represents the base fact table computed through the aggregation of all dimensions. All views of the lattice depend upon the root view. A view V_X is said to be dependent on another view V_Y, if queries on V_X can be answered using the view V_Y. Direct dependencies are represented by defining an edge between corresponding views, while indirect dependencies get captured transitively. For example, consider a 3-dimensional lattice shown in Fig. 1. The index of the view is shown in brackets alongside the name of the view. The size of the views is shown alongside the node in the lattice. From the lattice, it can be noted that all views directly or indirectly depend on the root view, i.e. V_{ABC}.

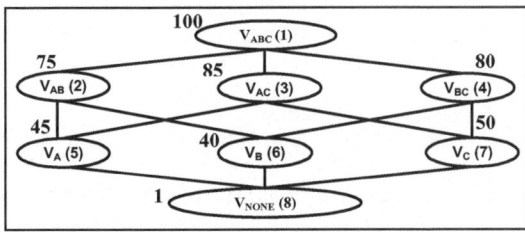

Fig. 1. 3-Dimensional Lattice

2.2   Genetic Algorithm

The genetic algorithm is an approach that mimics the biological process of evolution of living organisms into superior populations from one generation to the next. In GA, a random population of chromosomes, representing a candidate solution, is considered. Inspired by Darwin's theory of survival of the fittest, all chromosomes in the population are evaluated based on their fitness value, and the fitter ones are retained to generate a new population using the genetic operators of crossover and mutation. This process is repeated on the new population till a terminating condition is reached. The terminating condition can either be a pre-specified number of generations or when a satisfactory solution has been achieved or if no improvement is observed in the solution for a pre-specified number of generations. A general description of a simple genetic algorithm, as given in [3], is shown in Fig. 2.

> *initialize population*
> *evaluate population based on fitness function*
> *while TerminatingConditionNotSatisfied*
> *begin*
>> *select parents for reproduction*
>> *perform crossover and mutation*
>> *evaluate population based on fitness function*
> *end*

Fig. 2. Simple Genetic Algorithm

2.3   GA Based View Selection

The proposed GA based algorithm, as given in Fig. 3, takes a lattice of views with the size of each view, the probability of crossover, probability of mutation and the pre-defined number of generations as input and produces the top-T views as output.

Input: Lattice of Views with size of each view, P_c : Probability of crossover,
$\quad$ P_m : Probability of mutation, G : Pre-defined number of generations.
Output: Top-T Views.
Method:
$\quad$ Generate a random population of Top-T views V_{TopT} with chromosome length T and each gene represents a distinct view in the chromosome.
$\quad$ WHILE generation $\leq$ G DO
$\quad$ Use the following fitness function TVEC to evaluate each individual in V_{TopT}

$$TVEC = \sum_{i=1 \wedge SM_{V_i}=1}^{N} Size(V_i) + \sum_{i=1 \wedge SM_{V_i}=0}^{N} SizeSMA(V_i)$$

$\quad$ where
$\quad$ N is total number of Views in the Lattice
$\quad$ SM_{V_i} is Status Materialized of view V_i ($SM_{V_i} = 1$, if materialized, $SM_{V_i} = 0$, if not materialized)
$\quad$ Size(V_i) is size of view V_i
$\quad$ SizeSMA(V_i) is size of smallest materialized ancestor of view V_i
$\quad$ Select the set of Top-T views from the given population using tournament selection.
$\quad$ Apply crossover on the selected chromosomes at crossover rate P_c.
$\quad$ Apply mutation with the mutation rate P_m
$\quad$ Place the new population into V_{TopT}
$\quad$ Increment Generation by 1
$\quad$ END DO
$\quad$ Return Top-T Views

Fig. 3. GA based View Selection Algorithm

The algorithm starts by randomly generating an initial population of top-T views V_{TopT} from the given lattice of views. The population would consist of chromosomes, where each chromosome comprises of the top-T views. The first step in a GA based algorithm is to define the chromosome encoding scheme. This is discussed next.

2.3.1 Chromosome Representation

The encoding scheme used for chromosome representation is the first, and key, step in finding the solution to a problem using GA. This representation needs to be in a form that can ideally represent a solution to the problem being solved. The approach presented in this paper represents a chromosome for selecting top-T views, as a string of distinct T views from the multidimensional lattice with each gene in it having a view index as value. The chromosome representation for selecting top-5 views for materialization from the three dimensional lattice in Fig. 1, is shown in Fig. 4.

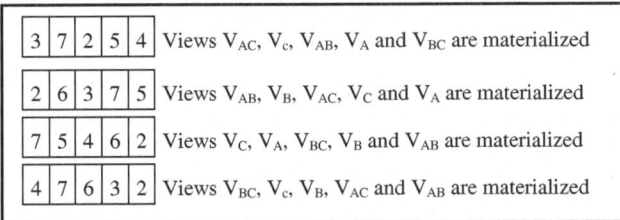

3	7	2	5	4	Views V_{AC}, V_c, V_{AB}, V_A and V_{BC} are materialized
2	6	3	7	5	Views V_{AB}, V_B, V_{AC}, V_C and V_A are materialized
7	5	4	6	2	Views V_C, V_A, V_{BC}, V_B and V_{AB} are materialized
4	7	6	3	2	Views V_{BC}, V_c, V_B, V_{AC} and V_{AB} are materialized

Fig. 4. Chromosome representation for selecting top-5 views

The next step in the GA based algorithm is to evaluate the top-T views in the population using a fitness function. The fitness function used by the algorithm is discussed next.

2.3.2 Fitness Function

A fitness function is used to evaluate the degree of fitness of each chromosome for a given objective. It is used to measure the goodness of the represented solution and is required to be consistent with the problem being solved. The quality of the GA based solution depends upon the correctness and appropriateness of the fitness function defined for the problem. In case of selection of views from a multi-dimensional lattice, the major objective is to reduce the total cost of evaluating all the views[7], referred to as Total View Evaluation Cost (TVEC), due to the selected views. Therefore, the approach aims to evaluate the fitness of the chromosome, representing the top-T views, based on the value of TVEC. The corresponding fitness function is given below:

$$TVEC = \sum_{i=1 \wedge SM_{V_i}=1}^{N} Size\ (V_i) + \sum_{i=1 \wedge SM_{V_i}=0}^{N} SizeSMA\ (V_i)$$

where

N is total number of Views in the Lattice

SM_{V_i} is Status Materialized of view V_i ($SM_{V_i} = 1$, if materialized, $SM_{V_i} = 0$, if not materialized)

Size(Vi) is size of view Vi

SizeSMA(Vi) is size of smallest materialized ancestor of view Vi

For the three dimensional lattice shown in Fig. 1, if views V_{ABC}, V_{AB}, V_B and V_C are selected for materialization then their fitness value TVEC is computed as shown in Fig. 5.

$$\sum_{i=1 \wedge SM_{V_i}=1}^{8} Size\ (V_i) = (Size\ (V_{ABC}) + Size\ (V_{AB}) + Size\ (V_B) + Size\ (V_C))$$

$$= (100 + 75 + 40 + 50)$$

$$= 265$$

$$\sum_{i=1 \wedge SM_{V_i}=0}^{8} SizeSMA\ (V_i) = (SizeSMA\ (V_{BC}) + SizeSMA\ (V_{AC}) + SizeSMA\ (V_A) + SizeSMA\ (V_{NONE}))$$

$$= (100 + 100 + 75 + 40)$$

$$= 315$$

$$TVEC = \sum_{i=1 \wedge SM_{V_i}=1}^{8} Size\ (V_i) + \sum_{i=1 \wedge SM_{V_i}=0}^{8} SizeSMA\ (V_i) = 265 + 315 = 580$$

Fig. 5. TVEC computation if views V_{ABC}, V_{AB}, V_B and V_C are selected for materialization

The algorithm proceeds by selecting a set of top-T views for crossover. This is discussed next.

2.3.3 Selection

Selection is a process of choosing individuals from a population for performing crossover. The fitter individuals are more likely to produce fitter offspring's in the subsequent generations. Selecting only fitter individuals might hinder exploration of the search space thereby leading to early convergence. Therefore, there is a need to randomly select individuals where individuals, having higher fitness value, have greater likelihood of being selected for crossover. The approach uses binary tournament selection method [4] where two individuals are randomly selected from the population and a tournament is conducted among them. A value r is randomly generated between 0 and 1. If r is less than the pre-defined value of k (say k=0.75), taken between 0 and 1, the individual having lower TVEC is selected else the individual with higher TVEC is selected. The binary tournament selection method [4] used by the approach is shown in Fig. 6.

> Given: a parameter **k** (say **k**=0.75)
> Choose two individuals randomly from the population
> Choose a random number **r** between 0 and 1.
> If **r** < **k**
>   Select the fitter individual among the two individuals
> Else
>   Select the less fitter individual among the two individuals

Fig. 6. Binary Tournament Selection Method

The next step is to perform crossover between the pair of selected top-T views.

2.3.4 Crossover

The crossover operation is used to exchange genetic materials in two individuals, as parents, to produce two offspring. The idea of the crossover operation is to produce offspring that enable exploration of promising areas in the search space. Several crossover operators have been mentioned in literature, of which the approach has used the single point crossover [13], where a point is randomly selected with crossover probability P_c. Thereafter considering this crossover point in the two individuals, cyclic crossover[16] is used for exchanging genetic materials between them to produce two offspring. The crossover operation used by the algorithm is illustrated in Fig. 7.

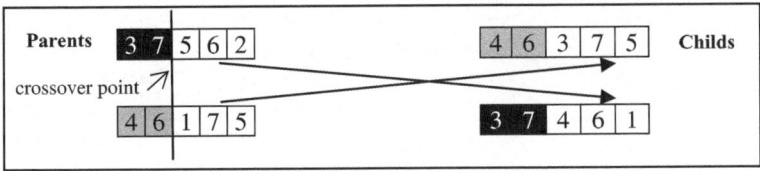

Fig. 7. Single-Point Cyclic Crossover

Thereafter, the chromosomes in the population undergo mutation, which is discussed next.

2.3.5 Mutation

The mutation operation is used to alter one or more gene in a chromosome from its initial state. Mutation is performed in order to add more genetic diversity and thus preventing the search process from stagnating at any local optima. It may be used to exploit the search space to arrive at a better solution than was previously possible. The proposed GA based algorithm carries out random mutations[13] in individuals with probability P_m. It ensures that there is no duplication in views in the individual chromosome. The mutation operation used by the algorithm is illustrated in Fig. 8.

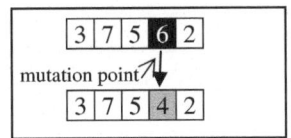

Fig. 8. Mutation

The new population i.e. the population of top-T views after mutation replaces the old population V_{TopT} whereafter the same steps, mentioned above, are repeated until the algorithm has run for G generations. After G generations, the top-T views, having minimum TVEC are produced as output. These views are selected for materialization.

The algorithm can be further illustrated with the help of an example given next.

3   An Example

Consider a four dimensional lattice shown in Fig. 9. The view index is shown in parenthesis alongside the name of the view. The size of the views is shown alongside the node in the lattice. Suppose there is a need to select top-T views (T=10) for materialization from the given four dimensional lattice of views.

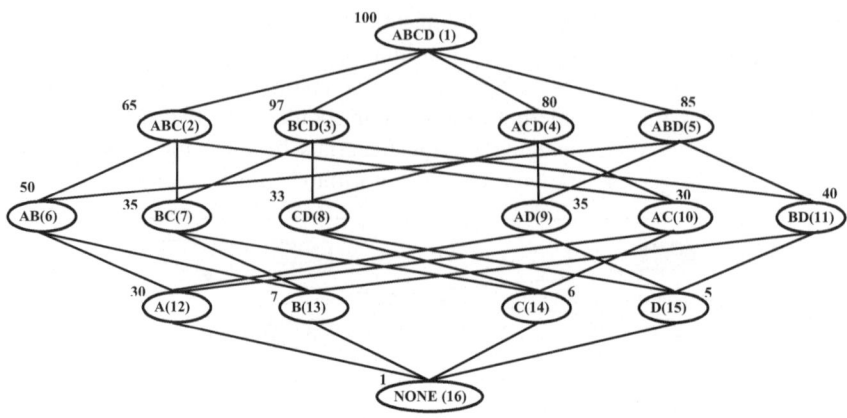

Fig. 9. Four-Dimensional Lattice of Views

First, an initial population of top-T views V_{TopT} is generated randomly from the given four dimensional lattice. These are shown in Fig. 10.

Top-T Views	Chromosomes (top-T Views)									
ACD, BD, ABC, AB, ABD, AC, AD, C, D, B	4	11	2	6	5	10	9	14	15	13
BCD, BD, CD, BC, AB, ABC, AC, C, A, D	3	11	8	7	6	2	10	14	12	15
ACD, BCD, BD, CD, BC, AB, ABD, C, D, B	4	3	11	8	7	6	5	14	15	13
ACD, BD, ABC, CD, BC, ABD, AD, D, A, B	4	11	2	8	7	5	9	15	12	13
BCD, ABC, CD, BC, ABD, AB, AC, D, A, C	3	2	8	7	5	6	10	15	12	14
BCD, ABC, BD, CD, ABD, BC, AD, C, D, B	3	2	11	8	5	7	9	14	15	13
ACD, BCD, BD, CD, BC, AC, ABD, AD, C, A	4	3	11	8	7	10	5	9	14	12
ACD, BCD, ABC, BC, ABD, BD, AC, AD, C, A	4	3	2	7	5	11	10	9	14	12

Fig. 10. Initial population of top-T views

The fitness function, defined in Fig. 3, is then used to evaluate the fitness of top-T views in V_{TopT}. The fitness, i.e. TVEC, computation of top-T views (4, 11, 2, 6, 5, 10, 9, 14, 15, 13) in V_{TopT} is shown in Fig. 11.

$$\sum_{i=1 \wedge SM_{V_i}=1}^{16} Size(V_i) = (Size(ACD) + Size(BD) + Size(ABC) + Size(AB) + Size(ABD) + Size(AC) + Size(AD) + Size(C) + Size(D) + Size(B))$$

$$= (100 + 80 + 40 + 65 + 50 + 85 + 30 + 35 + 6 + 5 + 7) = 503$$

$$\sum_{i=1 \wedge SM_{V_i}=0}^{16} SizeSMA \ (V_i) = (SizeSMA \ (BCD \ ) + SizeSMA \ (BC \ ) + SizeSMA \ (CD \ ) + SizeSMA \ (A \ ) + SizeSMA \ (V_{NONE} \ ))$$

$$= (100 \ + 65 \ + 80 \ + 30 \ + 5 \ ) = 280$$

$$TVEC = \sum_{i=1 \wedge SM_{V_i}=1}^{16} Size \ (V_i) + \sum_{i=1 \wedge SM_{V_i}=0}^{16} SizeSMA \ (V_i) = 503 \ + 280 \ = 783$$

Fig. 11. TVEC computation of top-T views (4, 11, 2, 6, 5, 10, 9, 14, 15, 13)

In a similar manner, TVEC of the remaining 7 top-T views in V_{TopT} is computed. The fitness values of each top-T views in V_{TopT} is shown in Fig. 12. The binary tournament selection is then applied (k=0.75) as shown in Fig. 13.

Chromosomes (top-T Views)										Fitness Value (TVEC)
4	11	2	6	5	10	9	14	15	13	783
3	11	8	7	6	2	10	14	12	15	831
4	3	11	8	7	6	5	14	15	13	763
4	11	2	8	7	5	9	15	12	13	690
3	2	8	7	5	6	10	15	12	14	751
3	2	11	8	5	7	9	14	15	13	688
4	3	11	8	7	10	5	9	14	12	740
4	3	2	7	5	11	10	9	14	12	824

Fig. 12. TVEC of top-T views in V_{TopT}

Randomly generated indexes [i] [j]	Tournament between individuals [P(i)] [P(j)]	Fitness [TVEC(P(i)] [TVEC(P(j)]	Random (r)	Individual Selected
[1] [4]	[4, 11, 2, 6, 5, 10, 9, 14, 15, 13] [4, 11, 2, 8, 7, 5, 9, 15, 12, 13]	783 690	0.54	[4, 11, 2, 6, 5, 10, 9, 14, 15, 13]
[1] [7]	[4, 11, 2, 6, 5, 10, 9, 14, 15, 13] [4, 3, 11, 8, 7, 10, 5, 9, 14, 12]	783 740	0.84	[4, 3, 11, 8, 7, 10, 5, 9, 14, 12]
[3] [6]	[4, 3, 11, 8, 7, 6, 5, 14, 15, 13] [3, 2, 11, 8, 5, 7, 9, 14, 15, 13]	763 688	0.32	[4, 3, 11, 8, 7, 6, 5, 14, 15, 13]
[4] [5]	[4, 11, 2, 8, 7, 5, 9, 15, 12, 13] [3, 2, 8, 7, 5, 6, 10, 15, 12, 14]	690 751	0.95	[4, 11, 2, 8, 7, 5, 9, 15, 12, 13]

Fig. 13. Selection of top-T views using Binary Tournament Selection

The selected individuals undergo cyclic crossover with crossover probability P_c=0.5, implying that two individuals would be selected randomly for crossover. The crossover is shown in Fig. 14.

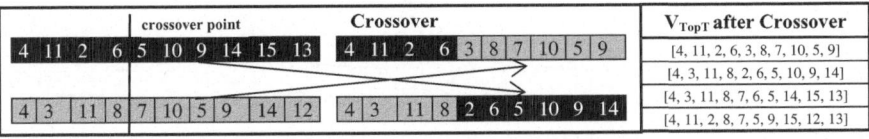

Fig. 14. Crossover betweeb top-T views [4, 11, 2, 6, 5, 10, 9, 14, 15, 13] and [4, 3, 11, 8, 7, 10, 5, 9, 14, 12]

Next, mutation is applied on the selected individuals with mutation probability P_m=0.025, implying that one bit in the population is changed. The mutation is shown in Fig. 15.

The new population V_{TopT}, after mutation, replaces the old population and the same steps mentioned above are repeated until the algorithm has run for G generations.

mutation point	Mutation	V_{TopT} after Mutation
4 **3** 11 8 7 6 5 14 15 13		[4, 11, 2, 6, 3, 8, 7, 10, 5, 9]
		[4, 3, 11, 8, 2, 6, 5, 10, 9, 14]
4 **2** 11 8 7 6 5 14 15 13		[4, 2, 11, 8, 7, 6, 5, 14, 15, 13]
		[4, 11, 2, 8, 7, 5, 9, 15, 12, 13]

Fig. 15. Mutation of top-T views [4, 3, 11, 8, 7, 6, 5, 14, 15, 13]

4   Experimental Results

The proposed GA based view selection algorithm (PA) and the greedy algorithm HRUA, were implemented using JDK 1.6 in a Windows-XP environment. The two algorithms were compared by conducting experiments on an Intel based 2 GHz PC having 3 GB RAM. The comparisons were carried out on TVEC due to views selected by the two algorithms. The experiments were performed for selecting the top-10 views for materialization for dimensions 4 to 10 over 1000 generations.

First, the graphs showing TVEC, for different crossover and mutation probabilities for selecting top-10 views, were plotted and compared with TVEC of selecting top-10 views using HRUA. These graphs, plotted for pair of crossover and mutation probabilities (0.6, 0.05), (0.6, 0.1), (0.65, 0.05), (0.65, 0.1), (0.7, 0.05), (0.7, 0.1), (0.75, 0.05), (0.75, 0.1), are shown in Fig. 16.

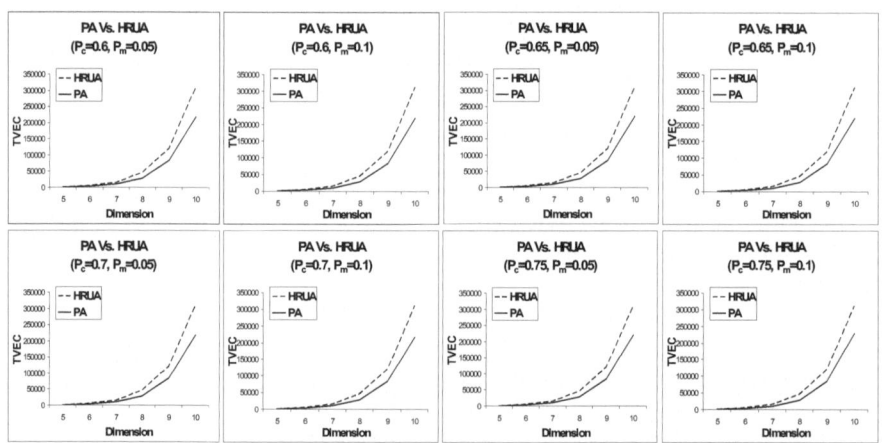

Fig. 16. Comparison of PA and HRUA – TVEC Vs. Dimensions for different P_c's and P_m's

The graphs show that the GA-based view selection algorithm, in comparison to HRUA, is able to select views at lower TVEC for different crossover and mutation probabilities. This difference in TVEC becomes significant for higher dimensional data sets. Further, it can be observed from the graph that, for crossover probability 0.6 and mutation probability 0.05, the GA-based approach is able to select views with maximum total difference in the TVEC value across all dimensions. Accordingly, for crossover and mutation probability 0.6 and 0.05 respectively, graphs showing TVEC versus top-T views for dimensions 5, 6, 7, 8, 9, 10 are plotted. These graphs are shown in Fig. 17. It can be noted from the graph that TVEC of views selected using PA is lesser than those selected using HRUA for each value of T in the top-T views. This difference becomes significant for higher values of T. Thus it can be stated that the observed value of crossover and mutation probability of 0.6 and 0.05 respectively are the most fitting with respect to selecting top-T views with minimum TVEC. Further, PA performs better than HRUA with respect to quality of views selected for materialization.

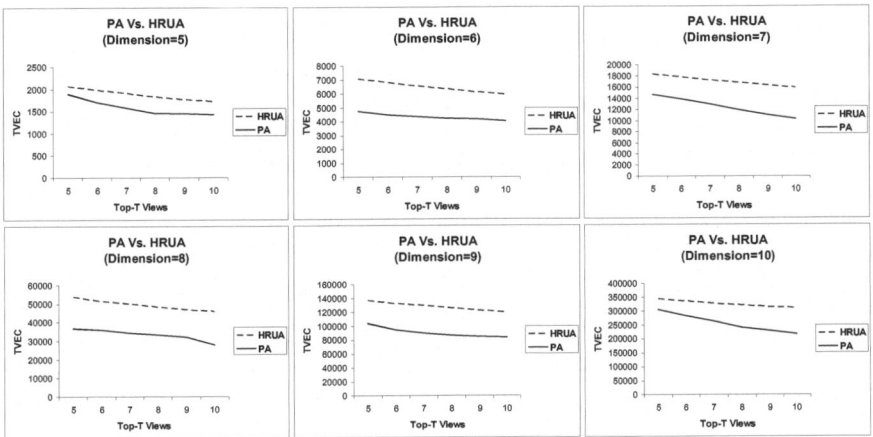

Fig. 17. Comparison of PA and HRUA – TVEC Vs. Top-T Views for P_c=0.6 and P_m=0.05

5   Conclusion

A GA-based algorithm for view selection that selects top-T views from a multi-dimensional lattice has been proposed in this paper. The algorithm first randomly selects a population of chromosomes, each comprising of the top-T views. The individual in the population undergoes selection, followed by crossover and mutation, within pre-specified probabilities, to generate a population for the subsequent generation. The algorithm terminates after it has run for a pre-specified number of generations and the chromosome representing the top-T views, having minimum TVEC, is produced as output. Using GA for selecting views enables exploration and exploitation of the search space. As a result, the views so selected are likely to have a lesser TVEC. Further experimental results show that the views selected using the proposed GA-based algorithm have a comparatively lower TVEC to those selected using HRUA for the observed crossover and mutation probabilities. That is, the GA-based algorithm is able to select comparatively better quality views. This in turn results in reduced query response time enabling efficient decision making.

References

1. Baralis E., Paraboschi S., Teniente E.: Materialized view selection in a multidimensional database, In Proceeding of 23rd VLDB Conference Greece, pp. 156–165, 1997
2. Chirkova, R., Halevy, A. Y., Suciu, D.: A formal perspective on the view selection problem, 27 VLDB Conference, Italy; 2001
3. Goldberg, D. E.: Genetic Algorithms in Search, Optimization, and Machine Learning, Addison-Wesley,1989
4. Goldberg, D.E., Deb, K.: A comparative analysis of selection schemes used in Genetic Algorithms, Foundations of Genetic Algorithms, MK, pp.69-93, 1991
5. Gupta, H., Mumick, I.: Selection of Views to Materialize in a Data Warehouse, IEEE Transactions Knowledge and Data Engineering, 17(1), pp. 24–43, 2005
6. Haider, M., Vijay Kumar, T.V.: Materialised Views Selection using Size and Query Frequency, International Journal of Value Chain Management (IJVCM), Inderscience Publishers, Vol. 5, No. 2, pp. 95-105, 2011
7. Harinarayan, V., Rajaraman, A., Ullman, J. D.: Implementing data cubes efficiently, ACM SIGMOD International Conference on Management of Data, pages 205-227, 1996
8. Horng, J.T., Chang, Y.J., Liu, B.J., Kao, C.Y.: Materialized view selection using genetic algorithms in a data warehouse system, in Proceedings of the World Congress on Evolutionary Computation, Washington, pp. 2221–2227, 1999
9. Horng, J.T., Chang, Y.J., Liu, B.J.: Applying evolutionary algorithms to materialized view selection in a data warehouse, Soft Computing.2003, Vol.7, pp.574–581, 2003
10. Inmon, W.H.: Building the Data Warehouse, Third Edition, Wiley Dreamtech, 2003
11. Lee, M., Hammer, J.: Speeding Up Materialized View Selection in Data Warehouses Using A Randomized Algorithm, in the International Journal of Cooperative Information Systems, Vol. 10, Nos. 3, pp. 327-353, 2001
12. Lin, W.Y., Kuo, I.C.: A genetic selection algorithm for OLAP data cubes, Knowledge and Information Systems 6 (1) pp. 83–102, 2004
13. Mitchell, M.: An Introduction to Genetic Algorithms, The MIT Press, 1999
14. Mohania, M., Samtani, S., Roddick, J. and Kambayshi, Y.: Advances and Research Directions in Data Warehousing Technology, Australian Journal of Information Systems, Vol 7, No 1; 1999
15. Shukla, A., Deshpande, P. M., Naughton, J. F.: Materialized view selection for Multidimensional Datasets, In Proceedings of VLDB, pages 488 – 500, 1998
16. Sivanandan, S.N., Deepa, S.N.: Introduction to Genetic Algorithms, Springer- Verlag, Berlin Heidelberg 2008
17. Vijay Kumar, T.V., Ghoshal, A..: A Reduced Lattice Greedy Algorithm for Selecting Materialized Views, Communications in Computer and Information Science (CCIS), Volume 31, Springer Verlag, pp. 6-18, 2009
18. Vijay Kumar, T.V., Haider, M., Kumar, S.: Proposing Candidate Views for Materialization, Communications in Computer and Information Science (CCIS), Volume 54, Springer Verlag, pp. 89-98, 2010
19. Vijay Kumar, T.V., Haider, M.: A Query Answering Greedy Algorithm for Selecting Materialized Views, Lecture Notes in Artificial Intelligence (LNAI), Volume 6422, Springer Verlag, pp. 153-162, 2010
20. Vijay Kumar, T.V., Haider, M.: Greedy Views Selection using Size and Query Frequency, Communications in Computer and Information Science (CCIS), Volume 125, Springer Verlag, pp. 11-17, 2011

21. Vijay Kumar, T.V., Haider, M., Kumar, S.: A View Recommendation Greedy Algorithm for Materialized Views Selection, Communications in Computer and Information Science (CCIS), Volume 141, Springer Verlag, pp. 61-70 , 2011
22. Wang, Z., Zhang D.: Optimal Genetic View Selection Algorithm Under Space Constraint, In International Journal of Information Technology, vol. 11, no. 5, pp. 44 - 51, 2005.
23. Widom, J.: Research Problems in Data Warehousing, In Proceedings of ICIKM, pp. 25–30, 1995
24. Yu, J. X., Yao, Y. X., Choi, C., Gou, G.: Materialized view selection as constrained evolutionary optimization, in the Journal of IEEE Transactions on Systems, Man, and Cybernetics - TSMC , vol. 33, no. 4, pp. 458-467, 2003

Routing Table Implementation Using Integer Data Structure

P. Manasa, M.R. Prasad, and T. Sobha Rani

Department of Computer and Information Sciences
University of Hyderabad
Hyderabad-500046
India
{mrprassad,t.sobharani.cs}@gmail.com

Abstract. Tremendous growth in traffic is witnessed over the Internet where backbone links of several gigabits per second are commonly deployed. In order to handle these gigabit-per-second traffic rates, backbone routers must forward millions of packets per second on each of their ports. Routing tables of the core routers consists of IP addresses of the order of 200,000-500,000 and changes dynamically. A major challenge is to determine the next-hop address with as low as possible number of accesses of the routing table. IP address lookup in the routers uses the packets destination address to determine the next hop for each packet and is therefore crucial to achieve the required packet forwarding rates. IP address lookup is difficult because it requires a longest common prefix (LCP) match search. In the last couple of years, various algorithms for high-performance IP address lookup have been proposed. The objective of this paper is to use a specific data structure and develop the lookup algorithm that is required to meet the demands like fast lookup, memory efficiency and fast incremental updates. We have used a novel data structure y-fast trie for the routing table in this work. We adapted the algorithm for predecessor/successor search in x-fast trie via dynamic perfect hashing technique to find the longest common prefix between the incoming packets destination address and the next-hop address. By looking at this longest common prefix, we identify the next-hop address. As an improvement over this method, we also have used indirection using balanced BSTs (y-fast trie). On average the routing table creation takes $51703\mu sec$ for 100000 IP addresses in the method using indirection. Average lookup time using dynamic perfect table takes $0.83\mu sec$.

Keywords: IP address lookup, routing, next hop, destination IP address and packets, y-fast trie, longest common prefix.

1 Introduction

Routers are responsible for forwarding packets on an IP network. Each router accepts packets from a variety of sources, examines the IP address of the destination and decides the next hop that the packet needs to take to get to its final destination. A router has to knows where to send different packets.

M. Parashar et al. (Eds.): IC3 2012, CCIS 306, pp. 238–249, 2012.
© Springer-Verlag Berlin Heidelberg 2012

Table 1. A Routing table

Destination address prefix	Next-hop	Output interface
48.240.32/20	192.41.77.148	2
30.82.6/16	201.41.177.181	6
108.12.116/20	192.41.177.241	4
208.12.21/24	201.41.177.196	1

Each router maintains information that provides a mapping between different network IDs and the other routers to which it is connected in a data structure called a routing table. Each entry in the table, called a routing entry, provides information about one network (or subnetwork, or host). Routing table is consulted to decide about the next hop address if the destination of this packet is known. Each time a packet is received the router checks it's destination IP address against the routing entries in its table to decide where to send the packet, and then sends it on its next hop. Router computes this route based on the information gathered by routing protocols and stores it in the routing table. To consult the routing table, the router uses the packets destination address as a key; this operation is called address lookup. Once the routing information is retrieved, the router can transfer the packet from the incoming link to the appropriate outgoing link, in a process called switching. A typical routing table is shown in Table 1.

Internet consists of hundreds of thousands of networks and routers. It is not only enough to determine the local connections to use for each network, but also the best connection to use for each network. Since routers are interconnected in a mesh there are usually multiple routes between any two devices, but the best route should be chosen whenever possible. This information is maintained in the forwarding table. This task is very important but a very complex job. Routers must plan routes and exchange information about routes and networks, which can be done in a variety of ways. This is accomplished in IP using special IP routing protocols. This may be the shortest route, the least congested, or the route considered optimal based on other criteria. An estimation of lookup time for a link having speed of 2.5 Gb/s and packet length of 64 bytes turns out to be 200 nanoseconds or 20 clock cycles [1]. This is the rate at which lookup has to happen to forward the packets without any delay.

In this paper we implement the routing table using y-fast tree. Using y-fast tree the lookup operation time is decreased and such kind of routing table would be efficient to route the packets as lookup time is less.

2   Existing Methods

The exponential growth of the Internet makes routing system very difficult to manage. The data rates of links have also increased in accordance with the increase in traffic. It has become very difficult for the packet processing capacity of routers to keep up with these increased data rates. Specifically, the address lookup operation is a major problem in the forwarding performance of the routers. In literature we find many methods being used to manage the routing tables. They can be broadly classified as software based approaches and hardware based methods [3]. Under software based approaches, trie and tree data structures [4–6, 9, 10, 12, 13], different search mechanisms on hash data structures [7, 8] and exploitation of caching can be considered. Hardware approaches depends on CAM [11] and specifically designed hardware for fast lookup. Number of algorithms for high-performance IP address lookup have been proposed in recent literature. A survey of some of the algorithms with their time complexity [2] is given by Sanchez et al. Comparison of binary trie versus the LC trie for lookup is better in LC trie ($O(W/K)$) but update is worse in LC trie $O(2^k)$. When range search is considered lookup is the same for binary range search, multiway range search and multiway range trees ($O(\log_2 N)$) but multiway range trees have better update complexity of the order of $O(k \log_k N)$. CAM has a lookup time of $O(1)$. Binary search on prefix length has a lookup time of the order of $O(\log_2 W)$ and update of the order of $O(N \log_2 W)$.

3   Prposed Approach

In order to implement the routing table we have chosen x-fast trie data structure [16, 17]. A x-fast trie is a binary trie with some modifications. Each element is viewed as a root-to-leaf path, which gives the bits of the number in order.inte Nodes which are on an active root-to-leaf path (corresponding to some element in S, where S are the set of addresses in the routing table) are marked by 1. Alternatively, a node is set to 1 if a leaf under it corresponds to an element in S.

Basic steps followed in constructing the routing table using x-fast trie and dynamic perfect hashing:

1. Construction of x-fast trie.
2. Store all prefixes of the binary representation of $y \epsilon S$ (All the addresses in the routing table) in a hash table (using dynamic perfect hashing).
3. Use binary search to find the longest common prefix of **x** (incoming packet's destination address) in the hash table.
4. Look at the min or max of the subtree to find either the successor or predecessor (next hop address) of the incoming packet.

We also implemented x-fast trie using indirection where the IP addresses are clustered and addresses that are clustered maintained as balanced BSTs. This particular implementation is known as y-fast trie [16, 17]. We have carried out experiments with synthetic data in Section 4.

4   Routing Table Construction Using X-Fast Trie and Dynamic Perfect Hashing

4.1   Construction of X-Fast Trie

X-fast trie represents a trie over a universe of size u. A trie, or prefix tree, is a binary trie used. Unlike a binary search tree, no node in the tree stores the

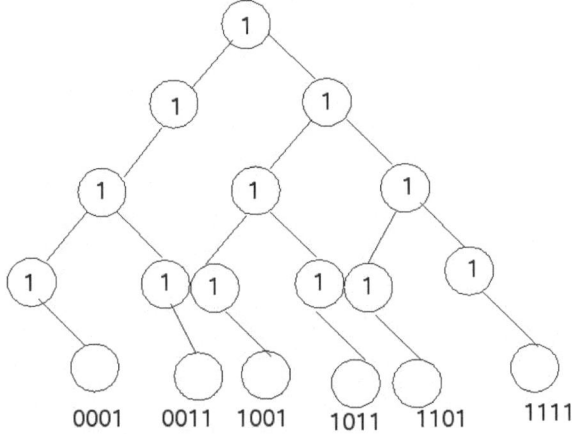

Fig. 1. x-fast trie

key associated with that node; instead, its position in the tree shows what key it is associated with. All the descendants of a node have a common prefix of the string associated with that node, and the root is associated with the empty string. Values are normally not associated with every node, only with leaves and some inner nodes that correspond to keys of interest.

An example x-fast trie is shown in Figure 1 which is constructed for 4-bit. The trie is constructed for { 0001,0011,1001,1011,1101 and 1111 } keys and these values are stored in the leaf nodes. Each edge is having values as 0 (for left edge) and 1 (for right edge). After constructing x-fast trie, we have to store all the prefixes of the binary numbers (which are IP addresses) in a hash table using dynamic perfect hashing.

4.2 Storage of Prefixes of all IP Addresses in Dynamic Perfect Hash Table

Dynamic perfect hash table [18] is a hash table of hash tables i.e it has 2-levels of hash tables (the second level hash table is pointer from each slot of the first level of hash table).

Here dynamic perfect hashing is used to store all the prefixes of the IP addresses stored in a x-fast trie. In this method, the entries that hash to the same slot of the table are organized into a separate second-level hash table. If there are k entries in this set, the second-level table is allocated with $2k$ slots, and its hash function is selected randomly from a universal hash function set so that it is collision-free (i.e. a perfect hash function). Therefore, the lookup cost is guaranteed to be constant in the worst-case.

Whenever theres a collision at the second-level hash table, rearrange the entire second-level table with a new choice of hash function. This may not happen very often, so amortized cost is low. Whenever a particular second level hash table is

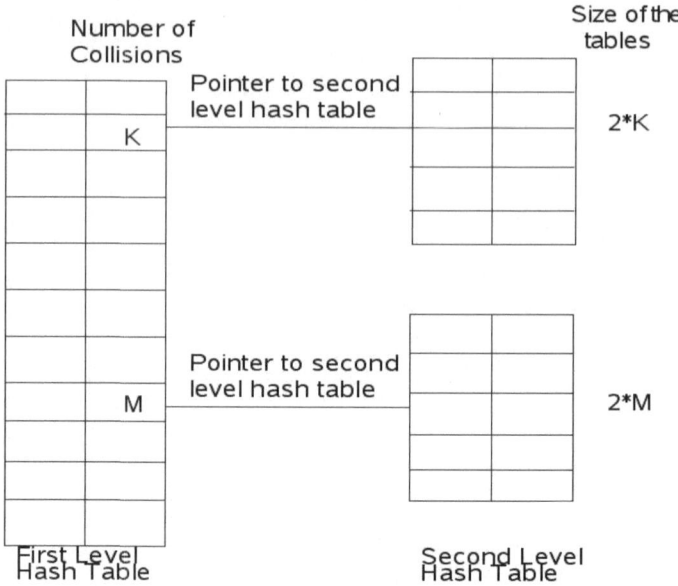

Fig. 2. Dynamic perfect hash table

full and other element comes to that hash table then we have to rehash. That
is double the size of the second level hash table and rehash all the entries using
another hash function which is selected at random from a universal hash function
set so that it is collision-free and insert the new entry. To store the prefixes (i.e.
store all prefixes of the binary representation of IP address) in the hash table
of x-fast tree, first traverse the tree from root to all leaf nodes along that path.
As soon as you reach the next node the position of that node is stored in hash
table.

Storing is done in the following way: First the slot into which a prefix has
to be placed at the first level in the hash table is computed. Let us denote this
as *first-level-location* using hash function which is selected at random from a
universal hash function set. To find *first-level-location*, the function which can
be used is given in Equation 1.

$$first - level - location = ((a * value + b) mod p) mod N \qquad (1)$$

where a & b are constants, p is prime greater than all the numbers in the hash
table, N is the size of the first-level hash table and *value* is the value of the
prefix which we are storing in hash table. As prefixes are in binary form it is
converted into integer value using convert function given in 2.

$$value = \sum_{i=0}^{length} x[i] * 2^{length-i-1} \qquad (2)$$

where *length* is length of the prefix, *x[i]* contains 24-bit binary address. so here
instead of 0, 2 is assigned and for 1, 1 is assigned.

If that particular first-level-location is empty then insert it in that slot of first level hash table, if collisions occur at that slot then find the slot in second level hash table (which is a pointer from first-level-location of first level hash table). Second-level-location is found using another hash function which is selected at random from a universal hash function set. To find *second-level-location*, Equation 3 is used.

$$second - level - location = (value1)mod2 \qquad (3)$$

where *value1* is the the value of the prefix which we are storing in the hash table. Since prefixes are in binary form it is converted into integer value using convert function which is as follows.

$$value1 = \sum_{i=0}^{length} x[i] * 2^{length-i-1} \qquad (4)$$

where *length* is length of the prefix, *x[i]* contains 24-bit binary address, so here for 0, 0 is assigned and for 1, 1 is assigned.

If collisions occur at that *second-level-location* of the second level hash table too then go to next slot in second level hash table where it is empty and insert it and rearrange all the elements in that second level hash table i.e., calculate slots for all the elements in that second level hash table using hash function which is selected at random from a universal hash function set. The function which is used is

$$second - level - location = (value)mod(second - level - count) \qquad (5)$$

where *second-level-count* is number of slots in that second-level-table. Whenever a particular second level hash table is full and other element comes to that hash table then we have to rehash that is double the size of the second level hash table and rehash all the entries using another hash function which is selected at random from a universal hash function set so that it is collision-free and insert new entry. The function which is used to hash is

$$second - level - location = (value)mod(2 * second - level - count) \qquad (6)$$

Where *second-level-count* is number of slot in second-level-table. This is how all the prefixes of x-fast tree are stored in a hash table using dynamic perfect hashing.

If we delete elements until we have $k/4$, we rebuild for k instead of $2k$. (If we delete enough, we rebuild at half the size.) All operations take amortized $O(1)$ time. Prefixes of the strings shown in **??** are { 0,00,000,0001,001,0011,1,10,100,1001,101,1011,11,110,1101,111,1111}. These are to be stored in the hash table as shown in Figure 3.

4.3   Finding the Longest Common Prefix of Destination Address

Here we have considered the prefixes maximum size as 24 bits. In order to find the longest common prefix of destination IP address, first compute the prefixes

Prefixes
0
00
000
0001
001
0011
1
10
100
1001
101
1011
11
110
1101
111
1111

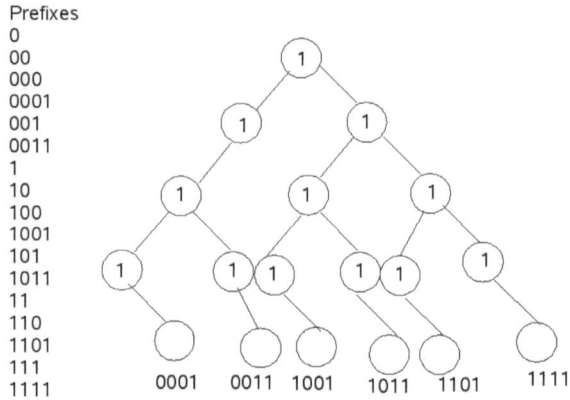

0001   0011 1001   1011   1101   1111

Fig. 3. Prefixes of all addresses of Figure ?? are stored in hash table

(according to sorted order) of 24-bit binary format of destination IP address. Now we have to perform binary search on these prefixes. As we have chosen the mask as 24 bits, we will get 24 prefixes. Choose the 12th prefix and search for this prefix in dynamic perfect hash table. If it is present in the hash table we will next perform binary search on the higher half of the prefixes (i.e from 13th prefix to 24th prefix) or else if we don't find it in the hash table perform binary search on lower half of the prefixes (i.e from 1st prefix to 11th prefix). Suppose 12th prefix is present in the hash table we will next perform binary search on the higher half of the prefixes. Now take middle prefix from higher half of prefixes i.e 18th prefix, and again search for this prefix in hash table. If it is present in the hash table we will next perform binary search on the higher half of the prefixes (i.e from 19th prefix to 24th prefix), or else if we don't find it in the hash table perform binary search on lower half of the prefixes (i.e from 13th prefix to 17th prefix) and so on. So we will perform binary search in this way and return longest matching prefix.

In the figure 3 the destination address is 0111 so its prefixes are { 0,01,011,0111}. So the node whose position is a longest matching prefix here 0 is showed in black color, in Figure 4.

4.4   Finding the Next Hop Address

To find a successor or predecessor which is nothing but a next-hop address, we have to maintain a minimum and maximum values (i.e IP address which are values of leaf nodes on the path of the subtree) for every subtree of x-fast tree, and these minimum and maximum values are stored in the hash table along with the prefixes, which are predecessor and successor respectively. After finding longest matching prefix in the hash table in a particular slot along with the prefixes, we search for the address which has the longest common prefix as the

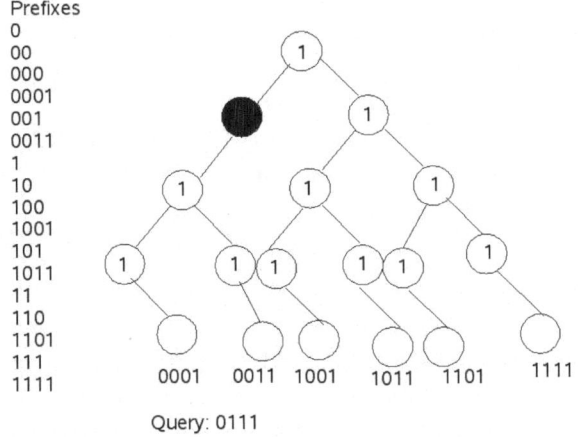

Fig. 4. Finding the longest common prefix of *Query* (i.e 0111) in the tree

starting address, which is nothing but our next-hop address. Hence the time taken to find next hop will be reduced. Figure 5 the next-hop of the destination address is the leaf node. An example of this method is shown in Figure 5.

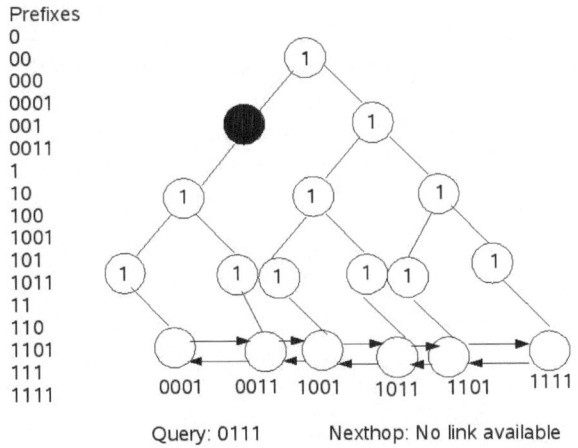

Fig. 5. Find the longest prefix, and next-hop address for *Query*(0111) in the tree

5   Implementation of a Routing Table Using Indirection with Y-Fast Trie

x-fast trie represents a trie over a universe of size u, u=$2^W - 1$. Lookup operation time is independent of the routing table size here. Because the search happens over the prefixes for the query string only. Even when we move into IPv6, it takes one more search than the existing structure. Unfortunately, the implementation of x-fast tries leaves us with the problem that updates take $O(logu)$ time (they may need to insert w nodes in the hash table), and the hash table takes $O(nlogu)$ space. To overcome this we can go for indirection[7]. This particular data structure is known as y-fast tree.

Indirection method is used is as follows: First elements of S (IP addresses in the y-fast trie) are clustered into consecutive groups of size $(logu)$ each. Then IP addresses of each cluster are maintained as a balanced BST. Thirdly, a set of representative IP addresses (one per cluster) are stored in the y-fast trie. These IP addresses are not necessarily in S, but they separate the clusters. A cluster representative is between the maximum IP address in the cluster (inclusively) and the minimum IP address in the next cluster (exclusively).

Indirection would make the requirement for space linear. Lookup time takes $O(loglogu)$ time which is same as y-fast tree method and insert or delete within the subtree takes $O(loglogu)$ time. If a subtree becomes too large, it is split and new item are inserted into the trie. This would take $O(logu)$ but we perform it once for $O(logu)$ insertions.

6   Results

We use two files, one consisting of IP addresses to build the routing table and the other consisting of destination IP addresses respectively. We conducted experiments for 19 different sets of IP address(and number of IP address in each set are 1000 to 10000, 20000, 30000, 40000 to 100000 receptively) to build the routing table and same set of 1000 destination IP addresses used to search for the next hop in these routing tables. We determine the next-hop IP address and the time taken for lookup for each IP address in the set. Using dynamic perfect hash table the time taken to search for few destination IP addresses increases because if we do not find prefix in the first level hash table then we have to search for the prefixes in the second level of the hash table. So average time taken for lookup operation is increased. Time taken for constructing routing tables using data sets of different sizes and average time taken for lookup operation using same set of 1000 destination IP addresses for each of data sets of different sizes are shown in figures 6 and 7. We also present the results for search and construction using indirection with balanced BSTs in the same figures to provide a comparison between the methods.

The graph for average time taken for lookup operation to find next-hop for destination IP address, for data sets of different sizes (i.e IP address) in x-fast trie using dynamic perfect hashing and y-fast trie using indirection are shown in Figure 7. The time taken is almost constant. The graph for time taken to insert data sets of different sizes (i.e IP address) in x-fast trie using dynamic perfect hashing and y-fast trie using indirection are shown in Figure 6. The time is of the order of O(n).

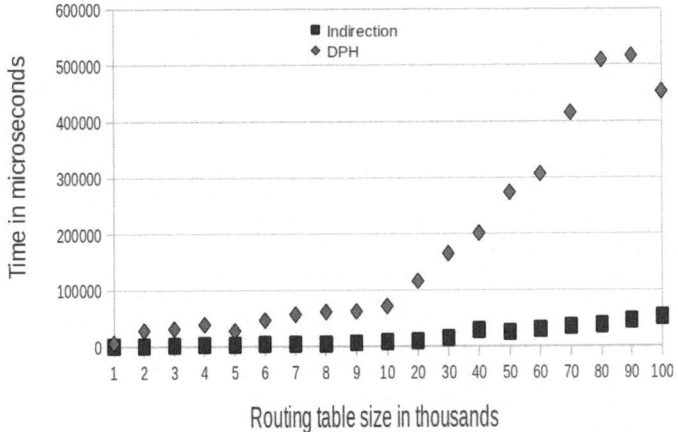

Fig. 6. Time taken to insert data sets of different sizes (i.e IP address) in x-fast trie using dynamic perfect hashing and y-fast trie using indirection using BSTs

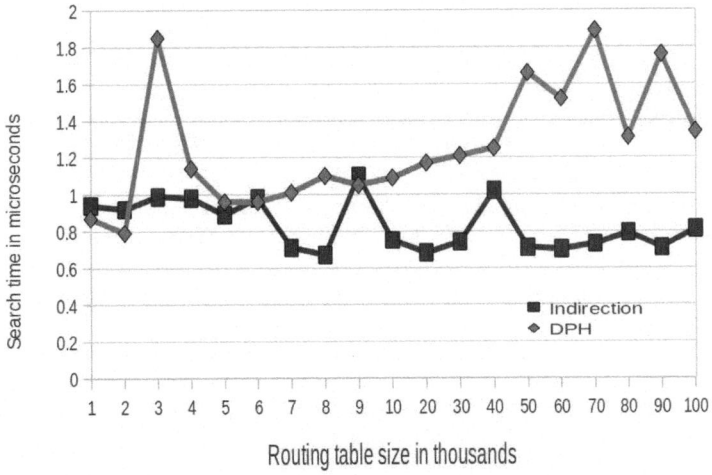

Fig. 7. Average time taken for lookup operation for different sizes of data sets (i.e IP address) using dynamic perfect hash table and indirection using BSTs

7   Conclusions

In this paper we presented ways of using x and y-fast trie data structures for the construction of the routing table. Y-fast treis have an advantage in the implementation of routing tables. We have tried two methods for lookup, one using dynamic perfect hashing and the other indirection using balanced BSTs. Method using indirection with balanced BSTs outperforms dynamic perfect hashing both in construction and lookup time of the routing table. Especially in construction of routing table, dynamic perfect hashing fares very badly. The reason could be the computation of hash value for all the prefixes of the IP addresses in the routing table. In indirection method, we have to sort the data and cluster about 64 of them and find the represenatives for the data. This would reduce the the number of addresses stored in the y-fast tree by two orders of magnitude. Indirection has the added advantage of reducing update from $O(logu)$ to $O(loglogu)$. This scheme is easily extendabe to IPv6 addresses also. since we are not concerned with the number of bits here.

References

1. Yazdani, N., Min, P.S.: Fast and Scalable schemes for the IP address Lookup Problem. In: Proceedings of the IEEE Conference on High Performance Switching and Routing, ATM 2000 (2000)
2. Ruiz-Sanchez, M.A., Biersack, E.W., Dabbous, W.: Survey and taxonomy of IP address lookup algorithms. IEEE Network, 8–23 (2001)
3. Zitterbart, M.: High-Performance Routing-Table Lookup. Philosophical Transactions of Royal Society of London A 358, 2217–2231 (2000)
4. Nilsson, S., Karlsson, G.: IP-address lookup using LC-tries. IEEE Journal on Selected Areas in Communications 17, 1083–1092 (1999)
5. Olsson, R., Nilsson, S.: TRASH A dynamic LC-trie and hash data structure. Trita-CSC-TCS series
6. Eatherton, W., Varghese, G., Dittia, Z.: Tree Bitmap: Hardware/Software IP Lookups with Incremental Updates. ACM SIGCOMM Computer Communications Review 34, 97–122 (2004)
7. Song, H., Hao, F., Kodialam, M., Lakshman, T.V.: IPv6 Lookups using Distributed and Load Balanced Bloom Filters for 100Gbps Core Router Line Cards. In: Proceedings of IEEE INFOCOM (2009)
8. Yim, C., Lee, B., Lim, H.: Efficient Binary Search for IP Address Lookup. IEEE Communications Letters 9, 652–654 (2005)
9. Bando, M., Chao, H.J.: FlashTrie: Hash-based Prefix-Compressed Trie for IP Route Lookup Beyond 100Gbps. In: Proceedings of IEEE INFOCOM (2010)
10. Pan, M., Lu, H.: Build shape-shifting tries for fast IP lookup in O(n) time. Computer Communications 30, 3787–3795 (2007)
11. Chan, C., Wang, P., Hu, S., Lee, C., Chen, R.: Scalable IP Routing Lookup in Next Generation Network. In: Kahng, H.-K. (ed.) ICOIN 2003. LNCS, vol. 2662, Springer, Heidelberg (2003)
12. Sahni, S., Kim, K.S.: An O(log n) Dynamic Router-Table Design. IEEE Transactions on Computers 53, 351–363 (2004)
13. Pao, D., Li, Y.K.: Enabling incremental updates to LC-tries for efficient management of IP forwarding tables. IEEE Commun. Lett. 7, 245–247 (2003)
14. Li, Y.K., Pao, D.: Address lookup algorithms for IPv6. IEE Proc. Commun. 153, 909–918 (2006)
15. BGP table statistics, http://bgp.potaroo.net
16. Willard, D.E.: Log-logarithmic worst-case range queries are possible in space (log logN). Information Processing Letters 17, 81–84 (1983)

17. Willard, D.E.: New trie data structures which support very fast search operations. Journal of Computer and System Sciences 28, 379–394 (1984)
18. Dietzfelbinger, M., Karlin, A., Mehlhorn, K., Meyer auf der Heide, F., Rohnert, H., Tarjan, R.E.: Dynamic Perfect Hashing: Upper and Lower Bounds. SIAM J. Comput. 23, 738–761 (1994)
19. http://courses.csail.mit.edu/6.897/spring03/scribe_notes/L2/lecture2.pdf
20. http://www.math.tau.ac.il/~haimk/adv-ds-2005/veb.ppt

Real Life Emotion Classification from Speech Using Gaussian Mixture Models

Shashidhar G. Koolagudi[1], Anurag Barthwal[1], Swati Devliyal[1],
and K. Sreenivasa Rao[2]

[1] School of Computing, Graphic Era University,
Dehradun - 248002, Uttarakhand, India
[2] School of Information Technology, Indian Institute of Technology Kharagpur,
Kharagpur - 721302, West Bengal, India
koolagudi@{ieee.org,yahoo.com}, {anubarthwal,swatidevliyal}@gmail.com,
ksrao@iitkgp.ac.in

Abstract. In this work, spectral features are extracted from speech to perform emotion classification. Linear prediction cepstral coefficients, Mel frequency cepstral coefficients and their derivatives (velocity and acceleration coefficients) are explored as features. Gaussian mixture models are proposed as classifiers. The emotions considered in this study are anger, fear, happiness, neutral, sadness and surprise. The emotional speech database used in this work is both simulated and semi-natural in nature. The semi-natural database has been collected from the dialogues of actors/actresses in popular Hindi movies. Average emotion recognition performance, in the case of male and female speaker is observed to be around 65.3% and 72% respectively. Recognition performance for semi-natural and simulated databases has been compared.

Keywords: emotion classification, velocity and acceleration coefficients, spectral features, GMM, LFPC, LPCC, MFCC, Emo-DB, IITKGP-SESC, text dependent emotion recognition, text independent emotion recognition.

1 Introduction

Speech has been used as an important mode of communication since the time immemorial. Emotions are an essential part of natural speech communication. Most of the present speech systems can process studio recorded neutral speech with greater accuracy. Therefore, a need is felt to update speech processing systems with the capability to process emotions. The component of emotion processing makes the existing speech systems more realistic and meaningful. Emotion recognition from speech utterances may be useful in different applications such as call center conversation analysis, entertainment, indexing of audio files based on emotions, development of effective human computer interaction and so on. Speech features may be basically extracted from excitation source, vocal tract or prosodic points of view, to accomplish different speech tasks. This work confines

M. Parashar et al. (Eds.): IC3 2012, CCIS 306, pp. 250–261, 2012.
© Springer-Verlag Berlin Heidelberg 2012

its scope to the use of spectral features for recognising emotions. Spectral features represent vocal tract information such as formant frequencies, sequential variation in the shapes/sizes of vocal tracts, spectral bandwidths, spectral rolloff and so on. Generally, most of the speech tasks are accomplished successfully using spectral features. Various spectral features have also been explored for emotion analysis. To distinguish anger from neutral speech in Mandarin language, a combination of MFCCs, LPCCs, Rasta PLP coefficients and log frequency power coefficients (LFPCs) has been used as the features [1]. Combination of features (MFCC+LFPC+LPCC) has been used for emotion recognition while employing simulated database but improvement observed is poor [13]. Excitation source features have also been explored as features in some experiments. LP residual is derived by inverse filtering of the speech signal, and the process is known as LP analysis. LP residual mainly contains higher order relations among the samples. For capturing the emotion specific information from these higher order relations, auto associative neural networks (AANN) and Gaussian mixture models (GMM) have been explored. The decrease in the error during training phase of AANN and the emotion recognition performance of the models demonstrate that the excitation source component of speech contains emotion-specific information and is indeed being captured by the AANN and GMM models. But excitation source features alone have failed to impress as a researcher's choice of features [17].

Text, age of speaker, gender and type of database have significant effect on the performance of emotion recognition systems, along with the choice of classifiers and features [14]. Recognition performance of emotions using segmental level prosodic features is not found to be appreciable, but by combining spectral features along with prosodic features, emotion recognition performance is considerably improved [15]. Epoch parameters extracted from LP (Linear Prediction) residual and zero frequency filtered speech signal have also been explored for recognition of emotions present in speech. Instant of glottal closure within pitch period of LP residual is known as an epoch. The significant excitation of vocal tract usually takes place at the instant of glottal closure. Epoch parameters namely strength of epoch, instantaneous frequency, sharpness of epochs and slope of strength of epochs have been used as features for classification of emotions, but their performance with simulated databases (Telugu database IITKGP-Simulated Emotion Speech Corpus (IITKGP-SESC) and Berlin Database of Emotional Speech (Emo-DB)) is not at par with spectral features [16].

In this work, MFCC features from lower frequency components (20 Hz to 300 Hz) of speech signal have been used to model pitch variations [2]. Normally, spectral features are extracted through block processing approach. Entire speech signal is processed frame by frame, considering the frame size of around 20 ms, and a shift of 10 ms. It is assumed that with in this frame, speech signal is stationary in nature. Mel frequency cepstral coefficients (MFCCs) and linear prediction cepstral coefficients (LPCCs) are extracted as spectral features and used in this work for emotion analysis.

In this work, semi-natural database (GEU-SNESC), collected from Hindi movies has been explored. Single and multiple male and female speakers are considered for classifying the emotions. Simulated emotion speech corpus (IITKGP-SESC) and semi-natural emotion speech database (GEU-SNESC) are used in this study [3].

The rest of the paper is organized as follows : Next section briefs about the databases used. Section 3 provides the details of feature extraction and use of MFCCs, LPCCs and their velocity/acceleration coefficients as feature vectors. An overview of classifiers (GMMs) is provided in section 4. Development of emotion recognition models (ERMs) and results are described in sections 5. The paper concludes with summary (section 6) followed by important citations.

2   Databases

From the available literature, three types of databases are used for analysis of speech emotions. They are : simulated, elicited and natural and semi-natural speech databases. Emotional speech extracted from dialogues of actors and actresses of Hindi movies has been used to create semi natural emotion speech corpus known as Graphic Era University Semi Natural Emotion Speech Corpus (GEU-SNESC). The emotions expressed by actors in Hindi movies are close to real life emotion expression observed in the case of normal Hindi speaking Indian population.

For the creation of the database, dialogues of the popular male and female actors and actresses have been extracted from Hindi movies. This database contains single and multi-speaker emotional utterances for both male and female speakers. The emotions collected for this database are anger, fear, happiness, neutral, sadness and surprise. For single speaker database, video clips of different Hindi movies acted by the same actor are used. Later, audio tracks are separated and concatenated to make a single file. Adobe Audition is used to extract audio with mono channel frequency of 16 KHz and 16 bit resolution. Emotional speech has been extracted carefully, containing no background music and disturbances. Long silence regions have been removed with the help of wavesurfer without affecting the embedded emotions. Fifteen minutes of effective data is collected in this way for each emotion for both female and male speakers. For multi-speaker database, the video clips of different Hindi movies are chosen irrespective of actors, but of the same gender and emotions.

The Indian Institute of Technology Kharagpur Simulated Emotion Speech Corpus (IITKGP-SESC) has been collected by simulating eight emotions using neutral statements. Professional artists from All India Radio (AIR), Vijayawada, India have recorded this database in Telugu language. As the speakers are professional artists, they can simulate the appropriate emotions close to the real and practical situations. Since, all the artists are from the same organization, it ensures the coherence in the quality of the collected speech data. The quality of the emotions present in the database is evaluated using subjective listening tests.IITKGP-SESC is the first database developed in an Indian language

(Telugu) for analyzing the basic emotions present in speech. This database is sufficiently large to analyze the emotions in view of speaker, gender, text and session variability [3].

3   Feature Extraction

Proper feature extraction eliminates irrelevant features that hinder the recognition rates; it reduces the input dimensionality (and therefore improves generalization); it saves up the computational resources [4]. Feature vectors can be long-time or short-time in nature. Long-time features are estimated over the entire utterance length. Short-time features are determined in a smaller time window (usually 20 to 30 msec). Contemporary research approach favors the long-time features for analysis of emotions [5], since the long time features correlate emotions better than short time ones.

Figure 1 shows the unique spectral characteristics for 5 emotions. The spectra shown in Fig. 1 represent the steady region of a vowel /A/ from Telugu utterance 'anni dAnamulalo vidyA dAnamu minnA', expressed in five different emotions. It is observed from the figure that the sharpness of formant peaks, positions of formants, formant bandwidths and spectral tilt have distinctive properties for different emotions. This basic observation is the motivation for using spectral features for characterising and classifying the emotions. It indicates that finer spectral variations maybe treated to be emotion specific [6]. Therefore, MFCCs and LPCCs are used as the features in this study.

The extraction of individual features and their use in developing the models has been discussed in the following paragraphs. Mel frequency cepstral coefficients (MFCCs), linear prediction cepstral coefficients (LPCCs) and their derivatives, known as velocity (Δ) and acceleration (Δ-Δ) coefficients are separately used for emotion analysis. 6, 8, 13, 21, 29 and 35 MFCCs and LPCCs are extracted from speech signal. The above mentioned number of features used separately for developing emotion recognition models. Δ and $\Delta - \Delta$ coefficients are used in concatenation with respective basic features to form the feature vectors. Hamming window has been used while framing the speech signal. The general block diagram of development of emotion recognition models (ERMs) is given in Fig. 2.

Human auditory system is assumed to process a speech signal in a non-linear fashion. It is well known that lower frequency components of a speech signal contain more information. Therefore, non-linear mel scale filter has been designed to emphasize lower frequency components over higher ones [7]. In speech processing mel frequency cepstrum is a representation of the short time power spectrum of a speech frame using linear cosine transform of log power spectrum on a non-linear mel frequency scale [8]. Conversion from normal frequency f to mel frequency m is given by the equation :

$$m = 2595 \log_{10} \left(\frac{f}{700} + 1 \right)$$

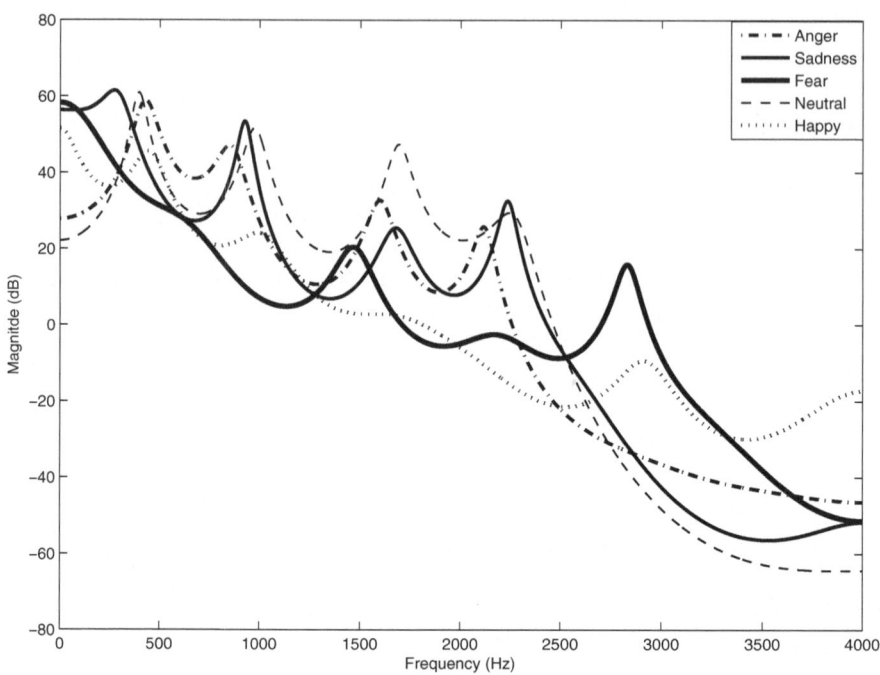

Fig. 1. Frequency Response of Speech for different Emotions

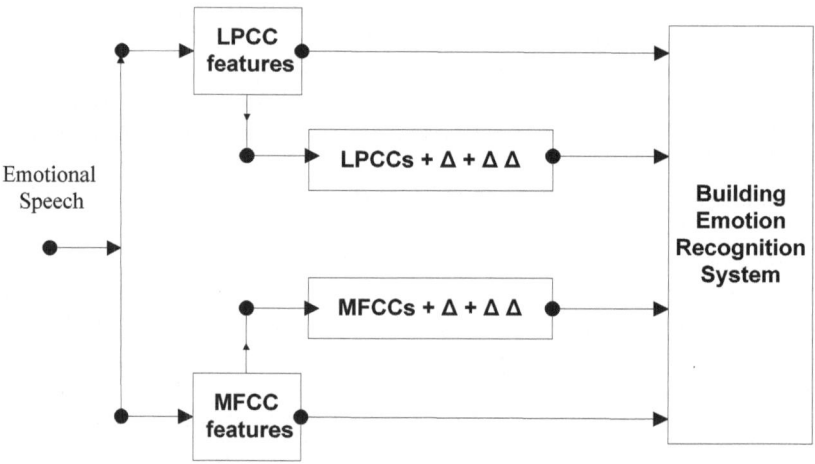

Fig. 2. Development of Emotion Recognition Models (ERMs)

The algorithm used in this work for obtaining mel frequency cepstral coefficients (MFCCs) from speech signal is as follows :

– Obtain Fourier transform of a speech segment to get short time spectrum.
– Compute powers of the above spectrum within the triangular overlapping windows placed according to mel scale.
– Compute the magnitude spectrum for each windowed frame by applying DFT.
– Take logs of the power at each of the mel frequencies.
– Compute the discrete cosine transform (DCT) of the list of mel log powers as if it were a signal. (Note: Basically one of the important applications of DCT is to discard negligible number of high frequency components during compression.)
– The amplitudes of resulting spectrum give MFCCs [9].

4   Gaussian Mixture Models (GMMs) as Classifiers

Different pattern classifiers such as artificial neural networks, Gaussian mixture models, hidden Markov models, decision trees, Kozinecs algorithm, non-linear (smooth) SVM, K-nearest neighbor algorithm, polynomial classifiers, logistic regression, least square methods, perceptron classifiers or linear support vector machines (SVM) may be used for different speech processing tasks, such as speech recognition, speaker recognition, emotion classification, speaker verification and so on [10]. Gaussian mixture models have been found to perform well with MFCCs, their derivatives and LPCCs as feature vectors and hence, have been used as classifiers. GMMs are used to develop emotion recognition models (ERMs) in this work, using spectral features. GMMs capture distribution of data points from the input feature space.

In this work, one GMM is developed to capture the information about one emotion. The components within each GMM capture finer level details among the feature vectors of each emotion. Depending on the number of data points, number of components may be varied in each GMM. Presence of few components in GMM, and trained with large number of data points may lead to more generalized clusters, failing to capture specific details related to each class. On the other hand over fitting of the data points may happen, if too many components represent few data points. Obviously the complexity of the models will increase, if they contain higher number of components. Number of Gausses in the mixture model is known as number of components. They indicate the number of clusters in which data points are to be classified [11].

In this work, one GMM is developed to capture the information about one emotion. The components within each GMM capture finer level details among the feature vectors of each emotion. Depending on the number of data points, number of components may be varied in each GMM. Presence of few components in GMM and trained using large number of data points may lead to more generalized clusters, failing to capture specific details related to each class. On the other hand over fitting of the data points may happen, if too many components represent few data points. Obviously the complexity of the models increases, if they contain higher number of components. In this work, GMMs are designed with 64 components and iterated for 100 times to attain convergence of weights. The decision regarding the emotion category of the feature vector is taken based on its probability of coming from feature vectors of the specific model. Gaussian mixture models (GMMs) are among the most statistically matured methods for clustering and for density estimation. They model the probability density function of observed data points using a multivariate Gaussian mixture density. Given a set of inputs, GMM refines the weights of each distribution through expectation-maximization algorithm. Once a model is generated, conditional probabilities can be computed for test patterns (unknown data points) [12].

5   Emotion Recognition Models (ERMs)

Emotion recognition models are developed using male, female and male+female speaker utterances. 90% of the data is used for training the emotion recognition models and 10% is used for validation. Figure 3 illustrates the overall methodology of an emotion recognition system. The process is divided into two parts: feature extraction phase and emotion recognition phase. From each speech utterance features (MFCCs or LPCCs) are extracted. Subsequently, feature vectors are formed. These feature vectors are given as input to the emotion recognition development phase. In the training stage, the feature vectors are used to train the GMM models. In the recognition stage, the feature vectors of test utterances are given to already trained models. Validation is done by giving test utterances to already trained models. Emotion Recognition Models are developed using MFCCS, LPCCs and their Δ and $\Delta - \Delta$ features obtained from the speech signal.

While using GEU-SNESC, the text of the dialogues recorded from different movies was not same. Hence, the emotional utterances used for training and testing the GMM models contains different text. This is the reason that the recognition performance is quoted as text independent. In this case, it may be noted that the influence of phonetic information on emotion recognition is least.

Table 1 shows the results of emotion recognition using 29 MFCCs in the form of confusion matrix. In the confusion matrix, diagonal elements represent correct classification of emotions whereas other members in the row give us misclassification pattern. As shown in Table 1, 76% of happy utterances are classified as happiness, 4% are detected as neutral and 20% are identified as surprise. Emotions like surprise are not expressed alone in real life, but come interlaced with other emotions like anger, happiness and fear. Similarly, fear is mostly expressed along with surprise. So, for such emotions, results obtained are comparatively less.

Table 2 shows the average emotion recognition performance for 6 emotions using semi natural database (GEU-SNESC). Emotion recognition performance is calculated using 6, 8, 13, 21 and 29 LPCCs and MFCCs as feature vectors as well as derivatives (Δ and $\Delta - \Delta$ coefficients) of MFCCs. Emotion recognition

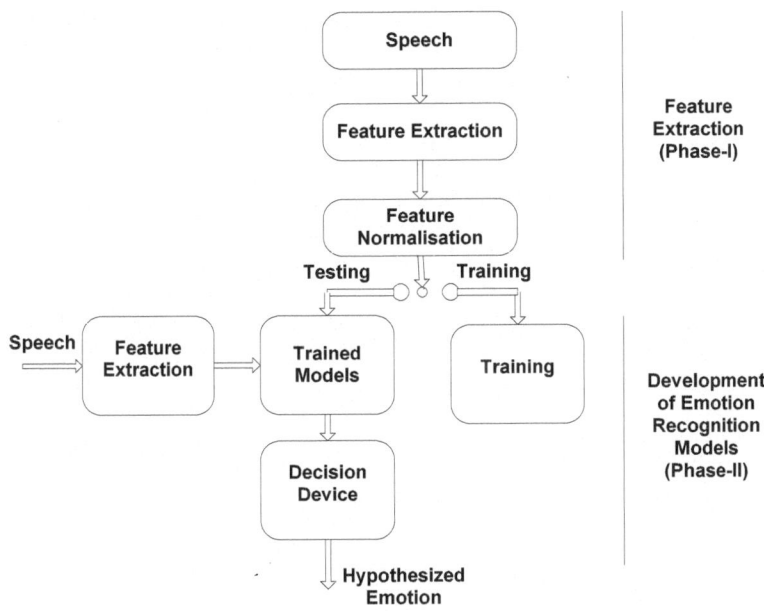

Fig. 3. Development of Emotion Recognition System

Table 1. Confusion matrix for single male speaker using 29 MFCCs (GEU-SNESC)

	Anger	Fear	Happy	Neutral	Sad	Surprise
Anger	72	4	0	0	4	20
Fear	12	60	0	0	0	28
Happy	0	0	76	4	0	20
Neutral	0	0	0	68	24	8
Sad	0	0	0	16	84	0
Surprise	16	20	12	20	0	32

performance for five emotions with 6, 8, 13, 21 and 29 LPCCs is observed to be 30.5%, 31.7%, 34.3%, 32.3% and 25.2% respectively. When 6, 8, 13, 21 and 29 MFCCs are used as feature vectors, average emotion recognition is found to be 48.7%, 51%, 46.8%, 46% and 65.3% respectively. It is observed that emotion recognition performance is better with MFCCs as compared with LPCCs. Highest emotion recognition performance of 65.3% is achieved with 29 MFCCs. Recognition of neutral emotion is significantly poor as in case of natural speech conversation, utterances of humans are never neutral, but always contain some emotion.

Table 3 shows the emotion recognition performance using velocity and acceleration coefficients of MFCCs and LPCCS. Average text independent emotion recognition performance for 6 emotions (64 centres, 100 iterations) is compared for semi-natural database (GEU-SNESC) and simulated database

Table 2.   Average emotion classification performance with seminatural database (GEU-SNESC) using varying number of spectral features and their derivatives

Emotion recognition models	No. of LPCCs					No. of MFCCs				
	6	8	13	21	29	6	8	13	21	29
	Recognition performance (in %)					Recognition performance (in %)				
Anger	14	12	20	18	4	35	39	26	30	72
Fear	31	29	36	32	22	46	50	47	43	60
Happy	88	76	83	77	79	58	58	71	71	76
Neutral	4	9	12	7	4	13	17	9	17	68
Sad	22	43	35	39	17	88	92	74	66	84
Surprise	24	21	20	21	25	52	50	54	49	32
Average	30.5	31.7	34.3	32.3	25.2	48.7	51	46.8	46	65.3

Table 3. Emotion classification performance (in %), using velocity and acceleration coefficients of MFCC and LPCC features for single male speaker (64 centres and 100 iterations), employing block processing approach

	29 LPCCs + Δ + $(\Delta - \Delta)$	29 MFCCs + Δ + $(\Delta - \Delta)$
Anger	64	84
Fear	32	60
Happy	31	76
Neutral	43	68
Sad	28	80
Surprise	34	40
Average	38.7	68

(IITKGP-SESC) in Table 4. For sigle male and female speaker, using semi-natural database, it is observed to be 65.3% and 72% (29 MFCCs+Δ+$(\Delta - \Delta)$) respectively. For simulated database, it is observed to be 63.50% and 77.83% respectively (13 MFCCs). Slight improvement in performance is observed by using velocity and acceleration coefficients.

The numbers shown in the Table 4 indicate the emotion recognition performance of 6 common emotions of two speech corpora using 13 and 29 MFCC features and their velocity and acceleration coefficients respectively. Utterances used used for training the Emotion Recognition Models are chosen to represent different speakers and both the genders. Hence the classification is purely performed on the basis of underlying emotions.

In case of simulated databases, emotions are artificially emulated by artists, while in case of semi-natural databases, emotions expressed are more natural. Therefore, the results obtained with simulated database are better than those obtained with semi-natural database. Results obtained using semi natural Hindi movie database are compared for male, female, male+female speakers. As the number of emotions to be classified increase, the complexity of system increases and there are more chances of an utterance being detected as some other emotion. Combination of features (LFPC+LPCC+MFCC) has also been experimented

Table 4. Emotion classification performance (in %), of 6 common emotions of two speech corpora using 13 and 29 MFCC features and their velocity and acceleration coefficients respectively (64 centres and 100 iterations), employing block processing approach

Emotion	IITKGP-SESC	GEU-SNESC
Male	63.50	65.3
Female	77.83	72
Male+Female	60.3	52

upon, but not much improvement is observed [13]. Emotions like surprise and fear are better expressed by professional artists in simulated databases but combined with other emotions in real life situations and hence, can't be distinguished well [14]. Table 5 gives a summary of average emotion recognition performance with single speaker, while using different features, classifiers and databases. The databases used are IITKGP-SESC and Emo-DB. It is observed that emotion recognition performance with MFCCs and their velocity and acceleration coefficients is the best. Gaussian Mixture Models have fared better than other classifiers in speech emotion classification. The classifier, GMM basically categorises the data points based on their distribution, whereas SVM categorises them on the basis of their discriminating properties. Therefore, an emotion recognition system that uses both GMM and SVM in supplementary manner, may perform better [16][18].

Table 5. Emotion classification performance (in %), using different features, classifiers and databases. LVQ : Learning Vector Quantiser, Emo-DB : Berlin Database of Emotional speech, SVM : Support Vector Machines, s.l. : subjective listening, t.i. : text independent, t.d. : text dependent.

Features	Classifiers	Databases	Performance	Ref.
LFPCs+LPCCs+MFCCs	LVQ	IITKGP-SESC	40%	[13]
LPCCs+MFCCs	LVQ	IITKGP-SESC	36%	[13]
LPCCs+MFCCs	LVQ	IITKGP-SESC	60% (s. l.)	[13]
MFCCs+Δ+Δ-Δ	GMM	IITKGP-SESC	72% (t. i.)	[14]
MFCCs+Δ+Δ-Δ	GMM	IITKGP-SESC	82% (t. d.)	[14]
LPCCs+VOPs	GMM+SVM	IITKGP-SESC	63.75%	[15]
Epoch parameters	GMM	IITKGP-SESC	61%	[16]
Epoch parameters	GMM	Emo-DB	59%	[16]
Epoch parameters	SVM	IITKGP-SESC	58%	[16]
Epoch parameters	SVM	Emo-DB	60%	[16]
L P Residual	AANN	IITKGP-SESC	48.21%	[17]
LP Residual	GMM	IITKGP-SESC	56.49%	[17]

6   Summary and Conclusion

In this work, semi natural speech corpus, collected from Hindi movies has been
used to characterize and classify the emotions. MFCC and LPCC features along
with their velocity and acceleration coefficients are used to capture emotion specific information from vocal tract of the speaker. The purpose of this study is to
investigate the spectral features for their containment of emotion specific information. Gaussian mixture models, known to capture the distribution pattern of
feature vectors are used as emotion classifiers. From the obtained results, it may
be observed that 29 MFCCs, along with their Δ and $\Delta - \Delta$ features have given
better results. It indicates that higher order spectral features contain better emotion specific information. The average emotion recognition performance for the
same emotions in the case of simulated emotion speech corpus (IITKGP-SESC)
is considerably high compared to the results of GEU-SNESC mostly due to the
influence of phonetic information on emotion recognition. As a continuance of
these studies, prosodic features may be used in combination with spectral features to further improve the emotion recognition performance of the models.
SVM and AANN may be explored as classifiers to further enhance the performance of ERMs. Emotion recognition in real world scenario expects language
independent emotion recognition. Therefore, there is a need to develop language
independent emotion recognition systems as well.

References

1. Pao, T.-L., Chen, Y.-T., Yeh, J.-H., Liao, W.-Y.: Combining Acoustic Features for
   Improved Emotion Recognition in Mandarin Speech. In: Tao, J., Tan, T., Picard,
   R.W. (eds.) ACII 2005. LNCS, vol. 3784, pp. 279–285. Springer, Heidelberg (2005)
2. Koolagudi, S.G., Maity, S., Kumar, V.A., Chakrabarti, S., Sreenivasa Rao, K.:
   IITKGP-SESC: Speech Database for Emotion Analysis. In: Ranka, S., Aluru, S.,
   Buyya, R., Chung, Y.-C., Dua, S., Grama, A., Gupta, S.K.S., Kumar, R., Phoha,
   V.V. (eds.) IC3 2009. CCIS, vol. 40, pp. 485–492. Springer, Heidelberg (2009)
3. Neiberg, D., Elenius, K., Laskowski, K.: Emotion recognition in spontaneous speech
   using gmms. In: INTERSPEECH 2006 - ICSLP, Pittsburgh, Pennsylvania, September 17-19, pp. 809–812 (2006)
4. Li, Y., Zhao, Y.: Recognizing emotions in speech using short-term and long-term
   features. In: Proc. of the International Conference on Speech and Language Processing, pp. 2255–2258 (1998)
5. Koolagudi, S.G., Maity, S., Kumar, V.A., Chakrabarti, S., Sreenivasa Rao, K.:
   Characterization of Emotions Using The Dynamics of Prosodic Features. CCIS,
   vol. 40. Springer (August 2009)
6. Sreenivasa Rao, K., Yegnanarayana, B.: Duration modification using glottal closure
   instants and vowel onset points. Speech Communication 51, 1263–1269 (2009),
   doi:10.1016/j.specom.2009.06.004
7. Koolagudi, S.G., Maity, S., Kumar, V.A., Chakrabarti, S., Sreenivasa Rao, K.:
   IITKGP-SESC: Speech Database for Emotion Analysis. In: Ranka, S., Aluru, S.,
   Buyya, R., Chung, Y.-C., Dua, S., Grama, A., Gupta, S.K.S., Kumar, R., Phoha,
   V.V. (eds.) IC3 2009. CCIS, vol. 40, pp. 485–492. Springer, Heidelberg (2009)

8. Chauhan, R., Yadav, J., Koolagudi, S.G., Sreenivasa Rao, K.: Text Independent Emotion Recognition Using Spectral Features. In: Aluru, S., Bandyopadhyay, S., Catalyurek, U.V., Dubhashi, D.P., Jones, P.H., Parashar, M., Schmidt, B. (eds.) IC3 2011. CCIS, vol. 168, pp. 359–370. Springer, Heidelberg (2011)
9. Rabiner, L.R., Juang, B.H.: Fundamentals of Speech Recognition. Prentice-Hall, Englewood Cliffs (1993)
10. Prasanna, S.R.M., Reddy, B.V.S., Krishnamoorthy, P.: Vowel onset point detection using source, spectral peaks, and modulation spectrum energies. IEEE Trans. Audio, Speech, and Language Processing 17, 556–565 (2009)
11. Murty, K., Yegnanarayana, B.: Epoch extraction from speech signals. IEEE Trans. Audio, Speech, and Language Processing 16, 1602–1613 (2008)
12. Koolagudi, S.G., Kumar, N., Sreenivasa Rao, K.: Speech emotion recognition using segmental level prosodic analysis. In: IEEE International Confernce on device Communication BIT MESRA, India (2011)
13. Koolagudi, S.G., Nandy, S., Sreenivasa Rao, K.: Spectral Features for Emotion Classification. In: IEEE International Confernce on Device Communication BIT MESRA, India (2011)
14. Chauhan, R., Yadav, J., Koolagudi, S.G., Sreenivasa Rao, K.: Text Independent Emotion Recognition Using Spectral Features. In: Aluru, S., Bandyopadhyay, S., Catalyurek, U.V., Dubhashi, D.P., Jones, P.H., Parashar, M., Schmidt, B. (eds.) IC3 2011. CCIS, vol. 168, pp. 359–370. Springer, Heidelberg (2011)
15. Koolagudi, S.G., Kumar, N., Sreenivasa Rao, K.: Speech Emotion Recognition Using Segmental Level Prosodic Analysis. In: 2011 International Conference on Devices and Communications (ICDeCom), February 24-25, pp. 1–5 (2011)
16. Koolagudi, S.G., Reddy, R., Sreenivasa Rao, K.: Emotion recognition from speech signal using epoch parameters. In: 2010 International Conference on Signal Processing and Communications (SPCOM), July 18-21, pp. 1–5 (2010)
17. Chauhan, A., Koolagudi, S.G., Kafley, S., Sreenivasa Rao, K.: Emotion recognition using LP residual. In: 2010 IEEE Students' Technology Symposium (TechSym), April 3-4, pp. 255–261 (2010)
18. Iliev, A.I., Michael, S.S.: Spoken emotion recognition using glottal symmetry. EURASIP Journal on Advances in Signal Processing 1-11 (2011)

Storage and Retrieval of Large Data Sets: Dimensionality Reduction and Nearest Neighbour Search

A. Poorna Chandrasekhar and T. Sobha Rani

Department of Computer and Information Sciences,
University of Hyderabad,
Hyderabad, India
tsrcs@uohyd.ernet.in

Abstract. Storing and querying are two important issues that need to be addressed while designing an information retrieval system for a large and high-dimensional data set. In this work, we discuss about tackling such data, specifically about the nearest neighbour search and the efficient storage layout to store such data. The data set used in the current work has been taken from an online source called ZINC, a repository for drug like chemical structures. Processing a high dimensional data is a tough task hence dimensionality reduction should be employed. Here for dimensionality reduction is achieved through a filter-based feature selection method, based on correlation fractal dimension (CFD) discrimination measure, is used. The number of dimensions using the correlation fractal dimension are reduced from 58 to 7. To identify the nearest neighbours for a given chemical structure Tanimoto similarity coefficient is used with these reduced set of features. The nearest neighbours identified using the Tanimoto measure are stored in a storage layout known as modified inverted file. Nearest neighbours for a query can be retrieved back from the storage layout, with just one read operation from the data file thereby reducing the time for retrieval.

Keywords: Correlation Fractal Dimension, Modified inverted file, Nearest neighbour, Dimensionality reduction.

1 Introduction

In recent years, there is a tremendous increase in data generation and storage and this vast amount of storage is termed as large storage. Many corporates and servicing systems such as social networking sites, railway reservation systems, banks, insurance companies, etc. are maintaining millions of records which amount to terabytes of memory or even more. Efficient management of this storage is essential in order to obtain information from this huge data. The higher the number of dimensions more complex the management will be. Some applications that use large high dimensional data are content based image retrieval, searching for similar chemical structures and so on.

M. Parashar et al. (Eds.): IC3 2012, CCIS 306, pp. 262–272, 2012.
© Springer-Verlag Berlin Heidelberg 2012

The retrieval and insertion operations on such data are of great importance. They should be performed efficiently so that their time complexity and space complexity is within the manageable limits. This work is an attempt to deal with this topic that is how to get nearest neighbours efficiently when the data is large and high dimensional and how to store such a data and which storage layout is to be used.

In content based image retrieval and searching for chemical structures of similar nature, we have to identify the entries close or similar to the given query. One method to identify the similar things close to the given query could be a nearest neighbour search. The nearest neighbours obtained by this nearest neighbour search will become the results for the given query. Since data is very high dimensional, nearest neighbour search in this high dimensional space is not at all efficient, because of the curse of dimensionality. Hence before doing operations on such data we have to reduce the number of dimensions that is we have to perform dimensionality reduction. After dimensionality reduction is done, using the reduced feature set we perform the operations on the data to retrieve the nearest neighbours. Operations that are performed using the reduced features will not cost much. But the reduced features should not lose the behaviour of the whole data, if so there is no point in using the reduced features. The major contributing features should be selected omitting the remaining features. We have to be careful about choosing a particular dimensionality reduction algorithm. The algorithm that we choose should not take much time and also it should cull features in a meaningful manner.

In order to find nearest neighbours for a particular reference, a variety of similarity metrics are available to quantify the similarity between reference and database item. Tanimoto Coefficient continues to be the most popular metric because of its ability to quantify the similarity between two items. The range of Tanimoto Coefficient is from 0 to 1. For highly similar cases Tanimoto Coefficient is very near to 1 and for any pair of dissimilar cases it is close to 0.

The storage layout that we use, should take less time for any operation such as insertion or deletion. Consider a binary search tree, for which any operation will take $O(\log_2 n)$ time whereas for a B-tree of minimum degree 't' the time required will be $O(\log_t n)$ time [1]. There are some new advanced storage layouts that will reduce this time further to $O(\log \log u)$ time, where u is the size of the universe. Here our data size should not be far less than u, if so it will not be effective. The other issue is that the storage layout that we use should also have higher storage utilization, means that it should not have sparsely filled nodes. If so, we have to spend on the cost of additional storage.

1.1 Dimensionality Reduction

We may require a large number of examples which grows exponentially with the number of features to analyze or make predictions. But, this may not be feasible in real life data sets. In order to reduce the computational complexity we will attempt to reduce the number of features. Dimensionality reduction not only reduces the computational cost but also can increase the accuracy by removing noise and redundant attributes/features. Usually the reduced number of features should match the intrinsic dimensionality of the data [2]. Dimensionality reduction techniques can viewed as linear and non-linear techniques.

Principal component analysis (PCA) [3], factor analysis [4], classical scaling [5], Partial least squares (PLS) [6] are some of the the linear techniques. These traditional techniques may not be able to handle complex real world problems. Hence a set of non-linear methods are developed. There are several non-linear techniques available in the literature. Maaten et al. have done a comparative study of some of these techniques with PCA [7]. They have evaluated the reduction using the generalization errors of 1-NN classifer trained on the low dimensional data and trust worthiness and continuity of low dimensional embeddings. They have conclluded that despite the ability of the non-linear techniques to learn the data better, they are unable to outperform PCA.

Several researchers working in this area proposed new ways to tackle this problem. H. Lejsek, et al. proposed a disk based data structure known as NV-tree, Nearest Vector tree [8] which can give good approximate answers to nearest neighbour queries with a single disk operation, even for large data. But a lot of work of projecting and partitioning is needed here. H.Y. Lin, et al. proposed a new data insertion algorithm to KDB-tree with a better splitting policy [9]. But it takes more than one disk read for retrieval operation.

We proposed a storage layout for this problem which is similar to inverted file, used as a storage structure for search engines, thus we call it as "modified inverted file". It is easy to create and we need just one read operation to retrieve the nearest neighbours from it, for the given query, after the query is mapped to key.

The remaining part of the paper is organized as below. In Section 2, the data set that we used is explained. Our approach is explained in Section 3 and the results along with implementation details are explained in Section 4. The conclusions are given in Section 5.

2   Data Set

We require a large and high dimensional data set to conduct experiments. So for such data, a data set of drug like chemical structures has been taken from an online source ZINC [10]. ZINC which stands for ZINC is not commercial, is a free database of commercially available chemical compounds for virtual screenng and it contains over 13 million purchasable compounds. The different formats for chemical structures that ZINC provides are SMILES, mol2, 3D SDF, and DOCK flexibase formats. For each chemical structure, ZINCID and SMILES notation of the chemical structure are also noted. **SMILES(Simplified Molecular Input Line Entry System)** representation is one of the many ways to write a chemical structure in linear format. It is a chemical information system that gives a string representation for a 2D or 3D molecule.

In ZINC, there are different subsets of chemical structures like drug like, fragment like, lead like, etc. The present data set belongs to "drug like" chemical structures. The data set contains a total of 8,783,230 chemical structures. It also provides 9 calculated properties - molecular Weight, logP, apolar desolvation, polar desolvation, No. of HBA, No. of HBD, tPSA, Charge, NRB and ZINCID for each molecule. Apart from these 9 physical properties provided by ZINC, 49 other features have been extracted from the SMILES notation of the chemical structures by Sankara et al. [11]. There are 58 features in total from different classes of features such as physical, atom count, structural and functional groups. These are listed in Table 1.

Table 1. 58 features [10], [11]

Physical(9)	Atom Count(10)	Structural(9)
1. Mol. Weight	10. Br Count	20. Cyclic
2. logP	11. C Count	21. Acyclic
3. De_apolar	12. Cl Count	22. Mono Cyclic
4. De_polar	13. F Count	23. Bi CYclic
5. HBD	14. I Count	24.Tri Cyclic
6. HBA	15. N Count	26. Hi cyclic($>$5 cycles)
7. tPSA	16. Na Count	27. Hetero cyclic
8. Charge	17. O Count	28. Chiral Centers
9. NRB	18. P Count	
	19. S Count	
Functional Groups(30)		
29. -Cl	39. -COOH	49. -CHO
30. -Br	40. -COOR	50. Ketone
31. -F	41. -COOCl	51. Thiketone
32. -O	42. Cyano	52. Peptide
33. -S	43. Isocynate	53. Nitroso
34. -N	44. –C=N-R	54. Nitro
35. Alkylamino	45. Acetyne	55. Furon
36. Dialkylamino	46. Ethylene	
37. Amide	47. Azo N#N	56. Pynol
38. Amide2	48. Phenol	57. Aromatic
		58. Phenyl

3   Approach

3.1   Dimensionality Reduction

It is difficult to process high dimensional data, hence first we need to reduce the dimensionality. Traditional methods available in literature are PCA, wavelets and so on. It is often difficult to interpret the features obtained through these methods and also they are not suitable for huge amounts of data. If the data is huge, numerosity reduction can be done using stratified selection, clustering, random undersampling or random oversampling etc. Each of these can introduce their own peculiarities into the picture. For this a feature selection algorithm based on correlation fractal dimension (CFD) is used [12].

Correlation Fractal Dimension. Fractal dimension is nothing but a non-integer dimension in contrast to the topological dimension which is always an integer. Correlation fractal dimension [12] is one of the generalized dimensions and is defined below which captures the probability of finding pairs of points within a distance of r.

Let an optimal n-dimenS.D.sional box be chosen such that it contains the entire n-dimensional data set. The box is divided into a grid of cells of size r and let $p_{k,r}$ denote the probability with which the points of the data set fall inside cell k. The correlation fractal dimension is given below.

$$CFD = \lim_{r \to 0} \frac{\log \sum_k p_{k,r}^2}{-\log r} \tag{1}$$

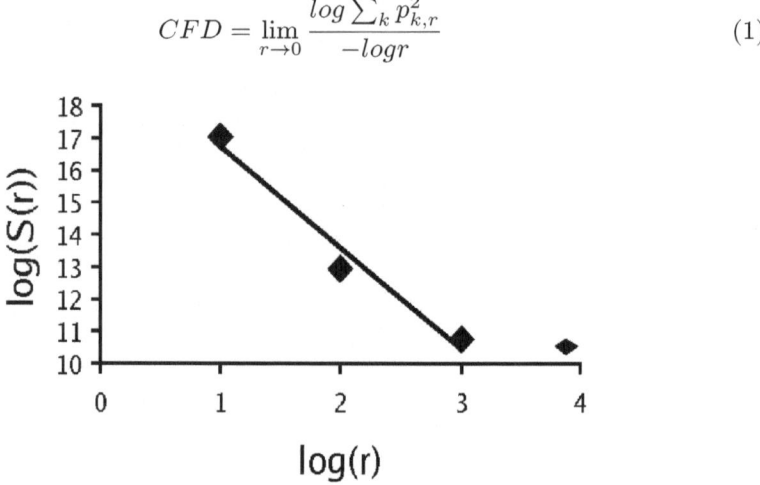

Fig. 1. Slope of the line gives the correlation fractal dimension

Figure 1 shows the plot of $\log S(r)$ where $S(r) = \sum_k p_{k,r}^2$ and $\log(r)$, where r is the grid scale resolution. CFD is approximately equal to the slope of the line that fits best to the plot of the values of $\log \sum_k p_{k,r}^2$ for each log r.

Given an N dimensional data set that is, with N attributes, the CFD will be a number less than or equal to N. For a one-dimensional data set of points, the value of CFD would be within the range 0 to 1 giving some measure of the distribution of points. The higher the CFD value, the higher is the distribution of points. So to do dimensionality reduction, we have to find CFD value for each feature in the data set and filter the features which do not contribute much i.e., the features which have less CFD value. Here we select top contributing features which results in dimensionality reduction. These selected features should perform as well as the original set of features. We have to filter the features to achieve this goal.

The reason for using this algorithm for dimensionality reduction is that it is a filter-based feature selection method, based on correlation fractal dimension (CFD) discrimination measure. It does not give new features. CFD value is based on the distribution of the data only. So weakly distributed features will have less value. And then we filter the features with less CFD value. So we will get the features that contribute in a large way.

3.2   Calculation of Nearest Neighbours

Tanimoto Similarity Coefficient. To calculate nearest neighbours for all the chemical structures in the data set, first we should be able to measure the similarity between each pair. For that, a similarity coefficient known as Tanimoto coefficient [11] is used. It gives the similarity for any pair of data points in the range 0 to 1. The similarity value of 1 means that both data points are exactly similar and in the same way the similarity value of 0 means that both data points are exactly dissimilar. For any two given data points A and B, Tanimoto coefficient is defined as:

$$TC(A, B) = \frac{\sum_{i=1}^{n} a_i b_i}{\sum_{i=1}^{n} a_i^2 + \sum_{i=1}^{n} b_i^2 - \sum_{i=1}^{n} a_i b_i} \tag{2}$$

Here a_i and b_i represent i^{th} feature value of A and B respectively.

In this approach, we need to find the Tanimoto similarity coefficient for each pair of chemical structures which is a very laborious task and takes much time especially when n, size of the data set is large.

3.3   Storage Layout

Modified Inverted File. An efficient storage layout is needed to store the nearest neighbours obtained for retrieval efficiency. Here a storage layout is used which is similar to **inverted file** [13] or **inverted index** and it can be called as **modified inverted file**.

An inverted file [13], which is used in search engines, consists of an index and a number of postings lists. The index contains a list of all the distinct keywords in the collection. Each keyword has a pointer to a postings list, which is a list of document identifiers to documents that contain the keyword.

The storage layout used in this work is similar to it and contains an index and a data file. We have a key value for each chemical structure. The index contains all these key values. The data file contains all the nearest neighbours for each chemical stucture. In the index, each key value has a pointer to the corresponding nearest neighbours in the data file.

In the inverted file, the size of a postings list is not fixed. Different keywords may have postings lists of different sizes. But in our case, each chemical structure has same number of nearest neighbours and a nearest neighbour needs a fixed memory. So any chemical structure needs a fixed amount of memory here. It enables us in a way that, just by having a key value we can find out the location of the corresponding nearest neighbours in the data file. For example, suppose that a chemical structure requires 1300 bytes to store all its nearest neighbours. Then we can calculate that, in the data file, the starting location of nearest neighbours of a chemical structure with key 2386 as byte number: (2385*1300)+1. So we no longer need index to locate the required address in the data file for a given key. So in our storage layout, it is enough to maintain only the data file as we are able to locate the required address in the data file automatically based on the key itself. It means that, here the index is implicitly maintained.

Space Complexity
In the modified inverted file we do not need this additional storage, in fact we need not store the key values also, it is enough to store the nearest neighbours alone.

Time Complexity
The time required to retrive the nearest neighbours is less for modified inverted file. The reason for this is that there is no need to traverse the tree to know the offset corresponding to the given key instead we need to perform a simple mathematical calculation to know the offset to find the nearest neighbours.

Updation
For modified inverted file, it is enough to simply add the nearest neighbours of new chemical structures at the end of the file.

4   Experiments and Results

4.1   Dimensionality Reduction Using CFD

The CFD (Correlation fractal dimension) algorithm is implemented in C language. A sample data set of size 50000 was taken from the actual data set. This data set is divided feature wise using statistical package R. Each of these feature wise sets are normalized. The CFD algorithm is run on each of these normalized feature wise sets and a CFD value was obtained for each feature. CFD values for all the 58 features in decreasing order of the CFD value are shown in Table 2.

Here the features like log P, De_apolar, tPSA, De_polar, MWT. etc. got higher CFD values as they are distributed well in their domain and in the same way features like I, Na, Phenol, etc. got lower CFD values as they are sparsely distributed in their domain and do not contribute much in decision making about the chemical structures. The graphs of the distribution of the features MWT which has high correlation fractal dimension and I which has low correlation fractal dimension are shown in Figure 2.

Based on the CFD value, now all the features can be ranked and the top ranked features can be selected for dimensionality reduction. Here the top six features and the feature "Cyclic" which represents number of cycles are selected reducing the number of features from 58 to 7. The remaining 51 features were filtered by this approach. The reason for selecting these 7 features is that these are supposed to find the more meaningful nearest neighbours for a given query. The feature "Cyclic" is ranked relatively less when compared to the features: number of rotatable bonds, number of oxygens, number of nitrogens but "Cyclic" is selected ahead of them, for the reason that, any two similar chemical structures are likely to contain same number of cycles than same number of oxygens or nitrogens. The reduced features and their CFD values are shown in bold in Table 2.

To find out the efficacy of these features we have extracted the nearest neighbours based on Tanimoto measure from these 50000 test data set. We have extracted the nearest neighbours using 28 features other than the functional groups and also the nearest neighnours using the reduced set of features mentioned in

Table 2. CFD values of all the 58 features

Feature	CFD value	Feature	CFD value
log P	**0.9874**	-Br	0
De_apolar	**0.9075**	-F	0
tPSA	**0.8504**	-O	0
De_polar	**0.8419**	-S	0
MWT	**0.8204**	-N	0
C	**0.7678**	Alkylamino	0
NRB	0.7312	Dialkylamino	0
O	0.7210	Amide	0
N	0.7059	Amide2	0
Cyclic	**0.6188**	-COOH	0
HBA	0.5931	-COOR	0
HBD	0.5856	-COOCl	0
S	0.5425	Cyano	0
Cl	0.3035	Isocynate	0
Charge	0.2682	–C=N-R	0
Br	0.2097	Acetyne	0
F	0.1357	Ethylene	0
I	0	Azo N#N	0
Na	0	Phenol	0
P	0	-CHO	0
Acyclic	0	Ketone	0
Mono	0	Thiketone	0
BiCy	0	Peptide	0
TriCy	0	Nitroso	0
TetCy	0	Nitro	0
HiCy	0	Furon	0
HeteroCy	0	Pynol	0
Chiral	0	Aromatic S	0
-Cl	0	Phenyl	0

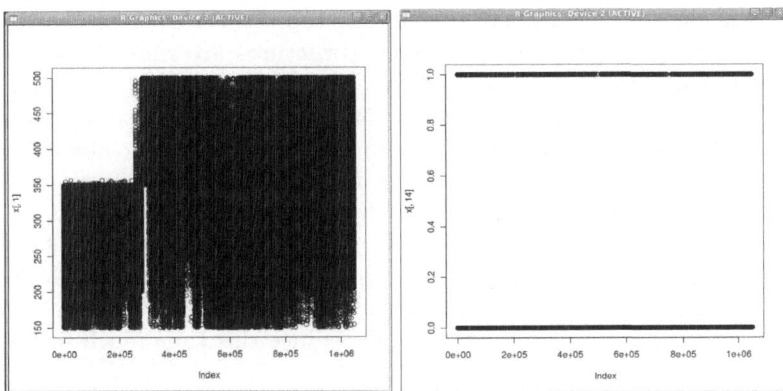

Fig. 2. Distribution of Molecular weight(MWT), Iodine(I) respectively

the Table 2. We have tried to match the number of nearest neighbours extracted using both sets of features and the number of matches. Figure 3 gives the results of this comparison with x-axis denoting the number of nearest neighbours and the y-axis denoting the number matches between nearest neighbours extracted using 28 dimensions and 7 reduced dimensions. The relationship is almost linear, thereby indicating that the dimensionality reduction is picking up good features for nearest neighbour search.

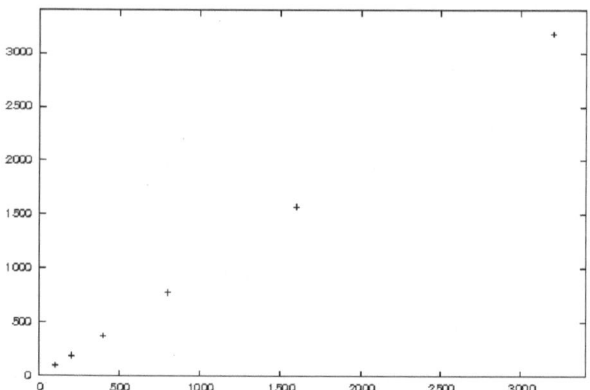

Fig. 3. Number of matches between nearest neighbours retrieved by using 28 dimensions and 7 dimensions culled out using correlation fractal dimension

4.2   Calculation of Nearest Neighbours

A sample data set of size 262,143 was taken from the actual data set. Now using the Tanimoto coefficient, similarity value is found out for each pair of chemical structures of the sample data set considering top 6 features only. Now for each chemical structure, all the other chemical structures are ranked based on the pairwise similarity value and top 100 were selected as the nearest neighbours. Here ranking was given only when number of cycles are same in both the chemical structures, otherwise it would be skipped from the ranking. One advantage with scheme is that the k-nearest neighbours can be any number in fact since we do a sorting based on the similarity score to find the k nearest neighbours.

To calculate 100 nearest neighbours for a given query on this data set, the time needed was approximately 2.3 seconds and thus to calculate nearest neighbours for all the chemical structures it took 262143 multiplied by 2.3 seconds which is almost 167 hours. A parallel processing will reduce this time much further.

4.3   Modified Inverted File

After calculating 100 nearest neighbours for all the chemical structures, they are written to the data file. Here for every chemical structure, its 100 nearest neighbours were written to disk as a whole, so that this data will be in a single location on the disk if available. The advantage of it is that when we retrieve nearest neighbours for the given query, we read as a whole once again leading to just one disk read. Each chemical structure was assigned unique key value in the range of 1 to 262,143. That is the creation of the modified inverted file.

Now the modified inverted file is ready with all the precomputed nearest neighbours for each chemical structure. Now one can retrieve nearest neighbours for any chemical structure just by one read operation. Here the input will be the ZINCID of the query chemical structure which is mapped to the key using which we can calculate the location of the corresponding nearest neighbours in the data file. So we go to the location directly and perform one read operation to read all the 100 nearest neighbours.

5   Conclusions

A large and high dimensional data set of drug like chemical structures was taken which is of size 8,783,230 and represented using 58 features. Dimensionality reduction is done using a filter-based feature selection method, based on correlation fractal dimension (CFD) discrimination measure and the data set is reduced to 7 features. One caution is that the CFD works well with real values rather than with quantized values. Hundred nearest neighbours were calculated for each chemical structure of the data set of size 262,143 which is sampled from the actual data set. These nearest neighbours were kept in a storage layout known as modified inverted file. Using just one read operation after mapping the query to its key, we can retrieve the nearest neighbours of a chemical structure from the storage layout.

Whatever is the size of the data set, we need just one read operation from the data file after mapping the query to key, to retrieve the nearest neighbours. Without using any precomputation and any storage layout we need approximately 100 seconds to calculate 100 nearest neighbours for a given chemical structure when the data set of size 8,783,230 is used. Our approach takes less than a second for this. So it is greatly helpful when we have to find the nearest neighbours very frequently, when we have to find nearest neighbours for thousands of chemical structures. It is highly advantageous to maintain online chemical databases.

Nearest neighbours are to be calculated for left over chemical structures also and these are to be kept in the storage layout. Deeper analysis is to be done in filtering the features because sometimes a relatively low ranked feature also is quite useful. Precomputation of nearest neighbours is a major time hogging process here. We would like to explore the possibility of generating an index scheme using the reduced features to identify the nearest neighbours automatically without having to resort to the precomputation.

We can in fact extend this scheme to any type of data such as image data, finacial data, biomedical data etc. We have to determine the features that are required to represent the data and the similrity measure required to compute the similar data items in the data base. Then we can apply the CFD algorithm to find the relevent features. Using these relevant features we do a one time search of nearest neighbours for all the data in the database. These nearest neighbours can be stored as modified inverted files. Searching for a query then will just reduces to fetching the relevant modified inverted file.

References

1. Cormen, T.H., Leiserson, C.E., Rivest, R.L.: Introduction to algorithms. The MIT Press, London (2000)
2. Fukunaga, K.: Introduction to Statistical Pattern Recognition. Academic Press Professional, Inc., San Diego (1990)
3. Pearson, K.: On lines and planes of closest t to systems of points in space. Philiosophical Magazine 2, 559–572 (1901)
4. Spearman, C.: General intelligence objectively determined and measured. American Journal of Psychology 15, 206–221 (1904)
5. Torgerson, W.S.: Multidimensional scaling I: Theory and method. Psychometrika 17, 401–419 (1952)
6. Nguyen, D.V., Rocke, D.M.: Tumor classication by partial least squares using microarray gene expression data. Bioinformatics 18, 39–50 (2002)
7. Maaten, L.V., Postma, E., Herik, J.V.: Dimensionality Reduction: A Comparative Review. Technical report: TiCC TR 2009-005 (2009)
8. Lejsek, H., Asmundsson, F.H., Jonsson, B.P., Amsaleg, L.: NV-Tree: An Efficient Disk-Based Index for Approximate Search in Very Large High-Dimensional Collections. IEEE Transactions on Pattern Analysis and Machine Intelligence 31, 869–883 (2009)
9. Lin, H.-Y., Huang, P.-W., Hsu, K.-H.: A new indexing method with high storage utilization and retrieval efficiency for large spatial databases. Information and Software Technology 49, 817–826 (2007)
10. ZINC- A free database for virtual screening, http://www.zinc.docking.org
11. Sankara Rao, A., Durga Bhavani, S., Sobha Rani, T., Bapi, R.S., Narahari Sastry, G.: Study of Diversity and Similarity of Large Chemical Databases Using Tanimoto Measure. In: Venugopal, K.R., Patnaik, L.M. (eds.) ICIP 2011. CCIS, vol. 157, pp. 40–50. Springer, Heidelberg (2011)
12. Bhavani, S.D., Rani, T.S., Bapi, R.S.: Feature selection using correlation fractal dimension: Issues and applications in binary classification problems. Applied Soft Computing 8, 555–563 (2008)
13. Garratt, A., Jackson, M., Burden, P., Wallis, J.: A survey of alternative designs for a search engine storage structure. Information and Software Technology 43, 661–677 (2001)

Emotion Recognition from Semi Natural Speech Using Artificial Neural Networks and Excitation Source Features

Shashidhar G. Koolagudi[1], Swati Devliyal[1],
Anurag Barthwal[1], and K. Sreenivasa Rao[2]

[1] School of Computing, Graphic Era University,
Dehradun -248002, Uttarakhand, India
[2] Indian Institute of Technology Kharagpur,
Kharagpur - 721302, West Bengal, India
koolagudi@yahoo.com, {swatidevliyal,anubarthwal,ksrao1969}@gmail.com

Abstract. This paper proposes Linear Prediction (LP) residual of speech signal for characterizing the basic emotions. LP residual is extracted from speech signal by LP analysis, by inverse filtering of the speech signal. LP residual basically contains higher order relations among the samples. Instant of glottal closure in a speech signal is known as an epoch. The significant excitation of vocal tract usually takes place at the instant of glottal closure. For analysing speech emotions, the LP residual samples chosen around glottal closure instants are used. A semi-natural database GEU-SNESC (Graphic Era University Semi Natural Emotion Speech Corpus) is used for modeling the emotions. This database is collected by recording dialogs of film actors from Hindi movies. In the study four emotions namely anger, happy, neutral and sadness are used. Auto-associative neural network models are used for characterizing the basic emotions present in the speech. Average emotion recognition of 66% and 59% is observed respectively for the epoch based and entire LP residual samples.

Keywords: Emotion Recognition, Epoch, Excitation Source information, LP residual, AANN (Auto-associative neural network).

1   Introduction

Speech signal contains information about textual message, speaker identity and intended emotion. In addition to the message conveyed through text, the manner in which these words are spoken also conveys essential non linguistic information. A sentence or a word in a speech may have several different meanings, depending on how it is said. For example, using the word *'What'* in English, a speaker can ask a question, express either admiration or disbelief. Therefore it may be said that it is important to interpret the meaning of a spoken word/sentence by understanding embedded emotion. So, it is important that speech systems would be able to process the underlying emotions along with the textual message. Emotion recognition in speech has many real life applications. Emotion processing can be used

M. Parashar et al. (Eds.): IC3 2012, CCIS 306, pp. 273–282, 2012.

for enhancing naturalness in speech based human machine interaction [1][2][3]. In call centers, emotion recognition system are helpful for examining the behavior of call attendants with their customers for improving quality of service [4]. For keeping the driver alert during driving to avoid accidents this system may be used as an on board car driving system, where information about mental state of a driver may be captured. Applications like interactive movie [5], story-telling [6] and e-tutoring [7] would be more practical, if they can adapt themselves to listener's emotional states. Emotional contents of a patient's speech can be used as one of the diagnosing tools by doctors for various ailments [8]. Emotion analysis of telephone conversation between criminals would help crime investigation department for the investigation. Robotic pets and humanoid partner's conversations would be more realistic, if they are able to understand and express emotions like humans. Call analysis in emergency services like ambulance and fire brigade, may help to evaluate genuineness of requests.

1.1   Related Work

Speech is produced from a time varying vocal tract system excited by a time varying excitation source. Speech signal contains information about message, speaker, language and intended emotion. In literature, some of the known features used for emotion processing are pitch, duration, energy, articulation, voice quality and spectral shapes [9]. McGilloway *et al.* have used the peaks and troughs in the profile of fundamental frequency, intensity and duration of pauses for identifying anger, fear, joy and sadness. They reported 55% of average emotion recognition rate using discriminant analysis [10]. Dellaert *et al.* used only F0 information and reported 79.5% of recognition rate for 4 emotions using k-nearest neighbor classifier [11]. Nicholas *et al.* used both prosodic and phonetic (power, intonation pattern, LPCs and delta LPC features) information for classifying 8 simulated emotions, and reported 50% recognition performance using neural network classifiers [12]. Ververidis *et al.* used short time prosodic features (pitch, energy, formant locations, formant band widths extracted frame wise) and statistics of their dynamic behavior [13]. Iida *et al.* exploited the complex relations between pitch, duration and energy for detecting the emotions [14]. Gobl et al combined vocal tract features, voice overtones and pitch dynamics to detect emotions [15]. Along with pitch related information Kwon *et al.* used log energy, formants, Mel based energy, MFCCs, delta MFCCs, delta-delta MFCCs for classifying the emotions [16]. Wang *et al.* used 55 dimensional feature vector (25-prosodic, 24-MFCCs and 6-formant frequencies) for recognizing 6 emotions [17]. It can be seen from the literature that, most of the emotion recognition systems are developed using the spectral and prosodic features. Excitation source information is not much used for recognizing the emotions. Therefore in this work the excitation source information is used for recognizing the emotions present in a speech.

There are several issues in emotion recognition such as availability of large, generalized emotion database, identifying emotion specific information in speech signal, extracting suitable emotion specific features, use of suitable classifiers for recognizing the emotions and so on. It can be said based on above lines that basically there are three main issues in developing emotional speech systems:- databases, features and models. In this study semi-natural database collected from Hindi movies is used, which is more closer to real world speech. Choosing suitable speech features is a crucial decision. Different features represents different information. So in speech research feature are selected on experimental basis or based on some mathematical approaches. In literature very few attempts were made to use the excitation source information in developing emotion recognition systems. The reasons for this may be: popularity of spectral features, linear prediction (LP) residual is mostly treated as an error signal, capturing higher order relations from LP residual samples is not properly known. However excitation source signal may contain the emotion specific information, in the form of unique features such as higher order relations among linear prediction (LP) residual samples. In this study, firstly complete LP residual signal is used as a feature for emotion recognition. Further LP residual signal, chosen around glottal closure instants are used to capture emotion specific information. LP residual signal is obtained by first extracting the vocal tract information from the speech signal and then suppressing it by inverse filter formulation. Resulting signal is termed as LP residual and contains mostly information about the excitation source. From the human speech production mechanism, it may be observed that vocal folds vibration, plays a important role in speech production. Epoch is an instant of vocal folds closure. In this study an effort has been made to parameterize the epoch events. It is believed that, the features extracted from excitation source related to epochs may contain some useful information about the emotion. So epoch related LP residual samples are used here as the features during emotion classification.

There are several pattern classifiers being used for development of speech system. In this study auto-associative neural network (AANN) is used. In excitation source features, basically higher order relations are present which are highly nonlinear in nature. The intension is to capture there higher order relationships through AANN models.

Remaining paper is organized as follows: Section 2 describes the database used. Section 3 contains the details about feature extraction. Section 4 explains the classifier being used in this study. Section 5 discusses the development of emotion recognition models. Section 6 contains the summary and conclusion. Section 7 concludes the paper, followed by references.

2   Database : GEU-SNESC

In this work a new semi natural database is introduced for categorizing speech emotions. This database is collected from the dialogs of Hindi movies and expressions of emotions is close to the real and practical situations. The conversations in movies are generally acceptable by listener as natural he/she can easily categorizes these emotion by listening the dialogs spoken by the speaker. This database is collected from Hindi movies for single (male+female) and multi (male+female) speakers. This semi natural database is named as Graphic Era University Semi Natural Emotion Speech Corpus (GEU-SNESC). The emotions collected in this database (GEU Semi Natural Emotion Speech Corpus) are sadness, anger, happiness and neutral. For single speaker, one popular male/female actor/actress and for multi-speaker, multiple male and female actor/actress are considered. Male and female dialogs are separately extracted from movies to collect desired emotions. For each emotion, different clips are collected from various hindi movies and then combined to form a single file of 15 minutes. From the databases, 70% of the data is used for training the emotion recognition model and 30% is used for testing the trained models. Initially the audio is extracted from the video with the help of Adobe Audition, in which the sampling rate of 16KHz and mono channel with 16 bit resolution are chosen. After that different speech sentences without background music are separated carefully be a part of the database based on the contextual emotion present. Then these sentences are edited with the help of wave surfer for removing the longer silence regions between the words without affecting the emotions. Table 1 shows the details of speaker database.

Table 1. Details of Speakers

S.No.		No of speakers contributed	Amount of data in minutes
1	Male Speaker (single)	1	35
2	Female Speaker (single)	1	30
3	Male Speaker	30	43
4	Female Speaker	25	13

3   Feature Extraction

Linear prediction (LP) predict current sample based on linear combination of past p samples. The difference between the actual and predicted sample values is known as the prediction error or residual. The residual is obtained by passing the speech signal through the inverse filter A (z) given by,

$$S(n) = 1 + \sum_{k=1}^{p} a_k S(n - k)$$

where $S(n)$ is current speech sample, p is order of prediction, a'_ks are the filter coefficients and $S(n - k)$ is the $(n - k)^{th}$ sample of speech.

LP (linear prediction) starts with the assumption that a speech signal is produced by a buzzer at the end of a tube (voiced sounds), with occasionally added hissing and popping sound. The glottis (the space between the vocal folds) produces the buzz, which is characterized by its intensity (loudness) and frequency (pitch). The vocal tract (the throat and mouth) forms the tube, which is characterized by its resonances, which give rise to formants or enhanced frequency bands in the sound produced. Hisses and pops are generated by the action of the tongue, lips and throat. LP analysis the speech signal by estimating the formants, removing their effects from the speech signal, and estimating the intensity and frequency of the remaining buzz. The process of removing the formants is called inverse filtering, and the remaining signal after the subtraction of the filtered modeled signal is called the residue. At the time of glottal closure the prediction is poor in the LP analysis, and results into larger error. Therefore this paper also explores the properties of excitation source signal in the vicinity of instants of glottal closure to capture the emotion specific information. Feature vectors are formed from LP residual of speech signal in following way.

In this study LP analysis is carried out on speech signal using an, LP order of 13 and frame size of 320 ms with a shift of 160 ms every time. The impulse like signal caused due to vocal folds closure, within a pitch period is known as an 'epoch'. Though entire glottal pulse is responsible for the excitation of vocal tract, significant excitation takes place at epoch locations [18]. So excitation information may play an important role in emotion recognition. In this work glottal closure or epoch location are located using zero frequency resonator [18]. Speech signal is passed two times through zero frequency resonator to locate epoch locations. 'Zero frequency' is used to nullify the resonance effect of vocal tract. In this work feature vectors are constructed in two different ways. In the first method a frame of 40 LP residual samples within overlap of single sample is directly used as feature vector. For a speech of pitch value around 200Hz approximately continuous 40 samples contribute to less than the pitch period. This help to avoid repeated information being considered for feature extraction from consecutive cycles. In the second method the LP residual samples only around gci locations are used to form the feature vectors. 32 samples of LP residual (10 samples before GCI and 22 after GCI) are used to construct feature vectors. 32 samples are used to avoid the overlap between the consecutive feature vectors.

4 Classifier

The task of pattern classifier is to capture the characteristics of each category from feature vectors of the training data. In literature, different pattern classifiers are used for developing different speech systems namely, speech recognition, speaker recognition, emotion classification, speaker verification and so on. But the justification for choosing a particular classifier to the specific speech task is rarely provided. Most of the time, suitable classifiers are chosen based on either thumb rule, or some past references. There are several classifiers such as artificial neural networks, Gaussian mixture models, hidden Markov models, decision trees, Kozinec's algorithm, Non-liner (smooth) SVM, k-nearest neighbor algorithm, polynomial classifiers, logistic regression, least square methods, perception classifiers, linear support vector machines (SVM) and so on.

In this work, auto-associative neural network (AANN) are used to model emotion specific non-linear information present in LP residual samples. As it is already known that LP residual contains higher order relations among the samples which are non-liner in nature.

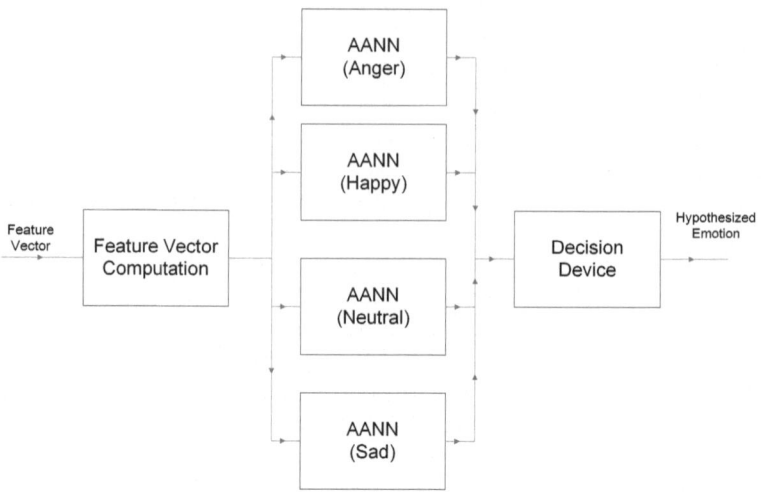

Fig. 1. Emotion recognition models using AANN

Fig.2 shows a five layer AANN structure (40L-60N-12N-60N-40L), where 40 represents the number of nodes in the input layer, which is the same as the size of feature vectors, L represents linear units and N represents nonlinear units. The decrease in the error during training phase of the AANN's shows that excitation source features contain some emotion specific information. The training error using samples of noise is found to be non-decreasing, indicating that there is no relation among the noise samples.

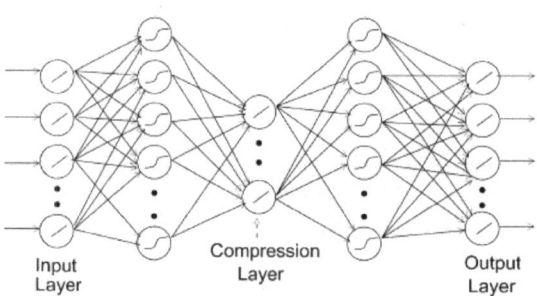

Fig. 2. AANN Structure

5   Devlopment of Emotion Recognition Models

Emotion recognition using pattern classifiers is basically a two stage process as shown in Fig.3. In the first stage emotion recognition models are developed by training the models using the feature vectors extracted from speech utterances of known emotions. It is known as supervised learning. Four AANN models individually for anger, sad, happy and neutral are created during training. In the second stage, testing (evaluation) of the trained models is performed by using the speech utterances of unknown emotions. The features extracted from unknown speech is given to all trained models. Then the decision device checks the Eucilidian distance between the models and get the results. The model that gives the least distance is treated as the hypothesized emotion. Fig.3 shows the training and testing phases of developing emotion recognition models. In the training phase, four AANN models are trained, one for each emotion. As the classifier used in identify mapping neural network, the same 40 LP residual samples are used as both input and output. The weights are adjusted to transform input feature vector into the output. As inputs and outputs are same, the network is known as Auto-associative or identity mapping neural network. While training 70% of data is used and the process is iterated toward convergence rest 30% of data is used for validating the trained models.

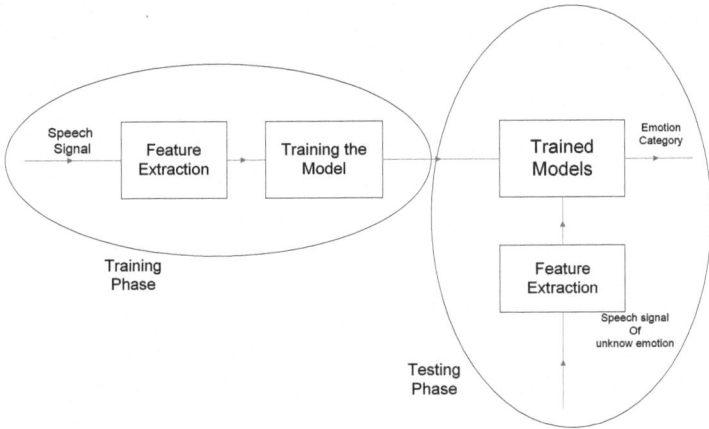

Fig. 3. Training and validation of Emotion Recognition Models

Table 2. Emotion classification performance (in %), using LP Residual(Database : GEU-SNESC Database)

	Anger	Happy	Neutral	Sad
Anger	60	10	16	14
Happy	16	70	0	14
Neutral	20	0	65	15
Sad	19	6	15	60

During testing phase, LP residual signal is obtained for the different test sentences. 40 samples of LP residual are given as input. The output of each model is compared with its input to compute the mean squared error of each block. The AANN model that produces highest confidence/lowest error value is hypothesized as the identified emotion. The result of emotion classification performance are presented in Table 2 in the form of confusion matrix. In this confusion matrix, diagonal elements show the correct classification and other elements in the row indicate misclassification percentages. Confusion matrix is named as confusion because in each emotion there are some misclassifications are also there. Table 2 shows some misclassifications also. The result present in this table are derived over a male dataset. From the table, it is observed that 60% of anger is classified as anger and similarly 70%, 65% and 55% of happy, neutral and sad emotions are recognized correctly. The misclassification pattern observed in the results of emotion may be due to several reasons important of them are-

a) Due to difficulty in emotion annotation there is a chance of mixing of utter-ances with different emotions into the same group either during training or during testing.
b) Similar acoustic properties of different emotions may lead to their mutual misclassification. For example anger and happy emotions share similar prop-erties along arousal and valence dimension [19].
c) Use of different features may lead to misclassification of emotions due to individual emotion specificity.

The average emotion recognition performance is 63%. The process is used sep-arately for female, male and male+female speakers. The consolidated emotion recognition performance is given in Table 3.

Table 3. Comparative study of emotion recognition using LPR and LPR around GCI for different types of speakers, Legend:LPR-Linear prediction residual, GCI-Glottal closure instant

Emotion	Male		Female		Male+Female	
	LPR	LPR around GCI	LPR	LPR around GCI	LPR	LPR around GCI
Anger	60	65	65	70	50	50
Happy	70	75	65	70	55	60
Neutral	65	80	50	80	60	65
Sadness	55	60	55	60	50	55
Average	70	70	58	63	59	54

As it is said earlier epoch is an important event and carried information is present around epochs. Therefore the LP residual samples chosen around epochs are used as feature vectors. In this case initially epoch locations are extracted from speech signal using zero frequency filtered speech signal. Then these glottal closure instants (epochs) are mapped with LP residual signal. Feature vectors are formed using 10 LP residual samples before GCI's and 22 values after GCI's. Using these 32 samples AANN models are trained for sad, happy, neutral and angry utterances. In the training phase, four AANN models are trained for each emotions.

In Table 3 the emotion recognition performance in case of epoch parameters has been observed to be 70%, 70% and 58% for male, female and male+female speakers respectively. The emotion recognition performance in case LP residual has been observed to be 63%, 59% and 54% for male, female and male+female speakers respectively. It is observed that in case of epoch parameters, better results are obtained as compared to LP residual. Because it is observed that at the time of glottal instant maximum emotion specific information is present. The misclassification that is observed between the emotions anger/neutral, happy/sad may be due to the reason a mentioned above. Misclassification in case of happy/anger, neutral/sad is due to b given above. Apart from this text, gender, age of the speaker may always have influence over the classification performance.

6   Summary and Conclusion

In this paper, excitation source features are derived from speech and are explored for characterizing emotions present in speech. The effort has been done through this work to explore the importance of epoch locations and LP residual for recognizing the emotions using speech utterances. Epoch locations are obtained from zero frequency filtered speech signal and the LP residual is obtained using inverse filtering. AANN model is used to capture emotion specific information from excitation source features. These feature vectors are used to train the AANN model. For testing same feature vectors are extracted for unknown speech sentences. GEU-SNESC database is used as a speech corpus, for this task. Four emotions used are anger, happy, neutral and sad. The average emotion recognition performance obtained in this study is better, indicating the presence of useful emotion specific information in the excitation source using epoch locations better emotion recognition results are obtained indicating the presence of emotion specific crucial information around GCI locations. The performance may be improved by combining the different features such as spectral and prosodic. GEU-SNESC database is evaluated using subjective listening tests. The discrimination of emotions can be investigated further by combining the evidence from different models such as- Gaussian mixture models, Hidden Markov models, Support Vector Machines developed at various levels like spectral features or prosodic features.

References

1. Schuller, B., Rigoll, G., Lang, M.: Speech emotion recognition combining acoustic features and linguistic information in a hybrid support vector machine-belief network architecture. In: Proc. IEEE Int. Conf. Acoust., Speech, Signal Processing, pp. 577–580. IEEE Press (May 2004)
2. Dellert, F., Polzin, T., Waibel, A.: Recognizing emotion in speech. In: Fourth International Conference on Spoken Language Processing, Philadelphia, PA, USA, pp. 1970–1973 (October 1996)

3. Koolagudi, S.G., Maity, S., Kumar, V.A., Chakrabarti, S., Rao, K.S.: IITKGP-SESC: Speech Database for Emotion Analysis. In: Ranka, S., Aluru, S., Buyya, R., Chung, Y.-C., Dua, S., Grama, A., Gupta, S.K.S., Kumar, R., Phoha, V.V. (eds.) IC3 2009. CCIS, vol. 40, pp. 485–492. Springer, Heidelberg (2009)
4. Lee, C.M., Narayanan, S.S.: Toward detecting emotions in spoken dialogs. IEEE Trans. Speech and Audio Processing 13, 293–303 (2005)
5. Nakatsu, R., Nicholson, J., Tosa, N.: Emotion recognition and its application to computer agents with spontaneous interactive capabilities. Knowledge Based Systems 13, 497–504 (2000)
6. Charles, F., Pizzi, D., Cavazza, M., Vogt, T., Andr, E.: Emoemma: Emotional speech input for interactive story telling. In: Decker, Sichman, Sierra, Castelfranchi (eds.) Eighth Int. Conf. on Autonomous Agents and Multiagent Systems (AAMAS 2009), Budapest, Hungary, pp. 1381–1382 (May 2009)
7. Ververidis, D., Kotropoulos, C.: A state of the art review on emotional speech databases. In: Eleventh Australasian International Conference on Speech Science and Technology, Auckland, New Zealand (December 2006)
8. France, D.J., Shiavi, R.G., Silverman, S., Silverman, M., Wilkes, M.: Acoustical properties of speech as indicators of depression and suicidal risk. IEEE Transactions on Biomedical Engg. 47(7), 829–837 (2000)
9. Nwe, T.L., Foo, S.W., Silva, L.C.D.: Speech emotion recognition using hidden Markov models. Speech Communication 41, 603–623 (2003)
10. McGilloway, S., Cowie, R., Douglas-Cowie, E., Gielen, S., Westerdijk, M., Stroeve, S.: Approaching automatic recognition of emotion from voice: A rough benchmark, Belfast (2000)
11. Dellaert, F., Polzin, T., Waibel, A.: Recognising emotions in speech. In: ICSLP 1996 (October 1996)
12. Nicholson, J., Takahashi, K., Nakatsu, R.: Emotion recognition in speech using neural networks. In: Sixth International Conference on Neural Information Processing, ICONIP 1999, pp. 495–501 (1999)
13. Ververidis, D., Kotropoulos, C., Pitas, I.: Automatic emotional speech classification. In: ICASSP 2004, pp. I593–I596. IEEE (2004)
14. Iida, A., Campbell, N., Higuchi, F., Yasumura, M.: A corpus-based speech synthesis system with emotion. Speech Communication 40, 161–187 (2003)
15. Gobl, C., Chasaide, A.: The role of voice quality in communicating emotion, mood and attitude. In: SPC, vol. 40, pp. 189–212 (2003)
16. Kwon, O., Chan, K., Hao, J., Lee, T.: Emotion recognition by speech signals. In: Eurospeech, Geneva, pp. 125–128 (2003)
17. Wang, Y., Guan, L.: An investigation of speech-based human emotion recognition. In: IEEE 6th Workshop on Multimedia Signal Processing, pp. 15–18 (2004)
18. Yegnanarayana, B., Murty, K.S.R.: Event-based instantaneous fundamental frequency estimation from speech signals. IEEE Trans. Audio, Speech, and Language Processing 17(4), 614–624 (2009)
19. Koolagudi, S.G., Sreenivasa Rao, K.: Exploring Speech Features for Classifying Emotions along Valence Dimension. In: Chaudhury, S., Mitra, S., Murthy, C.A., Sastry, P.S., Pal, S.K. (eds.) PReMI 2009. LNCS, vol. 5909, pp. 537–542. Springer, Heidelberg (2009)

Maximizing Automatic Code Generation: Using XML Based MDA

Atul Saurabh, Deepak Dahiya, and Rajni Mohana

Jaypee University of Information Technology Waknaghat,
Computer Science Department,
Solan 173215
atul.saurabh@gmail.com, {deepak.dahiya,rajni.mohana}@juit.ac.in

Abstract. Currently unified modelling language (UML) is widely used for the specification and modeling of software. Model driven approach uses unified modeling language as platform independent model and converts it into platform specific model by adopting different strategies in the form of stereotype and metadata. However non-uniformity in strategy makes UML based model driven architecture (MDA) a challanging job. Also very less number of platform specific code is generated when UML platform independent model (PIM) is converted to platform specific model (PSM). A tool is proposed for design and implementation which is using eXtensible markup language (XML) as PIM. XML provides uniformity in description of different components. It also provides interoperability which is otherwise not achieved. Code density and code gain significantly increase when XML PIM is converted to PSM. A case study demonstrates the applicability of this tool.

Keywords: eXtensible markup language (XML), Unified modelling language(UML), Model driven architecture(MDA), Software development process, Platform independent model(PIM), Platform specific model(PSM), Object Management Group(OMG).

1 Introduction

Software development process has become very challenging as the client's requirement specification keeps on changing. Business agility is another aspect which complicates the software development process. Traditional Software development life cycle like waterfall, spiral, iterative and other methodologies typically follow a linear approach and hence take time to develop and launch the software. Agile methodologies like scrum works faster as they are less restricted in the adoption of phases of software development life cycle(SDLC). Some phases in these methodologies can be skipped or can be worked out manually. Developing the same project on heterogeneous platform requires a lot of labor and hence the time consumptions get multiplied. The development of electronic based technology adds another type of complexity in software design and implementation. The

M. Parashar et al. (Eds.): IC3 2012, CCIS 306, pp. 283–293, 2012.

incredible increase in hardware cycle has forced a demand for better software.It is further observed that the software development methodologies consume a lot of time in testing the developed code which results in unacceptable development delays. The above mentioned complexities in software development requires the introduction of new innovative design methodologies with design automation at higher levels of abstraction. In 1996 the OMG group introduced unified modelling language (UML) [1] for pictorial representation of software components and their interrelations. Later on the same group came up with the idea of Model driven architecture(MDA) [1].

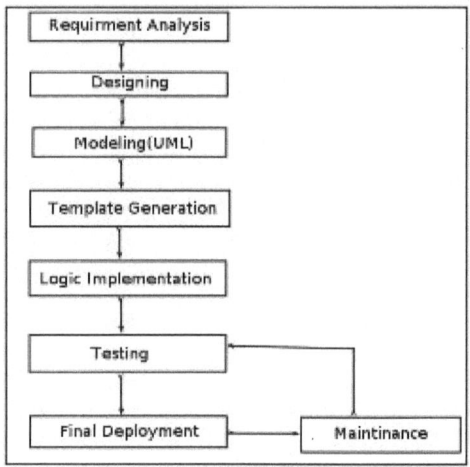

Fig. 1. UML based MDA scheme

The idea of MDA introduces different use of UML. Instead of using it only as the pictorial representation of software architecture, it can be used as a reusable component for the generation of code for the same.The automatic generation of tested code for different platform reduces the time factor drastically low and hence accelerates the software development process. The fig 1 shows the typical approach to software development when the UML is used as a modeling language. From the past experience on UML automatic code generation through UML has a limitation that it is not able to cope up with the current pace of software development. It generates very less executable code. Plenty of code is still developed manually and falls inside the cycle of testing. Agility can be achieved by generating more number of tested code automatically [3]. In this paper we are proposing the idea of introducing XML as PIM instead of UML. XML will overcome the limitation of UML and will go beyond the limitation of a diagram. It also provides interoprability between heterogeneous systems. Also transformation of XML PIM generates more number of executable code than UML PIM.

The remainder of this paper is organized as follows: Section 2 gives background on some of the well known software methodologies, section 3 discusses proposed methodology for solving the current problem including the implementation of a tool named Visual XML for generation of XML PIM. Section 4 describes the results and observations. Lastly, sections 5 and 6 describe the conclusion and scope of future work.

2   Related Study: Current Trends in MDA

In this fast growing software industry environment it is almost impossible to develop software systems and applications without adhering to a properly structured approach. Over the years, a number of rules of thumb or best practices have developed among enterprise software developers, both in-house and commercial or third-party vendors. Indeed, in the last 25 years, a large number of different approaches to software development have been introduced. Some of them are still surviving and some of them have met to their end. There are numerous best practice methodologies proposed for accomplishing the typical software development life cycle [3,15].

All the methodologies proposed adopt a linear approach at some stage of the software development life cycle. Basic steps are same in all methodologies. Agility can be achieved by reducing the time required at each phase [3]. Some phases like requirment analysis and feasibility study are few basic pahses where we can not put time constraint. One of the main phases where time constraint can be truly applied is the testing. There is no means by which we can cut down the time required in testing when we are following the above mentioned methodologies. In 1996, OMG group proposed UML [1], the unified modeling language. UML is basically used to represent the components of software and their interrelations like *has-a*, *is-a* and *uses-a* relationship. Later on in 2001 the same group came up with the idea of MDA [1]. MDA, the model driven architecture, uses a platform independent model (PIM) to represent the software architecture. After designing the PIM, it is converted to platform specific model (PSM) using some additional information about platform and software architecture. PSM is basically a platform dependent code which does not require repeated testing and hence reduces the time factor of testing. As plenty of code of code is generated automatically through PSM, the labor cost of software also decreases.

Currently UML is used as de facto standard of generating PIM which has certain advantages [1] . The introduction of UML as PIM language changes the SDLC resulting in code generation and automatic testing at the early design stage. The Fig: 5 show the UML based MDA scheme. The above mentioned advantages of UML as PIM are very useful for software industry and hence many scholars proposed different strategic scheme of using UML for generating different kind of software system.

1. [4] suggest how to generate and weave aspects at early design statge. AspectComponent is used to design aspects and wrapper component is used to weave aspects at proper place. UML 2.0 is used to design AspectComponent and wrapper.
2. [6] proposed an idea of generating web services using UML. The software paradigm is shifting from stand-alone development to distributed development. Web Services is a family of standards that provide a layer of abstraction above existing software systems. In distributed environment components are communicating with each other using web services. This paper suggests to adopt different stereotypes like $<<WSDLmessage>>$, $<<WSDLPortType>>$ and $<<XSDTopLevelElement>>$ to identify web service components. This paper also pointed out that existing MDA tools are not interoperatable with each other.
3. [5] propose a methodological approach for the model driven development of secure XML databases (DB). Currently XML database is used in various aspects. To develop a secure data PIM, a secure UML profile has been developed. User and data are classified using some classification criteria. Then designed PIM is converted to secure XML schema using some stereotype and metamodels.
4. [7] proposed an idea of generating and weaving of both dynamic and static AOSD using UML as PIM. Code generation is done by working from the UML XMI (XML Model Interchange) format, the standard UML serialization.

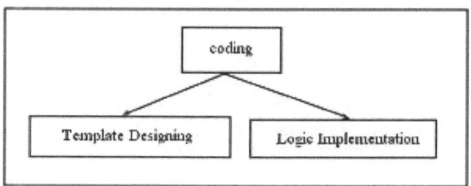

Fig. 2. Division of coding

A study of the above literature work led to the following observations:

1. Code generation for different platform is the main aspect of UML-based modeling. Software industry is flowing in one direction: generating maximum number of code automatically so that there should be less number of codes to be implemented and tested.
2. UML lacks a specialized syntax for generating different kind of software system. We need to change the way or adopt a different approach to convert PIM to PSM when we use UML as PIM. There are other issues related to UML which may be considered as the disadvantage of UML based modeling technique:
   (a) Interoperability [6]: There is much software available which supports MDA core functionality. But they store information in different formats. The formats are not compatible with each other. For instance,the UML

generated by Rational Rose is not supported by ArgoUML. So, both softwares are not compatible with each other. There is no platform neutral way to generate UML diagram.

(b) Require high bandwidth for network transmission: UML diagram is stored/saved in different binary format. In large enterprise application this diagram becomes huge in size. If it is required to send this diagram through network, then high bandwidth is required.

(c) Lack of template designing at method level: Template stands for basic architecture of software. It may possible that a certain function requires calling other function in a sequence. UML is unable to detect this sequence. Also there is no way to describe some non-traditional part of software e.g. there is no direct way to describe about web services [12,13] and aspect [11].

(d) Unable to identify the component: Software is composed of lot many components like aspect, web service etc. UML treats these component just like a normal class. So adaption of different strategies is required to identify the component and generate right code for that component.

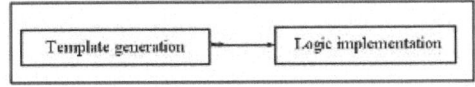

Fig. 3. Logic implementation follows template generation

3. It has also been observed that coding can be divided into two basic parts as shown in fig 2

(a) Template Designing: Template stands for basic architecture of the software. It is a reusable component. It includes classes, methods or functions (without definitions), interfaces etc.

(b) Logic Implementation: This is a part of coding which produces the main functionality. In this phase mainly definition of a method/function is provided. That means business logic is implemented in this phase. This phase basically answers the question: How a particular functionality can be enabled in the software?

The business logic of any software system is activated by implementing various algorithms and policies. As the client's requirment is not fixed the way of implementing business logic is also not fixed. Different algorithm and policies are used for different kind of software system. Even same kind of software system may vary in some policies. As for example the tax calculation process varies from place to place, the taxation policy may also vary. So we can conclude that as on date no tool can be designed which can generate 100% logic for a software system. On other side template has fixed patterns for one kind of software system. So template can be generated through software tool. Using UML and adopting some strategies only the template of the software system is generated. In UML based modeling the template is generated first and then logic is implemented as shown in fig3. Template and implementation are two disjoint sets which can't be merged when using UML based modeling.

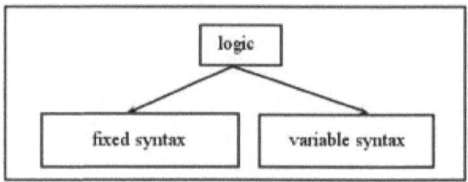

Fig. 4. Division of logic

In this paper an alternate approach is proposed which is based on XML. XML is a narrative language [2]. Software industry discovered and adopted it in quest of achieving interoperability in distributed environment where two different systems are communicating with each other [2].Currently many technologies are using XML or their derivatives for different purposes. The remote procedure call(RPC), is achieved using Simple Object Access Protocol (SOAP) [16], which is a XML family document [16].Web services are communicating with each other using XML which is known as web services definition language(WSDL) [13].Further Java web technology is using XML based configuration file named called web.xml for describing configuration of web project [8]. It is not only easy to generate XML data but is also easy to parse and fetch useful data from an XML file. Many technologies like XPath [2] and XQuery [2], adopted by w3c, are available for querying about any node in an XML file. Using XML as PIM we can remove many disadvantages of UML based modeling. Following are some of the advantages of XML:

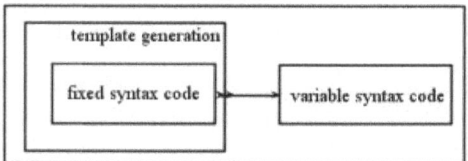

Fig. 5. Dragging of fixed syntax code into template generation

1. Interoperability: XML requires parser to fetch out information and do the job. Parser designing is very easy on any kind of environment. So, XML generated by JAVA based tool can easy be parsed by a tool designed on C#. So XML provides interoperability.
2. Template designing can be achieved: XML is all about tags. Further, We can design our own tag which can describe about web services and aspect. Also calling sequence of a method/function can be described easily. Also we can describe about aspect weaving syntax.

These advantages make XML a perfect choice for PIM.The only requirement for using XML is the parser. It is the parser which fetches information from XML document and does some useful job with that information. Designing a parser is not a very tough job. There are many technologies available for this purpose which makes this job easy. The document object model (DOM) and simple API for XML (SAX) technologies are handy in helping us in parsing an XML document. So developing a technology based on XML is not very hard.

3   Proposed Methodology for PIM

Section 2 highlighted various pros and cons of UML which makes it less useful when software will be developed using web services [12,13] and AOP [11]. Also XML provided ample evidence of its advantages over UML which makes it a perfect choice for PIM fig 4.

1. Fixed syntax logic : There are some codes which have fixed format in a particular programming language. As for example database connection code, file opening code, method/function call etc.
2. Variable Syntax Logic: There are codes which purely depend upon client's requirements. These can be categorized as variable syntax logic. e.g. Database reading, file manipulation, computing tax etc.

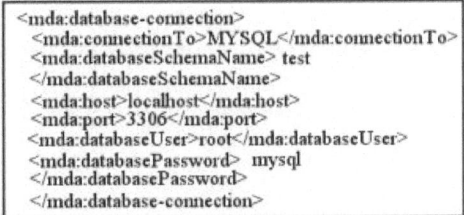

Fig. 6. Database connection code written in XML

Since variable syntax logic depends upon client's requirement, it will be implemented using different format in a different scenario. So we can't generate logic for generating variable syntax code. As in the case of template, fixed syntax code is always have fixed format of coding in all scenarios and hence can be generated through some tool. As XML is a narrative language fixed syntax logic can easily be described in terms of XML tag and attribute. Having fixed syntax code description in XML a template can be generated as well a fixed syntax pretested code. Hence some part of logic, along with template, can be generated through a tool which is using XML as a PIM.. Thus code density will increase a lot having fixed syntax code dragged inside template generation set as in fig5. Using XML gives us much flexibility than UML. Designing tags and then parsing can cause certain changes in traditional SDLC. Fixed syntax logic can easily described in terms of XML tags. Once the XML code is present, parsing it and generating code become an easy task. Thus, with the help of XML we can generate template as well as fixed syntax logic. Having fixed syntax concrete code we need not to implement and test the logic which is generated through modeling. Instead we only need to focus on variable syntax logic. Now SDLC focuses only on implementation and testing of variable syntax logic.

```
import java.sql.*;
public class DatabaseConnection
{
    private Connection connection;
    public Connection getDatabaseConnection()
    {
        try
        {
        Class.forName("com.mysql.jdbc.Driver");
        }
catch(ClassNotFoundException classNotFoundException)
{
//handle your exception
return null;
}
  try
  {
  String url="jdbc:mysql://localhost:3306/test";
  String username="root";
  String password="mysql";
connection=DriverManager.getConnection(url,username,password);
}
  catch(SQLException sqlException)
  {
    //handle sqlException
     return null;
  }
     return connection;
     }
}
```

Fig. 7. Code generated from XML listed in Figure[6]

Having fixed syntax code description in XML and parser designed for this kind of XML we can generate the code in various languages like JAVA, PHP, C++, C#, Python etc. The fig[7] shows an example of code of a class for database connection generated in JAVA using XML code described in fig[6].

3.1 Working of Visual XML

To implement the proposed work we designed a tool named Visual XML using java 1.6, swing, XML, XPath and MYSQL database. Swing is used as a frontend. MYSQL database is used as temporary storage. XML is used as PIM and XPath technology is used used for querying about any node.

Though we have designed a menu driven tool to generate XML model and transforming XML model into code, it is very easy to implement a tool which can use diagram in drag and drop manner to generate XML model.

4 Results and Observation

A submodule of Employee information System(EIS) was designed using Visual XML and eventually generated source code for the project and to do a further analysis of its performance over UML, we also designed the EIS using UML 8 and generated the code. The UML tool used for performance analysis was ArgoUML. The metric for performance analysis between the tools are code density and code gain. Code density and code gain is defined as follows: and code gain. Code density and code gain is defined as follows:

1. Code density : The code density of source i denoted as ∂_i and defined as the number of executable line per file generated by a tool i.

$$\partial_i = \frac{\sum_{i=1}^{i=n}(total\ executable\ code\ in\ i^{th}\ file)}{n} \qquad (1)$$

2. Code gain: The code gains of source i over the source j is denoted as $\triangle_{i \rightarrow j}$ and defined as the difference of code density of source i and j.

$$\triangle_{i \rightarrow j} = \partial_i - \partial_j \qquad (2)$$

It was observed that the total number of executable line in source code generated by UML based MDA is 57 and total number of files produced is 8. So code density is: $\partial_{uml} = \frac{57}{8} = 5.1818\ lines/file$.

The same project when designed using Visual XML generated 205 executable lines of code in source file and total number of files generated is 7. So, code density of XML based MDA is:

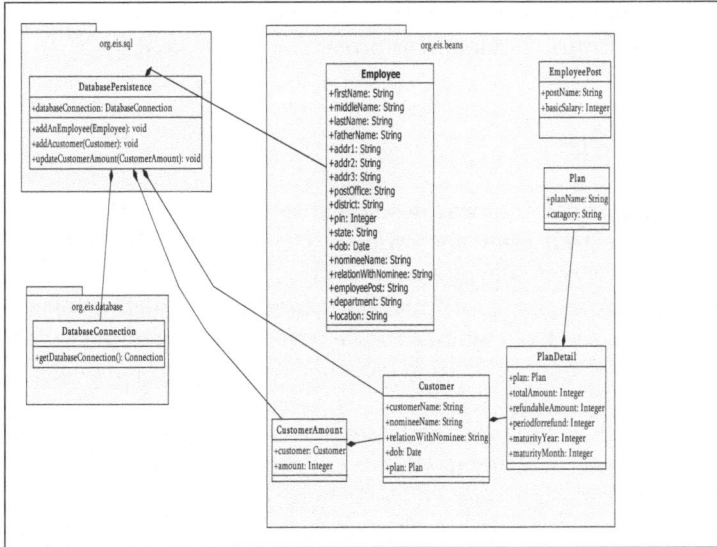

Fig. 8. UML diagram for EIS

$$\partial_{xml} = \tfrac{205}{7} = 29.2857\, lines/file$$

Hence code gain of source XML over source UML can be calculated as :
$\triangle_{xml \rightarrow uml} = 29.2857 - 501818 = 24.10\, lines/file$

(Note that all codes are generated in JAVA language only.)

5   Conclusion

Using UML as model is a great way to represent and generate a project, but as a diagram it can not describe each and every component of a software system. Components can be identified by adopting different approach for different component. UML provides no generalized syntax for different kind of components. UML based modeling lacks behind with respect to the current pace of software industries as it generates less number of executable code. Testing a maually generated code consumes a lot of time which result in software deployment delay. Client becomes unstisfied with this unusual delay. The main disadvantage of UML is that it does not recognize the fixed syntax code. The more fixed syntax code will be recognized, the more the executable code will be generated automatically and lesser the amount of time will be devoted to testing. This strategy will speed up the production rate and unusual delay can be minimized. The limitation of UML can be overcome if XML is used. Being a narrative language, a lot can be described about a project in terms of tags and attributes of XML i.e. about classes, methods, aspects etc by designing tag. The parser can be designed easily on any platform and hence interoperability can also be achieved which is otherwise not achieved. XML provides a tool independent approach to generate code regarding a project. As the fixed syntax code like database connection, file opening etc is generated automatically, very less number of code is required to be tested. Thus software development process is accelerated by XML if it is used as PIM.

6   Future Work

Currently a menu driven tool was developed to generate XML PIM as it is easy to implement. The tool does not provide a complete visual aspect of model. Also, there are many component available other than database connection code, file opening, calling sequence of function, aspects etc which a software system can use and which has fixed syntax to use. One of the example is web services. Currently the parser is limited to generating code in two languages JAVA and PHP only.

Future work will include an implementation of a tool which will provide a complete visual aspect which will similar to UML but will be more flexible than UML. Also we will design tags and attribute for all other fixed syntax code. Parser can be extended to many other programming language like C++, C#, Python etc so that we can achieve a generalized syntax for code generation for all components on all platform.

References

1. Object Management Group: OMG Unified Modeling Language Specification 2.4.1 (2012), http://www.omg.org/spec/UML/2.4.1/ (last accessed on November 2011)
2. World wide web consortium, http://www.w3.org (last accessed on November 2011)
3. Agile Methodology, http://agilemethodology.org/ (last accessed on June 2011)
4. Clemente, P.J., Hernandez, J., Sanchez, F.: An MDA Approach to Develop Systems Based on Components and Aspects, pp. 1033–1034. ACM, New York (2007)
5. Vela, B., Medina, E.F., Marcos, E., Piattini, M.: Model Driven Development of Secure XML Databases. SIGMOD Record 35(3) (2006)
6. Aho, P., Maki, M., Pakkala, D., Ovaska, E.: MDA-Based Tool Chain for Web Services Development, pp. 11–18. ACM, New York (2009)
7. Evermann, J., Fiech, A., Alam, F.E.: A Platform Independent UML Profile for Aspect-Oriented Development, pp. 25–34. ACM, New York (2011)
8. Hall, M., Brown, L., Chaikin, Y.: Core Servlet and Java Server Pages, 2nd edn., vol. 1. Pearson Education (2003)
9. McLaughlin, B.D., Edelson, J.: Java and XML, 3rd edn. O'Reilly publication (2006)
10. Walls, C., Breidenbach, R.: Spring in Action, 2nd edn. Dreamtech Manning publication (2007)
11. Laddad, R.: AspectJ in Action, 2nd edn. Manning publication (2009)
12. Sandoval, J.: RESTful Java Web Services. PACKT publication (2009)
13. Chappel, D.A., Jewell, T.: Java Web Services. O'Reilly publication (2002)
14. Hall, R.S., Pauls, K., McCulloch, S., Savage, D.: OSGi in Action. Manning (2011)
15. Jalote, P.: An Integrated Approach to Software Engineering, 3rd edn. Springer (2005)
16. Englander, R.: Java and Soap, 1st edn. O'Reilly publication (2002)
17. Spiral Model, http://www.ianswer4u.com/2011/12/ spiral-model-advantages-and.html#axzz1vi6f3ILT (last accessed on March 2012)

Proposed Mobile Controlled Handoff (MCHO) in 3GPP Long Term Evolution (LTE) System

Vikrant Chauhan[1], Juhi Gupta[1], and Chhavi Singla[2]

[1] Jaypee Institute of Information Technology University, Noida, India
vikrantchauhan22@gmail.com, juhi@jiit.ac.in
[2] HCE, Sonepat
chhavisingla2010@gmail.com

Abstract. LTE is a standard for wireless communication of high speed data rates, higher system throughput and lower latency for delay critical services. Basically belongs to 3GPP family and is based upon GSM and UMTS network technologies. Proper Handoff (HO) algorithm can make the system increased capacity, better coverage requirements. A new Handoff (HO) algorithm in LTE networks based on MCHO is being proposed in this paper for the improvement of performance in a fading environment based on cost-231 Walfisch Ikegami Model.

Keywords: Long Term Evolution (LTE), Handoff (HO), Relative Signal Strength Indices (RSSI), Third Generation Partnership Project (3GPP), eNodeB- Base Station, Mobile Controlled Handoff (MCHO).

1 Introduction to LTE System

With the fast changing landscape and coverage in all aspects of telecommunication, "seamless handover" is necessary for any technology to succeed. Operators and consumers both benefits from seamless handoff in terms of cost effectiveness, enhanced features, location independence and ease of use, not only with in a LTE network but also between other radio access technologies includes mainly UMTS, GSM and CDMA. LTE supports mobility for various mobile speeds up to 350 km/hour [1]. With moving speed even higher, the handoff will be more frequent. Therefore, handoff performance becomes more crucial, especially for real time service.

A major difference of LTE in comparison to its 3GPP ancestors is the radio interface; Orthogonal Frequency Division Multiplexing (OFDM) and Single Carrier Frequency Division Multiple Access (SC-FDMA) are used for the downlink and uplink respectively as radio access schemes [2], [3]. The radio interface is termed Enhanced UTRA (E-UTRA) and the radio network Enhanced UTRAN (E-UTRAN).The one major advantage of LTE system is its adaptability to other radio access technologies.

An evolved Node B - eNB - is the radio access part of the UMTS LTE system. Each eNB contains at least one radio transmitter, receiver, control section and power

M. Parashar et al. (Eds.): IC3 2012, CCIS 306, pp. 294–305, 2012.

supply. In addition to radio transmitters, and receivers, eNB contain resourcemanagement and logic control functions that have been traditionally separated into base station controllers (BSCs) or radio network controllers (RNCs). This added capability allows eNBs to directly communicate with each other, eliminating the need of mobile switching systems (MSCs) or controllers (BSCs or RNCs). MCHO extends the role of the UE by giving overall control to it. The UE and eNodeB, both, make the necessary measurements and the eNodeB sends them to the UE [20]. Then, the UE decides when to handoff based on the information gained from the eNodeB and itself.

In this paper, an algorithm is designed to provide the handoff service requested by the UE. The various sections of the paper are organized as follows: Section 2 outlines the Handoff overview. Objective of handoff is illustrated in Section 3. Fourth section describes the procedure of handoff in LTE networks. Section 5 introduces a proposed handoff algorithm that improves the performance of the system, followed by the simulation model and results in section 6. Finally we give a conclusion and discuss the future work to improve the performance of Handoff in LTE system.

2   Handoff Schemes and Its Techniques

Handoff is a basic mobile network capability for dynamic support of terminal migration. Handoff Management is the process of initiating and ensuring a seamless and lossless handoff of a mobile terminal from the region covered by one base station to another base station. A handoff mechanism must be defined to maintain uninterrupted user communication session during his/her movement from one location to another. This improvement in delay parameter is being focussed in the paper.

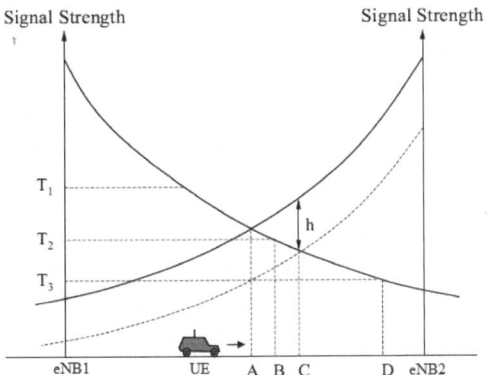

Fig. 1. Handoff Initiation

A hard handoff occurs when the old connection is broken before a new connection is activated. The performance evaluation of a hard handoff is based on various initiation criteria. It is assumed that the signal is averaged over time, so that rapid fluctuations due to the multipath nature of the radio environment can be eliminated.Numerous studies have been done to determine the shape as well as the length of the averaging window and the older measurements may be unreliable. Figure-1 shows a UE moving from one eNB (eNB1) to another eNB (eNB2). Where h represents the handoff hysteresis margin (HOM). The mean signal strength of eNB1 decreases as the UE moves away from it. Similarly, the mean signal strength of eNB2 increases as the UE approaches it.

There are numerous methods for performing handoff, at least as many as the kinds of state information that have been defined for UEs, as well as the kinds of network entities that maintain the state information [4]. The decision-making process of handoff may be centralized or decentralized (i.e., the handoff decision may be made at the UE or network). From the decision process point of view, one can find various kinds of handoff decisions [5].

3   Objectives of Handoff in LTE System

1. It is important that QOS is maintained not just before and after a Handoff but also during the Handoff as well.
2. The battery power should not be exhausted during the Handoff process.
3. Minimum handoff Latency
4. Seamless Handoff to 3G/2G, GSM and CDMA technologies.

Meanwhile handoff can be initiated by the eNodeB for several different reasons. When Radio Resource Control (RRC) entity in the base-station decides to initiate the Handoff it sends "mobility from E-UTRA" RRC message to UE. This message contains the Radio Access Technology (RAT) and other parameters required for the UE to establish a radio link with the target Handoff cell [6].

RRC, as specified in [7], is the protocol by which the E-UTRAN controls the UE behaviour in RRC_CONNECTED. RRC also specifies the control signalling applicable for a UE in RRC_IDLE, namely paging and system information. The UE behaviour in RRC_IDLE is specified in [8]. Mobility control in RRC_IDLE is UE-controlled (cell-reselection), while in RRC_CONNECTED it is controlled by the E-UTRAN (Handoff). However, the mechanisms used in the two states need to be consistent so as to avoid Ping-Pong between cells upon state transitions.

Different reasons for the initiation of Handoff are:

1. Quality Based Handoff-Typically these handoffs are initiated as a result of a UE measurement report indicating that the UE can communicate with a neighbour cell with a better channel quality than that of the current serving cell.
2. Coverage Based Handoff- These Handoff moves the connection to another RAT because UE is losing coverage for the current RAT.
3. Load Based Handoff- Balancing of load is the important criteria during the call management process [9].

A Handoff procedure can typically be divided into four parts: the measurements controls, the measurements reports, the Handoff decision and Handoff execution.The E-UTRAN architecture is comprised of eNodeB, Mobile Management Entity (MME) and System Architecture Evolution gateway (SAE) shown in Figure-2.

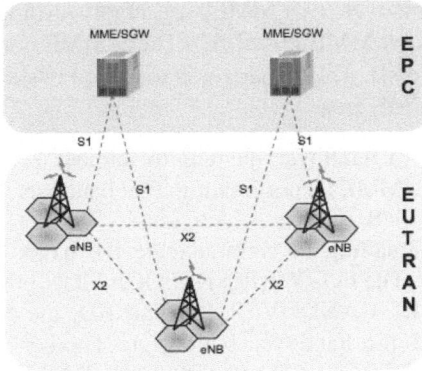

Fig. 2. E-UTRAN architecture

Handoff in LTE systems is performed over two important interface i.e. S1 interface(connects the eNodeB to the EPC) and X2 interface (it is the interface used to connect each and every eNodeB in a particular MME). LTE mobility in RRC-idle and RRC-connected are other two important factors determines during the Handoff process [10].In RRC_CONNECTED, the E-UTRAN decides to whichcell a UE should hand over in order to maintain the radio link. As with RRC_IDLE, EUTRAN may take into account not only the radio link quality but also factors such as UE capability, subscriber type and access restrictions.

4   Procedure of Handoff in LTE System

In 3G and LTE networks, a hybrid approach is used to decide on the handoff. In this case, the UE will assist in the handoff decision by measuring the neighbouring cells and reporting the measurements to the networks, which in turn decides the Handoff timing and target cell. The parameter to measure and the threshold for reporting are decided by the network. Basically LTE systems have three types of Handoff process which can be defined as:

1. Handoff within the same LTE network i.e. between same or within MME/SGW.
2. Handoff with other LTE system between existing MME/SGW and other MME/SGW.
3. Handoff between LTE and other RAT like GSM, CDMA [11].

Handoff technology has many decision criteria, the main are reference signal received power (RSRP), and reference signal received quality (RSRQ), received signal strength indicator (RSSI) and signal noise ratio. Among them received signal strength is most important criteria in the system.

Figure-3 gives a detail description of the inter-MME Handoff using the S-1 interfaces. This Handoff is triggered when the UE moves from one MME area to another MME area where both the MME are connected to the same SGW [15] [16].

In an inter-MME handover, two MMEs are involved in the handover, the source MME (S-MME) and target MME (T-MME). The S-MME controls the S-eNB and the T-MME controls the T-eNB. This handover is triggered when the UE moves from one MME area to another MME area.

1. The S-eNB decides to handover the UE to another eNodeB (T-eNB) with the involvement of two MMEs coordinating the handover signalling between the source and target eNodeB.
2. The S-MME uses signalling to communicate the handover signalling to the T-MME and vice versa. The FORWARD RELOCATION procedure is being used.
3. After receiving the S1 HANDOVER REQUIRED, the S-MME detects that the target cell requested for handover belongs to another MME and initiates the FORWARD RELOCATION REQ message to the T-MME.
4. The T-MME creates the S1 logical connection toward the T-eNB and sends the S1 HANDOVER REQ on it.
5. The T-eNB prepares the requested resources and responds with a HANDOVER REQ ACK to the T-MME.
6. The T-MME sends a FORWARD RELOCATION RESP to the S-MME, to notify the resource reservation at the T-eNB.

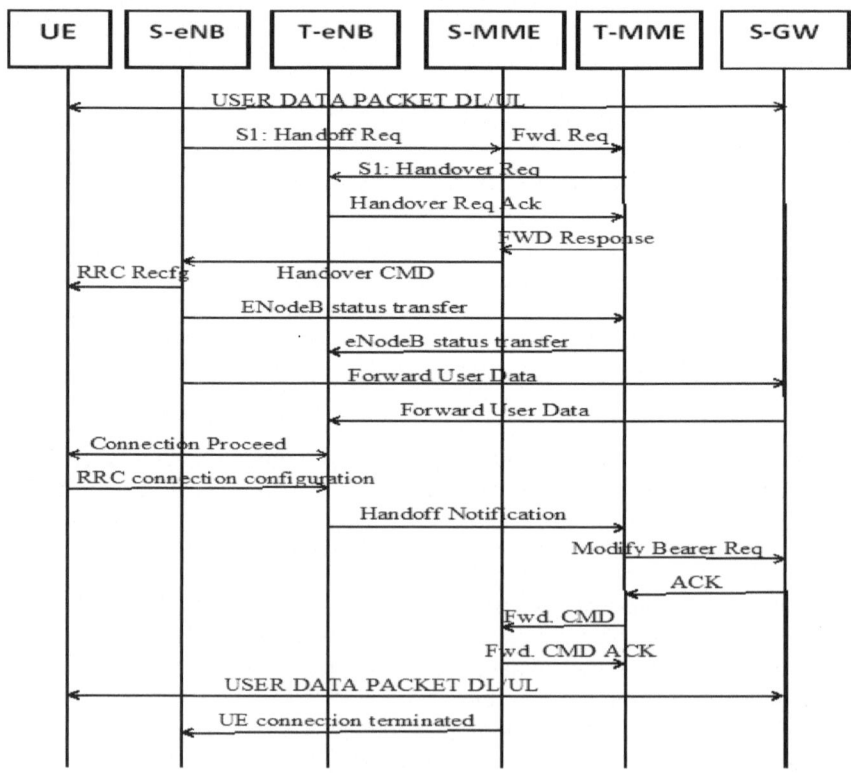

Fig. 3. Inter MME Handoff

7. DL data packets are forwarded from the S-eNB to T-eNB via the SGW during the handover as the SGW is not changed here.
8. Once the T-eNB detects the UE in its area, it notifies the T-MME with a S1 HANDOVER NOTIFY message.
9. The T-MME notifies the completion of the handover to the S-MME with a FORWARD RELOCATION COMPLETE NOTIFY message.
10. The S-MME acknowledges the GTP FORWARD RELOCAION COMPLETE NOTIFY to the T-MME and proceeds with clearing the S1 logical connection and the associated bearer resources.

In LTE systems, active mode mobility management are distributed, the eNodeB are making the handoff decision without involving MME/SGW.

5   Proposed Handoff Algorithm Model in LTE System

A handoff algorithm is proposed which minimizes the Time-to-Trigger and hence reduces the latency during handoff process which automatically reduces the delay parameter in the LTE system by comparing both the standard Handoff algorithm and the proposed Handoff algorithm.

Calculation of the relative signal strength in LTE network is basically a mutual concept which includes both UE and eNodeB in determining the best possible region for the UE. The RSS of serving eNodeB is compared with that of surrounding eNodeBs.

The cost-231 Walfisch Ikegami Model is used to compute the propagation loss, shadow fading taking Gaussian log normal distribution with zero mean and 12 dB standard deviation and non-frequency selective Rayleigh fading to calculate slow fading in order to calculate the relative signal strength of eNodeB[12] [13].

Hard Handoff is performed, the mobile periodically measure the received power from its serving eNodeB and from the neighbouring eNodeB. The main concept is to make the handoff decision by historical signal strength differences. The signal strength difference calculation in proposed handoff algorithm is described as follows:

$$RSSI\_LTE\_BS_1 < RSSI\_LTE{<}BS_n \qquad (1)$$

$$PBQ > \text{Handoff Margin (HOM)} \qquad (2)$$

$$(ST{=}1 \| ((LTE\_BS_1\_coverage) \,\&\&\, (LTE\_BS_N\_coverage))) \qquad (3)$$

$$PG_{TS} \geq PG_{SS} + HOM \qquad (4)$$

PBQ denotes power budget quantity which are being evaluated by the eNodeB and on the basis of the power being calculated by the serving eNodeB, it helps in determining whether a UE wanted to have handoff or not and accordingly eNodeB sends request to the target eNodeB to carry out handoff process.While ST denotes service type i.e. the UE is in idle state or connected state (for connected state ST=1).

The essential condition required is that the received power from the target eNodeB must be higher than a threshold and enough resources should be available in the target eNB. Algorithm for determining the PBQ is described as follows [17] [18] [19]:

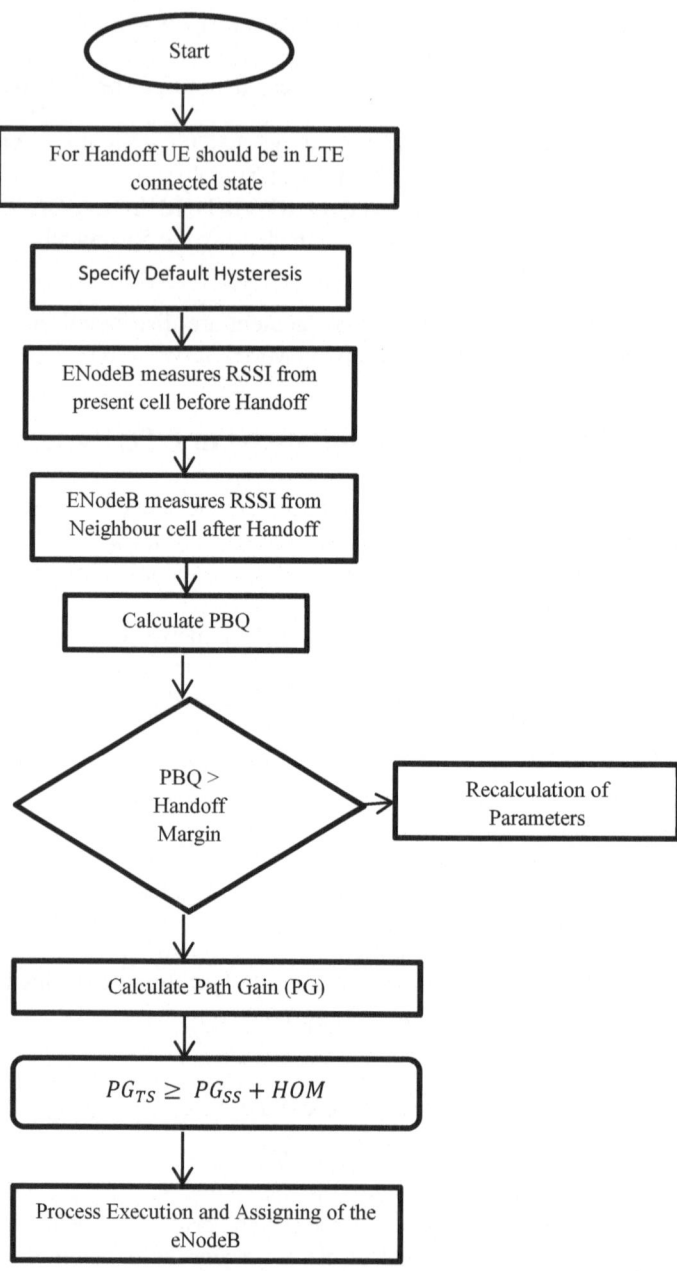

Fig. 4. Handoff Procedure in LTE Networks

1. Distance Calculation

The distance of the UEs from its serving eNodeB is calculated.

$$distance_{(x,y)} = \sqrt{distance_x{}^2 + distance_y{}^2} \tag{5}$$

2. Use of omnidirectional antennas in order to determine the PBQ values of each UE.

Firstly we calculate the Q-function

$$\text{Q-function= qfn } \left[\frac{10PL\ log\left[\min\left(\frac{distance(\Sigma i,j)}{distance_{(x,y)}}\right)\right]}{\sqrt{2}a}\right] - \sqrt{2}\log (a) \tag{6}$$

3. Now further we will be calculating the PBQ using Q-function

$$\text{PBQ= } [[(1+ (G_p/v)*(1/a)\text{-}q) \div (1+0.5*distance_{(x,y)})]\text{-}1]*10 \tag{7}$$

Here G_P is processing gain, v is the frequency of the channel, a is the standard deviation and q is AWGN to signal ratio, qfn is an error function. Thus by calculating the PBQ we can determine the UEs which needed to handoff as soon as the PBQ > Handoff margin (HOM).The path gain (PG) defines the relationship between transmitted power and received power between the UE and target eNodeB (PG_{TS}) and serving eNodeB (PG_{SS}). The Calculation of path gain is described below:

$$\text{PG= } (G_{eNodeB}*G_{UE}*\lambda^2) / (4\pi)^2 * distance_{(x,y)}{}^2) \tag{8}$$

Where G_{eNodeB} is the gain of antenna gain of base station, G_{UE} is the antenna gain of user equipment and λ is the wavelength and d is the distance between the antennas.

Table 1. Simulation Parameters

Parameters	Values
Carrier frequency	2 GHz
Bandwidth	1.4 MHz
eNodeB Tx Power	20 Watt
Propagation Model	Cost-231 Walfisch Ikegami Model
Channel Model	3GPP typical Urban
UE speed	{10, 50}; km/h
Shadow Fading	Gaussian log-normal distribution
Multi-path	Non-frequency selective Rayleigh fading
Scheduling Time	0.5 ms
Simulation Time	1000 ms
HOM range	1.6 dB
G_{UE}, G_{eNodeB}	5 dB, 18dB

6   Simulation Result

The performance of proposed handoff algorithm is evaluated, optimized and compared using a 7- hexagonal-cell scenario of 1.4 MHz bandwidth with 15 resource block and 2 GHz carrier frequency. User Equipment's (UE) are uniformly distributed within the hexagonal cell area as shown in Fig. 5. UEs are moving at speeds of 10 km/hr, 50 km/hr or 120 km/hr depend on each scenario. Direction for each user is randomly chosen initially and stays constant in whole simulation. Users are evaluated whenever they reach the edge.

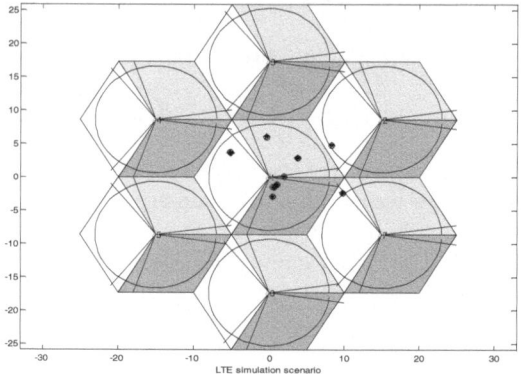

Fig. 5. LTE simulation Scenario

Figure-6 explains the detailed measurements of Power budget quantity (PBQ) of UEs by the eNodeB with respect to the location of UE. Star- shaped red dot represents randomly generated UEs with in a region of surrounding eNodeB. The PBQ measurements obtained are being compared with the handoff margin (HOM) and the value of PBQ will decide which UE will be requiring Handoff by the eNodeB and on the basis of that UE decides when to handoff based on the information gained from the eNodeB and itself.

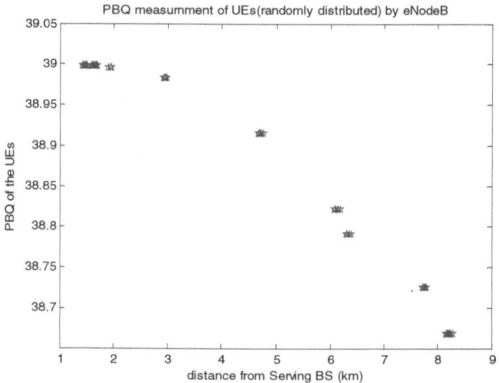

Fig. 6. PBQ measurements of UE by eNodeB

Figure-7 illustrates the signal strength vs time curve based on standard LTE hard handoff algorithm. Handoff is triggered when the triggering condition is fulfilled for the entire TTT time as shown in equation 5. [14]

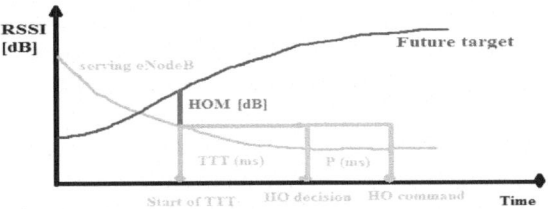

Fig. 7. Standard LTE Handoff Algorithm

$$RSSI_T > RSSI_S + HOM \tag{9}$$

Where $RSSI_T$ and $RSSI_S$ are the RSSI received from the target cell and the serving cell, respectively.

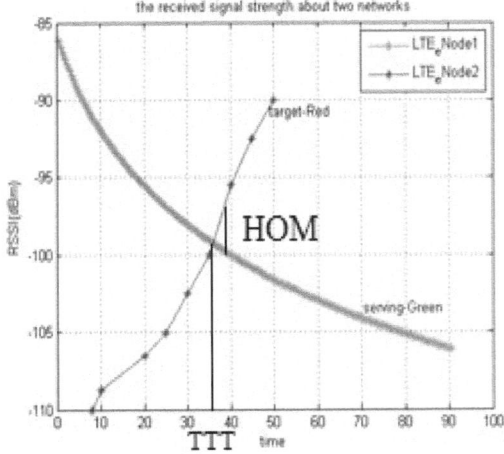

Fig. 8. RSS calculation by proposed Handoff algorithm

Figure-8 shows the relative signal strength vs time graph between two eNodeB based on the proposed handoff algorithm.

Thus in this paper a modification in RSS based algorithm with TTT window is proposed and also the delay factor in the proposed model is less as compared to standard Handoff model. Thus it will help in improving the performance of the system during Handoff process and Handoff decision can be taken early. The UE makes periodic measurements of RSSI based on the RSSI received from the serving cell and from the strongest adjacent cells. In case the handover algorithm is based on RSSI values, handover is triggered when the RSSI value from an adjacent cell is higher than the one from the serving cell by a number of dBs equal to HO hysteresis; this condition has to be satisfied for a period equal to the TTT.

It can be seen that higher the threshold level, the lower is the mean number of handoffs. Higher threshold values also reduce the mean number of handoffs. The measured parameters and the thresholds for reporting are decided by the user equipment (MCHO). This paper analyses the performance of both the algorithms in a LTE network by calculating the handoff parameters like TTT and relative signal strength.

After comparing the proposed model with the standard LTE handoff model there is a deduction of 12ms in the interruption time and also a 6 ms deduction in time to trigger in proposed handoff algorithm. TTT is directly proportional to the HOM. In the algorithm the value of HOM is coming out to be 1.46 as compared to that of standard algorithm (HOM value- 1.6dB).

7   Conclusion

The proposed handoff algorithm in the paper minimizes interruption time when compared to the standard LTE hard handoff algorithm. In this case, the UE will assist in the Handoff decision by measuring the neighbouring cells and reporting the measurements to the network, which in turn decides upon the handoff timing and the target cell/node. A modification in RSS based algorithm with the introduction of mobile controlled handoff (MCHO) yields better result in comparison to standard handoff algorithm. We can improve its performance even better by optimizing the different handoff parameters.

References

1. Requirement for Further Advancement for E-UTRA (LTE-Advanced), Version 8.0.0 (2008)
2. Evolved Universal Terrestrial Radio Access (E-UTRA) Physical Layer Measurements, Version 8.5.0 (2008)
3. Evolved Universal Terrestrial Radio Access (E-UTRA) Physical Layer Procedure (Release8), Version 8.5.0 (2008)
4. Aggeliki, S., Dimitrios, D.V.: Handoff Prioritization and Decision Schemes in Wireless Cellular Networks: a Survey. IEEE Communication Tutorial (2009)
5. Pollini, G.P.: Trend in Handover Design. IEEE Communication Magazine (1996)
6. Stefania, S., Issam, T., Matthew, B.: LTE – The UMTS Long Term Evolution: From Theory to Practice (2009)
7. Erik, D., Stefan, P., Johan, S., Per, B.: 3G Evolution: HSPA and LTE for Mobile Broadband. Academic Press (2008)
8. 3GPP Technical Specification: Base Station (BS) Radio Transmission and Reception (FDD), http://www.3gpp.org
9. Tiberwala, A., Pramanick, D., Dhar Roy, S., Kundu, S.: Signal Strength Radio Based Handoff Algorithms for Cellular Networks. IEEE

10. Nikaein, N., Krco, S.: Latency for Real-Time Machine-to-Machine Communication in LTE-Based System Architecture. Ericsson (2011)
11. Myung, H.G.: Technical Overview of 3GPP LTE (2008)
12. Gudmundson, M.: Correlation Model for Shadow Fading in Mobile Radio Systems. In: Electronics Letters, vol. 27, pp. 2145–2146. IEEE press, Paris (2005)
13. Komninakis, C.: A Fast and Accurate Rayleigh Fading Simulator. In: IEEE Globecom, San Francisco, CA (2003)
14. Yang, Y.: Optimization of Handoff Algorithm within 3GPP LTE. MSc Thesis Report, KTH (2009)
15. Rao, V.S., Gajula, S.: Interoperable UE Handovers in LTE (2011)
16. Spirent Landslide LTE Testing: Inter Handoff coverage (2009)
17. Ridha, N., Altman, Z.: Handover Adaptation for Dynamic Load Balancing in 3GPP Long Term Evolution Systems (2007)
18. Ekström, H., Furuskär, A., Karlsson, J., Meyer, M., Parkvall, S., Torsner, J., Wahlqvist, M.: Technical Solutions for the 3G Long-Term Evolution. IEEE Communication. Mag. 44(3) (2006)
19. Nasri, R., Altman, Z., Dubreil, H.: WCDMA downlink load sharing with dynamic control of soft handover parameters. In: IEEE International Symposium VTC, Melbourne, Australia (2006)
20. Nasıf, E., Tara, S., Sibel, K., Fidanboylu, G.: An Overview of Handoff Techniques in Cellular Networks. World Academy of Science, Engineering and Technology (2005)

A Different Approach of Addressing, Energy Efficient Routing and Data Aggregation for Enhanced Tree Routing Protocol

Sharad[1], Shailendra Mishra[2], Ashok Kumar Sharma[3], and D.S. Chauhan[4]

[1] Department of Computer Application, Bharat Institute of Technology, Meerut, UP, India
[2] Department of CSE, BCTKEC, Dwarahat, Uttrakhand, UK, India
[3] Department of CSE, YMCA Faridabad, India
[4] Uttrakhand Technical University, Dehradun, UK, India
{sharadzoom,skmishra1}@gmail.com, ashokkale@rediffmail.com

Abstract. Tree topology based sensor node deployment in a region is a common approach. The network has a root called sink node and leaves known as end-devices. The end-devices sense the environmental phenomenon and forward it to the sink by single-hopping or multi-hopping. For it, device can either follow a fixed parent-child path depicted by Tree Routing protocols, or can utilize neighbor table to identify shortest path to the destination. The Enhanced Tree Routing (ETR) protocol is such a protocol that uses a structured node address assignment scheme. It uses neighbor table to find alternative one-hop neighbors link with minimum computation, other than parent-child links, for packet forwarding. The protocol is well suited for small and static tree topology and performs well. However, it lacks in focusing some issues like, how data is forwarded to sink i.e. raw-data converge cast or aggregated-data converge cast at each node, how to resolve multiple shortest path problem if network density increases and how to deal with changeable network topology. We, in this paper thus resolve some of the issues related to ETR protocol by proposing some new ideas and improvements.

Keywords: ETR, Hop-count, Energy, Data-Aggregation, Ad-Hoc sensor.

1 Introduction

A sensor is a short-range radio device with a limited life time. The life time is totally dependent on the amount of processing performed by it and battery capacity. An ad-hoc sensor network [1], which is collection of sensors, can be deployed in a region where human intervention is not required in order to sense physical phenomena, such as sound, light, magnetic field, temperature etc. Finally, the sensed data is transmitted to a short range positioned sink node for processing. The data transmission can take place either through single-hop distance or multiple-hop communication link. A WSN is self-organizing, and can adapt to sensor failure and degradation and react to task changes. They are used in wide applications like battlefield surveillance, environment

M. Parashar et al. (Eds.): IC3 2012, CCIS 306, pp. 306–321, 2012.
© Springer-Verlag Berlin Heidelberg 2012

monitoring, animal tracking and chemical detection etc. The basic need of a sensor for sensing, processing and transmitting is accomplished by small batteries. Manually recharging batteries of deployed sensors is extremely difficult task. Therefore, solutions to increase the network lifetime are important. Moreover every aspect of design, deployment and management of WSN has to be energy-efficient [2] to meet stringent power requirements. Among various components of sensors, radio communication is the most energy consuming operation a node performs, and thus, it must be used sparingly and only as dictated by the task requirements [3]. Moreover, a direct long distance transmission consumes more power than short distance; a multi-hop technique can be superior to a single-hop technique. Topology creation, therefore, is an essential function of multi-hop WSN and routing is the method built into the firmware of each sensor node for finding paths between source and destination. The basic method of sensor network construction is to start with a root node and expand it, by joining new nodes as child nodes. Each node can have multiple children but only one parent. The resultant network structure is like a tree as depicted in Fig. 1.

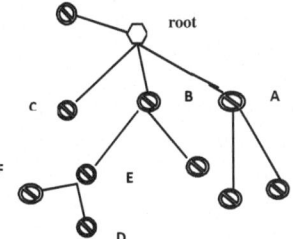

Fig. 1. Basic Tree Topology

In Fig. 1, nodes A, B and C are the child nodes of root node. Both root and C are the ancestors of node E and F while all nodes except root are descendants' nodes. The basic routing strategy in a tree is well depicted by Tree Routing (TR) [4], where inter-node communication is restricted to parent–child links only. It has no path searching and updating complexities, hence is suitable for networks consisting of small-memory, low-power and low-complexity lightweight nodes. The Enhanced Tree Routing (ETR) protocol [4] uses the links to other one-hop neighbors if it is found to be shorter (in terms of hop count) than the tree path. It uses minimum storage and computing cost to identify new paths by utilizing the systematic addressing structure. It takes advantage of neighbor table to improve performance of TR protocol. The protocol helps in identifying the shortest route for data forwarding from a sensor node to the sink node. But the protocol is well suited for static tree topology. For a changeable environment the count of sensor nodes can increase or decrease as per need of the applications. The alteration in count can increase or decrease in the density of the sensor network in the same region. However, the tree topology remains the same. An increase in sensor density may lead to, existence of more number of alternative paths to sink node. Here ETR cannot predict the best shortest path to the destination. It is illustrated in Fig. 2.

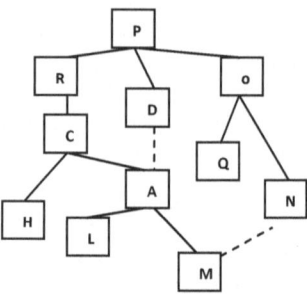

Fig. 2. ETR Tree Topology

The dashed lines in Fig. 2 represent neighbor relationships other than parent–child links. If D is selected as destination node than the TR route from node M to node D is M->A->C->R->P->D (hop-count = 5). For ETR, node M selects N as the next hop node according to the ETR Theorem leading to the ETR route M->N->O->P->D (hop-count = 4). The ETR protocol cannot predict that a better ETR route M->A->D (hop-count = 2) can be established. This is because the distance between M and N is shorter than the distance between M and A. ETR will select the shortest path i.e. M to N instead of M to A.

Further, in a densely deployed network the possibilities of more number of nearest neighbor nodes exist. In this case, data forwarding increases excessive hop-count from sensor node to the sink node. Therefore instead of saving energy the intermediate node consumes extra energy for data forwarding, though a comparatively large path can save energy having less hop-count. Further, data in a tree based topology can travel from sensor node to the sink node in two ways: firstly, every node generate a packet and send it directly to the sink node; secondly, every node generate a packet and send it to a nearby node designated as accumulator to buffer the packet and then forward them to sink node, as per some scheduling mechanism. The first method is refereed as raw-data convergecast and second is known as aggregate convergecast. ETR protocol does not depict such aspects of data forwarding.

In this paper we have proposed a new Non Orthogonal Variable Spreading Factor Based (NOVSF) [5] addressing technique to sensor nodes. The codes not only provide addressing to the sensor node but also are used to trace the location of sensor deployment to support flexible tree topology. To reduce excessive hop-count we have planned to place mobile gateways to some feasible sites in a region. Feasible sites are those locations where the maximum number of sensor has direct approach to either sink node or mobile gateway. These locations are identified by solving some formula and some ILPs described in further sections. The mobility of gateway is controlled by fixed sink node and is utilized only for repositioning it to feasible site whenever there is a change in the density of the sensor node is observed. After repositioning, the network becomes static. There-after the addresses are assigned to the sensor nodes as per the new scheme and links are created to transmit data. Every sensor generate single data packet and send it to the mobile gateway. The gateway performs the task of data aggregation and forwards it to the sink node.

This paper is organized as follows. Section 2 discusses about single hopping, multi hopping scenario, TDMA technique and some related work. Section 3 presents Improved ETR protocol deployment scheme. Section 4 gives addressing scheme for Improved ETR protocol. Section 5 discusses on data collection technique for improved ETR protocol. Section 6 focuses on power optimization concept of the Improved ETR protocol. The hop-count and energy comparison of ETR and Improved ETR is shown in section 7. Finally section 8 concludes the paper.

2   Background Discussions

Multi-hop topologies are superior to single-hop topologies in a dense ad-hoc sensor network. Multi-hopping is more energy efficient in wireless communication for short distances [6]. Short distances need less energy to transmit and have better signals resulting in fewer re-transmissions due to packet loss. Excessive Multi-hop networks have issues like congestion at the sink and unfair bandwidth allocation. The nodes at far distance have as fair a chance of getting their data to the base station as the nearest nodes. The chances of packets loss increases with increase in hopping due to lose nature of wireless links. Moreover, the traffic in sensor networks tends to be greatly correlated. Asynchronous events can cause sudden burst of traffic, leading to collision, congestion, and channel capture [7]. The slotted time division schemes are effective to solve these problems. They can leave traffic uncorrelated and provide end to end fairness. They are more energy efficient as it is known when to keep radio off to save power. Policies are generated to achieve bandwidth reservation from source to sink and from it, it is clear when to turn the radio on and off locally. Slotted time division scheme are centrally controlled having static global schedule, and needs fine-grain time synchronization.

Authors in [8] proposed TDMA-based protocols that are inherently energy efficient. In TDMA nodes turn on their radio only during their allotted time slots and switch-off for rest of the time. Therefore TDMA based protocols removes problems associated with medium interference among nodes. In data-centric routing [9], the node desiring certain types of information sends queries to certain regions and waits for data from the nodes located in the selected regions. Hierarchical protocols [10] group nodes into clusters where cluster heads are responsible for intra-cluster data aggregation and inter-cluster communication in order to save energy. Location based protocols utilize the position information to increase the energy efficiency in routing by relaying the data to the desired regions rather than the whole network [11]. Algorithms which search for alternatives to the parent–child links have recently been proposed specifically for ZigBee networks [12]. Most popular AODV protocol [13] uses hop-count as the metric and tries to find the shortest route possible. It establishes a route to a destination only on demand. It means, when a node requires a route, it initiates a route discovery procedure broadcasting route request (RREQ) messages. Tree routing (TR) [4] is a simple routing algorithm where a node only forwards packets to its parent or child nodes. It prevents energy by avoiding intensive message exchanges of path search/update processes. Emerging architecture for large-scale urban wireless networks employ TR schemes as well. Routing (ETR) [4] assumes that each node has an updated neighbor table having the address of its immediate one-hop neighbors. This neighbor table is utilized to identify the alternate path to the sink node with hop-count less than the actual path. For peer to peer communication each node has a unique identification number. This number is assigned to the node as it joins the network.

The method proposed in this paper uses distributed algorithm and no centralized control, and requires only coarse grain time synchronization. Because of distributed nature, there is no method to generate and distribute a network-wide global schedule. However, discovery can be achieved locally, as we are using constrained tree topology. A local schedule can be generated at each node by message exchanging and can be adapted to the changing need of the network. By adopting coarse grain schedule the medium does not become absolutely contention free, we need a MAC layer to handle traffic generated by different nodes at the same time. The coarse-grain schedule can coordinate transmission times and can distribute traffic. A MAC layer is still required to, but with less work to do.

3   Protocol Deployment Scheme

This section describes improved ETR Tree protocol for sensor node deployment and data communication. The entire region is considered to be consisting of *n* regions. Each region is supervised by a mobile gateway (*see* Fig. 3). The mobile gateway assigns and eliminates the relevant address to a sensor node, as it enters and leaves the specific region. The addressing to the sensor node is done by using orthogonal code scheme called NOVSF described in section 4. The scheme is adopted to avoid code blocking and code reassignment problem. The mobile gateway is assumed to be rich in power resources that buffer local data from the sensor nodes and forward it to the fixed sink node.

Each sensor uses a 16 bit of addressing scheme as specified in Zigbee 802.15.4 [14]. The first eight bits of address of the sensor node determine the location of the sensor and the parent mobile sink node address, and the rest eight bits are used as the sensor identity. MG1, MG2,...., MGn in Fig. 3 are the mobile gateways(1..n) placed at feasible sites. The count of the mobile gateway is determined by the orthogonal code spreading factor. As for a specific spreading factor we can generate a fix number of orthogonal codes. Theses orthogonal codes are used to find addresses of sensor node. Mobile gateway recognizes sensors by theses addresses.

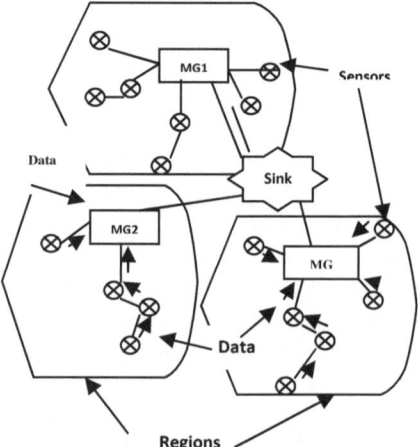

Fig. 3. Protocol Deployment Scheme

The feasible site is determined by solving some equations and ILPs described in section 6. For data transmission, each sensor utilizes a fixed TDMA slot provided by mobile gateway to send each data packet generated to the mobile gateway. The gateway collects the data and forwards it to the sink station as per some scheduling algorithm described in section 5. For our discussion and result comparison we have utilized spreading factor (SF)-8 NOVSF code for address assignment to the mobile sink stations and sensors. The various code addressing schemes are shown in Section 4, Table 1.

4   Addressing Scheme for Improved ETR

We have taken SF-8 for addressing. SF-8 can generate eight unique orthogonal codes [5], hence they can be assigned to eight mobile gateways only. Therefore, SF-8 can provide maximum of 8 mobile gateways in the region. The mobile gateway generates sensor node addresses by combining its assigned orthogonal code, with a continuous sequence number as shown in Fig. 4.

Node Address

Region Code (NOVSF Code)	Sensor Number (Sequence Number)

Example

8 bit		8 bit	
1111	1111	0000	0001

Fig. 4. Address Template

Table 1. Complete Addressing Scheme for 8 Gateways

Mobile Gateway	Region Identification Orthogonal Codes	Generated Node Addresses
MG1	1111 1111	1111 1111 **0000 0001** to 1111 1111 **1111 1111**
MG2	1111 -1-1-1-1	1111 -1-1-1-1 0000 0001 to 1111 -1-1-1-1 1111 1111
MG3	11-1-1 11-1-1	11-1-1 11-1-1 0000 0001 to 11-1-1 11-1-1 1111 1111
MG4	11-1-1 -1-111	11-1-1 -1-111 0000 0001 to 11-1-1 -1-111 1111 1111
MG5	1-11-1 1-11-1	1-11-1 1-11-1 0000 0001 to1-11-1 1-11-1 1111 1111
MG6	1-11-1 -11-11	1-11-1 -11-11 0000 0001 to 1-11-1 -11-11 1111 1111
MG7	1-1-11 1-1-11	1-1-11 1-1-11 0000 0001 to 1-1-11 1-1-11 1111 1111
MG8	1-1-11 -111-1	1-1-11 -111-1 0000 0001 to 1-1-11 -111-1 1111 1111

Like an example mobile gateway MG1 has NOVSF code as (1111 1111) it combines it with a sequence number in the range shown in Table 1 (e.g. 0000 0001) to get a complete address of a sensor node as (1111 1111 0000 0001, 1111 1111 0000 0002, 1111 1111 0000 0003 ....etc.). Therefore one mobile gateway can support a maximum number of 255 (0000 0001 to 1111 1111) sensor nodes. However as per application needs more number of mobile gateways can be deployed by extending spreading factor to 16, 32 or higher, to achieve more unique codes and to support more sensors in the region. The assigned regional code helps sink to identify the area of gateway deployment and data collected from it. The data segregation or collection according to the region becomes easy at sink node from this addressing scheme. Moreover generating a continuous sequence number, combining it with region code and assigning it to the sensor node required minimum computation and less processing power.

5   Data Aggregation and Collection in Improved ETR Protocol

The data collection approach can vary depending on application requirements. For instance, in disaster early warning applications, such as detection of forest fire [15] and gas/oil leaks [16], or structural damage identification [17], burst traffic generated by events needs to be delivered to the sink as quickly and as reliably as possible to prevent catastrophes. On the other hand, in applications where sensor nodes only report periodic data, such as animal habitat monitoring [18], energy-efficiency may become a more important concern as opposed to quick data collection. Moreover under regular, heavy traffic conditions, contention-free medium access control (MAC) protocols like Time Division Multiple Access (TDMA), where nodes communicate on different time slots to prevent conflicts, offer several advantages for data collection as compared to contention-based protocols [19]. They eliminate collisions, overhearing, and idle listening, which are the main sources of energy consumption in wireless communications. Moreover it also permits nodes to enter into sleep modes during inactive periods, thus, achieving low duty cycles and conserving energy. Furthermore, TDMA-based communications can provide provable guarantee on the completion time of data collection, for instance, in timely detection of events. Another key aspect of time-slotted communication is robustness during peak loads. When the number of source nodes is many or the data rates are high, carrier-sense multiple access protocols like, CSMA, may fail to allocate the medium successfully, causing in retransmissions and collisions.

TDMA-based scheduling algorithms are widely exploited for fast and timely delivery of data with the objective of minimizing the time to complete convergecast, i.e., minimizing the latency. In a TDMA schedule, time is slotted and each slot is long enough for transmission or reception of a single packet. Consecutive time slots are grouped into non-overlapping frames, and the schedule for each frame is repeated when data collection is periodic. It is assumed that some form of time synchronization exists among the nodes, which can be achieved using one of the protocols such as [20]. The minimum time required for data collection now depends on number of time slots required per frame. Further, multi-hop TDMA allows reuse of time slots, therefore more than one node can transmit simultaneously if their receivers are in non-conflicting parts of the network. There are two types of conflicts that arise: (i) primary conflict, and (ii) secondary conflict. Primary conflict occurs due to simultaneously transmitting and receiving at the same time, or receives more than one transmission destined to it at the same time. A secondary conflict arises when a node (*receiver*) of a particular transmission is also within the range of another transmission intended for other nodes.

Algorithm 1. Data collection in Improved ETR
1.   //Transmission from sensor node to Gateway Node
2.   *Initialize* node. Buffer = FULL
3.   If {node is gateway} then
4.   Among the eligible top-subtrees(i), choose the one with the largest number of packets.
5.   Select link (root(i), s)
6.   Else If {node. Buffer == EMPTY} then
7.   Select a random child c whose buffer is full
8.   Select link (c, node)
9.   c.Buffer = empty
10.   node. Buffer = full
11. End If
12. End If
13. //Transmission from Gateway to Sink Node
14. //Using TDMA to pick one gateway in a slot
15. For {i= No-of-gateways}
16. If {gateway (i).buffer == EMPTY}
17.   No aggregated data
18. Else
19.   Select link (gateway(i),Sink)
20.   Transfer data limited to allotted time slot
21. End if
22. End For

For Improved ETR-Tree protocol we propose two strategies, (i) parallel raw-data convergecast from sensor nodes to mobile gateway, (ii) transmission of aggregated-data to the fixed sink node called aggregated convergecast. The idea is formally presented in Algorithm 1. Each node maintains a buffer and its associated state, which can be either full or empty, depending on whether it contains a packet or not. Initially, all the buffers are full because every node has a packet to send. The first block of the algorithm in lines 3-5 gives the scheduling rules between the gateway and the roots of the top sub-trees. A top-sub-tree is defined as one whose root is a child of the gateway. It is eligible to send data if it has at least one packet to send. As shown in Fig. 5, the top sub-trees are {1, 4}, {2, 5, 6}, and {3, 7}. For a given time slot, the root of an eligible top sub-tree which has the largest number of total remaining packets is scheduled. If none of the top sub-trees are eligible, the gateway does not receive any packet during that time slot. Inside each top sub-tree, nodes are scheduled according to the rules in lines 6-12. A sub-tree is defined to be active if there are still packets left in it (excluding its root) to be relayed. If a node's buffer is empty and the sub-tree rooted at this node is active, one of its children is scheduled at random whose buffer is not empty. The algorithm guarantees that in an active sub-tree there will always be at least one child whose buffer is not empty, and so whenever a node empties its buffer, it will receive a packet in the next time slot, thus emptying buffers from the bottom of the sub-tree to the top.

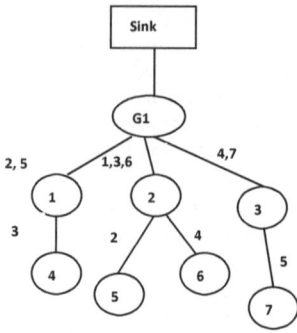

Fig. 5. Raw-data Convergecast and Aggregation at Gateway G1

Fig. 5 shows an illustration of the working of the algorithm. In slot 1, since the eligible top sub-tree containing the largest number of remaining packets is {2, 5, 6}, link (2, s) is scheduled and the sink receives a packet from node 2. In slot 2, the eligible top sub-trees are {1, 4} and {3, 7}, both of which have 2 remaining packets. One of them can be selected at random, say {1, 4}, and schedule the link (1, s). Also, in the same time slot since node 2's buffer is empty, it chooses one of its children at random, say node 5, and schedule the link (5, 2). In slot 3, the eligible top sub-trees are {2, 5, 6} and {3, 7}, both of which have 2 remaining packets. Again one of them is chosen randomly, let it is 2 and selected link is (2, s), and so the sink receives a packet from node 5 (relayed by node 2). We also schedule the link (4, 1) in slot 3 because node 1's buffer is empty at this point. This process continues until all the packets are delivered to the gateway, yielding an assignment that requires 7 time slots. Thus, the entire data is collected at the mobile gateway. The aggregated data from mobile gateway is transferred from them to the sink by using steps 15-22.

6   Formula and Proposed ILPs for Feasible Site Determination and Power Optimization

Following are the assumptions made for the proposed protocol:

1. Each sensor node has a unique address.
2. The data generated per unit time by each node is equal.
3. Each sensor has a definite transmission range.
4. The transceiver exhibits first order radio model characteristics, where energy dissipation for the transmitter or receiver circuitry is constant per bit communicated. Moreover the energy spent for a bit transmitting over a distance d is proportional to d^2.
5. A contention free MAC protocol is available for channel access.
6. The maximum limit to number of mobile gateway exists.
7. Rounds contain equal time periods. At the beginning of each round, the new location of the mobile gateway is determined.

Initially a sink node is placed at a location and sensors are placed randomly in the region. A logical polygon is created by combining the extreme sensors in the region and the centroid location is calculated using equations 1, 2 and 3.

$$A = \frac{1}{2} \sum_{i=0}^{N-1} (x_i y_{i+1} - x_{i+1} y_i) \tag{1}$$

$$X = \frac{1}{6A} \sum_{i=0}^{N-1} (x_i + x_{i+1})(x_i y_{i+1} - x_{i+1} y_i) \tag{2}$$

$$Y = \frac{1}{6A} \sum_{i=0}^{N-1} (y_i + y_{i+1})(x_i y_{i+1} - x_{i+1} y_i) \tag{3}$$

Here A is the area of the polygon; X and Y are the coordinates of the centroid of the polygon, x_i and y_i are the coordinates of the randomly deployed sensors. Thus $P(X, Y)$ will be feasible position for mobile gateway placement. Since a single sink can support maximum of 255 nodes and if the region expends, we need to place more than one mobile gateway in the region. Therefore in this case the complete area must be divided in to two sub-areas and two polygons will be created. Again the centroid for two regions will be computed by above equations. The process can be repeated maximum up to 8 (SF 8). At the beginning of each round, the location of the mobile gateway needs to be fixed at feasible sites. We referred this problem as MGL (Mobile Gateway Location) problem. We have devised some mathematical formulation to solve this problem known as Integer Linear Program (ILP) [21]. Let the sensor node is represented by a graph G(V, E) where V is the set of all vertex of the graph and E is the set of all edge connecting the various vertex. In our sensor network V and E are defined as:

a) $V = V_s \ U \ V_f$, where V_s is the set of the sensor nodes and V_f is the set of the feasible sites.

b) $E = V \ x \ V$ represents sets of all wireless links.

Let MG_{max} represents the maximum number of mobile gateway possible. T is the timeframe for a single round. Each sensor generates one packet of data in a single timeframe. Let a sensor node i has a residual energy RE_i . During a round the total energy spent by a sensor i is at most βRE_i , where $0 < \beta \leq 1$ is a parameter. Now we can describe an integer linear program formulation for MGL problem as:-

Let L_{loc} is a Boolean integer variable that can have values 0 or 1. It contains value 1 when mobile sink is placed successfully at some feasible site loc and 0 otherwise. E_{max} is the maximum energy spent in a round. Nbr (i) = {j: (i, j) $\in$ E}, here j is the neighbor node of i. Now for a given G (V, E), β, and MG_{max} the following ILPs can be formed.

Minimize E_{max}

$$\sum_{loc \in Vf} L_{loc} \leq MG_{max} \tag{4}$$

$$\sum_{j \in Nbr(i)} q_{ij} - \sum_{k \in Nbr(i)} q_{ki} = T \tag{5}$$

$$E_t \sum_{j \in Nbr(i)} q_{ij} + E_r \sum_{k \in Nbr(i)} q_{ki} \leq \beta RE_i \; ; i \in V \tag{6}$$

$$E_t \sum_{j \in Nbr(i)} q_{ij} + E_r \sum_{k \in Nbr(i)} q_{ki} \leq E_{max} \; ; i \in V \tag{7}$$

$$x_{ij} \geq 0, i \in V_s, j \in V; \; L_{loc} \in \{0, 1\}, k \in V_f \tag{8}$$

Equation (4) depicts the number of feasible sites to locate mobile station and should be less than MG_{max}. The messages produced and consumed ratio in the network is shown by equation (5), q_{ij} represents the messages sent from node i to node j and q_{ki} shows the message sent from node k to i. Let E_r is the energy consumed in receiving a message and E_t is the energy for message transmission. Both E_r and E_t are deterministic from antenna characteristics. Then total energy spent in a round can be determined from equation (6). Constraint (6) minimizes the maximum energy spent by any sensor node during the round. Equation (8) shows the constraint associated with the other equations. This problem thus can be referred as *Minimize* MGL (G, β, MG_{max}). Solving these equations, we can determine energy consumption and flow of messages.

7   Performance Evaluations of Improved ETR and ETR

To analyze the proposed improvement, we simulated a sensor network in NS-2 [22], of 50 nodes randomly deployed, randomly distributed in a 500 x 500 meter square sensor field. 15 feasible sites were located randomly on the sensor field. Using a SF 8, eight mobile gateways are made available. Each sensor node is provided with an initial energy of 0.5J. The transmitter range is set to 230 meters. The packet length is fixed to 200 bits. Each round lasts 100 time-frames. We have used CPLEX method to solve MGL (G, β, B_{max}) problem with a time limit of 4 minutes. For each instance, the value of β as 0.2 and incremented in step of 0.2 in case the instance is infeasible. On this simulated sensor network we have taken two cases namely, *case-1* of 4 mobile gateway with random positioning among 15 possible sites and *case-2* of 4 mobile gateway with location obtained by MGL (G, β, B_{max}).

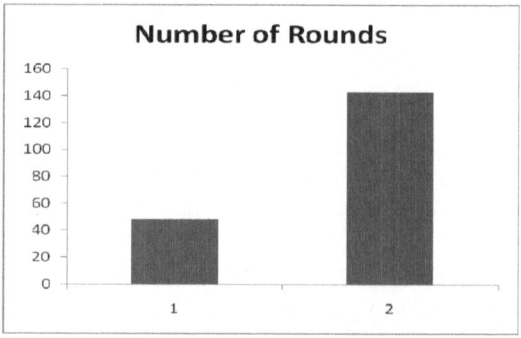

Fig. 6. Number of Rounds till First Node Die

It is evident from Fig. 6 that when the gateways are randomly deployed without finding the feasible site, the network is not able to sustain for a longer time and dies early as the number of rounds increases (case 1). While in case 2 where the mobile gateways are placed at feasible sites, the network is sustainable for a longer period of time. Hence, feasible site determination and placement of mobile gateway at those positions increases the life time of the sensor network. For hop-count and energy comparison a few dynamic network topologies are generated and two protocols are tested on it. In particular, after the nodes are deployed, the coordinator is powered on to start network. All the nodes then power on and search their neighbor-hood for parents. The new node and its identified parent exchange joining information, and a network address issued to the new node by the mobile gateway. The network is established when all the nodes join the network. An event is a transmission of packet from a source node to a destination node along the route determined by the protocol. For each event, number of hops and energy consumption of each hop is recorded. There is a sequential execution of events i.e. the second event triggers only when first one finishes. We have considered random deployment of the sensors in a fixed region of 500m by 500m. The energy consumption model specified by [23] is used. According to which the energy required by a single-hop transmission of a packet is computed as $(0.001 \times d^3)$. Where d is the distance between two nodes. We have considered eight network scenarios for the simulation having *(20, 25, 32, 40, 45, 50, 60, and 65)* randomly deployed sensor nodes respectively. The scenario is identified as *Sensors in the Networks (NWKS) = (20, 25, 32, 40, 45, 50, 60, and 65)*. A *RUN=10,000* runs are conducted for each instance. For each instance the hop-count and energy consumption are recorded. The results of network instances are average to find the metrics:

$$\text{Hops\_Average} = \frac{1}{NWKS*RUNS} \sum_{i=1}^{NWKS} \sum_{r=1}^{RUNS} h_{r.i} \qquad (9)$$

$$\text{Energy\_Average} = \frac{1}{NWKS*RUNS} \sum_{i=1}^{NWKS} \sum_{r=1}^{RUNS} e_{r.i} \qquad (10)$$

Where $h_{r.i}$ and $e_{r.i}$ are, the hop-count and energy consumption of the rth run for i^{th} network instance respectively. We have considered two network scenarios for the simulation:

Scenario 1: The transmitter range is set to 260m and the numbers of node deployed are taken in the range (20, 25, 32, 40, 45, 50, 60 and 65). The simulation results are shown in Fig. 7 and Fig. 8. As the network is firstly created with 20 nodes, ETR creates neighbor links in addition to regular parent-child links and Improved ETR-Tree finds a feasible site for mobile sink positioning. Mobile sinks assign addresses and time slots to sensor nodes for transmission. Each sensor in the network has some initial energy. Every sensor creates data packet, to send it to sink node. The data packet is delivered either through single-hopping or multi-hopping from one sensor to another sensor, till it reaches the fixed sink node. The round is supposed to complete when any of the sensor drain its' energy or reaches to a maximum of 10,000. The energy of a sensor is depreciated by a factor of $(\beta = 0.2)$ after a round. The average hops and average energy are computed from equations 9 and 10 for different number of sensors. The experiment is repeated for (25, 32, 40, 45, 50, 60 and 65) nodes. It can be seen from Fig. 7 that for 40 sensors both protocol have nearly same hop counts. At other points of instances the graph shows a noticeable depreciation in hop-count to the sink node. The difference is observed because with increase in number of sensors, the density of the network increases and the chances of more number of alternative shortest paths in the neighbor table. The shortest paths availability increase HOP-Count. On the other hand Improved ETR takes advantage of mobile gateway positioning in the network and thus helps in reducing excessive multi-hopping to single hopping. Moreover Improved ETR-Tree allows repositioning of mobile sinks in a dense dynamic network to feasible sites so as to cover maximum sensors, in the area, and convert excessive multi-hopping to single-hopping as far as possible.

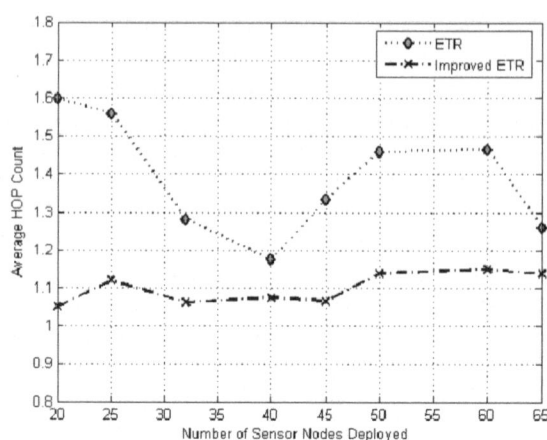

Fig. 7. HOP-Counts in Scenario 1

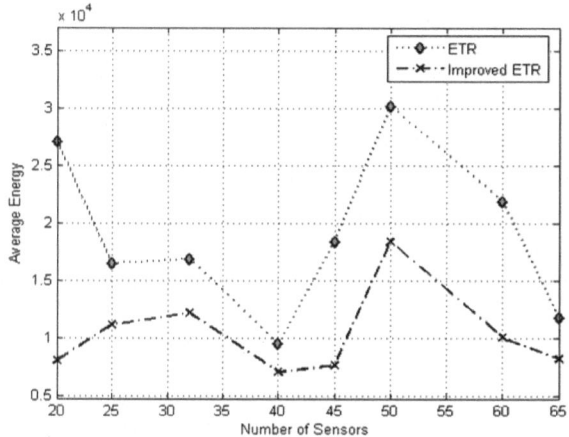

Fig. 8. Energy Consumption in Scenario 1

Since transmission energy is directly dependent on the distance between the two nodes, the ETR protocol seems to reduce energy consumption by considering shortest path from neighbor table. As the network density increases sensors become too closer and generates excessive multi-hopping, thus intermediate nodes drain their energy in forwarding their own data and data from other sensors. This can be seen in Fig. 8, that energy consumption reduces slowly to a certain point, as more number of sensors is deployed. This is because of multi-hopping of data packets. The energy consumption increases thereafter because of excessive hop-counts that outweigh any possible decrease in single-hop distances. In practice, dense deployment is used not for energy efficiency. Rather, it is used for providing the required measurement density, the radio connectivity redundancy needed to deal with issues such as node failure etc. The positioning of mobile gateway to the feasible location of the region reduces excessive multi-hopping created in ETR protocol. Hence sensors can sustain for a longer time in the network. Therefore Improved-ETR is observed to be more energy efficient than ETR protocol.

***Scenario 2*:** The number of nodes deployed is fixed to 45 (one selected value from the range in case 1) while the maximum radio range is taken in the range (230, 235, 240, 245, 250, 255 and 260). The simulation results are shown in Fig. 9 and Fig. 10. Starting from transmitter range 230, 45 nodes are deployed in the region. The three protocols are executed on the network scenario for *NWKS=45* and *ROUND=10,000*. Graph in Fig. 9 shows that increase in transmitter range extends coverage area of the sensors; hence, hop-counts are tending to decrease. For ETR, large transmission range means availability of more neighbors, and therefore chances of more number of shortest paths. In Improved ETR-Tree the increase in transmitter range causes direct attachment of sensors to the mobile gateway placed at the feasible site of the region where the sensors are densely deployed. This leads to reduction of multi-hopping to single-hopping and hence, reduction in hop-count. Therefore, for transmitter range 235 the two protocols have maximum hop-count and for 260 it is reduced to minimum.

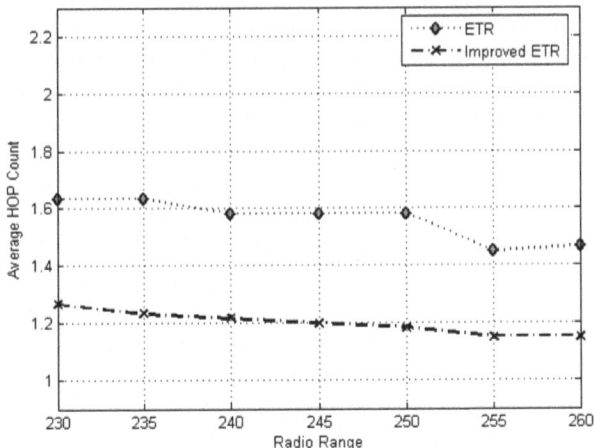

Fig. 9. HOP-Counts in Scenario 2

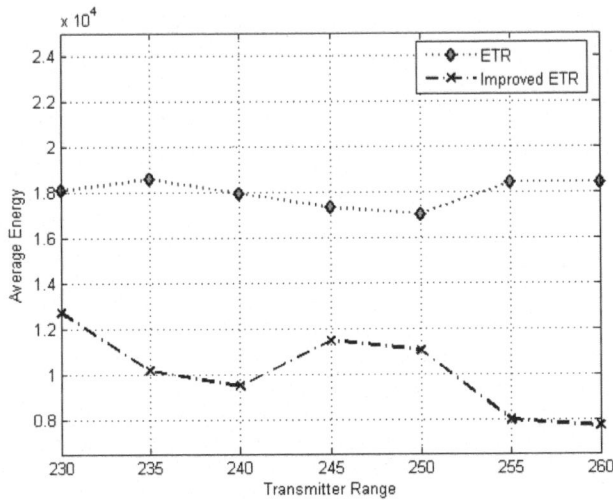

Fig. 10. Energy Consumption in Scenario 2

As for energy consumption, it is clear from Fig. 10 that with increase in transmitter range the energy consumption increases in both ETR and Improved-ETR protocols. Because transmission energy is directly dependent on distance, increase in transmitter range increases per hop distance. Improved ETR-Tree shows significantly low energy consumption because of relocation of mobile gateway to feasible location. Hence, Improved ETR-Tree is more energy efficient than ETR protocol.

8   Conclusions

Multi-hopping in sensor network is energy saving approach, but it causes adverse effect when the density of the sensor nodes increases. Since intermediate node has to consume more energy for data forwarding and to transmit their own data. Moreover, data collection is a challenging issue in a widely deployed sensor network. ETR protocol though found to be suitable and energy efficient for small sensor network but do not focuses on these issues. Therefore in this paper we have proposed some improvement to ETR protocol. The improved protocol provide a new orthogonal code NOVSF based addressing scheme to uniquely identify region of deployment of sensor nodes and also limits the count of mobile gateway, that can be employed in the region. Some ILPs are introduced for the protocol for determining feasible site and to minimize transmission power, so as to optimize power consumption. ETR becomes complex when the density of the sensor nodes increases. The orthogonal codes as addresses can be used further for spreading and de-spreading of signals so as to avoid disturbances occurring from the external environment. TDMA in improved ETR allows only one sensor to send data to the mobile gateway at a time hence, avoiding collision. The positioning of mobile gateway at feasible location in the region causes reduction in excessive hop-counts. Further we have proposed data collection method for improved ETR protocol. The method combines the approach of raw-data convergecast, where every sensor sends a single packet to the data collection point (gateway) and aggregated-data convergecast, where buffered data is forwarded from mobile gateway to the sink node. The data collection method as proposed causes less congestion in tree based topology and is more efficient. The Improved ETR Protocol is found to be more energy efficient and easy to implement than ETR.

References

1. Akyildiz, I., Su, W., Sankarasubramaniam, Y., Cayirci, E.: A Survey on Sensor Networks. IEEE Communications Magazine, 102–104 (2002)
2. Raghunathan, V., Schurghers, C., Park, S., Srivastava, M.: Energy-aware wireless micro sensor networks. IEEE Signal Processing Magazine 40–50 (2002)
3. Zhao, F., Guibas, L.: Wireless Sensor Networks: An Information Processing Approach. Elsevier-Morgan Kaufmann, Boston (2004)
4. Qiu, W., Skafidas, E., Hao, P.: Enhanced tree routing for wireless sensor networks. Elsevier- Ad Hoc Networks, 638–650 (2009)

5. Vadde, K., Cam, H.: A Code Assignment Algorithm for Non-blocking OVSF Codes in WCDMA. Telecommunication Systems 25(3,4), 417–431 (2004)
6. Pottie, G.J., Kaiser, W.J.: Wireless Integrated Network Sensors. Communication of ACM 4(5) (2000)
7. Raghavendra, C.S., Singh, S.: PAMAS- Power aware multi access protocol with signaling for ad-hoc networks. ACM Communication Review 28(33) (1998)
8. Rhee, I., Warrier, A., Aia, M., Min, J.: Z-MAC: A hybrid MAC for wireless sensor networks. In: Proc. ACM SenSys, San Diego, USA (November 2005)
9. Intanagonwiwat, C., Govindan, R., Estrin, D.: Directed diffusion: a scalable and robust communication paradigm for sensor networks. In: Proceedings of the Sixth Annual International Conference on Mobile Computing and Networks MobiCom, pp. 56–67. ACM Press, Boston (2000)
10. Heinzelman, W., Chandrakasan, A., Balsakrishnan, H.: Energy-efficient communication protocol for wireless sensor networks. In: Proceeding of the Hawaii International Conference System Sciences, Hawaii, p. 8020 (2000)
11. Sohrabi, K., et al.: Protocols for selforganization of a wireless sensor network. IEEE Personal Communications 7(5), 16–27 (2000)
12. Taehong, K., Daeyoung, K., Noseong, P., Seongeun, Y., Lopez, T.S.: Shortcut Tree Routing in ZigBee Networks. In: Proceedings of the Second International Symposium on Wireless Pervasive Computing (2007)
13. Perkins, C.E., Royer, E.M.: Ad hoc on-demand distance vector routing. In: Proceedings of Second IEEE Workshop Mobile Computing Systems and Applications, pp. 90–100 (1999)
14. ZigBee Specification Version 1.0, ZigBee Alliance (2005)
15. Yu, L., Wang, N., Meng, X.: Real-time forest fire detection with wireless sensor networks. In: WiCom, vol. 2, pp. 1214–1217 (2005)
16. Dalbro, M., Eikeland, E., Veld, A.J.I., Gjessing, S., Lande, T.S., Riis, H.K.: Wireless sensor networks for off-shore oil and gas installations. In: SENSORCOMM 2008, pp. 258–263 (2008)
17. Chintalapudi, K., Fu, T., Paek, J., Kothari, N., Rangwala, S., Caffrey, J., Govindan, R., Johnson, E., Masri, S.: Monitoring civil structures with a wireless sensor network. IEEE Internet Computing 10(2), 26–34 (2006)
18. Mainwaring, A., Culler, D., Polastre, J., Szewczyk, R., Anderson, J.: Wireless sensor networks for habitat monitoring. In: WSNA 2002, pp. 88–97 (2002)
19. Gandham, S., Zhang, Y., Huang, Q.: Distributed time-optimal scheduling for convergecast in wireless sensor networks. Computer Networks 52(3), 610–629 (2008)
20. Elson, J., Girod, L., Estrin, D.: Fine-grained network time synchronization using reference broadcasts. SIGOPS Oper. Syst. Rev. 36(SI), 147–163 (2002)
21. Nemhauser, G.L., Wolsey, L.A.: Integer Programming and Combinatorial Optimization. Wiley (1998)
22. NS-2 Simulator, http://isi.edu/nsnam/ns/
23. Park, J., Sahni, S.: An online heuristic for maximum lifetime routing in wireless sensor networks. IEEE Transactions on Computers 55(8), 1048–1056 (2006)

Packet and Flow Based Network Intrusion Dataset

Prasanta Gogoi[1], Monowar H. Bhuyan[1],
D.K. Bhattacharyya[1], and J.K. Kalita[2]

[1] Dept. of Comp. Sc. and Engg., Tezpur University, Tezpur-784028, India
[2] Dept. of Comp. Sc., University of Colorado, Colorado Springs, USA
{prasant,mhb,dkb}@tezu.ernet.in, jkalita@uccs.edu

Abstract. With exponential growth in the number of computer applications and the size of networks, the potential damage that can be caused by attacks launched over the internet keeps increasing dramatically. A number of network intrusion detection methods have been developed with their respective strengths and weaknesses. The majority of research in the area of network intrusion detection is still based on the simulated datasets because of non-availability of real datasets. A simulated dataset cannot represent the real network intrusion scenario. It is important to generate real and timely datasets to ensure accurate and consistent evaluation of methods. We propose a new *real dataset* to ameliorate this crucial shortcoming. We have set up a testbed to launch network traffic of both attack as well as normal nature using attack tools. We capture the network traffic in packet and flow format. The captured traffic is filtered and preprocessed to generate a featured dataset. The dataset is made available for research purpose.

Keywords: Testbed, Dataset, Packet, Netflow, Anomaly, NIDS.

1 Introduction

With the tremendous growth in size and use of computer networks and the enormous increase in the number of applications running on them, network security is becoming increasingly more important. Intrusion detection (ID) is an important component of any infrastructure protection mechanism. It is a type of security management system for computers and networks. Intrusion can be defined as a set of actions aimed to compromise the computer security goals such as confidentiality, integrity and availability [9]. An intrusion detection system (IDS) gathers and analyzes information from various areas within a computer or a network to identify possible security breaches, which include both types of intrusions - misuse and anomaly. A misuse intrusion detection approach uses information about known attacks and detects intrusions based on matches with existing attack patterns or signatures. On the other hand, an anomaly detection approach learns the normal behavior of the system or the network it monitors and reports when the monitored behavior deviates significantly from the normal profile. There exist various IDSs that are based on misuse as well as anomaly.

M. Parashar et al. (Eds.): IC3 2012, CCIS 306, pp. 322–334, 2012.

Examples include Bro [10], Snort [11], ADAM [4]. The effectiveness of an IDS is evaluated based on its true detection rate of intrusions. An intrusion dataset is important to find the effectiveness of a method for intrusion detection. The KDD Cup 1999 intrusion dataset [1] is an internationally accepted benchmark intrusion dataset.

1.1 Motivation

The majority of the research in the field of network intrusion detection is based on the synthetic datasets because of the lack of better datasets. With the knowledge of the shortcomings of the data, it is necessary and urgent to create datasets to ensure consistent and accurate evaluation of intrusion detection systems.

1.2 Objective

The objective of this paper is to set up a network testbed for generating normal network traffic as well as attack network traffic and capture the traffic in packet as well as flow modes in isolated environments. The captured traffic will be filtered, preprocessed, analyzed and will ultimately be used to produce two unbiased network intrusion datasets called *Packet Level* and *Flow Level TUIDS* datasets.

1.3 Organization of Paper

The remainder of the paper is organized as follows. The importance of datasets in evaluating an IDS is presented in Section 2. In Section 3, presents details of some existing datasets. Section 4, a performance comparison of existing IDSs is presented. In Section 5, the proposed dataset generation method is elaborated. In Section 6, the standard evaluation method for IDS is described. Finally, in Section 7, conclusion and future direction of research is given.

2 Importance of Datasets in Evaluating an IDS

There are a lot of intrusion detection systems that have been come into existence in the last three decades. The various techniques used in IDSs have their own strengths and weaknesses. A key aspect of any IDS is the nature of the input data. For a set of input data, different IDS techniques face different challenges. Input is generally a collection of data instances (also referred to as objects, records, points, vectors, patterns, events, cases, samples, observations or entities) [12]. The attributes can be of different types such as binary, categorical or continuous. Each data instance may consist of multiple attributes (multivariate). In the case of multivariate data instances, all attributes may be of the same type or may be a mixture of different data types. The nature of attributes determines the applicability of an IDS technique.

---

[1] http://kdd.ics.uci.edu

2.1   Data Labels

The labels associated with a data instance denote if that instance is normal or anomalous. It should be noted that obtaining labeled data, which is accurate as well as representative of all types of behaviors, is often prohibitively expensive. Labeling is often done manually by human experts and hence requires substantial effort. Typically, getting a labeled set of anomalous data instances which cover all possible type of anomalous behavior is more difficult than getting labels for normal behavior. Moreover, anomalous behavior is often dynamic in nature, e.g., new types of anomalies may arise, for which there is no labeled training data. Based on the extent to which the labels are available, anomaly detection techniques can operate in one of the following two modes: supervised and unsupervised.

Techniques [6] trained in supervised mode assume the availability of a training data set which has labeled instances for normal as well as anomalous classes. The typical approach in such cases is to build a predictive model for normal vs. anomalous classes. Any unseen data instance is compared against the model to determine which class it belongs to.

Techniques [2] that operate in unsupervised mode do not require training data, and thus are most widely applicable. The techniques in this category make the implicit assumption that normal instances are far more frequent than anomalies in the test data. If this assumption is not true, such techniques suffer from high false alarm rate.

3   Existing Datasets and Their Pros and Cons

Datasets play an important role in the testing and validation of any intrusion detection method. The quality of data not only allows us to identify a methods ability to detect anomalous behavior, but also shows its potential effectiveness during deployment in real operating environments. Several datasets are publicly available for testing and evaluation of intrusion detection. However, the most widely used evaluation datasets are the *KDD Cup 1999* and its modified version, the *NSL-KDD* dataset [13].

3.1   KDD Cup 1999 Dataset

The *KDD Cup 1999* dataset is the benchmark dataset for intrusion detection. Each record of the dataset represents a connection between two network hosts according to existing network protocol and is described by 41 attributes (38 continuous or discrete numerical attributes and 3 categorical attributes). Each record of the training data is labeled as either normal or a specific kind of attack. The attacks fall in one of four categories: Denial of Service (*DoS*), User to Root (*U2R*), Remote to local (*R2L*) and *Probe*.

- Denial of Service(*DoS*): An attacker tries to prevent legitimate users from using a service. For example, SYN flood, smurf and teardrop.

- User to Root (*U2R*): An attackers has local access to the victim machine and tries to gain super-user privilege. For example, buffer overflow attacks.
- Remote to Local (*R2L*): An attackers tries to gain access to victim machine without having an account on it. For example, password guessing attack.
- *Probe*: An attacker tries to gain information about the target host. For example, port-scan and ping-sweep.

The datasets consist of two types of data: training and testing. The training data contain a total of 22 attack types and an additional 15 attack types in the test data only. The numbers of samples of each category of attack in *Corrected KDD* and *10-percent KDD* training dataset are shown in Table 1.

Table 1. Attacks distribution in KDD Cup training dataset

Dataset	DoS	U2R	R2L	Probe	Normal	Total
Corrected KDD	2,29,853	70	16,347	4,166	60,593	3,11,029
10-percent Corrected KDD	3,91,458	52	1,126	4,107	97,278	4,94,021

3.2   NSL-KDD Dataset

NSL-KDD is a dataset for network-based intrusion detection systems. It is the new version of KDD Cup 1999 dataset. In the KDD Cup dataset, there are a large number of redundant records, which can cause learning algorithms to be biased towards frequent records. To address this issue, one unique copy of each record is kept in the NSL-KDD dataset. Though this dataset is not the perfect representation of real networks, it can be applied as an effective benchmark dataset to compare different intrusion detection methods. The description of two datasets $KDDTrain^+$ and $KDDTest^+$ of NSL-KDD with four categories of attacks *DoS*, *U2R*, *R2L*, *Probe* and *Normal*, is shown in Table 2.

Table 2. Attacks distribution in NSL-KDD dataset

Dataset	DoS	U2R	R2L	Probe	Normal	Total
$KDDTrain^+$	45,927	52	995	11,656	67,343	1,25,973
$KDDTest^+$	7458	67	2,887	2,422	9,710	22,544

The *KDD Cup 1999* and *NSL-KDD* dataset both are evaluation datasets. The records in the dataset may be distinctly different from real network traffic data. Besides, the nature of attack and normal instances may dynamically change. One of the most important deficiencies of the KDD dataset is the very large number of redundant records, which causes the learning algorithms to be biased towards frequent records, and thus prevent them from learning from infrequent records, which may be more harmful to network health. In addition, the existence of these repeated records in the test set causes the evaluation results to be biased positively toward methods which have better detection rates on the frequent records.

4   Performance of Detection Methods in the Context of These Datasets

Among the approaches surveyed in [14], the most prevalent approach to evaluation of the intrusion detection systems is based on the *KDD Cup 1999* dataset. The generation of this evaluation dataset consist of simulated host and network normal traffic and manually generated network-based attacks. A list of some existing intrusion detection systems validated with KDD cup 1999 intrusion dataset are summarized in [5].

5   Our Dataset

our method of dataset generation extracts various types of features from network packet and flow data captured using an isolated network. Using existing attack tools, we generate a group of attacks against a local network server and collect the produced traffic as known attack traffic. The attacks for which we capture data along with the corresponding tools for their generation are presented in Table 3 [2]. These attacks and tools are also used by Amini et al. [2].

5.1   Testbed Setup

The experimental setup of the testbed for network traffic capture includes one router, one L3 switch, two L2 switches, one server, two workstations and forty nodes. Six VLANs are created from the L3 switch and L2 switch; and nodes and workstations are connected to separated VLANs. The L3 switch is connected to a router through an internal IP router and the router is connected to the Internet through an external IP router. The server is connected to the L3 switch through a mirror port to observe traffic activity to the switch. Another LAN of 350 nodes is connected to other VLANs through five L3 and L2 switches and three routers. The attacks are launched within our testbed as well as from another LAN through the Internet. To launch attacks within the testbed, nodes of one VLAN are attacked from nodes of another VLAN as well as the same VLAN. Normal traffic is created within our testbed in a restricted manner condition after disconnecting the other LAN. Traffic activities to our testbed are observed on the computer connected to the mirror port. A diagram of the testbed for generation of TUIDS intrusion detection datasets is shown in *Fig. 1*.

The various features are extracted using an distributed feature extraction architecture as given in *Fig. 2*. The frame work is used for fast protocol specific (e.g. TCP, UDP, ICMP) feature extraction for packet and flow data separately. Servers ($S1$ and $S2$) are be used for the initial storage of the captured and preprocessed data as well as for the final formatted packet and flow feature data. Workstations ($WS1$ and $WS2$) are dedicated in the various types of feature extraction in a distributed manner using multiple nodes ($N1$, $N2$, ..., $N6$).

---

[2] http://packetstormsecurity.nl/index.html

Table 3. Attack List

Attack	Generation Tool	Attack	Generation Tool
bonk	*targa2.c*	1234	*targa2.c*
jolt	*targa2.c*	*saihyousen*	*targa2.c*
land	*targa2.c*	*oshare*	*targa2.c*
nestea	*targa2.c*	*window*	*targa2.c*
newtear	*targa2.c*	*syn*	*Nmap*
syndrop	*targa2.c*	*xmas*	*Nmap*
teardrop	*targa2.c*	*fraggle*	*fraggle.c*
winnuke	*targa2.c*	*smurf*	*smurf4.c*

Table 4. TUIDS intrusion detection datasets

Connection type	Dataset type			
	Training dataset		Testing dataset	
Packet level				
Normal	71785	58.87%	47895	55.52%
Attack	50142	41.13%	38370	44.48%
Total	121927		86265	
Flow level				
Normal	23120	43.75%	16770	41.17%
Attack	29723	56.25%	23955	58.83%
Total	52843		40725	

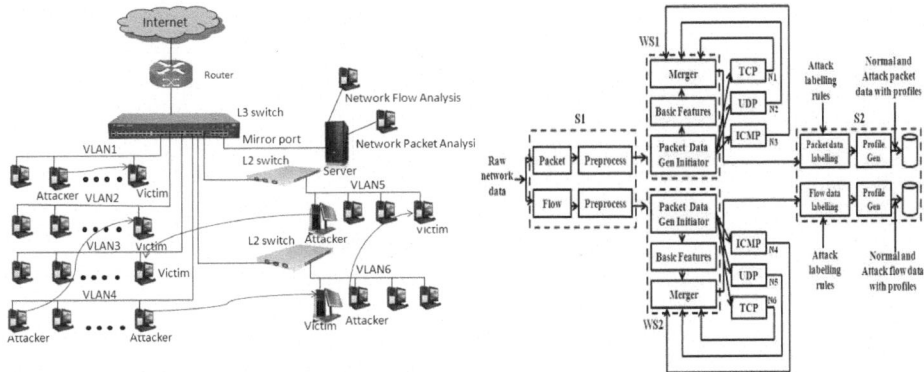

Fig. 1. Testbed for generation of TUIDS intrusion detection datasets

Fig. 2. Architecture of distributed feature extraction

5.2 Packet Network Traffic Feature Extraction

The packet level network traffic is captured using the open source software tool called *gulp* [3]. *Gulp* drop packets directly from the network and write to disk at high rate of packet capture. The packets are analyzed using the open source packet analyzing software *wireshark* [4]. The raw packet data is preprocessed and filtered before extracting and constructing new features. In the packet level network traffic, 50 types of features are extracted. To extract these features we use open source tool *tcptrace* [5], *C* programs and Perl scripts. These features are classified as *basic, content based, time-based* and *connection-based*. The list of features is given in Tables 5.

5.3 Network Flow Traffic Feature Extraction

The network flow data consists of a unidirectional sequence of packets passing through an observation point in the network during a certain time interval

---

[3] http://staff.washington.edu/corey/gulp/

[4] http://www.wireshark.org/

[5] http://www.tcptrace.org

Table 5. Packet level Features of TUIDS Intrusion dataset

Sl.	Feature Names	Type*	Feature Description
	Basic features		
1.	Duration	C	Time since occurrence of first frame
2.	Protocol	D	Protocol of layer 3- IP, TCP, UDP
3.	Src IP	C	Source IP address
4.	Dst IP	C	Destination IP address
5.	Src port	C	Source port of machine
6.	Dst port	C	Destination port of machine
7.	Service	D	Network service on the destination e.g., http, telnet etc.
8.	num-bytes-src-dst	C	No. of data bytes flowing from src to dst
9.	num-bytes-dst-src	C	No. of data bytes flowing from dst to src
10.	Fr-no.	C	Frame number
11.	Fr-length	C	Length of the frame
12.	Cap-length	C	Captured frame length
13.	Head-len	C	Header length of the packet
14.	Frag-offset	D	Fragment offset value
15.	TTL	C	Time to live
16.	Seq-no.	C	Sequence number
17.	CWR	D	Congestion Window Record
18.	ECN	D	Explicit Congestion Notification
19.	URG	D	Urgent TCP flag
20.	ACK	D	Ack flag
21.	PSH	D	Push TCP flag
22.	RST	D	Reset RST flag
23.	SYN	D	Syn TCP flag
24.	FIN	D	Fin TCP flag
25.	Land	D	1 if connection is from/to the same host/port; 0 otherwise
	Content-based features		
26.	Mss-src-dst-requested	C	Maximum segment size from src to dst requested
27.	Mss-dst-src-requested	C	Maximum segment size from dst to src requested
28.	Ttt-len-src-dst	C	Time to live length from src to dst
29.	Ttt-len-dst-src	C	Time to live length from dst to src
30.	Conn-status	C	Status of the connection (1-complete, 0-reset)
	Time-based features		
31.	count-fr-dst	C	No. of frames received by unique dst in the last T sec from the same src
32.	count-fr-src	C	No. of frames received by unique src in the last T sec to the same dst
33.	count-serv-src	C	No. of frames from the src to the same dst port in the last T sec
34.	count-serv-dst	C	No. of frames from dst to the same src port in the last T sec
35.	num-pushed-src-dst	C	No. of pushed pkts flowing from src to dst
36.	num-pushed-dst-src	C	No. of pushed pkts flowing from dst to src
37.	num-SYN-FIN-src-dst	C	No. of SYN/FIN pkts flowing from src to dst
38.	num-SYN-FIN-dst-src	C	No. of SYN/FIN pkts flowing from dst to src
39.	num-FIN-src-dst	C	No. of FIN pkts flowing from src to dst
40.	num-FIN-dst-src	C	No. of FIN pkts flowing from dst to src

Table 5. (*Continued*)

Sl. Feature Names	Type*	Feature Description
Connection-based features		
41. count-dst-conn	C	No. of frames to unique dst in the last N packets from the same src
42. count-src-conn	C	No. of frames from unique src in the last N packets to the same dst
43. count-serv-src-conn	C	No. of frames from the src to the same dst port in the last N packets
44. count-serv-dst-conn	C	No. of frames from the dst to the same src port in the last N packets
45. num-packets-src-dst	C	No. of packets flowing from src to dst
46. num-packets-dst-src	C	No. of packets flowing from dst to src
47. num-acks-src-dst	C	No. of ack packets flowing from src to dst
48. num-acks-dst-src	C	No. of ack packets flowing from dst to src
49. num-retransmit-src-dst	C	No. of retransmitted packets flowing from src to dst
50. num-retransmit-dst-src	C	No. of retransmitted packets flowing from dst to src

Note- *(C-Continuous, D-Discrete)

between source and destination hosts. All traffic belonging to a particular flow has a set of common properties. The NetFlow protocol (IPFIX standard) [6] provides a summarization of the router or switch traffic. Network flow is identified by source and destination IP addresses as well as by port numbers. To identify flow uniquely, NetFlow also uses several fields, viz., the type of protocol, the type of service (ToS) from the IP header, and the input logical interface of the router or the switch. The flows are stored in the router or the switch cache and exported to a collector under the following constraints. The frame work in *Fig. 2* is used in the feature extraction.

- Flows that have been idle for a specified time are expired where default setting of specified time is 15 seconds, or the user can configure this time to be between 10 to 600 seconds.
- Flows lived longer than 30 minutes are expired.
- If the cache reaches its maximum size, a number of heuristic expiry functions are applied to export flows.
- A TCP connection has finished with flag FIN or RST.

A flow collector tool, viz., *nfdump* [7] receives flow records from the flow exporter and stores them in a form suitable for further monitoring or analysis. A flow record is the information stored in the flow exporter cache. A flow exporter protocol defines how expired flows are transferred by the exporter to the collector. The information exported to the collector is referred to as flow record. NetFlow version 5 [8] is a simple protocol that exports flow records of fixed size (48 bytes in total).

---

[6] http://www.ietf.org/rfc/rfc3917.txt,http://www.ietf.org/rfc/rfc3954.txt
[7] http://nfdump.sourceforge.net/
[8] http://www.cisco.com

Table 6. Flow level Features of TUIDS Intrusion dataset

Sl. Feature Names	Type*	Feature Description
Basic features		
1. Duration	C	Length of the flow (in sec)
2. Protocol-type	D	Type of protocols- TCP, UDP, ICMP
3. src IP	C	Src node IP address
4. dst IP	C	Destination IP address
5. src port	C	Source port
6. dst port	C	Destination port
7. ToS	D	Type of service
8. URG	D	Urgent flag of TCP header
9. ACK	D	Ack flag
10. PSH	D	Push flag
11. RST	D	Reset flag
12. SYN	D	SYN flag
13. FIN	D	FIN flag
14. Source byte	C	No. of data bytes transfer from src IP to dst IP
15. dst byte	C	No. of data bytes transfer from dst IP to src IP
16. Land	D	Same src IP/src port are equal to dst IP/dst port
Time-window features		
17. count-dst	C	No. of flows to unique dst IP addr inside the network in the last T sec from the same src
18. count-src	C	No. of flows from unique src IP addr inside the network in the last T sec to the same dst
19. count-serv-src	C	No. of flows from the src IP to the same dst port in the last T sec
20. count-serv-dst	C	No. of flows to the dst IP using same src port in the last T sec
Connection-based features		
21. count-dst-conn	C	No. of flows to unique dst IP in the last N flows from the same src
22. count-src-conn	C	No. of flows from unique src IP in the last N flows to the same dst
23. count-serv-src-conn	C	No. of flows from the src IP to the same dst port in the last N flows.
24. count-serv-dst-conn	C	No. of flows to the dst IP to the same src port in the last N flows.

Note- *(C-Continuous, D-Discrete)

Table 7. Confusion matrix for *Packet level* dataset

		Predicted Class			
		Normal	Attack	Sum	Recall
Actual class	Normal	47363	532	47895	0.9889
	Attack	273	38097	38370	0.9929
	Sum	47636	38629	86265	

Table 8. Confusion matrix for *Flow level* dataset

		Predicted Class			
		Normal	Attack	Sum	Recall
Actual class	Normal	16620	150	16770	0.9911
	Attack	113	23842	23955	0.9953
	Sum	16733	23992	40725	

Table 9. Comparison of Results of method [7] with TUIDS intrusion dataset

Data sets	Total	Attacks	Normal	Detection Rate (%)	TPR (%)	FPR (%)
Corrected KDD	311029	250436	60593	97.55	90.01	2.45
10% KDD	494021	396743	97278	95.75	94.76	4.25
KDDTrain+	125973	58630	67343	97.65	93.89	2.35
KDDTest+	22544	12834	9710	98.88	96.55	1.12
Packet Level	86265	38370	47895	99.29	98.89	0.71
Flow Level	40725	23955	16770	99.53	99.11	0.47

All data is stored on disk before analyzing. This separates the process of storing and analyzing the data. The data is organized in a time based fashion. Nfdump has a flow record capturing daemon process $nfcapd$ which reads data from the network and stores the data into files. Automatically, after every n minutes, typically 5 minutes, $nfcapd$ rotates and renames each output file with the time stamp $nfcapd.YYYYMMddhhmm$. For example, $nfcapd.201012110845$ contains data from December 11th 2010 08:45 onward. Based on a 5 minutes time interval, this stores results in 288 files per day. The analysis of the data is performed by concatenating several files for a single run. The output is stored either in ASCII or in binary into a file and it is ready to be processed again with the same tool. We use C programs to filter the captured data to extract new features. Unnecessary parameters are removed and the retained parameters are flow-start, duration, protocol, source-IP, source-port, destination-IP, destination-port, flags, ToS, bytes, packets-per-second (pps), bits-per-second (bps) and bytes-per-packet (bps). Network traffic corresponding to attack and normal traffic is gathered using our local network within a 4 week period. A summary of the dataset is available in http://www.tezu.ernet.in/ dkb. The extracted features are of 24 types and are classified into three groups: (i) basic, (ii) time-window based, and (iii) connection based features. The list of features is given in Table 6. The network traffic data for attack and normal modes are captured using our local network. The attacks are generated using attack tools given in Table 3 against a local network server and the produced traffic is collected and labeled as known attack traffic. There are generated 16 different types of attacks. The network traffic data was captured at packet level and flow level through two separate port mirroring machines. The captured data was preprocessed and filtered to extract various types of features. The numbers of records in the datasets are given in Table 4. We call the two datasets: Packet Level and Flow Level TUIDS datasets.

6   Performance Evaluation of Intrusion Detection Methods Using TUIDS Intrusion Dataset

In this section we report the performance evaluation of three of our intrusion detection methods based on TUIDS intrusion dataset.

1. In the recent research work [7] an unsupervised method was proposed. The method is evaluated with *KDD Cup* 1999 dataset as well as *TUIDS* intrusion dataset. The confusion matrices for *Packet level* and *Flow level* dataset is given in Table 7 and Table 8 respectively. A performance comparison of detection rate (DR), true positive rate (TPR) and false positive rate (FPR) are given in Table 9 for method [7] with other dataset *KDD Cup* 1999 and *NSL-KDD*.

2. The *TUIDS* intrusion dataset is utilized in generating decision rules in [8] for intrusion detection. The results of *Flow level* dataset are given in Table 10. The detection performance over the dataset is excellent. A total of 29 rules were generated for the all-attacks and normal classes. The percentage of successful classification, (*PSC*) in case of the normal class, is 99.94% whereas for the all-attacks class, it is 96.21%.

Table 10. Results on Network Flow Intrusion Dataset

Class name	Records	Detection	Accuracy (PSC)
bonk	2680	2589	96.63%
jolt	282	277	98.57%
nestea	19	19	100%
newtear	28	27	99.27%
syndrop	13	12	98.48%
teardrop	27	27	100%
winnuke	2510	2417	96.33%
1234	6216	5994	96.43%
oshare	2500	2306	92.27%
saihyousen	52	51	98.07%
smurf	6	6	100%
fraggle	2500	2246	89.87%
syn	1650	1567	94.98%
xmas	2720	2707	99.55%
window	2766	2679	96.89%
land	2	2	100%
All attacks	23955	22926	95.70%
normal	16770	16759	99.94%

Table 11. Distribution of Normal and Attack connections instances in real time packet and flow level TUIDS intrusion datasets

Connection type	Dataset type			
	Training dataset		Testing dataset	
Packet level				
Normal	71785	58.87%	47895	55.52%
DoS	42592	34.93%	30613	35.49%
Probe	7550	6.19%	7757	8.99%
Total	121927		86265	
Flow level				
Normal	23120	43.75%	16770	41.17%
DoS	21441	40.57%	14475	35.54%
Probe	8282	15.67%	9480	23.28%
Total	52843		40725	

The accuracy of each experiment was measured based on the percentage of successful classification (PSC) [1] on the evaluated dataset, where

$$PSC = \frac{No.\ of\ Correctly\ Classified\ Instances}{No.\ of\ Instances\ in\ Dataset} \times 100. \tag{1}$$

3. We have also used *TUIDS* intrusion dataset to evaluate our method NADO [3] for its effectiveness in intrusion detection. Table 11 describes the distribution of the normal and attack instances in both packet and flow level TUIDS intrusion dataset. Table 12 presents the confusion matrix for each category of attack class in terms of precision, recall and F-measure.

Table 12. The Confusion matrix of the proposed scheme [3] over the packet and flow level TUIDS intrusion datasets

	Evaluation measures			Confusion matrix				
Connection type	Precision	Recall	F-measure	Value	Normal	DoS	Probe	Total
Packet level								
Normal	0.9607%	0.9813%	0.9708%	Normal	46011	1817	67	47895
DoS	1.0000%	0.9764%	0.9764%	DoS	720	29893	0	30613
Probe	0.9988%	0.8918%	0.9436%	Probe	838	8	6911	7757
Average	0.9865%	0.9498%	0.9636%	Total	47569	31718	6978	86265
Flow level								
Normal	0.9745%	0.9842%	0.9793%	Normal	16342	421	7	16770
DoS	0.9991%	0.9938%	0.9964%	DoS	89	14374	12	14475
Probe	0.9995%	0.9626%	0.9806%	Probe	354	5	9121	9480
Average	0.9910%	0.9802%	0.9854%	Total	16785	14800	9140	40725

7 Conclusion

In this paper, we provide high-level analysis of the *KDD Cup 1999* and *NSL-KDD* datasets. The analysis shows that these dataset are simulated and very old. In applying machine learning methods to intrusion detection, these datasets are not always suitable in current dynamic network scenarios. To address these issues, we create two real life network intrusion datasets: *Packet Level* and *Flow Level TUIDS* datasets. To create the datasets, we set up an isolated testbed to launch attacks and capture the traffic in two modes, and generate the dataset after rigorous preprocessing of the raw data. To establish the effectiveness of the datasets, we used them in evaluating the performance of some intrusion detection method. The results have been reported.

A Distributed Denial of Service (DDoS) attack uses many computers to launch a coordinated DoS attack against one or more targets. Using client/server technology, the perpetrator is able to multiply the effectiveness of the Denial of Service significantly by harnessing the resources of multiple unwitting accomplice computers which serve as attack platforms. In the future, we plan to generate one new intrusion dataset focussing on distributed denial of service (DDoS) attacks.

Acknowledgment. This work is supported by Department of Information Technology, MCIT Government of India. The authors are grateful to anonymous reviewer and the funding agencies.

References

1. Adetunmbi, A.O., Falaki, S.O., Adewale, O.S., Alese, B.K.: Network intrusion detection based on rough set and k-nearest neighbour. International Journal of Computing and ICT Research 2, 60–66 (2008)
2. Amini, M., Jalili, R., Shahriari, H.R.: Rt-unnid: A practical solution to real- time network-based intrusion detection using unsupervised neural networks. Computers & Security 25(6), 459–468 (2006)

3. Bhuyan, M.H., Bhattacharyya, D.K., Kalita, J.K.: NADO: network anomaly detection using outlier approach. In: Proceedings of the ACM International Conference on Communication, Computing & Security, New York, NY, USA, pp. 531–536 (2011)
4. Daniel, B., Julia, C., Sushil, J., Ningning, W.: Adam: a testbed for exploring the use of data mining in intrusion detection. SIGMOD Rec. 30(4), 15–24 (2001)
5. Gogoi, P., Borah, B., Bhattacharyya, D.K.: Anomaly detection analysis of intrusion data using supervised & unsupervised approach. Journal of Convergence Information Technology 5, 95–110 (2010)
6. Gogoi, P., Borah, B., Bhattacharyya, D.K.: Supervised anomaly detection using clustering based normal behaviour modeling. International Journal of Advances in Engineering Sciences 1, 12–17 (2011)
7. Gogoi, P., Borah, B., Bhattacharyya, D.K.: Network anomaly detection using unsupervised model. International Journal of Computer Applications (Special Issue on Network Security and Cryptography) NSC, 19–30 (2011)
8. Gogoi, P., Das, R., Borah, B., Bhattacharyya, D.K.: Efficient rule set generation using rough set theory for classification of high dimensional data. In: Proc. of Int'nl Conf. on Communication and Network Security (ICCNS 2011), Bhubaneswar, India, November 13-14, pp. 19–22 (2011)
9. Heady, R., Luger, G., Maccabe, A., Servilla, M.: The architecture of a network level intrusion detection system. Tech. rep., Computer Science Department, University of New Mexico, New Mexico (1990)
10. Paxson, V.: Bro: A system for detecting network intruders in real-time. In: Proceedings of the 7th USENIX Security Symposium, San Antonio,Texas (January 1998)
11. Roesch, M.: Snort-lightweight intrusion detection for networks. In: Proceedings of the 13th USENIX Conference on System Administration, pp. 229–238. USENIX, Seattle (1999)
12. Tan, P.N., Steinbach, M., Kumar, V.: Introduction to Data Mining. Addison-Wesley (2005)
13. Tavallaee, M., Bagheri, E., Lu, W., Ghorbani, A.A.: A detailed analysis of the kdd cup 99 data set (2009), http://nsl.cs.unb.ca/NSL-KDD/
14. Tavallaee, M., Stakhanova, N., Ghorbani, A.A.: Toward credible evaluation of anomaly-based intrusion-detection methods. IEEE Transactions on Systems, Man, and Cybernetics, Part C 40, 516–524 (2010)

Efficient Hierarchical Threshold Symmetric Group Key Management Protocol for Mobile Ad Hoc Networks

Adarsh Kumar, Alok Aggarwal, and Charu

Computer Science Engineering and Information Technology Department,
Jaypee Institute of Information Technology, Noida, India
{adarsh.kumar,alok.aggarwal,charu.kumar}@jiit.ac.in

Abstract. With rapid growth of Ad Hoc Networks consisting of low power computing devices, security will be an important factor for their full implementation. Because of scarcity of resources in terms of computing capability and energy efficiency, designing of computationally efficient group key management protocols with dynamic topology is a major concern. Teo and Tan [11] proposed an energy-efficient generalized circular hierarchical group model, but this approach suffers from: (i) exponential increase of key messages due to dynamic topology and (ii) energy loss because the vicinity of nodes in a subgroup is high. This work is an extension of Teo & Tan's circular hierarchical model for fixed number of group members. The proposed modification overcomes these two weaknesses of Teo & Tan's protocol. The proposed modifications make this protocol secure against replay, masquerading, spoofing, chosen ciphertext and impersonation attacks because of proper authentication and digital signatures. The comparative numerical and simulation analysis of proposed approach has been made with Teo & Tan, Wen-Lin-Hwang's (WLH) and along with Tseng's group key agreement approach. The analysis shows that proposed approach is well suited for low computational mobile devices with minimum delay. Through WLH protocol shows maximum throughput and minimum delay however it lacks in terms of security aspects.

Keywords: MANET, Symmetric Key, Key Management, Key Agreement, Key Distribution/Transport, Group Communication.

1   Introduction

Mobile Ad Hoc Network (MANET) works unlikely the cellular network because of its infrastructure-less nature [15]. Applications of MANETs are increasing day by day. Some of the important application areas are: Vehicular Ad Hoc Networks (VANETs), military based secure information transmission, remote operations for home or office appliances, cluster formation etc. Implementation of MANET has been a major area of research for the last few decades. Various challenges in this area are: robust and flexible routing, cross layer architectures, energy efficiency, scarcity of resources, dynamic topologies, Quality of Service (QoS), security etc. Various cryptography techniques have been designed to ensure secure transmission of information over MANETs.

M. Parashar et al. (Eds.): IC3 2012, CCIS 306, pp. 335–346, 2012.
© Springer-Verlag Berlin Heidelberg 2012

In order to secure the information over the networks, cryptographic aspects are classified into two broad categories: Symmetric and Asymmetric [16]. Each of these categories has key management and encryption/decryption protocols [23]-[33]. Key management protocols are further classified as key agreement and key distribution protocols. Key agreement protocols deal with contribution of two or more parties to generate a session key while key transport protocol decides how to transmit this session key to all parties. Major weaknesses of key management protocols are · forward or backward secrecy, authentication, authorization, non-repudiation, privacy, confidentiality, tampering etc. Another key management approach is a combination of (i) key agreement and key transport/distribution [17]-[21] or (ii) symmetric and asymmetric, called hybrid key management protocols [22]-[23], [38], [39].

A key can be generated and transmitted manually or automatically. Most of the protocols designed contemporary are automatic [1]-[2] because manual in billion nodes is awkward. Automatic key generation mechanism given by Arvid Damm in 1919 was also used in World War II. Later on various key agreement and distribution protocols were proposed. Asymmetric key management idea was started with the thought of James H. Ellis in 1970 and it was first published by W. Diffie and M. Hellman in 1976 with Clifford Cocks's large invertible prime number generation technique [3]. Three group key management protocols for low capacity devices are Teo & Tan, WLH and Tseng's protocol. Though all these protocols strive to achieve the target of low computational cost, Teo & Tan's protocol seems to be most efficient in terms of computational complexity. However, this protocol also fails to cater the problem of network dynamics and energy resources, computational cost of the protocol increases exponentially with change in network topology.

In this paper modifications have been done to Teo and Tan's protocol and the proposed approach is compared with Teo & Tan's protocol along with WLH & Tseng protocols. Authentication, digital signature, forward and backward secrecy are the parameters used for analysis. The proposed approach is simulated using three basic MANET routing protocols, Ad hoc On-demand Distance Vector (AODV), Dynamic Source Routing (DSR) and Destination Sequenced Distance Vector (DSDV) and their performance is compared with Teo and Tan, WLH, Tseng and proposed approach. Jitter and throughput parameters are used for performance evaluation.

The rest of this paper is organized as follows: Section 2 provides review of three key management protocols for low computing devices: Teo and Tan, WLH and Tseng. Proposed approach is presented in Section 3 based on two modifications on Teo & Tan's protocol: (i) mode of communication and (ii) integration of virtual node hierarchy for dynamic topology. Section 4 shows the simulation and numerical security analysis of three key management protocol taken with the proposed approach. Finally, Section 5 concludes the work.

2   Review of Protocols

2.1   Teo and Tan's Protocol

This is energy efficient key agreement protocol for large Ad Hoc Networks proposed by J. C. M. Teo and C. H. Tan in 2005 [11]. This protocol is based on Burmester Desmedt Group Key Agreement (BD GKA) protocol. The protocol runs as:

Protocol: Teo & Tan's Protocol

Premises: Let 'n' be the number of elements in each subgroup, 'h' is the height of hierarchical structure such that $m=n^h$, HL_i denote the ith hierarchical layer, $SG_j^{HL_i}$ is the jth subgroup at i^{th} layer for $j\epsilon\{0.....\ n^i-1\}$, $SG_{SC_j}^{HL_i}$ represent subgroup controller of jth subgroup at hierarchical layer HL_i, $SM_{(j,k)}^{HL_i}$ is the kth member of jth subgroup at hierarchical layer HL_i, where $k=jn+l$ for $l\epsilon\{0,.....n-1\}$ and 'H' is the hash function.

Goal: Share a symmetric group key 'K' using circular hierarchical group model.

Phase 1:-   Each subgroup will run BD-GKA protocol & compute key $K_{SG_j^{HL_{h-1}}}$.

Phase 2:-   a. From HL_{h-2} to HL_1, each subgroup member $SM_{(j,k)}^{HL_v}$ of subgroup $SG_j^{HL_v}$ for $j\epsilon\{0....n^v-1\}$ and $k=jn+l$ for $l\epsilon\{0..n-1\}$ and $v\epsilon\{h-2...1\}$ will run BD GKA protocol within its subgroup to obtain $K_{SG_j^{HL_v}}$.

              a. Unlike round 1 of BD GKA, it compute $Z_k^{HL_v} = \propto^{H(K_{SG_k}^{HL_{v+1}})}$mod p.

              b. Each user compute $X_i =(Z_{i+1}/Z_{i-1})^{Z_k^{HL_v}}$.

Phase 3:-   Key Computation

              a. Top group $SG_0^{HL_0}$ uses $K_{SG_k^{HL_1}}$ of next layer to compute $Z_k^{HL_0} = \propto^{H(K_{SG_k^{HL_1}})}$ mod p in first round of BD GKA.

              b. Subgroup key of the top group is $K_{SG_0^{HL_0}}$ and this group uses any symmetric encryption method $E_{K_{SG_k}^{HL_1}}(K)$ and send K to subgroup $SG_k^{HL_1}$.

Phase 4:-   Key Distribution

           a.   Next layer decrypt $D_{K_{SG_k}^{HL_1}}(K)$ and encrypt $E_{K_{SG_k}^{HL_2}}(K)$ for next layer.

           b.   Process continues until all layer HL_{h-1} receive the symmetric key 'K'.

Major strengths of this protocol are: (i) this is based on BD GKA protocol, which is proven to be secure for symmetric key exchange [22], (ii) subgroup members are secured against chosen ciphertext attack, (iii) J. Toe and C. Tan's calculated the computation and communication cost and it is efficient than any other protocol and (iv) provide strong backward secrecy. Weaknesses of this protocol are: (i) it provide moderate signature mechanism, (ii) forward secrecy is not strong and provide limited security against impersonation. Hierarchical structure of this protocol is shown in Figure 1(a).

2.2   WLH Protocol

This is a key exchange protocol proposed in 2005 for low computing devices [4], [5]. Two hybrid key exchange protocols were proposed to achieve mutual authentication. Weakness of this protocol is that it does not provide strong forward secrecy [5]. However the forward secrecy can be secured with the integration of Diffie-Hellman key exchange parameters. Strengths of this protocol are: lesser number of computations, authentication from both parties, and exchange of identity information prevent the key compromise and hashing function makes it impossible to find a wanted key value.

2.3   Tseng's Protocol

This is another little computational required key agreement protocol proposed in 2005 by Y. M. Tseng [6], [7]. Conference key management was extended in 2005 and 2007 [8]-[10]. Major strengths of this protocol are: (i) fault tolerant conference key agreement protocol, (ii) small message size and less number of key management rounds and (iii) provide dynamic topology. Weakness of this protocol is: (i) do not provide strong forward or backward secrecy against key attacks [10].

3   Our Approach

In this work, a symmetric key agreement and distributed hierarchy is proposed for low computational devices in MANET using modified form of J. Teo and C. Tan's centralized circular hierarchical (CCH) group model, as shown in Figure 1.

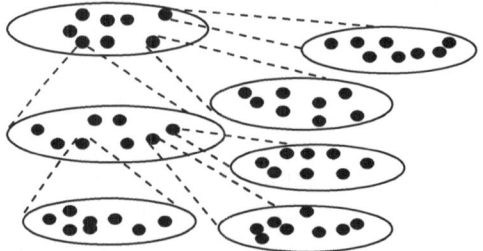

Fig. 1(c). Serial communication

Fig. 1(d). Ant's algorithm

Fig. 1(a). Toe and Tan's group/subgroup hierarchy

$C=\sum_{i=1}^{m}S_i$
S: share of each node
m: number of contributory nodes
& $m \leq n$.

Fig. 1(b). Circular Communication with both clockwise and anticlockwise

Fig. 1(e). Shamir's Threshold scheme

Fig. 1. Architecture to expedite the key management for low power devices in MANET

Modification 1(Change in Modes of Communication):

Method1 (serial communication rather than broadcast):- As shown in Figure 1(c), in first modification of Toe and Tan's protocol key message are transmitted serially using Dijkstra's algorithm [12]. The protocol runs as:

Protocol: Modified Teo & Tan's Protocol
Premises: Same as Teo &Tan's Protocol
Goal: Generate a common symmetric group key K and share it with all group members with lesser number of message exchanges.
Phase 1:-   Same as phase 1 of Teo and Tan's protocol to generate key $K_{SG_j}^{(HLh-1)}$.

Phase 2:-   Subgroup controller will generate $Z_K^{HLv} = \alpha^{H(K_{SG_j^{(HLv+1)}})} \bmod p$ and serially transmit message using Dijkstra's algorithm i.e. $SM_{(0,k)}^{HL_{h-1}}$ to $SM_{(1,k)}^{HL_{h-1}}$.

Phase 3:-   Same as phase 3 of Teo & Tan's protocol to generate and encrypt key 'K'.

Phase 4:-   a. Next layer decrypt the message using $D_{K_{SG_k}^{HL_1}}(K)$ and encrypt $E_{K_{SG_k}^{HL_2}}(K)$ and send it to next layer's $SG_{SC_j}^{HL_{l+1}}$. This $SG_{SC_j}^{HL_{l+1}}$ will use Dijkstra's algorithm to communicate message to other group members.

c. This process continues until all layers HL_{h-1} receive the key 'K'.

Table 1 shows the impact of modification on Teo and Tan's protocol. With this modification number of message and exponentiation operation reduces from layer 2 onward. Major strength of this proposed approach is the reduction of overhead on single subgroup controller of broadcasting. However it suffers from count to infinity problem in the network.

Table 1. Serial communication's cost

	Exponentiation	Message Sent	Message received
$SG_0^{L_0}$	3h	3h-1	h (n+1)
$SG_j^{L_v}$ $v \in [1, h-3]$	Lesser or same	Lesser or same	Lesser or same
$SG_j^{L_{h-2}}$	Lesser or same	Lesser or same	Lesser or same

Method 2 (circular communication):- As shown in Figure 1(b), in this method, subgroup controller will form the logical circle among mobile nodes using Spinrad algorithm [34]. The key messages in phase 2 and phase 4 of Teo and Tan's protocol are communicated with both clockwise and counterclockwise direction along with token 'T' to remove message duplicity on any node.

Protocol: Modified Teo & Tan's Protocol

Premises: Same as Teo &Tan's Protocol

Goal: Generate a common symmetric group key K and share it with all group members with lesser number of message exchanges and to remove count to infinity problem.

Phase 1:-   Same as phase 1 of Teo and Tan's protocol to generate subgroup key $K_{SG_j}^{(HL_h-1)}$.

Phase 2:-   Run Spinrad algorithm to form a circle.

Phase 3:-   Subgroup controller will generate $Z_K^{HLv} = \alpha^{H(K_{SG_j^{(Lv+1)}})} \bmod p$ and serially transmit message using Sprinrad's selected path.

Phase 4:-   Same as phase 3 of Teo & Tan's protocol to generate and encrypt key 'K'.

Phase 5:-   a. Check token 'T' for direction of message receive and duplicity.

b. If it passes check in step 5a then next layer decrypt the message using $D_{K_{SG_k}^{HL_1}}(K)$ and encrypt $E_{K_{SG_k}^{HL_2}}(K)$ and send it to next layer's $SG_{SC_j}^{HL_{l+1}}$. This $SG_{SC_j}^{HL_{l+1}}$ will use Spinrad to communicate to other group members.

c. $SG_{SC_j}^{HL_0}$ will also use Spinrad until all layers HL_{h-1} receive the key 'K'.

Table 2. Circular communication's cost

	Exponentiation	Message Sent	Message received
$SG_0^{L_0}$	3h	3h-1	h (n+1)
$SG_j^{L_v}$ v□ [1,h-3]	(3(h-v))/2	(2(h-v)+(h-(v+1)))/2	(((h-v)(n+1))+1)/2
$SG_j^{L_{h-2}}$	3	3	(2n+3)/2
Users	1	1	(n+2)/2

Token used to remove duplicity in a circle contains timestamp to remove replay attack, direction of communication i.e. clockwise or anti-clockwise and path traversed. Major strength of this proposed modification is that if destination node immediately respond to all its subgroup nodes with a light weight message K' then on an average it half the total number of communications, where size (K') < size (K), as shown in Table 2. Here, size (K') could be 1 bit in its best case. However it suffers from complete avoidance of count to infinity problem and if any intermediate mobile node is not active then predecessor and successor nodes have to wait for activation of node.

Method 3 (Ant's colony communication):- As shown in Figure 1(d), in order to avoid count to infinite problem in serial and group communication for Teo and Tan's protocol, Ant's algorithm is used [13]. Cost of communications is same as in serial communication, as shown in Table 2.

Protocol: Modified Teo & Tan's Protocol
Premises: Same as Teo &Tan's Protocol
Goal: Generate & share a common symmetric group key K with lesser number of message exchanges and to remove count to infinity problem.
Phase 1:-   Same as phase 1 of Teo and Tan's protocol to generate subgroup key $K_{SG_j}^{(HL_{h-1})}$.
Phase 2:-   Run Ant's colony optimization algorithm to find shortest path and remove count to infinity problem.
Phase 3:-   Subgroup controller will generate $Z_K^{HL_v} = \alpha^{H(K_{SG_j}^{(L_v+1)})} \bmod p$ and serially transmit message using Ant's algorithm of i.e. $SM_{(0,k)}^{HL_{h-1}}$ to $SM_{(1,k)}^{HL_{h-1}}$ so on.
Phase 4:-   Same as phase 3 of Teo & Tan's protocol to generate and encrypt key 'K'.
Phase 5:-   a. Next layer decrypt the message using $D_{K_{SG_k}^{HL_1}}(K)$ and encrypt $E_{K_{SG_k}^{HL_2}}(K)$ and send it to next layer's $SG_{SC_j}^{HL_{l+1}}$. This $SG_{SC_j}^{HL_{l+1}}$ will use Ant's algorithm to communicate message to other group members.
             b. $SG_{SC_j}^{HL_0}$ will also use Ant's algorithm to find HL_{h+1}'s subgroup controller and until all layers HL_{h-1} receive the shared symmetric key 'K'.

Strength of proposed modification is that it is able to remove count to infinity problem with less number of key messages. However it is unable to remove waiting delay if any intermediate mobile node is de-active. In case of deactivation, re-run of Ant's algorithm is required to fill the gap and it overhead the network.

Method 4 (Using Shamir's Threshold secret sharing communication):- As shown in Figure 1(e), in order to avoid waiting time during deactivation of any intermediate node,

Shamir's threshold secret sharing scheme is integrated with Teo and Tan's protocol [14]. Where a combiner function $C=\sum_{i=1}^{m} S_i$ is used to collect shares of 'm' mobile nodes out of 'n' nodes [36]. This solves the problem of deactivation of nodes and whenever any mobile node will be re-activated then it has to share the contributory symmetry key 'K' and only after mutual authentication. As $m \leq n$ thus number of message communication will always be less than Teo and Tan's cost, as shown in Table 3.

Protocol: Modified Teo & Tan's Protocol

Premises: Same as Teo &Tan's Protocol

Goal: Generate a common symmetric group key K and share it with all group members with lesser number of message exchanges and to remove count to infinity problem and waiting delays.

Phase 1:-   Same as phase 1 of Teo and Tan's protocol to generate subgroup key $K_{SG_j}^{(HL_h-1)}$.

Phase 2:-   Subgroup controller will generate $Z_K^{HL_v} = \alpha^{H(K_{SG_j^{(L_v+1)}})} \bmod p$ and it will broadcast message using Shamir's threshold's combiner function. This broadcast communication is with only those nodes that contributed to the combiner function 'C'. Any new node or regenerate node will establish a peer to peer communication with $SG_{SC_j}^{HL_i}$ for any further communication.

Phase 3:-   Same as phase 3 of Teo & Tan's protocol to generate and encrypt key 'K'.

Phase 4:-   a. Next layer decrypt the message using $D_{K_{SG_k}^{HL_1}}(K)$ and encrypt using $E_{K_{SG_k}^{HL_2}}(K)$ and send it to next layer's $SG_{SC_j}^{HL_{l+1}}$. This $SG_{SC_j}^{HL_{l+1}}$ will use threshold mechanism to communicate message to other $SG_{SC_j}^{HL_{l+2}}$ and $SM_{(j,k)}^{HL_{l+1}}$.

            b. $SG_{SC_j}^{HL_{l+2}}$ will also use threshold's algorithm to find HL_{h+1}'s subgroup controller and until all layers HL_{h-1} receive the shared symmetric key 'K'.

Table 3. Shamir's threshold key management cost

	Exponentiation	Message Sent	Message received
$SG_0^{L_0}$	<= 3h	<= 3h-1	h (m+1)
$SG_j^{L_v}$ v∈ [1,h-3]	<=3(h-v)	<=2(h-v)+(h-(v+1))	((h-v)(m+1))+1
$SG_j^{L_{h-2}}$	<= 6	<=5	2m+3
Users	<=3	<=2	m+2

Modification 2 (Virtual Empty Contributory Nodes):- As shown in Figure 2, Teo and Tan suggest construction of groups and subgroup with fixed number of mobile nodes however if fixed nodes are not in closer vicinity then energy loss in communication will be very high. To remove energy losses virtual nodes are supposed to be joining later and are considered to be the part of group or subgroup. These virtual nodes will do the same job as of existing nodes but carry a difference of joining and leaving phases to refresh a key for avoiding attacks. The communication and computation cost of joining/leaving members is an overhead for Teo and Tan's protocol but it is a natural process of real MANETs. The protocol runs as:

Protocol: Modified Teo & Tan's Protocol

Premises: Same as Teo &Tan's Protocol and $VN_{SM_j^k}^{HL_i}$ represents virtual node as j^{th} subgroup member in k^{th} subgroup and at i^{th} layer. $VN_{SC_j^k}^{HL_i}$ represents virtual j^{th} subgroup controller in k^{th} subgroup and at i^{th} layer. AL_{MN} is list of shared key algorithms supported by mobile node; SL_{VN} is shared key algorithm selected by entity virtual node. N_i is the nonce of ith node. One way hashing function H (x) is used over digital sign.

Goal: Generate a common symmetric group key 'K' and share it with all group members with lesser number of message exchanges and to remove energy losses using virtual nodes and threshold cryptosystem.

Phase 1:- Moderate radio range of mobile nodes decides the vicinity of group. If 'n' is not reached then consider 'w' $VN_{SM_j^k}^{HL_i}$ nodes exist in the network. Where, w≤n. $SG_{SC_j}^{HL_i}$ will select random secret value for these nodes and run the BD GKA and generate key $K_{SG_j}^{(HL_ih-1)}$ as in phase 1 of Teo & Tan's protocol.

Phase 2:- Same as phase 2 of method 4.

Phase 3:- Same as phase 3 of Teo & Tan's protocol to generate and encrypt key 'K'.

Phase 4:- a. Same as phase 4a of method 4.

b. Same as phase 4b of method 4.

Phase 5:- *Joining New Nodes*

As shown in Figure 2(b), whenever a new node wants to join the network then a fresh key is generated in order to make the new members to communicate within a network. According to energy level and vicinity of node subgroup is decided and virtual node will exchange its key parameter with new member using peer to peer Aziz Diffie (AD) algorithm [35].

a. $MN_{SM_{J+1}}^{HL_i} \rightarrow VN_{SM_j^k}^{HL_i}: Cert\left(MN_{SM_{J+1}}^{HL_i}\right), N_M, AL_M.$

b. $VN_{SM_j^k}^{HL_i} \rightarrow MN_{SM_{J+1}}^{HL_i}:$

$Cert\left(VN_{SM_j^k}^{HL_i}\right), E_{PK_M}\left\{SK_{VN_{SM_j^k}^{HL_i}}\right\}, SL_{VN},$

$E_{PR_{VN}}\{H\left(E_{PK_{VN_{SM_j^k}^{HL_i}}}\left\{SK_{MN_{SM_J}^{HL_i}}\right\}, SL_{VN_{SM_j^k}^{HL_i}}, N_{MN_{SM_J}^{HL_i}}, AL_{MN_{SM_J}^{HL_i}}\right)\}$

c. $MN_{SM_{J+1}}^{HL_i} \rightarrow VN_{SM_j^k}^{HL_i}:$

$E_{PK_{VN_{SM_j^k}^{HL_i}}}\left\{SK_{MN_{SM_{J+1}}^{HL_i}}\right\}, \{H\left(E_{PK_{VN_{SM_j^k}^{HL_i}}}\left\{SK_{MN_{SM_{J+1}}^{HL_i}}\right\}, E_{PK_{MN_{SM_{J+1}}^{HL_i}}}\left\{SK_{VN_{SM_j^k}^{HL_i}}\right\}\right)\}$

Phase 6:- *Leaving Existing Nodes:-*

As shown in Figure 2(c), every leaving node start the process of creating a virtual node as discussed in phase 1 and every new virtual node refreshes the shared key 'K' with subgroup controller.

a. $SG_{SM_j}^{HL_i} \rightarrow SG_{SC_k}^{HL_i}:$ "refresh".

b. $SG_{SC_k}^{HL_i} \rightarrow SG_{SC_k}^{HL_{i-1}}:$ "refresh and so on until top most subgroup controller receive the refresh singal.

c. $SG_{SC_k}^{HL_o}$ initiates the process of rekeying from phase1.

Let 'l' is total number of subgroups and 'o' is number of threshold selected subgroups such that o ≤ l. Table 4 shows the cost of joining and leaving a member.

Table 4. Cost of joining and leaving a member

	Joining	Leaving
Teo and Tan	h*n*l	h*n*l
Proposed approach	h*m*o	h*m*o

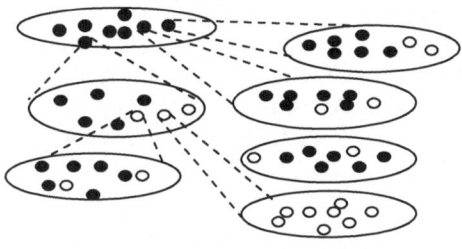

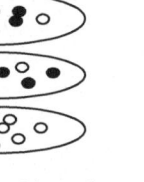

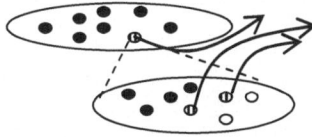

Fig. 2(b). Joining new member

Fig. 2(a). Virtual group/subgroup hierarchy

⊕   Leaving group member

●   Existing group member

○   Virtual group member   **Fig. 2(c).** Leaving existing members

⬭ Group or Sub-group

⟵⟶ Peer to peer communication

⟶ Leaving existing group member

Fig. 2. Dynamic virtual node topology

4   Results and Analysis

4.1   Security Analysis

In this work three key management protocols are discussed: (i) Teo and Tan, (ii) WLH and (ii) Tseng. Table 5 shows the security analysis of these protocols.

Table 5. Key Management Protocol's comparison

	Teo and Tan	WLH	Tseng	Proposed approach
Authentication	Moderate	Moderate	Moderate	Strong
Digital Signature	Weak	Weak	Weak	Strong
Forward Secrecy	Moderate	Weak	Moderate	Strong
Backward Secrecy	Strong	Weak	Moderate	Strong

In case of WLH, random variables are taken into consideration for low capacity devices. This random variable with client/server communication reduces the overall overhead of nodes but does not provide proper authentication or digital signature as compared to Teo and Tan or as in proposed approach. Without digital signature scheme, manipulation of old keys to generate future key (forward secrecy) or use of existing key to generate next key (backward secrecy) is comparatively easier [10]. Proposed approach used AD algorithm in peer to peer [35] and BD GKA in group communication thus provide more secured network.

4.2   Performance Analysis

Figure 3 and Figure 4 shows the comparative analysis of jitter and throughput for (i) Teo and Tan (ii) WLH, (iii) Tseng and (iv) Proposed approach. Three basic MANET routing protocols used in this comparison are: AODV, DSR and DSDV. This analysis is done for 1000 mobile nodes on NS-3 platform using python language [37]. The results show that WLH is having the minimum delay variation and maximum throughput but this is not the secure protocol. In term of jitter and other security consideration modified threshold group key Teo and Tan is the efficient protocol with AODV protocol, as shown in Figure 3. Teo and Tan with threshold key hierarchy scheme also provide the maximum throughput except WLH, which is not secured.

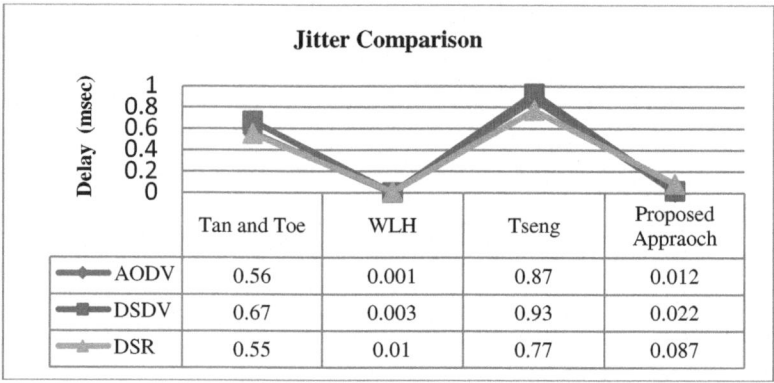

Fig. 3. Jitter comparison for 1000 nodes

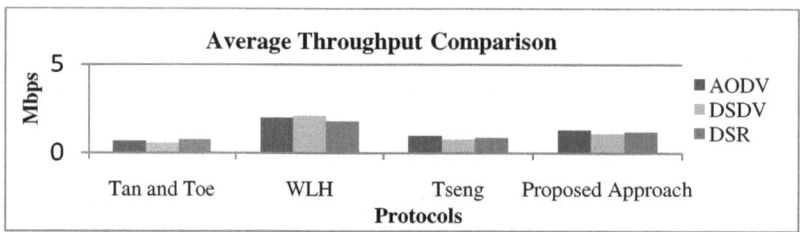

Fig. 4. Throughput comparison for 1000 nodes

5   Conclusion

In this work, a modified form of secure extended Teo & Tan's threshold group key management protocol is proposed for low power computation capability mobile devices. The proposed mechanism show that the modifications made on Teo & Tan's key management protocol make it fully contributory, more efficient in terms of energy efficiency & performance and make the protocol secure against different attacks because of AD peer to peer and BD GKA's mutual key authentication protocols. Construction of virtual nodes prevents the subgroups from energy losses therefore achieve fast and energy efficient subgroups. Modification of Dynamic leave and join adds the provision to Teo & Tan's protocol for making it open for new nodes. Cost and performance analysis shows that proposed scheme is the most energy efficient and dynamic as compared to three other group key management protocols for MANETs.

References

1. Boyd, C., Mathuria, A.: Protocols for Authentication and Key Establishment, 1st edn. Springer (2003)
2. van Tilborg, H.C.A.: Encyclopedia of Cryptography and Security. Springer (2005)
3. Hellman, M.E.: An Overview of Public Key Cryptography. IEEE Communications Society Magazine 16, 24–32 (1978)
4. Wen, H.A., Lin, C.L., Hwang, T.: Provably secure authenticated key exchange protocols for low power computing clients. Computers and Security 25, 106–113 (2006)
5. Vesteras, B.: Analysis of Key Agreement Protocols. Master's Thesis Report, Department of Computer Science and Media Technology, Gjovik University College (2006)
6. Tseng, Y.M.: Efficient authenticated key agreement protocols resistant to a denial of service attack. International Journal of Network Management 15, 193–202 (2005)
7. Tseng, Y.M.: Cryptanalysis and improvement of key distribution system for csat satellite communication. Informatica 13(3), 369–376 (2002)
8. Tseng, Y.M.: An improved conference key agreement protocol with forward secrecy. Informatica 16(2), 275–284 (2005)
9. Tseng, Y.M.: A communication efficient and fault tolerant conference key agreement protocol with forward secrecy. Journal of Systems and Software 80, 1091–1101 (2007)
10. Lee, S., Kim, J., Hong, S.J.: Security weakness of Tseng's fault tolerant conference key agreement protocol. Journal of Systems and Software 82, 1163–1167 (2009)
11. Teo, J.C.M., Tan, C.H.: Energy-Efficient and Scalable Group Key Agreement for Large Ad Hoc Networks. In: PE-WASUN's 2005, October 10-13, pp. 114–121 (2005)
12. Dijkstra, E.W.: A note on two problems in connexion with graphs. Numerische Mathematik 1, 269–271 (1959)
13. Gutjahr, W.J.: A graph-based Ant System and its convergence. Future Generation Computer Systems 16, 873–888 (2000)
14. Shamir, A.: How to share a secret. Communications of the ACM 22(11), 612–613 (1979)
15. Perkins, C.E.: Ad hoc Networking. Addison-Wesley, New York (2001)
16. Stallings, W.: Cryptography and Network Security: Principles and Practice, 5th edn. Prentice-Hall (2010)
17. Mao, W.: Modern Cryptography: Theory and Practice. Prentice Hall PTR (2004)
18. Krawczyk, H.: SKEME: A Versatile Secure Key Exchange Mechanism for Internet. In: Proc. of the Symposium on Network and Distributed System Security, pp. 114–127 (1996)
19. Harkins, D., Carrel, D.: The Internet Key Exchange Internet Request for Comments 2409 (November 1998)
20. Kaufman, C., Hoffman, P., Nir, Y., Eronen, P.: Internet Key Exchange Protocol version 2 (IKEv2), Internet Request for Comments 5996 (September 2010)
21. Arkko, J., Haverinen, H.: Extensible Authentication Protocol Method for 3rd Generation Authentication and Key Agreement (EAP-AKA), Internet Request for Comments 4187 (2006)

22. Katz, J., Yung, M.: Scalable Protocols for Authenticated Group Key Exchange. In: Boneh, D. (ed.) CRYPTO 2003. LNCS, vol. 2729, pp. 110–125. Springer, Heidelberg (2003)
23. Ingemarsson, I., Tang, D.T., Wong, C.K.: A Conference key distribution system. IEEE Transactions on Information Theory 28(5), 714–720 (1982)
24. Steiner, M., Tsudik, G., Waidner, M.: Diffie-Hellman Key Distribution Extended to Group Communication. In: ACM Conference on Computer and Communication Security, pp. 31–37 (1996)
25. Ateniese, G., Steiner, M., Tsudik, G.: Authenticated Group Key Agreement and Friends. In: International Conference on Computer and Communication Security, pp. 17–26 (1998)
26. Steiner, M., Tsudik, G., Waidner, M.: CLIQUES: A new approach to group key agreement. In: Proc. of the 18th International Conference on Distributed Computing Systems, pp. 380–387 (1998)
27. Steiner, M., Tsudik, G., Waidner, M.: Key agreement in dynamic peer groups. IEEE Transactions on Parallel and Distributed Systems 11(8), 769–780 (2000)
28. Burmester, M., Desmedt, Y.G.: A Secure and Efficient Conference Key Distribution System. In: De Santis, A. (ed.) EUROCRYPT 1994. LNCS, vol. 950, pp. 275–286. Springer, Heidelberg (1995)
29. Harney, H., Muckenhirn, C.: Group Key Management Protocol Architecture, Internet Request for Comments 2094 (July 1997)
30. Harney, H., Muckenhirn, C.: Group Key Management Protocol Specification, Internet Request for Comments 2093 (July 1997)
31. Harney, H., Meth, U., Colegrove A.: Group Secure Association Key Management Protocol, Internet Request for Comments 4535 (June 2006)
32. Weis, B., Rowles, S., Hardjono, T.: The Group Domain of Interpretation, Internet Request for Comments 6407 (October 2011)
33. Baugher, M., Weis, B., Hardjono, J., Harney, H.: The Group Domain of Interpretation, Internet Request for Comments 3547 (July 2003)
34. Spinrad, J.: Recognition of circle graphs. Journal of Algorithms 16(2), 264–282 (1994)
35. Aziz, A., Diffie, W.: Privacy and Authentication for Wireless Local Area Networks. IEEE Personal Communications 1, 25–31 (1994)
36. Merwe, J.V.D., Dowoud, D., McDonald, S.: A Survey on Peer to Peer key management for Mobile Ad Hoc Network. ACM Computing Surveys 39(1), Article 1 (2007)
37. NS3 Simulator, http://www.nsnam.org
38. Barker, E., Barker, W., Burr, W., Polk, W., Smid, M.: Recommendation for Key Management – Part 1:General. NIST Special Publication 800-57, Rev. 3, 1–143 (2011)
39. Lu, Y.F., Kuo, C.F., Pang, A.C.: A Novel Key Management Scheme for Wireless Embedded Systems. SIGAPP Applied Computing Review 12(1), 50–59 (2012)

A Cloud Based Robot Localization Technique

Faimy Q. Ansari, Jitendra Kumar Pal, Jainendra Shukla,
G.C. Nandi, and Pavan Chakraborty

Robotics & Artificial Intelligence Lab, Indian Institute of Information Technology
Allahabad (IIITA), Allahabad 21 10 12, U.P., India
{faimyqa,jpjitendrapal,jainendra08}@gmail.com,
{gcnandi,pavan}@iiita.ac.in

Abstract. Recently Cloud robotics is a very vibrant research area due to its strategic application potentials. In this paper we have developed a basic cloud based architecture for knowing the localization information of a robot in a dynamic environment. Subsequently, this information could be useful to guide the robot in the desired path as trained by the central cloud. In this paper, Artificial Neural Network (ANN) is used for the training of locations with Radial Basis Function (RBF). The idea is to establish the communication between the cloud and robot over a large environment using the JAVA-RMI interface and identify the location from the images sent by the robot .This paper describes the Cloud As Software As a Service(SAAS).

1 Introduction

The paper presents an architecture which deals with the concept of cloud robotics. This paper is focusing on the problem of localization of mobile robot on the cloud. The outlines are as follows:

1.1 Cloud Computing and Cloud Robotics

Cloud computing deals with the problem of assigning resources to the end over the internet or any network for the work being done. Such resources can be Processor, Memory, Hard Disk, Network infrastructure, application software etc. The end user is assumed to be unavailable with these resources but may have the requirement for the same. For this purpose the central cloud gets connected with it then performs the required task at its end and provides the end user abstraction of execution. Thus this reduces the work load on the end user connected to cloud. The cloud services are of three types: Infrastructure as a service (IaaS), Software as as Service (SaaS) and Plateform as a Service (PaaS)[1].

The cloud computing concept can also be used in robotics. This type of technique is known as Cloud Robotics. In Cloud Robotics the idea is to reduce the overall processing and computing burden of the clouds and shift all the loads to a central high computing cloud. In this aspect the cloud can be used as IaaS, Paas or Saas for the robots. The cloud robotics uses concept similar to Service Oriented Architecture(SOA)[2].The idea of cloud robotics can easily be understand by a small example

M. Parashar et al. (Eds.): IC3 2012, CCIS 306, pp. 347–357, 2012.

where a mobile robot is walking in an environment and suddenly it faced a huge car in front of it, but earlier it was not designed to avoid it so it fails. But if it was a cloud based robot, the cloud could easily get the control of the robot and downloads the program for avoiding the car. This concept is also well known as Remote Brain. This paper also deals with outlines of controlling the mobile robot from the central cloud, identify their locations and build a map to instruct the robot for further path follow.

2   Cloud Robotics Architecture

The cloud robotics architecture is very simple and is as shown in fig 1[4].

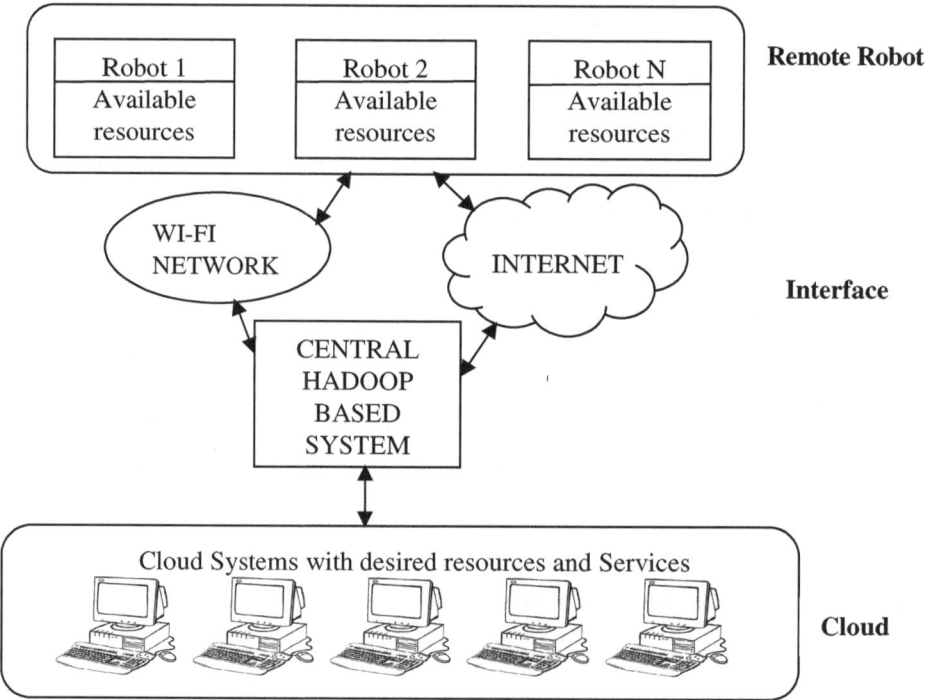

Fig. 1. Cloud Robotics Architecture

The cloud Based architecture consists of following three sections

1. Remote Robot
2. Interface and
3. Cloud

The Remote robots are the actual mobile robots which are around a large environment and need to be tracked or serviced. These robots lacks with the availability of resources for their need. The robot makes a connection to the central File System either via Wi-Fi network or Internet using Java-RMI [6] interface. This file system distributes the entire data and application throughout the cloud system and keeps the records for the same. This File System is similar to the Hadoop Distributed File System (HDFS)[4]. Depending on the request received from the robot the corresponding cloud is utilized and then get connected with the robot to perform the specific task. During the communication part the cloud id is hidden and user gets the abstraction of work being done on robot side which actually happens to occur at the other end.

This paper is written to focus the details of the localization problem related with the robots.

3   Basic Methodology

The basic methodology for the research is consists of following phases:

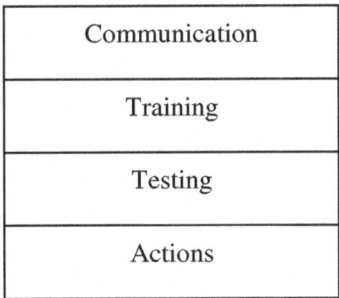

Fig. 2. Localization phases

3.1   Communication

This phase is used for establishing the communication between the cloud and the robots. Basically, the requirement for this paper is that the robot and the cloud should be in the same Wi-Fi Network. Now, the second program is the Java RMI Client side program [6]. This program takes the image generated by C program and sends it to the cloud via the network.

For connecting the two ends, we need to install JVM 1.6, JDK 1.6, Dev C++, Open CV 2.2. There are two program codes on robot side, the first code written in open CV executed in dev C++ to get the live images from the environment and store it.

The fig 3 shows the steps:

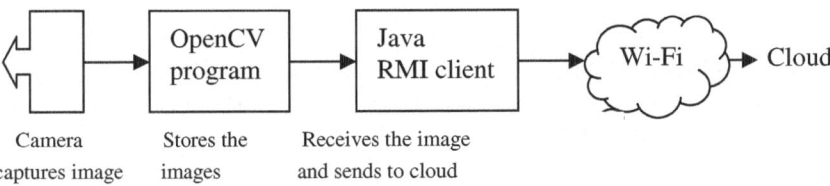

Fig. 3. Communication phase

The names of the images are also stored in a file.
The algorithmic steps for this phase are as follows:

1. At robot side capture the image from the camera
2. Save the image with a sequenced name and update the name of the image in the file out.txt.
3. Now start the cloud and make it available on the network.
4. Connect the robot to the cloud.
5. Convert the image to byte array form and then send it to the cloud by calling sendImage() method defined at the cloud side.
6. Together with the image data, robot ip address and other related parameters are also sent to uniquely identify the robot.
7. At the cloud side receive the image data and then convert it to image and then find the spatial histogram of this image [3].

3.2   Training

The cloud has to be trained with the histogram data of the images of locations to be identified. In this paper for the purpose of training, we are using Artificial Neural Network[1] with the Backpropogation algorithm[2]. The process is shown in the fig 4:

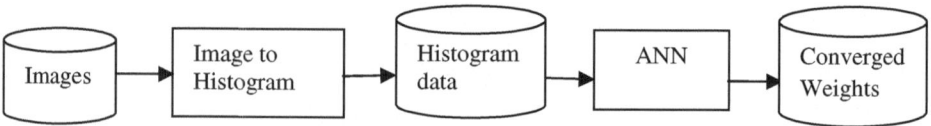

Fig. 4. Training the images on ANN

For training we have currently used 100 sample images of four locations each hence totaling 400 images. Now the histogram data of these images are calculated and stored in a file named "train.dat". Now another module takes this file as input and applies it on the ANN. As histogram data is the input to ANN hence the ANN has following initialization:

Number of input nodes:	256
Number of hidden nodes:	10
Number of output nodes:	02
Learning rate	0.02
Learning momentum	0.001

As the total locations are four so it can be identified with the codes 00, 01,10 and 11. Hence we have used two nodes at the output. The learning rate and momentum are the adjusted parameter for this system.

---

[1]   The Artificial Neural Network [5] is the algorithm used to simulate human brain working and the do the classification of dissimilar classes.

[2]   Back propagation algorithm [5] is used in ANN for training the neural network and transferring the changes in the output at the outer layer to middle layer.

A sample input data is as follows:

```
0.01,0.68,5.69,9.43,16.19,34.05,45.82,52.47,46.93,35.92,29.04,27.3,27.07
,32.22,38.3,42.8,43.34,38.31,31.41,32.26,36.38,43.53,37.56,28.8,23.91,21
.8,21.98,23.13,23.4,24.12,21.65,19.55,19.75,20.67,21.54,20.95,22.26,23.2
6,20.6,18.48,17.88,19.55,19.85,20.51,18.08,16.49,15.03,14.45,12.94,11.6,
12.07,12.9,13.17,15.29,15.8,17.06,16.94,15.3,13.62,14.35,14.4,15.41,18.1
8,20.35,24.21,26.09,26.12,23.84,24.06,20.73,19.56,15.61,13.14,11.38,11.8
3,12.26,14.55,12.64,10.31,11.2,11.82,12.44,12.23,11.47,12.27,12.37,11.29
,11.04,12.47,12.89,11.8,11.84,12.45,13.29,12.66,12.01,12.55,11.9,9.26,8.
41,7.31,7.33,7.31,7.9,8.01,7.66,6.95,7.11,8.37,10.23,9.7,8.71,8.79,8.99,
10.04,9.65,8.68,8.58,9.59,9.62,9.84,9.76,10.63,11.13,10.27,10.25,10.79,1
1.93,11.28,10.5,10.66,12.02,10.66,10.06,10.12,11.32,11.83,11.32,10.98,11
.6,9.79,8.7,8.02,9.11,9.51,8.81,8.92,8.19,7.84,6.43,6.6,6.04,5.56,5.44,5
.65,5.88,5.96,5.02,4.99,5.31,5.72,5.82,6.05,5.73,5.84,6.34,5.86,5.38,5.6
3,6.48,6.23,6.56,7.3,7.4,8.56,8.25,7.69,8.55,7.89,8.38,8.03,9.19,9.11,8.
59,8.26,7.55,7.23,7.55,8.02,9.77,8.11,6.8,6.37,5.76,5.81,5.65,6.16,5.61,
4.88,4.94,4.65,4.35,4.66,5.01,4.63,4.22,3.47,2.89,2.77,2.87,3.69,3.7,3.4
7,2.96,2.11,1.88,1.9,1.63,1.46,1.42,1.66,1.49,1.33,1.35,1.58,1.48,1.42,1
.76,2.02,2.11,2.61,3.15,2.89,2.01,1.55,1.3,1.26,1.34,1.35,1.32,1.03,1.4,
1.47,1.31,1.78,1.83,1.62,1.61,1.64,1.99,2.88,3.97,6.61,15.37,140.04,2.66
,1
```

The data are divided by 100 so they are in decimal. This data is of 256 dimensions, the last index '1' denotes that it belongs to class 1.

Once the system is trained with the data, the network finalizes its weights parameter for both the layers, so at this point the weights are again stored in a file weight.xls to use it afterwards when it is needed for testing the unknown location. In our system the two converged weights will be of 256x10 and 10x2 dimensions. The sample snapshot of the weights is:

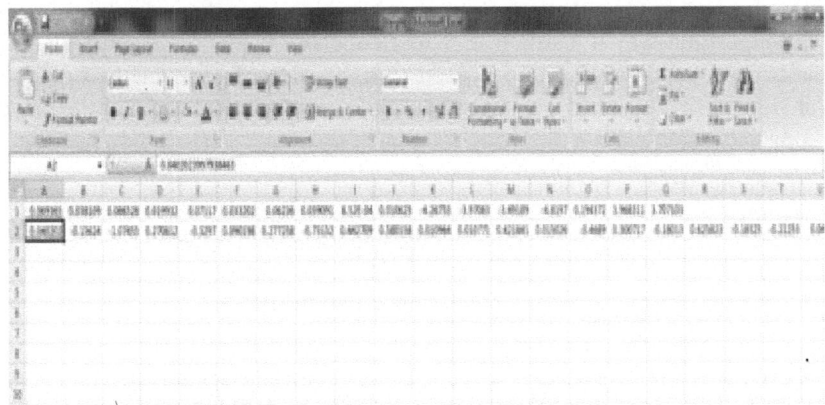

Fig. 5. Snapshot of weight.xls containing converged weights

3.3   Testing

The data received by the cloud is now converted to the image histogram and then fed to the neural network trained by the previous phase. Now, this time the network tests the input image against the four location images and finds the exact location of the robot. Cloud now plots that location on a predefined map and then it finds a path for robot to move. This phase can also be explained by the following figure:

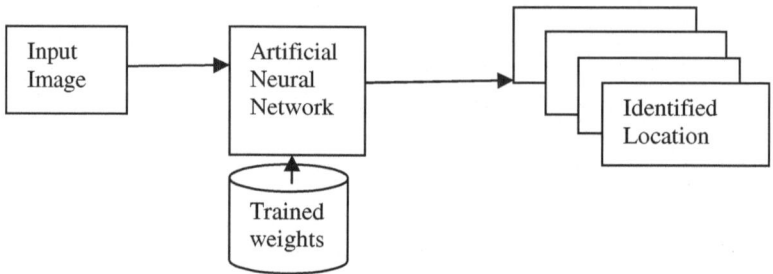

Fig. 6. Testing the current image

3.4   Action

Cloud now sends the signal to robot to move towards the goal. It also instructs it how much distance it has to go and in which direction as robot does not know anything. Now the robot turns its motor on for that time and moves to the final goal. Then it again sends the new location window to the cloud. Cloud goes back to the testing phase and identifies the new location to verify it. In this way, this process can be continued to plan a path or tour for the robot.

3.5   Artificial Neural Network

The algorithm which is used here is Artificial Neural Network with back-propgation algorithm. It is taken from the link [7]. The ANN is a network inspired from decision boundary algorithm which learns from experience and works on example and analogy. The backpropgation algorithm is used to train ANN. In this method outputs are calculated from first layer to last layer then difference is calculated and the errors are backpropgated to maintain to the correct output.

4   Results

We have used two robots SMART[3] and ANT[4] (Autonomous Navigation Test bed) available at Robotics and Artificial Intelligence Lab in IIIT-A:

---

[3]   SMART(A Social Mobile Advanced Robot Test bed for Humanoid Robot Researchers) is a Humanoid robot being developed as lab guide at Robotics & AI Lab , IIIT-Allahabad.

[4]   ANT (Autonomous Navigation Test Bed) is a test bed designed for R & D purpose at Robotics & AI Lab, IIIT-A.

Fig. 7. SMART (left) and ANT (right)

We have assumed our laptop as a cloud connected to Wi-Fi LAN. Now we are running the cloud side ANN training program for training against the four locations of our lab(shown in fig 8):

Fig. 8. The four locations on which the ANN is trained

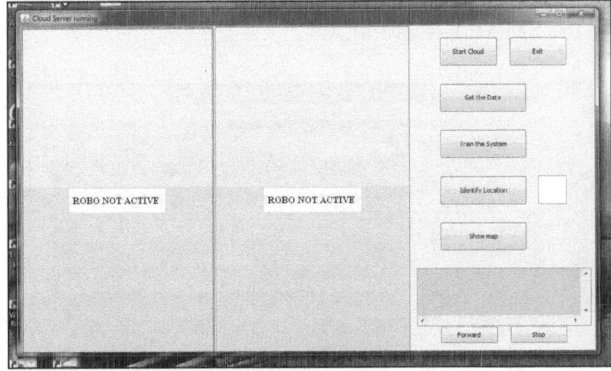

Fig. 9. First snapshot of Cloud GUI

We have taken 400 sample images of these locations. The GUI for our project is shown in fig 9.

This is showing in fig 9 that we have chosen two robots but they are not active now. As it can be seen that there are many options. The first option is Start cloud. When we click on "start cloud" the cloud get connected with the network and becomes available as shown in fig 10:

```
C:\Program Files\Java\jdk1.6.0\bin\Bismillah\server>java -Djava.security.policy=
mypolicy CloudServer
Cloud server is ready
Message Sending prepared
```

Fig. 10. Message sending prepared notification

Now we put the robots on the desired locations. Following are images taken from robot side:

Fig. 11. Image taken from robots

Now in fig 9 we click on the "Get the Data" button to convert the 400 images to the corresponding histograms and then click on the "Train the system" to train the neural network. Once the network is trained we start the programs on the robot side:

Snapshot from the SMART is as follows:

Fig. 12. Snapshot from the first robot

Snapshot from the ANT is in fig 13:

Fig. 13. Snapshot from the second robot

Now as these two robots have connected to the cloud so the snapshot from the cloud is as shown in fig 14:

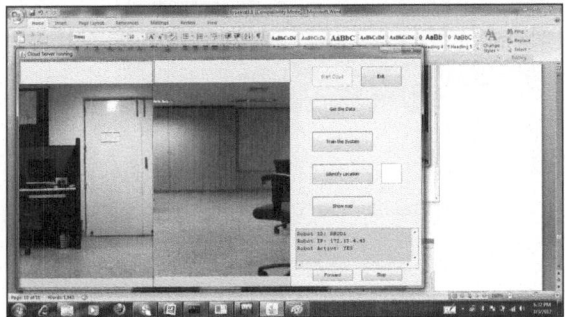

Fig. 14. Snapshot on cloud showing images from both the robots

Now if click on the show map button it shows the following image where spots denotes robots positions:

Fig. 15. Red shows SMART position and Green shows ANT position

This can also be verified by clicking identify location option from cloud window in fig 9:

Fig. 16. Left image is current image and right one is saved image

Now we can click on the forward button to move the robot to next location. This will send the forward signal to the robot's microcontroller (ATMEGA 16) via UART to move the robot. The snapshot is in fig 17:

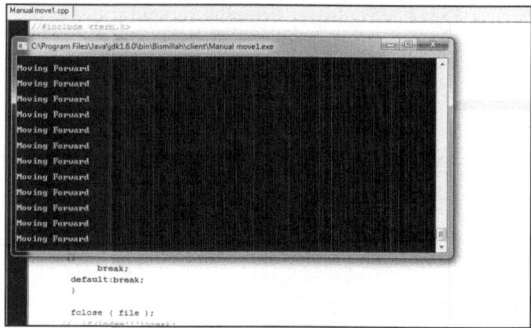

Fig. 17. Microcontroller program manualmove1.cpp got move signal from the cloud so sending it to the robot to move

We can now click on the "Stop" button on the cloud window to stop it otherwise it will stop itself after reaching the next location.

5   Conclusion and Future Scope

This paper is emphasizing on using cloud services for manipulating mobile robots in a dynamic environment. Using the approach discussed in this paper we can clearly identify the locations of the robots from a far away distance. This can be very useful in tracking the robots in a priori known environment. The other issue that is discussed in this paper is the shifting of processing load from the robot to the cloud which can be very helpful in case of very low processing, storage capable robot. The other works that can be done as a future work for this project are Obstacle detection, multi agent swarm optimization, Robot War planning, Robot Training etc. This work is using Wi-Fi network but in the future it can also be used with the internet connectivity as the JAVA-RMI provides connectivity on the internet. The method proposed here deal little with security like the services can be shared only if advertised by the cloud but it can also be extended in future for the authentication and confidentiality issues. Apart from this currently the research areas for the cloud robotics are as follows:

- Service availability and establishment
- Resource Sharing
- Robot Path planning
- Self Driving vehicle
- Robot Training

The robot motion planning is a huge challenging area which involves various problems like: Localization, Obstacle avoidance, Remote brain, Remote Gaming etc.

References

1. Du, Z., Yang, W., Chen, Y., Sun, X., Wang, X., Xu, C.: Design of a Robot Cloud Center. In: 2011 Tenth International Symposium on Autonomous Decentralized Systems (2011)
2. Chen, Y., Du, Z., García-Acosta, M.: Robot as a Service in Cloud Computing, Computer Science and Engineering, Arizona State University, Tempe, AZ 85287-8809, USA
3. Zhang, H., Gao, W., Chen, X., Zhao, D.: Object detection using spatial histogram features. Image and Vision Computing 24, 327–341 (2006)
4. Arumugam, R., Enti, V.R., Bingbing, L., Xiaojun, W., Baskaran, K., Kong, F.F., Senthil Kumar, A., Meng, K.D., Kit, G.W.: DAvinCi: A Cloud Computing Framework for Service Robots. In: 2010 IEEE International Conference on Robotics and Automation Anchorage Convention District, Alaska, USA, May 3-8 (2010)
5. Referred link for artificial neural network and back propagation algorithm (2012), http://www2.in.tu-clausthal.de/~hammer/lectures/...ml/ neural-network.ppt
6. http://docs.oracle.com/javase/tutorial/rmi/index.html (2012)

File Replication and Dereplication of Replica's in Distributed Environment

Manu Vardhan, Paras Gupta, and Dharmender Singh Kushwaha

Motilal Nehru National Institute of Technology Allahabad,
Department of Computer Science and Engineering,
Allahabad – 211004, U.P., India
{rcs1002,cs1006,dsk}@mnnit.ac.in

Abstract. Resource replication in distributed environment produces issues of secondary storage. Dereplication of resources is required when replication mechanism is hindered due to lack of secondary storage. This paper introduces dereplication approaches that depend upon last modification time, number of replica available and resource size. Comparative study shows that dereplication can be used to overcome the space overhead issue and reduces the dereplication time. Result shows that in case the space required is same but number of files to be dereplicated varies, dereplication time also varies depending on number of files to be dereplicated. Dereplication time will be more for case having large number of files. With the proposed approach, if file size increases by the multiple of 7, de-replication time will get increase just by the multiple of 1.5. This shows that dereplication time is decoupled from size of files that are dereplicated on the fly dynamically and does not increase proportionally with respect to file size.

Keywords: Dereplication, Distributed Systems, Replication.

1   Introduction

As the use of computer systems and internet is now becoming the part of our day to day life, requirement for services provided by them increases. To fulfill the requirement of services requested by an individual, service availability is an important issue. Distributed systems will take as the solution by various experts as compare to the centralized systems where services, resources, information are distributed over an environment and can be accessed by the members part of that environment.

A basic definition of distributed system in [1] is that a distributed system is a collection of independent entities that cooperate to solve a problem that cannot be individually solved. A term that describes a wide range of computers, from weakly coupled systems such as wide-area networks, to strongly coupled systems such as local area networks, to very strongly coupled systems such as multiprocessor systems [2].

Replication is a mechanism of service or resource placement to provide their availability in case of unavailability of resources and services. Replication is how to replicate data and request actors using adaptive and predictive techniques for selecting where, when and how fast replication should proceed [3].

M. Parashar et al. (Eds.): IC3 2012, CCIS 306, pp. 358–369, 2012.
© Springer-Verlag Berlin Heidelberg 2012

Dereplication is a mechanism to dereplicate / garbage-collect data or request actors and optimize utilization of distributed storage based on current system load and expected future demands for the object [3]. De-replication is done to optimize the utilization of storage space when the demand for a resource arises.The file to be dereplicated must be carefully taken into consideration of the future demands of a file. File currently being serviced cannot be dereplicated. The number of previously replicated files selected for dereplication can fulfill the requirement for storage space need of the upcoming file to be replicated. Dereplication is considered as a part of resource management process where as replication is considered as a part of resource placement process.

2   Related Work

Globally available various resource management policies and mechanisms represent a step towards efficient and adaptive resource management improving utilization of resources which results in improving the performance of system by reducing several overheads. Venkatasubramanian in [3] discuss about the security and timeliness application requirements using a using a customizable and safe middle ware framework called as CompOSE|Q. N. Venkatasubramanian describes the design and implementation of CompOSE|Q which is a QoS-enabled reflective middle ware framework. Also, to improve the performance of the system in the field of continuous media application, resource management technique is helpful in improving the utilization of resources. In [4], Chou Cheng-Fu et. al. describes various resource management policies on threshold basis in context of continuous media (CM) servers in the area of multimedia application. Venkatasubramanianet. al. in [5] discusses the two replication policies, these are static and dynamic. The division is based upon the number of copies of a file which is termed as degree of replication. In static replication policies, the degree of replication is constant while dynamic replication policies allow it to vary with time.

Santryet. al. in [6] identified four file retention policies for Elephant and have implemented these policies in their prototype. The policies are viz., Keep One, Keep All, Keep Safe and Keep Landmarks. Keep One provides the non-versioned semantics of a standard file system. Keep All retains every version of the file. Keep Safe provides versioning for undo but does not retain any long-term history. Keep Landmarks enhances Keep Safe to also retain a long-term history of landmark versions.

Hurley and Yeap [7] propose a file dereplication method based on β time interval that decides the frequency of invoking the dereplication operation. Over time, all files will eventually be candidates for migration/replication. Although many exist, the one we choose is as follows: every β time units (where β is a uniform time interval which defines the time between dereplication events), storage sites will decide which file qualifies for dereplication. The dereplication policy chosen applies the least recently used concept (i.e., the file selected for dereplication is the file which was not requested for the longest period of time at the storage site). Once the file has been selected, it will be removed from this storage site. Using β, it is possible to create a variety of dereplication policies: the smaller the value of β, the greater the frequency of dereplication, and the larger the value of β, the longer a file copy remains in the system. Similarly, Cabri et al. [10] proposed an adaptive file replication policy which is capable of reacting to changes by dynamically creating or deleting replicas.

Primary-copy (master-slave) approach for updating the replicas says that only one copy could be updated (the master), secondary copies are updated by the changes propagated from the master. There is only one replica which always has all the updates. Consequently the load of the primary copy is large. Domenici [11] discusses several replication and data consistency solutions, including Eager (Synchronous) replication and Lazy (Asynchronous) replication, Single-Master and Multi-Master Model, and pull-based and push-based. Author presented various replication and consistency maintenance algorithms to deal with huge scientific data. Jaechun [12] proposed two kinds of data replication techniques, called owner-initiated replication and client-initiated replication. Proposed replication techniques do not need to use file system-level locking functions, so that they can easily be ported to any of file systems. Guy [13] proposed a replica modification approach, a replica is designated either a master or a secondary replica. Only master replica is allowed to be modified whereas secondary replica is treated as read-only, i.e. modification permission on secondary replica is denied. A secondary replica is updated in accordance with the master replica if master replica is modified. Sun [14] proposes two coherence protocols viz., lazy-copy and aggressive-copy. Replicas are only updated as needed, if someone accesses it in the lazy-copy based protocol.

3 Problem Definition

During replication when a File Replicating Server (FRS) creates a replica of file on the peer nodes, space management issue arises i.e. whether space is available or not in the secondary storage of the peer nodes on which the file needs to be replicated. If space is available, the file will get copied, but if space is not available dereplication of previously replicated files needs to be done in the secondary storage of that peer node.

Dereplication of files will take place in a manner such that it will fulfill the size requirement of upcoming files. While maintaining the space management overhead, deletion of file should depend on the three criteria which will be discussed in section 3.1.

3.1 Parameters to Be Used

Solution to this problem will be represented on the basis of three parameters of a file which are last modification time of the file, number of replica available of a file and file size.

- *Last Modification Time of a File*: Last modification time is the time at which the file was last modified or last used.
- *Number of Replicas Available of a File*: Number of replicas available of a file is a count on number of copies available for a particular file. Whenever a copy of file is created, it will increase the number of replicas available of a file.
- *Size of a File*: File size is the size of a file required on a disk.

4   Proposed Solution

With everything being lodged on internet, computing paradigm is changing fast to harness this capability. Many information servers and files are resident on various machines and this can be effectively utilized by the users. We present a scenario discussed in section 4.1, although on a smaller scale where geographically disparate clusters interact with each other for information sharing through replication. Each of these cluster are owned by respective Institutes.

In proposed model, we talk about space overhead in replicating file on the storage site. If space is available, the file will get replicated, otherwise dereplication of previously replicated files needs to be done in that directory.

4.1   Architecture Used

One node in each cluster is designated as FRS. FRS can also be replicated on some other node in the cluster for backup and recovery. The scenario presented in the paper is illustrated in figure 1 and is elaborated subsequently.

The proposed architecture consists of loosely coupled systems, capable of providing various kinds of services like replication, storage, I/O specific, computation specific and discovery of resources. Based on the application requirement, the resources are made available to other nodes.

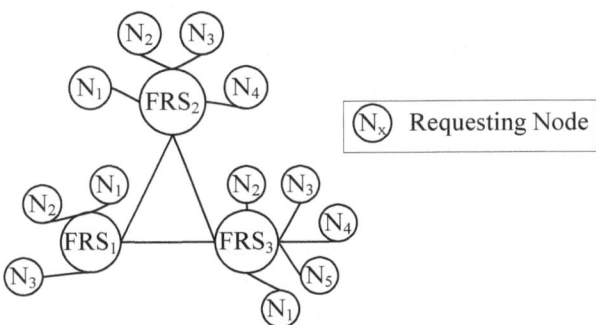

Fig. 1. Architecture

Figure 1 shows a network of three clusters that are connected to each other via intercommunication network. Each cluster consists of a group of trusted nodes and a File Replicating Server (FRS) assigned to these nodes. A FRS can be 'local' or 'remote'. A FRS is assigned to a subset of nodes known as local FRS and FRS positioned outside that cluster, will be called as remote FRS. Each subset of nodes (denoted as requesting nodes) receives the list having IP-address of remote FRS, to increase fault tolerance capability. But the nodes of a cluster will send the file request only to the local FRS. In case of the failure of the local FRS, a node can automatically select a remote FRS from the list and file request will be routed to the selected remote FRS. This makes the model robust and capable of handling crashes in case of local or even remote FRS fails. The system will keep functioning under all circumstances and will never come to halt. Each FRS maintains two tables:

1. File request count table with the following attributes: <file_id, file_name, request_count, meta data>.
2. Peer FRS table with the following attributes: <FRS_IP, FRS_PORT>.

Each FRS is informed whenever a new FRS is added to the network, to updates its peer FRS table. FRS does not monitor and maintains the status of remote FRS, instead FRS request for the current status of remote FRS on-demand. FRS status can either be 'busy' or 'ready'.

Threshold based file replication works as follows:

Each local FRS is responsible for accepting the file request and based on its current status (checks if the number of requests currently serving for a particular file is below the threshold or not), in the following manner:

1. If the status of local FRS is 'ready', the local FRS will fulfill the request.
2. If the status of local FRS is 'busy', it looks for a remote FRS that can handle the request, by one of the following manner, described as under:

The local FRS contacts the remote FRS that can handle the request by the available copy of the requested file i.e. the status of remote FRS is ready. If not so, the local FRS contacts those remote FRS on which the requested file is not available. In that case file replication will be initiated, by the local FRS of the cluster and the file replica will be created on remote FRS on which the file is not available. For both the cases mentioned above, IP address of the remote FRS that can handle the request will be send to the requesting node. On receiving the IP address, the requesting node will connect to the remote FRS and receives the file, without any user intervention. Thus the overhead of polling and broadcasting is reduced.

4.2   Approaches Proposed for Dereplication

Dereplication of files will take place in a manner such that it will fulfill the size requirement of upcoming files. While maintaining the space management overhead, three approaches for file dereplication are discussed below.

Last Modification Time Based Approach
In this approach, files are sorted on the usage basis file that was not requested for longest period of time will be selected for dereplication. A drawback of this approach is that if only one requested file is there before deletion, it causes loosing of information. So a check is performed before dereplication which will be done on number of replica available basis approach.

Number of Replicas Available of a File Based Approach
In this approach, files having many copies or the files with more than one replica are dereplicated only when there is not sufficient space available for new replicated files. Files with one replica are not dereplicated to avoid losing information of the file. In this case, before the dereplication of file, a check is performed, whether or not there are other copies of file available or not. If only single copy of file exists in the system,

in that case next probable file for dereplication will be selected from the sorted file list on the basis of last modification time.

File Size Based Approach

File size based dereplication approach is used when time required for dereplication considered as important factor. When there is a very little difference in the last modification time of the two files and number of replicas available of both files is more than one, dereplication of file with minimum file size among them will take place to avoid the delay in the process and complete it in the less time.

The proposed approach for dereplication will be described in Figure 2. The detailed description of the number labeled arcs will be described in sequential manner as follows:

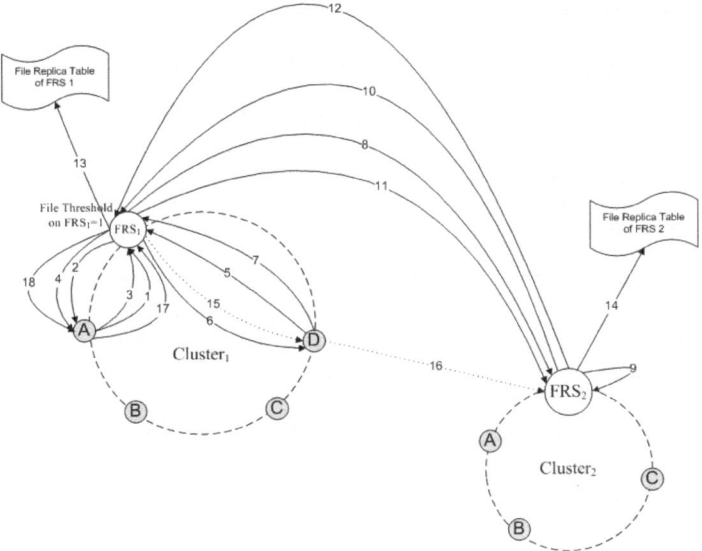

Fig. 2. Proposed Model

1. *Node A of cluster₁ sends connection request to FRS₁.*
2. *FRS₁ sends ip addresses of peer FRS and resource list to node A of cluster₁.*
3. *Node A of cluster₁ sends request for file f₁ to FRS₁ at time t₀.*
4. *Node A of cluster₁ starts receiving requested file f₁ from FRS₁.*
5. *Node D of cluster₁ sends connection request to FRS₁.*
6. *FRS₁ sends IP addresses of peer FRS and resource list to node D of cluster₁.*
7. *Node D of cluster₁ sends request for same file f₁ to FRS₁ at time t₁.*
8. As *FRS₁* can fulfill only one request at a time because the value of file threshold is *1* on *FRS₁*, so *node D of cluster₁* will look for another FRS in the system, here *FRS₂*, to fulfill its request. To fulfill the request of *node D of cluster₁* replication of requested files is initiated by *FRS₁* as the requested file is not present on *FRS₂*. FRS does not maintain any information about the "requesting node (e.g. *node D*)" at any point of time. So *FRS₁* will replicate the requested file to other FRS as its shared

resource information is being maintained, as discussed in section 4.1. Now, FRS_1 sends the size of the file to be replicated to FRS_2.

9. FRS_2 does not accept the file replication request because of space/storage scarcity. FRS_2 initiates dereplication operation on set of previously replicated files. The required amount of space is made available on FRS_2. If the secondary storage on FRS_2 did not contain any replicated files then user interruption will come, as dereplication of non-replicated file is not allowed.

10. FRS_2 sends message 'ready to receive file f_1' to FRS_1.

11. FRS_1 starts replicating the file f_1 to FRS_2.

12. FRS_2 sends message 'replication of file f_1 to be done successfully' to FRS_1.

13. FRS_1 updates its file replica table.

14. FRS_2 updates its file replica table.

15. FRS_1 sends IP address and port of FRS_2 to node D of $cluster_1$ informing that the file f_1 is now available on FRS_2.

16. Request of $node$ D of $cluster_1$ for file f_1 will now be fulfilled by peer FRS, FRS_2.

17. After some time $node$ A of $cluster_1$ request same file f_1 from FRS_1.

18. In case file with the same name already exists on the node A of $cluster_1$, file dereplication will be done on that node then the file transfer from FRS_1 to $node$ A of $cluster_1$ will be initiated.

4.3   Consistency

The most frequently used algorithms are *Write Update [8]* and *Write Invalidate [8]*. Hybrid Approach and Modification Propagation approach. Once the file replica is modified, one of the above discussed consistency maintenance algorithm will be used to update or invalidate the other replicas of the modified file.

Write Invalidate: Invalidates all the replicas of the file, once the file has been modified.

Write Update: This approach updates all the replicas of a file, once the file has been modified.

   The two approaches discussed above does not considers the number of file replicas available for a particular file, number of requests for a particular file and time required to update file replicas. Two approaches are mentioned below:

Hybrid Approach

Modification Propagation
This approach considers the factors that are discussed above.

Hybrid Approach: This approach will follow either write update or write invalidate mechanism to update or invalidate the replicas. Once the file replica has been modified, decision, whether to update or invalidate the file replica on other nodes depends on relationship between the file threshold value and number of requests for particular file on that node. The cases are discussed below:

Case 1: Number of requests for particular file $<<$ file threshold value on a node

Here write invalidate will be the best option as single updated file replica can handle all the requests as the number of request are quite less than the threshold value. So all the file requests will be transferred and processed by the node having the latest updated file replica. Thus updating only single file replica will fulfill the purpose in this case.

Case 2: Number of requests for particular file > file threshold value

Here write update policy is better as the number of on-demand updates will be minimized to null using this policy. All replicas will get updated as the number of requests for particular file is greater than the file threshold value.

Case 3: Unbalanced Load: Request Count is Uneven

Here the number of request on a particular node varies unevenly. In this case only those replicas will be updated where the number of file request is greater than the file threshold value. So using this approach on-demand updates are minimized to null, as the required replicas are already updated using hybrid mechanism.

Modification Propagation: This approach propagates only the modifications, to update the file replica. Complete file is never transmitted for updating a file replica. Timely modification are extracted and stored in a separate file and these modification are propagated on-demand, whenever there is request for updating a particular file replica.

4.4   Stability Analysis

According to Figure 3, the communication between a requesting node and a FRS (*Source* A and FRS$_1$) is described as follows: *Source* A sends a file request to FRS$_1$through$\overline{M_1}$.FRS$_1$ will receive the request of *Source*A represented as M$_1$. In return, FRS$_1$ sends file to *Source* A shown by M$_3$ received on *Source* A using $\overline{M_3}$.

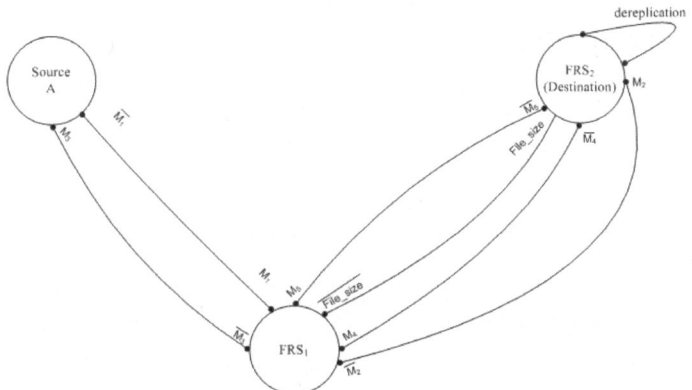

Fig. 3. File Dereplication Model Flow Graph in Process Algebraic Approach

The total communication between requesting node *Source* A and FRS$_1$ with internal actions (τ) will be given by equation 1 as follows:

$$SourceA \overset{\text{def}}{=} \overline{M_1}.M_3.\tau.SourceA \qquad (1)$$

Also as shown in Figure 3, communication between the two existing FRS in the architecture (FRS$_1$ and FRS$_2$) is described as follows: FRS$_1$ will send file size of the file to be replicated using $\overline{File\_size}$ which will be received at FRS$_2$ end by $File\_size$. When file size is received by FRS$_2$, it initiates dereplication operation on set of previously replicated files which will be represented by $\tau. derplicate\_file$, which is file dereplication with internal actions (τ). After the successful completion of dereplication operation, the required size for replication will be available on FRS$_2$. Now, FRS$_2$ will send 'ready to receive replicated file' message to FRS$_1$ represented through $\overline{M_4}$. FRS$_1$ received this message using M$_4$. After receiving the message, FRS$_1$ will send the file to be replicated to FRS$_2$ represented by message $\overline{M_2}$. FRS$_2$ will receive the file send by FRS$_1$ represented as M$_2$. When the file will be replicated successfully on FRS$_2$, it will send a message 'successful replication done' to FRS$_1$ by $\overline{M_5}$ which was received by FRS$_1$ using M$_5$.

As shown in Figure 3, FRS$_1$ and FRS$_2$ will act as source node and destination node respectively. From this, we can build the definition of FRS$_1$ and FRS$_2$ whichis defined as by the equation 2 and 3 respectively:

$$FRS_1 \overset{\text{def}}{=} M_1.\overline{File\_size}.M_4.\overline{M_2}.M_5.\overline{M_3}.FRS_1 \tag{2}$$

$$FRS_2 \overset{\text{def}}{=} File\_size.\tau.\overline{dereplicate\_file}.M_4.M_2.\overline{M_5}.FRS_2 \tag{3}$$

From the equations 1, 2 and 3, we can build the complete system as defined by the equation 4:

$$FDM \overset{\text{def}}{=} Source \parallel FRS \parallel Destination \tag{4}$$

5   Results and Discussion

To overcome from the overhead of space management issue, a data structure consisting of a table considered which is described in Table 1.

Table 1. Attributes

Attribute Name	Last Modification Date	Last Modification Time	File Name	File Size	File Replica
Type	yyyy-mm-dd	hh:mm	String	Long	Integer

Replicated files on the storage site will be sorted based on least recently used parameter which will be obtained using the combination of both last modification date and last modification time. The list of replicated files will be sorted in descending order. Example of a data structure of available files maintained at the storage site is described in Table 2.

Table 2. Data structure example for comparison between approaches

Last Modification Date	Last Modification Time	File Name	File Size (in MB)	File Replica
2011-12-21	20:08	a.mp3	3	4
2011-12-08	22:48	b.mp3	500	1
2011-11-23	16:36	c.mp3	100	2
2011-11-23	16:03	d.mp3	250	1
2011-11-09	20:11	e.mp3	50	1
2011-11-09	18:47	f.mp3	5	4
2011-11-09	18:43	g.mp3	10	2

The Figure 4 plots efficiency of all the three approaches versus load based on the data shown in Table 2 and the three approaches based on least recently used parameter, replica counts and file size parameters. Efficiency calculated is proportional to the reciprocal of extra memory size vacated during dereplication.

Unlike 2nd and 3rd approaches (i.e. number of replica available of a file basis and file size basis respectively), 1st approach(i.e. last modification time basis) is based only on least recently used parameter and disregards the replica counts and file size parameters. Thus it may even delete the last replica of file present in system. While 2nd approach is based on both least recently used and replica counts parameters and disregards the file size parameter. 3rd approach is based on all the three parameters, least recently used, replica counts parameters and file size parameter. Percentage efficiency of 2nd and 3rd approach is always better than 1st approach while in some cases percentage efficiency of 3rd approach is also better than 3rd approach. All the three approaches said to be 100% efficient only when space required before dereplication and after dereplication will be same.

Table 3. Dereplication time in required space

Number of Files dereplicated	Space Required (in MB)	Space Freed (in MB)	Dereplication Time (in msec)
1	6	6.0523	60
2	7.8607	13.1792	75
3	20.0399	21.0399	77
3	36.2634	39.7985	79
5	36.2634	59.7151	96
5	43.9405	51.0140	98

Dereplication time increases, as the number of files not accessed for the longest period and smaller in size, are more as compared to the files that are larger in size.Table 3 shows when the space required is same but the number of files to be dereplicated varies, dereplication time also varies depending on the number of files to be dereplicated. Dereplication time will be more for the case having large number of files.

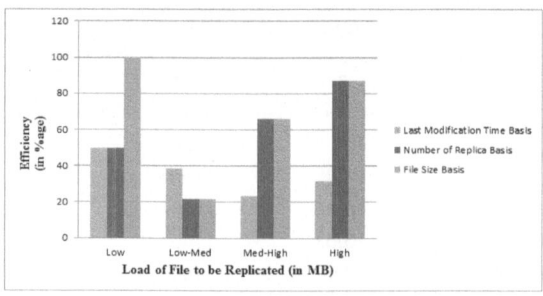

Fig. 4. Comparison of the Three Approaches

Table shows that if file size increases 7 times i.e. from 6 MB to 43.9405 MB, the increase in dereplication time is only 1.5 times i.e. from 60 milisec to 98 milisec. This shows that the dereplication time is decoupled from the size of files that are dereplicated dynamically and does not increase proportionally with respect to the file size.

6   Conclusion

This paper proposes approach that tackles the issue of space overhead in a distributed system environment. Proposed approach resolves this issue of space overhead. Dereplication time increases, as the number of files increasesthat are not accessed for the longest time period and smaller in size as compared to the files that are larger in size. Result shows that, in case when the space required is same but the number of files to be dereplicated varies, dereplication time also varies depending on the number of files to be dereplicated. Dereplication time will be more for the case having large number of files. If file size increases 7 times, the increase in dereplication time is only 1.5 times. This shows that the dereplication time is decoupled from the size of files that are dereplicated on the fly dynamically and does not increase proportionally with respect to the file size.

References

1. Kshemkalyani, A.D., Singhal, M.: Distributed Computing: Principles, Algorithms, and Systems, paperback edition, 756 p. Cambridge University Press (March 2011) ISBN: 9780521189842
2. Gupta, M., Ammar, M.H., Ahamad, M.: Trade-offs between reliability and overheads in peer-to-peer reputation tracking. Computer Networks 50(4), 501–522 (2006)
3. Venkatasubramanian, N.: CompOSE|Q - a QoS-enabled customizable middleware framework for distributed computing, Electronic Commerce and Web-based Applications/Middleware. In: 19th IEEE International Conference on Distributed Computing Systems, pp. 134–139 (1999)

4. Chou, C.-F., Golubchik, L., Lui, J.C.S.: Striping doesn't scale: how to achieve scalability for continuous media servers with replication. In: 20th International Conference on Distributed Computing Systems, pp. 64–71 (2000)
5. Venkatasubramanian, N., Deshpande, M., Mohapatra, S., Gutierrez-Nolasco, S., Wickramasuriya, J.: Design and implementation of a composable reflective middleware framework. In: 21st International Conference on Distributed Computing Systems, pp. 644–653 (April 2001)
6. Santry, D.S., Feeley, M.J., Hutchinson, N.C., Veitch, A.C., Carton, R.W., Ofir, J.: Deciding when to forget in the Elephant file system 33(5), 110–123 (1999)
7. Hurley, R.T., AunYeap, S.: File migration and file replication: a symbiotic relationship. IEEE Transactions on Parallel and Distributed Systems 7(6), 578–586 (1996)
8. Archibald, J., Baer, J.: Cache coherence protocols: evaluation using a multiprocessor simulation model. ACM Trans. Comput. 4(4), 273–298 (1986)
9. Hu, J., Xiao, N., Zhao, Y., Fu, W.: An Asynchronous Replica Consistency Model in Data Grid. In: Parallel and distributed processing and applications (ISPA 2005 Workshops), pp. 475–484 (2005)
10. Cabri, G., Corradi, A., Zambonelli, F.: Experience of Adaptive Replication in Distributed File Systems. In: IEEE Proc. of 22nd EUROMICRO Conf. on Beyond 2000: Hardware and Software Design Strategies, pp. 459–466 (1996)
11. Eason, G., Noble, B., Sneddon, I.N.: On certain integrals of Lipschitz-Hankel type involving products of Bessel functions. Phil. Trans. Roy. Soc. London A247, 529–551 (1955)
12. No, J.H., Park, C.W., Park, S.S.: Data Replication Techniques for Data-Intensive Applications. In: Alexandrov, V.N., van Albada, G.D., Sloot, P.M.A., Dongarra, J. (eds.) ICCS 2006, Part IV. LNCS, vol. 3994, pp. 1063–1070. Springer, Heidelberg (2006)
13. Guy, L., Kunszt, P., Laure, E., Stockinger, H., Stockinger, K.: Replica Management in Data Grids. Technical report, GGF5 Working Draft, Edinburgh, Scotland (July 2002)
14. Sun, Y., Xu, Z.: Grid Replication Coherence Protocol. In: The 18th International Parallel and Distributed Processing Symposium (IPDPS 2004) - Workshop, Santa Fe, USA, pp. 232–239 (April 2004)

Authentication and Authorization Interface Using Security Service Level Agreements for Accessing Cloud Services

Durgesh Bajpai, Manu Vardhan, and Dharmender Singh Kushwaha

Motilal Nehru National Institute of Technology Allahabad
Computer Science Engineering Department
Allahabad 211004, India
{is1023,rcs1002,dsk}@mnnit.ac.in

Abstract. Cloud computing is defined as delivering of computing resources as a service. Data security and access control are key components for any cloud service. The service level agreements are negotiated when service provider registers with an enterprise. This paper proposes an authentication and authorization interface to access a cloud service. Service selection is acquired via monitoring of security measures provided by a service provider through Security Service Level Agreements (Sec-SLAs). The enterprise and employee validation is performed through two level authentication mechanisms. Single sign on mechanisms for user and services makes the proposal more efficient. Features like denial of service, man in the middle attack and access control rights of employees are also handled. Security measures provided by service provider are handled by an enterprise, thereby, relieving the end user up to 20%-80% from the nitty-gritty of service providers in comparison to the approaches proposed in past, depending on application requirement.

Keywords: Authentication, Cloud, Denial of Service attack (DOS), Kerberos, Services, Service Level Agreement, Symmetric Encryption.

1 Introduction

Cloud computing has been envisioned as the next generation architecture of IT enterprise, due to its long list of unprecedented advantages in IT history. Problems like secure data storage, data transfer and access of data all depends upon the securing mechanisms used while using the cloud. Cloud consumers face various challenges such as security, privacy and discovery of reliable resource provider with the increase of public cloud providers.

A service level agreement (SLA) is maintained between the service provider and the consumer of the service about the quality parameters of the service which will be delivered by the service provider. In general SLAs consider the terms like packet loss,

M. Parashar et al. (Eds.): IC3 2012, CCIS 306, pp. 370–382, 2012.
© Springer-Verlag Berlin Heidelberg 2012

delay, throughput, etc. The security service level agreement (Sec-SLA) is a specific SLA that deals with metrics related to security instead of the traditional metrics of a service.

In the scenario as shown in Fig. 1where an enterprise wants to store its data on the cloud, to choose a right service provider is very critical. To eliminate the denial of service due to the traffic on a particular service provider, an enterprise registers with more than one service provider providing the same data storage as the service. Different service providers provide service with different security measures for example use different encryption mechanisms to store the data, thus provide different data confidentiality, integrity level.

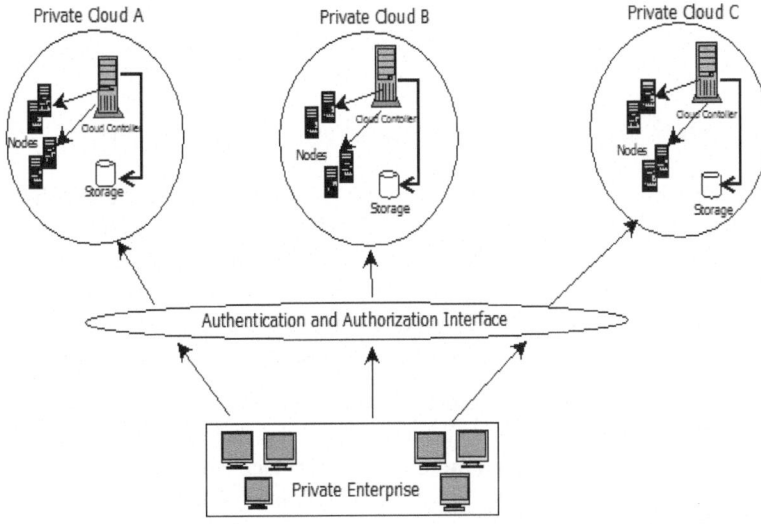

Fig. 1. Cloud computing Scenario

The security measures provided by the service provider has to be maintained by the help of the Sec-SLAs while using the service. Access rights are given to employees according to their role in an enterprise to access a service. For example an executive officer of an enterprise can access the data related to an enterprise policies but a database administer cannot.

A trusted third party plays the role of an authentication and authorization interface between an enterprise and cloud service provider to access a cloud service. In proposed approaches authentication tokens and passwords are used to access a cloud service by an end user. Message flow of previously proposed approaches while authenticating a user to access a cloud service is shown in Fig. 2.

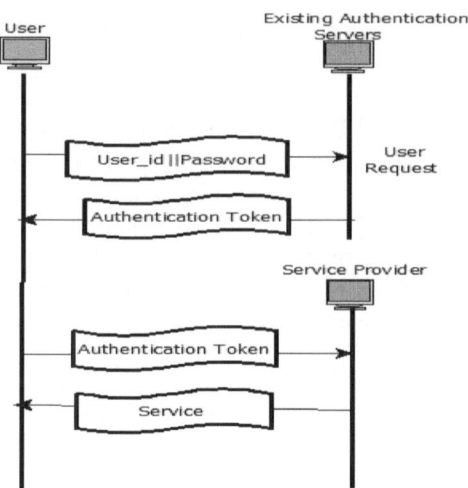

Fig. 2. Flow of control of messages in previously proposed models

A new authentication approach is proposed taking into account the security measures and their dynamic changes, provided by the service providers through the help of the Sec- SLAs. The proposed authentication and authorization interface is trusted third party trusted by the service provider and the enterprise. The access rights of an end user while accessing the cloud service are considered. The new approach tries to solve the following issues of previously proposed authentication approaches.

a.   In Pippal et al. [9] proposed approach the service authentication credentials are given to those employees also who don't have the access rights for the particular requested service. The possibility of denial of service attack increases, as service authentication credential granting server will get overloaded with the unauthorized employees demand.

b.   In Hota et al. [11] proposed model, an enterprise shares information regarding employee's credentials and access rights of employees with the service providers, proving as a source of leakage and misuse of employees information crucial to an enterprise.

c.   Authentication token is used in approach proposed by the Tao et al. [10] to resolve the problem of the single sign on of the user to access a service. If the same user wants to access the same service very frequently, the employee validity for the service is checked again and again through the authentication token, thus increasing the overhead.

d.   An employee has to check the trust level of a service provider before accessing the service. For this an employee should have all the information regarding the trust level and the features provided by a service provider increasing the load on an end user.

e.   Previously proposed models only consider SLAs while registering with cloud providers, don't consider security measures in general and their dynamic variations with time.

The rest of the paper is organized as follows. The next section discusses various related work done in the context of authenticating a user to access a cloud service and the service level agreements so far. Section 3 proposes a new trusted authentication and authorization interface between the service provider and an end user. In section 4 the proposed approach results are evaluated. The final section concludes the work followed by the references.

2   Related Work

Cloud Computing is the challenging area of research in IT field, many authors are working on it and tackling the various issues regarding the cloud. Cloud security is one of the more challenging one and need more attention as it is proving as a threat to the empowerment of the cloud computing. Chaves et al [1], Bernsmed et al. [2] and Kandukuri et al. [3] discusses the work done on the service level agreements and proposed an approach for the management of the service level agreements in the context of hybrid clouds. Authors discusses the security issues in the cloud computing and how they can be solved by the help of the service level agreements.

To fulfill the service requests in cloud, Ahuja et al. [4], Daniel and Lovesum [6] and Kubert and Wesner [7] discusses the usage of SLAs and their monitoring. Authors propose a service selection algorithm which allows re-provisioning of resources on the cloud in the event of failures. Author main focus is to provide a fair deal to the consumers, enhance quality of service delivered to the consumer as well as generation of optimal revenue. Clark et al. [5] proposed and designed a framework for secure and reliable monitoring of WS-Agreement specified service level agreements. In the Clark et al. framework WS-Agreement modifications are discussed as it is necessary for effective monitoring of service level agreements.

Liu et al. [8] and Pippal et al. [9] discuss approaches for mutual authentication and authorization, addressing the issue of establishing trust across heterogeneous domains. Pippal et al. [9] proposed a model CTES as an authentication and authorization module for the cloud. Through the CTES model they tried to overcome the problems associated with the Kerberos model like password guessing attack etc while using it in the cloud computing. Establishment of a trust across heterogeneous domains is very difficult due to different trust and security policies of different domains.

Tao et al. [10] discusses a generic authentication and authorization interface to allow the user to access the diverse Clouds in a unified way by the help of the authentication tokens. The proposed interface also combines different clouds enabling inter-cloud communications.

Hota et al. [11] addresses the challenge of data security and access control by using the capability based access control techniques. A modified Deffie-Hellman key exchange protocol was proposed by the Hota et al. [11] between the cloud service provider and the user for secretly sharing a symmetric key for secure data access. Zhang et al. [12] proposed a framework to ensure the data security in cloud storage system. Data storage safety issue is tried to address by dividing the various technologies to make the data storage safe roughly into the storage protect, transfer protect and authorize.

3   Proposed Approach

In the proposed model as shown in Fig. 3.an enterprise and the cloud service provider are present in different domains having different security policies. Assumptions made for the proposed model are:

- An employee is registered with his enterprise.
- A role is assigned to an employee and according to it the permissions to access a service that are registered with an enterprise.
- An enterprise is registered with the service providers which are providing the services of its need after negotiating the service level agreements.
- When an employee use a service, he records the security measures (like integrity of the data, backup frequency, reliability, confidentiality of the data, data store laws according to the domain) provided by the service provider and give feedback to the enterprise about the service provider.

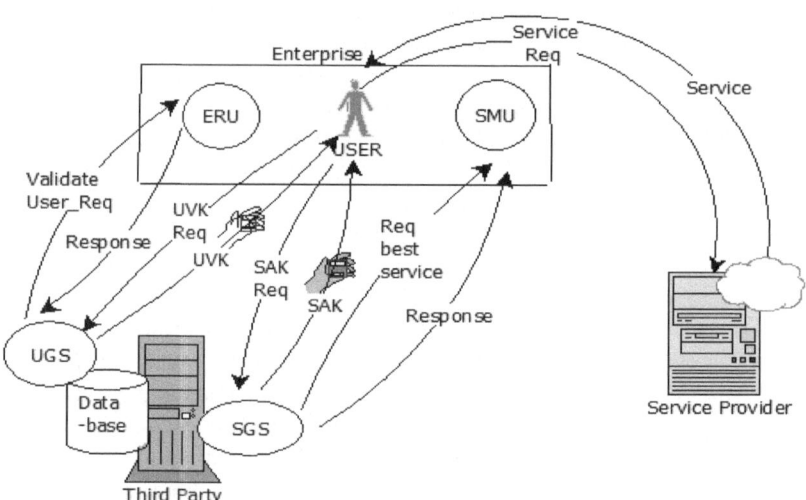

Fig. 3. Proposed Model

3.1   Proposed Model Units

The enterprise as shown in Fig. 3.consists of the following units:

Registry: Responsible for registering a service provider with an enterprise after negotiating the service level agreements.

Employee Registration Unit (ERU): An employee registers with an enterprise through this unit and it provides an employee with a unique employee id and a unique password. Records of employee credential (Password) are maintained, to check whether the employee is the registered employee of an enterprise or not before a user authentication credential i.e. User Validation Key (UVK) is granted.

Sec-SLA Management Unit (SMU): It keeps record of the security measures provided by the various service providers. A Sec-SLA is maintained about the service reliability, availability, backup frequency, data confidentiality, data integrity, domain where the data get store as the security policies change for different domains. Records of employee's access rights are maintained, to check the validity of employee to access a service, before a service access credential i.e. Service Access Key (SAK) is granted.

Third party authentication and authorization interface as shown in Fig. 3.consists of the following units:

User Validation Key Granting Server (UGS): It is responsible for granting UVK to an employee which works as an authentication token. The same authentication token can be used for single sign on till the lifetime of the UVK. Before granting the UVK, it takes the help of the Employee Registration Unit to validate an employee credentials as they are not shared with the third party because of security reasons. UVK is encrypted with the symmetric key K_u, known to the third party i.e. the authentication and authorization interface.

UVK: E (K_u [empid||special_code||timestamp|||lifetime||random_no])

Service Access Key Granting Server (SGS): It is responsible for granting a SAK to an employee to access a service after validating the UVK. Employee can use the same SAK to access the same service up to a certain time limit, till the SAK don't expire. SAK is encrypted with symmetric key Ks known to the third party i.e. the authentication and authorization interface and the service provider, shared between them initially by a secure procedure.

SAK: E (K_s [empid||special_code||timestamp|||lifetime||random_no])

3.2   Proposed Model Message Flow

In the Proposed model the message flows as shown in the Fig. 4. Total ten numbers of messages are required to access a service as described below.

1.   An employee sends a request to UGS for the UVK.
E→UGS: empid||password
2.   UGS asks the ERU for the validity of the employee.
3.   ERU returns a positive response if the employee pass correct credentials otherwise returns a negative response.
ERU→UGS: True/False
4.   UGS grants the UVK to the employee if the response of the ERU is true.
UGS→E: UVK
5.   Employee requests the SGS for SAK.
E→SGS: empid||special_code||UVK||serviceid
SGS verifies the validity of the UVK if its valid then goes to step 6.

6.   SGS requests the appropriate service provider reference from the SMU.
SGS→SMU: serviceid‖empid
7.   SMU gives the service provider reference to the SGS by checking out the security measures provided by the service providers and access rights of the employee.
8.   SGS grants the SAK to the employee for a particular service.
SGS→E: SAK
9.   The employee requests the service from the service provider.
E→SGS: SAK‖empid‖special_code‖serviceid
10.   The service provider checks the validity of the SAK and grants the service to the employee if SAK is valid.

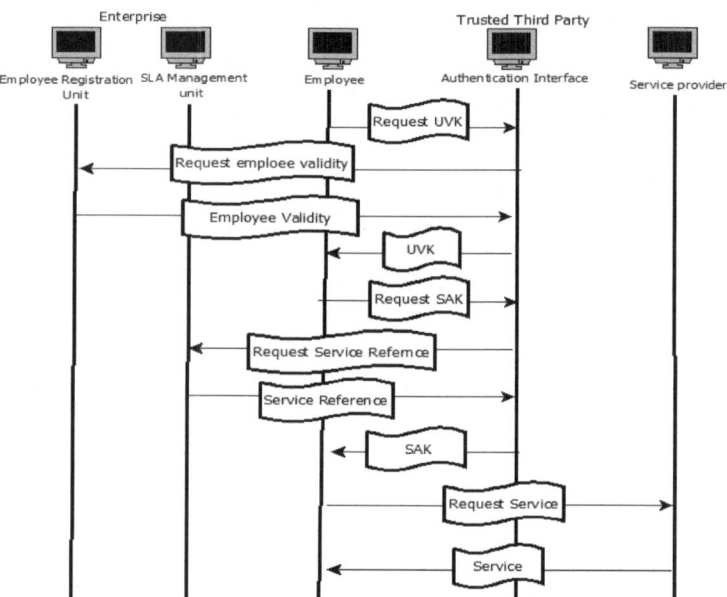

Fig. 4. Message flow sequence of the proposed model

3.3   Algorithms

A Rivest-Shamir-Adleman (RSA) based approach is used to make the UVK and SAK generation and validation algorithms more secure.

1.   Select two prime numbers p and q.
2.   n=p*q.
3.   φ (n) = (p-1)(q-1), where φ is Euler's Totient Function.
4.   Select an integer e such that $1 < e < φ(n)$ and greatest common divisor of (e, φ (n)) = 1, i.e. e and φ(n) are co prime, e will work as the public key.
5.   d = e-1 mod φ(n); i.e. d is the multiplicative inverse of e mod φ(n), where d will work as the private key.

Different private and public keys are generated and used for the SAK and the UVK generation and validation process. Private key d used for UVK is known to SGS and public key e used for UVK is known to UGS only. For SAK public key e_1 is known to the SGS and private key d_1 is known to the service provider providing the service for which the SAK is granted. A random number is included in the UVK and the SAK by the help of the d and e.

Algorithm to generate the UVK

1.   Generate a random number r, through random number generator function.
2.   K2= r^e mod n, by using standard cryptography Rivest-Shamir-Adleman (RSA) algorithm. Here e is the public key.
3.   Add a constant c. K3=K2+c.
4.   String=concatenation of the employee id and the special code passed by the user while requesting the UVK.
5.   Compute the substring KEY1 of 10 bytes from the symmetric key K_u using random number r.
6.   Encrypt the String with KEY1. enc = encrypt (KEY1, String).
7.   Compute Ticket1 i.e. the concatenation of the K3, current time T, lifetime L for which the UVK has to be valid and enc.
8.   Finally encrypt the Ticket1 with the symmetric key K_u to get the final authentication token UVK. UVK=encrypt (K_u, Ticket1).

Algorithm to check the validity of the UVK

1.   Decrypt the UVK with the symmetric key K_u . Ticket1= decrypt (K_u, UVK)
2.   Fetch the lifetime L and T from the Ticket1.
3.   Check the expiration of the lifetime of UVK by using the current time.
4.   Fetch K3 from the Ticket1.
5.   K2=K3- c
6.   r = $K2^d$ mod n; by using standard cryptography Rivest-Shamir-Adleman (RSA) algorithm. Here d is the private key.
7.   Compute KEY1 of 10 bytes from the symmetric key K_u using random number r.
8.   Fetch the enc from the Ticket1.
9.   Decrypt the enc with the KEY1, get the String. String= decrypt (KEY1, enc).
10.   Compare the String and the concatenation of the employee id and the special code provided by the user while using UVK. If both are same the UVK is valid otherwise not.

The algorithm to generate and validate the SAK is same as of UVK except the symmetric key K_s is used in place of K_u. K_s is shared between the service provider and the authentication and authorization interface initially by a secure means.

4   Results and Analysis

Number of Message. Proposed model uses total 10 numbers of messages for accessing a distributed cloud service. The comparison with other authentication models like Kerberos and Pippal et al. [9] based on the number of messages required to access a service is shown in Table 1. Based on the number of messages exchanged in different models, the load on the systems implementing the models due to message overhead varies as shown in the Fig. 5.

Table 1. Comparison based on the number of messages

		Kerberos	Pippal et al. Model [9]	Proposed Model
1.	Number of messages to get the User Authentication Key	2	4	4
2.	Number of messages to get the Service Access Key	4	6	8
3.	Number of messages to access the service	6	12	10
4.	Total number of messages	6	12	10

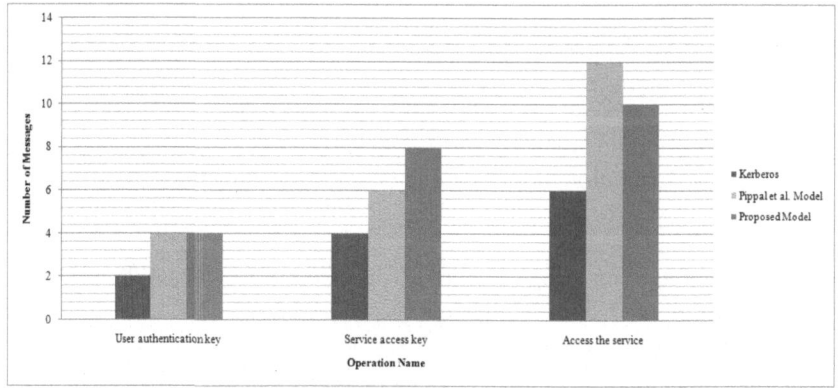

Fig. 5. Graph showing message overhead required in different models

In the proposed model the number of messages increases while acquiring the following benefits:

To acquire a user authentication credential i.e. UVK, two extra messages are used to validate the employee credentials by UGS as it takes help of the ERU, since the user credentials are stored at ERU only. This overcomes the problem of misusing the employee credentials by third party authentication and authorization interface, as they are stored at UGS and not shared with the third party.

To acquire a service access credential SAK, two extra messages are used to check the access rights of an employee and providing the reference of a service provider, considering security measures provided by the different service providers by SGS as it takes help of the SMU. This overcomes the chances of employee access rights alterations and misuse by third party authentication and authorization interface, a access rights of employees are stored at SMU and are not shared with the third party. All the information regarding the security measures provided by a service provider are handled by the SMU, thereby relieving the employee.

Implemented the proposed authentication and authorization interface with the help of the PHP, Apache server, MySQL and tried to measure the performance of the system, with the help of time required in acquiring the UVK, SAK and service by the employee.

Table 2. Average time required for acquiring keys and service

		UVK	SAK	Service
1.	In Proposed Model	30.666 sec	77.166 sec	114.833sec
2.	Without considering Sec-SLA and access rights and storing employee credentials at UGS	27.002sec	63.666 sec	97.667 sec

Security Service Level Agreements (Sec-SLAs)

Security measures provided by a service provider are handled by SGS without the intervention of an end user through the help of the Sec-SLAs, thereby relieving the end user of service providers as shown in Fig.6. in comparison to the Hota et al. [11] approach where all the information regarding a service provider are handled at the user end only. Selection of service provider is done by considering the Sec-SLAs maintained of different service providers.

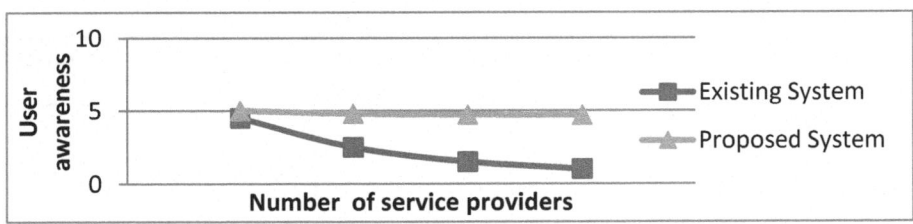

Fig. 6. Graph showing user awareness of service providers

Security Analysis

• *Denial of Service Attack (DOS):* Access rights of an employee for a particular service is checked before granting the SAK, the SAK granting server will not get overloaded by the requests of the unauthorized users, thus reducing DOS.

• *Access Control Rights:* Access rights of an employee are checked before providing him the SAK. Access rights are not shared with the authentication inter-face; there usage is done from the enterprise end only, increasing the trust level.

- *Man in the Middle Attack:* If a third person is able to capture SAK, then also he is not able to use that key because of the special code incorporated into the SAK known only to the valid user owning the SAK. A random number is used in SAK to make it more resistive from the security breaches.

- *Two Level Authentication:* Two level authentication is done at the authentication and authorization interface, first the enterprise authentication and after that the employee authentication.

- *Trust Level:* The user validation key (UVK) and service access key (SAK) are delivered by the use of a third party authentication and authorization interface trusted by both the service provider and the enterprise.

- *Encryption:* Encryption and decryption in the proposed model is used to encrypt and decrypt the UVK and the SAK with the help of the symmetric key. A RSA based asymmetric keys are also used to incorporate a encrypted random number into the UVK and SAK overcoming the issues of man-in-the middle attack. Use of symmetric and asymmetric keys while generating the UVK and SAK makes the proposed model more securely intact.

- *Security Measures:* The Security measures provided by a service provider and their dynamic change are considered in the proposed model while accessing a service.

- *Single sign on:* In the proposed model user authentication token UVK is used for user single sign on to authenticate the user, service authentication token SAK is used for the single sign on for a particular service making the approach more efficient.

On the various features a comparison of the proposed model with the Pippal et al. [9] and Tao et al.[10] proposed approaches is shown in Table 3.

The results show that the proposed model provides extra new features with the features already provided by the proposed models.

Table 3. Feature based comparison with previously proposed models

Particulars	Pippal et al. approach [9]	Tao et al. approach [10]	Proposed Model
User Single Sign on	Yes	Yes	Yes
Service Single Sign on	Yes	No	Yes
Checking of security Parameters	No	No	Yes
Adequate service registry Maintenance	Yes	Yes	Yes
Use of symmetric keys	Yes	Yes	Yes
Checking the access rights	No	Yes	Yes
Handling of Denial of Service Attack	No	No	Yes
Total	4	4	7

5   Conclusion

The proposed model explains the messages involved in the process of authenticating employees of an enterprise and providing them access of the distributed cloud services. The proposed model has been able to prove that it is more efficient than the previously proposed models. The trust is established between the end user and the service provider through the authentication and authorization interface. Access control rights of a user for a particular service are considered before granting the service access to the user of that service. Also to make the system more securely intact, the access rights are not shared with the authentication and authorization interface.

Security measures provided by a service provider are handled through the Sec-SLAs. Security measures are considered while referring the service to an end user in order to provide an end user more efficient cloud service. Denial of service attack, man in the middle attack and robustness of the system are efficiently handled by the proposed methodology that overcomes the drawbacks of previously defined models. In the initial authentication step enterprise handles the security measures provided by a service provider, thereby relieving the end user up to 80% from the nitty-gritty of service providers in subsequent phases as compared to the models proposed in the past that considers the handling of security measures through end users.

References

1. Chaves, S.A.D., Westphall, C.B., Lamin, F.R.: SLA Perspective in Security Management for Cloud Computing. In: Sixth International Conference on Networking and Services, pp. 212–217 (2010)
2. Bernsmed, K., Jaatun, M.G., Meland, P.H., Undheim, A.: Security SLAs for Federated Cloud Services. In: Sixth International Conference on Availability, Reliability and Security, pp. 202–209 (2011)
3. Kandukuri, B.R., Ramakrishna Paturi, V., Rakshit, A.: Cloud Security Issues. In: IEEE International Conference on Services Computing, pp. 517–520 (2009)
4. Ahuja, R., De, A., Gabrani, G.: SLA Based Scheduler for Cloud for Storage & Computational Services. In: International Conference on Computational Science and Its Applications, pp. 258–262 (2011)
5. Clark, K.P., Warnier, M.E., Brazier, F.M.T., Quillinan, T.B.: Secure Monitoring of Service Level Agreements. In: International Conference on Availability, Reliability and Security, pp. 454–461 (2010)
6. Daniel, D., Lovesum, S.P.J.: A novel approach for scheduling service request in cloud with trust monitor. In: Proceedings of 2011 International Conference on Signal Processing, Communication, Computing and Networking Technologies, ICSCCN, pp. 509–513 (2011)
7. Kubert, R., Wesner, S.: Service level agreements for job control in high performance computting. In: Proceedings of the International Multiconference on Computer Science and Information Technology, pp. 655–661. IEEE (2010)
8. Liu, P., Zong, R., Liu, S.: A new model for Authentication and Authorization across Heterogeneous Trust-Domain. In: International Conference on Computer Science and Software Engineering, vol. 03, pp. 789–792. IEEE Computer Society (2008)

9. Pippal, S.K., Kumari, A., Kushwaha, D.K.: CTES based Secure approach for Authentication and Authorization of Resource and Service in Clouds. In: International Conference on Computer & Communication Technology (ICCCT), pp. 444–449 (2011)
10. Tao, J., Marten, H., Kramer, D., Karl, W.: An Intuitive Framework for Accessing Computing Clouds. In: International Conference on Computational Science, ICCS, pp. 2049–2057 (2011)
11. Hota, C., Sanka, S., Rajarajan, M., Nair, S.K.: Capability-based Cryptographic Data Access Control in Cloud Computing. Int. J. Advanced Networking and Applications 03, 1152–1161 (2011)
12. Zhang, X., Hong-tao, D., Chen, J.Q., Lin, Y., Zeng, L.J.: Ensure Data Security in Cloud Storage. In: International Conference on Network Computing and Information Security, pp. 284–287 (2011)
13. Zhou, X., Tang, X.: Research and Implementation of RSA Algorithm for Encryption and Decryption. In: The 6th International Forum on Strategic Technology, pp. 1118–1121 (2011)
14. Alhamad, M., Tharam, D., Chang, E.: SLA-Based Trust Model for Cloud Computing. In: 13th International Conference on Network-Based Information Systems, pp. 321–324 (2010)
15. Sainan, L.: Task-role-based access control model and implementation. In: 2nd International Conference on Education Technology and Computer (ICETC), pp. 293–296 (2010)

A Non-iterative Learning Based Artificial Neural Network Classifier for Face Recognition under Varying Illuminations

Virendra P. Vishwakarma

Department of Computer Science and Engineering,
Jaypee Institute of Information Technology University,
Sector 128, Noida, Uttar Pradesh, India
`virendravishwa@rediffmail.com`, `vp.vishwakarma@jiit.ac.in`

Abstract. The performance of any face recognition system degrades severely under varying illumination conditions. In this paper, a new approach of face recognition under varying lighting conditions has been proposed, in which a non-iterative neural network based classification has been used. Adaptive histogram equalization along with logarithm transform has been used to enhance to face image contrast. Further, down scaling of low-frequency discrete cosine transform coefficients (LFDCT) has been applied to suppress the effect of variable illuminations. These illumination normalized face images have been recognized using a neural network classifier whose network parameters have been calculated analytically. The performance of the developed approach has been evaluated on Yale and CMU PIE face databases, which reveals significant performance improvement by our approach.

Keywords: Discrete cosine transform, face recognition, illumination normalization, neural network.

1 Introduction

Automatic face recognition by machines has emerged as one of the most successful applications of image analysis and understanding. This has attracted researchers from different disciplines such as image processing, pattern recognition, neural networks, computer vision, computer graphics and psychology. Major difficulties which may come across the automatic face recognition by machines; are primarily due to varying imaging conditions (lighting direction and viewpoint changes induced by body movement) along with other effects like facial expressions, aging, occlusions etc. [1], [2]. A face as a three-dimensional object, subject to varying constraints and it is to be identified based on its two-dimensional image, inherently limits the recognition rate [3].

Recognizing a 3D object from its 2D images generates many challenges. The illumination and pose problems are two prominent issues for appearance or image based approaches [3], [4]. Illumination is one of the most significant factors affecting the appearance of an image. It is the difference generated in frontal face images due to varying lighting conditions. The variations in illumination are the consequence of any

M. Parashar et al. (Eds.): IC3 2012, CCIS 306, pp. 383–394, 2012.
© Springer-Verlag Berlin Heidelberg 2012

variation in the positions and distribution of light sources, energy distribution of the ambient illumination, together with the 3D structure of the human face. These variations generate huge differences in the shading and shadows on the face. The shadows and highlights may change their position as the light intensity distribution varies. Such variations in the face appearance can be much larger than the differences between individuals [4], [5]. To solve the variable illumination problem, different approaches have been proposed [5]-[15]. These approaches can be broadly classified into two main categories. The first category is named as *passive* approach in which the visual spectrum images are analyzed to overcome this problem. The approaches belonging to other category named *active*, attempt to overcome this problem by employing active imaging techniques to obtain face images captured in consistent illumination condition, or images of illumination invariant modalities [16].

Different methods of *passive* approach can be broadly classified into three main categories. In first approach, the systems are exploiting "invariant feature extraction" method. A well established method for feature extraction is Fisher-face (based on linear discriminant analysis (LDA)), which maps the image space to a low dimensional subspace to ignore the variations in lighting etc. [6]. An illumination invariant signature image was generated using a bootstrap set [7]. This signature image is viewed as a quotient image, which can be used for face recognition under varying lighting conditions. This method needs a bootstrap database and the performance degrades when dominant features between the bootstrap set and the test set are misaligned. Second approach deals with face modeling methods which explores 3-D shape of human faces. Here the attempt is to construct a generative 3-D face model that can be used to render the face images with different poses and illuminations [5], [8]-[10]. A generative model called illumination cone was presented in [5], [8]. This method shows that an illumination convex cone can be constructed from a set of face images captured in fixed pose but under different illumination conditions. A low-dimensional linear subspace can be obtained by approximating this illumination cone. The measure drawback of model based approaches is that a training set containing face images of a subject under different lighting conditions is needed. Third approach is based on "preprocessing and normalization". The representative methods are histogram equalization, Gamma correction, logarithm transform, etc. for illumination normalization [3].

Based on discrete cosine transform (DCT), different approaches have been presented in [11]-[15] which efficiently handle the variable illumination problem. Discarding of low-frequency DCT coefficients in logarithm domain has been used by Chen et al. [11]. Input image contrast stretching was done by histogram equalization [12]-[14]. To suppress illumination variations, low-frequency DCT coefficients had been rescaled. Authors have shown very good recognition performance even with simple classification techniques [14]. For visual appearance enhancement, adaptive histogram equalization (AHE), logarithm transform along with down scaling of low-frequency DCT coefficients have been applied [15]. In these papers, the analyses had been performed on the databases which contain illumination variations only. With ample variations (illumination, pose, expression etc.) existing in the face images, the classification problem associated with face recognition is highly nonlinear and nonconvex. To deal with this, a good classification engine is required to be constructed. Artificial neural networks (ANN) based classifier can be used to resolve the nonlinearity imposed by different constraints of face recognition.

There are different variants of ANN based classifiers which are used for face recognition. For training of ANN, it mostly employs backpropagation (BP) algorithm. Using BP algorithm, the face recognition system can learn effectively on small training set. For large scale training set, it leads to slow convergence during the training and poor recognition rate. A variety of approaches are found to improve the performance of BP based classification [17], [18].

Haddadnia and Ahmadi used a hybrid N-feature neural network as an ensemble of classifiers, which extracts a set of different kind of features from face images with radial basis function networks. These are combined together for classification purpose through the majority rule. They have used three different feature domains for features extraction from input images [19]. Similarly in [20], in place of a single type of feature extractor and classifier, localized random facial features were constructed using internally randomized networks. The ensemble classifier was finally constructed by combining the multiple networks via a sum rule [20].

A hybrid neural network system for face recognition has been presented by Lawrence et al. which combine local image sampling, a self organizing map neural network and a convolutional neural network [21]. Similarly two variants of convolutional neural networks: neocognitron and NEO were used for face recognition in [22]. The topology of convolutional neural network is similar to that of biological networks and provides tolerance to local distortion. By weight sharing, the model complexity and number of weights is also efficiently reduced. It was found that both types of convolutional neural networks outperform the fully connected classifiers. Intrator et al. implemented a face recognition system using hybrid neural network based on supervised and unsupervised learning method [23]. BP network was integrated with fuzzy based feature extraction to utilize the feature-wise degree of belonging of patterns to all classes by Ghogh et al. [24].

In all the variants of neural network implementations, the network parameters are iteratively tuned to achieve the required performance index. These networks employ BP algorithm which is gradient descent based learning. The learning speed of this type of training algorithms is in general very slow. It leads to slow convergence during the training of the networks. Moreover, it suffers from some other issues like presence of local minima, imprecise learning rate, over fitting, and selection of number of hidden layer neurons.

To overcome the problem of iterative tuning based training algorithms, a new learning algorithm called extreme learning machine (ELM) has been proposed by Huang et al. [25]. The input weights and hidden layer neuron biases were arbitrarily (small random numbers) assigned. Though this makes fast learning speed, but the recognition rate varies with some standard deviation value. This makes the classification system nondeterministic. As the face recognition problem is highly non-linear and non-convex, ELM does not provide desirable performance, if the number of hidden layer neurons is small. To achieve less error rate, we require large hidden layer neurons for ELM. It also requires manual tuning for the number of hidden layer neurons to achieve faster training.

Authors have developed SLFN_BVOI learning algorithm for single-hidden layer feed forward neural network (SLFN), in which the input weights and biases are assigned from approximate basis vectors of input training space. The output weights and biases are decided through inverse operation on output matrix of hidden layer [26].

In this paper, we have done the performance evaluation of the proposed architecture which is an integration of illumination normalization technique and classification using a non-iterative learning algorithm (named SLFN_BVOI) based ANN classifier. The illumination normalization has been performed by rescaling of low-frequency DCT coefficient after preprocessing the input face images by AHE and logarithm transform. The experiments have been performed on the database which has all variations like pose and expression along with illumination variations.

The rest of the paper is organized as follows. The proposed architecture is described in Section 2. Section 3 presents the experimental results and discussions. Conclusions are drawn in Section 4.

2   Proposed Architecture of Face Recognition

The illumination variations are one of the significant factors affecting the performance of face recognition system. To solve this problem, AHE and logarithm transform have applied to increase the contrast of the input face images. Further, down scaling of low-frequency DCT coefficients has been done in order to suppress the effect of varying illumination. The classification has been performed using SLFN_BVOI. These modules have been explained in the following sub-sections.

2.1   Illumination Normalization

The face images captured under varying illumination may have low contrast. For contrast stretching, histogram equalization (HE) can be applied [27]. By histogram equalization, the local contrast of the object in the image is increased, especially when the usable data of the image is represented by close contrast values. Through this adjustment, the intensity can be better distributed on the histogram. This allows for areas of lower local contrast to gain a higher contrast without affecting the global contrast. The histogram equalization for a digital image is defined as a transformation on the input intensity levels (r_k) to obtain output intensity levels (s_k) as

$$s_k = T(r_k) = \sum_{j=1}^{k} p_r(r_j) = \sum_{j=1}^{k} \frac{n_j}{n} \tag{1}$$

for $k = 0, 1, 2, \ldots, L\text{-}1$.

Adaptive Histogram Equalization (AHE). In HE, the goal is to obtain a uniform histogram for the output image, so that an "optimal" overall contrast is perceived. However, the feature of interest in an image might need enhancement locally. AHE computes the histogram of a local window centered at a given pixel to determine the mapping for that pixel, which provides a local contrast enhancement. However, the enhancement can be so strong that two major problems may arise: noise amplification in "flat" regions of the image and "ring" artifacts at strong edges [28], [29].

A generalization of AHE, contrast limiting AHE (CLAHE) has more flexibility in choosing the local histogram mapping function. By selecting the clipping level of the histogram, undesired noise amplification can be reduced [30]. CLAHE operates on small regions in the image, called *tiles*, rather than entire image. Each tile's contrast is enhanced, so that the histogram of the output region approximately matches the histogram specified by a distribution parameter, which may be a uniform or a different shape histogram. The neighboring tiles are then combined using bilinear interpolation to eliminate artificially induced boundaries. The contrast, especially in homogeneous areas, can be limited to avoid amplifying any noise that might be present in the image.

Logarithm Transform. Logarithm transform is used to expand the values of dark pixels in an image as well as compressing the higher-level values [27]. If the values of pixels, before and after applying logarithm transform are denoted by r and s respectively, the relation between these values can be expressed by:

$$s = T(r) = c \log (1 + r) \tag{2}$$

where c is a positive nonzero constant. Due to logarithm operation, this transformation maps a narrow range of low intensity input values into a wider range of output levels and opposite mapping for higher values of input levels.

Illumination Normalization Using Discrete Cosine Transform (DCT). After HE, the illumination normalization has been performed based upon the relation of low-frequency DCT coefficients with illumination variations. The forward 2D-DCT [27] of a $M \times N$ block image is defined as:

$$C(u, v) = \alpha(u)\, \alpha(v) \sum_{x=0}^{M-1} \sum_{y=0}^{N-1} f(x, y) \times \cos\left[\frac{\pi(2x + 1)\, u}{2M}\right] \cos\left[\frac{\pi(2y + 1)\, v}{2N}\right] \tag{3}$$

The inverse transform is defined as

$$f(x, y) = \sum_{u=0}^{M-1} \sum_{v=0}^{N-1} \alpha(u)\, \alpha(v)\, C(u, v) \times \cos\left[\frac{\pi(2x + 1)\, u}{2M}\right] \cos\left[\frac{\pi(2y + 1)\, v}{2N}\right] \tag{4}$$

where
$$\alpha(u) = \begin{cases} \dfrac{1}{\sqrt{M}}; & u = 0 \\[2mm] \sqrt{\dfrac{2}{M}}; & u = 1, 2, ..., M\text{-}1 \end{cases}, \quad \alpha(v) = \begin{cases} \dfrac{1}{\sqrt{N}}; & v = 0 \\[2mm] \sqrt{\dfrac{2}{N}}; & v = 1, 2, ..., N\text{-}1 \end{cases}$$

x and y are spatial coordinates in the image block, u and v are coordinates in the DCT coefficients block. Although the total energy remains the same in the $M \times N$ blocks, the energy distribution changes with most energy being compacted to the low-frequency coefficients. We have taken the DCT coefficients in zigzag pattern [12], [14]. DCT is performed on the entire image obtained after processing the input face images by CLAHE along with logarithm transform. The first 6 low-frequency DCT coefficients is divided by a constant 50 [14]. After taking inverse DCT on the processed DCT coefficients, the illumination normalized face image is obtained, which is used for classification.

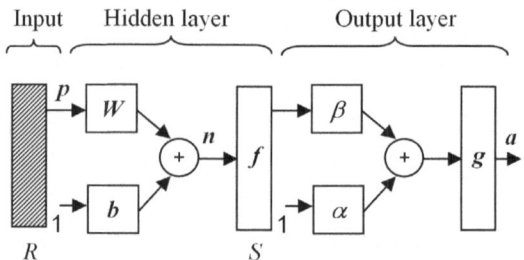

Fig. 1. Architecture of single hidden layer feedforward neural network

2.2   Classification Using SLFN_BVOI

Classification is a very crucial step in any pattern recognition application. ANN based classifier can be used to resolve the nonlinearity imposed by different constraints of face recognition. A multi layered feedforward neural network or simply feedforward neural network has *layers,* or subgroups of processing elements. A layer of processing elements makes independent computations on data that it receives and passes the results to another layer. Each processing element makes its computation based upon a weighted sum of its inputs. The first layer is the input layer and the last one is the output layer. The layers that are placed between the first and the last layers are the hidden layers. It has been shown by Tamura and Tateishi that the feedforward neural network with single hidden layer containing S neurons with arbitrarily chosen input weights can learn S distinct observations with arbitrarily small error [31]. Fig. 1 shows the architecture of SLFN with S hidden neurons. In supervised learning [17] of an ANN, a set of examples which represent proper network behavior is applied to the network:

$$\{p_1, t_1\}, \{p_2, t_2\}, \ldots, \{p_Q, t_Q\} \tag{5}$$

Here $p_q = [p_{q1}, p_{q2}, \ldots, p_{qr}, \ldots, p_{qR}]^T \in \Re^R$ is   an   input   to   the   network,   and $t_q = [t_{q1}, t_{q2}, \ldots, t_{qm}, \ldots, t_{qM}]^T \in \Re^M$ is the corresponding target. In appearance-based approach of face recognition, the input patterns are generated from training face images. All pixel values are read line by line to form an input pattern which is a column vector in $\Re^R$ dimensional real space. Here R is the total number of pixels or extracted features from the face image. p_{qr} is the intensity value of rth pixel or r^{th} feature value in the qth face image.

A Non-iterative Learning Algorithm (SLFN_BVOI) Based ANN Classifier

The detailed description of the non-iterative learning algorithm named SLFN_BVOI can be found in [26], its brief overview has been given here. Given a training set given by Equation (5) with Q arbitrary distinct samples $\{(p_i, t_i)$; for an SLFN with Q number of hidden layer neurons; and f as activation function for hidden layer; the SLFN can approximate these Q samples with zero error, if there exist β_i, w_i and b_i such that

$$\sum_{i=1}^{Q} \beta_i f(w_i^T . p_j + b_i) = t_j, \forall j = 1, 2, ..., Q; \tag{6}$$

Here w_i vector composed of the elements of ith row of input weight matrix W, such that $w_i = [w_{i1}, w_{i2}, ..., w_{ir}, ..., w_{iR}]^T$ w_{ir} is the weight of the connection between i^{th} neuron in hidden layer and r^{th} input.. The input weight matrix W is defined as

$$W = [w_1^T, w_2^T, ..., w_i^T, ..., w_S^T]^T \tag{7}$$

In SLFN_BVOI learning algorithm W has been obtained as

$$W = (cl^{1/2} P^T) / \| P^T.P \| \tag{8}$$

$$\text{and } b_i = \sum_{j=1}^{R} w_{ij} = E[w_i] \tag{9}$$

In Equation (8), $P = [p_1, p_2, ..., p_q, ..., p_Q]$ is the input matrix and input vector $p_q \in \Re^R$ represents the qth face image of training set. c is a positive constant and $\| . \|$ denotes the norm operation. l represents the number of training sample per class, i.e. the number of face images per subject used for training.

The Q equations given by Equation (6) can be rewritten compactly as:

$$H\beta = T \tag{10}$$

$$\text{where } H = \begin{bmatrix} f(w_1^T.p_1 + b_1) & \cdots & f(w_Q^T.p_1 + b_Q) \\ \vdots & & \vdots \\ f(w_1^T.p_Q + b_1) & \cdots & f(w_Q^T.p_Q + b_Q) \end{bmatrix} \tag{11}$$

$$\text{and } T = \begin{bmatrix} t_1^T \\ \vdots \\ t_Q^T \end{bmatrix} \tag{12}$$

The least square solution $\hat{\beta}$ of the linear system given by Equation (10) can be obtained with the help of Moore-Penrose generalized inverse [32] as

$$\hat{\beta} = H^* .T \qquad (13)$$

where H^* is Moore-Penrose generalized inverse of matrix H.

SLFN_BVOI learning algorithm can be given as:

Step 1: Assign the input weight w_i and bias b_i from approximate basis vector of input space P given by Equations (8) and (9); for $i = 1, 2, ..., Q$.

Step 2: Calculate the hidden layer output matrix H given by Equation (11).

Step 3: Determine the output weight matrix $\hat{\beta}$ using Equation (13) after calculating H^*.

3   Experimental Results and Discussions

To evaluate the proposed architecture, the experiments have been conducted on Yale face database [33]. The error rate variations have been calculated on this database for finding the performance improvement. Two set of experiments are performed, one with database image are used without illumination normalization and other with illumination normalization. The experiments are performed on the laptop pc with 1.73 GHz core 2, duo processor by using MATLAB 7.0.1.

3.1   Yale Face Database

There are 165 gray scale images of 15 subjects in GIF format in this database [33]. Original image size is 320 × 243 pixels. All images are manually cropped to include all internal structures (forehead with hairs, eye brow, eyes, nose, and mouth). After cropping the image size becomes 220 × 175 pixels. These images are further sub-sampled by 1.6 to get a resolution of 137 × 109 pixels. Fig. 2 shows all subjects of this database along with face images of subjects 1 and 2. As can be seen, the main challenge on this database is facial expressions (normal, happy, sad, sleepy, surprised, and wink), occlusion (with/without glasses) and misalignment along with illumination variations.

3.2   Illumination Normalization

The effect of contrast stretching and illumination normalization has been shown in Fig. 3. An example image has been shown in Fig 3(a), which is one of the images of subject one under non-uniform illumination. Fig. 3(b) and Fig. 3(c) show the output after CLAHE only and CLAHE along with logarithm transform respectively. To obtain bell shaped histogram of the input images, CLAHE has been applied with a distribution parameter as *'rayleigh'* in MATLAB function *adapthisteq*.

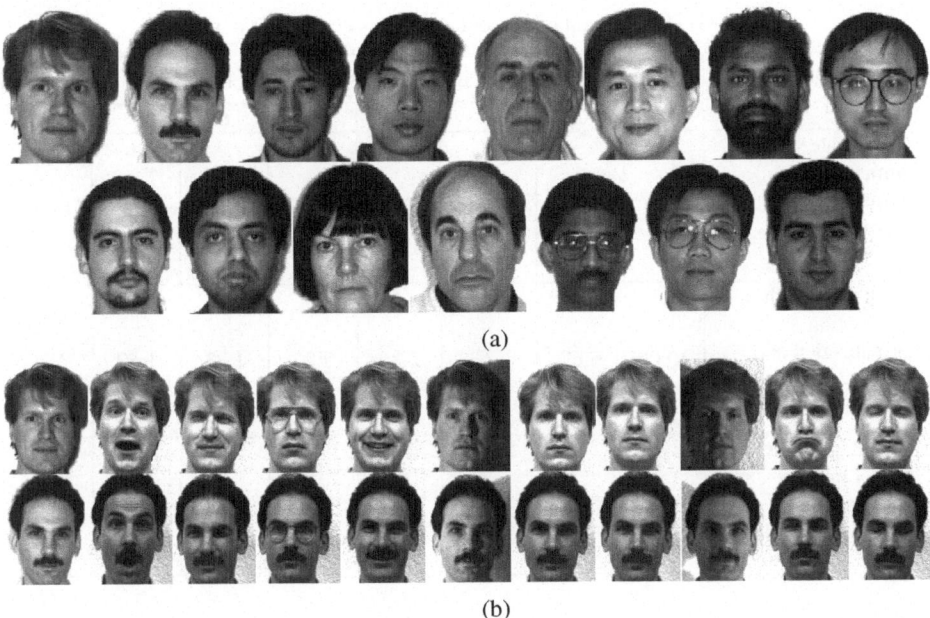

(a)

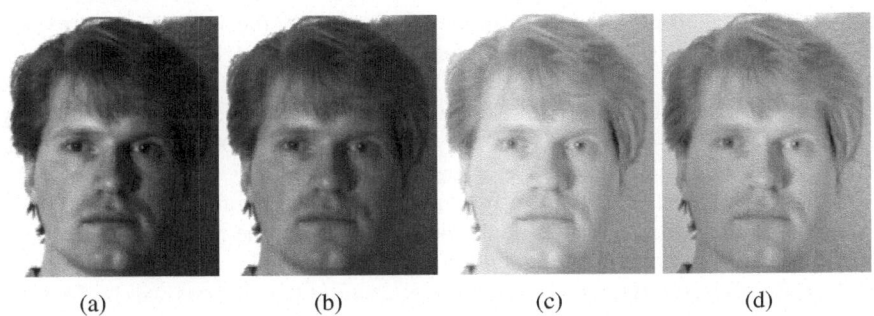

(b)

Fig. 2. (a) All subjects in Yale face database (b) subjects 1 and 2 under different variations from Yale face database

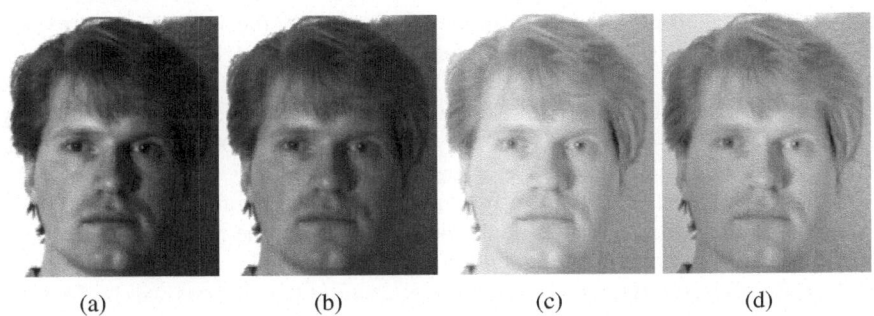

   (a)   (b)   (c)   (d)

Fig. 3. (a) An example image (Subject 1 under non-uniform illumination (b) after CLAHE; (c) after CLAHE along with logarithm transform; and (d)after CLAHE, logarithm transform and down scaling of 6 LFDCT coefficients

After CLAHE and logarithm transform, a high contrast image is obtained as shown in Fig. 3(c). But it is also visible from Figures 3.1(a), 3.1(b), 3.1(c) that the illumination variations are slightly affected. The illumination normalization is performed in DCT domain. It was shown by authors that that the illumination variations corresponds to mainly low-frequency DCT coefficients [12], [14]. The illumination normalization means to remove the effect of illumination variations on the low-frequency DCT coefficients as well as to retain the low-frequency details of a subject. This has been achieved by dividing the first 6 low-frequency DCT coefficients by a constant 50, as this database comprises small illumination variations.

Table 1. Comparison of percentage error rate on Yale database

% Error Rate and % Reduction	Number of images per subject used for training							
	1	2	3	4	5	6	7	8
% error rate without illumination normalization and classification by SLFN_BVOI	46.00	14.81	12.50	12.38	13.33	10.67	13.33	17.78
% error rate with illumination normalization and classification by SLFN_BVOI	30.00	6.67	6.67	2.86	2.22	1.33	1.67	2.22
Percentage reduction in error rate by illumination normalization with this classification	34.78	55.00	46.67	76.92	83.33	87.50	87.50	87.50

3.3   Error Rate Variations

Table 1 shows the percentage error rate variation with different size of training set. The size of training set is varying based on number of images per subject used for training. If we take one image per subject for training, the training set size is 15, similarly for two images per subject; the training set size is 30 and so on. The remaining images of the database are used for testing. The images are taken sequentially from database to build training set and test set, i.e. if number of images per subject for training is four, then the first four images per subject are used in training set and remaining seven images are used for testing.

The classification has been done using the neural network trained with SLFN_BVOI learning algorithm, which has been elaborate above. Here, the number of hidden layer neurons is assigned from the training set size. For example, if only one image per subject is used for training, then the number of training face images will be 15 for this database and that is the number of hidden layer neurons in SLFN_BVOI. The maximum number of hidden layer neurons is 120 for present investigation of SLFN_BVOI corresponding to 8 images per subject used for training. The activation function for the neurons in hidden layer has been chosen as *radial basis* (*radbas*) function.

The percentage error rate decreases as the number of images per subject used for training, increases. The percentage reduction in error rate by illumination normalization is also listed in Table 1. There is significant reduction in percentage error rates, when the database images are illumination normalized. The average reduction in error rate is 69.9%.

4   Conclusion

This paper presents a new architecture for face recognition system, when face images contains different variations along with illumination variations. First six low-frequency

DCT coefficients are scaled down by a factor 50 to compensate the effect of varying illumination, after processing the input face images by CLAHE along with logarithm transform. To handle other variations present in the database, classification has been performed using a non-iterative learning algorithm based ANN classifier. Experimental results show the effectiveness of illumination normalization with classification system using this ANN classifier.

References

1. Chellappa, R., Wilson, C.L., Sirohey, S.: Human and machine recognition of faces: a survey. Proc. IEEE 83(5), 705–740 (1995)
2. Zhao, W., Chellappa, R., Phillips, P.J., Rosenfeld, A.: Face Recognition: A Literature Survey. ACM Computing Surveys 35(4), 399–458 (2003)
3. Li, S.Z., Jain, A.K.: Handbook of Face Recognition. Springer (2005)
4. Phillips, P.J., Moon, H., Rijvi, S.A., Rauss, P.J.: The FERET Evaluation Methodology for Face-Recognition Algorithms. IEEE Trans. Pattern Anal. Mach. Intell. 22(10), 1090–1104 (2000)
5. Belhumeur, P.N., Kriegman, D.J.: What is the set of images of an object under all possible illumination conditions. International Journal of Computer Vision 28(3), 245–260 (1998)
6. Belhumeur, P.N., Hespanha, J.P., Kriegman, D.J.: Eigenfaces versus Fisherfaces: recognition using class specific linear projection. IEEE Trans. Pattern Anal. Mach. Intell. 19(7), 711–720 (1997)
7. Shashua, A., Riklin-Raviv, T.: The quotient image: class-based re-rendering and recognition with varying illuminations. IEEE Trans. Pattern Anal. Mach. Intell. 23(2), 129–139 (2001)
8. Georghiades, A.S., Belhumeur, P.N., Jacobs, D.W.: From few to many: illumination cone models for face recognition under variable lighting and pose. IEEE Trans. Pattern Anal. Mach. Intell. 23(6), 630–660 (2001)
9. Basri, R., Jacobs, D.W.: Lambertian reflectance and linear subspaces. IEEE Trans. Pattern Anal. Mach. Intell. 25(2), 218–233 (2003)
10. Zhang, L., Samaras, D.: Face recognition under variable lighting using harmonic image exemplars. In: Proc. IEEE Int. Conf. on Computer Vision and Pattern Recognition, vol. 1, pp. 19–25 (2003)
11. Chen, W., Joo, M., Wu, S.: Illumination Compensation and Normalization for Robust Face Recognition using Discrete Cosine Transform in Logarithm Domain. IEEE Trans. on Systems, Man, and Cybernetics-Part B: Cybernetics 36(2), 458–466 (2006)
12. Vishwakarma, V.P., Pandey, S., Gupta, M.N.: A Novel Approach for Face Recognition using DCT Coefficients Re-scaling for Illumination Normalization. In: Proc. IEEE 15th International Conference on Advanced Computing & Communication (ADCOM 2007), pp. 535–539 (December 2007)
13. Vishwakarma, V.P., Pandey, S., Gupta, M.N.: Illumination Normalization under Varying Illumination Conditions using Artificial Neural Network. In: Proc. 3rd International Conference on Advance Computing & Communication Technologies, pp. 455–460 (November 2008)
14. Vishwakarma, V.P., Pandey, S., Gupta, M.N.: An Illumination Invariant Accurate Face Recognition with Down Scaling of DCT Coefficients. Journal of Computing and Information Technology 18(1), 53–67 (2010)

15. Vishwakarma, V.P., Pandey, S., Gupta, M.N.: Adaptive Histogram Equalization and Logarithm Transform with Rescaled Low Frequency DCT Coefficients for Illumination Normalization. International Journal of Recent Trends in Engineering 1(1), 318–322 (2009)

16. Zou, X., Kittler, J., Messer, K.: Illumination Invariant Face Recognition: A Survey. In: Proc. of 1st IEEE Int. Conf. on Biometric: Theory, Application and Systems, pp. 1–8 (2007)

17. Haykin, S.: Neural Networks—A Comprehensive Foundation, 2nd edn. Prentice-Hall (1999)

18. Hagan, M.T., Demuth, H.B., Beale, M.: Neural Network Design. Thomson Learning (2002)

19. Haddadnia, J., Ahmadi, M.: N-feature neural network human face recognition. Image and Vision Computing 22(12), 1071–1082 (2004)

20. Choi, K., Toh, K.A., Byun, H.: A Random Network Ensemble for Face Recognition. In: Tistarelli, M., Nixon, M.S. (eds.) ICB 2009. LNCS, vol. 5558, pp. 92–101. Springer, Heidelberg (2009)

21. Lawrence, S., Giles, C.L., Tsoi, A.C., Back, A.D.: Face Recognition: A Convolutional Neural Network Approach. IEEE Trans. Neural Networks 8(1), 98–113 (1997)

22. Neubauer, C.: Evaluation of Convolutional Neural Networks for Visual Recognition. IEEE Trans. Neural Networks 9(4), 685–696 (1998)

23. Intrator, N., Reisfeld, D., Yeshurun, Y.: Face Recognition using a Hybrid Supervised/Unsupervised Neural Network. Pattern Recognition Letters 17(1), 67–76 (1996)

24. Ghosh, A., Shankar, B.U., Meher, S.K.: A novel approach to neuro-fuzzy classification. Neural Networks 22, 100–109 (2009)

25. Huang, G.B., Zhu, Q.Y., Siew, C.K.: Extreme Learning Machine: A New Learning Scheme of Feedforward Neural Networks. In: Proc. Int. Joint Conf. on Neural Networks, Budapest, Hungary, pp. 985–990 (July 2004)

26. Vishwakarma, V.P., Gupta, M.N.: A New Learning Algorithm for Single hidden Layer Feedforward Neural Networks. International Journal of Computer Applications 28(6), 26–33 (2011)

27. Gonzalez, R.C., Woods, R.E.: Digital Image Processing. Pearson Education (2006)

28. Pratt, W.K.: Digital Image Processing. John Wiley & Sons, New York (2001)

29. Stark, J.A.: Adaptive Image Contrast Enhancement Using Generalizations of Histogram Equalization. IEEE Transactions on Image Processing 9(5), 889–896 (2000)

30. MATLAB reference manual (2004),
    http://www.mathworks.com/access/helpdesk/help/toolbox/images

31. Tamura, S., Tateishi, M.: Capabilities of a Four-Layered Feedforward Neural Network: Four Layers Versus Three. IEEE Trans. Neural Networks 8(2), 251–255 (1997)

32. Israel, A.B., Greville, T.N.E.: Generalized Inverses: Theory and Applications, 2nd edn. Springer, New York (2002)

33. Yale face database (1997),
    http://cvc.yale.edu/projects/yalefaces/yalefaces.html

DDoS Detection with Daubechies

Gagandeep Kaur[1], Vikas Saxena[1], and J.P. Gupta[2]

[1] Deptt. of CSE and IT, JIIT, Noida, UP, India
{gagandeep.kaur,vikas.saxena}@jiit.ac.in
[2] Sharda University, Gr. Noida, UP, India
jaip.gupta@gmail.com

Abstract. Now a days the Internet has become common man's communication channel and due to that ensuring security at all levels has become tedious.Denial of Service (DoS) attacks have grown to give rise to Distributed Denial of Service (DDoS) attacks. Due to the open access of Internet the software tools for generating bots are easily available. This has increased the span of DDoS. The traditional methods of DDoS detection fail to detect this emerging breed of attacks. In the recent past Shannon entropy analysis has been done for detection of intrusions in the computer network. Shannon entropy however has limitations in failing to detect attacks of very short duration. Generalized form of Non extensive Tsallis entropy has been tested to look into weaknesses of Shannon entropy. Secondly, there has been growth in the area of application of wavelets to signal processing. Because of their inherent nature wavelets beautifully capture the nature of traffic at multiple scales. We have tried to use Daubechies wavelets to measure Tsallis entropy with different moments and have detected the sudden changes induced in the traffic pattern because of DDoS attacks.

Keywords: Self similarity, Non Extensive Tsallis Entropy, Wavelets, DDoS.

1 Introduction

The Internet is growing at an unprecedented rate. With its wide spread use amongst network users it has become the favorite platform for network criminals and hackers. The number of intrusions into computer systems is growing and raising concerns about computer security. The ever increasing list of Computer Emergency Research Team (CERT) [1] is proof enough of the urgency to look out for robust security mechanisms. Anomaly detection refers to looking for the abnormal behavior of data in a signal. The principal challenge in automatically detecting and classifying anomalies is that anomalies can span a vast range of events and even to new, previously unknown events. An anomaly detection system should therefore be able to detect not only the anomalous behaviour of data in the signal but shall also be able to categorize them.Considered as an alternative to the traditional network anomaly detection approaches or a data preprocessing for conventional detection approaches, recently signal processing techniques have been successfully applied to the network anomaly detection due to their ability in point change detection and data transformation [2, 16].

M. Parashar et al. (Eds.): IC3 2012, CCIS 306, pp. 395–406, 2012.
© Springer-Verlag Berlin Heidelberg 2012

2   Related Work

V.Alarcon-Aquino and J.A.Barria brought in the application of Wavelets into Network Intrusion Detection [3]. Many of the approaches rely on known statistical properties of normal traffic when the observed traffic deviates significantly from the normal behavior. Initial line of Intrusion Detection Systems (IDSs) used spectral techniques. Current applications of spectral techniques look for high-frequency occurrences to identify anomalous behavior [4] [5]. The wavelet tool allows a single signal to be decomposed in several signals representing different frequencies. High frequencies indicate spontaneous behavior by traffic while low frequencies exhibit global behavior by traffic. Methods of detection involve finding global and local variances in wavelet coefficients to detect respective short and long-term anomalies. Hussain et al. [7] apply spectral techniques to time series of packet arrival times. Based on spectral characteristics, they are able to distinguish between single- and multi-source attacks, and identify repeat attacks. Barford et al. use wavelets to analyze Simple Network Management Protocol (SNMP) and flow-level information to identify DoS attack and other high frequency anomalies [4]. Magnaghi et al. detect anomalies within TCP flows using a wavelet-based approach to identify network misconfigurations [8]. Spectral techniques have also been employed to identify bottleneck links [9] and routing information. G. Bartlett et al. in [14] look at periodicity between flows to identify hosts which maintain regular contact while considering low frequency behavior under long observation windows and use iterated filtering for full decomposition. Carl et al. in [10] applied wavelets transform for detecting change-points in the Cumulative SUM (CUSUM) statistic. Hamdi and Boudriga in [11], Xunyi et al. in [12], Dainotti et al. in [19] devise wavelet techniques for detecting DoS attacks. Lu et al. in [13] study intrusion detection performance with wavelet basis functions and state their impact on detection mechanisms.

3   Self Similarity, Energy and Wavelets

3.1   Long Range Dependence

The self similarity or long range dependence (LRD) of network traffic was found by Leland et al. [15] in 1993. The degree of self-similarity is measured with Hurst parameter, H [23]. The essence of self-similarity is that the same pattern is repeated at different levels of aggregation by time sequences. Therefore, if an object is self-similar, its parts, when magnified, resemble-in a suitable sense-the shape of the whole. All self-similar phenomena have two properties: a) there is pattern at the smallest of smallest scales. b) The pattern repeats. Therefore, a self-similar process contains replicas of itself at different scales. On the other hand stochastic process says that even if the initial condition is known, there are many possibilities the process might go to, but some paths may be more probable than the others. Therefore, we need to look out for stochastic nature of network traffic and self-similarity property of it. Network traffic does not possess exact resemblance of their parts with the whole at finer details. If we adopt a view that traffic series are sample paths of stochastic processes and relax the measure of resemblance of the rescaled time series, then it may be possible to expect similarity of mathematical object. Second order statistics are statistical properties that capture burstiness or variability, and the autocorrelation function is a vital parameter with respect to which scale-invariance can be defined.

Let $X=\{X(t), t \ \varepsilon \ \mathbb{Z}\}$ be a wide-sense stationary process with constant mean μ finite variance σ^2 and autocorrelation function $r(k)$ that depends only on $k, (k \ \varepsilon \ \mathbb{Z})$. Their measures as in [22] [24] can be calculated as $\{\mu = E[X(t)]\}$, $\{\sigma^2 = E[X(t) - \mu)]^2\}$ and $\{r(k) = \frac{E[(X(t)-\mu)(X(t+k)-\mu)]}{\sigma^2}\}$.

Let $X^{(m)} = \{ X^{(m)} (t), t \ \varepsilon \ \mathbb{Z}_+$ denote the aggregate process of X at aggregation level m, $m \ \varepsilon \ \mathbb{Z}_+$. That is, for each m, $X^{(m)}$ is given by $\{X^{(m)(t)} = \frac{1}{m} \sum_{l=m(t-1)+1}^{mt} X(l), t\epsilon\mathbb{Z}_+\}$ where V^m and $r^{(m)}(k)$ denote the variance and the auto correlation function of $X^{(m)}$, respectively. The second-order stationary process X is called *exactly second-order self-similar* with $\{H = 1 - \frac{\beta}{2}\}$ if its auto correlation function is $\{r(k) = g(k), k\epsilon\mathbb{Z}_+\}$ where $\{k\hat{=}\frac{[(k+1)^{2-\beta}-(2k)^{2-\beta}+(k-1)^{2-\beta}]}{2}\}$ and $\{0 < \beta < 1, k\epsilon\mathbb{Z}_+\}$.

Process X is called *long range dependent (LRD)* with $H=1-\frac{\beta}{2}$, $0<\beta< 1$ if its autocorrelation function satisfies $\{r(k) \sim ck^{-\beta}, k \rightarrow \infty\}$ where c is a positive constant. X is called strong *asymptotical second-order self-similar* with $H=1-\frac{\beta}{2}$, $0<\beta< 1$, if the variance of $X^{(m)}$ satisfies $V^m \sim cm^{-\beta}$, $m \rightarrow \infty$ where c is a positive constant. X is called *asymptotical second-order self-similar* with $H=1-\frac{\beta}{2}$, $0<\beta< 1$, if $lim_{m\rightarrow\infty}r^{(m)}(k) = g(k), k \ \epsilon \ \mathbb{Z}_+$.

3.2   Entropy

The Internet in its present size [29] is very complex. This system is difficult to measure and analyze. On the other hand statistical methods have proved to be useful in aggregation methods and analysis. Entropy statistics are one such measure. Entropy in general measures level of disorder in a system. A sudden increase or decrease in the system disperses its energy and hence increases its entropy. An entropy analysis of wavelet coefficients can therefore be used for attack detection. The three most popular entropies are Shannon, Renyi and Tsallis. The Shannon entropy $H(X)$ of a random variable X with a discrete probability distribution $p_i = p_1, p_2, \ldots, p_k$ is given by $\{H(X) = - \sum_{i=1}^{k} p_i \log_2 p_i\}$. Renyi entropy is given by $\{R_\alpha(X) = \frac{\log \sum_{i=1}^{k} p_i^\alpha}{1-\alpha}\}$ where $\sum_{i=-1}^{k} p_i = 1$ and $\lim_{\alpha\rightarrow 1} R_\alpha(X) = H(X)$. The Renyi divergence can be used as a measure of auto correlation. It is based on joint and marginal probabilities. However, the Renyi divergence cannot be expressed purely in terms of entropy, as it is in Shannon entropy. Other generalized entropy Tsallis entropy is given by $\{S_\alpha(X) = \frac{1-\sum_{i=1}^{k} p_i^\alpha}{1-\alpha}\}$ where $\alpha \geq 0$ and $\lim_{\alpha\rightarrow 1} S_\alpha(X) = H(X)$. It has been observed and quoted in [17] and [25]that Tsallis entropy is better suited to deal with non-Gaussian measures, which are well-known to characterize Internet traffic, while Shannons entropy is better adapted to Normal distributions. Tsallis has been successfully applied to various problems such as fractal random walks, complex high energy processes, cosmic rays, turbulence, earthquakes, stock markets and income, non linear maps at the edge of chaos, stochastic resonance, protein folding and biomolecules, citation networks of scientific papers, urban agglomeration, and linguistics [18]. Tsallis has a well defined concavity for all the values of α, being concave when $\alpha > 0$ and convex when $\alpha < 0$. It is important to note that using Shannon entropy; events with high or low probability do not have different weights in the entropy computation. However, using Tsallis entropy, for $\alpha > 1$, events with high probability contribute more than low probabilities ones for the entropy value.

Abe and Suzuki in their work [18] have studied the self similar behavior of ICMP ping packets with non extensive Tsallis entropy for time scales ranging from 10min to 1hr.They conclude that the network undergoes a series of transitions from one stationary state to another. Each state is scale invariant and maximizes the Tsallis entropy. The points of transition correspond to catastrophic changes in the time series e.g sudden-heavy congestion. Tsallis entropy statistics are therefore quite usefull for defining stationary states in the time series exhibited by complex systems.

Karmeshu and Sharma in their work [21] have discussed some of the salient features of non-extensive Tsallis entropy. They have given the Tsallis entropic framework in the context of network traffic characterization as an alternative approach to model the phenomenon of LRD. That in turn helps to study its impact on network performance and gain a better insight into the quality of service parameters e.g. network bandwidth attacks.For further details the reader can refer to [21].

3.3   Wavelet Transform and Entropy Measurement

Wavelets are an excellent tool suitable for long discrete data sequences. As per definition, any signal can be decomposed by using a dyadic discrete family $\{2^{\frac{j}{2}}\psi(2^j t - k\}$ which is an orthonormal basis in $L^2(\mathbb{R})$. The translation (k) and scale (j) functions are based on mother wavelet (ψ). Wavelet analysis therefore defines a collection of nested subspaces V_j that satisfy $\{\ldots V_{-2} \subset V_{-1} \subset V_0 \subset V_1 \subset V_2 \ldots\}$ where $\{\cup_{j\epsilon \mathbb{Z}} V_j = L^2(\mathbb{R}) and \cap_{j\epsilon \mathbb{Z}} V_j = \phi\}$.

The wavelet transform can therefore be represented as a pyramidal combination of low-pass (L_0) and high-pass (H_0) filters derived from scaling function and mother wavelet chosen for transformation. The outputs of the low-pass are termed as approximations $(Approx)$ and outputs from high-pass are termed as details (det). An input signal can therefore be represented in terms of wavelet function ψ and scaling function ϕ based on the given dilation equations:

$$\phi_{j,k}(t) = 2^{\frac{-j}{2}}\phi_0(2^{-j}t - k), k\epsilon \mathbb{Z} \tag{1}$$

$$\psi_{j,k}(t) = 2^{\frac{-j}{2}}\psi_0(2^{-j}t - k), k\epsilon \mathbb{Z} \tag{2}$$

The $Approx$ is given by $approx_j(t) = \sum_k a_x(j,k)\phi_{j,k}(t)$ and det is given by $detail_j(t) = \sum_k d_x(j,k)\psi_{j,k}(t)$.

Hence signal can be written as:

$$x(t) = approx_N(t) + \sum_{j=1}^{N} detail_j(t) = \sum_j a_x(N,j)\phi_{N,j}(t) + \sum_{j=1}^{N}\sum_k d_x(j,k)\psi_{j,k}(t)$$
(3)

Where $d_x(j,k)$ is the Discrete Wavelet Transform (DWT) of $x(t)$. We know from [22], [24] and [31] that for mean-zero stationary stochastic processes the variance of the DWT is $\{Ed_x^2(j,k) = \int_{-\infty}^{\infty} \Gamma(2^{-j}v) \mid \hat{\psi}(v) \mid^2 dv\}$ where $\{\hat{\psi}(v) = \int \psi(t)e^{-j2\pi vt}dt\}$.

For LRD processes the equation becomes $\{Ed_x^2(j,k) \sim 2^{j\alpha}C(\psi,\alpha),\}$ where $\{C(\psi,\alpha) = \int \mid v \mid^{-\alpha} \mid \hat{\psi}(v) \mid^2 dv\}$. Energy associated with every resolution can be estimated by performing time average of wavelet detail coefficients at a given resolution j, $E_j = \sum_k \mid d_x(j,k) \mid^2$. Similarly, for a signal of length N, the mean wavelet energy at resolution j comes out to be $\tilde{E}_j = \frac{\sum_k E\mid d_x(j,k)\mid^2}{N_j}$, where $j = 1,\ldots,\log_2 N$. From the wavelet energy and the total wavelet energy $\sum_j E_j$, relative wavelet energy has been calculated by [20] and is computed as $p_j = \frac{E_j}{E_{tot}}$ and the relative temporal average wavelet energy as $\tilde{p}_j = \frac{\tilde{E}_j}{\tilde{E}_{tot}}$. Remember that Tsallis entropy $S_\alpha(X) = \frac{1-\sum_{i=1}^{k}p_i^\alpha}{1-\alpha}$ is well suited for systems with long-range dependence. Applying the above wavelet average energy equations to Tsallis entropy equation Tsallis wavelet entropy for LRD processes can be calculated as $S_\alpha(X) = \frac{1-\sum_{j=1}^{k}(\frac{E_j}{E_{tot}})^\alpha}{1-\alpha}$.

3.4 Distributed Denial-of-Service (DDoS) and Pulsating Distributed Denial-of-Service Attacks (PDDoS)

In a computer network a denial of service (DoS) attack tries to degrade the quality of service available to the legitimate users. Distributed Denial of Service (DDoS) uses large number of DoS to attack the service providers from distributed nodes. Therefore DDoS attacks are very lethal and hamper the services within seconds of their deployment [30]. More recently a new breed of DDoS attacks has been discovered and is named as Low-rate DDoS attacks or LDoS [32]. Pulsating DoS or PDoS is a similar variation of the former attack. In LDoS instead of flooding the communication channels with large number of packets timed packet pulses of small duration are sent to the target machine.

Because there is sudden increase in the number of packets for a short duration of time these pulses help the attacker to disrupt TCP services. When combined with distributed architecture, these pulses of still shorter duration can be so generated such that on reaching their target the impact is very high number of packets for short duration. The challenge in detecting attacks of this kind is that the duration of the pulse is very small and hence the detection module has to be not only accurate but fast as well. Since Tsallis entropy is able to detect the sudden changes in the flow at different scales therefore we can use wavelet Tsallis entropy to detect slaughtering by DDoS attacks and can stop them.

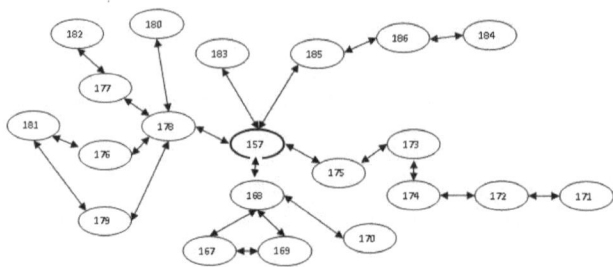

Fig. 1. Zoom in at nodes connected to the gateway node and the bottleneck link

4 Simulation Model

The works by Mirkovic in [26] have been referred to for creating the test environment. There are total of 200 nodes following three level hierarchies: domain, cluster, and nodes generated with GT-ITM topology generator. The edge nodes are host nodes and intermediate nodes act as access routers and core routers. Access routers are connected to core routers. Links between core to core routers are of 100Mbps, core to access router are of 10 Mbps and access router to edge nodes are of 5Mbps with edge probability of 0.85. Backbone link delays are of 0s. Figure 1 shows the simulation topology. The system consists of following components:

Clients We discuss two main cases.
Case 1: There are two types of clients in our network. Majority of the clients are legitimate users of the service whereas a small number of clients are illegitimate users or the attackers. According to [29] the traffic is application-based and more than 90 percent of it consists of web and P2P. We therefore have application-based traffic between legitimate clients and server from ftp, voip and http. There are three types of legitimate clients. Firstly, the clients that run FTP application on TCPReno(a type of TCP implementation), second ones are VoIP application and third ones are web based service based on HTTP. We used the following modules in NS-2 to generate the traffic: Pagepool/Webtraf for Web, Pagepool/Webtraf with *pagesize_* for ftp, UDP packets of packetsize 210 with burst time of 180ms and idle time of 50ms to simulate VoIP traffic. The attack traffic has been simulated using CBR packets following the bot attack pattern as per Moore [27].

Case 2: We have TCP senders $C_1 - to - C_n$ and attackers from $A_1 - to - A_n$. All senders and attackers have one sink S. The traffic goes through bottleneck link R1-R2-S. Bottleneck link bandwidth is 10Mbps and all other links have 100Mbps bandwidth. The start time of each TCP sender is a random variable uniformly distributed from 0 to 1500s. The attackers begin to send pulses at 20s and stop at 1000s. We have used traffic trace to simulate train of square pulses [32]. The size of attack packet is 50 bytes. As shown in Figure 2 the attacker nodes send small cooperative pulses such that when their pulses reach the router the combined effect is one large burst of traffic that inundates the router. The simulations were carried out for low, medium and high traffic rates. Different scenarios were studied for 5,20,50 and 100 DoS flows. Burst lengths consisted of 50, 100, 150 and 200ms for periods ranging from 2500 to 200,000ms.

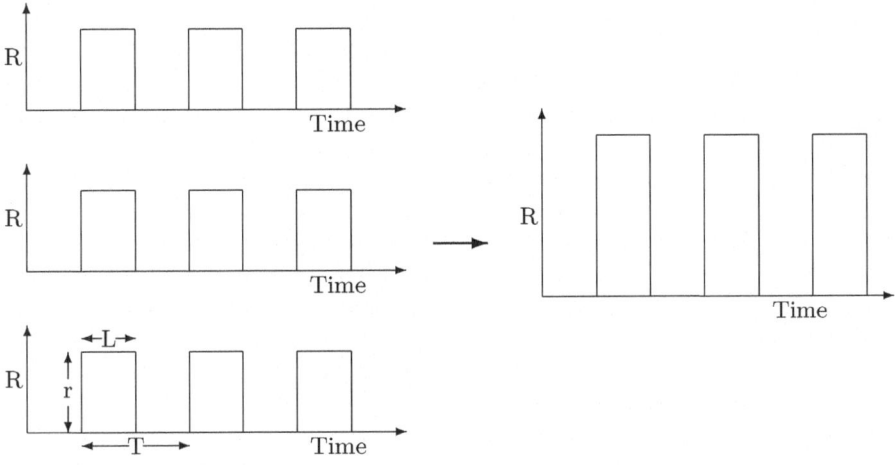

Fig. 2. Pulses from attacker nodes

Server. The simulation parameters for server side are mentioned below:
Case 1&2: The server provides generic TCP-based service. During normal scenario the legitimate clients connect to the server and avail satisfactory services from the server. When the network is under attack the zombies either send flooding packets or pulsating pulses towards the server and hence the network suffers congestion in its bottleneck links. Because of heavy amount of traffic on the links the routers drop packets. Since congestion control protocols are meant to tackle loss of packets in order to provide quality of service therefore their services are most affected due to packet loss. As a result the throughput decreases.

5   Detection Methodology

Our objective in this work is to detect DDoS attacks. We propose our detection methodology for the same. We have used Tsallis-entropy based detection mechanism for attack detection.The simulation is run for the required amount of time and trace file is obtained for the ingress traffic at the access router.The aggregated data values are output to the trace file every 10ms and stored in the tuple format $< timestamp, no.of bytes >$.The sampling sliding window is of 10ms and for each window Tsallis entropy is calculated.

5.1 Detection and Characterization of the Attacks

Detection of Attacks. Let us define total incoming traffic at the server as $ser\_tot(t)$ then we can say it to be equal to normal incoming traffic $normal(t)$ and incoming attack traffic $attack(t)$. Hence we can write it as : $ser\_tot(t) = normal(t) + attack(t)$ where t is time. Under normal conditions the incoming server traffic is due to regular legitimate users only but during attack this traffic is comprised of both normal traffic and DDoS traffic.

Mathematically, we can define the incoming traffic as a random process $\{X(t),$ $t = j\triangle, j\epsilon N, \triangle \epsilon N\}$, where $\triangle$ is a constant sliding factor, N is set of positive integers and for each $t, X(t)$ is a random variable. Here $X(t)$ represents count of incoming bytes of network traffic in $\{t - \triangle, t\}$ interval.

Phase I: We know that network traffic exhibits long range dependence and hurst parameter H is a measure of self-similarity. Under normal circumstances the network traffic follows the self similar behavior which can be measured with H. Whereas in the case of DDoS attacks the LRD nature of the traffic changes because DDoS attacks and their detection are short-range phenomena. It is because of the fact that the attackers emit packet bursts and attack the target for short periods of time only. This in turn changes the traffic behavior which deviates from the self-similar nature.

Let us consider the incoming traffic at the server as discrete time series of length P. Divide it into N non overlapping sections. Each section is divided into M non overlapping segments. Divide each segment into K non overlapping blocks. Each block is of L length. Let $m(n)$ be the hurst value at aggregation level L in the segment of the section ($m = 0, 1, \ldots, M - 1; n = 0, 1, \ldots, N - 1$). The H values for all the segments of the series are never the same so we can find the average H value $H(n)$ within a confidence interval. When the system is under attack we represent the changed hurst value as $H(c)$.

Let us assume that at time t_a the attackers start emitting attack packets and as a result the system comes under attack. We can therefore say that before time t_a the system is under normal state and is in attack state after that. Let t_D denote our estimate on t_a. At time t_D we have total incoming traffic at server as $serv_{tot}(t_D) = normal(t_D) + attack(t_D)$. As a result following event triggers attack detection:

$$\varphi > \delta \qquad attack\ detected \qquad (4)$$

where $\varphi = \parallel H_n - H_c \parallel$ represents the deviation of H of monitored traffic time series and $\delta > 0$ is threshold.

However $\Gamma = \parallel H_n - H_l \parallel > \delta$ means false alarm.

Phase II: For a given incoming traffic we generate a signal and find out the wavelet energy at resolution level j for the time window i as $\tilde{E}_j^{(l)} = \frac{\sum_{k=(i-1).L+1}^{i.L} C_j^2(k)}{N_j}$ with $i = 1, \ldots, N$, where N_j represents the number of coefficients at resolution j corresponding to time window i, whereas total energy estimator in this time window is $\tilde{E}_{tot}^{(l)} = \sum E_j^{(i)}$. The wavelet energy at resolution j is $< E_j > = \frac{\sum_{i=1}^{N} E_j^{(i)}}{N}$. Total wavelet energy average is therefore given as $< E_{tot} >= \sum < E_j >$.We can now find p as $p = \frac{<E_j>}{<E_{tot}>}$,with $\sum p_j = 1$. The corresponding Tsallis entropy can now be calculated as $S_\alpha(X) = \frac{1-\sum_{i=1}^{k} p_i^\alpha}{1-\alpha}$ for given values of α. The values of Tsallis entropy vary from 0 (maximum concentration) to S_α^{max} which indicates maximum dispersion, where $S_\alpha^{max} = \frac{1-k^{1-\alpha}}{\alpha-1}$. We know that when the system is under no threat the Entropy $< E_j >$ values at different scales j do not vary much and thus, traffic exhibits self-similar property. We take average of E_j and designate it as $< E_{tot}(n) >$. However during attack the self-similar nature of the traffic changes. To detect the on start of attack the changed entropy $S_c^\alpha(X)$ can be measured and whenever there is appreciable deviation from $S_n^\alpha(X)$ the system is considered under attack.

5.2   Pre Test Experiments

Wavelet Selection. We used data sets of Lawrence Berkeley Laboratory (lbl-pkt-4) [28] to choose an appropriate wavelet for our work. The trace captured on Fri 21, Jan94 is one hour long and has 1.3 million packets.We did extensive tests for 10ms sampling window with Wavelets family of Coiflet, Mexlet, Haar,Symlet and Daubechies. Based on the tests it was realized that Daubechies performs better to other wavelets. The H values for Db3 to Db18 were obtained as 0.829747, 0.817425, 0.801689, 0.813604, 0.819814, 0.810229, 0.797133, 0.802043, 0.808398, 0.80307, 0.790789, 0.798109, 0.79824, 0.791681, 0.791417 and 0.795235 respectively.We shortlisted Db6 for our experiments.

Selecting Scaling Parameter α. In order to select our scaling parameter α for computation of Tsallis entropy we performed large number of simulations for α values from $[-2, -1.75, -1.5, \ldots, 1.5, 1.75, 2]$ and shortlisted α to be -1.5 to 1.5 for our experiments.

5.3   Wavelet Entropy Visualizer

To be able to use the wavelet detail coefficients at different levels along with values of the Tsallis entropy scaling parameter   for detection of low rate as well as high rate DDoS attacks we introduce a new visualization method called Wavelet Entropy Visualizer (WaEV). The WaEV is a two axis plot that plots the entropy values over time (horizontal axis) and for different levels of resolution j (vertical axis). The entropy values have been mapped to a color range to view events ranging from low activity to high activity.

In total we tested approximately 56 variations of attacks for normal TCP flow.

6   Results and Discussion

Figure 3 $(a), (b)$ and (c) show the WaEV outputs for time periods 1200s to 1600 s. In our simulation the DDoS attacks start at 1300s . As we can see there is change in color of the bars from dark grey to light grey to almost white and so we can see the start of attack.Because of space constraint it is difficult to show

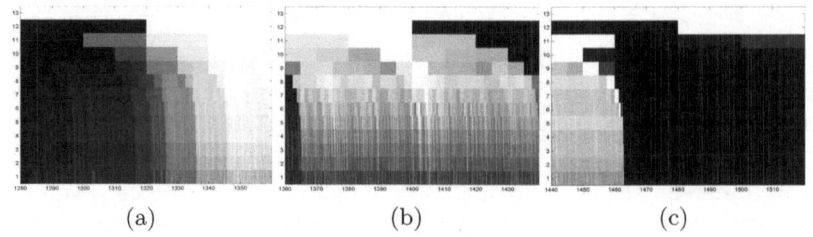

(a)   (b)   (c)

Fig. 3. WaEV outputs of Case 1

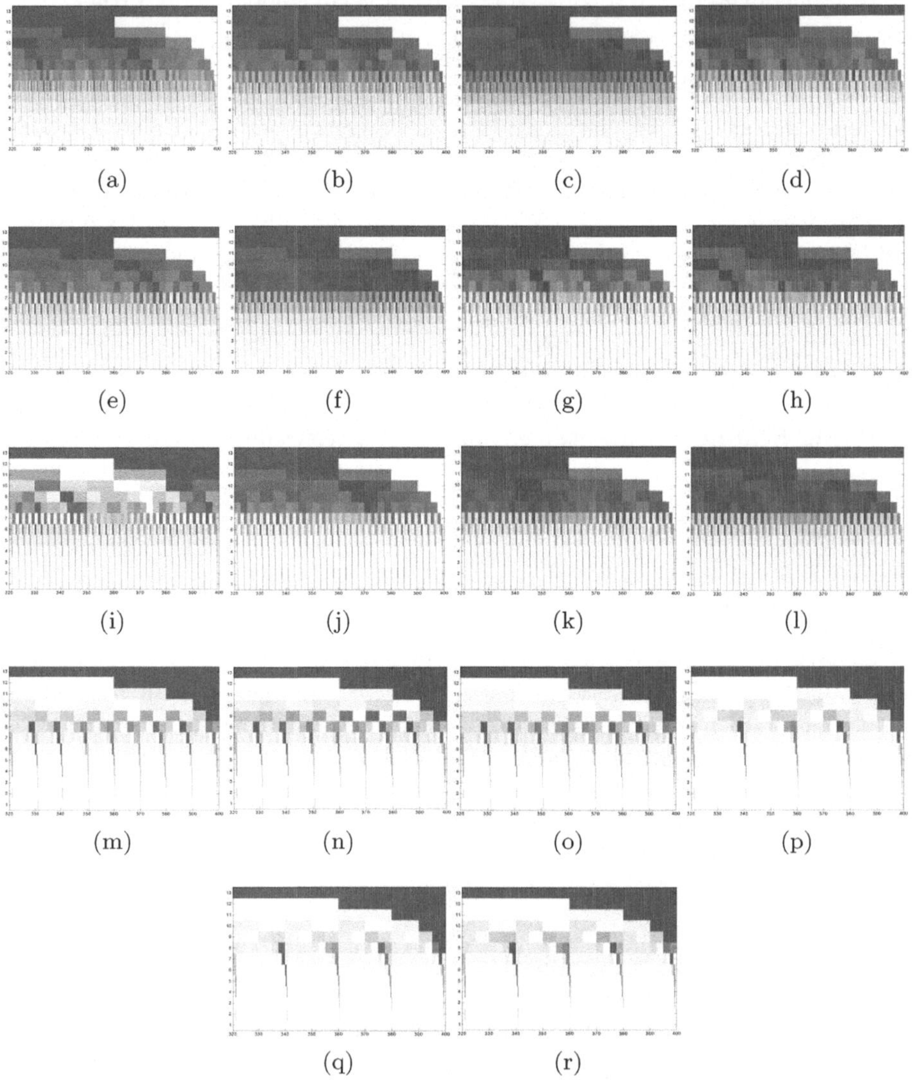

(a)   (b)   (c)   (d)

(e)   (f)   (g)   (h)

(i)   (j)   (k)   (l)

(m)   (n)   (o)   (p)

(q)   (r)

Fig. 4. WaEV outputs of Case 2

and discuss all the generated scenarios for case 2. Figure 4 has thumbnails for following outputs that we received through WaEV. Figure 4 (a), (b) and (c) are of 20/40/80 TCP 5 DoS 50 length 2500 period; (d), (e) and (f) are of 20/40/80 TCP 5 DoS 100 length 2500 period; (g), (h) and (i) are of 20/40/80 TCP 5 DoS 150 length 2500 period; (j), (k) and (l) are of 20/40/80 TCP 5 DoS 200 length 2500 period; (m), (n) and (o) are of 20/40/80 TCP 50 DoS 50 length 10000 period; (p), (q) and (r) are of 20/40/80 TCP 100 DoS 50 length 20000 period.

7   Conclusion

Wavelets can be successfully used for visualization of computer network traffic and detection of anomalous behavior in the traffic.

References

1. CERT.: Overview of Dos and DDoS attacks,
   http://www.us-cert.gov/cas/tips/ST04-015.html
2. Lu, W., Ghorbani, A.A.: Network Anomaly Detection Based on Wavelet Analysis. EURASIP Journal on Advances in Signal Processing 2009, 1–17 (2009)
3. Alarcon-Aquino, V., Barria, J.A.: Anomaly Detection in Communication networks using wavelets. In: IEE Proceedings-Communications, pp. 355–362 (2001)
4. Barford, P., Kline, J., Plonka, D., Ron, A.: A signal analysis of network traffic anomalies. In: ACM SIGCOMM Proceedings Internet Measurement Workshop (2002)
5. Cheng, C.M., Kung, H.T., Tan, K.S.: Use of spectral analysis in defense against DoS attacks. In: IEEE GLOBECOM Proceedings, pp. 2143–2148 (2002)
6. Limthong, K., Kensuke, F., Watanapongse, P.: Wavelet-Based Unwanted Traffic Time Series Analysis. In: IEEE International Conference on Computer and Electrical Engineering, pp. 445–449 (2008)
7. Hussain, A., Heidemann, J., Papadopoulos, C.: Identification of repeated denial of service attacks. In: Proceedings of the IEEE Infocom, pp. 1–15 (2006)
8. Magnaghi, A., Hamada, T., Katsuyama, T.: A Wavelet-Based Framework for Proactive Detection of Network Misconfigurations. In: Proceedings of ACM Workshop on Network Troubleshooting (2004)
9. He, X., Papadopoulos, C., Heidemann, J., Mitra, U., Riaz, U.: Remote detection of bottleneck links using spectral and statistical methods. In: ACM International Journal of Computer and Telecommunications Networking, pp. 279–298 (2009)
10. Carl, G., Brooks, R.R., Rai, S.: Wavelet based denial-of-service detection. ELSEVIER Journal on Computers & Security 25, 600–615 (2006)
11. Hamdi, M., Boudriga, N.: Detecting denial-of service attacks using the wavelet transform. ELSEVIER Computer Communications 30, 3203–3213 (2007)
12. Xunyi, R., Ruchuan, W., Haiyan, W.: Wavelet analysis method for detection of DDoS attack on the basis of self-similarity. Frontiers of Electrical and Electronic Engineering in China 2(1), 73–77 (2007)
13. Lu, W., Tavallaee, M., Ghorbani, A.A.: Detecting network anomalies using different wavelet basis functions. In: Proceedings of the Communication Networks and Services Research Conference, pp. 149–156 (2008)

14. Bartlett, G., Rey, M.D., Heidemann, J., Papadopoulos, C.: Using Low-Rate Flow Periodicities for Anomaly Detection Extended Technical Report ISI-TR-661 (2009)
15. Leland, W., Taqqu, M., Willinger, W., Wilson, D.: On the self-similar nature of Ethernet traffic. In: Proceedings of ACM SIGCOMM, pp. 183–193 (1993)
16. Li, L., Lee, G.: DDoS attack detection and wavelets. In: 12th International Conference on Computer Communications and Networks, pp. 421–427 (2003)
17. Pacheco, J.C.R., Roman, D.T.: Distinguishing fractal noises and motions using Tsallis Wavelet entropies. In: 2010 IEEE Latin/American Conference on Communications, pp. 1–5 (2010)
18. Abe, S., Suzuki, N.: Itineration of the Internet over Non-equilibrium Stationary States in Tsallis. Statistics in Physical Review E 67 (2003)
19. Dainotti, A., Pescapé, A., Ventre, G.: Wavelet-based Detection of DoS Attacks. In: IEEE Conference on Global Communications, pp. 1–6 (2006)
20. Perez, D.G., Zunino, L., Garavaglia, M., Rosso, O.A.: Wavelet entropy and fractional Brownian motion time series. Physica A 365(2), 282–288 (2006)
21. Karmeshu, Sharma, S.: Power Law and Tsallis Entropy: Network Traffic and Applications. In: Chaos, Nonliniearity and Complexity. STUDFUZZ, vol. 206, pp. 162–178. Springer (2006)
22. Abry, P., Veitch, D.: Wavelet analysis of long-range dependent trafic. IEEE Transactions on Information Theory 44, 1111–1124 (1998)
23. Stoev, S., Taqqu, M.S., Park, C., Marron, J.S.: On the Wavelet Spectrum Diagnostic for Hurst Parameter Estimation in the analysis of Internet Trafic. ACM Journal on Computer Networks 48, 423–445 (2005)
24. Abry, P., Veitch, D., Flandrin, P.: Long-Range Dependence: Revisiting Aggregation with Wavelets. Journal of Time Series Analysis 19(3), 253–266 (1998)
25. Tellenbach, B., Burkhart, M., Sornette, D., Maillart, T.: Beyond Shannon: Characterizing Internet Traffic with Generalized Entropy Metrics, pp. 239–248. Springer, Berlin (2009)
26. Mirkovic, J., Hussain, A., Fahmy, S., Reiher, P., Thomas, R.: Accurately Measuring Denial of Service in Simulation and Testbed Experiments. IEEE Transactions on Dependable & Secure Computing 6(2), 81–95 (2009)
27. Moore, D., Shannon, C., Brown, J.: Code-Red: A case study on the spread and victims of an Internet worm. In: Proceedings of Internet Measurement Workshop (2002)
28. The Internet Traffic Archives, http://ita.ee.lbl.gov/html/traces.html
29. Labovitz, C., Johnson, S.I., McPherson, D., Oberheide, J., Jahanian, F.: Internet inter-domain traffic. In: Proceedings of ACM SIGCOMM, vol. 40, pp. 75–86 (2010)
30. Peng, T., Leckie, C., Ramamohanrao, K.: Survey of Network-Based Defense Mechanisms Countering the DoS and DDoS Problems. ACM Computing Surveys 39(1) (2007)
31. Roghan, M., Veitch, D., Abry, P.: Real-time estimation of the parameters of long-range dependence. IEEE/ACM Transactions on Networking, 467–478 (2000)
32. Kuzmanovic, A., Knightly, E.: Low-Rate TCP-Targeted Denial of Service (The Shrew vs. the Mice and Elephants). In: ACM SIGCOMM Proceedings, pp. 75–86 (2003)

Rigorous Design of Lazy Replication System Using Event-B

Raghuraj Suryavanshi[1] and Divakar Yadav[2]

[1] Institute of Engineering and Technology, GBTU, Lucknow, India
[2] Faculty of Mathematics and Computer Science,
South Asian University, New Delhi 110067, India
suryavanshi.cse@ietlucknow.edu, dsyadav@cs.sau.ac.in

Abstract. Eager replication is a technique of replication that ensures high consistency. Unfortunately, it degrades the system performance by increasing the response time and sacrificing availability. Lazy replication is a technique that provides high availability and ensures that database will eventually be in a consistent state. A formal rigorous reasoning is required to precisely understand the behavior of such techniques and to understand how they achieve the objectives. Event-B is a formal technique that is used for specifying and reasoning about complex systems. In this paper, we present a formal development of lazy replication system using Event-B. We outline our model for distributed environment where same database is replicated at all the sites. After updating the database locally within transactional framework messages are broadcast to other sites so that they can change their replicas.

Keywords: Formal Methods, Replication, Event-B, formal specifications, Total order broadcast, Sequencer.

1 Introduction

Replication is technique for increasing fault tolerance and data availability. It provide fault tolerance because in case of failure of a site the data can be recovered from other sites. It also ensures availability because multiple copies of same database are stored at different sites [1]. The operations which are performed on replicas may be read or update transaction. Due to data availability reading local copies certainly increase the performance of system but if transaction involves update operation then replica updation at any site should reflect the changes at all the sites that have a copy of the same replica.

There are number of approaches for handling the replicas. The replica control mechanisms categorized on the basis of how updates are propagated between the copies. When the updates propagate within transaction boundaries then it is known as eager approach [2],[3]. This approach guaranties that replica will remain consistent, i.e., all the replicas will have the same value. But the limitation of this approach is that it sacrifice the availability of the data, thereby, increasing the response time, and decreasing system performance. On the other hand, when

M. Parashar et al. (Eds.): IC3 2012, CCIS 306, pp. 407–418, 2012.

the updates propagate outside the transaction boundaries then it is known as lazy approach [4],[5]. To improve the response time lazy replication delays the propagation of changes until the end of the transaction. After the commitment of the transaction, the update message is broadcast to all sites so that they can change their replicas.

In this paper, we develop a formal model of lazy replication system in B. We have considered the case of replication where same copy of database is replicated all over the sites. The model has conflict check event for checking whether the objects required by the transactions are available or not. In this model an update transaction modifies local copy of database through a single atomic event. After performing commitment of the transaction the updates are propagated to other sites and change their replica. Update messages are delivered to remote site following a total order broadcast. The ordering of messages can be done through group communication or broadcast primitives [6],[7],[8]. Total order broadcast is one such primitive that ensures that delivery order of update messages at all the destination sites will be same. It satisfies following requirement.

If site s and s' both deliver the messages m1 and m2 then s delivers m1 before m2 if and only if s' delivers m1 before m2.

The remainder of this paper is organized as follows: Section 2 describes the Event B and Rodin, Section 3 outline informal description of events, Section 4 presents Event−B Model of Lazy Replication System containing execution of transaction in distributed environment where same copy of database is replicated at all sites. It has the events for changing the replica due to commitment of transaction at any site, broadcasting and ordering of update messages, remote site replica updation. Section 5 concludes the paper.

2   Event-B and Rodin Platform

The B Method [9],[10],[11],[12],[13] is a model oriented state based method. It represent the complete mathematical development of a Discrete Transition System. It is made of several components of two kinds: machines and contexts. Machines represent the dynamic part of model. This part is used to provide behavioral properties of model. It contains the variables, invariants, theorems, and events of a project. Variables correspond to mathematical objects: sets, binary relations, functions, numbers, etc. These variables are constrained by invariants and these invariants are to be preserved while change the value of variables. The theorem of machine must follow from the context and the invariants of that machine. Moreover, a machine can be refined by other machines, but each machine can refine only one machine. Contexts contain the static part of model. It contains carrier sets, constants, axioms, theorems. Carrier sets may be enumerated or deferred. Axioms are used to describe the properties of those sets and constants. The context may be seen by machine directly or indirectly.

Event-B [14],[15],[16],[17],[18],[19] is event driven approach used to develop formal models of distributed systems through a series of refinement steps. An event is made up of three elements its name, guards and actions. The guards are the necessary conditions for the event to occur. An event known as initialization event has no guard and it gives initial position of the model. New variables, invariant, event may also add in the refinement step. The main purpose of adding new invariant and event is to find out more concrete specification. Event-B notations are set theoretic notations. The syntax and description of notations are outlined in [3].

The B Method requires the discharge of proof obligations for consistency checking and refinement checking. There are several B tools such as Rodin [18],[19], Click'n'Prove [20], Atelier B [21], B-Toolkit [22]. They provide an environment for generation and discharge of proof obligations. In this work, we have used Rodin platform. It is an open extensible tool for specification and verification of Event-B. It contains modeling element like event, variables, invariants and components like context and machines. It is embedded by various plugins such as proof-obligation generator, model checkers, provers, UML transformers, etc. This tool provide an environment for generation and discharge of proof obligation.

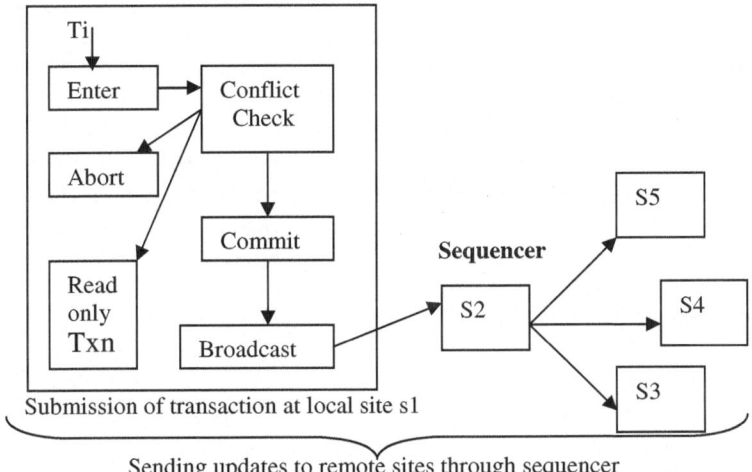

Fig. 1. Lazy Replication system

3   Informal Description of Events

We have considered a case of full replication, such that, a copy of entire database is available at all sites. Further, we assume that communication is asynchronous (no bound on transmission delays) and reliable (a message sent by site Si to Sj is eventually received by Sj). After the submission of transaction at any site it first check for conflict. If there is no conflict then transaction execution start and subsequently commits. After the commitment of update transaction at submission site (coordinator site) update messages are broadcast to other sites (remote site) so that they can also update their replicas to make them consistent (see Fig. 1). We have also introduced the notion of sequencer site. This site builds the total order on the delivered messages which ensures that the delivery order of the messages at all remote site will be same. The informal description of events are as follows:

1. *Start Transaction:* A transaction can be submitted at any site. This site is known as local site or coordinator site for that transaction. It creates an entry of submitted transaction and the objects need by this transaction.
2. *Conflict Check:* Before starting the execution of the transaction the transaction manager first perform conflict check at that site. If the objects needed by this submitted transaction are already acquired by those transaction which are active and performing execution then this transaction will have to wait until all the required objects are freed by them.
3. *Commitment of Transaction:* The transaction may be read-only transaction or update transaction. If the transaction is read only transaction then it reads the value of data object from the local site (submission site) and if it is an update transaction then it update data object and commit the transaction.
4. *Broadcast:* In distributed system, the sites communicate with each other by exchange of messages. As we have considered lazy replication so the updates propagate to other site after the commitment of the transaction. When the transaction commit at the local site it broadcast the messages to all the sites. To broadcast a message, local site sends an update message to the sequencer. Upon receiving the message, the sequencer builds the total order on them and then broadcast the message to all the sites with sequence number so that they can change their replicas.
5. *Total order Broadcast:* In our model of lazy replication, it is required that all messages are delivered to all sites in same order. This problem can be solved by group communication primitives that ensure ordering guarantees on the delivery of messages. A total order broadcast is a reliable broadcast that ensures delivery of messages to the sites in the same order.
6. *Updating Replica at remote site:* After the commitment of transaction at local site (coordinator site) the update messages are sent to remote sites through sequencer so that they can also change their replicas.

4   Event−B Model of Lazy Replication System

We begin with the transactional model where a copy of database known as replica is located at all over sites. The replica is updated atomically as a result of commitment of a transaction. In a context seen by the machine, *TRANSACTION*, *OBJECT* and *VALUE* represent carrier set. *TRANSSTATUS* is enumerated set containing the element *COMMIT, ABORT, PENDING. CONFLICTCHECK-STATUS* is also enumerated set and contain the element, *pending* and *complete*.

VARIABLES
trans, sitetransstatus, transeffect, transobject, replica, siteactivetransa,
siteconflictcheckstatus, sender, totalorder, tdeliver, coordinator.
INVARIANTS
inv1: trans $\in \mathbb{P}$(TRANSACTION)
inv2: sitetransstatus $\in$ (SITE$\leftrightarrow$trans) $\twoheadrightarrow$TRANSSTATUS
inv3: transeffect $\in$ trans$\rightarrow$((OBJECT$\twoheadrightarrow$VALUE)$\twoheadrightarrow$(OBJECT$\twoheadrightarrow$VALUE))
inv4: transobject $\in$ trans$\rightarrow \mathbb{P}1$(OBJECT)   inv5: replica$\in$ REPLICA
inv6: siteactivetransa $\in$ SITE$\leftrightarrow$trans
inv7: siteconflictcheckstatus $\in$ (SITE$\leftrightarrow$trans) $\twoheadrightarrow$CONFLICTCHECKSTATUS
inv8: coordinator $\in$ trans$\rightarrow$SITE   inv9: sender $\in$ MESSAGE$\twoheadrightarrow$SITE
inv10: totalorder $\in$MESSAGE$\leftrightarrow$MESSAGE   inv11: tdeliver $\in$ SITE$\leftrightarrow$MESSAGE
EVENTS
INITIALISATION $\hat{=}$
BEGIN
act1: trans $:= \varnothing$ act2: sitetransstatus $:=$\{ \}   act3: transeffect $:=$ \{ \}   act4: transobject $:=$ \{ \}
act5: replica $:=$rep0 act6: siteactivetransa $:= \varnothing$ act7: siteconflictcheckstatus $:= \varnothing$
act8: coordinator $:=\varnothing$ act9: sender $:= \varnothing$ act10: totalorder $:=\varnothing$ act11: tdeliver $:=\varnothing$
END

Fig. 2. Variables, Invariants and Initialization of Machine

Variable replica is modeled as $replica \in REPLICA$ and in the context $REPLICA$
is declared as:

$$REPLICA = SITE \rightarrow (OBJECT \rightarrow VALUE)$$

It maps a total function from SITE to *value function*. The value function maps
a total function from objects to value which means there are no such objects
which are undefined in replica located at any site thus all the objects should
be defined. The variable *transeffect* is defined as a total function from *trans* to
update function. The update function is defined as:

$$(OBJECT \twoheadrightarrow VALUE) \twoheadrightarrow (OBJECT \twoheadrightarrow VALUE)$$

The domain of this update function which is a partial function from $OBJECT$ to
$VALUE$ represent a *readset OBJECT*. The range of this update function which
is also a partial function from $OBJECT$ to $VALUE$ represent a *writeset*. The
update function is partial because it will write to a subset of readset it means
$writeset \subseteq readset$. If the transaction is read only transaction then $writeset = \phi$
i.e. for any read only transaction tt the $ran(transeffect(tt) = \phi)$. The $SITE$ and
$MESSAGE$ is defined as carrier set. The site where the transaction is submitted
is known as coordinator site for that transaction. After the commitment of update transaction the update messages are broadcasted by coordinator site. These
update messages should propagate to the other sites to make all the replicas consistent. To broadcast a message m, a sender (local site) sends update message
m to the sequencer. Upon receiving m, the sequencer builds the total order and
then broadcast the message to the destination. The transactional model of lazy

replication system is given in Fig. 2. The description of other variables are as follows:

(i) The variable *trans* represent a set of started transactions.

(ii) The variable *sitetransstatus* maps each started transaction at any particular site to *TRANSSTATUS*.

(iii) The variable *transobject* is a total function which maps a transaction to a set of objects. The set *transobject(t)* represents the set of data objects read by a transaction *t*. The set of objects written to by *t* will be a subset of *transobject(t)*.

(iv) The variable *siteactivetransa* represent a set of activated transactions at any particular site.

(v) The variable *siteconflictcheckstatus* maps each started transaction at any site to *CONFLICTCHECKSTATUS*.

(vi) The variable *coordinator* represent the site where the transaction is submitted.

(vii) The sender is defined as partial function from *MESSAGE* to *SITE*. The mapping $(m \mapsto s) \in sender$ indicates that message has sent from the site *s*.

(viii) The variable *totalorder* is defined as:

$$totalorder \in MESSAGE \leftrightarrow MESSAGE$$

Where $MESSAGE \leftrightarrow MESSAGE$ indicates set of relations between *MESSAGE* and *MESSAGE*. A mapping $(m1 \mapsto m2) \in totalorder$ indicate that message *m1* is totally order before *m2*

(ix) The variable *tdeliver* shows that the message is delivered following a total order. A mapping $(s \mapsto m) \in tdeliver$ represent that site *s* has delivered *m* following a total order.

Transaction Submission and Conflict Checking with other Transaction: The events of transaction submission (*StartTran*) and checking for conflicts (*CheckConflict*) are given in Fig. 3. Transaction *tt* is new transaction and submitted at site *ss*. This site work as coordinator site for *tt*. This event makes site *ss* as coordinator*(act4)* and set the transaction status for site *ss* as *PENDING (act5)*. It also makes *siteconflictcheckstatus* of *tt* transaction at site *ss* as *pending (act6)*.

The event *CheckConflict* checks that the object needed by this transaction *tt* at coordinator site *ss* is available or not because it may possible that the same object is acquired by other transaction which are active and performing some execution. It is represented by following guard:

$$\forall tz \cdot (tz \in trans \land (coordinator(tt) \mapsto tz) \in siteactivetransa \Rightarrow$$
$$transobject(tt) \cap transobject(tz) = \phi)$$

If all objects are freed then the status of conflict check at coordinator site is set be complete and *tt* is added to the *siteactivetransa* set *(act1 and act2)*.

StartTran ≙
ANY
tt, updates, objects, ss
WHERE
grd1: tt ∈ TRANSACTION   grd2: tt ∉ trans
grd3: objects ∈ ℙ1 (OBJECT)   grd4: ss ∈ SITE
grd5: updates ∈ ((OBJECT↦VALUE) ↦ (OBJECT↦VALUE))
THEN
act1: trans≔trans ∪ {tt}   act2: transobject(tt)≔objects   act3: transeffect(tt)≔updates
act4: coordinator(tt)≔ss   act5: sitetransstatus({ss↦tt})≔PENDING
act6: siteconflictcheckstatus({ss↦tt})≔pending
END

CheckConflict ≙
ANY tt
WHERE
grd1: tt ∈ trans   grd2: (coordinator(tt)↦tt)∉siteactivetransa
grd3: {coordinator(tt)↦tt} ∈ dom(sitetransstatus)
grd4: {coordinator(tt)↦tt} ∈ dom(siteconflictcheckstatus)
grd5: sitetransstatus({coordinator(tt)↦tt})=PENDING
grd6: siteconflictcheckstatus({coordinator(tt)↦tt})=pending
grd7: ∀ tz· (tz ∈ trans ∧ (coordinator(tt)↦tz) ∈ siteactivetransa ⇒ transobject(tt)∩transobject(tz)=∅)
THEN
act1:   siteconflictcheckstatus({coordinator(tt)↦tt})≔complete
act2:   siteactivetransa ≔ siteactivetransa ∪ {coordinator(tt)↦tt}
END

Fig. 3. Start Transaction and Check-Conflict event of Machine

Commit and Abort of Update Transaction: The event *CommitWriteTran* models the commitment of update transaction (see Fig. 4.). The transaction is active and it is update transaction is ensured by *grd2* and *grd3* respectively. This event update the replica at coordinator site *(act2)* and set the status of transaction as *COMMIT (act1)*. After the commitment of transaction it removes the transaction *tt* from *siteactivetransa* set *(act3)*.

AbortWriteTran event is given in Fig. 4. This event set the status of update transaction *(grd4)* at coordinator site as *ABORT (act1)* and removes the transaction from *siteactivetransa* set *(act2)*.

ReadTran event (Fig. 4.) models the commitment of read only transaction. Transaction *tt* is read only transaction is ensured by *grd3*. This event perform reading of the objects from the replica located at coordinator site. It set the status of transaction as *COMMIT (act1)* and remove the transaction from *siteactivetransa* set *(act2)*.

Ordering and Delivery of Messages: When the update transaction has performed commit at the local site (coordinator site) it broadcast a update message

CommitWriteTran ≜
ANY tt, pdb
WHERE
grd1: tt ∈ trans   grd2: coordinator(tt)↦tt ∈ siteactivetransa
grd3: ran(transeffect(tt))≠ {∅}   grd4: {coordinator(tt)↦tt} ∈ dom(sitetransstatus)
grd5: sitetransstatus({coordinator(tt)↦tt})=PENDING
grd6: pdb ∈ dom(transeffect(tt))   grd7: pdb=transobject(tt)◁replica(coordinator(tt))
THEN
act1: sitetransstatus({coordinator(tt)↦tt}) ≔ COMMIT
act2: replica(coordinator(tt)) ≔ replica(coordinator(tt)) ◁ transeffect(tt)(pdb)
act3: siteactivetransa≔siteactivetransa\{coordinator(tt)↦tt}
END

AbortWriteTran ≜
ANY tt
WHERE
grd1: tt∈trans   grd2: {coordinator(tt) ↦ tt} ∈ dom(sitetransstatus)
grd3: (coordinator(tt)↦tt) ∈ siteactivetransa   grd4: ran(transeffect(tt))≠{ ∅}
grd5: sitetransstatus({coordinator(tt)↦tt}) = PENDING
THEN
act1: sitetransstatus({coordinator(tt)↦tt})≔ ABORT
act2: siteactivetransa≔siteactivetransa\{coordinator(tt)↦tt}
END

ReadTran ≜
ANY tt, readval
WHERE
grd1: tt ∈ trans   grd2: (coordinator(tt)↦tt) ∈ siteactivetransa
grd3: ran(transeffect(tt))={∅}   grd4: {coordinator(tt)↦tt} ∈ dom(sitetransstatus)
grd5: sitetransstatus({coordinator(tt)↦tt})=PENDING
grd6: readval=transobject(tt)◁replica(coordinator(tt))
THEN
act1:   sitetransstatus({coordinator(tt)↦tt})≔COMMIT
act2:   siteactivetransa≔siteactivetransa\{coordinator(tt)↦tt}
END

Fig. 4. Commit, Abort and Read Transaction events of Machine

to other sites through sequencer. The broadcast event is given in Fig.5. As a Lazy system the transaction should perform commit before sending a message (this constraints is specified as *grd7*). The *grd8* ensures that the message has not been delivered yet.

The Order event, given in Fig. 5., models the ordering of update messages sent by the senders. The message has been sent is specified through *grd3*. The messages for which ordering is not performed should not be delivered by the sequencer *(grd5)*. After receiving the messages the sequencer builds the total order on received messages. The actions *act1* ensures delivery of message at sequencer site and *act2* builds the total order on received message.It also ensures

Broadcast $\hat{=}$
ANY tt, ss, mm
WHERE
grd1: tt $\in$ trans grd2: ss $\in$ SITE   grd3: ss=coordinator(tt) grd4: mm $\in$ MESSAGE
grd5: ({ss$\mapsto$tt}) $\in$ dom(sitetransstatus)   grd6: ran(transeffect(tt)) $\neq$ {$\varnothing$}
grd7: sitetransstatus({ss$\mapsto$tt})=COMMIT   grd8: mm$\notin$dom(sender)
THEN
act1: sender=sender $\cup$ {mm$\mapsto$ss}
END

Order $\hat{=}$
ANY ss, mm
WHERE
grd1: ss $\in$ SITE   grd2: mm $\in$ MESSAGE   grd3: mm$\in$dom(sender)
grd4: ss=sequencer   grd5: (sequencer$\mapsto$mm)$\notin$tdeliver
THEN
act1: tdeliver=tdeliver $\cup$ {ss$\mapsto$mm}   act2: totalorder=totalorder $\cup$ (ran(tdeliver)$\times${mm})
END

Todeliver $\hat{=}$
ANY ss, mm, tt
WHERE
grd1: ss $\in$ SITE grd2: tt$\in$trans   grd3: ss$\neq$coordinator(tt) grd4: mm $\in$ MESSAGE
grd5: mm$\in$dom(sender)   grd6: ss$\neq$sequencer
grd7: mm$\in$ran(tdeliver)   grd8: ss$\mapsto$mm $\notin$ tdeliver
grd9: $\forall$m$\cdot$(m$\in$MESSAGE $\wedge$ (m$\mapsto$mm) $\in$totalorder$\Rightarrow$(ss$\mapsto$m)$\in$tdeliver)
THEN
act1: tdeliver=tdeliver $\cup$ {ss$\mapsto$mm}
END

Fig. 5. Ordering and Delivery of messages

that all messages delivered at any process are ordered before the new message mm.

The event *ToDeliver* (see Fig. 5.) models the delivery of update message mm to the site ss following the total order. The guard *grd5* ensures that the message mm has been sent by the sender (coordinator) and guard *grd7* ensures that it has been delivered to at least one site and it also implies that the total order on the update message mm has been constructed. The guard *grd9* is expressed as:

$$\forall m\cdot(m\in MESSAGE\wedge(m\mapsto mm)\in totalorder\Rightarrow(ss\mapsto m)\in tdeliver$$

It state that if any message m is totally order before other message mm then delivery of message m at any site ss has already been done before the delivery of message mm.

Updating the Replica at Remote Site: The event *RemoteTranSubmit* (Fig. 6.) models the submission of transaction at remote sites for changing the replicas.

Remote_Tran_Submit ≜
ANY ss, mm, tt
WHERE
grd1: ss ∈ SITE   grd2: tt∈trans   grd3: ss≠coordinator(tt)
grd4: mm∈dom(sender)   grd5: ss↦mm ∈ tdeliver
grd6: ∀tx·(tx∈trans∧ (ss↦tx)∈siteactivetransa ⇒ transobject(tt)∩transobject(tx)=∅)
THEN
act1: siteactivetransa⁼siteactivetransa∪{ss↦tt}
act2: sitetransstatus({ss↦tt})⁼PENDING
END

Remote_Replica_Update ≜
ANY ss, tt, remotereplica
WHERE
grd1: ss ∈ SITE   grd2: tt∈trans   grd3: ss≠coordinator(tt)
grd4: ss↦tt∈ siteactivetransa   grd5: {ss ↦ tt}∈dom(sitetransstatus)
grd6: sitetransstatus({ss↦tt})=PENDING   grd7: remotereplica∈dom(transeffect(tt))
grd8: remotereplica=transobject(tt)◁ replica(ss)
THEN
act1: replica(ss) ⁼ replica(ss)◁ transeffect(tt)(remotereplica)
act2: sitetransstatus({ss↦tt})⁼COMMIT   act3: siteactivetransa⁼siteactivetransa\{ss↦tt}
END

Fig. 6. The events for Transaction Submission and Replica Updation at remote site

The remote site *ss* has received the update messages following the total order is ensured by *grd5*. The guard *grd6* ensures that the data objects which is required by transaction *tt* are available at site *ss*. The transaction is activated at site *ss* through *act1* and status of transaction is set to *PENDING* through *act2*.

The event *RemoteReplicaUpdate* is given in Fig. 6. This event update the replica at remote site due to execution of transaction *tt*. Site *ss* is not coordinator site for the transaction *tt* is ensured by *grd3*. Transaction *tt* is activated at site *ss* and its status is *PENDING* is ensured by *grd4* and *grd6* respectively. In this event *remotereplica* is partial database and defined as:

$$remotereplica = transobject(tt) \lhd replica(ss).$$

An update function takes current values of objects and generates new values of objects. It is represented by action *act1*:

$$replica(ss) := replica(ss) \Lleftarrow transeffect(tt)(remotereplica)$$

This event update the replica at remote site *(act1)*, set the status of *tt* at site *ss* as *COMMIT (act2)* and remove the transaction from *siteacivetransa (act3)*.

5   Conclusions

In replicated databases, an update transaction modifies data objects at different sites. Formal analysis of fault-tolerant transactions for replicated database systems based on eager approach is reported in [3]. In this approach execution of update transaction submitted at a site (coordinator site) doesn't perform commit until commit or abort confirmation messages are received by the coordinator site, thereby, data at coordinating and remote site remains unavailable until commit of the update transaction at coordinator site. In our model, the coordinating site broadcast update messages to remote site using total order broadcast [6],[8]. The update transaction at coordinator site commits by updating replica locally, while remote site start a fresh update transaction at remote site once they receive update message from coordinating site. For ensuring same delivery order, the messages are broadcast through sequencer. Sequencer builds a total order on delivered messages. These ordered update messages are delivered to all sites so that they update the replica and remains in a consistent state.

We have used Event-B for formal analysis of our model. It facilitates incremental development of model. We have given formal specifications of replication system. This is done by defining formal specification for abstract model and then stepwise refinement by adding more invariants. Modeling guideline as outlined in [16] has been adhered to in our model. As a result we obtained a high degree of automated proofs in this case study. This work has been carried out on Rodin tool [18],[19]. The tool provide an environment for generation and discharge of proof obligations arising due to consistency and refinement checking. In this case study 94% proof obligations were discharged automatically while other required interaction with the tool. The proofs and invariants together helped us to reason about the system design.

References

1. Helal, A., Heddya, A., Bhargava, B.: Replication Techniques in Distributed System. Kluwener Academic Publishers (1997)
2. Kemme, B., Alonso, G.: A new approach to developing and implementing eager database replication protocols. ACM Transaction Database System 25(3), 333–379 (2000)
3. Yadav, D., Butler, M.: Rigorous Design of Fault-Tolerant Transactions for Replicated Database Systems Using Event B. In: Butler, M., Jones, C.B., Romanovsky, A., Troubitsyna, E. (eds.) Fault-Tolerant Systems. LNCS, vol. 4157, pp. 343–363. Springer, Heidelberg (2006)
4. Pedone, F., Guerraoui, R., Schiper, A.: The database state machine approach. In: Distributed and Parallel Databases, vol. 14(1), pp. 71–98. Springer (2003)
5. Kemme, B.: Database replication for clusters of workstations. Dissertation No ETH 13864. Ph.D Thesis, Department of Computer Science, ETH Zurich (2000)
6. Baldoni, R., Cimmino, S., Marchetti, C.: Total Order Communications: A Practical Analysis. In: Dal Cin, M., Kaâniche, M., Pataricza, A. (eds.) EDCC 2005. LNCS, vol. 3463, pp. 38–54. Springer, Heidelberg (2005)
7. Birman, K., Schiper, A., Stephenson, P.: Lightweigt causal and atomic group multicast. ACM Trans. Comput. Syst. 9(3), 272–314 (1991)
8. Marchetti, C., Cimmino, S., Baldoni, R.: A classification of total order specifications and its application to fixed sequencer-based implementations. Journal of Parallel and Distributed Computing 66(1), 108–127 (2006)

9. Butler, M.: An Approach to Design of Distributed Systems with B AMN. In: Till, D., P. Bowen, J., Hinchey, M.G. (eds.) ZUM 1997. LNCS, vol. 1212, pp. 223–241. Springer, Heidelberg (1997)

10. Butler, M., Walden, M.: Distributed System Development in B. In: Proc. of Ist Conf. in B Method, Nantes, pp. 155–168 (1996)

11. Rezazadeh, A., Butler, M.: Some Guidelines for Formal Development of Web-Based Applications in B-Method. In: Treharne, H., King, S., C. Henson, M., Schneider, S. (eds.) ZB 2005. LNCS, vol. 3455, pp. 472–492. Springer, Heidelberg (2005)

12. Abrial, J.R.: The B-Book: Assigning programs to meanings. Cambridge University Press (1996)

13. Abrial, J.R.: Extending B without changing it (for developing distributed systems). In: Habrias, H. (ed.) First B Conference (November 1996)

14. Suryavanshi, R., Yadav, D.: Formal Development of Byzantine Immune Total Order Broadcast System using Event-B. In: Kannan, R., Andres, F. (eds.) ICDEM 2010. LNCS, vol. 6411, pp. 317–324. Springer, Heidelberg (2012)

15. Yadav, D., Butler, M.: Application of Event B to Global Causal Ordering for Fault Tolerant Transactions. In: Proc. of REFT 2005, Newcastle upon Tyne, pp. 93–103 (2005)

16. Butler, M., Yadav, D.: An incremental development of the mondex system in Event-B. Formal Aspects of Computing 20(1), 61–77 (2008)

17. Yadav, D., Butler, M.: Formal Development of a Total Order Broadcast for Distributed Transactions Using Event-B. In: Butler, M., Jones, C., Romanovsky, A., Troubitsyna, E. (eds.) Fault Tolerance. LNCS, vol. 5454, pp. 152–176. Springer, Heidelberg (2009)

18. Metayer, C., Abrial, J.R., Voison, L.: Event-B language. RODIN deliverables 3.2 (2005), http://rodin.cs.ncl.ac.uk/deliverables/D7.pdf

19. Abrial, J.-R.: A System Development Process with Event-B and the Rodin Platform. In: Butler, M., Hinchey, M.G., Larrondo-Petrie, M.M. (eds.) ICFEM 2007. LNCS, vol. 4789, pp. 1–3. Springer, Heidelberg (2007)

20. Abrial, J.R., Cansell, D.: Click'n'Prove - Interactive Proofs within Set Theory (2003)

21. Steria, Atelier-B User and Reference Manuals (1997)

22. B Core UK Ltd. B-Toolkit Manuals (1999)

Saturation Analysis of IEEE 802.11 EDCA
for Ad Hoc Networks

Ash Mohammad Abbas and Khaled Abdullah Mohammed Al Soufy

Department of Computer Engineering
Aligarh Muslim University, Aligarh - 202002, India
am.abbas.ce@amu.ac.in, kalsoufi@gmail.com

Abstract. IEEE 802.11e EDCA can be used to provide *Quality of Service* (QoS) in an ad hoc network at the *Medium Access Control* (MAC) layer. In this paper, we describe a model for the analysis of IEEE 802.11e EDCA for an ad hoc network. Our model is based on the differentiation among different classes of traffic based on the size of *Contention Window* (CW), and *Arbitration Inter-Frame Space* (AIFS). During our analysis, we focus on the following parameters: (i) average end-to-end delay, and (ii) throughput. To validate our analysis, we carried out simulations and found that the results obtained analytically are in accordance with those obtained through simulations.

Keywords: Ad hoc network, IEEE 802.11e EDCA, analysis, saturation.

1 Introduction

IEEE 802.11e is designed for applications that require *Quality of Service* (QoS). IEEE 802.11e enhances DCF and PCF through the use of a new coordination function called *Hybrid Coordination Function* (HCF), which consists of two methods of channel access: (i) *HCF Controlled Channel Access* (HCCA), and (ii) *Enhanced Distributed Channel Access (EDCA)*. The operation of HCCA is similar to PCF, however, instead of providing two separate periods CP and CFP (as in case of *PCF*), HCCA provides only one CFP period called *Controlled Access Phase* (CAP), which can be initiated at any time during the contention period. However, the support for HCCA is optional and a very few APs are available in which HCCA is enabled.

EDCA assigns different priorities to different types of traffic so that high priority traffic has higher chances of being sent than lower priority traffic. This is accomplished by using a shorter *Contention Window* (CW) and shorter *Arbitration Inter-Frame Space* (AIFS) for higher priority traffic as compared to lower priority traffic. Additionally, EDCA is capable of providing a contention-free access to the channel for a time duration called *Transmit Opportunities* (TXOP). If there is a large frame that cannot be transmitted in a single TXOP, it can be fragmented into smaller frames. The use of TXOP forces a node to access the channel only for a limited amount. A TXOP equal to 0 means that the node

M. Parashar et al. (Eds.): IC3 2012, CCIS 306, pp. 419–430, 2012.
© Springer-Verlag Berlin Heidelberg 2012

Table 1. Access categories for different types of traffic

AC	Traffic	CW_{min}	CW_{max}	AIFSN	TXOPlimit
0	Best Effort (BE)	31	1023	7	0
1	Background (BK)	31	1023	3	0
2	Video (VI)	15	31	2	3.008ms
3	Voice (VO)	7	15	2	1.504ms

is limited to transmit only for a single *MAC Service Data Unit* (MSDU). The classes of priorities in EDCA are called *Access Categories* (ACs). The ACs for different types of traffic are given in Table 1.

There are four access categories numbered from 0 through 3 in the increasing order of their priorities. In other words, the best effort traffic has the lowest priority, the background traffic has the next lowest priority. The voice traffic has the highest priority and the video traffic has the next highest priority. Depending on the type of traffic, the values of CW_{min}, CW_{max}, and *AIFSN* are different. Typical values of CW_{min}, CW_{max}, *AIFSN*, and *TXOPlimit* are shown in Table 1.

Many researchers have focused on the analysis of IEEE 802.11e EDCA such as [4], [9], [10], [11], [12], and [14]. A model for analyzing saturation throughput and delay performance of IEEE 802.11e EDCA assuming an ideal channel is presented in [7]. An analysis of the Medium Access Control (MAC) access delay for IEEE 802.11e Enhanced Distributed Channel Access (EDCA) mechanism under saturation is proposed in [8]. The model tries to incorporate the effect of AIFS, CW, TXOP and backoff multiplier differentiation on the MAC access delay.

A model for analysis of IEEE 802.11e EDCA is described in [7]. However, the model presented in [7] does not take into account, during the computation of the average one-hop delays and the throughput, the random number of empty slots a node has to wait before trying to transmit a packet. Our model is an improvement over the model presented in [7] because we take into account the above mentioned random number of empty slots. One more difference between the model presented herein and the model presented in [7] is that we compute the transmission attempt rate (or the transmission probability), τ_{ij}, using the *renewal-reward theorem* [5], however, in [7], the transmission probability is computed using *mean value analysis*. Further, the expression of the transmission probability presented in [7] does not consider a finite number of retransmission attempts (rather it assumes the number of transmission attempts to be infinite), however, our expression of the transmission probability or transmission attempt rate takes into account a finite number of transmission attempts. The models presented in [7] consider only a single hop WLAN, however, we here consider an ad hoc network where there can be multiple hops from a given source to destination.

In this paper, we analyze the performance of IEEE 802.11e EDCA in an ad hoc network where there can be multihop paths from a given source to a destination. During our analysis, we focus on the following parameters (i) average end-to-end delays, and (ii) throughput. We study the impact of the probability of collision and the transmission attempt rate on the average end-to-end delays and throughput of different access categories of IEEE 802.11 EDCA.

The rest of this paper is organized as follows. Section 2 contains an analysis of IEEE 802.11 EDCA. In Section 3, we present results and discussion. The last section is for conclusion.

2   Analysis of IEEE 802.11 EDCA

Let there be an ad hoc network with n nodes uniformly and randomly distributed in a region of area A. Each node is equipped with an omnidirectional antenna and has a transmission radius r. The carrier sense range of each node is denoted by r_{cs} and is assumed to be β times the transmission range. Let the node density be, $\zeta = \frac{n}{A}$. The number of nodes that are in the transmission range of a node including itself is $\nu_{ts} = \zeta \pi r^2$, and the number of nodes lying in the carrier sensing range is

$$\nu_{cs} = \zeta \pi r_{cs}^2. \tag{1}$$

EDCA provides differentiated access using the EDCA parameters AIFS[AC], $CW_{\min}[AC]$, $CW_{\max}[AC]$, and TXOPlimit[AC] for a corresponding AC, numbered from 0 to 3. The parameter AIFS[AC] is determined by

$$\text{AIFS[AC]} = \text{SIFS} + \sigma \times \text{AIFSN[AC]} \tag{2}$$

where σ is the slot time and AIFSN[AC] is the number of slots for which a station has to defer its transmission after an SIFS duration.

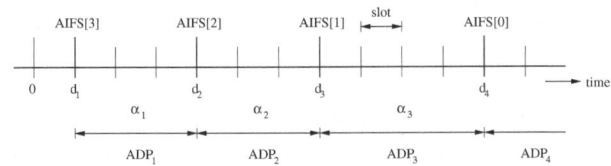

Fig. 1. AIFSs of different ACs and their differences

Let the EDCA parameters for a station with a given AC be AIFS[AC], $CW_{\min}[AC]$, and $CW_{\max}[AC]$. As shown in Table 1, AC = 3 has the highest priority, AC = 2 has the next higher priority, and so on, AC = 0 has the lowest priority. In other words, a larger priority number designates a higher priority of an AC. For the sake of simplifying the expressions, we transform the EDCA parameters as follows: (i) $d_i = \frac{AIFS[4-i]}{\sigma}$, (ii) $W_i = CW_{\min}[4 - i]$, (iii) $CW_{\max}[4 - i] = 2^{m_i} CW_{\min}[4 - i]$, and (iv) $n_i = N[4 - i]$ (i.e. number of stations with AC = $4 - i$). In other words, there are n_1 stations of AC = 3 (voice), n_2 stations of AC = 2 (video), n_3 stations of AC = 1 (best-effort), n_4 stations of AC = 0 (background). Using Table 1 and (2), we have,

$$AIFS[0] = SIFS + 7\sigma$$
$$AIFS[1] = SIFS + 3\sigma$$
$$AIFS[2] = SIFS + 2\sigma$$
$$AIFS[3] = SIFS + 2\sigma. \tag{3}$$

Clearly, $AIFS[0] \geq AIFS[1] \geq AIFS[2] \geq AIFS[3]$, therefore, $d_1 \leq d_2 \leq d_3 \leq d_4$.

In a network, many stations might be contending to access the wireless channel to transmit their frames using the procedure laid down for EDCA. When a station is in the backoff state, it does not transmit any frame and is considered to be idle. There can be a sequence of idle periods and transmission periods on the channel. For a station, an idle period followed by a transmission period is called a cycle. The length or duration of an idle period is random and can be divided into four subperiods that we call *Arbitration Difference Periods* (ADPs). The jth ADP is defined as the time difference between $AIFS[4-j]$ and $AIFS[3-j]$ for $j = 1, 2, 3$; and the fourth ADP is defined as the time duration greater than ADP[4]. Let $\alpha_j = d_{j+1} - d_j$, $j = 1, 2, 3$ be the length of ADP_j in terms of the number of slots.

We wish to model delays and throughput of IEEE 802.11e EDCA. As mentioned earlier, IEEE 802.11e EDCA has four ACs with their own AIFSs. In order to model the delays and throughput of IEEE 802.11e EDCA, let p_{ij} be the probability that a frame transmitted by a station with access category $4 - i$ collides with the transmissions of another station in the ADP_j (whose length is α_j).

Let R_{ij} be a random variable that represents the number of attempts to transmit a packet of an AC = $4 - i$ with $CW_{\max}[4 - i] = 2^{m_i} CW_{\min}[4 - i]$, assuming the collision probability p_{ij}, and the maximum number of transmissions for a packet for all ACs to be M. The expected number of transmission attempts is as follows [5].

$$E[R_{ij}] = 1 + p_{ij} + p_{ij}^2 + \cdots + p_{ij}^M$$
$$= \frac{1 - p_{ij}^{M+1}}{1 - p_{ij}}. \tag{4}$$

Let X_{ij} be a random variable that represents the number of backoff slots for a station with AC = $4 - i$ in ADP_j in a backoff stage. The expected number of backoff slots is as follows.

$$E[X_{ij}] = \left(\frac{W_i - \sum_{k=1}^{j-1} \alpha_k}{2} \right) + p_{ij} \left(\frac{2W_i - \sum_{k=1}^{j-1} \alpha_k}{2} \right)$$
$$+ p_{ij}^2 \left(\frac{2^2 W_i - \sum_{k=1}^{j-1} \alpha_k}{2} \right) + \cdots + p_{ij}^{m_i-1} \left(\frac{2^{m_i-1} W_i - \sum_{k=1}^{j-1} \alpha_k}{2} \right)$$
$$+ p_{ij}^{m_i} \left(\frac{2^{m_i} W_i - \sum_{k=1}^{j-1} \alpha_k}{2} \right) + p_{ij}^{m_i+1} \left(\frac{2^{m_i} W_i - \sum_{k=1}^{j-1} \alpha_k}{2} \right)$$

$$+ p_{ij}{}^{m_i+2} \left(\frac{2^{m_i} W_i - \sum_{k=1}^{j-1} \alpha_k}{2} \right) + \cdots + p_{ij}{}^M \left(\frac{2^{m_i} W_i - \sum_{k=1}^{j-1} \alpha_k}{2} \right)$$

$$= \frac{1}{2} \left\{ \left(\sum_{r=0}^{m_i-1} p_{ij}^r W_i^r \right) + \left(\sum_{r=m_i}^{M} p_{ij}^r W_i^{m_i} \right) \right\} - \frac{\sum_{k=1}^{j-1} \alpha_k}{2} \left\{ \sum_{r=0}^{M} p_{ij}{}^r \right\}$$

$$= \frac{W_i}{2} \left\{ \left(\frac{1 - (2p_{ij}^{m_i})}{1 - 2p_{ij}} \right) + 2^{m_i} p_{ij}{}^{m_i} \left(\frac{1 - p_{ij}{}^{M-m_i+1}}{1 - p_{ij}} \right) \right\}$$

$$- \frac{\sum_{k=1}^{j-1} \alpha_k}{2} \left\{ \frac{1 - p_{ij}{}^{M+1}}{1 - p_{ij}} \right\}. \tag{5}$$

Let τ_{ij} represents the average transmission attempt rate (or the transmission probability) of a station with $AC = 4 - i$ at a slot boundary in ADP_j, which is as follows.

$$\tau_{ij} = \frac{E[R_{ij}]}{E[X_{ij}]}. \tag{6}$$

Using (4) and (5), (6) can be written as follows.

$$\tau_{ij} = \frac{2(1 - 2p_{ij})(1 - p_{ij}^{M+1})}{W_i \left\{ (1 - 2^{m_i} p_{ij}{}^{m_i})(1 - p_{ij}) + 2^{m_i} p_{ij}{}^{m_i}(1 - p_{ij}{}^{M-m_i+1})(1 - 2p_{ij}) \right\} - (1 - 2p_{ij})(1 - p_{ij}{}^{M+1}) \sum_{k=1}^{j-1} \alpha_k}. \tag{7}$$

In what follows, we describe the computation of MAC delays using the transmission attempt rate.

2.1   MAC Delays

The MAC delays for a *head-of-line* (HOL) packet in IEEE 802.11 consist of backoff delays and transmission delays. We describe how to compute each of these components as follows.

As mentioned earlier, τ_{ij} represents the transmission probability (more accurately, the transmission attempt rate) of a station with $AC = 4 - i$ at a slot boundary in ADP_j. It may happen that none of the station from the whole network transmits in a slot. To incorporate it, let p_{tr_j} be the probability that there is at least one transmission in a slot, which is given by the following expression [3], [7].

$$p_{tr_j} = 1 - \prod_{i=1}^{j} (1 - \tau_{ij})^{n_i} \tag{8}$$

where, $j = 1, 2, 3, 4$ for the $AC = 4 - i$. The matrix for the four ACs is,

$$\mathbf{P_{tr}} = [p_{tr_1} \quad p_{tr_2} \quad p_{tr_3} \quad p_{tr_4}].$$

Note that an ADP may contain many slots, and in each slot, a station with an access category j can transmit with probability p_{tr_j}. We use another matrix that we call *ADP transmission probability matrix*, represented by $\mathbf{P}_\alpha = [p_{\alpha_1} \ p_{\alpha_2} \ p_{\alpha_3} \ p_{\alpha_4}]$. The jth element, p_{α_j}, of the matrix $\mathbf{P}_\alpha$ represents the probability that a transmission begins in ADP_j. Using the principle of independence, the jth element, p_{α_j}, of the matrix $\mathbf{P}_\alpha$, is given by the following expression [7].

$$p_{\alpha_j} = \left\{ 1 - \left(1 - p_{tr_j} \right)^{\alpha_j} \right\} \prod_{k=1}^{j-1} \left(1 - p_{tr_k} \right)^{\alpha_k}, \quad j = 1, 2, 3$$

$$p_{\alpha_4} = \prod_{k=1}^{3} \left(1 - p_{tr_k} \right)^{\alpha_k}. \tag{9}$$

In other words, (9) gives the probability that there is at least one transmission during the ADP_j while there is no transmission by a station with a higher priority AC (see the definition of ADP_j whose duration in terms of the number of slots is α_j).

Let $p_{suc_{ij}}$ be the probability that a transmission from a station with $AC = 4-i$ in ADP_j is successful, and is given by,

$$\begin{aligned} p_{suc_{ij}} &= \frac{\tau_{ij}}{p_{tr_j}} \frac{1 - p_{tr_j}}{1 - \tau_{ij}} \\ &= \frac{\tau_{ij}}{1 - \tau_{ij}} \frac{1 - p_{tr_j}}{p_{tr_j}}. \end{aligned} \tag{10}$$

Let p_{s_i} be the probability that a transmission from one of the n_i stations with $AC = 4 - i$ is successful. The probability p_{s_i} is given by

$$p_{s_i} = \sum_{j=1}^{4} p_{suc_{ij}} p_{\alpha_j}. \tag{11}$$

The average length of the slot time for $AC = 4 - i$ (including the idle time, transmission time, and collision time) is as follows [3].

$$E[slot_i] = (1 - p_{tr_i})\sigma + p_{tr_i} p_{s_i} T_{s_i} + p_{tr_i}(1 - p_{s_i}) T_{c_i}. \tag{12}$$

The average delay, $E[D_i]$, incurred by a packet of $AC = 4 - i$ is given by,

$$E[D_i] = E[X_i].E[slot_i]. \tag{13}$$

Adding to $E[D_i]$ the queuing delays, (say $E[Q_i]$), we get single hop delays for a packet of an access category i. In other words, the delays incurred by a packet of an AC i is,

$$\mathcal{D} = E[D_i] + E[Q_i], \tag{14}$$

where, $E[Q_i]$ depends upon the queuing discipline. We here assume an M/M/1/K priority queue model.

2.2   Multihop Delay

As mentioned earlier, each node in the network is assumed to have a transmission range of r and a carrier sensing range $r_{cs} = 2r$. A node can transmit to a neighboring node lying inside its transmission range, however, the transmissions of a node lying in its carrier sensing range may collide with its own transmissions. Assuming that all nodes in an ad hoc network, irrespective of their access categories, are distributed randomly in the region of its deployment, the expression of the number of nodes lying in the carrier sense range, ν_{cs}, is given by (1). In IEEE 802.11e EDCA, there are four access categories, and assuming that a node may belong to any one category, the average number of nodes belonging to an access category i is, $n_i = \frac{\nu_{cs}}{4}$.

However, there can be common nodes between the carrier sense areas of two or more adjacent nodes lying along a path. Therefore, there has to be an adjustment in the number of neighboring nodes whose transmissions may collide with the transmissions of a given node. Adjustment in the number of neighboring nodes of two or more adjacent nodes lying along a multihop path in a contention based MAC protocol is presented in [1]. Therein, an expression that relates the modified number of neighboring nodes after adjustment, ν'_{cs}, and the original number of neighboring nodes without such an adjustment, ν_{cs}, has been described, which is as follows.

$$\nu'_{cs} = (1 - \chi)\nu_{cs}. \tag{15}$$

where, $0 \leq \chi \leq 1$, is called an adjustment factor. An expression for χ in terms of the number of hops along the path is presented in [1]. Then, the modified number of nodes of each access categories can be taken to be $n'_i = \frac{\nu'_{cs}}{4}$. Let there be h hops along a path from a given source to a destination. Let $\mathcal{D}'$ be the single hop delay corresponding to the adjusted average number of neighbors, ν'_{cs}. Then, the average end-to-end delay from a given source to a destination is given by,

$$D_{\text{path}} = h\mathcal{D}'. \tag{16}$$

In what follows, we analyze the throughput of IEEE 802.11 EDCA.

2.3   Throughput

In this subsection, we analyze the throughput under saturation i.e. when the queue is assumed to be never empty. Let $E[P]$ be the expected length of the payload including the header. Let ϕ_i be the system throughput of AC[$4 - i$], which is given by the following expression.

$$\phi_i = \frac{p_{s_i} p_{tr_i} E[P]}{E[slot_i]} \tag{17}$$

where, $E[P]$ is the average length of the frame. Using (12), (17) can be written as,

$$\phi_i = \frac{p_{s_i} p_{tr_i} E[P]}{(1 - p_{tr_i})\sigma + p_{tr_i} p_{s_i} T_{s_i} + p_{tr_i}(1 - p_{s_i})T_{c_i}}. \tag{18}$$

Note that (18) gives an expression for the throughput of a node under saturation. In what follows, we present results and discussion.

Table 2. Different parameters and their values for IEEE 802.11e EDCA

Parameter	Value	Remark
MAC Hdr	$20.36\mu s$	28 bytes
PHY Hdr	$192\mu s$	24 bytes
t_{SIFS}	$10\mu s$	
σ	$20\mu s$	
t_{ACK}	$304\mu s$	$(112 + 192)$ bits
Data Channel	11 Mbps	
Control Channel	1 Mbps	
Propagation Delay ϵ	$1\mu s$	(Assumed)
Data	1024 bytes	(Assumed)
(UDP + IP) Header	$29.090\mu s$	40 bytes

3   Results and Discussion

Let there be 100 nodes distributed randomly in a region of area $1000m \times 1000m$. Each node has transmission range of $250m$ unless and otherwise stated explicitly, and the carrier sense range is assumed to be twice of the transmission range. We assume that each node is equipped with an omnidirectional antenna. The traffic is constant bit rate with a packet size of 1024 bytes. We have *queue load factor* $\rho = 0.1$. We have assumed a propagation delay of $1\mu s$. In case of IEEE 802.11e EDCA, the data channel is assumed to have a rate $11Mbps$ and the control channel is assumed to have a rate of $1Mbps$. A summary of the parameters and their corresponding values is given in Table 2. The carrier sensing range is assumed to be the twice of the transmission range. For the results obtained analytically and through simulations, we assume a node may send a packet of only one access category and the number of nodes sending packets of one category is one fourth of the total number of nodes in the network. However, all nodes, irrespective their access categories, are distributed randomly. For simulation results, each point represents an average of 100 simulation runs.

Figure 2 shows the average delay as a function of the collision probability when the transmission range of each node is set to $150m$. We observe that with an increase in the probability of collision, the average delay increases for all access categories of traffic. However, the amount of increase in the average delay incurred by packets of access categories with higher priorities is less as compared to the average delay incurred by packets of access categories with lower priorities. Specifically, the delays incurred by packets of different access categories are in the following order.

$$D_{AC_3} \leq D_{AC_2} \leq D_{AC_1} \leq D_{AC_0} \tag{19}$$

where, D_{AC_i} represents the average end-to-end delay of AC_i. Further, the above trend is observed for the average delays incurred by packets of different access categories computed analytically as well as obtained through simulations.

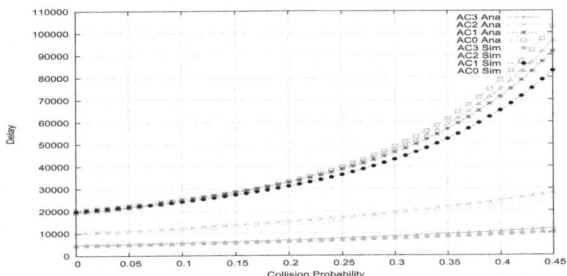

Fig. 2. Average end-to-end delay (in microseconds) as a function of the collision probability for transmission range 150m

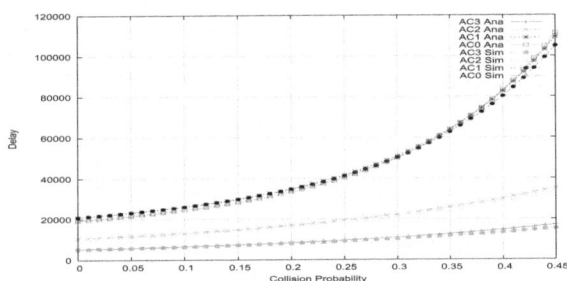

Fig. 3. Average end-to-end delay (in microseconds) as a function of the collision probability for transmission range 250m

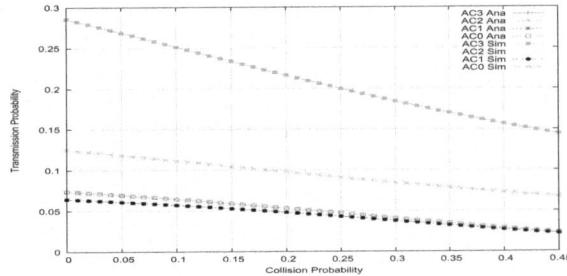

Fig. 4. Transmission probability as a function of collision probability for transmission range 250m

Figure 3 shows the average delay as a function of the collision probability for the transmission range of each node is set to 250m. We observe that the delays of all access categories increase with the increase in the collision probability. The trend of increase in the delays is similar to that of Figure 2. In other words, the delays incurred by the packets of different access categories are in accordance with (19). Comparing Figure 2 and Figure 3, we find that the delays for the transmission range 150m are smaller than the delays for 250m.

Figure 4 shows transmission probability (or transmission attempt rate) as a function of the collision probability when the transmission range of each node is set to 250m. We observe that with an increase in the collision probability, the transmission probability decreases. The reason is obvious, an increase in the number of collisions implies that a node that wishes to transmit has to increase its backoff window again and again, and as a result, the chances to successfully transmit the packet decrease, thereby, decreasing the transmission probability.

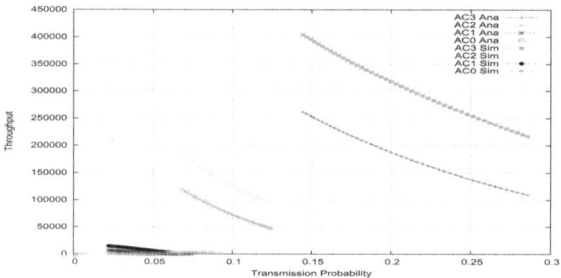

Fig. 5. Average throughput (in bits per second) as a function of transmission probability for transmission range 150m

Figure 5 shows the throughput as a function of the transmission probability (or transmission attempt rate) for the transmission range of each node to be 150m. We observe that as the transmission probability increases, the throughput of nodes of all access categories decreases. This is due to the fact that an increase in the transmission probability or the transmission attempt rate means that more number of nodes try to transmit simultaneously, thereby, decreasing the throughput. However, the throughput of the nodes that are part of an access category with higher priorities is higher than the nodes that belong to an access category with lower priorities. In other words, the throughput of nodes with different access categories satisfy the following inequality.

$$\phi_{AC_0} \le \phi_{AC_1} \le \phi_{AC_2} \le \phi_{AC_3} \tag{20}$$

where, ϕ_{AC_i} represents the throughput of AC_i.

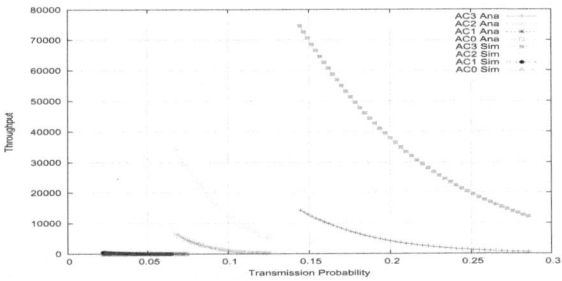

Fig. 6. Average throughput (in bits per second) as a function of transmission probability for transmission range $250m$

Figure 6 shows the throughput as a function of the transmission attempt rate for the transmission range, $r = 250m$. Similar to Figure 5, we observe that the throughput of nodes of all access categories decrease with an increase in the transmission attempt rate. The reason for this decrease is the same as for Figure 5. The throughput of nodes of all access categories decrease more rapidly when the nodes in the network are assigned a transmission range of $250m$ (see Figure 5) as compared to the transmission range of $150m$ (see Figure 6). This is due to the fact that increasing the transmission range increases the number of neighbouring nodes contending for the channel, which increases the number of collisions, and thereby, the throughput is decreased.

4   Conclusion

In this paper, we proposed a model for the analysis of IEEE 802.11e EDCA for an ad hoc network. The contributions made in this paper are as follows.

- Our model is based on the CW and AIFS differentiation. During the analysis, we focus on the average delays incurred by a packet along a path from a given source to a destination, and the average throughput.
- We studied the effect of collision probability on the average delays incurred by packets of different access categories. Also, we studied the effect of transmission attempt rate on the average throughput of a node that belongs to an access category.
- We observed that the average delays incurred by packets of different access categories increase with the collision probability and their throughput decrease with an increase in the transmission attempt rate.
- To validate the analysis, we carried out simulations. We found that the results obtained through simulations are in accordance with the results obtained analytically.

References

1. Abbas, A.M.: Multihop Adjustment for the Number of Nodes in Contention-Based MAC Protocols for Wireless Ad hoc Networks. Computing Research Repository, arXiv:1108.4035v1[cs.NI] (2011)
2. Abbas, A.M., AlSoufy, K.A.M.: Analysis of IEEE 802.11 DCF for Ad hoc Networks: Saturation. In: 5th IEEE International Conference on Internet Multimedia Services Architecture and Applications (IMSAA), pp. 306–311. IEEE Press, New York (2011)
3. Bianchi, G.: Performance Analysis of the IEEE 802.11 Distributed Coordination Function. IEEE Journal on Selected Areas in Communication 18, 535–547 (2000)
4. Tinnirello, I., Bianchi, G.: Rethinking the IEEE 802.11e EDCA Performance Modeling Methodology. IEEE/ACM Transactions on Networking 18, 540–553 (2010)
5. Kumar, A., Altman, E., Miorandi, D., Goyal, M.: New Insights from a Fixed Point Analysis of Single Cell IEEE 802.11 WLANs. IEEE/ACM Transactions on Networking 15, 588–601 (2007)
6. Duffy, K.R.: Mean Field Markov Models for Wireless Local Area Networks. Markov Processes and Related Fields 16, 295–328 (2010)
7. Hui, J., Devetsikiotis, M.: A Unified Model for the Performance Analysis of IEEE 802.11e EDCA. IEEE Transactions on Communications 53, 1498–1510 (2005)
8. Xu, D., Sakurai, T., Vu, H.L.: An Access Delay Model for IEEE 802.11e EDCA. IEEE Transactions on Mobile Computing 8, 261–275 (2009)
9. Kosek-Szott, K., Natkaniec, M., Bach, A.R.: A Simple But Accurate Throughput Model for IEEE 802.11 EDCA in Saturation and Non-saturation Conditions. Computer Networks 55, 622–635 (2011)
10. Serrano, P., Banchs, A., Azcorra, A.: A Throughput and Delay Model for IEEE 802.11 EDCA Under Non-saturation. Wireless Personal Communications: An International Journal 43, 467–479 (2007)
11. Robinson, J.W., Randhawa, T.S.: Saturation Throughput Analysis of IEEE 802.11e Enhanced Distributed Coordination Function. IEEE Journal on Selected Areas in Communications 22, 917–928 (2005)
12. Inan, I., Keceli, F., Ayanoglu, E.: A Capacity Analysis Framework for the IEEE 802.11e Contention-Based Infrastructure Basic Service Set. IEEE Transactions on Communications 57, 3433–3445 (2009)
13. Li, J., Li, Z., Mohapatra, P.: APHD: End-to-End Delay Assurance in 802.11e Based MANETs. In: 3rd IEEE International Conference on Mobile and Ubiquitous Systems: Networking and Services (MOBIQ), pp. 1–8. IEEE Press, New York (2006)
14. Lin, Y., Wong, V.W.S.: Saturation Throughput of IEEE 802.11e EDCA Based on Mean Value Analysis. In: IEEE Wireless Communication and Networking Conference (WCNC), pp. 475–480. IEEE Press, New York (2006)

Financial Option Pricing on APU

Matthew Doerksen, Steven Solomon, Parimala Thulasiraman,
and Ruppa K. Thulasiram

Computational Financial Derivatives Lab,
InterDisciplinary Evolving Algorithmic Sciences Lab, Department of Computer Science,
University of Manitoba, Winnipeg, MB, Canada
{umdoerk9,umsolom9,thulasir,tulsi}@cs.umanitoba.ca

Abstract. Financial option pricing is a compute-intensive problem that requires real-time pricing for making decisions on investment portfolios or studying the risk value of a company's assets. In this study, we report our experiences designing an algorithm for a complex option pricing problem on the Accelerated Processing Unit (APU), a state-of-the-art multi-core architecture. Using a naive algorithm, both the APU and GPU do not perform well as there is a non-optimal use of memory which limits our utilization of computational resources. To improve performance we examined two methods of optimization: (i) vectorization of the computational domain and (ii) loop unrolling of the computation. Through these two methods we achieve better performance and scalability with less powerful hardware than other GPU solutions currently available.

Keywords: Hybrid Multicore, APU, Option Pricing.

1 Introduction

A financial option, generally known as derivative, is a contract between two parties over a pre-specified period of time on an underlying asset such as a stock. The holder of the option contract gets the right to exercise this option during the contract period. The other party, the writer, is obliged to the decisions of the holder. There are two types of options, a Call (Put) option gives the holder right to buy (sell) the underlying asset at a pre-specified price (strike price). If the contract allows the holder to exercise the option only at the expiration time of the contract period, it is known as a European option. Alternatively, an American option can be exercised any time prior to the expiration period. In a *Lookback option (exotic option)* the option price depends on the maximum and minimum of the asset price attained during the contract period. In this paper we price American Lookback option.

The pricing of options is a fundamental problem in finance for various purposes such as risk analysis and portfolio management. In a dynamic and volatile market, pricing the options quickly is advantageous to the market players and, hence, high performance computing platforms are always in demand for real time pricing. Although there are many different algorithms to price an option, we consider the

M. Parashar et al. (Eds.): IC3 2012, CCIS 306, pp. 431–441, 2012.

binomial lattice algorithm. This algorithm builds a tree where each node in the tree can be regarded as a time period with the contract. The tree data structure allows us to make the problem fine-grained or coarse-grained, increasing or decreasing the number of computations. The problem is data parallel in nature, where there is parallelism within each level of the tree and synchronization between the levels. The algorithm works forward for a certain number of levels and traverses backwards from the last level of the tree to the root node.

Recently, AMD has fused CPU and GPU into a single chip with the Accelerated Processing Unit (APU). APUs have great potential in scientific as well as finance computing, positioning them as the next step in heterogeneous computing. Financial applications are computationally intensive and regular.

In this paper we exploit the large number of fine grained computations on the GPU cores and study the AMD Fusion architecture's advantages and disadvantages for a financial application. The algorithm is iterative and synchronous and therefore, can be efficiently implemented on an APU. We show the parallelization of the binomial lattice algorithm using three different implementations. We show that we gain improved performance if we explicitly use and manipulate the VLIW features of the APU architecture during the code development phase. We compare the performance of the APU implementation with that of Solomon et al. [7] implementation of discrete GPU.

The rest of the paper is organized as follows. Section 2 describes the American Lookback option followed by related work in option pricing on the GPU in Section 3. Section 4 presents the APU/GPU architecture. Sections 5 and 6 discuss the experimental results. Section 7 concludes.

2   Option Pricing

The binomial lattice is a popular method for approximating the asset price movements that enables pricing of an option [3], [8]. This lattice is essentially a binary tree with the root node representing the current date (in other words contract start date) and the leaf nodes at the maturity date of the option contract. This method discretizes the evolution of the asset price in small time steps. Though this structured way of price evolution may not completely represent the random walk followed by an asset, this method remains a popular method in the finance community for its easiness to study with any hardware or software such as Microsoft Excel.

Each step of the binomial tree captures the price movement up or down. The probability for the price to move up or down in the tree can be pre-specified or computed based on volatility estimation. A move upwards from a given node in the lattice will result in price going up by a factor u, whereas a move downwards will result in the price going down by a factor d. Figure 1 captures this scenario.

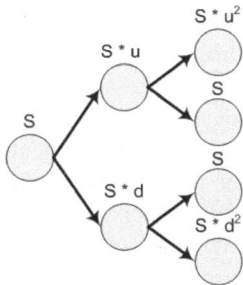

Fig. 1. Binomial Tree Structure for Option Pricing

2.1   American Lookback Options

Lookback options are a style of exotic option that depends on the path of the asset price to reach a particular node in the tree. The payoff of a lookback option is based on the maximum (put) or minimum (call) price of the underlying asset between the purchase date and maturity date of the option. In order to accomplish pricing lookback options, a new parameter $Y(t)$ is suggested in a couple of earlier studies [4], [5]. In essence, $Y(t)$'s value is derived from the following equation:

$$Y(t) = G(t) / S(t) \tag{1}$$

where $G(t)$ is the maximum price the asset achieves up to time t and $S(t)$ is the current stock price at t. The asset price is placed in each node of the binomial lattice through $Y(t)$ unlike in other options.

Figure 2 shows the structure of the binomial lattice for pricing lookback option. The top number at each node is the Y value computed using the following rules: (i) Y is 1 at the root node of the lattice; (ii) When moving to the next time step from a node where $Y = 1.0$, Y equals u if the movement is an upwards move, or 1 if the movement is a down move. Here $u=1.25$; (iii) When moving to the next time step from a node where $Y = u^m$ for $m \geq 1$, $Y = u^{m+1}$ for an upward move, or $Y = u^{m-1}$ for a downward move in the lattice.

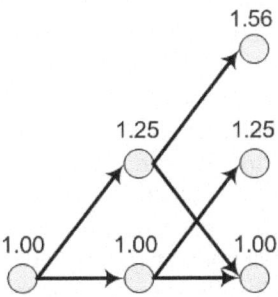

Fig. 2. Binomial Lattice Structure for Pricing Lookback Options

The above rules transforms the tree in such a way that the bottom"tier" of nodes always retain a $Y(t)$ value of 1. This is due to the nature of $Y(t)$. An *upward* movement in the lattice corresponds to an *upward* movement in Y(t) and, therefore, a *downward* movement in $S(t)$ (for $S(t)$ must decrease in order for $Y(t)$ to grow, as $G(t)$ cannot, by definition, decrease). Hence, a downward movement in the lattice means that $S(t)$ is increasing. If we move ``past" the initial value of S, then both $S(t)$ and $G(t)$ grow at the same rate, resulting in a $Y(t)$ value that is always 1.

While this strategy for pricing American Lookback options uses the binomial lattice structure as its base, the formula used to update the option payoff for each node differs is as follows:

$$C_{i,j} = \max(Y_{i,j} - 1, e^{-r\delta}((1-p)C_{i+1,j+1}d + pC_{i+1,j-1}u))$$
(2)

for $j \geq 1$, and

$$C_{i,j} = \max(Y_{i,j} - 1, e^{-r\delta}((1-p)C_{i+1,j+1}d + pC_{i+1,j}u))$$
(3)

for $j = 1$.

All of the parameters remain the same as in the binomial approach. The new additions of u and d represent the proportional movement of the asset price up or down at each time step (level in the lattice) respectively.

3   Related Work

To the best of our knowledge, there exists no study on pricing lookback options on the APU. Therefore, we discuss a few existing studies of opting pricing on GPUs in this section.

Podlozhnyuk [6] provides an example of the binomial lattice technique for option pricing on Nvidia GPUs. In this study sub-trees within the binomial lattice are computed independently in each thread block. This allows for computations to take place solely in shared memory. Podlozhnyuk describes the redundant computations across each thread block as a side-effect of this method. However, the improved speed of shared memory over the global memory of the GPU likely provides a greater degree of performance than a method that uses global memory to reduce redundancy.

As an extension to the work of Podlozhnyuk [6], Jauvion and Nguyen [2] describe an implementation of the trinomial lattice on the GPU. The authors' implementation is, for the most part, similar to the work of Podlozhnyuk. Jauvion and Nguyen, however, describe how each thread block in the GPU can be used to compute the value of one option. Thus, each of the thread blocks allocated in the thread grid are tasked with computing individual option prices for different options.

This approach proves to work well when the number of options requiring pricing is equal to the number of SMs. However, the approach fails to provide improved performance for lower numbers of options, as there too few thread blocks to saturate all SMs. Further, the options priced within each thread block are priced independently of one another. Because thread blocks cannot communicate with one another through shared memory, it is not possible to price portfolios with dependencies between assets/options using the exact strategy described by Jauvion and Nguyen.

Solomon et al. [7] reported design and implementation of a complex option. The particular option they studied was American lookback option. This study exploited the GPU architecture for expediting the pricing process.

4   System Details

4.1   APU/GPU Architecture

At a high level, an APU is comprised of four main components: the CPU cores, the GPU cores, the GPU's on-chip memory and the interconnect linking the CPU and GPU. Since this is not an in-depth review of the GPU architecture, we will only make note of the fact that the E-350 and A6-3400M APUs utilize a Single Instruction Multiple Threads (SIMT) architecture.

The APU's on-chip interconnect is both its greatest strength and weakness. On one hand, it enables quick data movement from the CPU to the GPU and vice versa and will eventually require no data transfer as a shared CPU/GPU address space is planned for future devices. The downside to this interconnect is that it means it is very quick to transfer data from the CPU to the GPU or vice versa, any data off the CPU must be accessed via the system bus which has lower bandwidth than a dedicated GPUs own global memory.

Continuing to the GPU (as the APU's memory is the same as the GPU's except global memory is emulated in system memory), there is a large global memory which is both read/write accessible from all threads executing across all Streaming Multiprocessors (SMs). While this is convenient, it does have a latency penalty of hundreds of cycles for every access [1].

Other memories in the GPU include the constant and texture memories which are emulated in global memory and are read-only but have the benefit of being cached memories. Next, there is the local memory which is a small memory on each SM that can be accessed as fast as a register provided no bank conflict exists. Last we have the private memory which is exclusive to each thread.

From this, it's simple to see that in order to hide the latency associated with global memory we must have a significant number of threads active (coalescing is another technique that can help minimize latency). This however is the GPU's greatest strength as the architecture was built for data parallel tasks, enabling us to exploit this finely-grained parallelism within our applications.

4.2   OpenCL Threading Model

OpenCL enforces a threading model almost identical to the CUDA model, using a different naming scheme and adding a new identifier. At the highest level we have the global workgroup which includes every thread that will execute the kernel.

Underneath, we have groups of threads referred to as workgroups. For identification purposes each workgroup is given a unique identifier and each thread in every workgroup is given both a local ID to mark its location in the workgroup and a global ID to mark its position in the global workgroup [9], [10], [11].

Unfortunately, due to this threading model, there are strict limitations on how data is shared between workgroups. In the context of GPUs (other devices will have these same memory types, though they may be emulated in the device's global memory which may reside in system memory if the device has no global memory, such as with APUs), communicating information in local memory between workgroups involves copying the data into global memory and then having the other workgroup copy that information into its own local memory. This type of forced access causes a large latency penalty which may result in performance degradation for the application. Fortunately, AMD does have a small global data share (similar to local memory except it is accessible from all workgroups), however, at this time it has not been enabled through an AMD specific OpenCL extension.

5   System Details

For performance comparisons we use the CPU and GPU results with the hybrid algorithm from the work of Solomon *et al.* [7]. Our hardware includes:

Device	Cores	Core/Shader Speed	Memory Speed	GPU Bandwidth	GFLOPS
Radeon 5870M	800	700 MHz	4 GHz	64 GB/s	1,120
E-350	80	492 MHz	1066 MHz	8.528 GB/s[1]	78.72
A6-3400M	320	400 MHz	1333 MHz	21.33 GB/s[1]	256
E8400	2	3 GHz	1333 MHz	-	24
GTX 260	216	576/1242 MHz	2000 MHz	111.9 GB/s	804

Note that all GPUs currently support OpenCL 1.1 with OpenCL 1.2 support expected upon the release of AMD's APP SDK 2.6 due in mid-December. All systems were running Windows 7 x64 with at least 4 GB of system memory. Programs were compiled using MS Visual Studio 2010's C++ compiler with AMD's APP SDK 2.5, Catalyst driver 11.11 and OpenCL runtime version 793.1. Results were averaged over 30 trials to ensure a fair comparison with as few outliers as possible.

6   Results and Discussions

For the pricing of American-style lookback options, we design a parallel algorithm based on the technique proposed in [4], [5], which is also described in [8]. We have

---

[1] As APU's do not have dedicated memory, the GPU's bandwidth is also the system bandwidth.

implemented our algorithm on the APU. This strategy makes use of a binomial lattice structure and is tailored for ``put" options. This allows for parallelization on the APU with multiple values (the *Y(t)* value and the option payoff) must be updated at each iteration rather than just the option value.

6.1   Naïve Implementation

Overall we see 5870M perform relatively well, but not as good as the GTX 260 executing the hybrid algorithm used by Solomon et al. [7]. This version however is naïve and doesn't use local memory as it was a first attempt at getting the algorithm to run on the device.

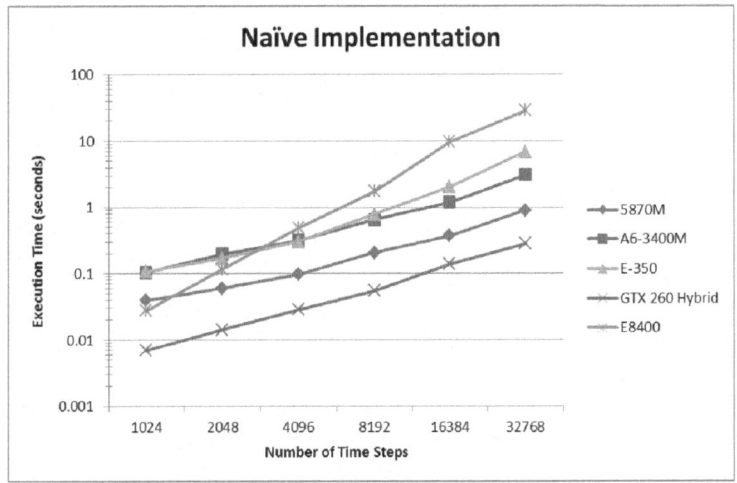

Fig. 3. Naïve implementation of Lookback option pricing algorithm on APU including the results of Solomon *et al.* [7]

Moving to the APUs, we see from Figure 3 that until 8192 time steps they both perform relatively similar to each other even though the A6-3400M has four times the number of Stream Processors (SPs) and slightly more than double the memory bandwidth (which is particularly important considering the APUs use system memory while the 5870M has its own on-chip memory). Even as we scale the problem upwards to 32768 time steps we see the 5870M holds a large lead over the A6-3400M and the E-350. This is somewhat odd to see as the number of SPs isn't scaling equally. If it was, we would see the 5870M being roughly two and a half times faster than the A6-3400M and the A6-3400M being roughly four times faster than the E-350. We believe this disparity is being caused by the memory subsystem being used in an un-optimized way. Since the 5870M has roughly three times the bandwidth of the A6-3400M, we see that is a good metric for how this algorithm scales with larger inputs. Likewise for the A6-3400M, it performs roughly 2.33 times better than the E-350, which is close to the bandwidth difference between the two systems. From this, we can see that, while adding more compute resources to this naïve implementation does increase performance, we end up being limited by memory bandwidth when using this algorithm.

6.2   Vectorization Technique

Vectorization involves packing multiple independent instructions together which can be run in parallel, increasing resource utilization and performance. We started with the naïve algorithm and modified it so that we could now calculate either 2 or 4 (based on implementation) data points in parallel. While this would result in fewer active threads for smaller data sizes, we theorized that for large data sizes we could increase performance by 2-4 times. Unfortunately, we found the necessary branching required for ensuring some array elements would not be updated resulted in no difference in execution time for executing two items in parallel. When executing four items in parallel, we found that execution time was actually worse than with two items because it required 3 branches as opposed to the 2 branches when executing 2 items in parallel[2].

While we did not achieve better performance with vectorization (execution times were within a 10-30 milliseconds), it did have enable us to compute up to 114688 time steps while still retaining accuracy comparable to the single-precision CPU implementation. We believe this increase in accuracy is caused by the compiler building a more complex instruction stream, forcing 32-bit precision instead of the standard 24-bit precision for multiplication. Due to this, we found it advantageous to continue using the vectorized code even though it did not perform any better. We also note that vectorization may cause problems when using local memory such as bank conflicts. When bank conflicts occur memory access is no longer as fast as a register. Instead, memory accesses become serialized which can drastically hurt performance. This was evident in our algorithm as with vectorization each memory location would hold two elements, and, when accessing either of them, would require serialization. However, using global memory enables us to avoid this penalty and use memory coalescing to give us good execution times.

6.3   Loop Unrolling Technique

We now look at the effect of a second optimization technique termed loop unrolling which involves executing multiple loop iterations at once on the device to increase utilization. To implement loop unrolling we compared two methods: a direct copy/paste of code to unroll the loop in the kernel and using a loop inside the kernel that would run multiple iterations. From our results, we found that using a loop did result in a slight penalty (10-30 milliseconds difference in execution time); it drastically simplified the code and reduced its size.

We now look at the same vectorized algorithm but instead of returning to the CPU after each iteration, we run multiple iterations on the APU/GPU. Note: we ran the

---

[2] Note: This comparison was made when executing 4 items total so as to ensure an equal amount of calculation was done between both versions.

program for 32,768 time steps on each device. Also, because we used a technique called double buffering in an attempt to avoid reading/writing to the same memory locations which would slow down our kernel, we did not include a version of the algorithm that only executed a single iteration in the figure. Instead, we must use the original naïve algorithm as the baseline for no loop unrolling, which should be fair as execution times between the naïve and vectorized versions were almost identical.

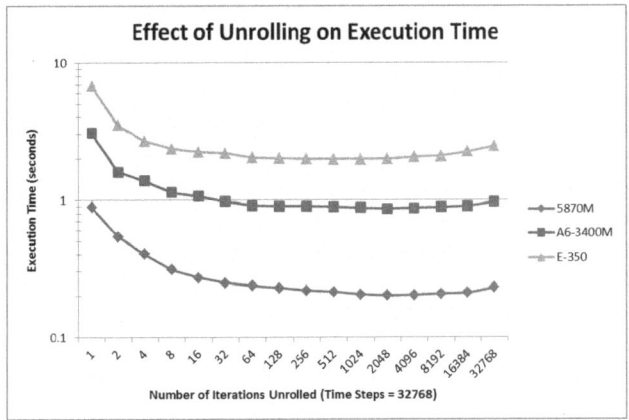

Fig. 4. Effect of Unrolling on execution time

From Figure 4, we see that the largest improvement in performance comes through unrolling two loop iterations as the execution time is cut roughly in half for 32,768 time steps. This is the result of less synchronization and kernel enqueuing overhead. However, after surpassing the optimal unrolling value, execution time increases. This is caused by more thread switching than necessary at which point, returning to the CPU is in fact more efficient because of its implicit synchronization. We see this when the best unrolling value is found (512 for the E-350 and 2048 for the 5870M and A6-3400M) as we achieve performance roughly four and a half times better than the original algorithm for the 5870M and approximately three and a half times better for the A6-3400M and E-350 APUs.

Looking further into the cause of this increase in execution time, we took some screen captures from AMD's System Monitor which shows APU resource allocation. From this, we have the one graph (Figure 5(a) which shows a saw-edge motion during execution with a low number of loop iterations unrolled. Comparing this to the other graph in Figure 5(b), during execution we don't see the same saw-edge graph (once we unroll more iterations than the optimal number). From monitoring APU resource allocation during runtime we believe that the cause of this is that when the GPU is under a large amount of stress, the CPU is able to clock down to give the GPU more headroom. In the case of a high number of unrolled iterations, the CPU is forced into a busy waiting period while the kernel finishes executing, not enabling it to save power, thus taking away headroom from the GPU. Then, with lower headroom, the GPU isn't able to increase its resources making it performs worse than with fewer unrolled iterations.

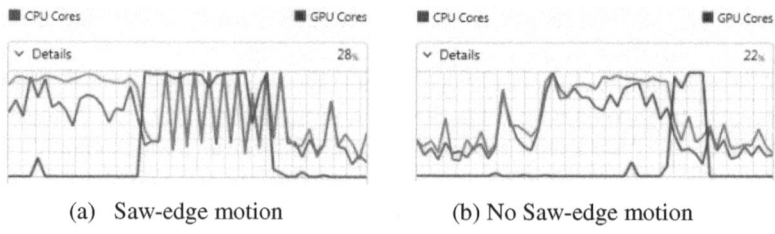

(a)   Saw-edge motion   (b) No Saw-edge motion

Fig. 5. Screen capture of the effect of loop unrolling

6.4   Vectorized and Unrolled Technique

Next we move to the execution times of our most optimized algorithm (vectorized and unrolled). Here we used the best unrolling value for each device when executing 32,768 time steps and used that as the unrolling value for our tests. For the 5870M and A6-3400M which have an unrolling value above the minimum number of time steps, we used the maximum number of iterations possible, 1024 in this case. We did not run the algorithm on the E-350 APU for any number of time steps greater than 65,536 simply because the execution time would be far too long.

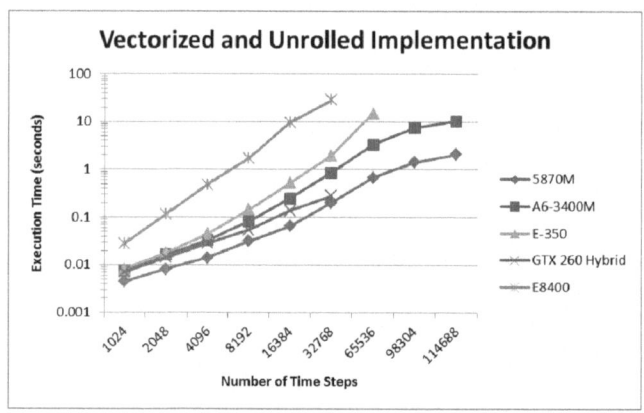

Fig. 6. Execution times for Vectorized and Unrolled Implementations

In Figure 6 we see that the 5870M once again execute much faster than the APUs for larger input sizes, even improving on the GTX 260's execution time. This is amazing as the GTX 260 not only has a 35% SP advantage in scalar code, but it is also clocked 77% higher! In this case, we actually have a larger difference than with the naïve algorithm, where the 5870M had a 3 and 7 times advantage over the A6-3400M and E-350 respectively due to its global memory which has 3 and 7 times the bandwidth of the APUs, again respectively. Now, this algorithm has been optimized so as to better take advantage of memory, partially removing the dependency, meaning the 5870M's advantage in SP count and clock speed enable it to achieve better performance. Getting into actual numbers, the 5870M is able to achieve a speedup of approximately 4.25 and 9.75 over the A6-3400M and E-350 respectively.

7   Conclusions

In this study we have proposed a pricing algorithm design for APU. We did a first design and implementation of pricing algorithm on APU for American Lookback put option. Though we do not discuss the actual pricing results, we have compared the pricing results for plain vanilla options from APU implementation against standard models such as Black-Scholes-Merton [8] and Binomial Lattice [3] before embarking on the actual APU implementations of lookback option. We have developed and implemented the binomial lattice algorithm by explicitly unrolling the loop and vectorizing instead of allowing the compiler to find the parallelism within the code. Vectorization did not improve performance due to branching. We noted that vectorization may cause problems when using local memory such as bank conflicts. We saw that the largest improvement in performance came through unrolling two loop iterations as the execution time was cut roughly in half for 32,768 time steps.

Acknowledgments. The last two authors acknowledge the partial financial support from the Natural Sciences and Engineering Research Council (NSERC) of Canada to do this research through Discovery Grants.

References

1. NVIDIA: CUDA 2.0 Programming Guide, Version 2.3.1. NVIDIA (2009)
2. Jauvion, G., Nguyen, T.: Parallelized Trinomial Option Pricing Model on GPU with Cuda (2008), http://www.arbitragis-research.com/cuda-in-computational-finance/coxross-gpu.pdf
3. Cox, J.C., Ross, S.A., Rubinstein, M.: Option pricing: A simplified approach. J. Fin. Econ. 7, 229–263 (1979)
4. Babbs, S.: Binomial valuation of lookback options. J. Econ. Dyn. and Con. 24, 1499–1525 (2000)
5. Cheuk, T., Vorst, T.: Currency lookback options and observation frequency: A binomial approach. J. Int. M. and Fin. 16, 173–187 (1997)
6. Podlozhnyuk, V.: Binomial option pricing model (2008), http://developer.download.nvidia.com/compute/cuda/sdk/website/projects/binomialOptions/doc/binomialOptions.pdf
7. Solomon, S., Thulasiram, R.K., Thulasiraman, P.: Option Pricing on the GPU. In: 12th IEEE International Conference on High Performance Computing and Communications, pp. 289–296. IEEE Press, New York (2010)
8. Hull, J.: Options, Futures, and Other Derivative Securities. Prentice-Hall, Upper Saddle river (2008)
9. OpenCL: The Open Standard for Parallel Programming of Heterogeneous Systems, http://www.khronos.org/opencl/
10. Hwu, W., Stone, J., Nandakumar, D.: The OpenCL Programming Model – Part 1: Basic Concepts, Illinois UPCRC Summer School (2010), http://www.ks.uiuc.edu/Research/gpu/files/upcrc_opencl_lec1.pdf
11. Hwu, W., Stone, J., Nandakumar, D.: The OpenCL Programming Model – Part 2: Case Studies, Illinois UPCRC Summer School (2010), http://www.ks.uiuc.edu/Research/gpu/files/upcrc_opencl_lec2.pdf

Object Oriented Software Maintenance in Presence of Indirect Coupling

Nirmal Kumar Gupta and Mukesh Kumar Rohil

Birla Institute of Technology and Science, Pilani, India
{nirmalgupta,rohil}@bits-pilani.ac.in

Abstract. Maintenance of deployed software is an important phase of software lifecycle. Estimation of maintenance effort in object oriented software engineering is one of the major challenges. In object oriented software the maintenance effort is highly correlated with coupling among classes. It is widely accepted that there is strong relationship between high coupling and poor maintainability. The existing metrics sometimes do not depict the effect of the key factors which contribute significantly towards maintenance effort. Indirect coupling which manifests between two seemingly unrelated classes through hidden connections plays a major role in determining maintenance effort. This research proposes metrics which estimates the maintenance effort for software having indirect coupling between classes.

Keywords: Software Quality, Object Oriented Software, Maintenance Effort, Indirect Coupling.

1 Introduction

Software maintenance is an important phase in lifecycle of software development. After the release of a software product the maintenance phase keeps the software up to date with the environment changes and user requirements [1]. The earlier phases particularly the design phase must be completed in such a manner that the product could be easily maintained. One major concern which affects a good object oriented software design is coupling between classes. Coupling is described as the degree to which one class is dependent on the other class [2]. If a class is having high coupling value then it is highly interdependent on other software classes and vice versa. If a class is highly interdependent then any change in the class requires significant changes in other classes to which it is coupled [3]. Hence highly coupled classes require high maintenance effort. It can be noted that a system cannot completely be devoid of coupling for the proper functioning of software. There is some need of some connections among various sub classes of software. Hence maintaining loose coupling among classes is desirable characteristics of good software design [4]. Previous research has shown that complex coupling relationships among OO software classes are among the critical factors that make testing and maintenance difficult and costly [5]. Therefore, analyzing and measuring software class relationship has gained increasing importance [6].

M. Parashar et al. (Eds.): IC3 2012, CCIS 306, pp. 442–451, 2012.
© Springer-Verlag Berlin Heidelberg 2012

Among the existing coupling measures, very few measures investigate indirect coupling [7] connections. Most of the research has applied only to direct coupling that is, coupling between modules that have some direct relationship. However little investigation has been done into indirect coupling which can be described as coupling between modules that have no direct relationship. We consider that indirect coupling is little more than the transitive closure of direct coupling which involves path of the data flow between classes also into account.

We propose the metrics based on this Indirect Coupling. The proposed metrics are modifications of established metrics. The established metrics will be discussed along with a unified way of representing these metrics. There is also a description of exactly which aspects of the system they attempt to measure.

We also have identified the limitations of existing metrics in defining the maintenance effort in terms of indirect coupling existing in a class cluster within an object oriented software system. We explore that indirect coupling minimization defined by considering coupling paths we are able to relate indirect coupling to maintenance effort. This gives us a clear idea, how indirect coupling affects maintenance effort.

2   Background

Although it is well known that evaluation and prediction of software quality must be based on design properties like coupling, but a little work has been done in this area. The most existing measures consider coupling between modules using source code which becomes available only after implementation phase [8]. Various researchers have put their efforts to define and measure various forms of couplings which can be identified in design phase itself. According to Fenton and Pfleeger[6] "There are no standard measures of coupling". Many of the researches use some variation of Yourdon and Constantine's [9] original definition which defines coupling as "a measure of the strength of interconnection" between modules. They suggests that coupling should be concretely defined in terms of the probability that coding, debugging, or modifying one module will necessary require consideration of changes of another module. Such kind of definitions is not formal definitions since they don't specify the meaning of "strength" or "interconnection". But such idea is an excellent heuristics for guiding the design of the software.

A descriptive survey for object oriented coupling has been done by Berard [10]. In his research coupling is divided into two basic categories which are internal coupling and interface coupling. Interface coupling exists when one object (client) makes use of another object (server) interface by calling its public method. In this case any change to the interface of server object enforces corresponding change in client object, but immune to any change occurs in the internals of classes of server object. Internal coupling occurs when an entity accesses an object's state, either from the "inside" or "outside". "Inside" Internal coupling occurs when that entity is a constituent of the accessed object, for example its method or a component object. "Outside" internal coupling occurs when that entity is a subclass or an unrelated object. He emphasizes that internal coupling is stronger and hence less desirable than interface coupling. Moreover, outside internal coupling is always stronger than its counterpart inside internal coupling.

Many researchers [11] [12] [8] have worked to understand object oriented coupling. Arisholm [13] distinguishes different types of couplings on the basis of its direction. In his framework there are two types of couplings namely import and export coupling. Harrison [11] has not discussed anything regarding direction of coupling. Sherif and his team [12] have explained import and export coupling with respect to total number of messages exchanged during scenario. Briand[8] and his team observed that many measures studied earlier have used the direct coupling but some of measures have used indirect coupling also. Consideration of direct or indirect measure is again a matter of discussion. Many authors have not defined direct and indirect coupling in detail. Yang et al. [7] studied the characteristics of indirect coupling that has not been studied in depth and suggested that its existence may be the source of unnecessary maintenance costs. Poor software designs having large number of indirect coupling relations must be detected and ultimately such connections must be reduced.

3   Limitations

Based on our literature study we identify following limitations within the established metrics.

1. There is a fundamental issue with the definition of CBO (Coupling Between Objects) i.e. it is not specific as to whether a couple is counted in terms of instances or the number of classes.
2. It is established that maintenance effort is proportional to the value of indirect coupling between any two classes in a class cluster, but a suitable metric which defines this relationship appropriately is missing.
3. When the two classes in a class cluster are indirectly coupled through multiple paths and if these paths are partially overlapping then exactly in what manner the indirect coupling between such classes should be computed is not clear.

Therefore the problem becomes how we can relate maintenance effort with the indirect coupling for a class cluster.

The objectives addressed in this research are:

1. Define Indirect coupling in terms of shared variables, function calls or data flows.
2. Development of metrics to relate maintenance effort and indirect coupling for a class cluster.
3. To develop an algorithm which can logically compute maintenance effort for two indirectly coupled classes which have multiple coupling paths.

In the next section we will describe maintenance effort in object oriented software engineering through indirect coupling.

4   Our Approach

Direct Coupling
The coupling metric that takes account of the degree of coupling, functional complexity and transitive (i.e. indirect) coupling between classes, an object-oriented software system can be regarded as a directed graph [3]. The classes comprising the system are the vertices in the graph. Suppose such a system comprises a set of classes $C \cong \{C_1, C_2 \ldots . C_m\}$. Let M_j be the set of methods of the class C_j, and V_j be the set of instance variables of class C_j. $MV_{j,i}$ is the set of methods and instance variables in class C_i invoked by class C_j for $j \neq i$ ($MV_{j,j}$ is defined to be null). Then the edge from C_j to C_i exists if and only if $MV_{j,i}$ is not null. Thus an edge of the graph reflects the direct coupling of one class to another. The graph is directed since $MV_{j,i}$ is not necessarily equal to $MV_{i,j}$. MV_j, the set of all methods and instance variables in other classes that are invoked by class C_j, can be defined as [3]:

$$MV_j = \bigcup_{1 \leq i \leq m} MV_{j,i} \tag{1}$$

The extent of direct coupling from class C_i to class C_j depends upon the number of methods and variables in the set $MV_{i,j}$. The class is said to be coupled strongly if this value is large.

Using the above notations we can define direct coupling from class C_i to class C_j as [3]:

$$C_D^{i,j} = \frac{|MV_{i,j}|}{|MV_i| + |M_i| + |V_i|} \tag{2}$$

In the above equation denominator represents the total number of methods and variables used by class C_i, which accounts for the total functionality of class C_i. This guarantees that the direct coupling from class C_i to class C_j, $C_D^{i,j}$ is independent of class size. As per the definition in equation (2) the value of $C_D^{i,j}$ will always be in the range from zero to one.

Indirect Coupling
Suppose that the two direct coupling values $C_D^{i,j}$ and $C_D^{j,k}$ for classes C_i, C_j and C_k, but the value of direct coupling $C_D^{i,k}$ is zero. Even though there is a dependency between classes C_i and C_k because C_i is *depending upon* C_j which in turn depends upon class C_k. Because of this indirect dependency any modification done in class C_k may affect class C_i. Therefore at the time of maintenance activities such indirect relations must be considered and the maintenance effort will depend upon the coupling path between C_k and C_i. This maintenance effort depends upon the fact that how strongly the individual classes are coupled together. Therefore we can define this effort as:

$$E_I^{i,k} = E(C_D^{i,j} + C_D^{j,k}) \tag{3}$$

A coupling between two classes exists if there is a path from one to the other made up edges whose direct coupling values C_D are all non-zero. The maintenance effort required depends upon the sum of all those C_D values. Thus we define effort required because of this indirect coupling between classes C_i and C_j due to a specific path p, as:

$$E_I^{i,k}(p) = E\left(\sum_{e_{s,t} \in p} C_D^{s,t}\right)$$

$$= E\left(\sum_{e_{s,t} \in p} \frac{|MV_{s,t}|}{|MV_s| + |M_s| + |V_s|}\right) \quad (4)$$

Here $e_{s,t}$ denotes the edge between vertices s and t.

We are assuming that coupling between any two classes will always be less than 1, so indirect dependency due to longer paths will lead to increase. Longer will be the path, higher will be the indirect coupling and vice versa. Here we measure Maintenance effort in terms of value of indirect coupling which is directly proportional to indirect coupling.

Effort α Indirect Coupling
Higher the value of indirect coupling, greater maintenance effort required in tracing and modification and vice versa.

Relationship between Indirect Coupling and Maintenance Effort

Effort α $\Sigma_{p \in \text{Chains}}$length(p)
Effort [10] is associated with the sum of direct coupling measured along each path in the set of paths or chains exist among different software classes [2]. We are using the chains notation defined by Yang [7]. This theory states that Effort is directly proportional to length of the path. Effort is associated with the sum of lengths (measured in terms of edges) of all chains in the set Edges. Therefore greater is the length of the chain, more effort will be required to trace it.

Effort α Number of Chains
Effort is associated with the number of chains or set of paths. This theory states that Effort is directly proportional to number of chains or path exists between different software classes. The length of path between any two classes having indirect coupling may or may not be same. Since, multiple path or relationship exists between source and destination, so effort required in getting the work done will be more. Similarly if there is multiple paths exist between different software classes, which may or may not have overlapping edge in common and even path length may vary, then maintenance effort required in tracing the path and modification will cost more.

Thus, effort required in this situation can be determined using the following algorithm. This algorithm considers that if there are multiple paths between two classes and partially they are overlapping then redundant effort for such common edges must be removed.

Assume for the two classes C_i and C_j various coupling paths p_s (s > 0) exist and partially they may be overlapping. Each path p_s consists of a certain number of edges e_{ks}, ($1 \leq k \leq n_s$). Each edge is formed between two classes if they are directly coupled. Here ns is the total number of edges along path ps. If the maintenance effort required along edge e_{ks} is denoted by $E(e_{ks})$ then the algorithm can be written as:

```
Initialize E₀=0
for each path pₛ
        initialize for all rₖ = false
        for each edge eₖₛ in path pₛ
                if rₖ == false
Eₒ(new) = Eₒ(old) + E(eₖₛ)
rₖ = true
endif
endfor
endfor
```

Fig. 1. Algorithm for computing maintenance effort when multiple, possibly overlapping coupling paths exist between two classes

Thus increasing the number of paths or connections between different software classes will increase indirect coupling productively which resulting in increase in the maintenance effort required in modification or extending the functionality of the class and tracing the path.

5   Experiment

We consider the case study with EasyMock v3.1 software for validation of our proposed metrics. EasyMock is open source library that provides an easy way to use Mock Objects for given interfaces. It helps to create mock objects which can be easily used in conjunction with JUnit. We have used a set of 37 classes from the source code of EasyMock. We identified coupling relations of different lengths between these classes. A coupling length of more than one involves more than two classes. The number of classes identified for different coupling lengths are summarized in Table 1. We have considered coupling lengths from 2 to 5 and identified the number of such paths existing in our class cluster.

Table 1. Number of paths and total number of classes involved for different path lengths

Path length (n)	Total Number of classes involved	Number of paths (N_n)
2	36	65
3	27	46
4	18	31
5	11	19

Table 2 summarizes the overall coupling of all individual paths having a path length of 2. The overall coupling along a path must be computed in such a manner that it must represent the overall effort required during maintenance activities following that path. This maintenance effort increases in an incremental manner along with the path length. Here p denotes the path number, C_{e1} and C_{e2} are coupling values of individual edges along the path and is computed using equation (2). C_o represents the overall coupling for the corresponding path.

Table 2. Summarizing coupling values for each path for a path length of 2

p	C_{e1}	C_{e2}	C_o	p	C_{e1}	C_{e2}	C_o
1	0.39	0.37	0.76	34	0.14	0.28	0.42
2	0.37	0.38	0.75	35	0.26	0.10	0.36
3	0.44	0.32	0.76	36	0.10	0.06	0.16
4	0.04	0.62	0.66	37	0.39	0.23	0.62
5	0.58	0.47	1.05	38	0.55	0.66	1.21
6	0.04	0.29	0.33	39	0.51	0.37	0.88
7	0.49	0.13	0.62	40	0.38	0.69	1.07
8	0.29	0.15	0.44	41	0.43	0.44	0.87
9	0.55	0.43	0.98	42	0.61	0.29	0.9
10	0.38	0.47	0.85	43	0.18	0.34	0.52
11	0.04	0.20	0.24	44	0.44	0.31	0.75
12	0.26	0.42	0.68	45	0.20	0.06	0.26
13	0.18	0.21	0.39	46	0.37	0.38	0.75
14	0.44	0.14	0.58	47	0.48	0.73	1.21
15	0.49	0.31	0.80	48	0.43	0.09	0.52
16	0.13	0.42	0.55	49	0.34	0.01	0.35
17	0.07	0.38	0.45	50	0.50	0.64	1.14
18	0.40	0.34	0.74	51	0.19	0.66	0.85
19	0.42	0.34	0.76	52	0.53	0.16	0.69
20	0.29	0.07	0.36	53	0.38	0.29	0.67
21	0.16	0.10	0.26	54	0.19	0.58	0.77
22	0.56	0.15	0.71	55	0.33	0.48	0.81
23	0.20	0.14	0.34	56	0.61	0.67	1.28
24	0.23	0.34	0.57	57	0.33	0.35	0.68
25	0.75	0.45	1.20	58	0.60	0.21	0.81
26	0.71	0.03	0.74	59	0.35	0.63	0.98
27	0.20	0.16	0.36	60	0.39	0.60	0.99
28	0.34	0.27	0.61	61	0.18	0.24	0.42
29	0.46	0.49	0.95	62	0.59	0.27	0.86
30	0.56	0.53	1.09	63	0.20	0.31	0.51
31	0.36	0.25	0.61	64	0.33	0.54	0.87
32	0.55	0.45	1.00	65	0.50	0.65	1.15
33	0.48	0.17	0.65				

$$\text{Mean of } C_o = \frac{\Sigma C_o}{N_2} = \frac{46.17}{65} = 0.71$$

Similarly we have Table 3 which summarizes the overall coupling of all paths having a path length of 3. We also compute mean of coupling values computed of all paths for different path lengths.

Table 3. Summarizing coupling values for each path for a path length of 3

p	C_{e1}	C_{e2}	C_{e3}	C_o	p	C_{e1}	C_{e2}	C_{e3}	C_o
1	0.31	0.46	0.40	1.17	24	0.26	0.63	0.81	1.70
2	0.49	0.56	0.59	1.64	25	0.70	0.35	0.03	1.08
3	0.57	0.15	0.14	0.86	26	0.27	0.11	0.69	1.07
4	0.95	0.30	0.34	1.59	27	0.11	0.28	0.52	0.91
5	0.13	0.13	0.67	0.93	28	0.47	0.20	0.37	1.04
6	0.40	0.32	0.30	1.02	29	0.78	0.09	0.76	1.63
7	0.42	0.39	0.37	1.18	30	0.68	0.01	0.37	1.06
8	0.12	0.64	0.47	1.23	31	0.47	0.11	0.25	0.83
9	0.53	0.57	0.59	1.69	32	0.18	0.76	0.17	1.11
10	0.78	0.71	0.48	1.97	33	0.57	0.96	0.25	1.78
11	0.56	0.58	0.83	1.97	34	0.71	0.50	0.55	1.76
12	0.21	0.76	0.29	1.26	35	0.07	0.40	0.54	1.01
13	0.55	0.80	0.40	1.75	36	0.64	0.75	0.10	1.49
14	0.60	0.32	0.15	1.07	37	0.15	0.59	0.42	1.16
15	0.64	0.47	0.30	1.41	38	0.51	0.16	0.44	1.11
16	0.61	0.65	0.70	1.96	39	0.67	0.28	0.52	1.47
17	0.63	0.51	0.81	1.95	40	0.27	0.23	0.61	1.11
18	0.50	0.66	0.46	1.62	41	0.25	0.19	0.76	1.20
19	0.20	0.54	0.60	1.34	42	0.31	0.30	0.70	1.31
20	0.21	0.44	0.18	0.83	43	0.20	0.65	0.33	1.18
21	0.65	0.49	0.16	1.30	44	0.76	0.96	0.82	2.54
22	0.03	0.75	0.03	0.81	45	0.04	0.37	0.63	1.04
23	0.34	0.66	0.64	1.64	46	0.60	0.68	0.68	1.96

$$\text{Mean of } C_o = \frac{\Sigma C_o}{N_3} = \frac{62.74}{46} = 1.36$$

In Table 4 we summarize the mean values of completed overall coupling values for different path lengths.

Table 4. Mean values of overall coupling values for different path lengths

Path length (n)	2	3	4	5
Mean of C_o	0.71	1.36	1.95	2.72

In Fig. 2 we draw the frequency of paths in paths in different coupling slots for path length of 2, 3, 4 and 5. In Fig. 2(a) we observe that there are more number of paths having a coupling value in the middle range. If there are more number of paths in the higher coupling range it would mean more maintenance effort will be needed.

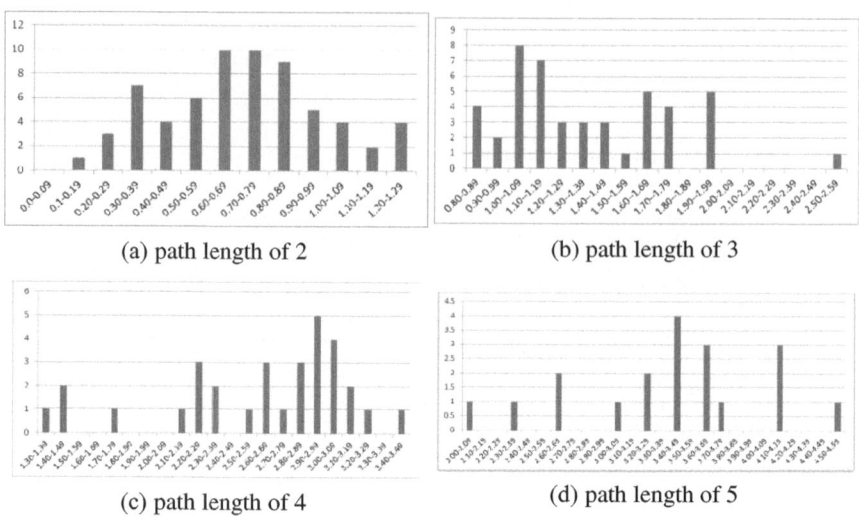

(a) path length of 2   (b) path length of 3

(c) path length of 4   (d) path length of 5

Fig. 2. Frequency of paths in different coupling slots for different path lengths

Since here it is in the middle range comparatively less maintenance effort will be needed for classes which are coupled with coupling path length of 2. In Fig. 2(b) many paths are in the lower coupling range that means overall maintenance effort will be less for path length 3 in taken case study. Similarly in Fig. 2(c) and Fig. 2(d) we observe that coupling range for C_o is larger and most of the paths are having larger values and fall at the end in these figures. Therefore, maintenance effort in this case is larger for classes coupled with these path lengths.

6   Conclusion

In this research we have identified some limitations of established coupling measurement metrics which measure the indirect coupling between any pair of classes in a class cluster. We have provided our metrics which is in relation with the maintenance effort required for these classes. In our experiment it is shown that as the path length increases between two classes the value of indirect coupling also increases as it is expected since the maintenance effort must increase. This increase in Indirect coupling value depends upon how strongly the classes are coupled together. Strongly coupled are expected to require more effort at the time of maintenance.

References

1. Erdil, K., Finn, E., Keating, K., Meattle, J., Park, S., Yoon, D.: Software Maintenance as Part of the Software Life Cycle, Comp180: Software Engineering Project, December 16 (2003)

2. Briand, L.C., Wust, J., Lounis, H.: Using coupling measurement for impact analysis in object-oriented systems. In: Proceedings of the International Conference on Software Maintenance (ICSM), Oxford, England, UK, pp. 475–482 (1999)
3. Weisfeld, M.: The Object-Oriented Thought Process. SAMS Publishing (2000)
4. Hitz, M., Montazeri, B.: Measuring coupling and cohesion in object-oriented systems. In: Proc. Int. Symposium on Applied Corporate Computing, Monterrey, Mexico (1995)
5. Li, W., Henry, S.: Object-oriented metrics that predict maintainability. Journal of Systems and Software 23(2), 111–122 (1993)
6. Fenton, N.E., Pfleeger, S.L.: Software Metrics: A Rigorous and Practical Approach, 2nd edn. International Thomson Computer Press (1996)
7. Yang, H.Y., Tempero, E., Berrigan, R.: Detecting indirect coupling. In: Proceedings of the Australian Software Engineering Conference (ASWEC), pp. 212–221. IEEE Computer Society, Los Alamitos (2005)
8. Briand, L., Daly, J., Wuest, J.: A Unified Framework for Coupling Measurement in Object-Oriented Systems. IEEE Transactions on Software Engineering 25(1), 91–121 (1999)
9. Yourdon, E., Constantine, L.: Structured Design: Fundamentals of a Discipline of Computer Program and System Design. Prentice-Hall (1979)
10. Berard, E.: Issues in the testing of object-oriented software. In: Electro 1994 International, pp. 211–219. IEEE Computer Society Press (1994)
11. Harrison, R., Counsell, S., Nithi, R.: An evaluation of Object-Oriented software metrics. IEEE Transactions on Software Engineering 23(1), 491–496 (1998)
12. Yacoub, S.M., Ammar, H.H., Robinson, T.: Dynamic metrics for object oriented designs. In: Proceedings of the 6th International Symposium on Software Metrics, p. 50. IEEE Computer Society (1999)
13. Arisholm, E., Briand, L.C., Foyen, A.: Dynamic coupling measurement for object-oriented software. IEEE Transactions on Software Engineering 30(8), 491–506 (2004)

Development of a Robust Microcontroller Based Intelligent Prosthetic Limb

Anup Nandy, Soumik Mondal, Pavan Chakraborty, and G.C. Nandi

Indian Institute of Information Technology Allahabad, Robotics & AI Laboratory, India
{nandy.anup,mondal.soumik}@gmail.com,
{pavan,gcnandi}@iiita.ac.in

Abstract. Adaptive Modular Active Leg (AMAL), a robotic Intelligent Prosthetic Limb has been developed at the Indian Institute of Information Technology Allahabad. The aim of the project was to provide the comfort of an intelligent prosthetic knee joint for differently abeled person with one leg amputated above the knee. AMAL provides him with the necessary shock absorption and a suitable bending of the knee joint oscillation. The bending and the shock absorption are provided by artificial muscles. In our case, it is the MR (Magneto Rheological) damper which controls the knee movement of an amputee. The feedback signal is provided by the heel's strike sensor. AMAL has been kept simple with minimal feedback sensors and controls so that the product is economically viable for the patients. In this paper we describe the mechanical design, the electronic control with its successful testing on differently abeled persons.

Keywords: Adaptive Modular Active Leg (AMAL), Robotic knee joint, Magneto-Rheological Damper, Prosthetic Leg, Heel strike sensor, Above knee amputee.

1 Introduction

The knee joint movement is an important aspect for a human biped locomotion [1], [2], [3]. An amputee with a prosthetic rigid leg is deprived of this knee movement. This leads to an uncomfortable walking gait and injuries due to lack of shock absorption which the knee joint provides during walking.

Several prosthetic limbs are available for amputee persons with different costs. The cost of below the knee prosthetics is between $6000 to $8000 and the cost of above the knee prosthetics is between $10,000 to $15,000 [4]. The C-Leg, manufactured by Otto Bock Health care is completely controlled by the microprocessor circuit. It provides better comfort to the trans-femoral amputee during locomotion. It facilitates multiple settings for running, walking, bicycling and even incline-skating. The cost of newest C-Leg is extremely high in the range of $30,000 to $40,000 to be fitted and delivered [5].

The Jaipur above knee prosthesis is built to help active knee amputees with different knee joints such as Exoskeleton (Plastic Knee joint), Endoskeleton (Pylon knee joint) and Exoskeleton (Oilone Axle knee joint) [6]. The mechanical design of this leg involves locking system at the knee joint which helps to oscillate the knee flexion and knee extension whenever required. No other microcontroller based

M. Parashar et al. (Eds.): IC3 2012, CCIS 306, pp. 452–462, 2012.

controller circuit has been put into this leg. It lacks of calculating the suitable damping force required to the knee joint.

Another Limb manufacturing organization named as Artificial Limb Manufacturing Corp. of India (ALIMCO) [7] is involved to fabricate the above knee prosthesis with conventional hip joint and above knee with Silesian suspension for the betterment of amputee's gait. The price of this leg is economically cheap compared to other prosthesis manufacturing organizations. This leg also deprives to have a damping controlling circuit.

The Endolite India Limited [8] is the leading manufacturing corporation to develop prosthetic limb. The characteristics of this leg are the knee movement is measured by the Orion sensors in real time and the microprocessor is used to process the sensory information. The knee speed is being controlled by Hydraulic/pneumatic dampers which allow the prosthetic patient to walk on slopes, stairs and flat terrain.

Indian Institute of Information Technology Allahabad has been involved in developing an Adaptive Prosthetic Limb to facilitate differently abled people whose one of the legs has been amputated above the knee. This robotic prosthetic limb [9] has been named as AMAL. It is an acronym for Adaptive Modular Active Leg. AMAL provides him with suitable comfort for walking, by providing a suitable bending of the knee joint and knee joint oscillation.

2   The Human Locomotion and the Use of the Knee

To design a prosthetic leg one should understand the human locomotion [10], [11] and the use of the knee joint. Human locomotion can be separated into two phases. The stance phase and the swing phase (Fig. 1a). Stance phase begins with the right heel strike. By shifting the center of gravity of the body, the body weight is transferred onto the right leg from the left leg. The momentum causes the human to rise on its standing right leg freeing the left leg which then swings into position. The left knee bends, stretched, bends and stretches, going through double oscillation with short and long amplitude. The knee finally straitens to take the left heel strike. The human falls forward naturally and catches itself on the left leg during the heel strike. As the swinging left leg touches the ground, the ground contact triggers the knee to tighten and get ready for the body weight transfer. The legs then swap roles. The Fig. 1b also shows the major muscles involved in human locomotion. The acting muscles are shaded in black.

The knee Joint has a complex structure. The skeleton view in Fig. 2a illustrates this joint. The knee joint connects a single (thigh bone) with the duel bone tibia and fibula which forms the lower part of the leg. The dual bones help to provide the necessary torque for the knee joint movement. The small circular bone patella in front of the knee prevents it from bending forward. The end surfaces of the femur and tibia are convex as well as concave. This surfaces move with respect to one another by simultaneously (1) rolling, (2) gliding, and (3) spinning. When the concave surface is fixed and the convex surface moves on it (Fig. 2b), the convex surface rolls and glides in opposite directions. When the convex surface is fixed and the concave surface moves on it (Fig. 2c), the concave surface rolls and glides in the same direction.

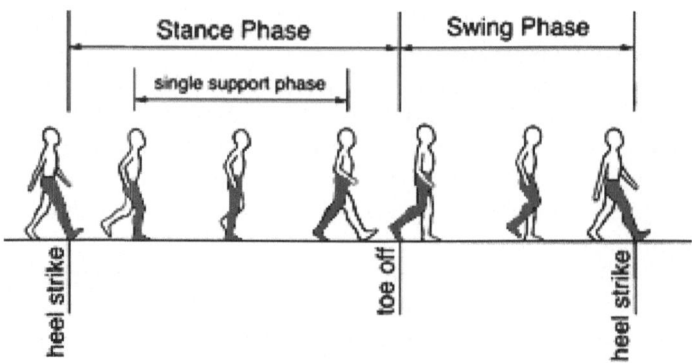

(a) Different phases of Human Locomotion

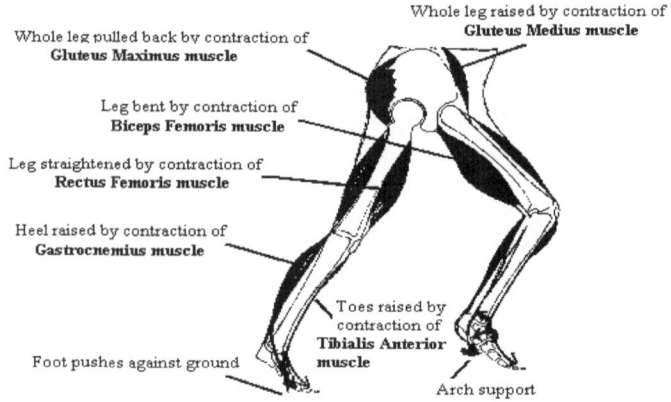

(b) Different muscles involved in human locomotion

Fig. 1.

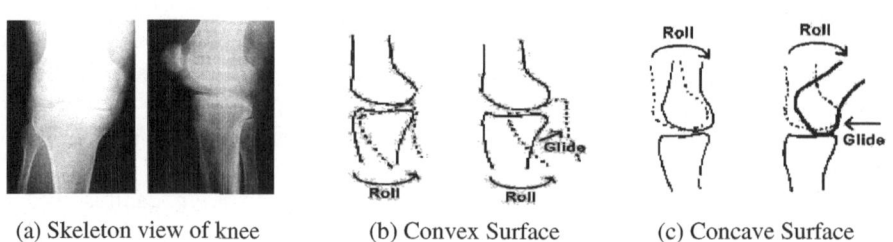

(a) Skeleton view of knee   (b) Convex Surface   (c) Concave Surface

Fig. 2.

3   Mechanical Design of AMAL

AMAL, has been designed to be very rugged, easy to use and maintain. The mechanical parts of AMAL are made with strengthened steel and stainless steel. Some of these steel parts can be replaced with strengthened aluminum or advance carbon fiber structure to reduce the weight. The design is modular and it may be altered for people with different height. As per our design, the mechanical structure of AMAL was manufactured at the mechanical workshop of the Artificial Limb Manufacturing Corporation of India (ALIMCO), Kanpur, India. An MOU was signed between IIIT-Allahabad and ALIMCO for manufacturing and marketing of AMAL. After satisfactory testing, the technology has been transferred to ALIMCO for mass producing the prosthetic limb and doing the required field study. Preliminary results by this field study have been extremely positive.

While designing AMAL, the human knee has been kept in mind. Fig. 1b illustrates the major muscles involved in human locomotion. We see that there are multiple muscles involved in the process which makes it extremely complicated. It is assumed that the patient will have a thighs stub with quadriceps femoris muscle sufficiently intact and having the capacity to move his hip joint. Fig. 3a shows an MRI picture of a healthy leg. The MRI picture shows the major bones, Femur, Tibia and Fibula and the inner muscles that connects the Femur with the Tibia. Our MR damper will simulate and work, as this muscle. The working of the MR damper is explained in the next section. We also notice from the MRI picture that the central axis of Femur and Tibia have an offset. This allow and additional torque which helps in bending of the knee. The frontward bending of the knee is prevented by the Patella. In our design we have maintained an offset of 11.5 mm (Fig. 3b). The frontward bending is automatically prevented by the maximum limit of the piston of the MR Damper. This piston is also offset from the rotation axis by 35mm. This provides the additional necessary torque and a full bending capability up to crouching/squatting. Fig. 3c shows the front view of the AMAL's knee. The knee should be able to bear the weight of the person and a higher backward force during heel strike. Earlier design had a thin axel of 5 mm which gave way during trials. Therefore the joint was redesigned with a thicker axel and with 2 heavy-duty bearings. The separation between the bearings had to be less than what is seen in Fig. 3c. This separation was

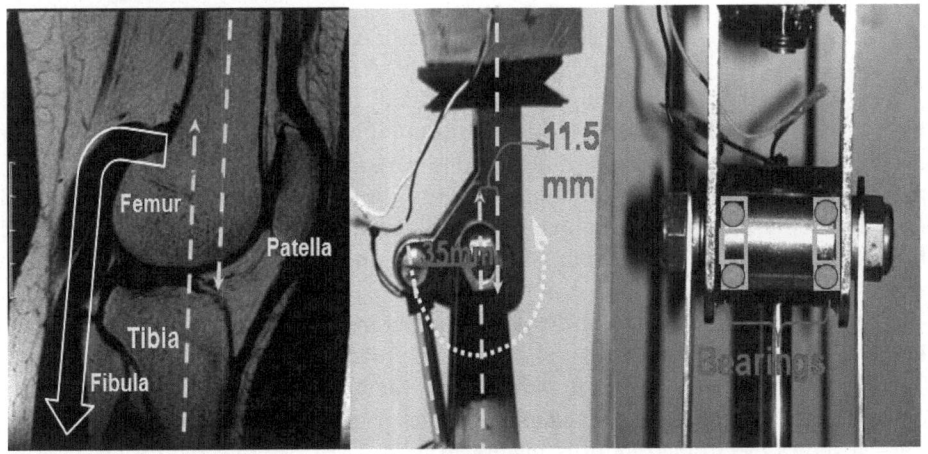

(a) Knee joint muscles   (b) Knee joint socket   (c) Bearing hinge joints

Fig. 3.

increased during manufacturing at ALIMCO. A readily available axel of the dimension was used. This has prevented the twisting motion that a human knee has for negotiating uneven terrain.

The mechanical design of AMAL has been kept simple and made it economically viable. The price at which AMAL is being marketed is approximate. $300. The knee joint movement of AMAL using the MR damper should be controlled, synchronized and coordinated with the knee joint movement of the other healthy leg. A control circuit which has been developed at IIIT-Allahabad provides the required current in the MR damper which tightens or relaxes as a normal human muscle involved in knee joint movement.

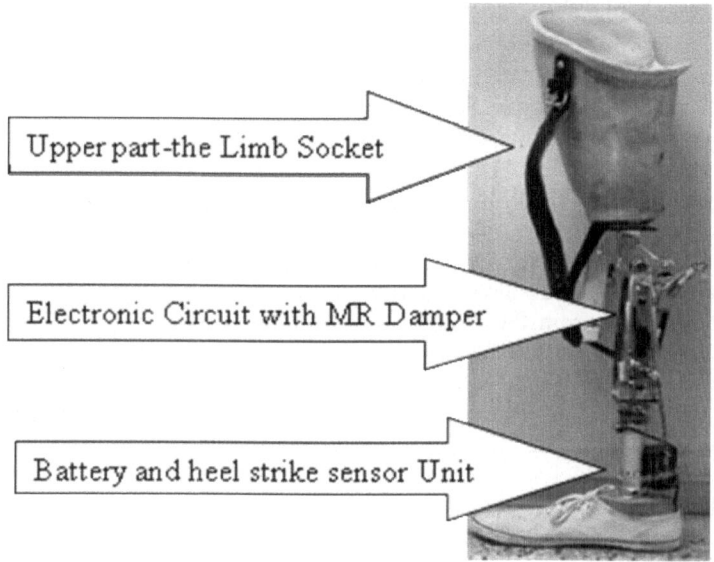

Upper part-the Limb Socket

Electronic Circuit with MR Damper

Battery and heel strike sensor Unit

Fig. 4. The total layout of AMAL

The AMAL mechanical design can be divided into two parts; the upper and the lower. The upper part of the AMAL which is the limb socket (Fig. 4) has to be tailor made for the amputee. It has to be designed to the specification of the amputated limb and should be comfortable and tightly fitted to the amputee and giving him a good grip. The lower part of AMAL contains the MR damper; the electronic controller and battery; which will be common to all patients except the foot size may be changed to match the other feet.

The upper and lower parts of the AMAL structure can move freely back and forth in the same way as that of a natural limb of a human can move along the knee joint. The MR damper is placed such that the free movement of the AMAL structure can be controlled by the changing the damping profile of the MR liquid inside the damper. Fig. 5a shows electronic circuit is integrated with AMAL before field trials. AMAL has been tested on actual patient (Fig. 5b) whose one of the legs has been amputated from above the knee. The impressive result has been obtained from testing field.

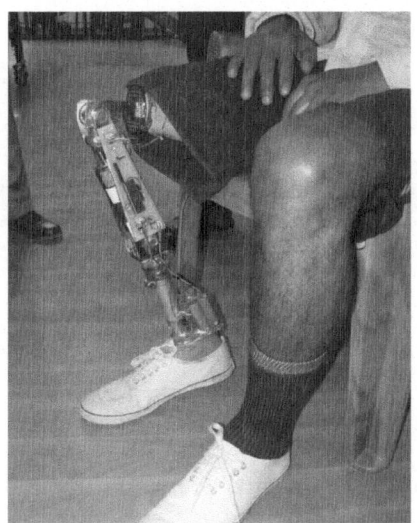

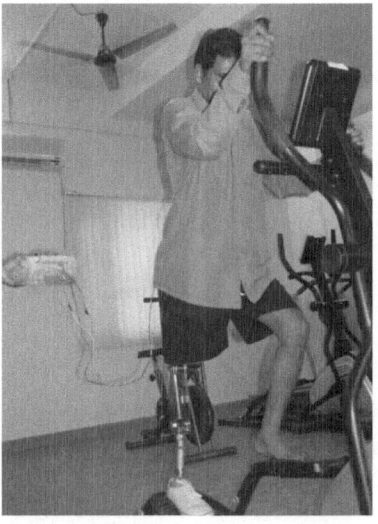

(a) Electronic circuit integrated with AMAL   (b) Field testing on actual amputee

Fig. 5.

4   MR Damper Specifications

A Magneto-Rheological (MR) Damper [12] simulates the natural knee joint for a human being. The MR damper is a sophisticated shock absorber whose damping profile can be accurately adjusted as required at a very fast rate (few milliseconds). The MR damper (Fig. 6) is filled with the Magneto-Rheological fluid which is a smart fluid. It is a colloidal mixture of microscopic magnetic particle and carrier liquid (oil) (Fig. 7a). During un-biased conditions the smart fluid behaves like any other viscous oil, free to flow in any direction.

Fig. 6. MR Damper designed by LORD's corporation

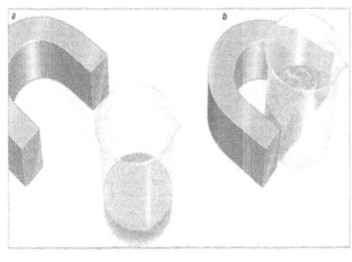 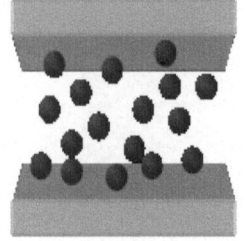 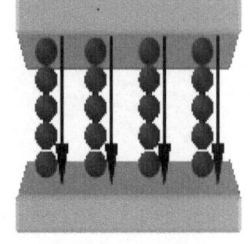

(a) MR Damper with liquid   (b) Without Magnetic Field   (c) With Magnetic Field

Fig. 7.

Fig. 7b shows the MR damper without magnetic field. Fig. 7c shows the MR damper whose fluid's viscosity changes with the applied magnetic field. Iron/magnetic particles are suspension in glycol and get aligned with the magnetic field and thus increase its viscosity [13].

When subjected to a magnetic field the micrometer sized magnetic particles align themselves according to the magnetic line of force and transform into a viscoelastic solid. Therefore, the viscosity of the smart fluid can be varied over a wide range, from free flowing to fully rigid, by changing the strength of the applied magnetic field. An electro-magnet is used to apply the magnetic field. The electro-magnet coil can be excited using a battery. The damping profile of the MR damper is controlled using an advanced electronic circuit.

A typical Magneto-Rheological (MR) fluid consists of 20-40% by volume of relatively pure, 3-10 micron diameter iron particles, suspended in a carrier liquid such as mineral oil, synthetic oil, water or glycol.

Iron particles in suspension align and develop yield strength in the presence of a magnetic field. The change from a free-flowing liquid to a semi-solid when a magnetic field is applied is rapid and reversible.

5   Controller Circuit Description

We have designed and built a new control circuit (Fig. 8) using commonly available components in India. The circuit has been successfully tested and deployed on the AMAL.

The AMAL electronic controller works on 12V D.C and drains 2 Amps of current at full load. The power going to the MR damper is controlled using an advanced power management IC and it can extent the battery life three folds. Essentially it works in a pulse mode. Peak power is only applied for about 50μs over an average gait cycle of one second. The approximate consumption is about 1miliwatt/second. This drastically reduces the battery consumption. With a high capacity modern NiMH rechargeable cells which has a rating of 60 – 120 watt-hr the leg can easily perform for more than 8hrs of continuous working. However the power efficiency always been

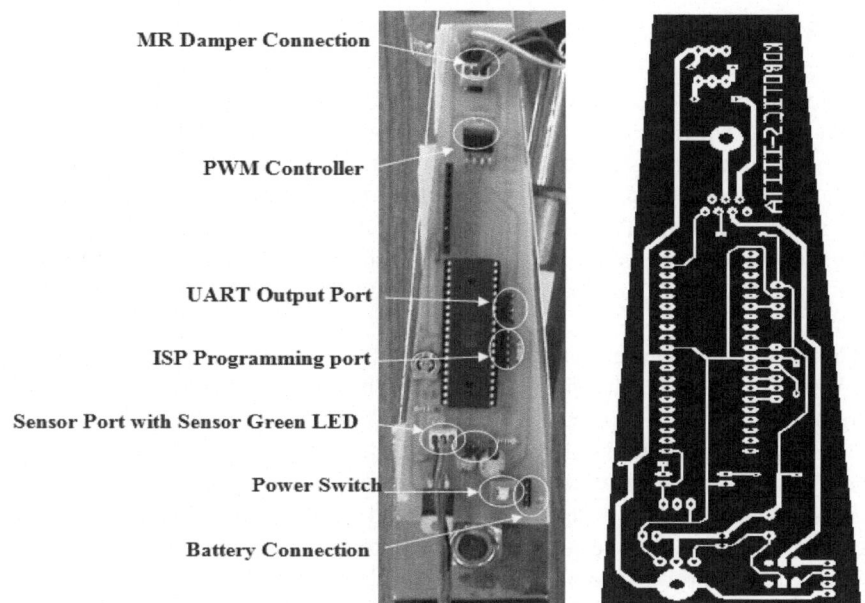

Fig. 8. AMAL controller circuit and PCB design

the major concern in such endeavor. The control circuit employs a microcontroller – AVR Atmel Mega32 for computational needs. The microcontroller is used to process the data coming from the hell strike sensor. The heel strike sensor provides a pulse as the heel strikes the ground. It is essentially a rugged switch. This pulse is used as start and stop for computations of gait period. The output of microcontroller is directed to the input pin of the MR damper controller and the damping profile is controlled.

The input from the heel strike sensor is attached to the "Sensor IN" of the electronics circuit. There is no polarity of connecting MR Damper. The battery unit is connected to the PCB (Fig. 8) using "Battery". The toggle switch is the ON/OFF switch for the circuit. The electronics circuit is powered using a battery pack of 12.6V. The 7V line is tapped from the same battery unit. A standard voltage regulator IC (IC7805) is used to regulate supply to 5V. The 5V is used to power the microcontroller circuit. The 500 ohms reference potentiometer is used to supply the analog reference voltage to the microcontroller for A/D conversion. Its screw should be set in the middle for 250 Ohms drop. The microcontroller is programmed using a PC serial port and the 6 pin ISP PORT. The output of the microcontroller can be viewed on a PC computer using a serial port and UART PORT on the PCB. The Red LED shows the ON/OFF status of the circuit. The yellow LED on the PCB shows the over temperature or over current protection enable. The MR damper controller has an inbuilt over-temperature and over-current protection. The IC DRV102 and IC 7805 are expected to heat when used continuously and therefore need heat sinks. The Fig. 8 shows the electronic circuit.

6   Working of AMAL

The control of AMAL is done by a specially designed sophisticated electronics control circuit which is fixed to the support bars of the MR Damper. The electronics should be hermetically sealed and properly cushioned to keep it safe. The control circuit consists of the AMAL electronics circuit and the batteries. The battery is fixed at the ankle joint of the AMAL. It solves two purposes, firstly the battery unit is near to the electronics circuit and secondly the weight of the battery will help the AMAL to retrieve the stable position quickly while walking (like head mass effect in a hammer).

The electronic control circuit is powered by advanced rechargeable NiMH rechargeable cells. The charging of the NiMH battery needs an advanced intelligent charging circuit which is provided with the pack. The control circuit can be switched ON/OFF by a toggle button on the circuit board. There is a status LED on the circuit which indicates the normal working of the circuit. The control circuit uses a latest microcontroller to analyze the heel strike and produce digital output signal. The microcontroller has advance software written into its memory.

The active control of AMAL is initiated by the foot heel strike of the AMAL. The heel strike sensor (Switch, Foot, Small, IP67, and Black) is pressure detector. The sensor detects the pressure applied on the heel of the foot while natural walking; it sends digital signals to the microcontroller. The microcontroller analysis the signal using the software and sends the control signal to the PWM controller. The PWM damper controller changes the stiffness of the MR Damper and thus changing the free movement of the AMAL Knee. If the control circuit detects the heel strike it energizes the MR Damper to its maximum value. The moment pressure is removed from the heel sensor the MR damper returns to its flexible condition. This gives amputee a comfortable gait and a stable standing position. All the above mentioned process happens in split of a second and the amputee will never feel any lag in the response.

7   Conclusion and Future Work

AMAL is now being manufactured by ALIMCO and tested on different patients. The feedback has been extremely positive. The likely impact of this innovation will be to the physically challenged persons whose one of the legs has been amputated above the knee. AMAL provides the suitable comfort for walking, by providing the required bending of the knee joint and knee joint oscillation. The robotic leg coordinates excellently with the other healthy leg in an extremely synchronized fashion. The heel strike follows essentially the hip joint movement of the subject. The hip joint is part of the subject's natural hip which follows the will of the subject. Thus the will of the subject is captured through the heel strike pulse obtained from the heel strike sensor and sent to the microcontroller which provides the excellent coordination with the healthy leg. The Knee joint movement is controlled by an MR Damper which simulates a human muscle. A control circuit which has been developed at IIIT-Allahabad provides the required current in the MR damper which tightens or relaxes as a normal human muscle involved in knee joint movement. The robustness of the design is by minimal use of sensors (only heel strike) and economical use of battery. The mechanical design provides the required gravity aided torque which reduces the power consumption. The mechanical lock bears the weight of the patient and the knee does not buckle during stand still mode. During this period the electronics goes into hibernation which further reduces the power consumption.

After satisfactory testing, the technology has been transferred to ALIMCO for mass producing the prosthetic limb and doing the required field study. Preliminary results by this field study have been extremely positive. AMAL was also tried on a female patient and was found successful. The only complain was the weight of the prosthetic limb. Though the prosthetic limb weight much less than an actual leg would, it feels as an additional weight. This weight could easily be reduced by replacing some of the heavy steel with the much lighter carbon fiber material. This will however escalate the price of AMAL. The weight of the prosthetic limb is a factor that one needs to gets accustomed and acclimatized with.

From field studies we have realized that AMAL requires further modifications and improvement. In our present design we have only considered the rotation aspect of the knee joint. The gliding and rolling aspect of a normal human knee joint is not provided in the prosthetic knee. This aspect of rolling and gliding will be implemented in our next design. The knee pivot and the linking with the human stub will be modified to provide the required rolling and gliding.

Acknowledgments. This work was fully supported by Indian Institute of Information Technology, Allahabad. We would like to thank to Dr. M.D. Tiwari, Director of IIIT-Allahabad to bring this project from Department of Science of Technology (DST), Govt. of India. We would also like to thank to ALIMCO, Kanpur, India for supporting field testing of AMAL on actual patients. Mr. Mahendra Singh Khuswa had lost his right leg in a railway mishap. Almost all of our testing and field trials were made on him. We are extremely indebted to him for all his support and feedback from the patient's point of view. We also thank Mr. Advitiya Saxena for the help of electronics part related to the project.

References

1. QiDi, W., ChengJu, L., JiaQi, Z., QiJun, C.: Survey of locomotion control of legged robot inspired by biological concept. In: Information Science. Springer, Science in China Series F, pp. 1715–1729 (2009)
2. Marzani, F., Calais, E., Legrand, L.: A 3-D marker-free system for the analysis of movement disabilities - an application to the legs. IEEE Transactions on Information Technology in Biomedicine 5(1), 18–26 (2001)
3. Dejnabadi, H., Jolles, B.M., Aminian, K.: A New Approach for Quantitative Analysis of Inter-Joint Coordination During Gait. IEEE Transactions on Biomedical Engineering 55(2), 755–764 (2008)
4. Prosthetic leg costs, http://www.scipolicy.net/prosthetic-legs/
5. ottobock C-Leg, http://c-leg.ottobock.com/en/

6. Jaipur Foot, http://www.jaipurfoot.org/
   04_Services_Above_Knee_Prosthesis.asp
7. Artificial Limb Manufacturing Corporation of India,
   http://www.artlimbs.com/lower_limb_prosthetics.htm
8. Endolite India Limited, http://endoliteindia.com/home/main.aspx
9. Nandi, G.C., Ijspeert, A.J., Chakraborty, P., Nandi, A.: Development of Adaptive Modular Active Leg (AMAL) using bipedal robotics technology. In: Robotics and Autonomous Systems, vol. 57, pp. 603–616 (2009)
10. Mondal, S., Nandy, A., Chakrabarti, A., Chakraborty, P., Nandi, G.C.: A Framework for Synthesis of Human Gait Oscillation Using Intelligent Gait Oscillation Detector (IGOD). In: Ranka, S., Banerjee, A., Biswas, K.K., Dua, S., Mishra, P., Moona, R., Poon, S.-H., Wang, C.-L. (eds.) IC3 2010, Part I. CCIS, vol. 94, pp. 340–349. Springer, Heidelberg (2010)
11. Mondal, S., Nandy, A., Chandrapal, Chakraborty, P., Nandi, G.C.: A Central Pattern Generator based Nonlinear Controller to Simulate Biped Locomotion with a Stable Human Gait Oscillation. International Journal of Robotics and Automation (IJRA) 2(2), 93–106 (2011)
12. LORD MR Damper, http://www.lord.com/
    products-and-solutions/magneto-rheological-%28mr%29.xml
13. Magnetorheological Fluids,
    http://www.hs-owl.de/fb5/labor/rt/en/mrf_aktorik_en.html

SMART- A Social Mobile Advanced Robot Test Bed for Humanoid Robot Researchers

Jainendra Shukla, Jitendra Kumar Pal, Faimy Q. Ansari,
G.C. Nandi, and Pavan Chakraborty

Robotics & Artificial Intelligence Lab,
Indian Institute of Information Technology Allahabad (IIITA),
Allahabad 211012, U.P., India
{jainendra08,jpjitendrapal,faimyqa}@gmail.com
{gcnandi,pavan}@iiita.ac.in

Abstract. We envision that in near future, Humanoid Robots will enter in the household. They have capability to change the quality of life and advance the human civilizations further. For this thing to happen, humanoid robot researchers need to solve many challenging problems. Towards this we have taken a significant step in developing indigenously a low cost research test bed where researchers can develop and test many technologies for Human Robot interactions. The basic issue which has been addressed is the development of a cost effective platform which will be stable and robust, having an open architecture so that various technologies like speech, vision, intelligence can be integrated with physical gestures. First we have described the developmental architecture of the SMART, and then the application of SMART as an intelligent robot which, for the time being, is capable of demonstrating our robotics and artificial intelligence laboratory to the visitors as a lab guide in an interactive manner.

1 Introduction

This research describes about a humanoid robot named SMART, developed to work as lab guide in a structured environment. The acronym SMART stands for **S**ocial **M**obile **A**dvanced **R**obot **T**est-bed. SMART is Social as it is having ability to interact with people, Mobile as it can be programmed to move in given area, Advanced as it houses standard and sophisticated techniques for vision, interaction and locomotion, and Testbed because having an open and flexible architecture that can be easily used to develop, test and implement techniques in direction of humanoid robotics. Although SMART is developed to work mainly as lab guide, but simultaneously SMART is equipped with facilities which enables it to act as a test bed for research and development in robotics discipline. The building of the robot is done indigenously from scratch in Robotics & Artificial Intelligence laboratory only. SMART has 6 degree of freedom and 2 additional degrees of mobility with 3 degree of freedom in both the arms. SMART weighs 24 kg and is 127 cm tall. Hardware and software of SMART is fully disclosed and is completely open source. It enables anyone to add his/her creativity to SMART and to develop and test new or existing algorithms on SMART.

M. Parashar et al. (Eds.): IC3 2012, CCIS 306, pp. 463–470, 2012.

The body & base of the SMART is made of plywood & aluminum profiles. The motion in SMART is achieved by using powerful wiper motors. SMART moves its arms using low rpm DC motors. SMART is equipped with a laptop to acquire the data from sensors, to do the required planning and to instruct the actuators.

SMART uses camera as its only sensor to sense environment around it. Planning requires extensive image processing to achieve real time performance e.g. in obstacle avoidance. SMART is also able to narrate the things to the visitors, using its speech generation ability. While explaining the technical details, the SMART is capable of making various simple hand gestures.

SMART can be easily deployed at many public places easily.

2   System Architecture

The architecture of SMART can be understood by figure 1 [1].

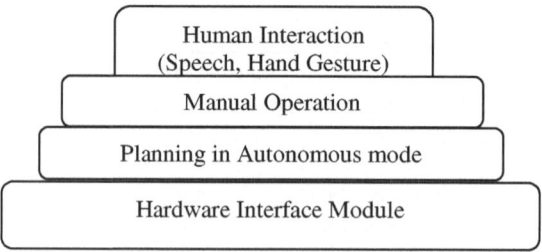

Fig. 1. SMART Complete Layered Architecture

After complete development of robot body frame, actuators have been placed. Two high torque are motors used to provide the robot locomotion. And for arms, low rpm DC 12V geared motors are used. To control heavy torque wiper motor as well as geared motors, "Dual Motor Driver electronic circuit" made by robokits is used. It provides up to 5Amp current to the motor. One driver circuit can drive two motors in both the directions (clock wise or anti clock wise) [2]. In both the arms SMART has 3 DOF; to achieve this we are using 6 geared motors. And for controlling these motors same "Dual Motor Driver electronic circuit" has been used. So, for total 8 motors (2 for locomotion+6 in arms) 4 driver circuits are required. On the mother circuit 5 Dual Motor Driver circuits has been installed to add additional DOF in future. Using its 3 DOF in both the hands SMART is able to pick and place objects from anywhere in its surrounding.

To control actuators of SMART, laptop, which has configuration (1GB RAM, Intel Dual-Core processor) is used. Laptop sends the controlling signals, which is then received by microcontroller. To accomplish this task, AVR 40 pin Development board has been used, in which atmega16 µcontroller is used. To control 10 motors in both directions, 20 pins of µcontroller send control signal to all 5 driver circuits. For this PORTA 8 pins, PORTB 8 pins & PORTC 4 pins are used.

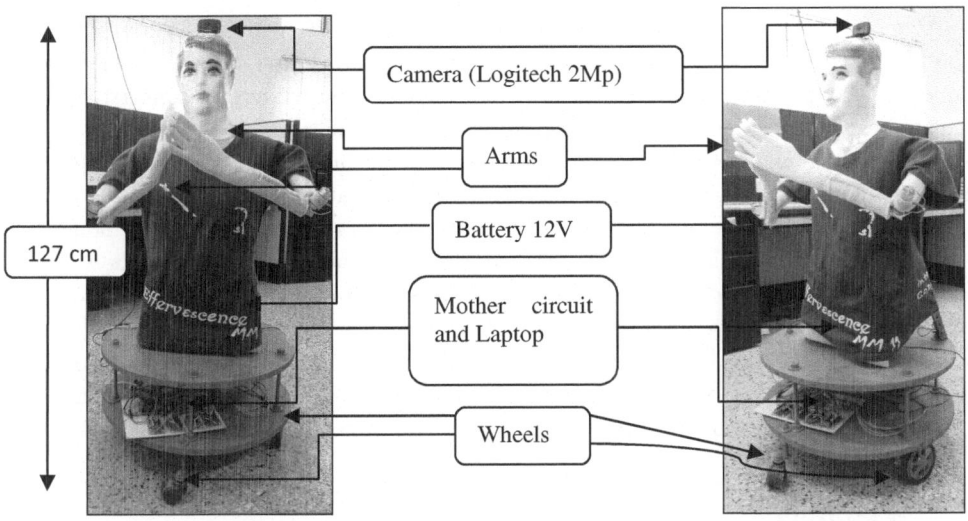

Fig. 2. Illustration of complete robot

Controlling signals are being sent through USB port to the UART of the microcontroller Atmega16.

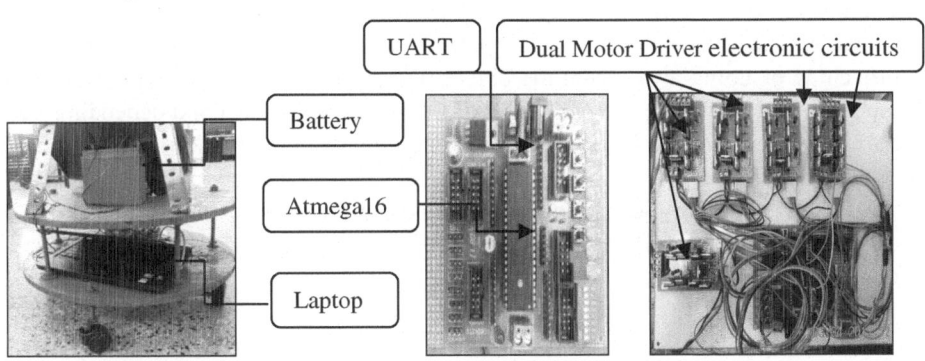

Fig. 3. [Battery, Laptop in robot, Interface circuit using atmega16 µcontroller & Mother Circuit]

Locomotion is provided to the robot by controlling two base motors. SMART is able to move forward, backward, it can also take left and right turns. These turns are achieved by turning off only one side motor.

3   Software Description

SMART's software is developed entirely in C using OpenCV and GSL libraries. It consists of around 10 modules, which communicates according to their hierarchy as shown in figure 1.

At the primary level, hardware interface module interacts with the vision sensor and the actuators (driving IC's & motors). On the top of that navigational planning is done by vision module using the information provided by the vision sensors. At a higher level, interaction module of the software determines what SMART says i.e. speech & sound and how SMART expresses its hand gestures. Finally at the top most level, integration and synchronization between different modules is achieved.

Software architecture of SMART makes it possible to run SMART in two modes: Autonomous and Manual. In autonomous mode SMART works as lab guide but when operated in manual mode SMART can be used to perform much other different kind of tasks such as pick and place some object.

SMART's software is completely open source which enables anyone to modify and update SMART's working. This enables SMART simultaneously to work as a test bed for research and development in robotics discipline.

4   Planning

4.1   Localization

SMART's planning capability makes it possible to move SMART autonomously in the lab, avoiding obstacles. As SMART uses only one sensor i.e. single camera, planning requires extensive image processing to achieve real time performance.

When we see objects they appear larger or smaller depending upon whether we are approaching or going away from the object (Fig 4 and Fig 5). This is the basic idea behind the working of the SMART. SMART first sees the object and depending upon the area of the size of the object, it decides that how much it should move to reach to the object.

To facilitate smooth localization of objects in lab in an efficient manner, different checkpoints are created which are marked with a colored paper, as shown in figure 6 and in figure 7.

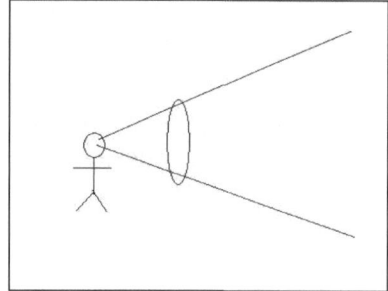   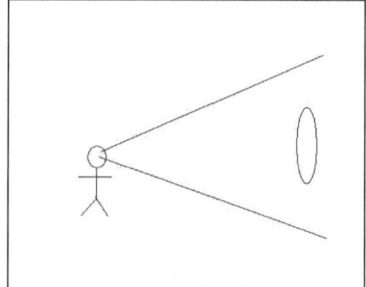

Fig. 4. Object as seen when nearer   **Fig. 5.** Object as seen when far

Now as shown in figure 6 & figure 7, if SMART wants to go to HOAP-2[1] (or PLC[2]) it checks for the above colour. Upon seeing this colour SMART knows that HOAP-2 (or PLC) is here. In this manner, localization of different objects is done.

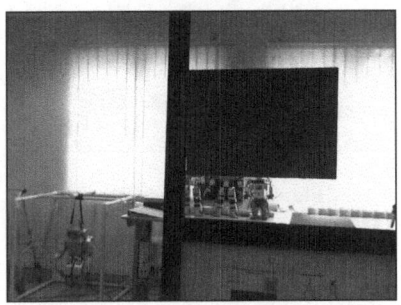   

Fig. 6. Check point at HOAP-2   **Fig. 7.** Check point at PLC

Algorithm for object localization is as follows:

- Image is captured from the camera.
- Image is converted to HSV plane.
- Thresholding is applied to the image on a range of HSV values of the object colour.
- Spatial moments of the threshold image are calculated.
- Area of the threshold image is calculated using zero order moment. This is the area of the object.
  Area A= moment (0, 0);
- Now centre of gravity is found by dividing spatial moments of first order m(1,0) and m (0,1) by the zero order moment m (0,0) (i.e. the area A of the object).
  X=moment (1, 0)/A=moment (1, 0)/moment (0, 0);
  Y=moment (0, 1)/A=moment (1, 0)/moment (0, 0);

4.2   Navigation

To move towards any localized object SMART sees the checkpoint it needs to visit as per the lab visit plan. Visiting order of objects in lab is predetermined. Now if SMART is far from the checkpoint it sees an image like figure 8 and if it is near, it sees an image as in figure 9.

---

[1] HOAP-2 is an advanced humanoid robot developed by Fujitsu Automation, Japan is kept in Robotics & AI Lab, IIIT-A for demonstration and R&D purpose.

[2] PLC is programmable logic controller kept at lab for industrial automation demonstration.

Fig. 8. Checkpoint as SMART sees it being far   **Fig. 9.** Image when it is near

Vision module applies a thresholding to the captured image and it gets a thresholded image like figure 10 (or figure 11, if it is near). From this thresholded image, using spatial moments, area of the image is calculated [3]. Now depending upon pre calibrated values SMART decides up to when it has to move towards the checkpoint. Some thresholded images showing their distance from SMART is shown in table 1.

Table 1. Pre Calibrated Distance of SMART from object as calculated from images

Serial NO	Image	Distance (in meter)
1	Figure 7	2.4 Meters
2	Figure 8	6.2 Meters
3	Figure 9	0.8 Meters

As shown in figure 10 and figure 11, colors have been thresholded and we are calculating area as well as center of this color in the image. So whether SMART has to turn right or left that entirely depends on the center of the color. For example if center of color is in left side in the image it means SMART has to take turn right or anti clock wise.

Fig. 10. Threshold image of figure 8   **Fig. 11.** Threshold image of figure 9

5   Speech Generation

SMART narrates about different things using its speech generation ability. For this purpose, first the speech about different objects which are to be demonstrated is prepared. Then this speech is converted to voice using text to speech convertor provided by Smart Link Corporation [4]. Male voice is used by this convertor and is in USA English ascent. Voice file generated by this convertor is in the form of shock wave file (.swf). To play this type of sound file a suitable audio player, "Media Player" is used. This audio player is invoked from the controller C program, with the name of voice file to be played as an argument.

To enable SMART to generate speech while doing image processing, multiprocessing is done using createProcess () function [5]. It takes following arguments:

1: Path to executable file, media player in our case.
2: Command string, which in our case the media file that the robot has to play.
3: Process handle not inherited.
4: Thread handle not inherited.
5: No inheritance of handles.
6: No special flags.
7: Same environment block as this program.
8: Current directory - no separate path.
9: Pointer to STARTUPINFO.
10: Pointer to PROCESS_INFORMATION.

6   Conclusion and Future Research

We have developed a vision-guided Intelligent Humanoid lab guide robot. Our robot is efficient and intelligent enough to work as lab guide in a structured environment. Structured environments do not impose any restrictions on working of the robot, as labs usually provide a structured environment. The algorithm developed for robots navigation is computationally efficient and yet good enough to work in labs. Our robot uses digital camera as the only sensor, which provides the robot enough information for detecting obstacles and to achieve a robust behavior. Our robots control strategy is very reactive. The robot reacts to only immediate sensing of the camera. The robot is deployed in Robotics and Artificial Intelligence Lab, IIITA and is performing very well. Because of its adaptive nature, SMART can be deployed at any required place very easily.

Colour based object detection suffers very much from the problem of calibration. To perform efficiently, the vision module is required to calibrate before each operation.   This pre calibration is very time consuming and hence, a robot which can be deployed in any environment without prior calibration is very much required. Robots equipped with auto calibration are next challenge for such robots.

Robot equipped with such auto calibration ability will calibrate itself automatically before each operation and hence, manual calibration will be no more needed. For auto calibration, robot will take pictures of the lab and the floor. In another approach, proximity sensors can be added with the camera. The correlation between the proximity and vision sensors can be learnt, which then could be used for auto calibration of the robot.

This robot can be made more useful if it recognizes the lab members, the way members of the lab recognize each other. In addition to lab members, if the robot could recognize the prominent visitors and could welcome them with their names, it would be very fascinating. So, to equip the robot with the real time face recognition capability is another task to achieve in future.

Acknowledgements. We are deeply indebted to the Hon'ble Director, Indian Institute of Information Technology- Allahabad for his kind support, making this project completion successful. This research is fully sponsored by IIITA.

We also thank to Ms. Manisha Tiwari for providing her valuable support in managing our project.

References

[1] Thrun, S., Bennewitz, M., Burgard, W.: MINERVA: A Second-Generation Museum Tour-Guide Robot. In: IEEE International Conference on Robotics and Automation (1999)
[2] Robokits, http://www.robokits.co.in
[3] Kilian, J.: Simple Image Analysis by Moments, 0.2 Version (2001)
[4] Smart Link Corporation, http://www.text-to-speech.imtranslator.net
[5] MSDN Library, http://www.msdn.microsoft.com

Skin Infection Identification Using Color and Euclidean Distance Algorithm

Manish Kumar Sharma[1], Rohit Maurya[2], Ajay Shankar Shukla[3], and P.R. Gupta[4]

[1] GNIT Greater Noida
[2] Gameloft India Pvt. Ltd
[3] ABV- IIITM Gwalior
[4] CDAC Noida

Abstract. In this paper we have discussed the method to detect skin identification. This method includes three main steps: First segmentation based on the pixel values, in which when the particular pixel values lies in the range it is skin area. Second is the post processing stage in which some area which is not the skin color but counted as a skin area is eliminated and some which is not counted as skin is added as possible. Third the segmented area is masked with original image (input image) and Finally Euclidean Distance is applied to find out Color difference between the segmented skin and mean of reference image based on threshold values classify the skin is infected or not.

Keywords: Image Histogram, Pixel-Based Skin Detection, Morphological Processing, Masking, Euclidean Distance Algorithm.

1 Introduction

Skin detection and identification has been topics of extensive research for several past decades. Many researchers have been done work on the topic Skin Detection but very little has been done on the Skin identification to find out the skin having rashes or infection. The process of skin identification is very difficult due to the fact, there is no certainty of skin color, it may be of red, pink, white, black etc. And the skin color of the same person is not homogenous through his various body parts. [1]

Skin is an organ composed of several kinds of tissues, It is Largest organ, Performs many functions such as Prevents harmful substances, chemicals, microorganisms from entering body, water loss, Maintains temperature, Houses sensory receptors, Produces chemicals such as Vitamin D, Excretes wastes. There are two layers of skin. First: Epidermis- The outer layer of skin is epidermis, it is a thin layer and Second: Dermis- the Inner layer of skin is dermis (thicker than epidermis). Our Experiment is carried out on the Epidermis, which is the outer layer of skin. For many years, a premise has been accepted in the field of skin identification that in order to have a valid identification that the skin is infected or not, it can be obtained when we find dissimilarities or similarities respectively in the skin region.

M. Parashar et al. (Eds.): IC3 2012, CCIS 306, pp. 471–480, 2012.
© Springer-Verlag Berlin Heidelberg 2012

2   Methods

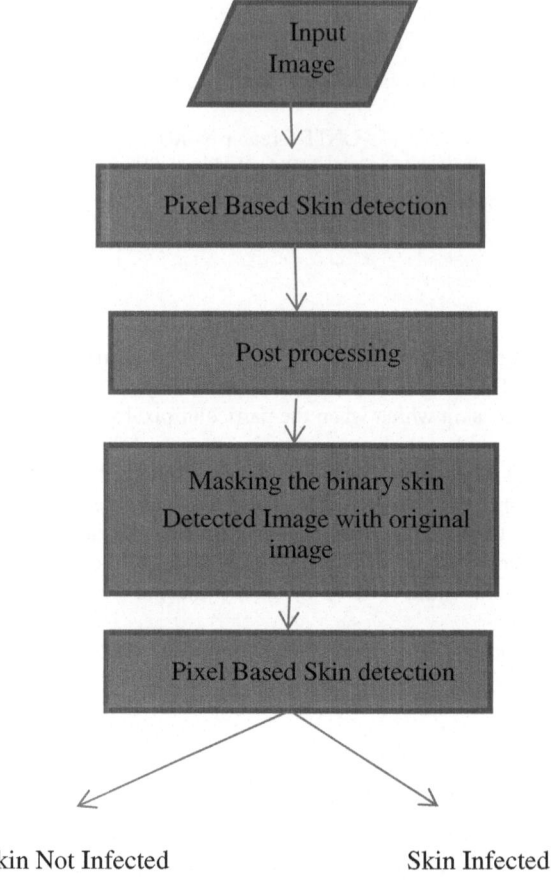

Fig. 1. The block diagram of the proposed system

2.1   Skin Detection

Skin detection process has two phases: a training phase and a detection phase.
Training a skin detector involves three basic steps:

1. Collecting a database of skin patches from different images. Such a database typically contains skin-colored patches from a variety of people under different illumination conditions.
2. Choosing a suitable color space.
3. Modeling the skin color distribution.

2.1.1. Pixel Based Skin Detection

2.1.1.1 Color Space for Skin Color Detection
The simplicity of transformation and the explicit separation of luminance and chrominance component make YCbCr attractive for Skin Color Modeling. The component Cb and Cr are the Red and Blue Chroma component in YCbCr Color Space. Y is responsible for the intensity change and the Cb, Cr are the pure colored irrespective to light change. [2]

2.1.1.2 Skin Color Modeling
Histogram is used for modeling different color space. [11].

Histogram of RGB Color Space: histogram of RGB skin sample.

Histogram of R   Histogram of G   Histogram of B

Fig. 2. Histogram of RGB skin sample

Histogram of YCbCr Color Space
Here, we can see in Figure 2: the RGB color space having high brightness in image, the intensity reach toward the gray level 255 (white) and when the light is not enough then the intensity goes toward the 0 (Black), But if we consider YCbCr color space, the range is not in varying nature for different condition of light and it model itself in very limited range as we can see in Figure 3. [5],[6],[7],[8]

Histogram of Cb   Histogram of Cr

Fig. 3. Histogram of YCbCr skin sample

Steps to Train the Skin Detector:

1. Take the skin samples.
2. Normalize the intensity level.
3. Convert normalized RGB to YCbCr Color Space.
4. Make histogram of skin samples Cb and Cr Component.
5. Find min and max of histogram value of each sample.
6. Now select the minimum and maximum value from all samples of Cb and Cr. With the help of this we can find out the Range of threshold value for skin classifier.
7. The range of threshold value gives the skin color and the rest will be non-skin color.

After all the steps performed, we get the Range of skin in the YCbCr color space is:

Cb >= 77 & Cb <= 127 & Cr >= 133 & Cr <= 173
i.e. 77 <= Cb <= 127
And 133 <= Cr <= 173

2.1.2   Post Processing Stage

The refining process is done in this stage. Refining means the removing the false position which is encountered as skin color and adding the true position which is not came in the range of the skin colored as possible.

Morphological Operation: In image processing, morphology is about regions and shapes. It is used as a tool for extracting image components that are useful in representing regions and shapes. It is explained below.

a.   Opening operation [4]

Morphological opening of an image is basically erosion followed by dilation, using the same structuring element.

$$OPEN (A, B) = D (E (A))$$

Where, D - Dilation, E - Erosion
And A - image, B - structuring element

Opening generally makes the contours of the image smooth and breaks down narrow bridge and eliminates thin protrusions.

b.   Closing operation [9]

Morphological closing of an image is basically dilation followed by erosion, using the same structuring element.

$$CLOSE (A, B) = E (D (A))$$

Where, D - Dilation, E - Erosion
And A - image, B - structuring element

Closing generally tends to fuse narrow breaks and eliminates small holes. This simplifies the process of assessing the separation of particles.

Here we should use the opening operation since its behavior is to eliminate the outer area. The false position lays outside the larger detected region. In the experiment we realized that the non-skin area is about the 1% of the total no of pixel in the image. So our aim to be removes those parts of detected region.

Connectivity: [10] There are 2 types of connectivity

a. 4 connectivity
b. 8 connectivity

Here, 8 connectivity is used for finding connected component, 8 connected concept is used due to the skin is of bulmerege shape [banana like structure]. It is used when we need to perform on particular area when there are many skin areas are detected. It can be illustrated below.

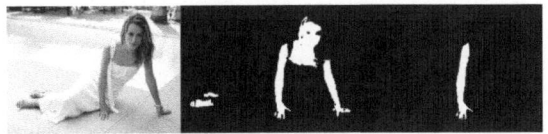

Input RGB   Image Detected Skin   Extracted Part

Fig. 4. Connected component is extracted

2.1.3   Masking

It is the procedure by which we extract the interested area in colored image using some mask, these masks is the binary skin detected area, the original RGB input image is multiplied with this binary image to find out the detected RGB colored image. The procedure of masking is illustrated in the figure 5.

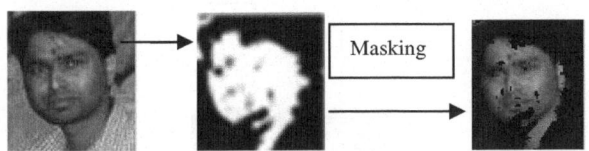

Input RGB Image   Detected Skin   Detected Colored Skin

Fig. 5. Masking operation of input RBG image with the Binary Detected Skin Area Image

2.2   Classification

Statistical Texture Measures

The statistical texture measures are required for the infected skin, which is helpful for the skin classification. For this purpose we have taken the numbers of infected skin samples and find out its mean, covariance, variance and standard deviation.

Suppose, we have taken 8 Infected skin samples then we should find out the mean image of the 8 samples and the mean value of the mean image after that the covariance is find out to derived the variance, which is the diagonal elements of the covariance then finally the standard deviation is derived from the square root of the variance. [3], [14]

Mean or Average: It is the Arithmetic mean of all infected skin samples. Also known as average intensity or average of color vectors.

Steps to find the mean image:

Step 1: Collecting a database of skin patches from different images. Such a database typically contains colored skin-infected patches from a variety of infected skin people.
Step 2: Convert each skin patches into color vector.
Step 3: Find mean color vector.
Step 4: Find the mean value of colour vector (which is the mean value of mean_infected image)
Step 5: Again convert the mean colour vector in to the mean image.

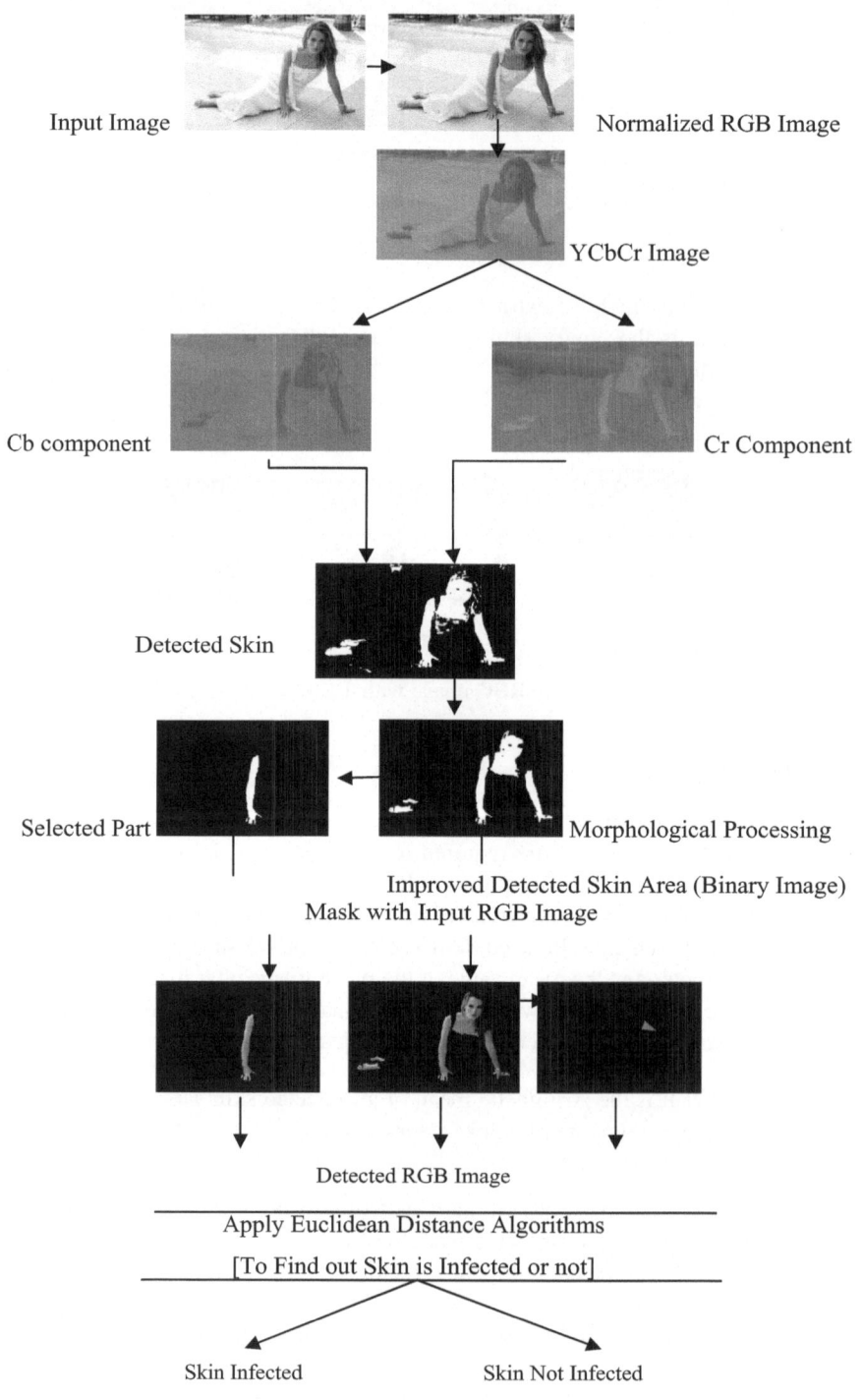

Fig. 6. Working model of Proposed System

Covariance- it can be obtained with the help of the mean_infected image and the mean value, it is the matrix of RED, GREEN and BLUE component.

Variance- diagonal of Covariance contains the variance of the RGB component.

Standard Deviation - measure of Average contrast, it can be obtained by the square root of the variance. When we obtained it for RGB image, we get the three standard deviation, which is for RED, GREEN and for BLUE. We select the highest value to set the threshold. [16], [17]

Uniformity- when the skin is infected then it's having the property coarse texture or grain texture. But the skin is not infected then it is uniform or homogeneous texture. So the pixel values of the non-infected skin will be the uniform type so variation will be negligible. But in case of infected skin pixel values differ from the neighbouring pixel.

Euclidean Distance Algorithms for Skin Classification: The Euclidean distance (DE) metric is usually used to compute distance in N dimensional vector space. It is defined as

$$D_E\,(\bar{v}_1, \bar{v}_2) = \parallel \bar{v}_1, \bar{v}_2 \parallel \tag{1}$$

Where $\parallel \bullet \parallel$ is the L_2 vector norm. For a three plane colour space, the distance calculated as

$$D_E(v_1, v_2) = \sqrt{(\,(v_{1,1} - v_{2,1})^2 + (\,v_{1,2} - v_{2,2})^2 + (\,v_{1,3} - v_{2,3})^2\,)} \tag{2}$$

Where $\bar{v}_1 = [\, v_{1,1}\; v_{1,2}\; v_{1,3}\,]^T$ is color triplet of the Detected skin in an image and $\bar{v}_2$ is the mean value of the mean vector (reference) image obtained by mean of the different samples of infected skin. [12]

If the Euclidean Distance $\bar{D}_E\,(v_1, v2)$ is less than the particular threshold values then the skin is infected otherwise skin is not infected. If the skin infection shows above 80% then the skin is not infected due to Uniformity and below is the infected skin. The Threshold value is the standard deviation calculated of the infected skin samples mean image.

The maximum value of standard deviation within Red, Green and Blue is set as the threshold value. [13], [15]

2.3   Result

2.3.1   Experimental Result
After morphological analysis

Table 1.

Method	TP	FP
Pixel Based Thresholding	88%-93.2%	2.3%-8.2%

2.3.2   Skin Identification Using Euclidean Distance Algorithm

Table 2.

No of images	True identification	False identification
60	54(90%)	6(10%)

Table 3.

Criterion	Skin detection	identification
Frontal face	88%-93.2%	96%
Tilted/rotated face	86.14%	91%
Complex background image	82.11%-84.41%	88%
Profile face	89.41%	96%
Time consumption	4sec	6sec

2.3.3   Results Analysis

In table 1: we can say that the detection phage of the proposed system is satisfactory since the true positions have a higher values and false positions have a lower value. The system can be more accurate if the texture property is also applied in skin detection phage.

In table 2 the improved version of skin is detected and the false position is removed as much as possible. We can see the detected skin range goes from 88% to 93.2% since some of the detected skin is small so they are removed and the range goes from 90% to 88% and some more pixel value is added due to the dilation process thus the result goes from 90% to 93.2%. While we talk about false position, the false position is not in large area if performed in control environment and can be removed easily. So we can see that it goes from 2.3 % to 8.2 %. That is useful for identification phage so that the false result cannot draw from the identification phage.

We have performed the experiment on various images. The result is giving 90% true identification and 10 % false identification it is due to the mean image calculated or due to the threshold value selected. If the mean image will obtained from more than 8 images then there can be better result and in the same way if the no of samples images will increase then the threshold value automatically will adjust in good figure.

In Table 3: we can see the result for the Frontal Face and Profile Face are good; it is due to the minimum no of non-skin area. The skin area also will detect in this in good format. The result is poor in complex background and Tilted / Rotated Face it is due to the maximum likelihood of skin like element in the figure and the tilted/ rotated faces will not cover the uniform distribution of light on face so the result is poor for detection as well as the identification.

3   Conclusions

The Detection and Identification is done. Skin detection in color images is a very efficient way to locate skin-colored pixels, which might indicate the existence of human faces and hands. However, many objects in the real world have skin-tone colors, such as some kinds of sand, wood, leather, fur, etc., which might be mistakenly detected by a skin detector. Therefore, skin detection can be very useful in finding human faces and hands in controlled environments where the background is guaranteed not to contain skin-tone colors. Since skin detection depends on locating skin-colored pixels, its use is limited to color images, i.e., it is not useful with gray-scale, infrared, or other types of image modalities that do not contain color information. There has been extensive research on finding human faces in images and using other cues such as finding local facial features or Skin Detection Using Color, Texture and Space Information.

Euclidean distance Algorithms is used as the skin classifier as a skin is infected or not. This is based on averaging the color vector of infected skin and finding out of the mean value, which was the responsible for the color differentiation and with the help of threshold value we said that the skin is infected or not but some type of infections which are not in the special class are not encountered, but if we talk about the particular class of infection then it is successfully extracted and quantified the abnormality. This technique is depending on the average pixel intensity or color vector and threshold. For medical images with abnormality as hotspot, these parameters can be standardized. Hence color image segmentation algorithm is a parameter independent, image independent technique that can be standardized for abnormalities exhibiting as hotspot.

3.1 Limitations

- Uniform distribution of light is required in the image.
- While taking the image, Background should have minimum skin similar objects.
- Not useful with gray-scale, infrared, or other types of image modalities that do not contain color information.
- Resolution of image should not be much less (should be good enough).
- The Application will not work when we apply completely damaged Skin image.

3.2 Future Work

We have Detected Skin and also done the Identification in number of images, which is having identical infection, but there can be more different types of infections which is not encounter due to its color and statistical texture properties. If we do the work on that also, this project can be helpful for the medical purpose to find which type of infection is in the skin. So the collection of different types of infection study is required for the extension of the project.

References

1. Vezhnevets, V., Sazonov, V., Alla, A.: A Survey on Pixel-Based Skin Color Detection Techniques. In: Proc. Graphicon 2003, Moscow, Russia, pp. 85–92 (September 2003)
2. Sajedi, H., Najafi, M., Kasaei, S.: A Boosted Skin Detection Method based on Pixel and Block Information. In: 5th International Symposium on Image and Signal Processing and Analysis, ISPA 2007, September 27-29, pp. 146–151 (2007)

3. Fotouhi, M., Rohban, M.H., Kasaei, S.: Skin Detection Using Contourlet-Based Texture Analysis. In: Fourth International Conference on Digital Telecommunications, ICDT 2009, July 20-25, pp. 59–64 (2009)
4. Monwar, M.M., Rezaei, S.: Pain Recognition Using Artificial Neural Network. In: 2006 IEEE International Symposium on Signal Processing and Information Technology, pp. 28–33 (August 2006)
5. Wesolkowski, S., Dony, R.D., Jernigan, M.E.: Global color image segmentation strategies. In: Proceedings of the 1999 IEEE Signal Processing Society Workshop on Euclidean Distance vs. Vector Angle: Neural Networks for Signal Processing IX, pp. 419–428 (August 1999)
6. Healey, C.G., Enns, J.T.: A Perceptual Colour Segmentation Algorithm: UBC CS Technical Report TR-96-09
7. Abdullah-Al-Wadud, M., Chae, O.: Region-of-Interest Selection for Skin Detection Based Applications. In: International Conference on Convergence Information Technology, November 21-23, pp. 1999–2004 (2007)
8. Chen, D.-S., Liu, Z.-K.: A survey of skin color detection. Chinese Journal of Computers (2006)
9. Fink, B., Grammer, K., Matts, P.J.: Visible skin color distribution plays a role in the perception of age, attractiveness, and health in female faces. Evolution and Human Behavior (2006)
10. Gonzalez, R.C., Woods, R.E.: Digital Image processing, 2nd edn.
11. Jones, M.J., Rehg, J.M.: Statistical color models with application to skin detection. In: IEEE Computer Society Conference on Computer Vision and Pattern Recognition, vol. 1(2), pp. xxiii+637+663 (1999)
12. Selvarasu, N., Nachiappan, A., Nandhitha, N.M.: Abnormality Detection from Medical Thermographs in Human Using Euclidean Distance Based Color Image Segmentation. In: International Conference on Signal Acquisition and Processing, ICSAP 2010, February 9-10, pp. 73–75 (2010)
13. Kelly, W., Donnellan, A., Molloy, D.: Screening for Objectionable Images: A Review of Skin Detection Techniques. In: International Conference on Machine Vision and Image Processing, IMVIP 2008, September 3-5, pp. 151–158 (2008)
14. Jiang, Z., Yao, M., Jiang, W.: Skin Detection Using Color, Texture and Space Information. In: Fourth International Conference on Fuzzy Systems and Knowledge Discovery, FSKD 2007, August 24-27, vol. 3, pp. 366–370 (2007)
15. Abdel-Mottaleb, M., Elgammal, A.: Face detection in complex environments from color images. In: Proceedings of the 1999 International Conference on Image Processing, ICIP 1999, vol. 3, pp. 622–626 (1999)
16. Jedynak, B., Zheng, H., Daoudi, M.: Statistical Models for Skin Detection. In: Conference on Computer Vision and Pattern Recognition Workshop, CVPRW 2003, June 16-22, vol. 8, p. 92 (2003)
17. Fleck, M.M., Forsyth, D.A., Bregler, C.: Finding Naked People. In: Buxton, B.F., Cipolla, R. (eds.) ECCV 1996, Part II. LNCS, vol. 1065, pp. 593–602. Springer, Heidelberg (1996)

Annotation of Human Genomic Sequence
by Combining Existing Gene Prediction Tools
Using Hybrid Approach

Anubhav Saxena, Gokulakrishnan Pitchaipillai, and Pritish Kumar Varadawaj

Indian Institute of Information Technology, Jhalwa, Allahabad, India
{ibi2010017,gokulakrishnan.p,pritish}@iiita.ac.in

Abstract. Various methods and tools are used for genomic sequences annotation, each of which needs training data set and hence their accuracy is confined to specific type of organism. To surmount this problem, we proposed a hybrid method in which weighted annotated binary DNA sequences from different tools are convolved independently with multi scaled modified Gaussian function that generates set of multi scaled sequences for each tool. All the sequences of the same scale values from different tools are added based on each nucleotide position. Then this multi scaled sequences are normalized, scaled and combined together for each nucleotide position. By combining best predicted ranges among different predicted ranges from individual gene prediction tool, our proposed tool increases Exon level accuracy by 10 – 12 % whereas 2-4 % of missed and wrong exons can be identified in comparison to accuracy given by single gene predicting tool.

Keywords: Hybrid, Modified Gaussian Function (MGF), Function approximation, Gene finding programs, combining Gene finding approach.

1   Introduction

In post genomic era, necessities of developing new automated gene annotation tool increased rapidly as annotation require to process a vast amount of genomic data. Some of the most widely used gene predictive tools are GENSCAN, HMMgene, FGENES, GeneMark.hmm, Genie, Morgan and MZEF. Genscan [1] is a gene finding program which uses probabilistic model based on explicit HMM approach which uses combination of weight matrices, weight arrays and maximal dependence decomposition. Genscan is used to predict single-gene and multi-genes that are either complete gene or partial gene. It can also predict suboptimal exons (potential exons with a higher probability).

HMMgene [2] program uses conditional maximum likelihood based HMM approach, to maximize the probability of correct prediction. If the sequence has identified to have sub-regions like hits with EST or protein database, then those sub-regions can be annotated as coding regions or non coding regions before submitting to HMMgene Server. It is used to predict either complete or partial genes in the genomic

M. Parashar et al. (Eds.): IC3 2012, CCIS 306, pp. 481–489, 2012.

sequence. FGENES [3] program is based on dynamic programming. It portends the optimal combination of promoters, exons and polyA sites using pattern recognition algorithms. It is very flexible and used to predict single-gene and multi-genes that are either having complete gene or partial gene information. GeneMark.hmm [4] is HMM and dynamic programming based gene finding program like Genie and Genscan. It also uses an algorithm based on recognition of ribosomal binding site to process optimal candidate genes which are predicted through HMM and dynamic programming approach. Genie [5] is generalized HMM based gene finding program which uses arbitrary length distributions in few part of model for gene prediction. The complete system follows modular architecture, because every single state is separately trained and new states can be easily added. The mechanisms of some states are based on neural network approach especially for splicing sites, with Markov chains for coding regions. Morgan [6] method is a combination of dynamic programming, decision trees and Markov chains. The decision tree uses a distinctive technique that classifies subsequences into three different classes: initial exon, internal exon, final exon. In MZEF [7] program a quadratic discriminant function is used to distinguish the sequence into two classes: coding and non-coding. MZEF can predict only the location of internal exons with a probability score. But MZEF only works for sequences shorter than 200 kb.

The entire Gene finding tools discussed above use either one or combination of both the following two approaches: i) Homology approach: Homology searching is an effective method for gene finding based on prior information of homologues sequence database. This approach [2,4,6] is based on database searching and scoring parts of genomic sequence as potential exon and intron regions. But major drawback of this method is it seldom works for novel sequence hence wide range annotation for new organism genome gives more false positive. ii) Pattern Recognition: It is estimated that ~ 50% of the newly discovered genes have no similar homologues in the databases so pattern recognition approach has been developed to annotate novel genome[1,3,5,7,8]. Pattern Recognition is a machine learning approach which is also having limitations like Sequence length, Generalization, requirement of Training Set. Preprocessing and similarity screening is required to nullify overtraining and biased training. Hence these methods are time consuming to do large scale annotation. Moreover since a confined set of sequences are used as training set hence chances of finding outlier is increased which results into wrong prediction. Therefore a combinatorial approach using both homology search and the pattern recognition is the need of the day.

2   Methods Adopted to Combine Gene Finding Programs

Murakami et. al. [9] proposed series of combination methods by utilizing logical screening like OR, AND & rule-based highest-policy methods which increases the accuracy by 3-5% in comparisons to single gene finding tool. Rogic et. al. [10] proposed combination method by using Exon Union and Intersection (EUI) , EUI Frame, Gene intersection of predicted exons regions based on probability score and reading frame consistency rules of different tools, which increase the accuracy by 7-9% in comparison to any single gene finding tool. Each combination approach has its own merits and demerits. To summarize: AND based method predicts the exons which are common in all programs, hence this method has lowest wrong exons. OR method gives more exon level sensitivity [9, 10]. Whereas rule based method which is introduced by burset and Guigo [11] and boundary method [9] follows probability of coding and non coding boundary information.

To utilize the best advantages of each program, set of gene predicting Programs are identified based on following selection criteria

1) Selecting a set of gene predicting program based on performance i.e. choosing program higher accuracy.
2) Avoiding combining similar program: like the human gene structure prediction program FGENEH [3], human exon prediction program FEXH [12].
3) Selecting Gene predicting tool based on its computational time
4) Program which processes results based on diverse sequence features.

Above mentioned criteria were followed to select gene predicting program GENSCAN and HMMGENE for our study.

2.1   Hybrid Approach Protocol

This protocol is divided into three phases: in the first phase accuracy parameters such as Sensitivity, Specificity, Exon Sensitivity and Exon specificity are taken for selected genomic sequence dataset from Gene prediction tools of interest i.e. GENSCAN and HMMGENE. All available Human genomic sequences from HMR195 dataset [13] have been used for the study. For each accuracy parameters weights are selected based on the tool which provides highest accuracy. To provide suitable weight for each tool, weight vector (Y) of accuracy parameters is initialized by using linear feed forward ANN tool and optimized by least mean square error difference of accuracy parameters among different tool using the formula:

$$E = Min \sum_{i=1}^{N_t-1} [(X_i \times Y) - (X_{i+1} \times Y)]^2 \qquad (1)$$

Where N_t – Number of tools

Optimized weights of accuracy parameters Y, are multiplied with accuracy parameters of each tool using the formula

$$W_i = X_i \times Y \qquad (2)$$

Where i = 1 to N_t, where N_t – No. of tools
X_i- Vector of Accuracy parameters for the ith tool
Y- Vector of weights of Accuracy parameters
Wi- Tool specific optimized Weight of ith tool

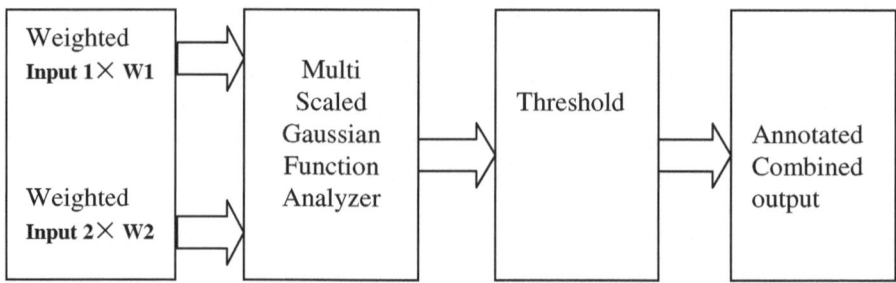

Fig. 1. Shows the block diagram of Hybrid approach to process and annotate the input DNA sequences from different tools where W1 and W2 are tool specific weights

Once specific weight for each tool is estimated, this weight is multiplied with the annotated output from each tool which is represented as 0 and 1 for intron and exon respectively. In the second phase, weighted annotated DNA sequences is given to Multi scaled Gaussian function analyzer block in which annotated sequences from each tool are analyzed with Multi scaled Modified Gaussian function. This function usually used for function approximation, interpolation etc [14]. This function also helps to find out best predicted values among different predicted values. Here each weighted DNA sequence from each tool is convolved independently with multi scaled Modified Gaussian function that generates set of multi scaled sequences for each tool. Usually Gaussian functions are rotated with different centers for function approximation and interpolation. In our approach as exon has some specific frequency, modified Gaussian function has been used with constant centre but variable width (Scale values).

$$\Psi = \alpha \times e^{-a(x-b)^2/2} \tag{3}$$

a - Scale values

b - Constant Center of Gaussian function

α - Peak of Gaussian function = $\sqrt{2\pi}$

Here Approximately 5 Modified Gaussian function with different width (Scale values) between the ranges 0.1 to 0.90 is used. Values of each nucleotide of the same scale value from different tools are added based on nucleotide position. Now this multi scaled sequences are normalized, scaled and combined together for each nucleotide position. This Modified Gaussian function analyzer used to approximate the underlying function. This method decrease Number of Missed exons and wrong exons and give good exon level sensitivity and specificity. Procedure to implement this algorithm is follows.

2.2   Algorithm Steps

1. I_1 – Annotated Binary DNA sequence from first tool as input
   I_2 – Annotated Binary DNA sequence from second tool as input

2. I_1 and I_2 are multiplied with tool specific weight. Weighted sequence from each tool will be calculated using the formula,

$$B_1 = (W_1 \times I_1)^2 \qquad (4)$$

$$B_2 = (W_2 \times I_2)^2 \qquad (5)$$

B_1-Weighted Annotated binary DNA sequence from the tool 1
B_2-Weighted Annotated binary DNA sequence from the tool 2

3. B_1 and B_2 are convolved with 5 multi scaled Modified Gaussian function which is generated with different linear width (Scale values) between the ranges 0.1 and 0.90 (Eg. 0.1, 0.3, 0.5, 0.7, 0.9). This generates 5 scaled sequences for each weighted annotated DNA sequences of two tools namely B_1 {Scale values} and B_2 {Scale values}.

4. All the sequences of the same scale values from different tools are added based on each nucleotide position.

$$B_{\{k\}} = B_{1\{k\}} + B_{2\{k\}} \qquad (6)$$

B_k – combined annotated sequence for the kth scale value.
For example, the scale value 0.2 generate two sequences for each tool

$B_{1\{0.2\}} = [0 \qquad 0 \qquad 0.2132]$
$B_{2\{0.2\}} = [0 \qquad 0 \qquad 0.2132]$
$B_{\{0.2\}} = [0 \qquad 0 \qquad 0.4264]$

We do the same for different scale values.

5. Then all 5 multi scaled sequences are normalized using the equation (7) scaled and combined together for each nucleotide position.

$$\phi_k(P) = B_k(P) / \sum_{s=1}^{NS} B_k(P) \qquad (7)$$

$\phi_k(P)$ - Normalized value for k_{th} scale value and P_{th} nucleotide position.
$B_k(P)$ - combined annotated sequence for the k_{th} scale value and P_{th} nucleotide position.

$B_{0.1} = [0 \qquad 0 \qquad 0.21 \qquad]$
$B_{0.3} = [0 \qquad 0.21 \qquad 0 \qquad]$
$B_{0.5} = [0.21 \qquad 0 \qquad 0 \qquad]$
$B_{0.7} = [0 \qquad 0 \qquad 0.21 \qquad]$
$B_{0.9} = [0 \qquad 0.21 \qquad 0 \qquad]$

Then normalized sequences are

$B_{0.1} = [0 \qquad 0 \qquad 0.5 \qquad]$
$B_{0.3} = [0 \qquad 0.5 \qquad 0 \qquad]$

$$B_{0.5}= [1 \qquad 0 \qquad 0 \qquad]$$
$$B_{0.7}= [0 \qquad 0 \qquad 0.5 \qquad]$$
$$B_{0.9}= [0 \qquad 0.5 \qquad 0 \qquad]$$

6. By giving proper weight to each normalized multi scaled sequence, the accuracy has improved notably. It is better to select the weights proportional to scale values of MGF.
7. In the final step, threshold has been applied based on the mode value of the sequence which is based on probability distribution of nucleotide value for different scale values.
8. Annotate the sequence as exons and introns.

2.3   Pseudo Code

```
for    index (1 TO Number of scale values)
       a   = escalas(index);
       w0  = (limit/2);
       w   = linspace(0,limit,limit);
       W   = sqrt(5*pi)*exp(-(a^3)*((w-w0).^2)/7);
       R1(index,:)= abs( convn(I1,W,'same').^2);
       R2(index,:)= abs( convn(I2,W,'same').^2);
end

R=R1+R2;

O = (H1*0.02)+(H2*.04)+(H3*.1)+(H4*.08)+(H5*.1);
```

3   Result and Discussion

3.1   Performance Analysis

To calculate exon level prediction performance; following parameters namely: Accuracy, Esn, Esp, ME and WE, are calculated as follows

TP: True Positive: (Exon predicted as Exon)
FN: False Negative: (Exon predicted as Intron)
TN: True Negative: (Intron Predicted as Intron)
FP: False Negative: (Intron predicted as Exons)

Accuracy can be calculated using the formula

$$ACC=TP+TN / (TP+FP+TN+FN) \qquad (8)$$

Based on the above method, accuracy of few individual DNA sequences from human sequences in HMR195 has been shown below (Table 1) for which accuracy of hybrid approach is better than single gene predicting tool.

Table 1. Accuracy of few human DNA sequences from HMR195 Dataset

S.No	Acc. No.	GenScan Accuracy	HMMgene Accuracy	Hybrid method
1	AB016625	90	90	95
2	AF096303	90	85	95
3	AF082802	81	90	95
4	AF099730	0	0	50
5	AF059675	92	96	98
6	AF016898	66	66	83.3
7	AF076214	73	66	83
8	AF053455	0	0	50
9	AF051160	80	70	100
10	AF009356	80	80	90
11	AF019409	83	83.33	91.66
12	AF015224	50	50	66.66
13	AF042782	50	50	75
14	AF065396	90	90	95
15	AB002059	87.5	87.5	95

The complete list of all sequences validated and tested and results therein have been given in supplementary file (result.xls).

3.2   Comparison of Accuracy for HMR195 Dataset for Different Tools

Here Exon level Accuracy parameters have been compared. To calculate over all exon level sensitivity, specificity, missed exons and wrong exons for all human sequences in HMR195 dataset, following formula has been used

1. Esn: Exon level Sensitivity: No. of correct exons/ No. of actual exons
2. Esp: Exon level Specificity: No. of correct exons/No. of predicted exons
3. Percentage of missed exons: No. of missed exons / No. of actual exons
4. Percentage of wrong exons: No. of wrong exons / No. of actual exons

Table 2. Exon level accuracy of different tools

S.No	Tool	Exon Level Accuracy			
		Esn	Esp	ME	WE
1	GenScan	0.82	0.78	0.13	0.10
2	HMMgene	0.76	0.77	0.18	0.09
3	Hybrid Approach	0.90	0.86	0.09	0.09

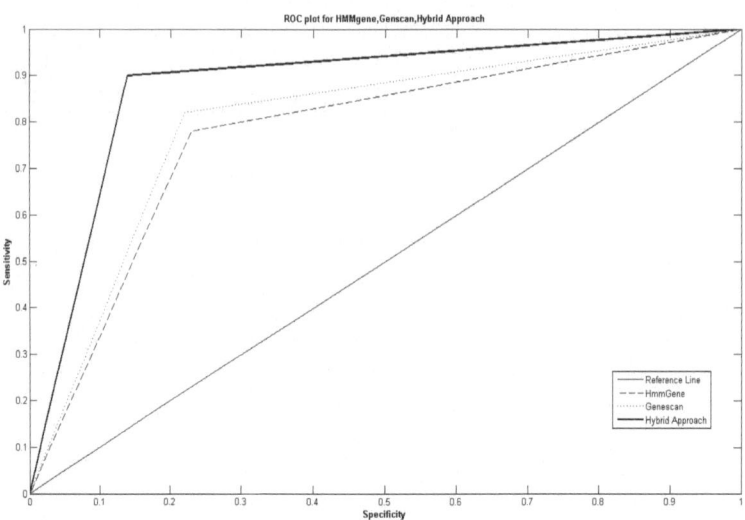

Fig. 2. Shows the ROC plot of HMM Gene, Genscan and Hybrid Approach based on sensitivity and specificity of each tool

Our Hybrid approach is tested with all human DNA sequences of HMR195 Dataset. Since we have selected tools which are specially designed for human Genome, our proposed algorithm has been tested and validated on human genomic sequences.

From table 1 and 2, it is pretty interesting to observe that Hybrid approach is giving promising higher exon level sensitivity and specificity approximately 10 – 12 % than existing single gene prediction tools and also prediction of missed exons and identification of wrong exons is improved in proposed hybrid approach by 4 % and 1% respectively.

4   Conclusion

Most of the Gene prediction tools combing approaches are being developed based on a set of rules that are created based on co-relation between different gene prediction tools and require large amount of training data and time. Proposed new hybrid combining approach in which we used position based nucleotide analysis using multi scaled MGF function with different scales values to overcome this limitation and this approach showed new way to analysis and combines multiple tools. As an initial step, we achieved 10 - 12 % higher exon level accuracy and prediction of missed exons and identification of wrong exons are improved in our hybrid approach by 4 % and 1 % respectively. In future we like to improve the prediction further by including more tools; which are designed for different vertebrates and invertebrates so that we will make a universal gene prediction tool without compromising with accuracy. We further like to utilize the advantages of multi scaled analysis using Gabor wavelet function to combine different tools that will provide better nucleotide accuracy and exon level accuracy for all dataset.

Acknowledgement. We are thankful to Indian Institute of Information Technology - Allahabad for providing the infrastructure and resources to carry out the work.

References

1. Burge, C., Karlin, S.: Prediction of complete gene structure in human genomic DNA. J. Mol. Biol. 268, 78–94 (1997)
2. Krogh, A.: Two methods for improving performance of an HMM and their application for gene-finding. In: Gaasterland, T., et al. (eds.) Proceedings of the Fifth International Conference on Intelligent Systems for Molecular Biology, pp. 179–186. AAAI Press, Menlo Park (1997)
3. Solovyev, V.V., Salamov, A.A., Lawrence, C.B.: Identification of human gene structure using linear discriminant functions and dynamic programming. In: Rawling, C., et al. (eds.) Proceedings of the Third International Conference on Intelligent Systems for Molecular Biology, pp. 367–375. AAAI Press, Menlo Park (1995)
4. Lukashin, A.V., Borodovsky, M.: School of Biology and Schools of Biology and Mathematics, Georgia Institute of Technology, Atlanta, GA 30332-0230, USA GeneMark. hmm: New solutions for gene-finding. Nucleic Acids Res. 26, 1107–1115 (1998)
5. Kulp, D., Haussler, D., Reese, M.G., Eeckman, F.H.: A generalized hidden markov model for the recognition of human genes in DNA. In: States, D., et al. (eds.) Proceedings of the Fourth International Conference on Intelligent Systems for Molecular Biology, pp. 134–142. AAAI Press, Menlo Park (1996)
6. Salzberg, S., Delcher, A., Fasman, K., Henderson, J.: A decision tree system for finding genes in DNA. J. Comp. Biol. 5, 667–680 (1998)
7. Zhang, M.Q.: Identification of protein coding regions in the human genome by quadratic discriminant analysis. Proc. Natl. Acad. Sci. 94, 565–568 (1997)
8. Uberbacher, E.C., Xu, Y., Mural, R.J.: Discovering and understanding genes in human DNA sequence using GRAIL. Methods Enzymol. 266, 259–281 (1996)
9. Murakami, K., Takagi, T.: Gene recognition by combination of several gene-finding programs. Bioinformatics 14(8), 665–675 (1998)
10. Rogic, S., Francis Ouellette, B.F., Mackworth, A.K.: Improving gene recognition accuracy by combining predictions from two gene-finding programs. Bioinformatics (2002)
11. Burset, M., Guigó, R.: Evaluation of gene structure prediction programs. Genomics 34(3), 353–367 (1996)
12. Solovyev, V., Salamov, A.: The Gene-Finder computer tools for analysis of human and model organisms genome sequences. In: ISMB 1997 Proceedings (1997)
13. Rogic, S., Mackworth, A.K., Ouellette, F.B.F.: Evaluation of genefinding programs on mammalian sequences. Genome Res. 11, 817–832 (2001)
14. Bors, A.G.: Introduction of the Radial Basis Function. Department of Computer science University of York (1994)
15. Mathé, C., Sagot, M., Schiex, T., Rouze, P.: Current methods of gene prediction, their strengths and weaknesses. Nucleic Acids Res. (2002)
16. Web, https://ccrma.stanford.edu/~jos/sasp/Gaussian_Function_Properties.html
17. Web, http://mathworld.wolfram.com/GaussianFunction.html

A Comparison of the DCT JPEG
and Wavelet Image Compression Encoder
for Medical Images

Farah Jamal Ansari and Aleem Ali

Section of Computer Engineering, University Polytechnic,
Faculty of Engineering and Technology,
Jamia Millia Islamia (A Central University), New Delhi-110025

Abstract. Compression is becoming very necessary in today's time especially in the medical field. The reason for this is that the current analog film based medical images are very difficult to manage and can be easily damaged if exposed to sunlight. Digital images are more reliable and easier to manage but occupy a lot of computer space. Compressed medical images occupy less space and can be easily transmitted over the network in lesser amount of time. In this paper two algorithms have been discussed: The JPEG DCT image compression and the JPEG wavelet compression. The algorithms have been compared on the values obtained for the Mean Square Error and Peak Signal to Noise Ratio. The results show that wavelet compression gives better quality for the same compression ratio in comparison to DCT compression.

Keywords: Medical Images, Compression, JPEG, Wavelet, MSE.

1   Introduction

Goal of medical image compression is to reduce the data volume required to represent different types of medical images without loss in image quality. [1] Standard compression algorithms include the Discrete Cosine Transform (DCT) and Discrete Wavelet Transform (DWT) , both of which belong to the class of lossy compression techniques. [2,3] The performance of these coders is degrading at low bit rates as they use the block based DCT compression. [5]The wavelet transform is very promising as it has shown improvements in image quality at higher compression ratio.[6]

2   JPEG Using DCT

The baseline standard based on DCT algorithms are lossy in nature and are applicable only to continuous tone images where the inter pixel difference is minutely small. In JPEG each picture is divided into blocks of 8*8 and each of these blocks is then DCT transformed, quantized and reduced further by entropy encoding .JPEG using DCT introduces blocking artifacts.

M. Parashar et al. (Eds.): IC3 2012, CCIS 306, pp. 490–491, 2012.
© Springer-Verlag Berlin Heidelberg 2012

3   JPEG Using DWT

Wavelets are mathematical functions that break up signals into different frequency components, and then study each component with a resolution matching to its scale. DWT transforms discrete signal from the time domain into time frequency domain. DWT unlike DCT does not divide the picture into blocks. This removes the blocking artifacts introduced by JPEG. The steps are digitization, thresholding, quantization and finally entropy encoding.

4   Results and Conclusion

The results in table 1 are a comparison of the values for Mean Square Error (MSE), Peak Signal to Noise Ratio (PSNR) obtained for both the algorithms for the same Compression Ratio (CR). Three images have been compared on the basis of both low and high CR.

Table 1. Comparison Of different Images for wavelet and DCT compression

Original Image	CR	MSE(wavelet)	PSNR(wavelet)	MSE(DCT)	PSNR dct)
Ct scan brain	1.2121	0.1413	56.6294	0.6062	50.3046
Ct scan brain	6.3158	37.1864	32.4270	46.9875	31.4110
MRI Brain	1.0952	4.9022	41.2269	5.2120	40.9608
MRI Brain	4.8261	43.8292	31.7152	46.9665	31.4129
Chest Xray	1.0455	26.0375	29.1971	28.1516	28.1516
Chest Xray	1.6429	56.2020	29.7452	56.2020	70.5681

As seen from table 1 wavelet compression is giving lower MSE and high PSNR for the same compression Ratios. This shows that the picture quality obtained through wavelet compression is better than DCT compression.

References

1. Abdullah, B.J.J., Ng, K.H., Pathmanathan, R.R.: The Impact of Teleradiology in Clinical Practice –A Malaysian Perspective. Med. J. Malaysia 54, 169–174.45 (1999)
2. Erickson, B.J., Manduca, A., Palisson, P., et al.: Wavelet compression of medical images. Radiology 206, 599–607 (1998)
3. Iyriboz, T.A., Zukoski, M.J., Hopper, K.D., Stag, P.L.: A comparison of wavelet and Joint Photographic Experts Group lossy compression methods applied to medical images. J. Digit Imaging 12, 14–17 (1999)
4. Ahmed, N., Natarjan, T.: Discrete Cosine Transforms. IEEE Trans. Computers C-23, 90–93 (1974)
5. Vetterli, M., Kovacevic, J.: Wavelet and Subband Coding. Prentice-Hall, Englewood Cliffs (1995)

Depth Map Based Recognition of Activities Involving Two Persons

Anupam, K.K. Biswas, Achyut Shukla, and Rajesh Kumar Pandey

Department of Computer Science and Engineering,
Indian Institute of Technology Delhi,
New Delhi 110016, India
{cs5070211,kkb}@cse.iitd.ac.in, {achyut89,28047rajesh}@gmail.com

Abstract. This paper presents a novel technique of using depth maps to recognize activities involving two persons. Very simple depth map based features are used to reduce processing power requirement. Kinect®SDK is used to identify the skeleton of up to two persons in the scene. Shape and temporal features are extracted from the region of interest. These features are subsequently passed to SVM Classifier for training and classification.

1 Introduction

In recent times with the availability of commodity hardware to capture depth maps (for example Microsoft Kinect®) it has become possible to capture 3-d data directly from scene. In this paper we demonstrate a method to recognize two people interaction using sequence of depth maps captured at various time intervals. Previous works on 3-d data focus on single person actions [2].

2 Method

Broadly there are 4 steps involved: (1) Image/Video acquisition, (2) Preprocessing of the image sequence obtained, (3) Feature extraction and (4) Classification.

Image Acquisition and Preprocessing. We have used Microsoft Research Kinect®SDK beta to capture depth images. We detect human body in the depth frame using Microsoft NUI library. Information of the human actors is separated and the region of interest is identified around the two actors.

Feature Extraction and Classification. The features we have extracted can be categorized broadly into shape features and temporal features.

For shape features, we divide the RoI (Region of Interest) around the silhouette of each person into a grid of 8x5. We create a histogram corresponding to the pixel values in each block by creating 5 bins. Hence, we obtain 200 values for this feature. Distance between centroids and average depth of the two person is

M. Parashar et al. (Eds.): IC3 2012, CCIS 306, pp. 492–493, 2012.
© Springer-Verlag Berlin Heidelberg 2012

used as another feature to incorporate the interaction between them. Fraction of foreground pixels in image is used as another feature.

For temporal features, we take the difference of each frame from the previous frame corresponding to each person. We then calculate the fraction of white pixels in the difference image and use it as a feature. Final feature vector is of size 205.

For classification, we have used multi class SVM (Support Vector Machines) with polynomial kernel. We use the svm-km toolbox [1] for this purpose. 15 labeled videos each corresponding to 9 activities are used to train the classifier. These videos correspond to 4 to 6 people in various combinations. We use the trained classifier to classify any unknown depth map sequence into one of the activity classes. The results and accuracies are discussed in the next section.

3   Results

We have picked 5 videos at random for each activity to do the testing. The results obtained after testing are tabulated in Table 1.

Feature extraction takes 1 sec for 10 frames and the classifier takes 18 sec to train on 8000 frames on MATLAB®. Hence, such a method can be used for real-time applications.

Table 1. Results: Frame wise accuracy

Activity	No. of frames	Percentage Accuracy
Fighting	500	100
Person A passes bottle Person B drinks	385	98.7
Waving Bye Bye	445	66.3
Japanese Greeting	500	100
Handshake	500	91
Person A drops object Person B picks	313	100
Person A reads while Person B stands	301	67.8
Sitting and talking	724	100
Person A walks up to Person B	400	89.7

References

1. Canu, S., Grandvalet, Y., Guigue, V., Rakotomamonjy, A.: Svm and kernel methods matlab toolbox. Perception Systmes et Information, INSA de Rouen, Rouen, France (2005)
2. Li, W., Zhang, Z., Liu, Z.: Action recognition based on a bag of 3d points. In: 2010 IEEE Computer Society Conference on Computer Vision and Pattern Recognition Workshops (CVPRW), pp. 9–14 (June 2010)

Real-Time Depth Estimation
from a Monocular Moving Camera

Aniket Handa and Prateek Sharma

Jaypee Institute of Information Technology, Noida 210301, Uttar Pradesh, India
{atneik,prat2007eek}@gmail.com

Abstract. A unique approach for estimating the depth from a monocular moving camera has been synthesized. Good interest points are obtained using the Shi-Tomasi technique for every frame in real time. Lucas-Kanade method is applied on these interest points of two consecutive frames which computes feature of the frames and the maps the interest points. It utilizes mainly the Lucas approach for estimation of depth from continuous input of frames from the moving camera which helps in estimating relative depth amongst various objects in the scene. Two approaches have been designed to solve this problem.

Keywords: Depth estimation, monocular camera, relative depth map, point cloud, 3D interest cloud.

1 Introduction

The term optical flow is referred to a visual phenomenon experienced when an object is moving at a different speed than the observer. It could be defined as the motion of every pixel in the image between two consecutive camera frames. Inspired by human ability to generate depth from visual cues either monocular or binocular, it is desired to develop an approach to support the need of depth of the real space in various forms such as relative depth-map from a typical camera generally found in notebooks or mobile phones. The aim is to provide the developer(s) with a robust approach which will enable them to create applications pertaining to 3D space, depth perception, or augmented reality and use their creativity to interact with the real world.

2 Approaches to Problem

As the camera moves and rotates in 3D around, individual features will be displaced and this will be mapped, and accordingly 3D point cloud will be generated. Two approaches have been developed for a stable solution to the problem. The first approach involves comparison between consecutive frames and a moving camera may lead to fair results but accompanied by a lot of noise. The second approach called "first frame differential" involved takes the first frame on capture start as the reference frame for all subsequent frames. All succeeding frames are then matched to the first frame contrary to the first approach.

M. Parashar et al. (Eds.): IC3 2012, CCIS 306, pp. 494–495, 2012.
© Springer-Verlag Berlin Heidelberg 2012

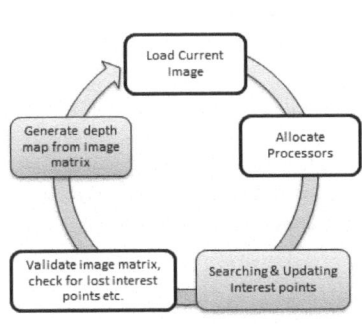

Fig. 1. Functional flow

(a)

(b)

Fig. 2. Sample test cases. (a) Total points=113, correct points = 104 (b) Total points = 104, correct points = 97, Metric=0.63

3   Conclusions

It can be concluded that no one cue is superb or indispensable for depth perception. Each cue has its own advantages and disadvantages. It is necessary to combine the suitable depth cues in order to achieve a robust all-round conversion algorithm. Some depth cues produce less detailed surface while some provide better results.

Acknowledgments. We would like to thank our supervisor Dr. Sanjay Goel for his continuous guidance in our research and his continuous help and support.

References

1. Furukawa, Y., Sethi, A., Ponce, J., Kriegman, D.: Robust Structure and Motion from Outlines of Smooth Curved Surfaces. In: PAMI, vol. 28(2), pp. 302–315 (2006)
2. Rieger, J.H., Lawton, D.T.: Sensor Motion and Relative Depth from Difference Fields of Optic Flows. Computer and Information Science Department, University of Massachusetts, Amherst, Massachusetts (1983)
3. Fua, P.: A parallel stereo algorithm that produces dense depth maps and preserves image features. In: Machine Vision and Applications, vol. 6, pp. 35–49. Springer (1993)
4. Dellaert, F., Seitz, S.M., Thorpe, C.E., Thrun, S.: Structure from Motion without Correspondences. In: Proc. Computer Vision and Pattern Recognition Conf. (CVPR) (2000)

Spoken Language Identification Using Spectral Features

Shashidhar G. Koolagudi[1], Deepika Rastogi[1], and K. Sreenivasa Rao[2]

[1] School of Computing, Graphic Era University, Dehradun -248002, UK, India
[2] Indian Institute of Technology Kharagpur, Kharagpur-721302, West Bengal, India
koolagudi@yahoo.com, {deepikarastogi17,ksrao1969}@gmail.com

1 Introduction

Spoken Language Identification (SLI) is the process of identifying the language spoken by a speaker. Language identification has several applications in day-to-day life. It may be used in call centers (e.g., emergency and customer services), information directories (e.g., airport, hotel, and tourist attractions) dealing with speakers speaking different languages[1]. Humans perform language identification mainly based on the specific words(phonetic information) and pattern of pronunciation. Spectral features are known well to capture phonetic information from the speech utterances[2]. Therefore, in this work MFCC's(Mel Frequency Cepstral Coefficients) are used. Language identification is mainly done using some pattern classifier namely GMM, SVM, ANN and HMM[3].

2 Development of Language Identification Model

For developing the language identification model creation of database is crucial task. In this work, semi-natural spoken database is collected from various TV shows and movies in six different Indian languages. Spoken language identification system has been developed with the help of Gaussian mixture models. The probability density function of observed variables has been modeled by using multivariate Gaussian mixture density[4]. Mel frequency cepstral coefficients are used to represent spectral characteristics of different languages. Different number of MFCC features are studied from the point of view and their contribution towards language identification. Once a GMM models are trained with MFCC's for six different Indian languages namely Assamese, Gujarathi, Hindi, Marathi, Tamil and Telugu, validation of these language identification models is done by testing the same. The percentage of language identification with different number of MFCC's is given in the following Table 1.

According to the Table 1 one can observe that certain languages are recognized well with lower order MFCC feature like Assamese, Gujarati on the other hand some languages are better recognized by higher order MFCC features like Hindi, Malayalam.

M. Parashar et al. (Eds.): IC3 2012, CCIS 306, pp. 496–497, 2012.

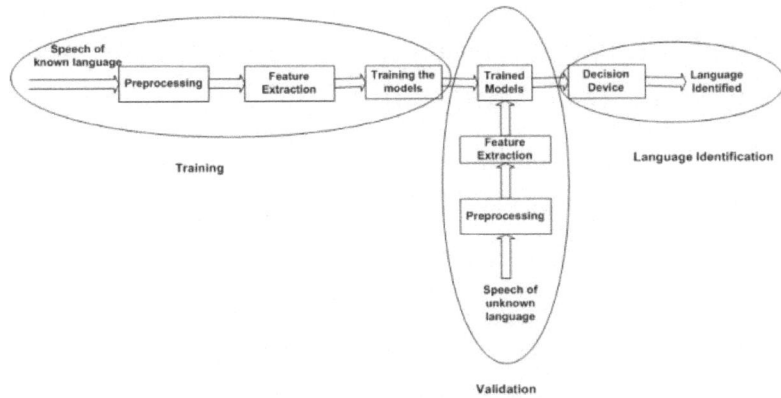

Fig. 1. Spoken Language Identification Model

Table 1. Language Classification Performance(in %) using different number of MFCCs

Language	Number of MFCC Features						
	6	8	13	19	21	29	35
Assamese	100	100	100	100	100	100	100
Gujarati	80	80	80	87	87	80	87
Hindi	33	34	40	47	47	60	80
Marathi	100	100	100	100	100	100	100
Telugu	93	93	100	100	100	100	100
Tamil	100	100	100	100	100	100	100
Average	87.9	86.2	87.4	88.4	88	87.6	88.4

3   Summary and Conclusion

In this paper, spoken database has been used for identifying the languages from speech signal. MFCC are used as spectral features. Six separate language identification models are developed using Gaussian mixture models. The influence of higher order and lower order spectral features is studied. The results obtained by using different number of spectral features are then compared. The study may be extended to use natural database for language identification.

References

1. Kumar, P., Biswas, A., Mishra, A.N., Chandra, M.: Spoken Language Identification Using Hybrid Feature Extraction Methods. Journal of Telecommunications 1(2) (March 2010)
2. Hieronymus, J.L., Kadambe, S.: Spoken Language Identification using large Vocabulary Speech Recognition. Bell Laboratories, 700 Mountain Avenue, Murray Hill, NJ 07974 Atlantic Aerospace Elect. Corp., 6404 Ivy Lane,Greenbelt, MD 20906
3. Savic, M., Acosta, E., Gupta, S.K.: An Automatic Language Identification System. In: International Conference on Acoustics, Speech and Signal Processing, vol. 2, pp. 817–820 (1991)
4. Muthusamy, Y.K., Barnard, E., Cole, R.: Reviewing Automatic Language Identification. IEEE Signal Processing Magazine 11(4), 33–41 (1994)

A Hybrid Intrusion Detection Architecture for Defense against DDoS Attacks in Cloud Environment

Sanchika Gupta, Susmita Horrow, and Anjali Sardana

E&CE Department
IIT Roorkee
Roorkee, India
sanchigr8@gmail.com, dr.anjalisardana@gmail.com

Abstract. Cloud Computing is emerging out as the future of next generation architecture for information technology enterprises. But due to its popularity, it is vulnerable to various unwanted attacks. One of the solutions is intrusion detection system. The Existing architectures of IDS in cloud environment are deployed on the network periphery of each guest OS that offers high attack resistance at the cost of visibility. In this paper, we propose hybrid architecture for deployment of intrusion detection system which takes into account security at both the front end and the clusters. This Paper also includes a critical review of previously proposed architectures on deployment of Intrusion Detection Systems in Cloud Environment and a detailed description of the research Gaps identified. Our approach leverages VMware virtualization techniques using open nebula as a test bed for deploying our proposed system.

1   Introduction and Literature Review

Cloud Computing provides the means through which computing infrastructure, applications, business processes to personal collaboration can be delivered as a service. These services expose cloud to the risk of security attack. One of the major attacks field is DDoS attacks.

In [1], an IDS system is deployed in each cloud computing region. These IDSs will cooperate with each other by exchanging alerts to reduce the impact of the DoS attack. However vulnerability to attacks is high as there is no central control. [2] Provides a generic model in which each instance of IDS has to monitor only a single user but has no cooperation.

2   Proposed Architecture, Results and Conclusions

We identified that providing full control to the users is risky and Location of deployment of IDS in cloud is a major decision factor for accurate detection and response to attacks An IDS framework for defense against DDoS attacks in cloud is shown in Fig 1, which is hybrid architecture. It consists of Cloud service users (CSU's) and a cloud service provider (CSP). A third party provides authentication to the cloud users.

M. Parashar et al. (Eds.): IC3 2012, CCIS 306, pp. 498–499, 2012.
© Springer-Verlag Berlin Heidelberg 2012

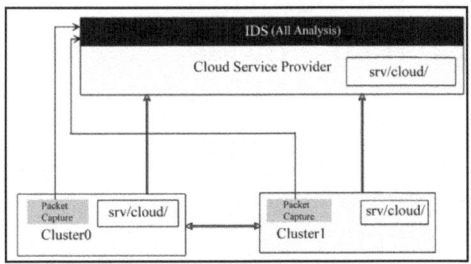

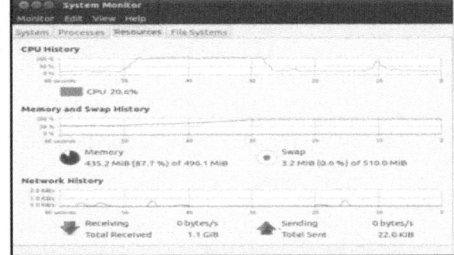

Fig. 1. Hybrid IDS Architecture   **Fig. 2.** CPU usage at Front end

Each Cluster node and Front-End are connected in mesh topology. The Front-End provides the NAT services. Hence, all the traffic flowing to and coming from the cluster nodes has to traverse the Front End. A single IDS is deployed at the Front End. IDS will be able to see all the traffic related to the virtual hosts in the cloud, and prove a very good point of observation. This IDS alerts, are stored in a common shared file system (NFS). The IDS deployed is Snort [3], it is a signature based NIDS. Attacks are generated using a Distributed- Internet Traffic Generator (D-ITG) [4] and using nmap port scan. The IDS at Front end sniffs the traffic from the Front-End and external traffic moving in and out of the cluster nodes. At each cluster node wire shark capture the traffic in a .pcap file, which is stored in the shared directory. This .pcap file is read by Snort as if packets are directly coming off the wire. Fig. 2 shows us the results of deployment where packets are captured at the Virtual Hosts and analyzed at the Front-End.

In this proposal, various deployment strategies of Snort have been analyzed in an open source cloud computing environment namely Open Nebula. Finally in the proposed architecture, packets are captured at the virtual hosts using wire shark which act as a sensor and later these packets are analyzed at front end. Moreover in the proposed architecture, deployment is done to provide security only for Infrastructure layer using open nebula.

References

1. Lo, C.-C., Huang, C.-C., Ku, J.: A Cooperative Intrusion Detection System Framework for Cloud Computing Networks. In: IEEE 39th International Conference on Parallel Processing Workshops, pp. 1–5. IEEE press (2010)
2. Dhage, S.N., Meshram, B.B., Rawat, R., Padawe, S., Paingokar, M., Mishra, A.: Intrusion Detection system in Cloud Computing Environment. In: ICWET 2011 Proceedings of the International Conference & Workshop on Emerging Trends in Technology, pp. 235–238. ACM, NY (2011)
3. Ranchal, R., Bhargava, B., Othmane, L.B., Lilien, L., Angin, P.: An Entity-centric Approach for Privacy and Identity Management in Cloud Computing. In: 29th IEEE symposium on Reliable Distributed Systems, pp. 177–183. IEEE press (2010)
4. Bugiel, S., Nürnberger, S., Sadeghi, A., Schneider, T.: Twin Clouds: An Architecture for Secure Cloud Computing. In: Workshop on Cryptography and Security in Clouds, ECRYPT II, the European Network of Excellence in Cryptology, and TClouds (2011)

Telephonic Vowel Recognition
in the Case of English Vowels

Sujata Negi Thakur[1], Manoj Kumar Singh[1], and Anurag Barthwal[2]

[1] Department of Computer Applications,
Graphic Era Hill University, Dehradun, UK, India
[2] School of Computing, Graphic Era University,
Dehradun, Uttarakhand, India
{sujatathakur1987,anubarthwal}@gmail.com, manojthakur1984@rediffmail.com

1 Introduction

Vowel recognition is the focus of automatic speech recognition (ASR) and speaker identification systems because of spectrally well defined characteristics of vowels. The ability to recognize speech improves significantly by efficient vowel recognition, both by humans as well as by ASR systems [1]. Therefore vowel recognition has an important role in speech processing systems. Now-a-days telephonic vowel recognition has gain lot of research interest as telephones have been revolutionized the personal and professional communication. Therefore, in this work emphasis is given to vowel recognition from telephonic speech. Telephonic vowel recognition of English language is a challenging task as the same vowel has got different contextual pronounciation. Telephonic speech recognition is greatly benefitted by efficient vowel recognition. Recognition of vowels from telephonic speech has applications in speaker recognition for critical banking transactions, identification of criminals, access control systems and forensic applications. In the field like Biometrics, goal of vowel recognition is to verify an individual's identity based on his or her voice. This is one of the trusted means of authentication as voice is one of the most natural forms of the communication.

2 Development of Vowel Recognition Models

Proper database is an important resource in any of the speech processing tasks. It is necessary to consider all possible vowel pronounciations while collecting data for specific vowel. For instance vowel /a/ has different pronounciation in different context such as career, cart, cat, similarly different pronounciation pattern are recorded using various context. Further a speech editing tool 'wave surfer' is used to separate cut vowel portion from the speech signal based on human marking. In this manner 30 speakers comprising of 15 males and 15 females are recorded. The similar data is recorded in an echoic room using microphone and the received call from a mobile telephone set. Call recording facility of a mobile set is used for the purpose. All vowel pronounciations of /a/, /e/, /i/, /o/, /u/ are grouped separately. From the literature, spectral features are proved to be better correlates of phonetic information of speech [2]. Therefore, in this work

M. Parashar et al. (Eds.): IC3 2012, CCIS 306, pp. 500–501, 2012.
© Springer-Verlag Berlin Heidelberg 2012

mel frequency cepstral coefficients (MFCCs) features that represent spectral information are used as features. Gaussian mixture models are matured pattern classifiers those work on probability density function. Their performance is good when sufficient number of feature vectors are available. Therefore, in this work Gaussian mixture models (GMMs) are used to develop vowel recognition models. One GMM is developed to capture the information about vowel. GMMs are designed with 64 components and iterated 100 times to attain convergence of weights. The decision regarding the vowel category of feature vector is taken based on its probability of coming from feature vectors of the specific model [3].

The Vowel Classification results obtained from studio recorded speech and mobile telephone recorded speech are shown in Table 1 and Table 2 respectively. The average recognition rate from studio recorded speech is 93.2% and for telephonic recorded speech is 89.4%.

Table 1. Vowel classification performance with studio recorded speech

	a	e	i	o	u
a	93	0	0	7	0
e	0	100	0	0	0
i	0	13	87	0	0
o	7	0	0	93	0
u	7	0	0	0	93

Table 2. Vowel classification performance with telephone recorded speech

	a	e	i	o	u
a	87	0	0	13	0
e	0	93	7	0	0
i	0	13	87	0	0
o	7	0	0	93	0
u	13	0	0	0	87

In the case of telephonic speech, vowel recognition performance is less mainly due to the effect of speech coding applied while transmission.

3   Conclusion

Though vowel recognition performance depends on category of vowels, their pronunciation, speaker, gender and languages. From the above results, it may be observed that, even in telephonic speech, vowels are recognised with good recognition rate. Further investigation is required to understand the effect of coding and transmission on vowel recognition. The vowel recognition performance can be improved further by combining the evidence from excitation source and prosodic parameters.

References

1. Gheidi, M., Sayadian, A.: Vowel Detection and Classification using Support Vector Machines (SVM). In: 4th International Conference: Sciences of Electronic, Technologies of Information and Telecommunications, TUNISIA, March 25-29 (2007)
2. Kocharov, D.A.: Automatic Vowel Recognition in Fluent Speech (on the Material of the Russian Language). In: SPECOM 2004: 9th Conference Speech and Computer (2004)
3. Murthy, K., Yegnanarayana, B.: Epoch extraction from speech signals. IEEE Trans. Audio, Speech and Language Processing 16, 1602–1613 (2008)

Application of 2D OVSF Codes in OFCDM for Downlink Communication in 4G Systems

Parul Puri[1] and Neetu Singh[2]

Department of Electronics & Communication Engineering,
Jaypee Institute of Information Technology, Noida, India
{parulpuri9,ntu.sgh}@gmail.com

Abstract. Orthogonal frequency and code division multiplexing (OFCDM) technique has shown promising results in achieving high data rate while simultaneously combating multipath fading. The novelty of an OFCDM system is two-dimensional spreading and code multiplexing. These are achieved by using 1D-OVSF codes. Here, 2D-OVSF codes are applied in the OFCDM system to reduce multi code interference amongst code multiplexed channels.

Keywords: OFDM, Multipath Fading, Two-dimensional spreading, OVSF codes, OFCDM.

1 Introduction

High speed data transmission is one of the biggest challenges in wireless communications. Multi-carrier techniques have helped to achieve high data rate while simultaneously combating multipath fading. Orthogonal frequency and code division multiplexing (OFCDM) is an OFDM based technique [1]. It is basically an OFDM system with two-dimensional spreading. 2D-spreading provides diversity gains in time and frequency domains and allows flexible and higher data rates.

The developed OFCDM system uses one-dimensional Orthogonal Variable Spreading Factor (OVSF) codes. However, it has been studied that 1D spreading sequences do not possess zero cyclic auto-correlation side lobes and cross-correlation functions. Hence, by using an alternative code set the system performance can be increased. Two-dimensional codes such as 2D-OVSF codes possess zero cross-correlation properties; hence, they can mitigate multipath and multiuser interference. Here, we study the performance of OFCDM system using 2D-OVSF codes.

2 OFCDM System

Y. Zhou et. al discuss the transceiver model of OFCDM system in [2]. It is similar to an OFDM transceiver with the addition of 2D spreading and code multiplexing. It has a net spreading factor, $SF = N_T \times N_F$. In order to obtain the same data rate as an OFDM system, $Ch = N_T \times N_F$, channels are code multiplexed. 1D-OVSF codes are used for this purpose. 1D-OVSF codes allow the combinational use of WH sequences with different lengths according to the chosen SF.

M. Parashar et al. (Eds.): IC3 2012, CCIS 306, pp. 502–503, 2012.

2.1   Multi-Code Interference

It is studied, that the orthogonality between the code multiplexed channels is maintained in presence of AWGN, however, in a fast fading channel the orthogonality amongst these channels is lost. This introduces multi code interference (MCI). Loss in orthogonality introduces imperfection in auto-correlation and cross-correlation properties of the code. Hence, 2D-OVSF [3] codes are introduced which possess better correlation properties.

3   Results

Fig. 1-2 show the results of the OFCDM system simulated on MATLAB. A downlink bandwidth of 100 MHz and 1024 subcarriers is considered. Channel considered is a frequency selective Rayleigh fading channel. Fig. 1 clearly indicates the performance enhancement of OFCDM system using 2D-OVSF codes in comparison to OFCDM with 1D-OVSF codes. Further, from Fig. 2, improvement in system performance is observed with increasing N_T as compared to an OFDM system where N_T is 1. This is mainly due to the increase in gain in time domain. However, a low N_T is desired when Doppler effects are prominent in the channel.

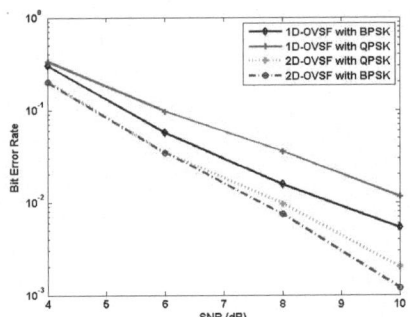
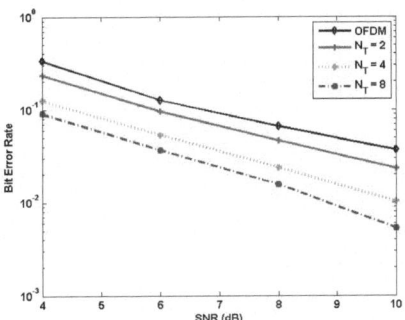

Fig. 1. OFCDM system performance using 1D OVSF and 2D OVSF codes with BPSK and QPSK modulation schemes and SF = 8 x 4

Fig. 2. OFCDM system performance keeping $N_F = 4$ constant, and varying N_T from 2, 4, and 8 with QPSK modulation scheme

References

1. Atarashi, H., Abeta, S., Sawahashi, M.: Variable spreading factor orthogonal frequency and code division multiplexing (VSF-OFCDM) for broadband packet wireless access. IEICE Trans. Commun. E86-B(1), 291–299 (2003)
2. Zhou, Y., Ng, T.-S., et al.: OFCDM: A promising broadband wireless access technique. IEEE Comm. Mag. 46(3), 38–49 (2008)
3. Wu, D., Spasojevic, P., Seskar, I.: Two-dimensional orthogonal variable-spreading-factor codes for multichannel DS-UWB. In: Conf. Record of the 38th Asilomar Conference on Signals, Systems and Computers, pp. 627–631 (2004)

Erratum: Dynamic Optimization Algorithm for Fast Job Completion in Grid Scheduling Environment

Monika Choudhary and Sateesh Kumar Peddoju

Electronics and Computer Science Department, IIT Roorkee, Roorkee, India
monika.ch13@gmail.com, drpskfrc@iitr.ernet.in

M. Parashar et al. (Eds.): IC3 2012, CCIS 306, pp. 86–94, 2012.
© Springer-Verlag Berlin Heidelberg 2012

DOI 10.1007/978-3-642-32129-0_56

The paper "Dynamic Optimization Algorithm for Fast Job Completion in Grid Scheduling Environment" authored by Monika Choudhary and Sateesh Kumar Peddoju, DOI 10.1007/978-3-642-32129-0_14, appearing on pages 86-94 of this publication has been retracted due to plagiarism. It is a duplicate of the paper titled "Turnaround time based job scheduling algorithm in dynamic grid computing environment" by the same authors, published in Proceedings of the CUBE International Information Technology Conference (CUBE 2012): DOI 10.1145/2381716.2381809.

The original online version for this chapter can be found at
http://dx.doi.org/10.1007/978-3-642-32129-0_14

Author Index